AMERICAN
ARBITRATION ASSOCIATION

HANDBOOK ON COMMERCIAL ARBITRATION

Thomas E. Carbonneau
Executive Editor
Orlando Distinguished Professor of Law
Penn State University

ASSISTANT EDITORS

Jeanette Jaeggi
Assistant Director of the Center for Dispute Resolution
Penn State University

Sandra K. Partridge
Penn State Center for Dispute Resolution

Questions About This Publication

For assistance with shipments, billing or other customer service matters, please call our Customer Services Department at:

1-631-350-0200

To obtain a copy of this book, call our Sales Department:

1-631-351-5430
Fax: 1-631-351-5712

Toll Free Order Line:

1-800-887-4064 (United States & Canada)

See our web page about this book:
http://www.arbitrationlaw.com

COPYRIGHT © 2006
by JurisNet, LLC

All Rights Reserved
Printed in the United States of America
ISBN 1-929446-47-0

JurisNet, LLC
71 New Street
Huntington, New York 11743
USA
www.arbitrationlaw.com

INTRODUCTION

It is with both pride and pleasure that the Penn State University Dickinson School of Law and the Institute of Dispute Resolution present the first of the AAA GUIDES on arbitration and ADR. The GUIDES contain recent important publications on the subject matter of each GUIDE written by authors who are recognized specialists in that area. Often the authors have both national and international reputations in the area. The contributions cover a wide array of topics that are of substantial interest in the field and provide analytically thorough, professional, and practical answers to problems that have emerged in the field.

The articles were selected from an extensive body of writings and, in the main, represent world class assessments of arbitration and practice. All the major facets of the field are addressed. The articles provide the reader with comprehensive and accurate information, lucid evaluations, and an indication of future developments. They not only acquaint, but also ground the reader in the field.

The American Arbitration Association, Juris Publishing, Inc., and Penn State welcome the opportunity to provide readers with a body of knowledge and interpretation that will allow them to take an active and effective part in arbitration and ADR. Arbitration and ADR are rapidly emerging as the new vehicles for legality and fairness in the social order—both domestically and internationally.

Thomas E. Carbonneau
Orlando Distinguished
Professor of Law
Penn State University

TABLE OF CONTENTS

Introduction i

Chapter One: Introduction to Arbitration

    I.   **AAA Looks at the Next Century** 1

        Past, Present & Future: Building on 70 Years of Innovation—
The AAA Looks to the 21st Century
        By The American Arbitration Association

    II.   **Top Developments of Last Decade** 15

        Top Ten Developments in Arbitration in the 1990s
        By Stephen K. Huber & E. Wendy Trachte-Huber

    III.   **The Fairness of Arbitration** 41

        Judging Arbitration: The Findings of Procedural
Justice Research
        By Deborah R. Hensler

    IV.   **The Benefits of Business Arbitration** 51

        Commercial Arbitration: Winning Over the Skeptics
        By Larry Engel

    V.   **Identifying the Parties to an Arbitration** 61

        Agency, Alter Ego and Other Identity Issues
Nonsignatories and Arbitration
        By John M. Townsend

    VI.   **Arbitration Agreements and Non-Signatories** 73

        What Arbitration Agreement? Compelling
Non-Signatories to Arbitrate
        By Charles Lee Eisen

Chapter Two: Arbitration Today—Recent Developments

I. Reassessing the Role of Arbitrators 83
Behind the Neutral: A Look at Provider Issues
By Thomas J. Stipanowich

II. The Consolidation of Arbitral Proceedings 89
Consolidated Arbitration: Will It Result in Increased Efficiency Or an Affront to Party Autonomy?
By Michael F. Hoellering

III. New Techniques to Manage Complex Commercial Disputes 107
Streamlining Arbitration of the Complex Case
By John Wilkinson

Chapter Three: Drafting Arbitration Clauses and Agreements

I. Drafting Clauses for Consumer and Employment Arbitration 115
Specs & the Single Arbitration Clause
By Thomas W. Lyons

II. Careful Use of "Arising" in Drafting Narrow Arbitration Clauses 127
Ambiguity in "Arising" Phrases: Caution for Drafters of Intended Narrow Arbitration Clauses
By Barry H. Garfinkel and James D. Fry

III. Arbitration Clauses and the Internet 133
Arbitration Clauses May Cure Internet Jurisdiction Woes
By Steven C. Bennett

IV. Drafting Effective Collective Bargaining Arbitration Agreements 141
Arbitration Agreements in the Wake of Wright: The Importance of Drafting
By Marshall H. Tanick

TABLE OF CONTENTS

Chapter Four: Selecting Service Providers and Arbitrators

I. Conducting a Successful Arbitration 149

The Ten Commandments of Arbitration: Some Guidelines for Arbitrators

By Lee M. Finkel and Robert F. Oberstein

II. Effective Procedural Management in Arbitration 153

Administered vs. Non-Administered Arbitration

By Glen H. Spencer

III. The Benefits of Independent Arbitration Administration 165

Engalla's Legacy to Arbitration: Why Independent Administration Is Important

By Edward A. Dauer

IV. The Essential Qualities of an Arbitrator 175

Striving for Excellence

By Richard Mittenthal

V. Counsel's Role in the Selection of an Arbitrator 181

Selecting the Arbitrator: What Counsel Can Do

By Francis O. Spalding

Chapter Five: Arbitration for Arbitrators

I. Attorneys Appearing Before Non-Attorney Arbitrators 189

Problems and Solutions: The Attorney and the Non-Attorney Arbitrator

By Raoul Drapeau

II. Issues Surrounding Party-Appointed Arbitrators 199

The Role of Party-Appointed Arbitrators

By Richard M. Mosk

III. Political Correctness—A Barrier to Arbitration Efficiency 211
The Problem of the "Politically Correct" Arbitrator
By Steven J. Stein

IV. Filling an Arbitrator Vacancy 215
When Arbitrator Vacancies Arise
By John Wilkinson

V. The Arbitrator's Role: Questioning 223
What Kind of Questions Should Arbitrators Ask?
By Sharon T. Nelson

VI. Arbitrators Testifying in Court 229
Must They Be Required to Testify? Arbitrators in Court
By Norman M. Fera

Chapter Six: Preliminary Arbitral Proceedings

I. Preliminary Conferences: Setting Up the First Meetings 239
Setting Up the Preliminary Conference: The Tribunal's Initial Communication to Counsel
By Tom Arnold

II. Discovery 249
Discovery in Arbitration: How Much Is Enough?
By Alfred G. Feliu

III. The Power to Subpoena Third Parties for Prehearing Discovery 257
Arbitral Subpoena Powers and Prehearing Discovery
By Paul M. Lurie

IV. Procedural and Interim Orders 263
The Arbitrator's Power to Issue: Procedural and Interim Orders
By Donald Francis Donovan

TABLE OF CONTENTS

Chapter Seven: Effective Arbitrations

I. Preparing Witnesses 275

Preparing a Witness for Arbitration
By Daniel I. Small

II. Expert Testimony 281

When Experts Testify: Exploiting the Advantages of Arbitration
By Norman Brand

III. Tandem Witnesses 289

Innovations in Arbitration: Using the Tandem Witness Examination When Experts Collide
By Stanley P. Sklar

IV. Effective Cross-Examination in Arbitration 293

Managing Cross-Examination: The Arbitrator's Perspective
By William L.D. Barrett

V. Improving Presentation to Win at Arbitration 299

Presentation Skills: A Quick Reference Guide for Advocates
By Morley R. Gorsky

Chapter Eight: Arbitration and Professional Responsibility

I. Arbitration Confidentiality 311

Confidentiality During and After Arbitration
By Edward Dolido

II. The Use of Sanctions in Arbitration 321

Sanctions & Arbitration Proceedings
By Georgene M. Vairo

III. Attorney-Client Privilege 329

The Attorney-Client Privilege and Arbitration
By James H. Carter

Chapter Nine: Arbitral Awards

I. Writing Arbitration Awards 337

    The Art of Communicating Arbitral Judgments
    By Charles J. Coleman and Gladys Gershenfeld

II. Arbitrators' Broad Authority to Grant Remedies 353

    Another Look at Remedies in Arbitration
    By Harvey Berman

III. Punitive Damages 363

    Punitive Damages in Arbitration: The Debate Continues
    By Lorenzo Marinuzzi

IV. Clarifying an Award: The Third Circuit's View 377

    Remanding an Award for Clarification:
    A Common Sense Approach to Functus Officio
    By Richard H. Porter

V. "Final" Interim Awards for Liability 383

    The "Finality" Principle and Partial Awards
    By John Wilkinson

VI. Post-Decision Debriefing—Point and Counter-Point 393

    The Case for Post-Decision Debriefing in Arbitration
    By David J. Hickton and Kelly B. Bakayza

    The Case Against Post-Decision Debriefing in Arbitration
    By Steven A. Arbittier

Chapter Ten: Arbitration and Court Proceedings

I. Venue Under the FAA 403

    Lessons from the High Court's Broad Reading of FAA Venue
    By Cary R. Singletary

TABLE OF CONTENTS

II. Waivers **407**

    Waiver of the Contractual Right to Arbitrate
    By Terry L. Trantina

III. State Arbitration Law **415**

    Does State Arbitration Law Matter at All?
    Part I: Federal Preemption
    By Alan Scott Rau

    Does State Arbitration Law Matter at All?
    Part II: A Continuing Role for State Law
    By Alan Scott Rau

Chapter Eleven: Judicial Review of Arbitration

I. A Discussion in Two-Parts of Judicial Review of Arbitration **435**

    Part I: Contractual Expansion & Limitation of Judicial Review of Arbitral Awards
    By Kenneth M. Curtin

    Part II: Contractual Expansion & Limitation of Judicial Review of Arbitral Awards
    By Kenneth M. Curtin

II. Judicial Review and Arbitration **463**

    Can Arbitration Coexist with Judicial Review?
    A Critique of LaPine v. Kyocera
    By Andreas F. Lowenfeld

Index **479**

CHAPTER ONE

INTRODUCTION TO ARBITRATION

I. AAA Looks at the Next Century

Past, Present & Future:
Building on 70 Years of Innovation

The AAA Looks to the 21st Century

The American Arbitration Association's history is the story of dispute resolution: a problem looking for a better solution. The AAA's roster of expert neutrals, spectrum of advanced dispute resolution techniques, and case administration skills, developed since those early days, reflect the changing history and needs of a nation. The AAA continues the quest for new advances in conflict management.

The businessmen, lawyers, tradesmen and academics who founded the American Arbitration Association in 1926 sought to avoid the costs, delays, and risks of a litigation system unresponsive to the needs of a busy industrial age. Today's information age requires a swifter and more finely tuned means of conflict resolution. The spotlight in the following pages on developments of the last 70 years tells the story not only of the past but of momentum toward the future. The timeline, launched with the first modern U.S. arbitration statute, highlights events up to the ADR cyberclause of today. Along the way are the rapid new expansions of the use of ADR into diverse areas of conflict, the revolutions in public policy support for these processes, and the growing international thrust. The American Arbitration Association now looks toward an age of conflict management that is both more digital and more humanistic, focused on dispute prevention as well as resolution, and fully integrated into the consciousness of our business and personal lives. What is the history of an organization? A series of beginnings, something to learn from and to build on, an identity that engages purpose and experience in the quest to meet the challenges of the future.

Chronology of Important Events in the History of Arbitration and ADR and the AAA

1920

The New York State Arbitration statute, the first modern arbitration statute in the United States, was enacted. The statute allowed enforcement of agreements to arbitrate future disputes.

1922

Business leaders created the Arbitration Society of America with a strictly educational mission to advance the use of arbitration.

1925

Congress enacted the United States Arbitration Act (also known as the Federal Arbitration Act), which enforced arbitration clauses in interstate contracts. The Act, which was based on the New York State Arbitration statute, provided a firm foundation for modern business arbitration as it is known today.

The Arbitration Foundation was established by business leaders, mainly devoting its efforts to research.

The Arbitration Conference was organized by representatives of trade and professional groups to promote arbitration.

1926

The American Arbitration Association was founded through the consolidation of the Arbitration Society of America, the Arbitration Foundation and the Arbitration Conference. Its main purpose was to promote knowledge of arbitration and its application to the settlement of disputes.

The AAA's National Panel of Arbitrators was created with 480 arbitrators.

The Actors' Equity Association's Basic Minimum Contract provided that controversies arising between actors and managers be referred to the AAA.

The Rules of the Arbitration Committee of the AAA were formulated, which later evolved into the AAA's Commercial Arbitration Rules.

1931

The First Code of Arbitration Practice and Procedure of the American Arbitration Association was published.

1932

The AAA's Accident Claims Tribunal was established.

1934

The Inter-American Commercial Arbitration Commission was established.

1936

The AAA's National Panel of Arbitrators grew to 7,000.

1937

The AAA's Voluntary Industrial Arbitration Tribunal was established. The Tribunal's General Principles, Organization and Administration, and Rules of Procedure were developed. The rules became the basis of the Labor Arbitration Rules.

The American Institute of Architects adopted a new arbitration procedure for standard building contracts and provided for administration by the AAA.

1938

The first course ever in arbitration law was offered by the New York University School of Law.

1940

AAA facilities were established in 31 cities in the U.S. to handle a Motion Picture Arbitration System for disagreements between producers and exhibitors following an anti-trust consent decree that severed film production from distribution.

1941

American Defense Fund promoted the use of arbitration clauses in munitions contracts.

1943

The AAA administered its first election.

1944

The Bureau of Labor Statistics reported that 75% of collective bargaining agreements in leading industries in the country provide for arbitration as the terminal point in the grievance process.

1945

The first course ever in industrial arbitration was offered by the New York University's Graduate School of Business Administration.

1946

The AAA's National Panel of Arbitrators reached 10,821.
    The AAA published its Code of Ethics for Arbitrators.
    A course in arbitration law was offered by Yale Law School.

1947

The International Court of Justice handled its first case: *Great Britain v. Albania*, for the destruction of British destroyers in the Corfu Channel in the previous year.

1948

Labor cases constituted more than 62% of all cases administered by the AAA.

1951

Frances Kellor, a founder and first vice president of the AAA (from 1926-1951), died.
    AAA's international commercial caseload increased 86% with parties from 43 countries.

1952

The AAA and the Japan Commercial Arbitration Association signed an agreement providing for the use of arbitration clauses in Japan-U.S. trade contracts and for two tribunals in New York and Tokyo, where disputes could be resolved.

1953

The AAA's National Panel of Arbitrators reached 13,000.

1954

Dedication ceremonies were held at the AAA for its new arbitration library consisting of more than 1,000 books, pamphlets, articles and unpublished manuscripts.

1955

The Commissioners on Uniform State Laws adopted a Uniform Arbitration Act (UAA), under which an agreement to arbitrate future disputes was enforceable. Today, all but two states support the Act.

The AAA developed its Accident Claims Arbitration Rules.

1957

Minnesota became the first state to adopt the Uniform Arbitration Act. Maine and Florida became the second and the third states, respectively, to adopt modern arbitration laws.

A major U.S. Supreme Court decision in *Textile Workers Union of America v. Lincoln Mills* of Alabama held that specific performance of promises to arbitrate grievances is enforceable under federal law.

1958

The United Nations Conference on International Commercial Arbitration in New York adopted the Convention on the Recognition and Enforcement of Foreign Arbitral Awards which was drafted to further international trade.

1960

In a series of three landmark decisions known as the Steelworkers Trilogy, the U.S. Supreme Court ruled that doubts about arbitrability of labor-management grievances should be resolved in favor of arbitration and that courts should permit arbitrators to exercise flexibility in awarding remedies for violations of collective bargaining agreements. The three cases were: *United Steelworkers of America v. American Manufacturing Co.*, the *United Steelworkers of America v. Enterprise Wheel & Car Corp.*, and the *United Steelworkers of America v. Warrior & Gulf Navigation Co.*

1962

Three decisions of the U.S. Supreme Court delivered simultaneously, often referred to as the Second Trilogy, were concerned with breach of the no-strike clause and the further availability of arbitration to resolve such disputes. The cases were: *Sinclair Refining Co. v. Samuel M. Atkinson et al.*; *Drake Bakeries Inc. v. Local 50, American Bakery and Confectionery Workers International, AFL-CIO*; and the *Atkinson v. Sinclair Refining Co.*

1964

In *John Wiley and Sons Inc. v. David Livingston*, the U.S. Supreme Court held that Wiley was required to arbitrate with the union under the agreement between the union and the interscience corporation which merged with John Wiley.

1966

The AAA's total caseload reached 12, 957.
  The AAA's Construction Industry Arbitration Rules were developed.

1967

In *Vaca v. Sipes*, the U.S. Supreme Court held that a union may refuse to process a worker's claim to arbitration and cannot subsequently be sued unless the worker can prove that the union failed in its duty of fair representation.

1968

The AAA established its Center for Dispute Settlement to ease urban crises through arbitration, mediation and fact-finding.

1970

The U.S. ratified the United Nations Convention on the Recognition and Enforcement of Foreign Arbitral Awards of 1958.
  In *The Boys Market Inc. v. Retail Clerks Union, Local 770*, the U.S. Supreme Court held that the anti-injunction provisions of the Norris-La Guardia Act did not preclude a federal district court from enjoining a strike in breach of a no-strike obligation as long as the bargaining agreement provided for binding arbitration of the grievance that led to the strike.

1971

In *Collyer Insulated Wire*, the National Labor Relations Board ruled that it would require exhaustion of the grievance procedure, including arbitration, before it would consider unfair labor practice claims. The issue of pre-arbitration deferral arose from a charge of refusal to bargain over an alleged unilateral change in the workday.

1974

In *Harrell Alexander Sr. v. Gardner-Denver Co.*, the U.S. Supreme Court held that an employee's statutory right to trial *de novo* under Title VII of the Civil Rights Act is not foreclosed by prior submission of the employee's claim to arbitration.

In *Scherk v. Alberto-Culver*, the U.S. Supreme Court upheld international trade arbitration.

1976

The United Nations Commission on International Trade Law adopted the UNCITRAL Arbitration Rules for worldwide use.

The AAA's Procedures for Cases under the UNCITRAL Arbitration Rules were developed.

The AAA's total caseload reached 35,156.

The AAA's National Panel of Arbitrators reached 37,000.

1978

The AAA developed the Employment Dispute Arbitration Rules.

1979

The first National Women's Arbitrator Development Program, co-sponsored by the AAA, the Federal Mediation and Conciliation Service and the New York State School of Industrial and Labor Relations, was established as a method of recruiting and training qualified women arbitrators.

1980

The AAA developed the Construction Mediation Rules.

1981

Inaugural ceremony was held July 1 for the U.S.-Iranian Claims Tribunal.

The AAA developed its Real Estate Valuation Arbitration Rules.

1982

President Ronald Reagan signed a bill authorizing the arbitration of patent disputes.

Chief Justice Warren E. Burger issued a nationwide call for greater use of private arbitration as an alternative to litigation.

The AAA's National Panel of Arbitrators and Mediators reached an all-time high of 60,000.

1983

The AAA's Patent Arbitration Rules were developed.

In *Charles v. Bowen v. United States Postal Service et al.*, the U.S. Supreme Court ruled that where an employee proves that his employer violated a bargaining agreement and the union breached its duty of fair representation, liability is to be apportioned between the employer and the union according to the damages caused by the fault of each.

In *Bergesen v. Joseph Muller Corp.*, the Second Circuit Court of Appeals affirmed the decision of the district court in New York, which held that the United Nations Convention applied to arbitration awards rendered in the U.S. involving foreign interests.

1984

In *Southland v. Keating*, the U.S. Supreme Court held that state laws, such as California's Franchise Investment Act, which purport to void arbitration agreements in contracts involving interstate commerce, are pre-empted by the federal substantive law embodied in the U.S. Arbitration Act.

The AAA developed the Alternative Dispute Resolution Procedures for Insurance Claims, and the Commercial Mediation Rules.

1985

Chief Justice Warren E. Burger, speaking before the AAA and the Minnesota State Bar Association, endorsed the use of private arbitration. "My own experience persuades me that in terms of cost, time and human wear and tear, arbitration is vastly better than conventional litigation for many kinds of cases," he said.

The UNCITRAL Model Law on International Commercial Arbitration was adopted at UNCITRAL's 18th session held in Vienna.

In *Dean Witters Reynolds Inc. v. Byrd*, the U.S. Supreme Court rejected the Ninth Circuit Court of Appeals' interpretation of the U.S. Arbitration Act, saying that it is an error to deny a motion to compel arbitration of arbitrable state law claims because they are intertwined with non-arbitrable federal law claims. Rather, under the Arbitration Act, the courts must compel arbitration of all arbitrable claims at the request of a party, where there is a valid agreement to arbitrate.

In *Mitsubishi Motors Corp. v. Soler Chrysler-Plymouth Inc.*, the U.S. Supreme Court held that the anti-trust dispute at issue was subject to arbitration under the U.S. Arbitration Act.

1986

The AAA's total caseload grew to 46,683.

In *AT&T Technologies v. Communications Workers of America*, the U.S. Supreme Court ruled that arbitrability is unquestionably a matter for judicial determination, saying "... It was for the court, not the arbitrator, to decide in the first instance whether the dispute was to be resolved through arbitration."

1987

The AAA's Dispute Resolution Journal celebrated its 50th anniversary.

The AAA's Securities Arbitration Rules were developed.

In *United Paperworkers International Union, AFL-CIO v. MISCO Inc.*, the U.S. Supreme Court held that the court of appeals exceeded the limited authority possessed by a court reviewing an arbitrator's award under a collective bargaining agreement.

In *Shearson/American Express Inc. v. McMahon*, the U.S. Supreme Court ruled that agreements to arbitrate future disputes raising statutory claims, such as those under the Securities and Exchange Act and the Racketeer Influenced and Corrupt Organization Act, are enforceable under the Federal Arbitration Act absent clear expression of Congressional intent to the contrary.

1989

In *Rodriguez de Quijas v. Shearson/American Express Inc.*, the U.S. Supreme Court held that an agreement to arbitrate claims arising under the Securities Act is enforceable. This overruled *Wilko v. Swan,* which the court deemed inconsistent with the prevailing uniform construction of other federal statutes governing arbitration agreements in business transactions.

1990

The Administrative Dispute Resolution Act was enacted, making explicit federal agencies' broad authority to use ADR in almost any type of dispute in which they were involved.

The Civil Justice Reform Act was enacted.

Florida became the first state to require brokers to give customers the option of taking cases to the AAA rather than using an industry-sponsored forum.

A Texas bankruptcy court ruled that Greyhound Lines could adopt an ADR program offered by the AAA to resolve injury and property damage claims resulting from traffic accidents involving Greyhound vehicles.

1991

The AAA developed the AAA International Arbitration Rules and the Grievance Mediation Procedures.

At the American Bar Association's annual meeting, Vice President Dan Quayle endorsed the use of ADR methods to alleviate the glut of lawsuits hampering American competitiveness in world markets. Quayle's views were based on recommendations made by the President's Council on Competitiveness, which Quayle chaired. The council recommended that ADR could be made available by creating a "multi-door courthouse" that would offer parties different methods for resolving their disputes.

In *Gilmer v. Interstate/Johnson Lane Corp.*, the U.S. Supreme Court enforced an arbitration agreement in a securities representative registration, thereby rendering Age Discrimination in Employment Act (ADEA) claims arbitrable.

1992

The AAA's Health Care Claim Settlement Procedures were developed.

The AAA reached a milestone when it handled case no. 1,000,000 in August.

The Insurance Commissioner of Florida designated the AAA as administrator of an ADR program for thousands of insurance claims disputes involving victims of Hurricane Andrew.

1993

The AAA established the Large, Complex Case Program to meet the special needs of larger, more complex business disputes, using Supplementary Procedures for Large, Complex Disputes.

The AAA developed several other important procedures: the Construction Industry Dispute Review Board Procedures; the Construction Industry Dispute Avoidance/Partnering Process; the Model Sexual Harassment Claim Resolution Process; the Arbitration Rules for Professional Accounting and Related Services Disputes; and the Environmental Dispute Avoidance and Resolution Guidelines.

The AAA helped resolve thousands of insurance claims disputes in the aftermath of Hurricane Iniki in Hawaii.

The first mandatory training requirement was established for all new AAA securities arbitrators before serving on a case. Mandatory training was later required for all neutrals in other caseloads.

ADR came into its own within the American Bar Association with the creation of the ABA's Section of Dispute Resolution to replace its Standing Committee on Dispute Resolution.

The National Performance Review (NPR), headed by Vice President Al Gore, strongly recommended that federal agencies expand their use of ADR techniques. President Clinton later issued an executive order directing government agencies to "explore, and where appropriate, use consensual mechanisms for developing regulations, including negotiated rulemaking."

1994

Twenty-four federal agencies pledged to review existing contract disputes and consider using ADR in accordance with recommendations by the National Performance Review, which studied government operations.

Total AAA caseload reached 59,424.

The Geneva-based World Intellectual Property Organization (WIPO), a specialized agency of the U.N., opened a center for resolution of intellectual property disputes between private parties through arbitration and mediation.

A federal fact-finding commission led by former Labor Secretary John T. Dunlop encouraged the use of voluntary ADR processes to resolve disputes in the workplace in an important report on the future of worker-management relations.

A joint committee established by the AAA, the American Bar Association and the Society of Professionals in Dispute Resolution released the Model Standards of Conduct for Mediators to serve as a general framework for the practice of mediation.

In a hearing on Dec. 16, AAA President William K. Slate II told the Committee on Long-Range Planning of the Judicial Conference of the United States that federal courts must be encouraged to consider and pursue ADR services to help alleviate a backlog in the federal court system.

1995

The AAA developed the California Employment Dispute Resolution Rules as a pilot program. It also developed the Arbitration Rules for Wills and Trusts, and the Excelleration Program, a fast-track arbitration process for the labor-management community.

The AAA convened the National Employment Conclave to focus on critical issues affecting ADR practitioners in the field of employment dispute resolution.

The AAA launched a World Wide Web site that provides instant information 24 hours a day to millions of Internet users throughout the world.

The AAA's National Construction ADR Task Force issued a major report calling for sweeping changes to enhance the Association's services for the construction industry.

The Judicial Conference of the United States, the policy-making arm of the federal judiciary, issued the Long-Range Plan for the Federal Courts, which included several recommendations on the use of ADR in the federal court system.

In *Allied-Bruce Terminix v. Dobson*, the U.S. Supreme Court provided authoritative support for the applicability of the U.S. Arbitration Act in state courts, even in the face of state law to the contrary.

In *Mastrobuono v. Shearson Lehman Hutton Inc.*, the U.S. Supreme Court's ruling reaffirmed the concept that, under the U.S. Arbitration Act, private arbitration is a creature of the agreement between the parties.

The Commercial Arbitration and Mediation Center for the Americas (CAMCA) was established by the AAA, the British Columbia International Commercial Arbitration Center, the Mexico City National Chamber of Commerce, and the Quebec National and International Commercial Arbitration Centre. The center is devoted to resolving private, cross-border commercial disputes related to the North American Free Trade Agreement.

Martindale-Hubbell published a Dispute Resolution Directory in cooperation with the AAA listing some 70,000 arbitrators, mediators, judges, attorneys, law firms and other practitioners of ADR.

1996

The AAA created the National Task Force on Alternative Dispute Resolution and Mass Torts to develop a blueprint on how courts may use ADR effectively in resolving mass torts. Supreme Court Justice Stephen G. Breyer joined the task force's first meeting in Washington.

The AAA announced the reconstitution of its commercial panels in response to the growing and changing needs of parties and their counsel.

Instant information about the AAA became available on America Online's Legal Pad channel which has five million subscribers.

AAA announces "virtual magistrate" pilot to arbitrate computer network-related disputes through electronic mail.

America Online named the AAA as ADR provider in disputes arising from a promotional contest affiliated with "24 Hours in Cyberspace."

II. Top Developments of Last Decade

Top Ten Developments in Arbitration in the 1990s

by Stephen K. Huber & E. Wendy Trachte-Huber[*]

The 1990s was a period of extraordinary growth in the use of arbitration in the United States. In the following article, Stephen Huber and Wendy Trachte-Huber analyze the evolution of arbitration law and practice during that decade. They also cast a discerning eye on the criticisms that have been leveled at arbitration, particularly in the context of employment and consumer disputes, and what they could mean to arbitration's future development.

When Samuel Gompers, the first president of the American Federation of Labor, was asked what organized labor wanted, he simply said: "more."[1] This word can also be used to describe what has happened in the area of arbitration during the last decade. The following is a look at what we see as the top ten developments in American arbitration law in the 1990s.

1. Uniform National Arbitration Law: FAA Preemption of State Law

The basis for federal arbitration law is the commerce clause of the U.S. Constitution, which allows federal control of foreign and interstate

---

[*] Stephen Huber is Law Foundation Professor at the University of Houston, Texas. Huber received a B.A. from Earlham College, J.D. from the University of Chicago, and LLM from Yale University.

Wendy Trachte-Huber is the former CEO of the Dow Corning Settlement Facility and the former Vice President, Educational Services, at the American Arbitration Association. She is also a Fellow of the American College of Civil Trial Mediators.

Huber and Trachte-Huber are the authors of Alternative Dispute Resolution: Strategies for Law and Business (1996), Mediation and Negotiation: Reaching Agreement in Law and Business (Anderson 1998) and Commercial Arbitration: Cases and Materials (Anderson 1998).

[1] "When I am asked if this eight-hour movement is my alpha and omega of the labor problem, I simply answer, we want more, and when we get it we shall still want more....We want more, and if I read the signs rightly, we are going to get more." Samuel Gompers' speech to the Trades and Labor Assembly of Chicago on April 23, 1890. THE SAMUEL GOMPERS PAPERS, 301, 302-303, (Samuel B. Kaufman, ed., Univ. Ill. Press 1987).

commerce, or activities "involving" such commerce. Virtually all activity that can be characterized as economic is subject to federal control under the commerce clause. The "separability doctrine" prohibits states from applying substantive law regarding voidable contracts to prevent enforcement of an arbitration agreement.[2] The commerce clause provides the basis for federal preemption of state arbitration law.

Two important Supreme Court arbitration cases decided in the 1990s serve to illustrate the scope and importance of the preemption of state law. One is based on a consumer contract and the other is based on a business transaction.

Allied-Bruce Terminix Companies, Inc. v. Dobson arose out of a contract between a locally owned pest control company (but also a franchisee of a national firm) and a homeowner, that provided for arbitration of disputes.[3] Subsequently, termite infestation was discovered. The homeowner brought suit, and the pest control company sought to have the state court enforce the arbitration provision. An Alabama statute prohibited the enforcement of pre-dispute arbitration agreements. While such broad anti-arbitration legislation is rare, many states have adopted statutes that seek to protect consumers, franchisees, and local firms by limiting the scope and application of arbitration and of forum selection clauses.

The Supreme Court held that the Alabama statute was preempted by the Federal Arbitration Act (FAA), and therefore the dispute was to be decided by arbitration rather than judicial trial. The Court reached this decision despite an extraordinary amicus brief filed by twenty state attorneys general, which argued that the Court should uphold the state statute. The Court also gave the broadest possible preemptive scope to the commerce power in the arbitration context. Few if any contracts have less connection with interstate commerce than a transaction between a small, locally owned business and an individual homeowner.

Doctor's Associates, Inc. v. Casarotto grew out of an arbitration term in a printed-form contract between the franchisor of the Subway sandwich shops and its Great Falls, Mass., franchisee.[4] The contract

---

[2] Prima Paint Corp. v. Flood & Conklin Manufacturing Co., 388 U.S. 395 (1967). The consequence of the separability doctrine is not to reject claims that an apparently binding agreement should not be enforced due to fraud in the inducement or other theories. Rather, these claims must be raised in arbitration, as provided in the contested agreement, rather than before a court.

[3] 513 U.S. 265 (1995).

[4] 517 U.S. 681 (1996).

specified that arbitration proceedings were to take place in Bridgeport, Conn.—the location of DAI's home office—under Connecticut law. A Montana statute expressly called for the enforcement of arbitration provisions in written contracts, but required that the arbitration term be written "in underlined capital letters on the first page of the contract."[5] None of the requirements were satisfied: the arbitration provision was on page nine, not capitalized, and not underlined.

The State of Montana, appearing to defend the statute, argued that the legislation was not hostile to arbitration because it merely channeled the use of the arbitration process in a manner that ensured an informed decision by persons signing arbitration agreements. This attempt to distinguish *Casarotto* from *Dobson* (the Alabama statute contained a general prohibition on the enforcement of pre-dispute arbitration provisions) was dispatched with ease by the Supreme Court. The principle adopted by the Court in *Casarotto* is that a state may not single out arbitration provisions for adverse treatment.

An additional factor which may have swayed the Court is that efforts to achieve the "informed consent" objective differ from state to state. In response to a question at oral argument by Justice Ginsburg—the author of the *Casarotto* opinion—counsel for DAI offered some of the following examples: New York requires 12-point type; California requires 10-point type; Iowa requires that arbitration terms be separately signed by the parties; and Texas requires the arbitration provision to be initialed by the lawyers for each party. To have adopted the Montana position would have undermined the important goal of promoting national uniformity in commercial laws and practices.

The *Casarotto* opinion is notable for its brevity, and for its thinly disguised irritation that some state courts are unwilling to heed the law of the land.[6] States are permitted to regulate arbitration provisions based on general principles of contract law. States may not, however, decide that the basic contract terms, such as price, quantity, quality, delivery, and credit, are fair enough to enforce, but that the arbitration term is not. This principle applies equally to legislative enactments and judge-made law.

That the Supreme Court saw *Casarotto* as an easy case, and dispatched it summarily, is the best evidence of the strength of the favorable view of arbitration by American courts. Indeed, the Supreme

---

[5] Mont. Code Ann. 27-5-114(4).
[6] "We have several times said...."; "It bears reiteration that...."; "Repeating our observation in Perry...."; "The Montana Supreme Court misread our Volt decision...."; "In *Allied-Bruce*, we restated...."

Court decided the case only after having returned it to the Montana Supreme Court for reconsideration in light of the *Dobson* decision. The Montana court failed to heed this hint to reverse its prior decision, whereupon the Supreme Court heard the case and reversed on the basis of *Dobson*.

2. The Arbitrability of Federal Statutory Claims

The scope of arbitrable claims had long been limited to those over which the parties had contractual power. These included statutory provisions subject to waiver, or default rules. Standard examples of areas that were excluded from arbitration included matters governed by civil rights, consumer protection, antitrust, and securities statutes. American law has taken a dramatic step away from the tradition that statutory claims are inarbitrable in the last decade, with arbitration now viewed as an alternative forum for raising statutory as well as contractual claims. This new approach originated with the Supreme Court's *Mitsubishi*[7] decision, in which the Court made the following statement:

By agreeing to arbitrate a statutory claim, a party does not forgo the substantive rights afforded by the statute; it only submits the resolution to an arbitral rather than a judicial forum. It trades the procedures and opportunity for review of the courtroom for the simplicity, informality, and expedition of arbitration. Nothing prevents a party from excluding statutory claims from the scope of an agreement to arbitrate.[8]

After *Mitsubishi*, other decisions followed that enforced pre-dispute arbitration provisions—commonly boilerplate terms in contracts of adhesion—in the context of securities fraud claims[9] and employment discrimination claims.[10] The securities area is of particular note because of the importance of the 1933 and 1934 Acts, and because the Court had to overrule a prior decision which explicitly declared that federal securities law claims could not be the subject of a pre-dispute arbitration agreement.[11] The practical consequence of the securities decisions is that all customer-broker disputes are now subject to arbitration.

The FAA calls for the arbitration of statutory claims because its general provisions contain no exemption for such claims. Of course,

---

[7] Mitsubishi Motors Corp. v. Soler Chrysler-Plymouth, Inc., 473 U.S. 614, 627 (1985).
[8] *Id.*
[9] Shearson/American Express, Inc. v. McMahon, 482 U.S. 220 (1987); Rodriguez de Quijas v. Shearson, Inc., 490 U.S. 477 (1989).
[10] Gilmer v. Interstate/Johnson Lane Corp. 500 U.S. 20 (1991).
[11] Wilko v. Swan, 346 U.S. 427 (1953).

Congress has the power to specifically provide that specified claims are inarbitrable.[12] The burden of demonstrating such an intention is a heavy one, and it rests with the party resisting arbitration. To meet this burden, the moving party must show, based on the text or legislative history of a statute that Congress affirmatively intended to preclude the waiver of a judicial forum.

The decisions that enforce contract provisions mandating the arbitration of claims arising under federal statutes result in the arbitration of more claims, and the proceedings are more complex. If closer and more law-oriented judicial review is to take place, such proceedings may also require the arbitrators—many of whom are not lawyers—to apply specific statutes, potentially followed by some level of serious judicial review to ensure that the arbitration did not deprive a party of substantive statutory rights. This, in turn, would necessitate the creation of an arbitration record, perhaps even a full transcript of the proceedings, and a reasoned written opinion with findings of fact and conclusions of law. This approach, if taken seriously, would fundamentally alter the very nature and practice of arbitration as we know it.

3. Statutory Rights and Arbitration Remedies

The power of arbitrators to fashion remedies appropriate to the situation is extremely broad. This power is further enhanced by the fact that judicial review of arbitration awards is extremely limited under the FAA. Here, however, we examine the converse situation, where a party seeks judicial review because the arbitrator underutilized his or her remedial authority by failing to award relief mandated by an applicable statute.

Attempts to limit damages or other relief in an arbitration agreement, when such relief is specified by statute, will bind the arbitrators to allow a judicial trial of some or all of the issues in dispute between the parties. In *Paladino v. Avnet Computer Technologies*, the Court refused to compel arbitration of an employment discrimination claim because the agreement allowed only contract damages, while Title VII specifically provides for back pay, reinstatement, and other relief not permitted under the agreement.[13] Many other federal and state statutes include specific provisions regarding recoverable damages, other monies associated with

---

[12] *See for example* Vessel Owners Liability Act, 46 U.S.C.App. § 183c, *discussed in* Carnival Cruise Lines, Inc. v. Shute, 499 U.S. 585 (1991).

[13] 134 F.3d 1054 (11th Cir. 1998).

making a claim, and attorneys' fees. While the FAA often preempts state law that would preclude arbitration, the FAA does not change the substantive state law to be applied by the arbitrators.

Numerous federal and state statutes mandate the recovery of attorneys' fees by a prevailing party. In Texas, for example, the awarding of attorneys' fees is specified in a variety of cases, including the breach of "an oral or written contract."[14] The tension between honoring the twin goals of (1) ensuring that statutory remedies are in fact awarded to prevailing parties, and (2) the limited judicial review of arbitration awards mandated by the New York Convention and the FAA, can be seen in *DiRussa v. Dean Witter Reynolds*.[15] DiRussa brought a successful claim under the Age Discrimination in Employment Act (ADEA). The ADEA provides for the recovery of attorneys' fees by a prevailing party, but the arbitrators did not award such fees to DiRussa.

The arbitration award specified that the claimant sought attorney's fees pursuant to the ADEA. Nevertheless, the Second Circuit confirmed the arbitration award. The court observed that knowing the law is a "daunting task," even for judges, and that while DiRussa admittedly sought attorney's fees under the ADEA, she had failed to inform the arbitrators that the ADEA required the award of attorney's fees. Accordingly, the decision of the arbitrators was not in manifest disregard of the law, and did not violate public policy, so the court confirmed the arbitration award.

The Second Circuit adopted this approach because it saw a decision in favor of DiRussa as presenting a serious slippery-slope problem. However innocent DiRussa's argument seems on its face, it could allow a court to vacate an arbitration award any time it disagreed with the arbitrator's interpretation of federal statutory law.[16]

One might respond that the arbitrators did not "interpret" the ADEA, but simply failed to award the attorney's fees required by the statute. Even if the Second Circuit overstated the danger of a decision on behalf of DiRussa, the court is clearly right in recognizing the fundamental tension between enforcement of full statutory rights and limited judicial review of arbitration awards. We are confident in predicting that the courts will have many more opportunities to address this dilemma.[17]

---

[14] Tex. Civ. Proc. & Rem. Code § 38.001(8). This provision "shall be liberally construed to promote its underlying purposes." *Id.* at § 38.005.
[15] 121 F.3d 818 (2d Cir. 1997).
[16] Cadence Design Sys., Inc. v. Avant Corp., 125 F.3d 825 (9th Cir. 1997).
[17] *See* Philip McConnaughay, *The Risks and Virtues of Lawlessness: A 'Second Look' at International Commercial Arbitration*, 93 Nw. L. Rev. 453 (1999)

4. Choice of Law and Choice of Forum Provisions

Contractual choice of forum[18] provisions traditionally were not enforced by American courts. The demise of this approach can be traced directly to the 1972 Supreme Court decision in *M/S Bremen v. Zapata Off-Shore Company* (Bremen).[19] The underlying contract was for the German company Bremen to tow an ocean-going drilling rig owned by Zapata from the Gulf of Mexico to the Adriatic Sea, near Italy. The contract included a judicial forum-selection clause-not an arbitration provision—specifying that any disputes were to be heard in London. The rig was damaged during a storm, and then taken into a Florida port per Zapata's instructions. Zapata brought suit in a Florida federal court, seeking damages of $3.5 million.

The Supreme Court recognized that forum-selection clauses have not been favored by American courts, but proceeded to apply the forum selection provision agreed to by the parties on these facts.[20] The Court noted that this case presented a clearly international transaction between two large firms, one American and one foreign, with specialized expertise. A single transaction was contemplated, and not a purchase or sale in the ordinary course of business where form contracts are commonly used. Furthermore, the transaction contemplated that during the course of performing the contract the rig would pass through international waters and the territorial waters of several nations. Finally, enforcing the forum selection provision promoted the intention of the parties to the contract by preventing either one from obtaining a "home court" advantage. The Court recognized that wider policy issues were implicated:

> The expansion of American business and industry will hardly be encouraged if, notwithstanding solemn contracts, we insist on a parochial concept that all disputes must be resolved under our laws and in our courts. [Such an approach] would be a heavy hand indeed on the future development of international commercial dealings by Americans. We cannot have trade and

---

[18] Arbitration terms are sometimes regarded as a type of choice of forum provision, but for present purposes choice of forum refers exclusively to the place where an adjudicatory proceeding, whether trial or arbitration, takes place

[19] 407 U.S. 1 (1972)

[20] Strictly speaking, the only question before the court was whether the Florida suit should be dismissed because of the forum selection term, and not the enforcement thereof

commerce in world markets and international waters exclusively on our terms, governed by our laws and resolved in our courts.[21]

Zapata's desire for an American forum was result oriented, as opposed to manifesting a concern about convenience. The contract included a limitation of remedies provision that made the owner responsible for any damage to the rig during transportation-even if caused by the negligence of the towing company. The limitation of remedy term would be enforced under English law, while it probably would not have been enforced under American law.

The next important forum selection decision, *Carnival Cruise Lines, Inc. v. Shute*,[22] also was a court rather than an arbitration case. Mr. and Mrs. Shute, who lived in the state of Washington, purchased passage for a cruise from Carnival, a major operator of cruise ships headquartered in Miami. Most of Carnival's cruises begin (and end) in Florida, but the cruise purchased by the Shutes started and ended in Los Angeles. Mrs. Shute was injured in a shipboard "slip and fall" accident, whereupon she brought suit in a Washington court. Carnival sought dismissal on the basis of a provision in the contract of passage which specified that all disputes incident to the contract were to be litigated in the state of Florida.

The contract did not provide for arbitration, because the Limitation of Vessel Owners Liability Act prohibited the use of such a provision. It specifies that a claimant is entitled "to a trial by court of competent jurisdiction" on the question of liability.[23] The primary purpose of the Act was to prohibit owners of vessels from limiting their tort liability to passengers.[24]

It was apparent to the Supreme Court, as well as to both of the litigants, that *Shute* was a domestic version of the *Bremen* case, but with a consumer instead of a commercial plaintiff. The Court enforced the forum selection term in the contract, as drafted by Carnival, and required the parties to litigate their dispute in Florida. The dissenting opinion of Justice Stevens highlighted the issues.

---

[21] *Bremen*, 407 U.S. at 24-25
[22] 499 U.S. 585 (1991)
[23] 46 U.S.C.App. § 183c(2); 49 Stat. 1480 (1936).
[24] The act did not address the use of forum selection clauses, but that may have been because they were so clearly unenforceable at the time. The major practice at which the act was aimed was disclaimers of liability, an approach that precluded any need for owners to specify a forum.

Stevens argued against enforcement of the forum clause because of the factual differences from *Bremen*. Instead of a contract between two expert parties, the contract in *Shute* was between a merchant and a consumer. Instead of a negotiated agreement, the *Shute* contract was a form document, with the forum selection clause found in the eighth of twenty-five small-print paragraphs appended to a ticket that was not delivered until after payment by the purchaser. While planning for the processing of a liability claim is a matter of real importance in hauling an oil rig thousands of miles across an ocean, forum selection in the event of a legal claim arising is not even a peripheral consideration in the purchase of a vacation cruise. Review of contracts by counsel is the norm for businesses, but not for consumers. Both parties in *Shute* were American, while a major justification for the Bremen decision was that the transaction was international. Bremen resulted in sending the parties to a mutually convenient neutral forum, while the result in *Shute* allowed one of the parties to dictate both the forum and the applicable law.

The Court recognized the factual differences between *Bremen* and *Shute* but still enforced the forum selection term, finding it to be reasonable. Not all contracts of adhesion are unenforceable-only those that are unreasonable. The Court noted two benefits that arise from a uniform forum selection term. (1) In the case of an event that gives rise to multiple claims—e.g., cancellation of a cruise, late return of a cruise, food poisoning, or other event that causes injury to multiple passengers, litigation in a single location promotes judicial economy and avoids the risk of inconsistent decisions in trials growing out of common facts. This benefit, however, apparently accrues to Carnival rather than its customers. Indeed, the inconvenience of litigating in several places might cause Carnival to make more generous settlements with suing customers. The Court responded with a resort to economic theory: forum selection clauses are beneficial to Carnival, which in turn achieves cost savings that are passed on to customers in the form of reduced fares. No evidence was adduced in support of this proposition: it simply "stands to reason." (2) The second benefit is "the salutary effect of dispelling any confusion about where suits arising from the contract must be brought and defended."[25] It is difficult to see how these "benefits" will accrue to plaintiffs who sue Carnival. The Court refers to the expense of pretrial motions, but the costs associated with such a motion in a Washington court would fall almost entirely on Carnival. And, this problem would

---

[25] 499 U.S. at 593-594.

arise only if Carnival objected to jurisdiction in Washington, presumably on the questionable theory that it does not do business in Washington.

Carnival chose a single forum to avoid the costs associated with claims in varied and far-flung jurisdictions. This would apply particularly where multiple claims arose from a single event. The Miami area was chosen because Carnival's head office, its legal department, and the passenger claims processing personnel are all located there. Also it is the point of origin and completion for most Carnival cruises. The same forum selection provision was used in all customer contracts, without regard to the residence of the customer or the itinerary of the cruise.[26]

Finally, the Court noted that forum selection clauses are subject to "judicial scrutiny for fundamental fairness." Forum selection terms are therefore enforced unless they are fundamentally unfair. Thus, the burden of proof is on the party that claims unfairness, and that burden is a heavy one.

One might suppose that the reach of the *Shute* decision at least is limited to choice of forum provisions within the United States, but the Second Circuit has gone so far as to enforce a choice of forum provision in a cruise case that sent a New York resident to litigate in Athens, Greece.[27] Even the widely admired Judge Guido Calabresi, although troubled, concurred: "Were we writing on a clean slate, I would want to examine the issue with great care. However, existing case law is as the majority describes it [so] the result reached is appropriate."[28]

Choice of law provisions are common in arbitration contracts, but the particular law chosen is of little substantive importance. The primary, if not the sole objective, is to have all disputes governed by the law of a single jurisdiction, rather than seeking a strategic advantage by selecting the law of a particular jurisdiction. Contract and commercial law is largely the same throughout the U.S. The best evidence is provided by DAI-the franchisor of the Subway shops-because when it moved its headquarters from Connecticut to Florida it changed the choice of law provision in its contracts to incorporate Florida law instead of Connecticut law.

---

[26] Carnival Cruise Lines, Inc. v. Superior Court, 234 Cal.App.3d 1019, 286 Cal.Rptr. 323 (1991) (sworn declaration of Lawrence D. Wilson, general counsel of Carnival Cruise lines). There is no reason to disbelieve this admittedly self-serving rationale; it is consistent with rational firm maximizer theory.

[27] Effron v. Sun Cruise Lines, Inc., 67 F.3d 7 (2d Cir. 1995).

[28] *Supra*, note 11.

5. *Explosion in Consumer and Employment Arbitration*

The common characteristic among consumers and employees is that they are the general public, and constitute the vast majority of the populace that, before the 1990s, was not subject to any regime of binding arbitration.[29] There was, however, an explosion of growth in arbitration in employment and consumer arbitration during the last decade.

A. *Consumer Arbitration*

Today, arbitration provisions are found everywhere in the world of consumer transactions. For example, the documentation accompanying a Gateway computer specifies that any disputes will be settled by arbitration in Chicago, based on South Dakota law.[30] The contests sponsored by McDonald's fast food restaurants call for arbitration of disputes. Contracts for the provision of pest control services commonly call for arbitration to settle all disputes.[31] Arbitration provisions are common in first-party insurance claims (i.e., claims by an insured against an insurer), and in a growing number of bank-customer agreements.[32]

Arbitration increasingly governs relationships in the medical field: between physician and patient; physician and provider organization; and provider organization and patients (often indirectly, through the employer that purchases health coverage on behalf of its employees).[33] Contracts between attorneys and their clients often provide for arbitration, both for malpractice claims and fee disputes, despite concern about whether this approach is consistent with the rules of professional

---

[29] Unionized workers were part of an important arbitration system, but as members of a group rather than as individuals.

[30] Gateway formerly required ICC arbitration, which involved the advance payment of $4,000 (one half of which was nonrefundable), and payment of the loser's attorney's fees. This approach was held to be unconscionable in Brower vs. Gateway 2000, Inc., 676 N.Y.S2d 569 (1988).

[31] *See for example* Allied-Bruce Terminex Co., Inc. v. Kaplan, 465 U.S. 1 (1984); Terminex Int'l Co. v. Stabbs 930 S.W.2d 345 (Ark. 1996).

[32] Mark E. Budnitz, *Arbitration of Disputes Between Customers and Financial Institutions: A Serious Threat to Consumer Protection*, 10 OHIO ST. J. DISP. RES. 267 (1995).

[33] *See for example* Engalla v. Permanente Medical Group, 938 P.2d 903 (Cal. 1997); Buraczynski v. Eyring, 919 S.W.2d 314 (Tenn. 1996); Sosa v. Paulos, 924 P.2d 357 (Utah 1996).

responsibility.[34] The academic literature is mostly critical of the use of arbitration provisions by attorneys and physicians.[35]

The assessment of the increase in use of consumer arbitration has been mixed. One critic states that "The Supreme Court has created a monster" by enforcing consumer arbitration provisions in contracts of adhesion, and by preempting state consumer protection laws that limited the use or enforcement of such provisions.[36] Whatever one thinks of the inclusion of arbitration provisions in consumer contracts, it is clear that this trend, which began in the 1990s, has not yet run its course.

B. *Employment Arbitration*

The term "employment," as used here, is limited to workers who are not covered by a collective bargaining agreement. Under the "employment-at-will" doctrine, recognized throughout the U.S., an employer could change the terms and conditions of employment at any time for any reason—or for no reason whatsoever. In this legal environment, employers naturally sought to avoid binding commitments to employees, and they certainly were not interested in arbitration of workplace disputes. When a party has the power to make decisions unilaterally, shifting those decisions to a neutral third party for a binding determination is hardly an attractive option.

The calculus of employer interests changed with the enactment of federal and state statutes which prohibited adverse action against an employee based on status factors such as race, sex, age, disability, and similar categories. The effect of this legislation was to limit the employment-at-will doctrine, and to provide employees with a basis to get their case before a jury. In the union context, it was clear that a CBA could not mandate the arbitration of statutory-as opposed to contractual-claims.[37]

---

[34] *See* Powers v. Dickson, Carlson & Campillo, 63 Cal.Rptr.2d 261 (Cal.App. 1997); Miller v. Purvis, 921 P.2d 610 (Alaska 1996).

[35] *See for example* Mark G. Anderson, *Arbitration Clauses in Retainer Agreements: A Lawyer's License to Exploit the Client*, 1992 J. DISP. RES. 341; Lester Brickman, *Attorney-Client Fee Arbitration: A Dissenting View*, 1990 UTAH L. REV. 277; Jean Fleming Powers, Ethical Implications of *Attorneys Requiring Clients to Submit Malpractice Claims to ADR*, 38 S. TEXAS L. REV. 625 (1997).

[36] David S. Schwartz, *Enforcing Small Print to Protect Big Business: Employee and Consumer Rights Claims in an Age of Compelled Arbitration*, 1997 WISC. L. REV. 33.

[37] Alexander v. Gardner-Denver Co., 415 U.S. 36 (1974). More recent developments are discussed in Ronald Turner, Employment Discrimination, Labor and Employment

INTRODUCTION TO ARBITRATION

Then, in its 1991 *Gilmer* decision, the Supreme Court held that contract terms calling for the arbitration of statutory claims by individual employees were enforceable.[38] In response, many employers began to place arbitration provisions in employment contracts.[39] Sometimes, the availability of arbitration tilted the balance of employer interests towards entering serious contracts with their employees for the first time.

Hooters of America v. Phillips provides an example of a one-sided, "egregiously unfair" employee arbitration provision.[40] The plan was created entirely by Hooters, which could change the plan unilaterally (or even abolish it) upon 30 days' notice. Other one-sided provisions included the following:

- Three arbitrators were required for all claims. This was a major expense for employees.

- While each party selected one arbitrator, the third one had to come from a list created by the employer.

- The employee's initial claim had to specify the nature of the claim, and the specific acts or omissions that would support the claim, but no answer was required by Hooters.

- The employer, but not the employee, was entitled to move for summary judgment prior to the hearing.

- The employer, but not the employee, was entitled to make a formal record of the arbitration proceeding.

- Rights to judicial review were provided on behalf of the employer but not the employee.[41]

The court refused to enforce what it characterized as an "aberrational system"... of "warped rules"; a "sham system unworthy even of the name of arbitration."[42] Among the legal bases for this outcome were

---

Arbitration and the Case Against Union Waiver of the Individual Worker's Statutory Right to a Judicial Forum, 49 EMORY L.J. 135 (2000).

[38] Gilmer v. Interstate/Johnson Lane Corp., 500 U.S. 20 (1991).

[39] *Gilmer* and its aftermath are examined in Geraldine S. Moohr, *Arbitration and the Goals of Employment Discrimination Law*, 56 WASH. & LEE L. REV. 395 (1999).

[40] 173 F.3d 933 (4th Cir. 1999).

[41] The employee would retain such appeal rights as provided by statute, but this is one more instance of *Hooter's* rules being one-sided.

[42] *Supra*, note 38.

unconscionability, public policy, and the failure to carry out a contract provision in good faith.[43]

In practice, the most realistic source of leadership in the development of standards for consumer and employment arbitration is a professional organization with an interest in the particular field. To date, the most notable examples of such standards are the due process protocols for consumer and employment arbitration developed by the American Arbitration Association.[44] These standards have a real impact because they set the baseline for what classes of disputes will be arbitrated by the AAA. Umbrella organizations with an interest in the well-being of arbitration provide the best hope for the development of fair and meaningful standards for different types of arbitration.

6. RUAA on Uniform State Laws

In 1995, the National Conference of Commissioners on Uniform State Laws (NCCUSL) appointed a study committee and then a drafting body to consider and prepare a revision of the Uniform Arbitration Act (UAA), adopted by the Conference in 1955. The UAA has been enacted in thirty-five states, and nearly all of the other states have adopted a similar statute.

The FAA has not been revised since its enactment in 1925, and the substantive provisions of the UAA largely tracked the FAA-with changes to reflect that it was state legislation.

Thus, the work on a revised uniform (state) arbitration act (RUAA) has provided a forum for the first systematic rethinking of arbitration legislation and practice since the enactment of modern arbitration statutes in the 1920s-starting with the New York Arbitration Act adopted in 1920 that became the model for the FAA. The many discussion papers and drafts of the RUAA have examined every issue of consequence related to arbitration law and practice in the U.S.

The goals of the RUAA are to make arbitration an efficient, expeditious, and economical process that is fair to the parties, and produces finality, i.e., very limited judicial review of arbitral awards. Both the FAA and UAA are bare-bones statutes. The major innovation in the RUAA is to adopt provisions relating to a number of issues not

---

[43] *See* Restatement (Second) of Contracts, § 205.
[44] American Arbitration Association, A Due Process Protocol for Mediation and Arbitration of Consumer Disputes (1998); Due Process Protocol for Mediation and Arbitration of Statutory Disputes Arising Out of the Employment Relationship (1995)

already covered in arbitration statutes. These include the following (the RUAA section is provided in parenthesis):

- Giving and receiving notice in arbitration proceedings (2).
- Specification of non-waivable RUAA provisions (4).
- Arbitrability: forum (court or arbitrator) and criteria (6).
- Provisional remedies, including proper forum (8).
- Process for initiating an arbitration proceeding (9).
- Consolidation of arbitration proceedings (10).
- Arbitrator disclosures regarding potential conflicts (12).
- Immunity for arbitrators and arbitral organizations (14).
- Competency of arbitrators to testify regarding proceedings (14).
- Powers of arbitrator to manage arbitration process (15):
    a) prehearing conferences;
    b) discovery and depositions;
    c) protective orders; and
    d) motions for summary disposition.
- Subpoena of witnesses outside state of arbitration (17).
- Judicial enforcement of pre-award arbitral rulings (18).
- Arbitration remedies and related awards (21):
    a) punitive damages, other exemplary relief;
    b) attorneys' fees (by statute or contract);
    c) fees and expenses of arbitrators; and
    d) relief "just and appropriate under the circumstances."
- Vacatur of award for arbitrator nondisclosure (23, 12).

The final draft of the RUAA was "approved and recommended for enactment in all the states" by the NCCUSL on Aug. 9, 2000 at its annual meeting, "subject to revision by the Committee on Style."[45] It

---

[45] The text of the RUAA, plus drafts and background materials are available from the NCCUSL Web site. <http://www.nccusl.org>.

remains to be seen whether the RUAA will be widely adopted by the states. The following are some reasons for concern:

- State legislatures may decide that the status quo-UAA plus case law-adequately meets present needs.

- The RUAA does not address any burning problems that require a legislative solution, so there is little incentive for a legislator to expend political capital to promote the RUAA.

- Action taken at the state level may prove to be ineffective due to the preemptive effect of federal arbitration law.

- The RUAA does not address the use of arbitration provisions in contracts of adhesion, so the RUAA is likely to be opposed (and certainly not actively supported) by consumer and employee interests.

The RUAA thus faces the dual risks of legislative inaction in some states, and the enactment of an RUAA that includes non-uniform provisions in others. If the RUAA—without major amendments—does not replace the UAA in most states, the end result of the RUAA process effort could be to undermine the existing uniformity of state arbitration law.

7. Arbitration Developments Outside the U.S.

The New York Convention on the Recognition and Enforcement of Arbitration Awards has now been adopted in over 120 countries. Therefore, the international recognition of foreign arbitration agreements and awards is close to universal.[46] The growth in multinational commercial arbitration during the 1990s was less striking than the parallel development in the U.S., but that is largely because arbitration was already so well-established on the international scene.

The United Nations Commission on International Trade Law (UNCITRAL) promulgated a Model Law on International Commercial Arbitration that has been adopted during the '90s by about thirty-five

---

[46] 21 U.S.T. 2517 (1970). The Convention is examined at book length in Albert Jan van der Berg, THE NEW YORK ARBITRATION CONVENTION OF 1958 (Kluwer, 1981). The American legislation implementing the New York Convention is found at 9 U.S.C. §§ 201 et seq.

jurisdictions[47]-Singapore (1994), Hong Kong (1990, amended in 1996), and Brazil (1996) are among them.[48] Brazil is of particular significance, both because of its economic importance and because this was the first pro-arbitration statute enacted in Brazil.[49] In Canada, the Model Law has been adopted at the provincial rather than the national level. Even in those nations that explicitly decided not to adopt the Model Law, consideration of the UNCITRAL approach has influenced the shape and contents of the non-uniform legislation that was enacted. Sweden adopted a new arbitration act in 1999.[50] This is an important development because Stockholm is a commonly used situs for arbitration proceedings. Taiwan also adopted a new arbitration law recently.[51]

Perhaps the most important foreign legislative development is the enactment of the English Arbitration Act in 1996.[52] While some substantive changes were adopted, the main impact of this Act was to place together in one clear arbitration statute a body of rules and requirements that previously were scattered across several different laws.

The U.S. Supreme Court decided only one international arbitration case during the 1990s, *Vimar Seguros y Reaseguros, S.A. v. M/V Sky Reefer*.[53] This decision reflects a favorable disposition towards international arbitration, even where it is contrary to the interests of American parties. In *Sky Reefer*, the Court upheld a provision in a maritime contract calling for arbitration in Tokyo. The underlying contract was for the shipment of citrus fruit from Morocco to Massachusetts on a refrigerated ship time-chartered to a Japanese

---

[47] *See* Howard M. Holtzmann & Joseph E. Neuhaus, A Guide to the UNCITRAL Model Law on International Commercial Arbitration: Legislative History and Commentary (Kluwer, 1989).

[48] Jan K. Schaefer, *Borrowing and Cross-Fertilizing Arbitration Laws: Comparative Overview of the Development of Hong Kong and Singapore Legislation for International Commercial Arbitration*, 16:4 INT'L COMM. ARB. 41 (1999). Cristina Schwansee Romano, *The 1996 Brazilian Commercial Arbitration Law*, 5 ANN. SURV. INT'L & ARBITRATION LAW (SPRING 1999).

[49] Brazil also became a party to the Panama Convention in 1996; it is not a signatory of the New York Convention.

[50] Sigvard Jarvin & Briana Young, *A New Arbitration Regime in Sweden: The Swedish Arbitration Act 1999 and the Rules of the Stockholm Chamber of Commerce*, VOL. 16, NO. 3, J. INT'L ARB. 89 (1999).

[51] Catherine Li, *The New Arbitration Law of Taiwan—Up to International Level?*," 16:3, J. INT'L ARB. AT 127 (1999).

[52] *See* Adam Samuel, *Arbitration Statutes in England and the USA*, ARB. & DISP. RES. J. at 2 (March 1999).

[53] 515 U.S. 528, 115 S. Ct. 2322 (1995).

company by its owner, a Panamanian corporation. Thousands of boxes of fruit were damaged, with alleged losses running in excess of $1 million. Vimar Seguros, the insurer of the cargo, paid some $733,000 and so became a claimant by subrogation.

Unlike an ordinary international commercial contract, where the arbitration provision would clearly be enforced,[54] the *Sky Reefer* facts brought into play the Carriage of Goods by Sea Act (COGSA).[55] Section 3(8) of COGSA provides:

> Any [provision] in a contract of carriage relieving the carrier or the ship from liability for loss or damage to or in connection with the goods, arising from negligence, fault, or failure in the duties or obligations provided in this section, or lessening such liability otherwise than as provided in this article, shall be null and void and of no effect.

The Supreme Court ruled that this provision was limited to the lessening of specific liability as provided by the Act, but did not address the means of enforcing such liability.[56] Put another way, section 3(8) denies enforcement to substantive provisions that limit carrier liability, but it does not apply to the procedural matter of the forum where liability is determined. Lessening of liability simply did not encompass "increases in the transaction costs of litigation."

It should be noted that COGSA litigation commonly is insurer-driven. The parties are sophisticated businesses that purchase insurance as a matter of course, and the real parties in interest often are the insurance carriers. Even a critic of the *Sky Reefer* decision admitted that the decrease in domestic-cargo litigation is likely to result in lower freight rates.[57] ADR supporters refer to this as a "win-win" situation.

---

[54] The leading case is Mitsubishi Motors Corp. v. Soler Chrysler-Plymouth, Inc., 473 U.S. 614 (1985).

[55] 46 U.S.C.App. §§ 1300 et seq.

[56] The *Sky Reefer* decision rejected the established law regarding the meaning of section 3(8). The leading case was Indussa Corp. v S.S. Ranborg, 377 F.2d 200 (2d Cir. 1967), a unanimous, en banc decision by the 2nd Circuit court of appeals, with the opinion written by Judge Henry Friendly. Subsequent Court of appeals decisions, without exception, followed Indussa. In sum, the *Sky Reefer* plaintiffs, who sought to litigate before a U.S. court rather than arbitrate in Tokyo, could hardly have asked for a stronger or better established leading case and subsequent set of consistent precedents.

[57] Charles M. Davis, *Sky Reefer: Foreign Arbitration and Litigation under COGSA*, 8 U.S.F. MARITIME L.J. 73, 88 (1995).

8. Dominance of Securities Arbitration in Case Law

Most disputes get settled short of the filing of a claim with a court or arbitrator. In addition, many of the disputes that do get submitted for arbitration, like most lawsuits, are settled prior to trial.[58] Disputes between brokers and their customers, however, are different. Securities claims typically do not get resolved short of a final determination by the arbitrators, because all settlements become part of the brokerage firm's record and the individual brokers involved. Therefore, more is at stake than just money. This concern is not unique to brokers; considerations related to professional reputation also explain the relatively low percentage of settlements in malpractice claims against physicians and attorneys.

Securities arbitration, unlike most other arbitrations, does not provide the parties with a confidential adjudication process. In these circumstances, far more securities claims make their way to the courts than do other types of arbitration. By way of comparison, far more construction disputes than securities disputes are governed by arbitration provisions, yet nearly all construction disputes that are subject to arbitration are terminated without resort to the courts. Most construction disputes are settled without a request for arbitration being filed; where there is a filing, most cases are settled, and of those disputes that proceed to a final arbitration decision, few are appealed to the courts. Securities disputes also generate a far higher proportion of judicial proceedings related to arbitrability and interlocutory appeals than construction or other common types of arbitration.

Securities cases tend to dominate the case law of arbitration. For better or worse, the law of arbitration is being formed in the crucible of disputes between securities brokers and their customers. Does this deform the path of the law of arbitration? Should arbitration law developed in the context of securities disputes be modified for other types of arbitration? Such questions are worthy of reflection, and the dominance of securities cases in judicial decisions on arbitration bears watching.

9. Expanded Judicial Review of Arbitration Awards by Contract

Arbitration proceeded for many decades with judicial review based exclusively on the standards specified in the FAA. It was only during the

---

[58] *See generally*, Mark Galanter & Mia Cahill, *Most Cases Settle: Judicial Promotion and Regulation of Settlement*, 46 STAN. L. REV. 1339 (1994).

1990s that the idea of expanded review at the behest of arbitration parties was even broached by the courts. The federal courts of appeals are split 2-2 on the validity of such "opt-in" review provisions.[59] The few state cases, all from intermediate level courts, are dubious about the opt-in review.[60]

Even the leading case that recognizes opt-in review, *Lapine Technology v. Kyocera*,[61] admits to substantial limitations on what parties can do by contract. In *Lapine*, a dispute arose between the contracting parties. It went to arbitration. The losing party sought enhanced judicial review, for errors of law or absence of substantial evidence, as provided by the arbitration term of the parties' contract. The three court of appeals judges produced three different opinions.

Judge Fernandez for the court allowed enhanced judicial review as consistent with the strong policy favoring arbitration, and of honoring party agreements. Judge Mayer, in dissent, adopted the principle that the parameters for judicial review are established in the FAA, and are not subject to variation by contract. Judge Kozinski, in voting to allow opt-in review, noted that he found the question "closer than most."

Opt-in review can impose major burdens on district courts, as is demonstrated by the situation in *Lapine*. The district court was not reviewing a completed arbitration process, but only the first part of a bifurcated decision process. Even that proceeding took four years, and produced thousands of exhibits and documents. Standard practice for arbitrators is to admit all proffered documents and exhibits into evidence, thereby producing an expansive body of material that is, as the district judge noted, "apparently unaided by the various modalities available to district courts to narrow issues and facilitate ultimate disposition...."[62]

If parties can require district courts to review the findings of fact and conclusions of law made by an arbitrator, widespread adoption of such review provisions would noticeably increase the workload of district courts. This is contrary to what is often stated to be a major systemic benefit of arbitration—the reduction in the workload of courts. Even

---

[59] Chicago Typographical Union v. Chicago Sun-Times, 935 F.2d 1501 (7th Cir. 1991) (opposes heightened review) (Posner); Gateway, Inc. v. MCI Corp., 64 F.3d 993 (5th Cir. 1995) (supports heightened review); UHC v. Computer Sciences, 148 F.3d 992 (8th Cir. 1998) (opposes heightened review).

[60] *See for example* Dick v. Dick, 534 N.W.2d 185 (Mich. App. 1994); Southshore & South Bend R.R. v. Northern Indiana Commuter Trans. Dist., 682 N.E.2d 156 (Ill. App. 1997), *rev'd* on other grounds, 703 N.E. 2d.7 (Ill. 1998).

[61] 130 F.3d 884 (9th Cir. 1997).

[62] 909 F.Supp. 697 (N.D.Cal. 1995).

more serious is the timing of judicial review. The FAA provides for rapid and summary review of arbitration awards. The rationale for the "streamlined procedure found in the FAA and other modern arbitration statutes," is that such review is so limited.[63] The FAA states that "any application" made pursuant to the FAA "shall be heard in the manner provided by law for the making and hearing of motions...."[64] Motions get heard promptly, while cases must queue up behind other civil proceedings not favored by statute.

Also, for defective awards, the parties almost always must start the arbitration process anew before a different arbitrator. Courts have a permanent existence, so an appellate tribunal usually can send a case back to the same trial court for review of facts, short of a full trial before a new judge. Arbitration, however, is an ad hoc process, with the power of the arbitrator ending with the issuance of a decision—*functus officio*.

Of the few decisions that permit the parties opt-in review, none have examined the consequences of the freedom-of-contract rationale. If the judicial review provisions of the FAA are only default rules, is freedom of contract a two-way street that permits parties to contract for less judicial review? Symmetry would seem to suggest an affirmative answer, as might the public policy favoring arbitration, but no court has adopted this approach. A plausible alternative is to treat the FAA as establishing a minimum level of required judicial review, but not prohibiting parties from agreeing to greater review. Such asymmetry is a reasonable approach for a legislature to adopt, but there is no basis for a court to assert that Congress so intended.[65]

If judicial review of arbitration awards can be expanded by contract, there should be limits to the exercise of this power. On this topic, Judge Kozinski offers this viewpoint:

> I would call the case differently if the agreement provided that the district court would review the award by flipping a coin or studying the entrails of a dead fowl.[66]

---

[63] Ian R. Macneil, Richard E. Speidel & Thomas J. Stipanowich, *Federal Arbitration Law* § 38.1.1 (1994).

[64] 9 U.S.C. § 6.

[65] Congress adopted an asymmetrical position regarding judicial review in the context of arbitrability disputes. An order that denies arbitration is immediately appealable, but an order that sends a dispute to arbitration is not appealable. *Compare* 9 U.S.C. § 16(a)(1) and 16(b).

[66] *Lapine*, 130 F.3d at 891.

This concession, however, does not address the scope of freedom of contract to craft opt-in review? One can imagine a considerable array of reasonable opt-in review provisions that are different from "findings of fact and conclusions of law," yet are far short of "flipping a coin or studying the entrails of dead fowl." Also, if opt-in district court review by contract is permitted under the FAA, why not also opt-in review standards for courts of appeals?

A bright line rule—review pursuant to the FAA provisions, either more or less—best follows the statute, and also is the most sensible approach for the courts. The charting of a different course should be left to the legislative branch of government.

As regards the RUAA drafting committee, "no issue produced more discussion or debate."[67] The text of the RUAA does not address opt-in review, but the matter is discussed in commentary. It is clear, however, that the drafters were opposed to opt-in review. They stated the issue as follows:

> [whether] the standard for judicial review of commercial arbitration awards is a matter of law properly determined by Congress ... or can the parties properly instruct the courts as to the standards for vacatur- even if they conflict with the standards set down in the FAA?[68]

The answer to that is surely no.

The RUAA drafters envisioned that opt-in review could "effectively eviscerate arbitration as a true alternative to traditional litigation."[69] An opt-in review provision could easily become standard, because a lawyer who failed to provide for opt-in review would face sharp questions from a losing client in arbitration.

Arbitrators, in turn, would be obliged to make written findings of fact and conclusions of law, otherwise heightened judicial review could not take place. Even transcripts—with the attendant costs—might become common. And, presence of opt-in review provisions "would virtually insure"[70] an appeal in most cases of consequence.

Given these concerns, the surprise is not that the RUAA omits an opt-in provision, but that it fails to prohibit it. Instead, the issue is left for

---

[67] *Id.*
[68] *Id.*
[69] *Id.*
[70] RUAA, reporter's notes to section 23.

development through future case law. One might wonder about the point of producing a model law that does not address the single most discussed and debated issue faced by the drafters. It may be because, politically, the drafting of an uncontroversial model act that will be widely adopted is preferable to one that tackles the most controversial issues and will not be widely adopted.

10. Judicial Vacatur of Arbitration Awards

The central message about judicial review of arbitration awards is that there are hardly any developments important enough to merit discussion. Courts throughout the United States have implemented the FAA and state arbitration statutes by confirming arbitration awards in virtually all circumstances, and doing so with dispatch.[71]

The scope of judicial review authorized by the FAA and the UAA is extraordinarily narrow.[72] That "the arbitrators exceeded their powers" is the only commonly employed substantive statutory basis for vacatur of arbitration awards.[73] Apart from matters related to the arbitration proceeding itself, the other basis for vacatur of an award is arbitrator bias. On occasion, attempts to vacate arbitration awards migrate to this category because a direct assault on an arbitration award has such a small chance of success.

Many state courts are even stricter than the federal courts in limiting the use of non-statutory review. To take the most important example, the California Supreme Court has ruled that decisions by arbitrators "are not generally reviewable for error of fact or law, whether or not such error appears on the face of the award and causes substantial injustice to the parties."[74] The Court read the California Arbitration Act as limiting judicial review to the bases enumerated in the statute, and to preclude any and all forms of non-statutory review.

Courts occasionally make use of two non-statutory categories to review arbitration awards: manifest disregard of the law and public policy. Manifest disregard could easily be incorporated into the statutory category of exceeded authority. This approach is endorsed by the Macneil Treatise.[75] At least eleven states have recognized manifest

---

[71] *See* Stephen L. Hayford, Law in *Disarray: Judicial Standards for Vacatur of Commercial Arbitration Awards*, 30 GA. L. REV. 731 (1996).

[72] *See* FAA, § 10; UAA, § 12.

[73] FAA §10(a)(4); UAA §12(a)(3).

[74] Moncharsh v. Heily & Blaise, 832 P.2d 889 (Cal. 1992).

[75] I. Macneil, R. Speidel & T. Stipanowich, Federal Arbitration Law § 40.5.1.3 (1994).

disregard as a non-statutory basis for vacating arbitration awards.[76] The judicial and academic discussion of manifest disregard is largely theoretical because hardly any decisions have used this doctrine to actually overturn an arbitration award.[77]

The public policy limitation on the enforcement of arbitration awards has an independent basis, being a specific application of a general public policy limitation on contract enforcement long recognized as part of the general law of contracts.[78] At the same time, courts are aware that most problem situations have already been provided for by the law, and that, if given much reign, a basis for decision as amorphous as public policy is antithetical to the rule of law. In practice, the public policy approach in review of arbitration remedies is extremely narrow and is limited to the health and safety context in workplace arbitration. What is required is no less than an "explicit, well-defined, and dominant public policy ... that specifically militates against the relief ordered by the arbitrator."[79]

Conclusion

The American courts, led by the U.S. Supreme Court and the Federal Courts of Appeals, have charted a greatly expanded role for arbitration—where called for by contract—in both the domestic and international contexts. At almost every opportunity, the federal courts have strongly favored arbitration. Earlier federal case law that limited arbitration has been swept away, and almost all state law attempts to restrict the use of arbitration, whether grounded in legislation or judicial decisions, have been preempted under the commerce clause.

American contract-drafting practices are changing rapidly in response to these developments, and use of arbitration terms in contracts is now highly attractive—at least from the perspective of drafting parties. Parties to contracts with arbitration terms can be confident that they will be readily enforced, including the attendant choice of law and choice of forum provisions.

---

[76] Hunter, Keith Industries, Inc. v. Piper Capital Management, Inc., 575 N.W.2d 850 (1998); Geissler v. Sanem, 949 P.2d 234 (Mont. 1997).

[77] Brad A. Galbraith, *Vacatur of Commercial Arbitration Awards in Federal Court: Contemplating the Use and Utility of the 'Manifest Disregard of the Law' Standard*, 27 IND. L. REV. 241 (1993).

[78] *See for example* Knapp, Chrystal & Prince, Problems in Contract Law: Cases and Materials 704-744 (1999); Restatement 2d of Contracts, § 178 199 (1979).

[79] Arizona Electric Power Coop., Inc. v. Berkeley, 59 F.3d 988 (9th Cir. 1995); Paine Webber, Inc. v. Argon, 49 F.3d 347 (8th Cir. 1995).

The move from judicial to arbitration trials eliminates a variety of process protections, most notably trial by jury. The distributional consequences of this shift might be seen as favoring the powerful over the weak. One law review article noted:

> Those who have been prejudiced by the Court's handiwork include many American consumers, patients, workers, investors, shopkeepers, shippers, and passengers. Those whose interests have been served include all those engaged in interstate or international commerce deploying their economic power to evade enforcement of their contractual duties, or the lash of state or federal commercial laws that are privately enforced.[80]

Furthermore, it is well known that forum selection and arbitration terms are form terms that usually are not negotiated—and that is true of commercial as well as consumer contracts.

A backlash to the astonishing growth in the use of arbitration during the 1990s—particularly in the context of employment and consumer disputes—is a real possibility, and to some extent is already taking place. Even staunch supporters of arbitration have raised concerns about one-sided arbitration provisions imposed on weaker parties by stronger parties, as evidenced by the provisions of the AAA's consumer and employment due process protocols.

Federal arbitration legislation is another possible basis for changing the law.[81] Several academic proposals to this effect have been suggested, but they are too broad to have a realistic chance of being adopted.[82] However, the ideas they contain can be incorporated in less sweeping proposals.

Sen. Charles Grassley (R-Iowa) has proposed a Motor Vehicle Franchise Contract Fairness Act—a targeted bill that would make pre-dispute arbitration agreements in motor vehicle franchise agreements

---

[80] Paul D. Carrington & Paul H. Haagen, *Contract and Jurisdiction*, 1996 SUP. CT. REV. 331, 333 (1997); Katherine van Wetzel Stone, *Rustic Justice: Community and Coercion under the Federal Arbitration Act*, 77 N.C.L. REV. 931 (1999).

[81] The statutory options at the state level are severely limited due to federal preemption.

[82] *See* Paul D. Carrington, *Regulating Dispute Resolution Provisions in Adhesion Contracts*, 35 HARV. J. LEGIS. 225 (1998) (Draft Employee, Local Franchisee, and Consumer Rights Enforcement Act); Richard E. Speidel, *Consumer Arbitration of Statutory Claims: Has Pre-dispute (Mandatory) Arbitration Outlived its Welcome?*, 40 ARIZ. L. REV. 106 (1998) (Draft Federal Consumer Arbitration Act).

voidable.[83] His co-sponsor, Sen. Russell Feingold (D-Wis.), however, would support considerably broader legislation. Rep. Mary Bono (R-Calif.) introduced a bill that would make binding arbitration provisions voidable in "sales and service contracts."[84] The Bono bill would require that when such disputes are arbitrated, the arbitrator must provide the parties with "a written explanation of the factual and legal basis for the award."[85]

Any member of Congress can introduce legislation, but getting a bill enacted into law is a vastly more difficult matter. The FAA has remained essentially unchanged since its enactment in 1925; the likelihood of any amendments being adopted is therefore modest. Enactment of new federal arbitration legislation appears unlikely at present, but the adoption of even a narrowly focused limitation on the enforcement of pre-dispute arbitration agreements would have a profound impact on arbitration, and would open the door to many other proposals. Once the principle that the FAA applies equally to all contracts was breached, further such laws would almost surely follow.

---

[83] S. 1020 (106th Cong. 1st Sess. 1999).
[84] H.R. 534 (106th Cong. 1st Sess. 1999). This proposal is limited to agreements between wholesalers and retailers, where the wholesaler authorizes the retailer to repair and service the product after sale to the ultimate consumer—retail buyers are not covered.
[85] Id.

III. The Fairness of Arbitration

Judging Arbitration

The Findings of Procedural Justice Research

by Deborah R. Hensler[*]

A rich vein of psychological data reveals that people often use their observations about the procedural characteristics of a dispute resolution mechanism to assess the likely fairness of its outcome. This article examines the principal findings of what has come to be known as "procedural justice" research and discusses the implications for arbitration in the context of adhesion contracts.

Styles of Adjudication

Procedural justice research began in a laboratory about twenty-five years ago when social psychologist John Thibaut and lawyer Laurens Walker teamed up to study individual preferences for different forms of dispute resolution.[1] Initially, they focused on preferences concerning different styles of adjudication. Using conventional psychological experimentation methods and student research subjects who played the role of the disputing parties, they investigated whether individuals preferred an adversarial process like the one used in the United States or an inquisitorial process similar to that used in many European courts for deciding criminal cases.[2]

---

[*] The author is the Judge John W. Ford Professor of Dispute Resolution, Stanford Law School, and Fellow, American Academy of Political and Social Sciences. She received her A.B. from City U. of New York and her Ph.D. from MIT. Hensler is the author of *Suppose It's Not True: Challenging Mediation Ideology*, 2002 JOURNAL OF DISPUTE RESOLUTION 81-99 (2002).

[1] Most of the publications that derive from this research were co-authored by Thibaut and Walker and their students. By convention, the research is usually attributed to the former, even when they do not appear as lead authors. I follow this convention.

[2] Laurens Walker, Stephen LaTour, E. Allan Lind & John Thibaut, *Reactions of Participants and Observers to Modes of Adjudication*, 4 J. APP. SOC. PSYCHOL. 295 (1974). In the experimental manipulation, the adversarial procedure allowed student subjects who were playing the role of criminal defendants to choose their attorneys (played by law students), who then presented evidence on their behalf to a "judge." In the inquisitorial procedure, a single attorney was assigned to present both prosecutorial and defense evidence to the "judge." *Id.* at 300

Thibaut and Walker found that subjects assigned the role of defendant perceived the adversarial procedure to be fairer than the inquisitorial approach. The researchers acknowledged that these results might reflect the cultural expectations of American students whose familiarity with adjudication was probably limited to media reports of adversarial-style proceedings. But unpublished data from a French study found a similar preference for adversarial procedures among Parisian students, controverting this cultural hypothesis.[3]

Thibaut and Walker's finding regarding the preference for adversarial procedures held true whether the "defendants" were judged innocent or guilty in the simulated procedure. The researchers interpreted the results to mean that individuals prefer procedures that allow them to control the process (such as where the parties' counsel examines and cross-examines witnesses), over procedures in which control of the process is ceded to a third party, as in an inquisitorial procedure (where the arbitrator or judge does the questioning).

Party Control

Follow-up research broadened the investigation to include preferences regarding control over decision making. The researchers discovered that while individuals preferred procedures that allowed them to maintain control of the process, they also preferred procedures that gave decision-making power to a neutral third party. Research subjects attached greater fairness to procedures that placed decision making in the hands of a neutral person over procedures that offered other combinations of control over process and decision making.[4] The researchers reasoned that these preferences reflected the belief that controlling the process accorded the subjects the best opportunity to present evidence favoring their position, while ceding control over the outcome offered the best opportunity to resolve the conflict with an outcome that reflected the relative weight of the evidence on each side.[5]

---

[3] *Id.* at 309. Later procedural justice research has found remarkably little variation in results across cultures

[4] Pauline Houlden, S. LaTour, L. Walker & J. Thibaut, *Preferences for Modes of Dispute Resolution as a Function of Process and Decision Control*, 14 J. EXPER. SOC. PSYCHOL. 13 (1978). In this line of experiments the researchers investigated subjects' preferences in a civil dispute for bilateral bargaining, mediation, the "moot" (which requires decision by consensus), arbitration and an autocratic procedure in which a third party controlled the process and outcome. *Id.* at 14.

[5] *Id.* at 16-17

Procedural Fairness

This research suggests that individuals involved in disputes are attentive to procedural characteristics and form judgments about procedural fairness based on the amount of control they have over the dispute resolution process and the outcome.

Just how much do they care about these procedural characteristics? Most judges and lawyers seem to believe that people caught up in a conflict care mainly about whether they win or lose. A person who wins, they reason, will be happy; a person who loses will be unhappy. Moreover some judges and lawyers seem to think that litigants who lose will conclude that the system that produced this outcome is unfair or illegitimate.

A second generation of procedural justice scholars, led by social psychologists Allan Lind and Tom Tyler, intensively investigated this question.[6] They consistently found that the degree of satisfaction with the legal process is a function of an individual's perception of the fairness of both the process and the outcome. Moreover, when individuals perceive the process to be fair, they are more likely to view the decision maker as legitimate and accept and comply with the decision, even if they believe the outcome is unfair.[7]

The findings that the process matters and that satisfaction is linked to assessment of the process and outcome are not limited to laboratory experiments. They have been replicated numerous times in studies of actual criminal defendants[8] and parties to civil disputes,[9] as well as in studies of participants in other transactions.[10]

---

[6] Lind was a student of Prof. Thibaut. For a review of this long line of research through the 1980s, see E. A. LIND & TOM TYLER, THE SOCIAL PSYCHOLOGY OF PROCEDURAL JUSTICE (Plenum 1988). More recent research is reviewed in T. Tyler & E.A. Lind, *Procedural Justice*, in Joseph Sanders & V. Lee Hamilton, eds., HANDBOOK OF JUSTICE RESEARCH IN LAW (Kluwer/Plenum 2001) (hereinafter, Tyler & Lind, 2001).

[7] Tyler & Lind, 2001, n. 6, *supra*, at 68-9.

[8] *See, e.g.*, J. Casper, R. Tyler & B. Fisher, *Procedural Justice in Felony Cases*, 22 Law & Soc. Rev. 483 (1988); T. Tyler, WHY PEOPLE OBEY THE LAW (Yale Univ. Press 1990).

[9] E.A. LIND et al., *In the Eye of the Beholder: Tort Litigants' Evaluations of their Experiences in the Civil Justice System*," 24 LAW & SOC. REV. 953 (1990) (hereinafter, Lind et al., 1990); E.A. Lind et al., *Individual and Corporate Dispute Resolution Using Procedural Fairness as a Decision Heuristic*, 38 ADMIN. SCI. QUART. 224 (1993) (hereinafter Lind et al., 1993).

[10] *See, e.g.*, R. Bies & S. Moag, *Interactional Justice: Communication Criteria of Fairness*, R. LEWICKI, M. BAZERMAN & B. SHEPPARD, eds., RESEARCH ON NEGOTIATION IN ORGANIZATIONS, VOL. 1 (JAI); E.A. LIND et al., *The Winding Road from Employee to*

Three Hypotheses

Procedural justice researchers have devoted considerable effort trying to explain why individuals care so much about the process of dispute resolution. Their laboratory and field research suggest these hypotheses:

(1) The nature of a dispute resolution process determines whether the parties have an opportunity to voice their needs and opinions; a greater opportunity for voice enhances the likelihood of obtaining a satisfactory outcome. (The "process control" or "voice" hypothesis.)

(2) The nature of the process indicates the standing or relationship of the parties to the social group and to authority; when fair procedures are provided, an individual's perception of his or her standing in society and relation to the larger group is positive. (The "relational" or "dignitary values" hypothesis.)

(3) Individuals understand that they may be exploited by the social group or an authority but lack the information or ability to assess whether such exploitation is occurring. As a shortcut for determining whether or not they should be concerned about such exploitation, they rely on their evaluation of the fairness of the process. (The "fairness heuristic" hypothesis.)

The voice hypothesis derives directly from Thibaut and Walker's original research, which stressed the importance of "process control" and suggested that individuals have an instrumental interest in this factor. One might hypothesize from this that individuals care about the process because they believe it shapes outcomes. But this hypothesis was disputed by later findings suggesting that individuals care about the process even when they can control the outcome themselves (as in mediation).[11] Conversely, Lind and his associates found that individuals prefer procedures that permit them to voice their opinions even when

---

Complainant, ADMIN. SCI. QUART. (in press). *See also* Robert Lane, *Procedural Goods in a Democracy: How One is Treated vs. What One Gets*, 2 SOC. JUST. RES. 177 (1988).
  These findings also are not limited to the United States, but have been replicated in studies conducted in Asia and Europe. E.A. Lind, *Procedural Justice and Culture: Evidence for Ubiquitous Process Concerns*, 15 ZEITSCHRIFT FUR RECHTSSOZIOLOGIE 24 (1994)

[11] TYLER & LIND, n. 6, *supra*, at 75.

they have been told that their opinions would have no effect on the outcome.[12]

Lind and Tyler developed the relational or dignitary values hypothesis as a substitute for the voice hypothesis. They reasoned that if an individual's concern about the process was not driven solely or primarily by the desire to ensure a favorable outcome, it might be the result of a more fundamental concern about the individual's standing in society. This hypothesis seemed consistent with the observation that individuals prefer dispute resolution procedures in which the parties have an equal opportunity to present their case, decision makers appear to give equal consideration to both sides, and the proceeding is conducted with decorum. To Lind and Tyler, giving "due process" to the participants to disputes was equivalent to recognizing their dignity as members of society.

In more recent research Lind returned to a more instrumental explanation of the individual's concern about the process. Drawing on the work of cognitive scientists, he posited that individuals frequently use intellectual shortcuts ("heuristics") to make judgments that would otherwise require an unreasonable or unattainable factual investigation. In many instances, Lind argued, individuals have no basis for assessing the fairness or appropriateness of the outcome of a dispute. Hence, they use characteristics of the process, which they are comfortable assessing for themselves, as a pragmatic substitute to decide whether to accept and comply with the outcome.[13] The fairness heuristic hypothesis is consistent with laboratory research suggesting that when individuals are given information to assess the fairness of the outcome prior to the dispute resolution process, they use that information, rather than process-related information, to assess the fairness of the ultimate result.[14]

Whether or not any of these (or any other) hypotheses is correct, it is a well-established fact that process matters and the perception of fairness

---

[12] E.A. LIND, R. KANFER & C. EARLY, *Voice, Control and Procedural Justice*, 59 J. PERSONALITY & SOC. PSYCHOL. 952 (1990). This result is troubling because it suggests that individuals could be manipulated to accept outcomes by providing them with a "voice" but no real control over the process

[13] LIND et al., 1993, n. 9, *supra*.

[14] K. VAN DE BOS, E.A. LIND, R. VERMUNT & H. WILKE, *How Do I Judge My Outcome When I Do Not Know the Outcome of Others? The Psychology of the Fair Process Effect*, 72 J. OF PERSONALITY & SOC. PSYCHOL. 1034-46 (1997).

of the process (rather than, for example, its cost) appears to matter most.[15]

"Real-World" Research

The theories reviewed above may explain the deep underpinnings of procedural justice concerns, but they do not focus on certain pragmatic aspects of the dispute resolution process that can be shaped by institutions and third-party neutrals. Laboratory research is limited in its ability to explore the relationship between procedural features and perceived procedural fairness because in experimental research, one or only a few variables are manipulated at a time, while others are held constant; this manipulation may encourage research subjects to give more attention to specific features than they would in the richer and more ambiguous real-world environment.

Moving into the real world, Lind, myself and others[16] compared how tort litigants described and evaluated three common court procedures (trial, judicial settlement conferences, and court-annexed nonbinding arbitration), which we compared with their evaluation of the process of unassisted negotiation. The information was gathered in 30-minute telephone interviews with plaintiffs and defendants in recently resolved tort cases filed in three mid-Atlantic region suburban courts.

In the first court, litigants could reach trial within six months of the case being declared ready by the attorneys, meaning that trial was a viable alternative to settlement (at least with regard to timing). In the second court, trial was also available within a relative short period of time, but nonbinding court-annexed arbitration was mandated as a precondition for securing a place on the trial calendar. In this process, brief arbitration hearings were held in jury deliberation rooms before a panel of three arbitrators who were paid modest honoraria, the arbitrators delivered their decision in writing without findings of fact or law, and the parties were free to accept or reject that decision. In the third court, which had fairly serious congestion problems, it could take up to three

---

[15] Lind et al. investigated the relative effects of time to disposition, costs and procedural fairness on tort litigants' satisfaction with dispute resolution and the courts. Lind et al., 1989, n. 11, *supra*. Contrary to conventional wisdom, in Lind's research, actual costs and time to disposition had little effect on satisfaction. Perceived costs and delay—whether the cost was worth the outcome and whether the time to disposition appeared reasonable—did affect perceptions of the outcome but were unrelated to actual costs and time to disposition.

[16] LIND et al., 1990, n. 9, *supra*; LIND et al., 1989, n. 11, *supra*.

years to reach trial. Judicial settlement conferences were scheduled one month before trial.

All of the litigants were asked to describe their experiences in court, as well as negotiations outside of court, and to assess the procedures they were exposed to with regard to factors such as formality, carefulness, neutrality and fairness. By comparing responses across the courts, we were able to analyze differences in perceptions of procedures as well as the sources of these differences.

We found that the satisfaction of litigants with the dispute resolution procedures they experienced and with the court generally was strongly dependent on their perception of whether there was procedural fairness. Regardless of how the cases were resolved, litigants felt more positive about the system when they believed it was fair. (Litigants who were satisfied with the outcome and believed the process was fair were the most satisfied.)

Perceptions of procedural fairness were highest for trial and court-annexed nonbinding arbitration and lowest for judicial settlement conferences. Analysis revealed that the most important factors were the litigants' perception:

(1) of control over the process;

(2) that the process was unbiased, which was related to their belief that the decision maker was impartial and paid equal attention to all parties;

(3) that the process was careful and thorough; and

(4) that litigants were treated in a dignified fashion.

Such process characteristics as privacy and perceived formality or informality have received a good deal of attention in the dispute resolution literature. In our research, these particular characteristics were unrelated to perceptions of procedural fairness.

Conventional Wisdom Belied

This research contradicted the conventional wisdom that litigants dislike trials because they are emotionally burdensome. Litigants whose cases were tried were as comfortable with that procedure as were litigants whose cases were arbitrated. Defendants were pleased to have an opportunity to vindicate themselves publicly at trial even when they lost.

Litigants rated trials and nonbinding court-annexed arbitration equally on the dignity scale. Litigants whose cases were tried rated the trial process somewhat higher on the formality scale than did litigants who arbitrated. But the degree of formality did not seem important to them, as long as the decision makers seemed to proceed with care.

Litigants in the third court had rather negative perceptions of the fairness of judicial settlement conferences, from which they were almost always excluded. These conferences did not give them an opportunity to be heard or to observe the proceedings. Sitting outside the judge's chambers, they could only wonder what was going on and when they asked their attorney, they sometimes distrusted his or her account of what occurred behind closed doors. There was little reason for these litigants to think that they were regarded as important members of society—or even important participants in the dispute!

Taken together, the research that has been done concerning individuals' perceptions of dispute resolution procedures suggests that people carry a rough concept of "due process" in their head and use it as a benchmark to assess procedural fairness. They are concerned with the features of dispute resolution that seem to signal authentic consideration of their claims and equal treatment of parties.

Implications for Arbitration

I draw the following conclusions for arbitration from the procedural justice research that has been done. The first is that employees, consumers, borrowers and like individuals who are required to arbitrate, whether or not they are represented by counsel, will assess the fairness of arbitration on the basis of its procedural features, rather than on whether they win or lose. Like court litigants, arbitration litigants will be satisfied with arbitration if they think the process is fair and will be dissatisfied if they think the process is unfair.

Second, any assessments of the procedural fairness of arbitration by arbitration litigants will depend on several variables: whether they are allowed to participate in, or at least observe, the process firsthand; and whether they believe the arbitrator is unbiased, gave fair consideration to their evidence, treated all parties equally, and treated them in a dignified fashion.

Thus, if arbitration hearings are thorough and conducted with decorum, devoted to understanding the facts of the dispute, and afford equal consideration to all parties, and if litigants believe that the arbitrator selection process was fair and the arbitrator appeared to be neutral and independent, workers, consumers and like individuals who are compelled to arbitrate are likely to find the process fair. Whether or not they like the outcome, they will accept and comply with it, and view it as legitimate.

It may be inferred from the procedural fairness research that disputants will be insensitive to many differences between arbitration and litigation that arbitration critics have cited as unfair. Examples include differences pertaining to discovery (sometimes more limited in arbitration), ability to bring group claims, application of substantive legal doctrine (not required in arbitration), and appeal rights (very limited in arbitration). But when arbitration is compelled, rather than freely chosen, policymakers have a responsibility to assess how these differences affect the distribution of outcomes between individuals and corporations and among individuals of different socio-economic backgrounds, race, ethnicity and gender.

IV. The Benefits of Business Arbitration

Commercial Arbitration: Winning Over the Skeptics

*by Larry Engel**

"It is feasible to achieve arbitration results that are consistent with the contract and applicable law if one is careful to address the key variables in advance," says author Larry Engel. This article identifies these elements and addresses significant issues that any risk-averse party to an arbitration must consider.

Few commercial parties continue to be comfortable with the capacity of our jury system to reliably satisfy their goals in resolving civil suits.[1] The debate is usually between litigation with jury-trial waivers vs. arbitration.[2] The question becomes whether the commercial party is more likely to obtain predictable justice from the judges or from the arbitrators. (This discussion assumes that effective jury-trial waivers are

---

* The author is a partner at White & Case, in San Francisco, Calif. He is a member of the American College of Commercial Finance and the American College of Bankruptcy and is former chair of the ABA Business Law Section. Engel holds a cum laude J.D. from Northwestern University Law School.

[1] The problems with the jury system are beyond the scope of this article. Suffice it to say that the variables involved in the jury system make predictable justice on the merits too uncertain for many commercial parties. That concern exists even where there is a large pool of probably responsible jurors with the experience and capacity to understand the complex commercial issues and evidence. Whatever the risk of jurors failing to decide disputes correctly on the merits, that risk must be multiplied by the compound risk of judicial errors and other dysfunctions in the system and by the other innumerable litigation risks (e.g., key lender witnesses becoming hostile when they lose jobs in the consolidating financial-services industry).

[2] For the purposes of this discussion, it is assumed that formal or informal mediation has failed and that the dispute cannot be resolved by a reasonable settlement. In major financial services-lender liability disputes between borrowers and lenders, this situation usually occurs when the borrower's needs exceed any reasonable compromise, and when the borrower feels that it has little left to lose. For such borrowers, the dispute is often the last maneuver to attempt to compel additional concessions before the borrower files Chapter 11 in order to stay the lender's exercise of its creditor remedies. Indeed, the prospect of the borrower's ultimate bankruptcy tactics impairs the borrower's ability to achieve maximum concessions outside of bankruptcy. For example, when the workout compromise fails, the lender can suffer further problems in the borrower's Chapter 11, notwithstanding whatever waivers may be included for the lender's benefit in the workout agreements.

both possible and feasible for the lender to enforce them in the applicable jurisdiction.)

While this article does not attempt to resolve that debate between the merits of judges and arbitrators, at least the following factors deserve special consideration:

1. While parties to commercial disputes can reasonably specify the qualifications of arbitrators, assigned judges are typically hard to select individually for their qualifications. While forum shopping for a desirable judge is possible in various circumstances, even in those more predictable cases the parties can be surprised to find themselves with another, unexpected trial judge as a result of uncontrollable factors, such as conflicts of interest,[3] retirement from the bench, promotion to an appellate court, etc.

2. While the quality of arbitrator panels is improving,[4] the quality of the lesser-rated judges is often perceived to be declining. In some places there are too many judges neither party to the dispute would be willing to accept if they had a choice. There are even more judges one side or the other would reject, if that were possible.

3. While the quality of an arbitrator's performance is essential to maintaining his or her reputation and acceptability, judges are often selected or elected and retained on criteria unrelated to the quality of their performance in resolving commercial disputes. Even where there is a reported "merit-selection" process for selecting judges, the results can be disappointing to one or both sides to commercial disputes.

4. While the confidentiality of the arbitration process tends to shield arbitrators from "political" or "public-relations" pressures, some judges are likely to be more focused on the public-relations consequences of their decisions. For example, lenders may be

---

[3] The increasing consolidation of the financial-services industry and the mobility of individual lending officers and attorneys complicates the predictability of conflict-of-interest issues.

[4] The American Arbitration Association has substantially reduced its arbitration panels so as to focus on the most qualified persons. Moreover, the AAA has used peer-review processes to assist in identifying the best-qualified arbitrators. For example, the AAA's National Panel for Financial Services Disputes includes a substantial number of financial-services lawyers whose qualifications have been validated by their peer selection in an evaluation process by the prestigious American College of Commercial Finance Lawyers.

INTRODUCTION TO ARBITRATION

concerned about the judge's anxieties about deciding against a financially distressed borrower-plaintiff who is a substantial employer in the local community where the suit is filed.

5. Even where the judges are the equal of the arbitrators in all other criteria, their typical judicial experiences in criminal, personal-injury and other common disputes do not equip them to appreciate the subtleties of the commercial disputes. Thus, the parties to a commercial dispute can expect to be able to specify an arbitrator who is an expert on the issues involved in the dispute, rather than risking a judge with typically far less experience and knowledge regarding those issues.

6. Finally, while there are other relevant issues and differentiations, the fundamental question is the extent to which the party to the commercial dispute can reliably obtain a decision-maker who is impartial and intelligent, has integrity, possesses intellectual (and other) honesty, and has sufficient knowledge and experience to be able to make the correct decision on the merits. In many situations arbitration provides the best opportunity to reliably obtain such a decision-maker.

Qualified Arbitrators

One of the advantages of arbitration is the ability to require reasonable qualifications for the arbitrators. For the best results, it is important for a commercial lender not to abuse that power, because the courts in at least some states may use unconscionability and other doctrines to invalidate the arbitration agreement.[5] Thus, it is important that the neutral arbitrators have both the real and the apparent capacity for a fair decision on the merits.

On at least narrow issues arising in workouts, the parties may be able to agree upon a prioritized list of arbitrators with a general selection procedure in the event that such nominated persons are unable or

---

[5] *E.g.*, Graham v. Scissor-Tail, Inc., 28 Cal.3d 807 (1981). The Musician's Union form of contract provided for arbitration by the union in a manner unconscionably prejudicial to employers having a dispute with the Musician's Union members. The problem centered on the fact that the union arbitrators were perceived to be likely to favor the union members, thereby denying the other party the opportunity for a fair trial on the merits. *See, for example*, Stirlen v. Supercuts, Inc., 51 Cal. App.4th 1519 (1997) (generally describing how unconscionability operates under state law, despite the Federal Arbitration Act, in the context of an unconscionable employment-arbitration agreement).

unwilling to serve. However, in most situations, the parties can either leave the identity of the arbitrators to the standard American Arbitration Association (or alternative) procedure, or specify the minimum qualifications of the arbitrators, either individually or by reference to a special panel. For example, arbitration clauses in loan documentation may refer to the AAA's special National Panel for Commercial Financial Disputes,[6] as well as specify individual qualification standards. Reference in the arbitration agreement to such specialized panels and other factual qualification standards is very useful in the major cases. The attorneys on such special panels tend to place considerable importance in maintaining their reputations with their peers for both their capacity to reach the correct result on the merits (e.g., a function of applied knowledge, skill, experience and intelligence) and their reliability in providing swift justice on the merits (e.g., a function of integrity, intellectual honesty, etc.). While arbitrations are confidential, the loss of significant peer respect is an observable phenomenon to which other comparable peers can react without knowing the particulars of the case in which expectations for the arbitrator's excellence and honesty were disappointed.

In addition to specifying arbitrators from such special panels, the parties to commercial disputes should also consider specifying objective qualification standards for arbitrators. Reasonable persons can disagree as to which qualifications are the most appropriate. However, when the objective is predictable justice on the merits, the best-qualified decision-makers are generally the best able to decide the issues correctly on the merits. While qualified persons might disagree on which witness to believe about who said what to whom, the real experts in the applicable commercial transactions will usually have a consensus on the right result,

---

[6] The AAA has worked with the American College of Commercial Finance Lawyers and other peer-review groups in order to develop a specialized panel of the best transactional-finance lawyers in the country. The qualifications of these individuals is far higher than typically formulated in contractual minimum standards. Peer review adds a valuable ingredient of subjective quality assurance that is otherwise hard to define as for individual factors. Some parties have attempted to specify (for example) subjective quality requirements for individual arbitrations (e.g., an attorney whose reputation for excellence and expertise in commercial finance transactions is generally recognized within his or her state and who is a partner or member of a law firm nationally recognized for its excellence). However, those attempts can be problematic and tend to place the AAA or other administrators (and challenged arbitrators) in a difficult position in applying such subjective quality standards, especially in borderline cases and when the arbitration occurs in places where there may not be many persons who meet that standard (assuming the question were asked of qualifying lawyers in some of our larger cities).

even regarding which of the conflicting witnesses is the most plausible, given what the experts know about how particular deals are done.[7] To a real expert, evaluating the conflicting testimony of expert witnesses is consistent with their daily practice, and the course of performance provides many meaningful clues as to the credibility of the witnesses. Moreover, on issues where the reported decisional law or statutes appear inconclusive or in conflict, the real experts on such transactions are most likely to have a consensus in predicting the correct result, among other things, because they understand what the law must be in order for it to "work" consistently with commercial realities.

The issue sometimes arises as to which expert background to specify. For example, debates arise about whether to specify lawyers vs. nonlawyers or litigators vs. transactional lawyers, etc. However, general or vague qualification references are not helpful because they can produce surprising results and, arguably, mistakes.[8] Therefore, while there are other reasonable alternatives, one illustration for use in commercial-finance transactions could be as follows:

> Arbitrators must be active members of the State Bar with expertise in regularly representing borrowers or lenders in comparable transactions, either in negotiating or documenting such transactions or in restructuring or working out such transactions.[9] Such arbitrators shall have no less than 10 years'

---

[7] The author has significant experience in discussing various commercial issues with some of the nation's best attorneys representing either or both lenders and borrowers in commercial financial transactions. There is typically a commonality of view about what is correct in various contexts where disputes tend to arise. This reality is demonstrated daily by such experts interacting on key state bar or American Bar Association committees and in peer groups such as the American College of Commercial Finance Lawyers or the American College of Bankruptcy.

[8] Consider, for example, a reference to an attorney with 10 years of experience specializing in the "subject matter in dispute." While the lender in a commercial finance transaction would expect that standard to produce transactional lawyers, the borrower may attempt (arguably incorrectly) to argue that the subject matter of the arbitration is lender-liability law. Thus, a vague standard might result either in a transactional specialist in lending transactions or a litigator specializing in lender-liability litigation.

[9] In many respects the ideal arbitrators may often be the commercial-finance workout attorneys, because they often have more direct, firsthand experience with the reasons why the loan documentation provisions exist and the realities of many common disputes. Because the knowledge base of those workout lawyers must include more of what is typically argued or alleged in such financial-services disputes, such lawyers may need less briefing and other assistance from the parties in putting themselves in a position where they can promptly and correctly decide the issues on the merits.

experience in so representing parties to such transactions as a material portion of their law practices.[10] Such arbitrators shall also be recognized for that expertise by the selection to the American Arbitration Association's National Panel for Commercial Financial Disputes, if such arbitrators are available and otherwise qualified to service in this dispute.[11]

Three Arbitrators

A single qualified arbitrator is sufficient. Nevertheless, whatever risk may exist for an erroneous decision can be reduced significantly by requiring three arbitrators: one selected by each party from the qualified pool of candidates, and one selected by those two arbitrators (or by the AAA, if one party fails to nominate an arbitrator). Some commentators contend that each party already has an advocate and question what a party-appointed arbitrator adds besides expense. Those skeptics should consider the following advantages of the three-arbitrator process:

1. The expert arbitrators will typically know each other (or at least they will have professional friends in common), especially if one imposes high standards for the arbitrators. Thus, the neutral arbitrator will tend to perform at his or her best when working closely with his or her peers as co-arbitrators. That effort to maintain peer respect is the best assurance of a quality and just decision on the merits. (Even if the party advocates know the neutral arbitrator, the distance inherent in that relationship results

---

[10] While this excludes the commercial litigators, including the plaintiff and defense lender-liability litigators, the litigator's unique expertise is often not the central focus of such arbitration (e.g., civil procedure, evidence, trial strategies, tort law, etc.). Every qualified transactional-finance lawyer shares the common appreciation with such litigators of lender-liability law, the parol-evidence law and exceptions to the enforcement of oral agreements, implied obligations of good faith and fair dealing, etc. Those who actually participate in the prelitigation dealings among the parties appear often to be the best qualified to appreciate the commercial realities and to decide what is plausible and feasible in that context. As one expert observed, in order to avoid mistakes one often needs the experience sufficient to know when the expert witnesses are clearly wrong.

[11] As discussed above, it is important to have arbitrators who have not only the practice qualifications, but also the human qualifications, such as intellectual honesty, judicial temperament, etc. As in any field, there are acknowledged experts who for such human factors would be vetoed from selection as arbitrators by the peers who know them best. Those human factors also tend to disqualify the same persons from the peer respect required for selection to such peer-recognition groups.

in less psychological need for a single arbitrator to satisfy peer expectations than when the three arbitrators are collaborating.)

2. Three arbitrators is the only way to be sure that all issues and facts are fully developed for the neutral arbitrator. If there is a single arbitrator, he or she may be reluctant to ask questions about a "hole" or problem that he or she perceives with respect to one party's evidence or argument, because that might be perceived as helping the other side.[12] However, when there are three arbitrators, the neutral arbitrator can express his or her concerns to the co-arbitrators, and the party-selected arbitrators can ask the hard questions that enable the parties to better address those issues.

3. The three qualified minds attempting to work on the process tend to produce a less-extreme result if any error is made. If three experts collaborate on the problem and the neutral expert makes a mistake in siding with one party, the neutral expert's respect for the position advocated by the losing side's arbitrator can moderate the extent of the loss. (This is not a question of Solomonic "split the difference" decision-making, but rather is typical of what happens when two credible experts disagree strongly about their opinions on a disputed issue.)

4. There is an important difference between the nature and the quality of the debate among the three arbitrators vs. the advocacy by the parties. For example, during private deliberations one party's arbitrator can laugh at the preposterous damage calculation of the other party's paid "expert," while the advocate for that party is prudent to be more respectful. The party-appointed arbitrator can explain why that "expert" deserves no credibility in more persuasive ways than can the advocate.

5. Lastly, and especially where there are no required findings of fact or conclusions of law, the party advocate can require that rigorous consistency and logic be applied in the neutral

---

[12] Even with able advocates, litigators serving as arbitrators may not anticipate all of the concerns of a "been-there and-done-that" neutral arbitrator who is an expert on the issues. This is especially true where the party mistakenly relies on a smooth-talking expert witness whose performance does not equal his or her résumé and whose opinions on the particular issues have little merit. The best counter to the modern trend of "experts" providing questionable testimony, at best, is to use a better-qualified expert as the neutral arbitrator.

arbitrator's rationale for his or her decision. Many times cases might be decided by a neutral arbitrator another way but for a requirement of having to justify the decision logically and with legal consistency. Even if the neutral does not have to explain his or her reasoning to the parties, as a practical matter the neutral does have to explain himself or herself to the two co-arbitrators.

Compliance with the Contract and Law

Arbitrators are bound by the express provisions of the arbitration agreement. However, if the arbitration agreement does not clearly require the arbitrators to decide in accordance with applicable law, they may make decisions that are contrary to the applicable law (and, therefore, contrary to the expectation of the party that relied upon that applicable law when it negotiated the contract). As the California Supreme Court explained in its controversial decision in *Advanced Micro Devices, Inc. v. Intel Corporation*,[13] "Arbitrators, unless specifically restricted by the agreement to follow legal rules, may base their decisions upon broad principles of justice and equity...." Most horror stories about rare cases where arbitrators frustrated the reasonable commercial expectations of one party are attributable to such failure to expressly limit the arbitrators to applying the applicable law and complying with the contract. A useful example is when the arbitration agreement expressly prohibits the arbitrator from considering extrinsic evidence to the extent specified in the integration clause commonly included in the contract in dispute.[14]

Such evasions of the contract by an arbitrator may be undetectable where there is only a single arbitrator and where there is no requirement for findings of fact and conclusions of law. As noted above, three arbitrators enable the party-appointed arbitrator to generally require strict compliance with the contract and the applicable law. Requiring findings of fact and conclusions of law also support that compliance, as well as adding useful intellectual discipline in decision-making. While many commentators recommend not requiring findings of fact and conclusions of law, the issue may be decided based upon a comparative preference between finality of the arbitrator's decision vs. an arbitrator's decision being consistent with the contract and applicable law. The latter is often

---

[13] Advanced Micro Devices, Inc. v. Intel Corporation, 9 Cal.4th 362, 374-75 (1994).

[14] *See, for example*, Bonshire v. Thompson, 52 Cal.App.4th 803 (1997) (vacating an arbitration award for basing the decision on extrinsic evidence contrary to the agreement, because that exceeded the arbitrator's power and authority as specified in the contract, and because the arbitrator cannot arbitrarily remake the contract).

a more important consideration, although someone who prefers to gamble on "equitable results" outside the "rules" in the contract and law would have an opposite reaction.

Conclusion

It is possible to address the problems often cited by cynics who have been disappointed by arbitrations in certain cases. By applying the principles described in this article in the drafting of the arbitration agreement, those risks can be reduced. It is feasible to achieve arbitration results that are consistent with the contract and applicable law if one is careful to address the key variables in advance. For the reasons noted above, the most risk-averse parties will wish to consider: specifying qualifications designed to assure that the arbitrators have the desired expertise and human factors needed for decisions on the merits; requiring three arbitrators, so that the party-nominated arbitrators can assure quality control in decision-making and assist in making sure that the neutral arbitrator has all the information that he or she may need for a correct decision on the merits; and requiring the arbitrators to follow the applicable law and (in most cases) to submit findings of fact and conclusions of law.

V. Identifying the Parties to an Arbitration

Agency, Alter Ego and Other Identity Issues

Nonsignatories and Arbitration

by John M. Townsend[*]

While an arbitration agreement may require the parties to arbitrate disputes within the reach of the agreement, it is not always apparent who those parties are. Periodically an entity that is not a signatory to an arbitration agreement, such as a corporate affiliate, shareholder, or employee of a signatory, seeks to take advantage of the agreement to arbitrate, either offensively (to commence an arbitration against a signatory) or defensively (to trump a court proceeding commenced by a signatory). Alternatively, a signatory to an arbitration agreement may attempt to bring a nonsignatory within the agreement's reach, again either offensively or defensively.

Under U.S. law, courts decide whether a party may be required to arbitrate unless there is "'clear and unmistakable' evidence" that the parties intended an arbitrator to decide the question.[1] In deciding whether a particular nonsignatory should be brought within the reach of an arbitration clause, the courts must be mindful that "[a]rbitration is contractual by nature—'a party cannot be required to submit to arbitration any dispute which he has not agreed so to submit.'"[2] This rule follows from the Federal Arbitration Act's requirement that a court may

---

[*] The author, a partner in the Washington, D.C., office of Hughes Hubbard & Reed LLP, and chairs the firm's Arbitration and ADR Group. Townsend earned a cum laude B.A. from Yale University and a J.D. from Yale Law School. He is the author of *Revised Code of Ethics for Commercial Arbitrators* (with Bruce Meyerson) DISPUTE RESOLUTION JOURNAL (FEB.-APRIL 2004) and *Commentary on the July 2003 Revisions to the AAA Commercial Arbitration Rules* (with Paul D. Friedland) DISPUTE RESOLUTION JOURNAL (November 2003/January 2004). Jason Dillinger and Gideon Jurgens contributed to this article.

[1] First Options of Chicago v. Kaplan, 514 U.S. 928, 943 (1995), *quoting* AT&T Tech., Inc. v. Communications Workers, 475 U.S. 643, 649 (1986).

[2] Thompson-CSF, S.A. v. American Arbitration Ass'n, 64 F.3d 773, 776 (2d Cir. 1995), *quoting* United Steelworkers v. Warrior & Gulf Navig. Co., 363 U.S. 574, 582 (1960).

only compel arbitration when "the making of the agreement for arbitration" is established.[3]

The "liberal federal policy favoring arbitration" does not come into play here. The U.S. Supreme Court has made it clear that the deference given to an arbitrator's decision as to "whether a particular merits-related dispute is arbitrable" is not available when it comes to deciding who has agreed to arbitration in the first place.[4]

Courts have used six legal theories grounded in contract or agency law to require or permit nonsignatories to arbitrate: (1) incorporation by reference, (2) assumption by conduct, (3) third-party beneficiary, (4) agency, (5) equitable estoppel, and (6) piercing the corporate veil or alter ego. The first three theories are fairly straightforward; the second three, however, have proved more difficult for the courts to deal with and the boundaries between them are not always clearly marked. This resort to different rationales has made it somewhat difficult to distill general rules for predicting how such cases will be resolved.

Employing one or more of these theories, signatories to arbitration agreements have been required to arbitrate disputes with nonsignatories, and (more rarely) nonsignatories have been required to arbitrate under clauses contained in contracts they have not signed. The Second Circuit explained:

> "It does not follow...that under the [FAA] an obligation to arbitrate attaches only to one who has personally signed the written arbitration provision."...[A] nonsignatory party may be bound to an arbitration agreement if so dictated by the "ordinary principles of contract and agency."[5]

The FAA "merely requires that the arbitration provision itself be in writing," not that the party to be bound has signed it.[6]

This article surveys the current approaches to compelling arbitration when nonsignatories are involved. All of these approaches, however, remain respectful of the actual wording of the arbitration clause, so that

---

[3] 9 U.S.C. § 4. Essentially the same rule is established for international arbitrations by Article II(3) of the N.Y. Convention, implemented by 9 U.S.C. § 201 et seq. *See* J.J. Ryan & Sons, Inc. v. Rhone Poulenc Textile, S.A., 863 F.2d 315 (4th Cir. 1988).

[4] *First Options*, 514 U.S. at 943, *quoting* Mitsubishi Motors Corp. v. Soler Chrysler-Plymouth, Inc., 473 U.S. 614, 625 (1985).

[5] *Thompson*, 64 F.3d at 776, *quoting* Fisser v. International Bank, 282 F.2d 231, 233 (2d Cir. 1960); McAllister Bros., Inc. v. A & S Transp. Co., 621 F.2d 519, 524 (2d Cir. 1980).

[6] *Fisser*, 82 F.2d at 233.

parties who foresee the question arising can draft their clauses to provide the answers. The "language of the arbitration clause itself" is always the starting point, and often the end of the inquiry.[7]

Incorporation by Reference

When a contract containing an arbitration clause is incorporated by reference into a completely separate agreement which does not contain an arbitration clause, a nonsignatory to the former agreement may nevertheless be required to arbitrate if a dispute arises under the latter agreement.

An example is *Import Export Steel Corp. v. Mississippi Valley Barge Line Co.*[8] Here, a shipping company sublet a charter party from its agent and assumed all the agent's obligations and privileges under a subcharter contract. The bills of lading issued by the shipping company to the shipper of certain cargo referred to the subcharter and unequivocally incorporated its provisions, including an addendum containing an arbitration clause. The Second Circuit found that the charterer could compel the shipping company to arbitrate a claim for the loss of cargo, as both were signatories to the bill of lading. But the cargo owner could not be compelled to arbitrate, as it was not a signatory of the subcharter or the bill of lading.

Thirty years later, the same court cited this case for the proposition that incorporation by reference may be used "by a nonsignatory" to compel arbitration against a signatory to an arbitration agreement.[9] But this is too narrow a reading. As long as the party to be compelled to arbitrate has signed an agreement that incorporates the agreement to arbitrate, it need not have signed the original agreement.[10]

Whether an arbitration clause has been incorporated by reference often arises in connection with guarantees. The courts tend to require that any incorporation by reference into a guarantee be explicit. In *Grundstad v. Ritt*,[11] for example, the Seventh Circuit found that an arbitration clause was not incorporated by reference into a guarantee that appeared below the signatures at the end of the contract in which the arbitration clause

---

[7] Cara's Notions, Inc. v. Hallmark Cards, Inc., 140 F.3d 566 (4th Cir. 1998).
[8] 351 F.2d 503 (2d Cir. 1965).
[9] *Thompson, supra*, n. 2, 64 F.3d at 777.
[10] *See* Polytek Eng'g Co. v. Jacobson Cos., 984 F. Supp. 1238, 1241 (D. Minn. 1997).
[11] 106 F.3d 201 (7th Cir. 1997). *See also* Asplundh Tree Expert Co. v. Bates, 71 F.3d 592 (6th Cir. 1995); U.S. Fidelity & Guar. Co. v. West Point Constr. Co., 837 F.2d 1507 (11th Cir. 1988).

appeared. The court reasoned that the guarantee did not "unambiguously express" the guarantor's "intent to be personally bound by the arbitration clause." The arbitration clause referred to any dispute "between the parties," and the court concluded that "parties" did not mean "guarantors." "The federal policy favoring arbitration," the Seventh Circuit said, "does not serve to extend the reach of an arbitration agreement to parties who never agreed to arbitrate in the first place."

Assumption by Conduct

Absent a signature, a party nevertheless may be bound by an arbitration clause if its conduct indicates it is assuming the obligation to arbitrate. An example is *Gvozdenovic v. United Air Lines, Inc.*[12] This case arose out of United Airlines' acquisition of a division of Pan Am. At the time of the acquisition, a collective bargaining agreement providing for arbitration existed between United and its employees' union. Although Pan Am flight attendants were neither members of this union nor employed by United when the CBA was signed, the court held that they were bound by the results of an arbitration conducted after the acquisition. This was because they had actively and voluntarily participated in the arbitration by choosing a committee and counsel to represent them in the proceeding. The court said: "Although a party is bound by an arbitral award only where it has agreed to arbitrate, an agreement may be implied from the party's conduct."

Third-Party Beneficiary

An exception to the general rule that a contract does not confer enforceable rights upon nonsignatories arises when the contracting parties intend to confer benefits on a third party. The right to arbitrate is a right that can be conferred on a third party if the intention to do so can be discerned from the contract.

In *Spear, Leeds & Kellogg v. Central Life Assur. Co.*,[13] several insurance companies sought to arbitrate claims against a brokerage firm based on its alleged participation in a fraud perpetrated by their insured. The firm claimed there was no agreement, and thus no arbitration clause,

---

[12] 933 F.2d 1100 (2d Cir.), *cert. denied*, 502 U.S. 910 (1991). *See also* Matter of Arbitration Between Keystone Shipping Co. and Texport Oil Co., 782 F. Supp. 28, 31 (S.D.N.Y. 1992).

[13] 85 F.3d 21 (2d Cir. 1996). *See also* McCarthy v. Azure, 22 F.3d 351, 362 (1st Cir. 1994); Paine, Webber, Jackson & Curtis v. Chase Manhattan, 728 F.2d 577 (2d Cir. 1983).

between it and the insurance companies. The Second Circuit found the Constitution and Rules of the New York Stock Exchange, which require members to arbitrate controversies with nonmembers arising out of the members' business, to be equivalent to a contract between the NYSE and its members, and that the insurance companies should be considered third-party beneficiaries of the arbitration provision. Therefore, the insurance companies could compel the brokerage firm to arbitrate.

That a nonsignatory may be a third-party beneficiary of a contract does not alone make it a third-party beneficiary of the arbitration clause in that contract. *Collins v. International Dairy Queen, Inc.*[14] illustrates the point. Here, the court found a franchisor entitled, as a third-party beneficiary of one set of contracts between its franchisee and certain subfranchisees, to compel arbitration because the arbitration clause provided for arbitration of disputes "between the parties hereto." But the same franchisor was not entitled to compel arbitration of claims asserted by a second group of subfranchisees, even though it was also a third-party beneficiary of those contracts. The court so held because the arbitration clause in those contracts provided for arbitration of disputes "between Territory Operator and Licensee." Stressing that "determination of intent is the crucial element," the court concluded that neither term was intended to include the franchisor. This distinction illustrates the control the drafters of an arbitration clause can exert if they anticipate the controversy.

Agency

The picture becomes more complex when dealing with agency theory, which is probably the most common basis asserted by a nonsignatory claiming the benefit of an agreement to arbitrate. This theory holds that, when a principal is bound under the terms of a valid arbitration clause, its agents, employees and representatives are also covered under the agreement's terms.

In *Pritzker v. Merrill Lynch, Pierce, Fenner & Smith*,[15] the Third Circuit required a party to an arbitration agreement to arbitrate claims against nonsignatory agents of the other party. This case involved a suit by a pension plan trustee against (1) a brokerage firm, (2) an employee of the firm, and (3) a sister corporation of the firm. The defendants moved to stay court proceedings and to compel arbitration pursuant to the

---

[14] *CCH Business Franchise Guide* ¶ 11,368 at 30,447-449 (M.D.Ga. Mar. 23, 1998).
[15] 7 F.3d 1110 (3d Cir. 1993).

agreement between the firm and the pension fund, to which neither the employee nor the sister corporation was a signatory. The court stayed the suit on agency principles. The court explained that an "entity such as Merrill Lynch can only act through its employees, and an arbitration agreement would be of little value if it did not extend to them."

For less clear reasons, the *Pritzker* court held that "agency logic" also mandated application of the arbitration clause to the sister corporation. Although the sister corporation's role was not clear, the court found that corporation was "obligated to perform certain services" in connection with the trustees' accounts and that its interests were "directly related to, if not predicated upon," the broker's conduct.[16] The court summed up: "Where the parties to [an arbitration] clause unmistakably intend to arbitrate all controversies which might arise between them, their agreement should be applied to all claims against agents or entities related to the signatories."

When applying agency concepts, some courts have required that a nexus be shown between the acts of the agent and the agreement containing the arbitration clause. The Sixth Circuit found such a nexus in *Arnold v. Arnold*,[17] a case in which a party to an arbitration agreement (a stock purchaser) sought to escape its reach by having its securities law claims decided in court. The defendants—the officers and directors of the issuer—moved to stay the suit pending arbitration. The court found the alleged wrongdoing by the officers and directors was related to the stock purchase agreement. Because of the agency relationship between the corporation and its officers and directors (who did not sign the stock purchase agreement), the court applied the "well-settled principle affording agents the benefit of arbitration clauses made by their principal." In reaching that conclusion, the court was clearly concerned that if parties "can avoid the practical consequences of an agreement to arbitrate by naming nonsignatory parties as [defendants]...the effect of the rule requiring arbitration would, in effect, be nullified."

A similar securities fraud case in the Ninth Circuit also emphasizes the importance of how the arbitration agreement is written. In *Letizia v. Prudential Bache Securities, Inc.*,[18] the court held that nonsignatory

---

[16] Since the two companies were under the same ownership, the court said the sister company "may be an alter-ego of" the broker. Later 3rd Circuit cases have ignored this allusion to alter ego doctrine and have required an agency relationship before binding nonsignatories to an arbitration agreement. See cases cited in notes 28-31.

[17] 920 F.2d 1269 (6th Cir. 1990).

[18] 802 F.2d 1185 (9th Cir. 1986).

employees of the defendant securities firm were entitled to the benefit of the arbitration clause in the customer agreement, both because their allegedly wrongful acts were related to their handling of the investor's security account, and because the agreement itself made it clear that the firm intended the agreement to protect its employees.

Where there is no nexus between the alleged acts and the contract containing the arbitration clause, some courts have declined to allow nonsignatory agents to take advantage of the arbitration clause. In *Britton v. Co-op Banking Group*,[19] investors in an allegedly fraudulent tax shelter investment sued the seller and its owner, a nonsignatory to the investment contract containing an arbitration clause. The owner had purchased the seller after the investment contract was executed. Although the Ninth Circuit found that the new owner became an agent, officer and employee of the original contracting party, the acts with which he was charged were "subsequent, independent acts of fraud, unrelated to any provision or interpretation of the contract." The court, therefore, denied his attempt to compel arbitration based solely on his agency relationship with a signatory.

Equitable Estoppel

Some courts have applied the doctrine of equitable estoppel to prevent a signatory from avoiding arbitration with a nonsignatory when the issues the nonsignatory seeks to resolve in arbitration are intertwined with an agreement that the estopped party has signed. Equitable estoppel has generally not been applied to compel a nonsignatory to arbitrate.

Equitable estoppel is usually used defensively, as a response to a suit in which the signatory claims tort damages against an affiliate of a party to an arbitration agreement. Court decisions applying this theory tend to rely heavily on the well-established rule that parties cannot avoid their obligations to arbitrate by bringing claims sounding in tort rather than in contract.

An early application of this theory is the Seventh Circuit's decision in *Hughes Masonry Co. v. Greater Clark County School Building Corp.*[20] A masonry contractor sued a construction manager for interference with

---

[19] 4 F.3d 742 (9th Cir. 1993).
[20] 659 F.2d 836 (7th Cir. 1981). *See also* McBro Planning & Dev. Co. v. Triangle Elec. Constr Co., 741 F.2d 342 (11th Cir. 1984); S. McKinnis, *Enforcing Arbitration with a Nonsignatory: Equitable Estoppel and Defensive Piercing of the Corporate Veil*, J. DISP. RESOL. 197, 210 (1995)(arguing that, because invocation of equitable estoppel is often uncertain and arbitrary, alter ego theory may be a better vehicle).

its contractual relationship with a building owner. The contractor and the manager each had separate contracts with the owner, but only the contractor's agreement contained an arbitration clause. The manager moved to compel arbitration. The contractor argued that the manager could not invoke the arbitration provision because it was not a party to the agreement.

The Seventh Circuit held that the contractor was "equitably estopped" from refusing to arbitrate, because the "very basis of [its] claim [was] that [the manager] breached the duties and responsibilities assigned and ascribed to [the manager] under the agreement" that contained the arbitration clause. The court reasoned that the tort claims against the manager were actually claims of a breach of the manager's contractual obligations, and that the manager was specifically named and its duties were outlined in the underlying contract. Thus, it would have been "manifestly inequitable" to allow the contractor both to claim that the manager was liable for a failure to perform under the contract, and at the same time to deny that the manager was a party to the contract in order to avoid arbitration. Although there was no affiliate relationship between the manager and any signatory party, there was a clear nexus between the dispute and the agreement to arbitrate.

This reasoning was applied in *Sunkist Soft Drinks, Inc. v. Sunkist Growers, Inc.*[21] In this case, the licensor of a soft drink trademark sued a licensee's parent corporation for allegedly managing the licensee in a manner that caused the licensee to violate the licensing agreement. The parent argued that, under the terms of that agreement, the licensor should be compelled to pursue its claims through arbitration. The Eleventh Circuit agreed. In view of the "close relationship between the entities involved as well as the relationship of the alleged wrongs to the nonsignatory's obligations and duties in the contract," the court held that the licensor was equitably estopped from asserting the lack of a written agreement between itself and the parent.

A panel of the Fifth Circuit rejected a defensive use of equitable estoppel on jurisdictional grounds in a recently vacated decision in *Marathon Oil Co. v. Ruhrgas, A.G.*[22] Marathon Oil and two affiliates sued Ruhrgas, a German company with which a third affiliate of Marathon had a contract containing an arbitration clause, for fraud in Texas state court. The case was removed to federal court, where Ruhrgas

---

[21] 10 F.3d 753 (11th Cir. 1993).
[22] 115 F.3d 315 (5th Cir.), *cert. denied*, 118 S. Ct. 413 (1997), *vacated en banc*, 1998 U.S. App. LEXIS 13358 (5th Cir. June 22, 1998).

sought a stay pending arbitration based on an arbitration clause in the contract between Ruhrgas and Marathon's third affiliate. Reasoning that federal jurisdiction under the U.N. Convention and 9 U.S.C. § 205 rests on "whether any relevant arbitration agreement exists between the parties," and finding that "no contracts exist between [the plaintiffs] and Ruhrgas," the panel concluded that the district court lacked subject matter jurisdiction to consider whether Marathon should be required to arbitrate its claims. The Fifth Circuit en banc vacated that decision on procedural grounds unrelated to arbitration and sent the case back to the district court for a new determination as to subject matter jurisdiction.

Piercing the Corporate Veil

Several courts have discussed the possibility of piercing the corporate veil or using alter ego theory to bind nonsignatory parties to, or to give them the benefit of, arbitration clauses in contracts entered into by their affiliates. When the courts have done so, the claims against the nonsignatory and its affiliate have been closely related. For instance, the Fourth Circuit said:

> When the charges against a parent company and its subsidiary are based on the same facts and are inherently inseparable, a court may refer claims against the parent to arbitration even though the parent is not formally a party to the arbitration agreement.... "[i]f the parent corporation was forced to try the case, the arbitration proceedings would be rendered meaningless and the federal policy in favor of arbitration effectively thwarted."[23]

Demonstrating how interchangeable the rationales for including nonsignatories can be, the same court observed: "The same result has been reached under a theory of equitable estoppel."[24]

---

[23] J.J. Ryan & Sons v. Rhone Poulenc Textile, S.A., 863 F.2d 315, 320-21 (4th Cir. 1988), *quoting* Sam Reisfield & Son Import Co., v. S.A. Eteco, 530 F.2d 679, 680-81 (5th Cir. 1979). *See also* Interocean Shipping Co. v. National Shipping & Trading Corp., 523 F.2d 527, 539 (2d Cir. 1975), *cert. denied*, 423 U.S. 1054 (1976).

[24] The 3rd Circuit has not expressly considered equitable estoppel as an alternative to piercing the corporate veil. The 3rd Circuit cases discussed below involved closely related nonsignatories, and the claims in each appeared to be intertwined with the underlying contracts.

It is important to note that a corporate relationship alone is not sufficient to bind a nonsignatory to an arbitration agreement.[25] In *United Int'l Holdings, Inc. v. Wharf (Holdings) Ltd.*,[26] the Tenth Circuit refused to extend the effect of an arbitration clause in a contract between one of a group of defendant companies and one of a group of plaintiff companies to all of the defendant companies. The court reasoned, "Wharf Cable was a separate legal entity from the other Wharf companies and Wharf Cable alone, not its affiliates or parent companies, signed" the contract containing the arbitration clause. The Tenth Circuit said, "Courts do not lightly pierce the corporate veil, even in deference to the strong policy favoring arbitration."

The Third Circuit has been particularly resistant to extending the corporate veil theory beyond its narrow purpose of dealing with fraud.[27] In *Kaplan v. First Options of Chicago, Inc.*,[28] the court declined to allow one party to a contract containing an arbitration clause to pierce the corporate veil to force a corporate president (and sole shareholder) of the other party to arbitrate. The Third Circuit emphasized that in signing a loan agreement in his corporate capacity and a letter agreement in his personal capacity, both as part of a work-out agreement, the corporate president never agreed or intended to be bound personally by the arbitration clause in the loan agreement.

The Supreme Court affirmed, but its opinion dealt primarily with the question of whether courts or arbitrators should decide who has agreed to be bound by an arbitration clause. It concluded that the answer "turns upon what the parties agreed."[29] In doing so, the Court emphasized the broader importance of looking to the agreement of the parties: "[A]rbitration is simply a matter of contract between the parties; it is a way to resolve those disputes—but only those disputes that the parties have agreed to submit to arbitration...[A] party can be forced to arbitrate only those issues it specifically has agreed to submit to arbitration."

---

[25] *Thomson, supra*, n. 2, 64 F.3d at 777.
[26] 210 F.3d 1207 (2000), *cert. denied*, 116 S. Ct. 2524 (1996).
[27] The 2nd Circuit has suggested it would allow the corporate veil to be pierced merely "where a parent dominates or controls a subsidiary." *Thomson, supra*, n. 2. The court's discussion in *Fisser, supra*, n. 5, however, makes it clear that three elements must be shown in the 2nd Circuit: (1) control in the sense of "complete domination," (2) use of such control to commit fraud or worse, and (3) that the misuse of control has caused the injury complained of. 282 F.2d at 237.
[28] 19 F.3d 1503 (3d Cir. 1994), *aff'd*, 115 S. Ct. 1920 (1995).
[29] 115 S. Ct. 1920, 1923 (1995).

In *Dayhoff v. H.J. Heinz Co.*,[30] the Third Circuit construed *First Options* to mean that no party can be compelled to arbitrate unless it specifically and expressly agreed to arbitration, taking *First Options* further than the Supreme Court's decision requires. The case involved a suit by Dayhoff, a candy distributor, based on the termination of one license and two distributorship agreements incident to the sale of its candy supplier. The purchaser of the candy supplier made the deal contingent on the prior termination of the agreements with Dayhoff. Dayhoff sued the candy supplier, its new owner and its former parent companies. The present and former owners attempted to stay the suit and compel arbitration based on an arbitration clause in the license agreement. The court refused. It reasoned that the new owner was not a party to the license agreement, and as to the former parent corporations, "there [was] no more reason to disregard the corporate structure with regard to such claims [than] there would be to disregard it with respect to other legal matters." If the nonsignatory affiliates had wanted the benefit of the arbitration clause, the Third Circuit reasoned, they should have directed the subsidiary to include appropriate language in the contract.

More recently, in *Ceska Sporitelna, A.S. v. Unisys Corp.*,[31] the Third Circuit affirmed without an opinion a district court decision that refused to allow a parent company to pierce its own corporate veil. The parent sought to compel arbitration of a fraud claim closely related to its subsidiary's contract (which contained an arbitration clause) to provide a foreign bank with a computer system. When the computer system failed to operate as agreed, the bank sued the parent for misrepresentation and fraud in inducing the bank to enter into the contract. The district court, relying on *Dayhoff*, denied the parent's petition to compel arbitration. "[O]nly where the signatories and nonsignatories first share a principal/agent relationship," the district court concluded, does it matter whether "their interests are co-extensive so as to make the arbitration clause applicable to the nonsignatory."

Courts have been particularly unsympathetic to efforts by a corporation to cite its own misconduct as a reason to pierce its corporate veil in order to take advantage of an arbitration clause signed by an affiliated corporation.[32] There is nothing peculiar to arbitration about this. It is simply a useful reminder that both equitable estoppel and

---

[30] 86 F.3d 1287 (3d Cir. 1996).
[31] 1996 U.S. Dist. LEXIS 15435 (E.D. Pa.), *aff'd without op.* 116 F.3d 467 (3d Cir. 1997), *cert. denied*, 118 S. Ct. 739.
[32] *McCarthy, supra*, n. 13, 22 F.3d at 362.

piercing the corporate veil are derived from theories developed in equity to soften the hard lines of contract law. Therefore, one would be well advised to consider how the equities are likely to strike a court before seeking to take advantage of either of them.

Conclusion

We return to the contract. Courts asked to compel a nonsignatory to arbitrate will look first to the arbitration clause. If it explicitly provides for, or excludes, arbitration of disputes involving affiliates or agents, the courts will enforce the language as written. And if the clause makes a nonsignatory a third-party beneficiary, or is incorporated by reference into another contract, or is assumed by the conduct of a nonsignatory, the courts have little difficulty requiring arbitration.

When the connection between the nonsignatory and the arbitration agreement is more remote, the other theories discussed above may come into play. Then, a court will need to be convinced that it is fair to overcome the rule that a party may only be compelled to arbitrate disputes that it has agreed to arbitrate. The equities that appear from the underlying facts are likely to be far more important to the outcome than which theory of law is advanced.

VI. Arbitration Agreements and Non-Signatories

What Arbitration Agreement?

Compelling Non-Signatories to Arbitrate

by Charles Lee Eisen[*]

The obligation to arbitrate a dispute is rooted in the contract. But this obligation is not limited to the parties who signed the contract. Sometimes such obligation extends to others who are non-signatories, but are nevertheless linked to the dispute covered by the contract. The following article discusses the underlying legal principles and theories that explain why some non-signatory parties are bound to arbitration agreements. Caution: parties should be aware of possible situations which might lead to a backdoor obligation to arbitrate.

It frequently surprises those involved in business transactions to learn that they may be bound to arbitrate a dispute while never having signed an arbitration agreement. There are a number of circumstances under which such an unexpected arbitration obligation may arise. Some may be avoided (or caused) by artful drafting. Others may result as a matter of law from the facts of the case. Often, this is an issue that is off the radar screen of those charged with counseling their clients in response to the question: "do we arbitrate or do we litigate?"

This article will examine the historical context in which this issue arises. It will be seen that while courts strongly favor arbitration, the obligation is still rooted in contract. Consequently, a party cannot ordinarily be compelled against its will to arbitrate a dispute that it has not agreed to submit to arbitration. Nonetheless, an obligation to arbitrate does not attach only to one who has signed an arbitration agreement. On the contrary, a non-signatory may be bound to arbitrate if that result is dictated by ordinary principles of contract and agency law. Finally, it will be demonstrated that based on such common law principles, there

---

[*] The author is a partner and trial lawyer with Kirkpatrick & Lockhart LLP in their Washington office. He is a member of the National Panel of Arbitrators of the American Arbitration Association and is a Fellow of the American College of Trial Lawyers. Eisen holds a magna cum laude B.A. from Princeton University and an LL.B. from Yale Law School.

are at least five legal theories that have been recognized by the courts under which non-signatories may be bound to arbitration agreements.

Arbitration Law

The centerpiece of arbitration involving interstate commerce is the Federal Arbitration Act (FAA).[1] When interstate commerce is not involved, disputes are often arbitrated pursuant to various state laws governing arbitration. As of this writing, at least thirty-four states and the District of Columbia have enacted the Uniform Arbitration Act (UAA). An additional thirteen states and Puerto Rico have enacted modern arbitration statutes which provide for the enforcement of agreements to arbitrate both existing controversies and any disputes arising in the future.

Both the FAA and the UAA mandate that a written agreement in any contract to submit an existing or future controversy to arbitration is valid, enforceable, and irrevocable except upon such grounds as exist at law or in equity for the revocation of any contract. The principles described in this article are equally applicable to arbitration proceedings whether they arise under the FAA, the UAA, or other modern arbitration statutes.

The United States Supreme Court has held that the liberal policy favoring arbitration agreements "is at bottom a policy guaranteeing the enforcement of private contractual arrangements: the [FAA] simply 'creates a body of federal substantive law establishing and regulating the duty to honor an agreement to arbitrate.'"[2]

The Supreme Court has held that the FAA reflects "a congressional declaration of a liberal federal policy favoring arbitration agreements, notwithstanding any state substantive or procedural policies to the contrary."[3] This liberal federal policy translates into a presumption that "any doubts concerning the scope of arbitrable issues should be resolved in favor of arbitration, whether the problem at hand is the construction of the contract language itself or an allegation of waiver, delay, or a like defense to arbitrability."[4]

However, a presumption in favor of arbitration does not mean that a court is free to compel a party to arbitrate when it has not agreed to do

---

[1] 9 U.S.C. § 1, et seq.

[2] Mitsubishi Motors, Corp. v. Soler Chrysler-Plymouth, Inc.473 U.S. 614, 625 (1985) (*citing* Moses H. Cone Memorial Hosp. v. Mercury Const. Corp., 460 U.S. 1, 25, n.32 (1983)).

[3] *Moses H .Cone,* 460 U.S.., at 24.

[4] *Id.* at 24-25.

so. Arbitration, at its core, is contractual by nature. Arbitrators derive their authority to resolve disputes only from the parties' advance agreement to submit their disputes to arbitration. Therefore, a party cannot be required to arbitrate a dispute that it has not agreed to submit to arbitration.

But it does not follow from these principles that an obligation to arbitrate attaches only to one who has personally signed an arbitration agreement. Indeed, a non-signatory may be bound to arbitrate if dictated by ordinary principles of contract and agency law.[5]

Five Theories

There are five theories that have been recognized by the courts, arising out of common law principles of contract and agency, under which non-signatories may be bound to (or may bind signatories to) arbitration agreements: 1) alter ego or veil-piercing; 2) incorporation by reference; 3) assumption; 4) agency; and 5) equitable estoppel.[6]

A. Alter Ego

One of the more creative ways in which a non-signatory may be bound to arbitrate is by means of piercing the corporate veil of the entity that agreed to arbitrate. By this means, a claimant may compel arbitration from a non-signatory individual or entity for which the corporation is merely an alter ego.[7] This can be an effective practice in circumstances where a claimant has an arbitration agreement with a corporate subsidiary that is or becomes judgment proof and the only relief available is to join the parent corporation as a co-respondent in the arbitration proceeding or to proceed against the parent in a post-award action.

Generally, a parent corporation and its corporate subsidiary are separate and distinct legal entities and, therefore, an agreement by the subsidiary to arbitrate is not an agreement by the parent to do so. However, where a showing of fraud or other legal wrong can be made, or where the affairs of the subsidiary have been so dominated by the parent

---

[5] McAllister Bros., Inc. v. A&S Transp. Co., 621 F.2d 519, 524 (2d Cir. 1980).

[6] American Bureau of Shipping v. Tencara Shipyard S.P.A., 170 F. 3d 349, 352 (2d. Cir. 1999); Thomson-CSF, S.A. v. American Arbitration Ass'n, 64 F.3d 773, 776 (2d Cir. 1995).

[7] TNS Holdings, Inc. v. MKI Securities Corp., 92 N.Y.2d 335, 703 N.E. 2d 749, 751 (N.Y. Ct. App. 1998).

that the parent is effectively controlling the subsidiary, the corporate veil of the parent is pierced and the parent may be compelled to arbitrate notwithstanding that it did not execute the arbitration agreement.[8]

It is also possible under the right circumstances to add an officer or shareholder of the corporate entity as a party to the arbitration proceeding notwithstanding that the individual in his or her personal capacity is a non-signatory to the arbitration agreement. Courts have held that to pierce the corporate veil under such circumstances there must be a unity of ownership and interest between the corporate entity and the individual such that the distinct personalities of the corporation and the individual no longer exist and to adhere to that separateness would promote a fraud or work an injustice.[9]

Although the inquiry is fact-specific in each case, courts will look to whether corporate formalities, such as regular maintenance of board minutes, books, and records have been disregarded, whether the same office space was used by the corporate entity and the individual shareholders, whether there has been a commingling of funds and other assets of the corporation with those of the individual officers or shareholders, and whether corporate funds or assets have been diverted to non-corporate uses such as the personal uses of the corporation's officers or shareholders.

Piercing the veil of a corporate entity to compel a non-signatory to arbitrate is an equitable doctrine, and, therefore, considerations of justice and equity apply. Some courts have rejected the contention that only a showing of fraud will justify piercing the corporate veil and have held that "when the notion of legal entity is used to defeat public convenience, justify wrong, protect fraud, or defend crime, the law will regard the corporation as [merely] an association of persons."[10]

Moreover, because this doctrine is an equitable one, courts have rejected the notion that in order to pierce the veil there must be a showing of fraud "directly tainting the obligation on which the plaintiff is suing."[11]

---

[8] Carte Blanche (Singapore) Pte., Ltd. v. Diners Club Int'l, Inc., 2 F.3d 24, 26 (2d Cir. 1993).

[9] C.F. Trust, Inc. v. First Flight Ltd Partnership, 111 F. Supp. 2d 734, 742 (E.D.Va. 2000); Camacho v. 1440 Rhode Island Ave. Corp., 620 A.2d 242, 249 (D.C. App. 1993) (*citing* McAuliffe v. C&K Builders, Inc., 142 A.2d 605, 607 (1958)).

[10] Callas v. Independent Taxi Owners Ass'n, 66 F.2d 192, 193 (D.C. App. 1933) (*citing* U.S. v. Milwaukee Refrigerator Transit Co., 142 F. 247, 255 (1905)).

[11] Vuitch v. Furr, 482 A.2d 811, 815 (D.C. App. 1984) (*citing* Harris v. Wagshal, 343 A.2d 283, 287-88 (D.C.1975)).

B. Incorporation by Reference

A non-signatory may also compel arbitration against a party to an arbitration agreement under circumstances where the signatory party has executed a different contract with the non-signatory that arguably incorporates by reference the existing arbitration clause.[12]

C. Assumption

A party who has not executed an arbitration agreement may also bind itself to arbitrate by its conduct. In *Gvozdenovic v. United Air Lines, Inc.*,[13] the plaintiffs were a group of former Pan Am flight attendants who had commenced employment with United Airlines following its purchase of Pan Am. The flight attendants appealed from a judgment of the trial court dismissing a class action they had brought against their trade union and United in which they sought to vacate an arbitral award granting them only partial credit in the seniority list for their time of employment with Pan Am. The record demonstrated that the attendants had designated a committee to represent them in the arbitration and the committee had, in turn, selected counsel to represent them and argued vigorously that they should receive full credit for their prior employment.

On appeal, the flight attendants argued that the trial court improperly dismissed their petition for vacatur of the arbitration award because they were not parties to the agreement providing for arbitration. Holding that an agreement to arbitrate "may be implied from a party's conduct," the Second Circuit found that because the flight attendants voluntarily and actively participated in the arbitration process they were bound by its outcome.[14]

Conversely, when a non-signatory receives notice of an arbitration clause contained in an agreement that directly benefits the non-signatory, and it fails to object to the agreement, it may also be bound by its terms.

---

[12] *See* Import Export Steel Corp. v. Mississippi Valley Barge Line Co., 351 F.2d 503, 505-06 (2d Cir. 1965) (different contract with non-signatory incorporating by reference the obligations and privileges of the signatory party under the contract containing the arbitration provision is grounds for enforcement of the arbitration clause by the non-signatory); Continental U.K. Ltd. v. Anagel Confidence Compania Naviera, S.A., 658 F. Supp. 809, 813 (S.D.N.Y. 1987) (when a party's arbitration clause is incorporated into a bill of lading, non-signatories who are linked to that bill of lading through general common law principles of contract or agency may be bound to arbitrate).

[13] 933 F.2d 1100 (2d Cir. 1991), *cert. denied*, 502 U.S. 910 (1991).

[14] *Id.* at 1105.

In *Deloitte Noraudit A/S v. Deloitte Haskins & Sells*,[15] "Deloitte-U.S." appealed an order from the district court denying its motion to compel arbitration of claims asserted against it by "Deloitte-Norway" that the latter had the right to use the Deloitte name in that country. Deloitte-Norway based its claim, in part, on its membership in an international association of Deloitte-U.S. and its worldwide affiliates known as DHSI. The facts revealed that as a result of a 1990 settlement of certain related disputes, the chairman of DHSI executed an agreement on behalf of all DHSI member firms that contained an arbitration clause. Each member of DHSI, including Deloitte-Norway, received a copy of the agreement and each was asked to approve or object to it. Deloitte-Norway did not object to the agreement. Several years later, Deloitte-Norway brought an action in federal district court in New York against Deloitte-U.S. which then sought to compel arbitration. Deloitte-Norway successfully contended at the district court level that because it was not a signatory to the 1990 agreement it was not bound by the arbitration clause contained in the agreement.

On appeal, the Second Circuit reversed and noted that the agreement expressly conditioned the continuing right of DHSI member firms to use the name "Deloitte" on their compliance with the terms of the agreement. The court assumed, as Deloitte-Norway had contended, that it did not receive a copy of the agreement until after it had been executed, but noted it was undisputed that Deloitte-Norway did ultimately receive a copy and never objected to it. The Second Circuit held that Deloitte-Norway was bound by the arbitration clause contained in the agreement based on its receipt of a copy of the agreement without objection and because it knowingly accepted the benefits of the agreement through its continuing use of the name "Deloitte."

D. *Agency*

Traditional principles of agency law may also bind a non-signatory to an arbitration agreement. In *Interbras Cayman Co. v. Orient Victory Shipping Co.*,[16] a shipping company named Frota entered into an agreement to charter a vessel from Orient. The agreement contained a standard arbitration clause. Frota subsequently sub-chartered the vessel to Interbras. A dispute concerning the vessel arose and Interbras demanded arbitration. Interbras originally claimed a right to arbitrate as

---

[15] *Deloitte*, 9 F.3d 1060, 1064 (2d Cir. 1993).
[16] 663 F.2d 4 (2d Cir. 1981).

the assignee of Frota, but it later changed its theory to one of agency, claiming that Frota had entered into the charter agreement that contained the arbitration clause as an undisclosed agent of Interbras. Although the appellate court remanded for a trial on the issue of agency, it held that an undisclosed principal may enforce a contract made for its benefit by an agent even though the signatory to the arbitration clause was unaware of the existence of an undisclosed principal.[17]

Additionally, when an agent executes a contract containing an arbitration clause and fails to reveal that he or she is signing as an agent on behalf of a disclosed principal, then the agent is deemed to be acting on his or her own behalf and may be compelled to arbitrate.[18]

Conversely, it is generally held that an agent who executes an agreement on behalf of a disclosed principal will not be individually bound to the terms of the agreement in the absence of clear evidence of the agent's intention to bind himself instead of or as well as the principal.[19]

E. *Equitable Estoppel*

1. *Permitting non-signatories to compel arbitration by signatories.*

Courts have permitted non-signatories to compel arbitration from signatories under the doctrine of equitable estoppel in two circumstances. First, equitable estoppel applies when the signatory must rely on the terms of the written agreement containing an arbitration clause in asserting its claims against the non-signatory. Second, equitable estoppel may be argued when the signatory alleges interdependent and concerted misconduct by both the non-signatory and one or more of the signatories to the agreement containing an arbitration clause.[20]

An example of the first circumstance is *Sunkist Soft Drinks, Inc. v. Sunkist Growers, Inc.*[21] Defendant Sunkist had entered into a license

---

[17] *Id.* at 6 (*citing* Morris v. Chesapeake & O.S.S. Co., 125 F. 62, 66 (S.D.N.Y. 1903), *aff'd*, 148 F. 11 (2d Cir. 1906, *cert. denied*, 203 US 592 (1906)).

[18] Cosmotek Mumessillik Ve Ticaret Ltd. Sirkketi v. Cosmotek USA, Inc., 942 F. Supp. 757, 760 (D. Conn. 1996) (*citing* Becks v. Suro Textiles Ltd., 612 F. Supp. 1193, 1194 (S.D.N.Y. 1985)).

[19] Lerner v. Amalgamated Clothing & Textile Workers Union, 938 F.2d 2, 5 (2d Cir. 1991).

[20] Grigson, v. Creative Artists Agency, L.L.C., 210 F.3d 524 (5th Cir. 2000), *cert. denied*, 121 S. Ct. 570 (2000).

[21] 10 F.3d 753, 757 (11th Cir. 1993), *cert. denied*, 513 U.S. 869 (1994).

agreement with a licensee providing a detailed framework for marketing its soft drinks. Del Monte subsequently acquired the licensee and absorbed it into its own operating division. Thereafter, a dispute arose between Del Monte and Sunkist that Del Monte sought to arbitrate. Sunkist objected on the ground that Del Monte was a non-signatory to the arbitration agreement between Sunkist and the licensee. The Court of Appeals affirmed the trial court's order to arbitrate. Noting that Sunkist's claims against Del Monte were based on alleged breaches of the license agreement and that the licensee had lost its independent operating status upon being merged into Del Monte, the court concluded that Sunkist's claims "are intimately founded in and intertwined with the license agreement." The court held, therefore, that Sunkist was equitably estopped from avoiding arbitration of its claims.

An example of the second circumstance is *Sam Reisfeld & Son Imp. Co. v. S.A. Eteco*.[22] Reisfeld had acted as the exclusive sales agent of Eteco, a Belgian concern, pursuant to a 1960 agreement containing an arbitration clause. Twelve years later, Eteco notified Reisfeld that it was terminating the arrangement and Reisfeld filed suit against Eteco's successor, Bekaert Overseas, and its parent corporation Bekaert, S.A. The defendants moved to dismiss for lack of jurisdiction and the court treated the motion as one seeking a stay pending arbitration. The Court of Appeals held that the trial court had discretion to include Eteco's parent and successor corporations in its stay order although they were not parties to the 1960 arbitration agreement. The court stated: "The charges against these two [non-signatory] defendants were based on the same operative facts and were inherently inseparable from the claims against Eteco. If the parent corporation was forced to try the case, the arbitration proceedings would be rendered meaningless and the federal policy in favor of arbitration effectively thwarted."

2. *Permitting signatories to compel arbitration by non-signatories.*

Courts have also held that under the doctrine of equitable estoppel a non-signatory may be bound to arbitrate claims that it is pursuing which are "inextricably intertwined" or "inherently inseparable" from other claims the party is pursuing that are subject to arbitration. For example, in *McBro Planning and Development Co. v. Triangle Electronic*

---

[22] 530 F.2d 679 (5th Cir. 1976).

Construction Co., Inc.,[23] plaintiff McBro contracted with a hospital to act as construction manager for a renovation project and defendant Triangle separately contracted with the hospital to perform electrical work for the same project. Both McBro and Triangle had arbitration provisions in their respective contracts with the hospital but the two parties had no contract with each other. Moreover, Triangle's contract with the hospital even provided that nothing contained therein would create any contractual relationship between McBro and Triangle.

Disputes arose between McBro and Triangle pertaining to the hospital construction and, when McBro was sued by Triangle, McBro moved to compel arbitration of Triangle's claims. The Eleventh Circuit held that although Triangle's concerns about being compelled to arbitrate absent a written agreement, and its resulting loss of a jury trial "are well taken," Triangle was equitably estopped from asserting this argument because its claims were "intimately founded in and intertwined with [McBro's] underlying contract obligations" between McBro and the hospital.

The courts have applied similar principles in the context of international arbitration. In *J.J. Ryan & Sons, Inc., v. Rhone Poulenc Textile, S.A., et al.*,[24] Ryan brought tort and contract claims against Rhone and four of its foreign affiliates arising out of the importation of products manufactured by Rhone's affiliates. Ryan had no contractual relations with Rhone; however, it had entered into several contracts with the Rhone affiliates including distribution agreements, security agreements, compensation agreements, and purchase orders. While the distribution contracts between Ryan and the Rhone affiliates contained arbitration clauses, the other agreements did not.

Ryan brought suit against Rhone and its four affiliates alleging a number of contract and tort-based claims. The trial court ordered arbitration of the principal claims against the affiliates under all the contracts notwithstanding the absence of an arbitration clause in the security agreements, the compensation agreements, and the purchase orders. The Fourth Circuit affirmed the order on the ground that although those agreements did not contain arbitration provisions they implemented the distribution agreement that did contain an arbitration provision. The court found that "[w]ithout the ancillary agreements pertaining to the

---

[23] 741 F.2d 342 (11th Cir. 1984).
[24] 863 F.2d 315 (4th Cir. 1988).

details of actual importation of the affiliates' products, the exclusive distribution agreements would be largely illusory."

Moreover, although Rhone was not a party to the distribution contract, it was willing to submit Ryan's claims against it to arbitration. However, Ryan contended that because it had no contract at all with Rhone, the trial court erred in referring its claims against Rhone to arbitration. The Court of Appeals affirmed this arbitration referral as well, holding that when claims against a parent company and its subsidiary "are based on the same facts and are inherently inseparable, a court may refer claims against the parent to arbitration even though the parent is not formally a party to the arbitration agreement."

In short, while a party ordinarily cannot be compelled to arbitrate a dispute against its will or in the absence of its signature on an arbitration agreement, a non-signatory may be bound to arbitrate, or may bind others to arbitrate, under a number of common law principles of contract and agency. Attorneys and company officials should be alert to the possibility that creative arguments based on the principles of alter ego or veil piercing, incorporation by reference, assumption, agency, and equitable estoppel may dictate that their disputes will be resolved in arbitration rather than in court although they have never signed an arbitration agreement.

CHAPTER TWO

ARBITRATION TODAY—RECENT DEVELOPMENTS

I.   Reassessing the Role of Arbitrators

Behind the Neutral:
A Look At Provider Issues

by Thomas J. Stipanowich[*]

In a world where conflict resolution services are rapidly proliferating, one may look wistfully back at a time not so long ago when we stood wide-eyed on the threshold of a universe of dispute resolution possibilities. It is in the nature of things that the innocent rapture of discovery must give way to cold-eyed appraisal of the methods we have embraced, to a more considered assessment of their relative benefits and burdens. Thus, even as many are drawn to ADR by fortune, philosophy or financial need, there is an unprecedented impetus to re-evaluate and possibly to reform.

A few examples. As the National Conference of Commissioners on Uniform State Laws sets to work on a new model mediation act, another NCCUSL committee is revising the venerable Uniform Arbitration Act. Major institutional sponsors of international arbitration, including the American Arbitration Association and the International Chamber of Commerce, recently made significant procedural changes in their international arbitration rules, a development mirrored on the domestic scene. As a result of numerous cases in federal and state courts challenging arbitration provisions in employment, health care and consumer contracts, three new national protocols addressing due process concerns in these arenas have been developed by commissions formed at the impetus of the AAA. In the wake of a report issued by a blue ribbon

---

[*] The author is the President of the CPR Institute for Dispute Resolution and is the former W.L. Matthews Professor of Law at the University of Kentucky. Stipanowich chaired the CPR's Commission on the Future of Arbitration and edited *Commercial Arbitration at Its Best: Successful Strategies for Business Users,* jointly published by the CPR and the American Bar Association (2001).

commission appointed by the National Association of Securities Dealers, many changes, some hotly debated, are occurring in customer/broker arbitration. In addition, several groups are developing ethical standards for neutrals and other participants in ADR. These are only some of the activities inspired by the perceived need for structure, certainty or fairness in conflict resolution.

The thing about reassessment-depending on your point of view, a laudable or a maddening thing-is that it tends to cast a new light on realities that were previously taken for granted, including verities which may not have been on the original agenda for change. Thus, the increasing preoccupation with standards for neutrals and procedural reform has drawn attention to the role played by providers of ADR services–the organizations or programs standing behind the mediator, arbitrator or evaluator.

The Role Providers Play

Since the days when the AAA was virtually unique as an institutional provider of conflict resolution services, much has changed. The contemporary landscape of ADR ranges from complex, multi-faceted organizations of national and international scope to ad hoc arrangements among individuals. Somewhere in between are more specialized services marketing particular procedures (such as adherence to rules of law and evidence, and written arbitration awards) or "celebrity" panelists (e.g., emeritus judges); groups that have evolved to serve the special needs of a community, industry, or business sector; and mom-and-pop mediation services.

The provider's "administrative" role varies greatly: in NASD arbitrations, case managers routinely sit in on hearings; at the AAA, case administrators facilitate many aspects of the ADR process, while the CPR Institute for Dispute Resolution offers "non-administered" procedures with minimal involvement by its employees. All providers, whether for-profit or non-profit, facilitate or implement ADR in one or more forms and, for good or ill, they all compete in the marketplace without significant outside regulation.

Many providers have acted responsibly. In the context of mandatory contractual arbitration, however, particularly in employer-administered employment and health care programs, there have been attacks based on alleged unfairness in the process. For this and other reasons, the provider's role has become the object of some reform efforts. For example, providers are mentioned in the latest drafts of the revised UAA.

The AAA has spearheaded some of the process improvements with the due process protocols in employment, health care and consumer disputes, the latter two of which address the need for independent administration.

Emerging Issues

Why do we care about providers of ADR services? And why have they been drawn into the ongoing debate over the nature and quality of ADR?

Setting the Playing Field. Providers inevitably play a primary role in determining the quality of the user's ADR experience. They often play a critical part in designing the ADR process and fine-tuning the procedural rules that will apply. In administered arbitration, a provider's case administrators or case managers may not only provide information to the parties, they may possess discretion concerning the scheduling of some procedures, such as the timing of preliminary discussions among the parties or the scheduling and location of initial hearings. They may also advise the parties on procedural options and "troubleshoot" problems which the neutrals cannot or will not address, including payment issues.

Neutral Screening. Of all of the ways in which provider organizations may affect the user's experience, none is as likely to be as critical as their role in screening and facilitating the selection of neutrals. Establishing and maintaining a pool of neutrals who meet its requirements for listing is usually a core competency of providers. They often assist in the neutral selection process by identifying prospective neutrals based on criteria provided by the parties and, in some cases, making the appointment. Moreover, providers may be empowered to consider and rule upon challenges to an appointee. At the conclusion of the proceeding, providers may furnish a mechanism for evaluation of the neutral and the process.

Promotional Activities. In the increasingly competitive ADR marketplace, many providers use an assortment of media outlets to advertise their services (including their procedures and the quality of their neutrals) to the general public or to a targeted audience. Because most members of the public (and many members of the bar) are unlikely to have more than the barest notion of what mediation and arbitration entail, they may rely more on a provider's statements about its procedures and panelists than they would on the promises of purveyors of other goods and services.

In this milieu and in light of the vast differences in the scope and type of services available from different providers, potential users of

ADR services need objective help to make a meaningful choice of providers. For commercial users, some guidance may be obtained from industry, trade or professional groups, which may work with a particular provider to develop standard ADR procedures for their constituency. Guidance on ADR standards for employment, health care and consumer disputes may be found in the three due process protocols referred to above (all available from the AAA). Other guidance is in the works. The CPR-sponsored Commission on the Future of Arbitration is considering the kinds of questions prospective users might ask ADR providers. An initiative by the CPR-Georgetown Ethics Commission is focusing on ethical standards for providers.

Provider Immunity. Like the arbitrators who act under their imprimatur, providers are cloaked with quasi-judicial immunity to preserve the integrity of the arbitration process. The principle of arbitral immunity is well established in the courts, along with a "penumbra" of immunity for providers. Current efforts to revise the UAA have inspired a debate over whether such immunity should be limited to so-called "independent" arbitral institutions.

The existence of provider immunity raises the question of alternative ways to ensure accountability. Some providers, to be sure, are making efforts to self-regulate. The AAA, for example, recently announced a new internal ethics policy for all of its staff.

Provider Independence and Interaction with Parties. The establishment of ADR programs at individual companies, such as employment or consumer ADR programs, would seem naturally to result in considerable interaction between the ADR provider and the party. This interaction seems to be regarded with relative casualness by providers, which may view the interaction as appropriate. First, they may perceive great value in preserving an informal interface and buffer between the party and the neutrals who will hear the disputes, particularly in arbitration and other processes limiting *ex parte* contacts. Second, providers often rely to a great extent on their users for input through advisory panel and committees.

But providers should recognize that an ongoing, close connection between a provider and regular user may be a source of concern to the incidental user who is drawn into an ADR process by a pre-dispute ADR clause in a contract of the other party's devising. Even if some interchange between a provider and a party is inevitable, what constitutes inappropriate *ex parte* communication? For example, is it alright for a provider to pass along to a "client," summaries of a particular arbitrator's determinations or of mediator settlement rates, without making them available to the other party? Obviously not. Should there be a presumption of non-independence by a provider that "goes along" with essentially one-sided substantive terms in a standardized agreement?

Although challenges of "systemic bias" in mandatory contractual arbitration programs have tended to receive short shrift in the courts, a number of recent developments suggest that, at least for employees and parties to "adhesion" transactions, the relationships between companies whose contracts call for mandatory binding ADR and their providers may be more closely scrutinized. Recently, several courts have closely examined the relationship between the employer and the institution administering the arbitration services in assessing the sufficiency of the program as a mechanism for guaranteeing the statutory rights of employees. In light of such developments, some providers are reviewing their policies regarding employment ADR.

In the consumer and health care arena, the broad-based national groups that drafted the due process protocols for consumer and health care disputes each concluded that contractually mandated private conflict resolution should be independently administered—a consensus shared by a blue-ribbon panel appointed by the nation's largest HMO in the wake of a California court decision refusing to enforce its in-house arbitration program. Moreover, the Health Care Due Process Protocol provides that "the agreement to use ADR should be knowing and voluntary," and "in disputes involving patients, binding forms of dispute resolution should be used only where the parties agree to do so after a dispute arises." These important developments reflect the good that can come of cooperative efforts by providers and user groups.

Conclusion

The focus on providers has already led to significant process and provider improvements. The trend may lead to further changes, either in the form of additional self-regulation from the ADR community, or from the community at large. Will broad-based, ADR community self-regulation, backed up by court decisions, be sufficient to avoid legislative solutions? (Our experience with securities arbitration indicates that extensive government regulation can be a costly alternative with its own systemic imperfections.) Only time will tell, but much will depend upon the care and discretion with which providers approach their role in the facilitation of out-of-court conflict resolution. They are wise to remember that for an entity holding itself out as the handmaiden of justice, being above reproach, like Caesar's wife, isn't a bad idea.

II. The Consolidation of Arbitral Proceedings

Consolidated Arbitration:
Will It Result in Increased Efficiency
Or an Affront to Party Autonomy?

by Michael F. Hoellering[*]

Multiparty contracts and even multicontract business arrangements frequently lead to multiple unforeseen problems when disputes arise. Three issues predominate: Will an arbitration agreement be enforced when some of the parties are not bound to arbitrate? Should there be joinder of the parties and consolidation of the claims, and how may this be effected? How will procedural matters, such as arbitrator selection, be handled under such complex circumstances? Hoellering offers a comprehensive examination of the relevant court perspective on these and related issues.

The majority of arbitrations involve two parties and are governed by one contract with one arbitration clause. At the same time, however, arbitration encompasses the resolution of multiparty disputes, arising in the context of the more complex international transactions, in the maritime, insurance and construction fields, and where buyers and retailers operate as a chain. In some such controversies the parties will all be signatories to the contract(s) containing an arbitration clause which outlines the procedures for each party to follow should a dispute arise. More often different contracts will be involved, the arbitration provisions will not be integrated, and certainly the parties will not have the same interests at stake.

Under such circumstances, three types of issues tend to arise: (1) those relating to the enforcement of arbitration when not all parties to the dispute are bound to arbitrate; (2) whether, and how to effectuate the joinder of parties and consolidation of claims into a single proceeding; and (3) if such occurs, the method of handling problematic procedural issues, such as arbitrator selection.

---

[*] This article is authored by the late Michael Hoellering, former General Counsel of the American Arbitration Association and President of the International Federation of Commercial Arbitration.

Effect of Arbitration Agreement

Frequently, not all parties to a dispute, or only a portion of the disputed claims, will be the subject of the applicable arbitration agreement(s). In such cases, what is the effect of the arbitration agreement and how will it impact on related litigation? Both aspects of the issue were the subject of recent decisions of the U.S. Supreme Court. The first case involved a dispute between two contracting parties, where some of the claims fell within the scope of the arbitration clause and some did not. In a securities case, *Dean Witter Reynolds, Inc. v. Byrd*,[1] the court had to decide whether, when a complaint raises both non-arbitrable federal securities claims and arbitrable pendent state claims, a federal district court may deny arbitration of the state law claims despite the parties' agreement to arbitrate their disputes. It was argued that when arbitrable and non-arbitrable claims arise out of the same transaction, and are sufficiently intertwined factually and legally, the district court may in its discretion deny arbitration as to the arbitrable claims and try all the claims together in federal court. The proponents asserted, inter alia, "that by declining to compel arbitration, the court avoids bifurcated proceedings and perhaps redundant efforts to litigate the same factual questions twice."[2]

The court rejected this argument and concluded that a court must compel arbitration of otherwise arbitrable claims when a motion to compel is made, and noted that "[t]he legislative history of the [Federal Arbitration Act] establishes that the purpose behind its passage was to ensure judicial enforcement of privately made agreements to arbitrate. We therefore reject the suggestion that the overriding goal of the Arbitration Act was to promote the expeditious resolution of claims."[3] The court further expounded, "[t]he preeminent concern of Congress in passing the Act was to enforce private agreements into which parties had entered, and that concern requires that we rigorously enforce agreements to arbitrate, even if the result is 'piecemeal' litigation, at least absent a countervailing policy manifested in another federal statute."[4]

In the second case, *Volt Information Sciences, Inc. v. Board of Trustees of Leland Stanford Junior University*,[5] the parties entered into a construction contract which contained an agreement to arbitrate all

---

[1] 105 S. Ct. 1238 (1985).
[2] *Id.* at 1240.
[3] *Id.* at 1242.
[4] *Id.*
[5] 109 S. Ct. 1248 (1989).

disputes between the parties "arising out of or relating to this contract or the breach thereof." They also agreed that their arbitration agreement would be governed by the law of the place of the project, California.

A dispute arose concerning compensation of additional work and Volt made a formal demand for arbitration. Stanford responded by filing an action against Volt in California Superior court and sought indemnity from two other companies involved in the project with whom it did not have arbitration agreements. Volt petitioned the court to compel arbitration of the dispute while Stanford moved to stay the arbitration pursuant to California Civil Procedure Code § 1281.2(c), which permits a court to stay arbitration pending resolution of related litigation between a party to the arbitration agreement and third parties not bound by it, where "there is a possibility of conflicting rulings on a common issue of law or fact."[6]

The court was asked to determine whether the FAA preempted the state civil code. In enacting the FAA, Congress' purpose was to ensure that private arbitration agreements are enforced according to their terms, and this court has held that the FAA preempts state laws which "require a judicial forum for the resolution of claims which the contracting parties agreed to resolve by arbitration."[7] It follows that the "FAA does not require parties to arbitrate when they have not agreed to do so, ...nor does it prevent parties who do agree to arbitrate from excluding certain claims from the scope of their arbitration agreement."[8]

The Supreme Court ultimately affirmed the stay of the arbitration proceedings noting that, "where, as here, the parties have agreed to abide by state rules of arbitration, enforcing those rules according to the terms of the agreement is fully consistent with the goals of the FAA, even if the result is that arbitration is stayed where the Act would otherwise permit it to go forward." It is important to note that this is a domestic case, not arising under the New York Convention, and that California has since enacted an International Arbitration Law[9] that would likely preempt and make inapplicable the stay provision of the California Code.

Another relevant issue in the context of multiparty arbitration is the extent to which the existence of a pending bankruptcy can pose an obstacle to related arbitration proceedings. In the past, U.S. courts have generally subordinated enforcement of privately negotiated arbitration

---

[6] *Id.* at 1251.
[7] *Id.* at 1255.
[8] *Id.*
[9] Cal. Civ. Proc. Code §§ 1297.11-1297.432.

provisions to the broader goals of the Bankruptcy Code and interests of creditors, who would not be a party to an arbitration, by deferring to the jurisdiction of the bankruptcy courts. More recently, particularly in international cases in which core bankruptcy issues were not involved, the courts have tipped the judicial scale in favor of arbitration.

An early example was the *Distrigas* case, wherein the court upheld a contractual arbitration provision and permitted the creditor foreign state enterprise to proceed in the international arbitration against a Chapter 7 debtor.[10] It should be noted that the debtor had filed a Chapter 11 proceeding but was unable to obtain approval of a reorganization plan. At issue was the liability, if any, and the valuation of contract damages arising from the debtor's rejection of a long-term supply contract for the purchase and sale of Algerian liquefied natural gas. The court found that (1) the arbitration of contract damages does not implicate any core bankruptcy issues; (2) there is a strong national policy favoring international arbitration; and (3) the arbitration of the instant dispute did not conflict with bankruptcy policies in a liquidation proceeding.

In another such case, *In re Dollar Corporation*,[11] the court held that the duty to enforce an international arbitration agreement under the FAA is not diminished when one of the parties to the contract files for relief in bankruptcy court. Hyundai Motor Company and Dollar Corporation entered into a contract wherein Dollar agreed to supply and install floor plan assembly equipment at Hyundai's automobile manufacturing plant in Korea. The contract provided for the arbitration of disputes in Seoul, Korea. Design specifications were changed during the course of performance which caused damages to both parties. Disputes over this matter were not yet resolved when Dollar filed a voluntary petition under Chapter 11 of the Bankruptcy Code (Code). A court order was issued granting the Unsecured Creditor's Committee of Dollar Corporation full authority to pursue Dollar's claims against Hyundai. After the committee filed a complaint, Hyundai moved for a stay pending arbitration pursuant to the FAA.

At issue was whether the Code conflicted with the FAA. The court noted several bankruptcy cases that have held that the duty to enforce an international arbitration agreement under the FAA is not diminished, nor is there any conflict which arises between the FAA and the Code, when

---

[10] Societe Nationale Algerienne Pour La Recherche, La Production, Le Transport, La Transformation el La Commercialisation des Hydrocarbures, 80 B.R. 606 (D. Mass. 1987).

[11] In re Dollar Corporation (Unsecured Creditor's Committee of Dollar Corporation v. Hyundai Motor Company), 88-08473-5, slip op. (Bankr. E.D. Mich. Jan. 30, 1992).

one of the parties to the contract files for relief in bankruptcy court. The court concluded that the reasoning in those cases applied to the case at bar because the proceeding involved is not a core matter, the issues were within the broad scope of the arbitration clause, and that nothing in the Code and its legislative history would prevent the arbitration panel from determining whether Hyundai had breached the agreement. Specifically, "the fact that the issue in the proceeding ar[o]se in the context of a bankruptcy does not invalidate the clause in the agreement of the parties to have any disputes or claims submitted and settled by a panel of arbitrators in Korea."[12]

The court also distinguished cases holding that the Code superseded the pro-arbitration policy of the FAA from the case at bar, finding that those cases are limited and do not control where the dispute contains a significant international dimension. Finally, the court considered the standard utilized by courts in cases involving domestic arbitration: whether the issue can be resolved more expeditiously by the bankruptcy court judge than by the arbitration process; whether or not special expertise is necessary in deciding the issue; whether arbitration threatens the assets of the estate; and the impact on creditors of the debtor who were never parties to the agreement containing the arbitration clause. Because these four factors were resolved in favor of arbitration in this case, and in accordance with its other findings, the court granted Hyundai's motion for the stay.

In *In re Mor-Ben*,[13] the court similarly held that, in the absence of congressional intent to exclude arbitration from bankruptcy matters or a compelling circumstance seriously affecting the rights of creditors, the bankruptcy court properly ordered arbitration to proceed in London pursuant to a valid arbitration clause in an international agreement.

Mor-Ben entered into an agreement with three insurers giving Mor-Ben the authority to bind property insurance on their behalf. A dispute arose regarding Mor-Ben's entitlement to reimbursements after it filed a Chapter 11 petition. The insurers filed proofs of claim and Mor-Ben subsequently initiated adversary proceedings. The bankruptcy court stayed the adversary proceedings and compelled arbitration against Mor-Ben. On appeal, the court determined that the evidence supported the bankruptcy court's finding that London was the most expeditious site for resolving the dispute between the parties. It was the parties' original

---

[12] *Id.* slip. op., at 6.
[13] 73 B.R. 644 (Bankr. 9th Cir. 1987).

intent to arbitrate the dispute in London, and London was the principal place of business for the majority of the parties.

A contrary result was obtained in *Corcoran v. Ardra Insurance Company, Ltd.*[14] The issue raised was whether the liquidator of an insolvent insurance company can be compelled to arbitrate the insolvent's claims against a foreign reinsurer. The court held that he could not, even though the reinsurance agreements fell within the broad terms of the United Nations Convention on the Recognition and Enforcement of Foreign Arbitral Awards (Convention),[15] because the arbitration clauses and the dispute alleged to be subject to them are not capable of performance and settlement under New York law. Because U.S. law provides that insurance matters are governed by the laws of the individual states since it is a matter of state concern, the court determined that New York Insurance Law is the law to be applied in interpreting the Convention's exceptions.

The court found that Corcoran "ha[d] no authority to pursue the commercial interests which motivated the original parties to conclude the reinsurance agreements,"[16] since he stepped into Nassau's shoes only because Nassau no longer existed. Since the "statutory scheme does not authorize his participation in arbitration proceedings... [t]he arbitration clause is 'incapable of being performed'"[17] under Article II of the Convention. Consequently, the claims are not "capable of settlement by arbitration" under the applicable domestic law per Article I of the Convention.[18] The court further reasoned that an arbitration award need not be enforced under Article V of the Convention if the subject matter of the dispute is not capable of settlement by arbitration under the law of the country in which recognition and enforcement is being sought.

Effectuating Consolidation and Joinder

There appears to be a consensus that in the appropriate case, where common issues of law and fact exist, for reasons of economy and consistency of result, the dispute resolution process will benefit from the consolidation of proceedings and/or claims. Thus, it has been noted that the policies in favor of consolidated arbitration proceedings generally outweigh competing concerns, and that it should be permitted in

---

[14] 77 N.Y.2d 225, 567 N.E.2d 969, 566 N.Y.S.2d 575 (1990).
[15] 21 U.S.T. 2517, T.I.A.S. No. 6997, 330 U.N.T.S. 4739 (June 10, 1958).
[16] *Id.* at 578.
[17] *Id.* at 578-79.
[18] *Id.* at 579.

appropriate circumstances.[19] "It can promote efficiency, economy and expedience by resolving related disputes in one proceeding rather than two or more."[20] Moreover, one uniform award may be more equitable than subjecting parties to the risk of inconsistent or even contradictory awards in multiple proceedings.[21] Nevertheless, there are some who believe that "it is far from clear that one single multiparty arbitration can be conducted in shorter time and with lower costs than two or more separate proceedings."[22] And, if imposed by a court or arbitral tribunal, rather than voluntarily agreed to by the parties, consolidated arbitration may be deemed to represent a fundamental invasion of the consensual nature of arbitration. These divergent views are also reflected in U.S. court decisions on consolidation and joinder.

Case Law

In 1975, the Second Circuit Court of Appeals held that under the FAA, arbitration cases could be consolidated without the consent of the parties.[23] The *Nereus* case involved a multiparty dispute over a petroleum shipping concern. The contract between the ship's owner and the charterer contained a broad arbitration clause, directing that "any and all differences and disputes of whatsoever nature arising out of this Charter shall be put to arbitration..." Later, the owner, the charterer and a third party/guarantor all signed an addendum to the charter contracts in which the third party agreed to guarantee the obligations of the charterer and would do so "on the same terms and conditions as contained in the Charter Party" and which did not refer to arbitration.

Disputes arose and the owner declared the charterer in default and initiated separate arbitrations against the charterer and the guarantor. The charterer petitioned the court to consolidate the proceedings and over objections from the owner, the lower court consolidated the two arbitrations. On appeal the court ruled that under the Federal Rules of Civil Procedure and more significantly under the Federal Arbitration Act,

---

[19] Thomas J. Stipanowich, Arbitration and the Multiparty Dispute: The Search for Workable Solutions, 72 IOWA L. REV. 473, 523 (MARCH 1987).

[20] Richard E. Wallace, Consolidated Arbitration in the United States-Recent Authority Requires Consent of the Parties, 10 JOURNAL OF INT. ARB. 5, 17 (DEC. 1993).

[21] *Id.*

[22] Andreas Austmann, *Commercial Multi-Party Arbitration: Case-By-Case Approach*, THE AMERICAN REVIEW OF INTERNATIONAL ARBITRATION, FALL 1990.

[23] Compania Espanola de Petroleos, S.A.v. Neretts Shipping, S.A., 527 F.2d 966 (2d Cir. 1975), *cert. denied*, 426 U.S. 936 (1976).

courts have authority to forcibly consolidate arbitrations involving common questions of fact or law, at least where separate arbitrations would pose a risk of inconsistent awards. Specifically, the court noted "[w]e think the liberal purposes of the Federal Arbitration Act clearly require that this Act be interpreted so as to permit and even to encourage the consolidation of arbitration proceedings in proper cases, such as the one before us."[24]

For many years after the *Nereus* holding, the lower courts within the Second Circuit continued to order the consolidation of related cases without regard to party consent. This was so until 1993 when the Second Circuit shifted its rule on consolidation in *United Kingdom v. Boeing Co.*,[25] reversed the *Nereus* decision and prohibited consolidated arbitrations absent consent of the parties.

The *Boeing* case involved losses incurred by the United Kingdom as a result of a helicopter testing incident. Boeing manufactured the helicopter and Textron manufactured its engine and developed the fuel control system that was being tested at the time of the incident. The companies both had separate contracts with the United Kingdom providing for arbitration of disputes by a three-member panel in New York, under AAA rules. Boeing rejected consolidated arbitration and the United Kingdom petitioned for an order to consolidate the two proceedings.

The court, after reviewing several recent U.S. Supreme Court decisions, concluded that under the FAA, private arbitration agreements are to be treated as other contracts negotiated between private parties, and that district courts should be concerned with enforcing the parties' agreement as written, regardless of potential inefficiencies created by such enforcement. The Courts of Appeal for the Fifth,[26] Sixth,[27] Eighth,[28] Ninth[29] and Eleventh[30] Circuits have generally followed this proposition. These two significant decisions demonstrate a clear shift in the policy of the courts when determining questions of consolidation. Prior to *Boeing*, courts looked primarily to the liberal purposes of the FAA when ordering

---

[24] *Nereus, supra*, note 20.
[25] 998 F.2d 68, 74 (2d Cir. 1993).
[26] Del E. Webb Constr. v. Richardson Hosp. Auth., 823 F.2d 145, 150 (5th Cir. 1987).
[27] American Centennial Ins. v. National Cas. Co., 951 F.2d 107, 108 (6th Cir. 1991).
[28] Baesler v. Continental Grain Co., 900 F.2d 1193, 1195 (8th Cir. 1990).
[29] Weyerhaeuser Co. v. Western Seas Shipping Co., 743 F.2d 635, 637 (9th Cir. 1984), *cert. den.*, 469 U.S. 1061 (1984).
[30] Protective Life Ins. Co. v. Lincoln Nat'l Life Ins. Corp., 873 F.2d 281, 282 (11th Cir. 1989) (per curiam).

consolidation over the objections of the parties, whereas now courts principally look to the agreement of the parties and whether they intended to and/or did agree to consolidate such disputes.

In a more recent case, *North River Ins. Co. v. Philadelphia Reins. Corp.*,[31] the Second Circuit Court of Appeals was again confronted with the issue of the validity of consolidation of claims into a single arbitration proceeding. In this case, however, the circuit court reversed the district court's decision vacating the award and upheld the decision to consolidate, despite lack of consent by all of the parties. North River commenced two separate arbitration proceedings against two separate reinsurers. After North River chose the same arbitrator for the two proceedings, and each of the reinsurers chose the same arbitrator for their individual arbitration proceedings, and the two arbitrators could not agree on a third, North River petitioned the court under the FAA for an order consolidating the two proceedings. Although the reinsurers objected, no appeal followed from the district court's decision ordering the consolidation.

Upon motion to confirm the award in North River's favor, the reinsurers cross-moved to vacate the award based upon the holding in *Boeing*. The court distinguished the facts in *Boeing* from *Nereus*, and noted that *Boeing* did "not disturb *Nereus* to the extent it is based on the general equitable powers of the court and principles of contract law"[32] and held that "equitable principles allow for confirmation of an award in a consolidated proceeding already had, especially when the parties did not appeal from the order of consolidation."[33] Perhaps, on a theory of implied consent to joinder, we are now beginning to see another shift in the judicial attitude towards consolidation.

An alternative source of judicial authority to consolidate related arbitration proceedings may be found in certain state statutes, such as those of Massachusetts[34] and California.[35] Thus, in *New England Energy, Inc. v. Keystone Shipping Co.*,[36] the court held that the FAA does not preclude a district court from ordering consolidation of arbitrations pursuant to state law providing for such where the agreement between the parties is silent on the issue.

---

[31] 63 F.3d 160 (2d Cir. 1995).
[32] *Supra*, note 25, at 74.
[33] *Supra*, note 31, at 165.
[34] Mass. Ann. Laws Chap. 251, § 2A.
[35] *See supra*, note 9, at § 1297.272.
[36] 855 F.2d 1 (1st Cir. 1988).

New England Energy and Keystone Shipping were signatories to one of two maritime contracts. Each contract contained an arbitration clause providing for the arbitration of disputes in Boston "pursuant to the laws relating to arbitration there in force."[37] One contract involved the creation of a joint venture for the purpose of owning and operating a coal-carrying ship, and the other involved the chartering of the ship from the joint venture. After separate arbitration actions were filed pursuant to the two contracts, one of the parties filed in state court seeking a consolidation of the two arbitrations.

The appellate court held that federal courts have the power to order consolidation of arbitrations when the agreement of the parties is silent on the issue. It rejected Keystone's argument that ordering consolidation pursuant to a state statute constituted a modification of the arbitration agreement in violation of § 4 of the FAA. The court also noted that the FAA has never been construed to preempt state law on arbitration. Since the FAA is silent on the issue of consolidation, the court concluded that the Massachusetts provision allowing consolidation of arbitrations was not in conflict with the FAA.

It should be noted that, for purposes of international arbitration, some such state provisions have now been superseded by state enactments of the UNCITRAL Model Law. To the extent that these provide for court assistance in consolidating arbitrations, they do so only where the parties have so agreed, in their respective arbitration agreements or otherwise.

AAA Policy

The question of whether multiple claims involving the same general transaction but separate agreements should be arbitrated jointly or separately arises with some frequency in AAA-administered cases. The AAA's administrative policy on consolidation and joinder is to initiate the arbitration as filed by the moving party, even though separate contracts may be involved, thereby providing parties with an opportunity to proceed jointly if they so desire. Should one or more parties object to such a procedure, the cases will be separated and processed individually unless a court orders otherwise. Separately instituted cases may be consolidated whenever all parties mutually agree or consolidation is ordered by the courts.

---

[37] *Id.* at 3.

In its efforts to facilitate an efficient arbitration process, the AAA routinely seeks to assist parties in resolving contested threshold consolidation and joinder issues. Based on the experience gained in a large number of construction cases, such efforts frequently succeed in vertical disputes, involving the owner, general contractor, and one or more subcontractors. They have been less successful in horizontal disputes, involving the owner, contractor, and architect or engineer. The reluctance of design professionals to participate in consolidated proceedings is reflected in the standard American Institute of Architects (AIA) agreement which expressly precludes the inclusion of the architect, or his employees or consultants, in any consolidated proceeding without the consent of all parties. There are other parties, however, who anticipate multiparty arbitration and expressly provide for consolidation or permit the intervention of a third party, by drafting a clause such as the following:

The owner, the contractor, and all subcontractors, specialty contractors, material suppliers, engineers, designers, architects, construction lenders, bonding companies, and other parties concerned with the construction of the structure are bound, each to each other, by this arbitration clause, provided that they have signed this contract or a contract that incorporates by reference this contract or signed any other agreement to be bound by this arbitration clause.

An even broader clause providing for the consolidation of separate arbitrations might read as follows:

> Arbitration proceedings under this agreement may be consolidated with arbitration proceedings pending between other parties if the arbitration proceedings arise from the same transaction or relate to the same subject matter. Consolidation will be by an order of the arbitrator in any of the pending cases or, if the arbitrator fails to make such an order, the parties may apply to any court of competent jurisdiction for such an order.

In the absence of governing contractual provisions, multiparty arbitration in AAA cases is currently being facilitated in several ways. At the outset, the AAA case administrator will attempt to negotiate an acceptable course of action and procedure to be followed. In maritime and construction cases, the parties generally experience a smoothly-run consolidated proceeding.

Aside from scheduling difficulties, they have commonly viewed such proceedings as "not particularly difficult." One explanation for this may be that the parties are all from the same industry, wish to maintain working relationships with one another, and are aware of the potential advantages of a consolidated proceeding. Further, they will be familiar with the kinds of disputes and arguments which the arbitration is intended to resolve.

When issues of consolidation and joinder cannot be resolved on an administrative level, the use of a neutral expert-mediator or arbitrator-to assist the parties in devising a procedure which accommodates participation by all relevant parties, may achieve the desired result. Resort to mediation or conciliation, if not contributing to a resolution of the entire dispute, should serve to lessen the procedural and practical difficulties which attend multiparty proceedings, particularly between parties from diverse legal and economic systems.[38] Another frequently utilized approach is to submit the consolidation issues to the arbitrator(s) for resolution, as a preliminary matter. For instance, when related demands for arbitration under the Commercial Rules are filed with the AAA, and all parties have signed the same contract with a broad arbitration clause, a list for the selection of the arbitrator(s) in the first case will be submitted to all parties, with a notice that the questions of consolidation will be submitted to the arbitrator(s) in that case.

A variation of this approach, employed in several recent cases with the approval by the parties, is to appoint an arbitrator for the sole purpose of deciding the consolidation or joinder issues. This may not be a viable option in the more complex and highly contested cases calling for a comprehensive evaluation of contractual relationships, or raising jurisdictional issues bearing on the identity of proper parties, piercing the corporate veil, etc., which are the very issues that the arbitral tribunal dealing with the merits of the dispute will need to decide.

Another possibility is to conduct parallel proceedings, with the same arbitral tribunal in two or more cases. This occurs rarely, perhaps because the same arbitrators are seldom chosen and the parties, whose cooperation is required, prefer a single consolidated proceeding. It has been pointed out that this approach "may give rise to difficulties because

---

[38] Howard M. Holtzmann, *Conciliation: A Promising Procedure for Resolving Multiparty Disputes*, International Arbitration Symposium Sponsored by International Council for Commercial Arbitration and Polish Chamber of Foreign Trade (Warsaw, 1980).

such arbitrators may be inclined to use in the second proceedings information acquired in the first."[39]

Arbitrator Selection

Among the most difficult issues of consolidated arbitration is that of determining the procedure for arbitrator selection, which can be rather complex, depending on the number of parties, contractual relationships, nature of respective claims, and the stage to which the selection process has progressed. Many features of the original arbitration agreement will be altered in a consolidated proceeding, e.g., the method for selecting arbitrators will have to be modified in order to accommodate the interests of the increased number of parties. Thus, in the Nereus case, the court directed each of the three parties to appoint one arbitrator, and then selected two additional court-appointed arbitrators.

Generally, when ordering consolidation, the courts have been quite willing to alter contractual appointment provisions to make them fit the needs of a unified procedure. Arbitral institutions, in the absence of governing provisions in the applicable rules, do not have such powers. Nevertheless, the problem will arise whenever separate arbitration agreements specify different methods of choosing the arbitrators; e.g., international arbitration clauses often provide that each party appoint an arbitrator, and that those two then appoint the presiding arbitrator. The parties may also specify in their agreement one or more particular arbitrators, or they may designate institutional rules, such as those of the AAA, to govern arbitrator selection.

Where multiple parties' agreements specify multiple methods by which to select arbitrators, these invariably will have to be changed to accommodate a multiparty proceeding. One author suggests a way to resolve this dilemma: Since parties may have different views and contrasting interests as to how the selection process should take place, "one approach is for the parties to relinquish the right to individually appoint arbitrators, leaving the appointment of all arbitrators to an appointing authority, such as an arbitral institution."[40] In fact, current proposals for the amendment of both ICC and AAA Rules to deal with this problem are very much along these lines.

---

[39] Mauro Rubino Sammartano, International Arbitration Law 185 (Kluwer Law & Taxation Publishers, 1990) p. 185.

[40] Lawrence W. Newman and Michael Burrows, *Arbitration and Disputes Involving Multiple Parties*, ARBITRATION & THE LAW 1993-94: AAA GENERAL COUNSEL'S ANNUAL REPORT, pp. 135, 145.

At present, AAA administrators deal with the arbitrator selection process on a case by case basis, exploring with the parties and their representatives the possibility of resolving such difficulties. To avoid costs and unduly complicated proceedings, every effort is made to limit the reconstituted tribunal to no more than three arbitrators. It will be more difficult to deal with this issue if one or all three of the arbitrators, or the panels in the proceedings to be consolidated, have been appointed at the time of consolidation, as some of the newly joined or rearranged parties will not have had an opportunity to select the arbitrator(s). For the most part, it does not pose a problem in construction cases, for the arbitrators are usually not yet appointed when consolidation occurs. This is because the parties to be included are generally involved early on, and those that do join in after the selection process has taken place are parties with nominal claims who accept and are willing to work with the tribunal already in place.

Procedurally, AAA administrators generally inform a new party of the identity of the tribunal and proceed with the case, unless the new party raises an objection to the existing tribunal. If an objection is raised and not resolved, and all parties fail to agree on a revised procedure or have not mutually agreed on the designation of the arbitrator(s), the administrator, pursuant to Article 6 of the AAA International Rules, shall administratively appoint the arbitrator(s) and designate the presiding arbitrator. In cases governed by the AAA commercial, construction, patent or other such rules, the traditional list procedure is employed to constitute a new arbitral tribunal.

Legislation

As previously described, some more recent U.S. case law and state arbitration enactments anchor the power of courts to direct consolidation and/or joinder on the agreement of all concerned parties. Such is also the case with the new English Arbitration Act which permits parties to agree on the consolidation of related arbitrations or concurrent hearings but specifies that unless the parties confer such power on the arbitral tribunal, it cannot order same.[41] Hong Kong, usually in the forefront of arbitration practice, limits non-consensual consolidation only to domestic arbitration.

Sweden has refrained from inserting any provision on multiparty arbitration or consolidation into its law, mainly because of their

---

[41] Article 35, English Arbitration Act.

complexity: "[R]espect for party autonomy is said to prevent any proposal of mandatory consolidation absent consent of the parties."[42] Canadian enactments provide that on application of all the parties to two or more arbitral proceedings the court may order consolidation on the terms it considers just. Several U.S. states, in their international acts, have included consolidation provisions,[43] one of which specifies that, upon application by one party with the consent of all other parties to those arbitration agreements, where the parties to two or more arbitration agreements have agreed, in their respective agreements, to consolidate the proceedings arising out of those arbitration agreements, the court may: (1) order the arbitrations to be consolidated; (2) appoint an arbitral tribunal for the consolidated arbitration (where all parties cannot agree on such); or (3) make any orders it deems necessary, where parties cannot agree on other necessary matters relating to the conduct of the consolidated arbitration.[44] The UNCITRAL Model Law on International Commercial Arbitration itself does not include any provisions on the subject of consolidation.

A notable exception to the general reluctance to impose non-consensual consolidation is The Netherlands Arbitration Act of 1986, which provides for the consolidation, without party consent, of arbitral proceedings taking place in The Netherlands by a single court, i.e., the Amsterdam District Court. The parties may, however, opt out of this possibility. It has been suggested that mandatory arbitration which disrupts the agreed-upon arbitrator selection procedure may well jeopardize the enforcement of arbitral awards, by reason of Article V(I)(d) of the New York Convention. Such should not be the case, however, where non-consensual consolidation is the result of the law of the place of arbitration, which the parties themselves have chosen.

Arbitration Rules

Given the complex nature of modern commercial transactions, it may not always be possible, or it may require extraordinary drafting, for parties to regulate in advance the modalities of multiparty arbitration in their arbitration clause(s). It has been suggested, therefore, that specific authority for consolidation and joinder should be provided by institutional arbitration rules.

---

[42] 42 Draft of New Swedish Arbitration Act, A Presentation, June 1994.
[43] *See supra*, notes 9 and 25.
[44] *See supra*, note 9, at § 2297.272.

At present, except for automobile accident arbitrations, only the AAA Grain Arbitration Rules provide for consolidation when contracts are interrelated or the parties or disputes so interdependent "that consolidation will result in a more economic or efficient disposal of the issues..."[45] The decision on whether or not to consolidate is made by a panel of arbitrators who may then continue to adjudicate the consolidated case. Its members are appointed from a predetermined list of experts, designated in rotation. To a large extent, the relatively smooth operation of this procedure is attributable to the simple arbitrator selection process, a requirement that all arbitrations be held in New York City, and the established practices and customs of the grain export trade.

The construction industry also has considered extensively whether the Construction Arbitration Rules should be amended to provide for the consolidation of claims arising under separate agreements between the parties, but involving the same construction project. The conclusion reached, based on surveys indicating that consolidation might be appropriate in some instances but not in others, was that the parties themselves should regulate, in their arbitration agreement or at the time of arbitration, the question of whether multiple claims involving the same project but separate agreements should be arbitrated jointly or separately.

More recently, the AAA Case Administration Advisory Committee has proposed to amend the Commercial Arbitration Rules so as to "...make the existing case administration system more desirable to its users, more efficient, and less costly for the AAA to deliver." Among the many proposals is a provision concerning consolidation/ joinder:

Consolidation, of two or more arbitrations, or joinder of one or more parties to an existing arbitration, shall be had where all of the following circumstances exist:

(a) each of the parties has agreed to arbitrate under these rules or the AAA's auspices, provided there is no provision in the arbitration clauses excluding consolidation;

(b) there exist common issues of law or fact involved in each of the arbitrations to be consolidated or joined;

(c) consolidation or joinder may result in a more economical or efficient resolution of the issues presented; and

---

[45] Rule 7, AAA Grain Arbitration Rules.

(d) no party shall be substantially prejudiced by the consolidation or joinder.

A party to an arbitration wishing consolidation or joinder shall notify in writing all interested parties and the AAA of its desire for consolidation or joinder. Any party that does not object within 10 days after transmittal of the notice shall be deemed to have agreed to consolidation or joinder. If any party objects during the 10-day period, the matter shall be referred to the arbitrator of the first arbitration filed.

No consolidation or joinder may be requested later than twenty days before the first date on which hearings in any affected arbitration are scheduled to commence. The AAA is empowered to take reasonable administrative action to accomplish consolidation or joinder.

Given that national legislators and the courts are reluctant to impose consolidation on the parties without their consent, it seems sensible to explore whether a workable consolidation/joinder mechanism cannot be incorporated in institutional rules. While issues of consolidation and joinder do not arise in a large number of arbitrated cases, empowering arbitrators under well-defined criteria to resolve such issues would reduce the need for court intervention in the arbitral process; also, by being "consensual," it should reduce potential complications at the award enforcement stage.

With respect to the above quoted draft, one might ask whether (1) an automatic generally applicable provision is suitable for the many different types of disputes arbitrated under the Commercial Rules; and (2) whether according jurisdiction to an arbitrator in whose selection an affected party did not have an opportunity to participate is legally permissible. Only recently in *Dutco*, the French Cour de Cassation[46] has ruled that the imposition of a joint arbitrator nomination on two defendants violated the principle of equality of the parties and the public policy of the forum. While not every jurisdiction may share this view, the ICC is now reconsidering its practice of requiring multiple claimant or defendant parties to jointly agree on the nomination of one arbitrator. For the same reason it has also been proposed that the AAA's International Rules include the following new section: "If two or more claimants or two or more respondents are named in the Statement of Claim, the administrator shall appoint all the arbitrators unless the parties have agreed otherwise no later than forty-five days after the commencement of the arbitration."

---

[46] First Civil Chamber, 7 January 1992.

Conclusion

It has been suggested that to accommodate the concept of consolidation in the arbitration process, effort is required on many levels—through clarification of the authority of the courts to order consolidation and joinder; the amendment of institutional rules to provide systematic treatment of the problem, and above all, through carefully drafted arbitration clauses which take into account the issues of multiparty arbitration. At the same time, it is well to remember that arbitration is a consensual process, and that disregard of a party's contractual rights to force consolidated arbitration is not likely to enhance the ultimate enforceability of the arbitral award.

III. New Techniques to Manage Complex Commercial Disputes

Streamlining Arbitration of the Complex Case

*by John Wilkinson**

As increasing numbers of complex commercial disputes are submitted to arbitration, it becomes imperative that the handling of such cases be cost-effective and expeditious while at the same time achieve a fair and complete hearing that will inspire confidence in the process. What steps should be taken to ensure this? The effective management of complex disputes is a progression that should commence at the first prehearing conference and continue through to the submission of posthearing briefs.

The primary reason for the mushrooming popularity of arbitration for large cases is that business managers and their general counsel have increasingly recognized that this form of dispute resolution provides a faster, more cost-effective result than litigation. And, perhaps most importantly, it provides a result that is at least as fair as a decision by an impartial jury or judge.

While these benefits are achieved in the great majority of complex arbitrations, they must never be assumed or taken for granted since effective case management is invariably required for an arbitration to be as brief as possible while affording a fair hearing to both sides. In assessing whether an arbitration of a complex dispute has been effectively managed, one must consider a number of important factors, in addition to counting the number of hearing days, since hearings in complex cases are necessarily quite extensive-even when handled in the most cost-effective way possible.

Arbitrators who serve on the AAA's newly qualified roster of neutrals, and have undergone its recently enhanced arbitrator-training program, are well equipped to achieve a cost-effective, fair result in a complex commercial dispute. Still, arbitrators can and should strive to

---

* The author is of counsel at Fulton, Rowe, Hart & Coon in New York City. He has served on the American Arbitration Association's Large, Complex Case Panel and on its Greater New York Advisory Council for Large Complex Cases. He is the editor co-author of CONOVAN LEISURE ADR PRACTICE BOOK, John Wiley & Sons (1991) is a member of the Board of Editors of the American Arbitration Association's ADR Currents.

improve the process. This article suggests some specific approaches that can shorten the arbitration process in certain circumstances without sacrificing fairness.

The Prehearing Phase

Steps taken at the first prehearing conference can save time later on and can shorten the entire process.

Comprehensive Schedule

An item critical to the agenda of the first prehearing conference is to prepare an encompassing schedule that sets forth deadlines for the various phases of the arbitration process. The schedule would include, for example, the deadlines for: serving and responding to document requests; submitting to the arbitrators discovery disputes the parties could not resolve themselves; exchanging expert reports and witness and exhibit lists; and filing prehearing memoranda. The schedule would also establish the dates for the hearings.

Absent such a schedule, the process lacks firmness and direction and can wander on for far too long. However, if the arbitrators work with the parties' counsel to establish an overall schedule at the outset, and if the arbitrators make clear that departures from the schedule will only be permitted for good cause shown, it is more likely that the process will conclude in a reasonable time frame.

Hearing Days

At the first prehearing conference, the parties almost always underestimate the number of hearing days that will be needed. And while the arbitrators may be skeptical about such estimates, they often are willing to schedule only the estimated number of hearing days since arbitrators have no wish to tie up their future calendars any more than necessary. However, when the hearings commence a few months after the first prehearing conference, it often becomes apparent that additional hearing days must be scheduled. But at that late date, it probably will not be possible to find any "open" dates during the next few months when all parties, counsel, and the arbitrators can participate in a hearing. And if the parties again underestimate the needed hearing time at that point, there will be yet another two-to-three month scheduling delay down the road.

The solution to this problem is to prepare a realistic, complete hearing schedule at the first prehearing conference. If the schedule is done properly and it is taken into account that parties almost always underestimate their time requirements, the arbitration process can be shortened by as much as six months, sometimes even more.

Motion Practice

Arbitrators may consider dispositive motions, such as a motion for summary judgment or a motion to dismiss all or some of the claims, early in the arbitration. The granting of such a motion can dramatically curtail the whole proceeding, but it is not without risk. First, an arbitrator who grants a dispositive motion greatly increases the chance that a court might reverse the award. Second, the award granting the motion must be supported by an airtight opinion, which can take substantial time to craft. And third, even if the award were ultimately upheld, it would take more time to wend its way through the courts than a relatively "bullet proof" award handed down after a full hearing.

As a general rule, it makes sense for arbitrators to grant a dispositive motion only when it is meritorious to a degree that is almost beyond dispute. Additionally, I believe that it may well be counterproductive for arbitrators to grant even a clearly meritorious motion unless such action would avert a substantial number of hearing days-certainly more than four.

Depositions

It is almost heretical to advocate depositions in advance of an arbitration hearing. After all, depositions have traditionally not been part of the arbitration process and according to many, their use in arbitration would so liken it to litigation that there would be little distinction between the two.

While respecting this argument, I have witnessed many cross-examinations at arbitration hearings that plod down one dead-end street after another, while the questioner endlessly gropes for any testimony that might be of help. In other words, the arbitration hearing can sometimes resemble a discovery deposition and when it does, it goes on too long with testimony that is largely unimportant, if not entirely irrelevant.

The arbitration hearing in a complex case can be greatly streamlined if prehearing depositions of some witnesses are permitted. This is not to suggest countless depositions of unending duration, which are often encountered when litigating a complex case in court. What I am advocating is a very limited number of depositions in advance of a complex arbitration hearing. Each side might be allocated ten, fifteen, or twenty hours for depositions to be taken during a limited period. Or each party might be permitted to take two-hour depositions of a limited number of people. Either way, objections at the depositions should not be permitted except for nonspeaking objections grounded on form privilege, or confidentiality. This precludes the lawyer defending the deposition from using all or most of the allotted deposition time with objections.

In short, the use of a controlled deposition program in advance of a complex arbitration hearing may reduce the ultimate length of the hearing with no significant lengthening of the discovery process.

Role of the Chair

Delays in resolving discovery disputes can grind the prehearing phase of a complex arbitration to a virtual halt. Further, the logjam can often grow worse as the arbitration proceeds since a party seeking delay quickly learns that this goal can be achieved by raising a discovery dispute at every turn. The result is a need to revise the entire arbitration schedule, but given the difficulty of rescheduling when everyone's calendars are already filled, a postponement of six months or more can easily occur.

One reason discovery disputes delay proceedings is the difficulty in arranging a telephone hearing with all three arbitrators on short notice. It is not uncommon to find that the first date the arbitrators are all available is two weeks or more down the road. If this happens more than twice, the entire arbitration schedule can be in serious jeopardy.

One step that can minimize if not eliminate such delays is to have the chair of the panel hear and resolve discovery matters. Everyone must agree to this procedure at the prehearing conference. While this can save a great deal of time, there is one pitfall. Certain rulings on the relevance of requested discovery can carve large, substantive areas out of the case. Clearly, the entire panel must decide matters such as these. As long as the chair exercises good judgment in consulting the entire panel when necessary-having him or her resolve non-substantive discovery issues-can significantly expedite the proceeding.

Bifurcation and Limited Hearings

In some instances, time can be saved by bifurcating the hearing to address liability first and, if necessary, damages later. If there is a finding for the respondent on liability, then the arbitration would be over, saving the time that would have been spent on proving damages.

Bifurcating the hearing can be counterproductive in certain instances. Since the effort required to effect a bifurcated hearing can take considerable time, its use should be limited to instances when proof of damages is expected to be voluminous. Also, bifurcation makes no sense if a significant amount of evidence goes both to liability and damages-as it often does-since the panel could end up hearing large amounts of the same evidence twice.

A refinement on the concept of bifurcation is to conduct an early hearing on a discreet, potentially dispositive issue, such as the meaning of a controlling contract provision. This procedure can save time in the right circumstances. But that is not always the case. If initial discovery is confined to the issue to be decided in the limited hearing, and if that hearing does not dispose of the case, then the parties will suffer a delay in their ability to pursue general discovery, and an overall final result may be substantially delayed. The early hearing also could develop into a more encompassing event than was originally anticipated if the parties argue-as they often do-that substantial background proof is necessary to decide the limited issue at hand. And if it ultimately proves necessary to hold a "general" hearing, the panel may then see a lot of the same witnesses and hear much of the same evidence (albeit in somewhat different packaging).

While an early hearing on a potentially dispositive issue can reap great benefits, it has a significant downside that must be considered if the overall result is to be an increase in efficiency and cost effectiveness.

Early Guidelines

Given the informality and flexibility of arbitration, it is not surprising that different arbitrators may take widely varying approaches in some key areas. For example, some arbitrators apply at least some form of the hearsay rule while others exclude virtually nothing on hearsay grounds. Some arbitrators limit document discovery to the bare essentials while others are more permissive. Some arbitrators require complete supporting materials for charts and summaries while others do not.

Uncertainty about which approach the arbitrators will take can lead to delay. The unexpected exclusion of large amounts of hearsay evidence, for example, can require a party to rethink its entire case right in the middle of the arbitration hearing. The point is that surprises cause delays and should be avoided. Thus, it is good practice to discuss at the first prehearing conference what the ground rules are going to be on such subjects as hearsay, scope of discovery, and requests for adjournment of the hearings. If the arbitrators plan to reject a party's application for postponement of the hearings except for good cause shown, they should clearly impart this message to the parties at the outset. Doing so will put everyone on notice and make it easier for the arbitrators to take an uncompromising position on postponement requests when they are made—as they surely will be.

The Hearing

Handling Documents

The process of finding, marking, authenticating, and introducing large quantities of documents in evidence at an arbitration hearing can greatly elongate the process. This is where the flexibility of arbitration can be used to promote brevity and cost effectiveness. To shorten the process the arbitrators might require that all exhibits be placed in tabbed binders, and that a set of binders be furnished to each arbitrator in advance of the hearing. The binder provides instant access to any given document. This averts the time-consuming process of marking and identifying each exhibit at the hearing.

The authentication and introduction of exhibits into evidence can also cause substantial delay. One shortcut is to direct that:

1. all documents used at the hearing will be automatically admitted in evidence in the absence of a specific objection raised when the document is first used; and

2. parties need not authenticate exhibits at the hearing unless a specific, serious objection is raised as to authenticity.

Written Direct Testimony

A growing practice among arbitrators of complex cases is to require that direct testimony be submitted in writing and that oral testimony at the hearing be limited to cross-examination. This practice can save significant amounts of time, but arbitrators should exercise some restraint in imposing such a requirement. Written direct testimony is useful and prejudices no one when used with witnesses of secondary importance. The same is not necessarily true when written direct testimony is obtained from key witnesses on whose testimony the case will likely turn. The arbitrators for example can often benefit from hearing direct testimony from those primary witnesses, which they can use to assess credibility in a very different context from that of cross-examination. Another factor that favors judicious use of this technique is that there may be a perceived or real disadvantage to the side presenting a key witness whose first oral testimony is in response to hostile questions.

Secondary Witnesses

Another way of saving hearing time is to forego altogether the testimony of at least some of the secondary witnesses. Instead, they can be deposed outside the presence of the arbitrators in the evenings or during adjournments in the hearing, with any important aspects of their testimony being incorporated in the posthearing briefs. This approach can save large amounts of time, but it does require the cooperation of counsel.

Two Arbitrators

We have already discussed how difficult it can be to find commonly open hearing dates in the schedules of three busy arbitrators. Arbitrator William Barrett (a former AAA board member) has devised a way of ameliorating if not eliminating this problem. His approach is to allow two arbitrators to hold a videotaped hearing that will be viewed at a later time by the unavailable arbitrator, who will later represent on the record that he or she has viewed the entire videotape. The parties' consent must be obtained to pursue this procedure. While they may not agree to it with respect to their vital witnesses, they may agree with regard to less important witnesses.

Communicate with Counsel

Counsel often pound a point relentlessly even after the arbitrators have digested the issue and are ready to move on. But counsel will not know how much or how little proof the arbitrators might want in a given area unless they make their wishes known. If the arbitrators say nothing, counsel tend to take the safe approach by droning on and on. But if the arbitrators are in regular communication with counsel and tell them when they have had enough proof on an issue, counsel will get the message. This can save a great deal of time over the course of a long arbitration.

Time can also be saved if the arbitrators regularly ask counsel how much more time they need with a witness. While the arbitrators probably should not hold counsel to their initial estimates—which are invariably understated—their repeated questions along these lines should gradually lay the groundwork for the panel to later impose a time limit on the witness' testimony. It should also make counsel aware that to please the panel, they should streamline the testimony as much as possible.

Time Limits

One way for the arbitrators to control the length of the hearing is to set a limit on the time for the direct case, for the respondent's case, and for rebuttal. A time limit on the claimant's direct case, however, can be undermined if the respondent uses up most of claimant's allotted time with extensive cross-examination. This problem can be avoided by an order from the panel directing that the length of a witness' cross-examination not exceed the length of the direct examination.

The panel should seriously consider placing time limits on the hearing if, for example, it has gone on for too long and large amounts of unnecessary proof are being introduced. An effective way of intervening is for the panel to "negotiate" with counsel and agree on how much more time is needed. A directive that each side is then limited to the negotiated amount of time can bring a rambling proceeding to a much earlier closing. And all this will have been accomplished with the agreement of the parties.

While time limits can be an effective tool, they should not be imposed loosely or too early in the proceeding. In the early stages of an arbitration, counsel notoriously underestimate their time requirements, and at that point, the arbitrators do not know enough about the dispute to impose realistic time limits. Thus, setting such limits at too early a point will likely result in the need to later extend them, rendering the whole exercise useless—and even counterproductive.

Conclusion

These are not the only steps that can be taken to shorten a complex arbitration. There are no limits to what resourceful arbitrators might do to streamline complex arbitration and make it more efficient and cost-effective while maintaining the overall goal of a fundamentally fair result.

CHAPTER THREE

DRAFTING ARBITRATION CLAUSES AND AGREEMENTS

I. Drafting Clauses for Consumer and Employment Arbitration

Specs & the Single Arbitration Clause

by Thomas W. Lyons[*]

While it is common practice for businesses to include an arbitration clause in their standard contracts, not everybody understands the obligations imposed by such clauses. Worse, some parties simply don't bother to read the part of the contract that requires arbitration in case of a dispute. This article explores the problems stemming from a "unilateral" arbitration clause or when an arbitration clause comes as an "unfair surprise." The article notes some cases showing that the courts are generally split over this issue.

Many businesses prefer to resolve commercial disputes through arbitration rather than a trial. They include in their transaction forms a provision requiring arbitration of all disputes arising from the transaction. For example, a form may say, "This contract is subject to all the terms and conditions printed on the reverse side." The back of the form will typically include a clause such as:

Arbitration: Any controversy arising under, or in relation to, this contract shall be settled by arbitration. If the parties are unable to agree respecting the time, place, method or rules of the arbitration, then such arbitration shall be held in the City of New York, in accordance with the

---

[*] The author is a partner with Strauss, Factor, Laing & Lyons, Providence, RI. He holds an A.B. from Colgate University and a J.D. from Case Western Reserve University Law School. His experience includes positions as vice chair of the Defense Research Institute's Business Litigation Committee and editor-in-chief of the Rhode Island Bar Journal. The article is reprinted with permission from The Business Suit, the quarterly newsletter of the Defense Research Institute's Business Litigation Committee.

laws of the State of New York and the rules of the American Arbitration Association.

However, other businesses do not include such a provision and may prefer to avoid arbitration, generally or selectively.

Typically, these two views will clash when one business sends out a standardized form specifying goods or services it offers to purchase. The seller sends back its standardized form agreeing to fill the order, oftentimes with the goods requested. The so-called "battle of the forms" can occur when the parties' preprinted terms and conditions, including arbitration provisions, are not in complete agreement. The documents rarely mirror each other. However, many businesspeople do not pay much attention until the deal goes sour.[1] The question then arises whether the party which prefers arbitration can enforce its clause.

The Supreme Court has held that the Federal Arbitration Act[2] preempts any state statute which imposes special requirements on the enforceability of arbitration clauses.[3] State laws which apply generally to all contractual provisions are not preempted.[4] The Act does not address whether a unilateral arbitration clause becomes part of the parties' agreement. State commercial law decides the issue.

The Uniform Commercial Code

Most courts hold under the Uniform Commercial Code that if the initial written specification or similar offer contains an arbitration clause, it becomes part of the contract unless the offeree explicitly rejects it.[5] However, if only the offeree's written acceptance contains an arbitration clause, the clause does not necessarily become part of the bargain.

Article 2 of the Code devotes Section 2076 to this question. It provides in part:

1. A definite and seasonable expression of acceptance or a written confirmation which is sent within a reasonable time operates as an acceptance even though it states terms additional to or different from those offered or agreed upon, unless acceptance is

---

[1] *See*, Ionics, Inc. v. Elmwood Sensors, Inc., 110 F.3d 184, 189 (1st Cir. 1997) ("The reality of modern commercial dealings....is that not all participants read their forms.").
[2] 9 U.S.C.§ 1, et seq.
[3] Doctor's Associates, Inc. v. Casarotto, 517 U.S. 689, 116 S.Ct. 1652 (1996).
[4] *Id.*
[5] *See for example* Southeastern Enameling Corp. v. General Bronze Corp., 434 F.2d 330, 333-34 (5th Cir. 1970); Polyclad Laminates, Inc. v. Vits Maschinenbau Gmbh, 749 F. Supp. 342, 345 (D.N.H. 1990).

expressly conditional on assent to the additional or different terms.

2. The additional terms are to be construed as proposals for addition to the contract. Between merchants such terms become part of the contract unless:

   (a) the offer expressly limits acceptance to the terms of the offer;

   (b) they materially alter it; or

   (c) notification of objection to them has already been given or is given within a reasonable time after notice of them is received.[6]

Thus, in the usual course, an arbitration provision in the acceptance becomes part of the contract when the offeree expressly conditions its acceptance on inclusion of the clause or when the clause is not considered a "material" alteration.

If, as sometimes happens, both parties' forms state the transaction depends on the other's acceptance of their terms or there are explicitly conflicting provisions, then "[t]he contract…consists of the terms originally agreed to, terms on which the confirmations agree, and terms supplied by [the UCC], including subsection 2 [of Section 207]."[7]

Accordingly, under either of these two scenarios, whether a unilateral arbitration provision becomes part of the contract usually still depends on whether it materially alters the agreement.

The Code does not define what constitutes a "material" alteration. Instead, it gives hints and examples in the Official Comments to Section 207. Comment 4 indicates that material alterations are clauses which "result in surprise or hardship if incorporated without express awareness by the other party." Examples include:

- clauses negating standard warranties such as merchantability or fitness for purpose in circumstances in which the warranties normally apply;

- clauses reserving to the seller the power to cancel upon the buyer's failure to meet any invoice when due; and,

---

[6] U.C.C. § 2-207.
[7] Official Comment 6.

- a clause requiring that complaints be made in time materially shorter than customary or reasonable.

Comment 5 states that clauses which "involve no element of unreasonable surprise" are incorporated in the contract unless the other party gives a seasonable objection. Examples of these are:

- clauses fixing a reasonable time for complaints;
- clauses providing for interest on overdue invoices;
- clauses limiting the right of rejection; or
- clauses otherwise limiting remedy in a "reasonable manner" under Section 2-718 and 2-719.

Section 2-207—"Murky Prose"

Suffice to say, the Comments do little to clarify what is a material alteration in other circumstances. One court has described Section 2-207 as a "murky bit of prose."[8] Professors White and Summers use more colorful language:

Unfortunately, the section is like the amphibious tank that was originally designed to fight in the swamps but was sent to fight in the desert. The original drafter of 2-207 designed it mostly to keep the welsher in the contract...Where preprinted forms are used to structure deals, they rarely mirror each other, yet the parties usually assume they have a binding contract and act accordingly. Section 2-207 rejects the common law mirror image rule and converts many common law counteroffers into acceptances under 2-207(1)....Here the courts are not deciding whether there is a contract. They are answering a different question: What are its terms? This is not only a different but a more difficult question for the law than that of keeping the welsher in.[9] Notably, in the circumstance where the buyer's standard order form contains an arbitration clause but the seller's standard acceptance form has some sort of no-arbitration provision the professors themselves cannot agree whether the arbitration clause becomes part of the contract.[10]

They do concur that if the parties reach an oral or other informal agreement and the offeree's written confirmation contains a unilateral

---

[8] Southwest Engineering Co. v. Martin Tractor Co., 205 Kan. 684, 694, 473 P.2d 18, 25 (1970).
[9] White and Summers, Uniform Commercial Code, Vol. 1, 8-9 (4th ed. 1995).
[10] *Id.* at 10-14.

arbitration clause, the clause, standing alone, is a material alteration. They add that course of dealing or trade usage are relevant to determine whether arbitration is implied in the parties' initial informal agreement.[11] They also note:

> Acceptors rarely win the argument that their additional terms are only immaterial alterations under 2-207(2). A principal reason for their losing record is that their non-verbal acts contradict their verbal argument. Who goes to the appellate court with lawyers hired at hundreds of dollars per hour to dispute a term that is not material?[12]

The problem with this argument is that it confuses the common law meaning of "material," i.e., substantively important, with the Section 2-207 meaning, i.e. "result[ing] in surprise or hardship." Comment 5 uses the adjective "unreasonable" indicating these terms have objective, not subjective, meaning. A businessperson's subjective surprise or hardship is irrelevant under Section 2-207 (unless he or she makes a seasonable objection). In any event, a contractual term can be surprising, objectively or subjectively, without being substantively important to the formation of the contract, and vice versa.

In other words, a businessperson might not have expected the other side to propose an unusual term but would have willingly agreed to it during negotiations. Nevertheless, this term is material under 2-207. Conversely, a businessperson might object to a term which is otherwise common in the industry. In this situation, the term is not "material" and Section 2-207(c) puts the burden on the objector to respond to the term in the other's form.

For example, Professors White and Summers include in a footnote two appellate decisions holding that provisions establishing choice of law and shortening the statute of limitations to one year are not material alterations.[13] Both these provisions are far more likely to be dispute dispositive, and, thus, more "material" in a substantive sense, than an arbitration clause. However, they are not objectively surprising which is

---

[11] *Id.* at 27-28 (*citing* Schubtex, Inc. v. Allen Snyder, Inc., 49 N.Y.2d 1, 424 N.Y.S. 2d 1154, 399 N.E.2d 1154 (1979)).

[12] *Id.* at 19.

[13] *Id.* at 36 (*citing* Coastal Industries, Inc. v. Automatic Steam Products Corp., 654 F.2d 375 (5th Cir. 1981) and Thermo-Coustics Manufacturing Co. Inc. v. Borden Inc., 167 Cal.App.3d 282, 213 Cal.Rptr. 611 (1985), respectively.)

why they are not material under Section 2-207. As we shall see, the professors' assumption that an arbitration clause is material in the Section 2-207 sense seems factually unsupported.

The New York Rule

The courts are split on whether the offeree's unilateral arbitration clause is a material alteration. Those courts following the "New York" rule usually hold that an arbitration requirement is per se "material."[14] Indeed, in *Diskin v. J.P. Stevens & Co., Inc.*, the court indicated that a "vague, unspecific reference" to the textile industries' custom of arbitrating disputes was not an acceptable substitute for a specific agreement to arbitrate.[15]

However, some New York decisions indicate the "New York" rule may not be absolute. In *Hatzlachh Supply Inc. v. Moishe's Electronics, Inc.*,[16] the court found the applicable Code provisions of New York and Texas law to be similar in all respects. The court rejected the "New York" rule as contrary to the spirit of both the Uniform Commercial Code and the Federal Arbitration Act.[17] It held that the purchaser could not have been surprised by the seller's standard arbitration provision when the seller had used the identical invoice in forty-two previous transactions over two years.[18] It also noted the purchaser used arbitration provisions in its invoices.

In *Schubtex, Inc. v. Allen Snyder, Inc.*,[19] the New York Court of Appeals reaffirmed its holding in Marlene that an arbitration provision on the back of a standard acknowledgment form did not bind the purchaser. The court went on to state that while a course of dealing could result in a provision becoming part of the parties' agreement, such forms alone did not establish a course of dealing no matter how many times the

---

[14] Diskin v. J.P. Stevens & Co., Inc., 836 F.2d 47, 50-51 (1st Cir. 1987)(applying New York law); Coastal Industries, Inc. v. Automatic Steam Products Corp., 654 F.2d 375, 379 (5th Cir. 1981)(applying New York law); Supak & Sons Manufacturing Co. v. Pervel Industries, Inc., 593 F.2d 135 (4th Cir. 1979)(applying New York and North Carolina law); Stanley-Bostitch, Inc. v. Regenerative Environmental Equipment Co., Inc., 697 A.2d 323, 329 (R.I. 1997); Marlene Industries Corp. v. Carnac, 45 N.Y.2d 327, 380 N.E.2d 239 (1978).

[15] *Supra*, note 14, at 51-52 (*quoting* Jones Apparel Group, Inc. v. Petit, 75 A.D.2d 504, 426 N.Y.S.2d 799 (1st Dept. 1980)).

[16] 828 F. Supp. 178 (S.D.N.Y. 1993).

[17] *Id.* at 183-84.

[18] *Id.* at 184.

[19] 49 N.Y.2d 1, 399 N.E.2d 1154, 424 N.Y.S.2d 133 (1979).

seller sent them to the buyer.[20] It indicated that relevant evidence of a course of dealing would be that the parties had previously arbitrated or that the arbitration provision was "material" in the parties' negotiations. (This reasoning appears to be a misuse of the Section 2-207 meaning of "material.")

Other courts, including the Seventh Circuit, sharply disagree with the New York rule and hold materiality must be determined on a case by case basis.[21]

In *Schulze and Burch Biscuit Co.*, the Seventh Circuit considered facts similar to those in *Schubtex*. The parties had nine prior transactions each involving the identical confirmation form. The court said the purchaser had "ample notice" the arbitration provision would also be in the tenth form and could have objected within a reasonable time. The court held the tenth identical form was not "unfair surprise" and, therefore, the arbitration provision was not a material alteration.[22]

The courts also disagree on whether the party favoring inclusion of the clause bears the burden of proof. One court has held it was the burden of the party opposing arbitration to establish that it was surprised by the inclusion of the arbitration provision.[23] The same court also held that where inclusion of the arbitration provision in the parties' agreement depends on trade custom or course of dealings there may be a question of fact which must be resolved by a jury. However, it appears most courts have said the party seeking to include the arbitration provision has the burden of proving it is part of the agreement.[24] Given the language of Section 2-207, i.e., that the additional terms become part of the contract unless they are a material alteration, it seems the objecting party should bear the burden.

Those decisions which apply the New York rule do so based on a perceived public policy which enforces arbitration clauses only when the

---

[20] *Id.* at 1156.

[21] Schulze and Burch Biscuit Co. v. Tree Top, Inc., 831 F.2d 704, 715 (7th Cir. 1987) (applying Illinois law); Dorton v. Collins & Aikman Corp., 453 F.2d 1161 (6th Cir. 1972) (Georgia and Tennessee law); Bergquist Co. v. Sunroc Corp., 777 F. Supp. 1236, 1245 (E.D. Penn. 1991) (Pennsylvania and Minnesota law); Dixie Aluminum Products Co. Inc. v. Mitsubishi International Corp., 785 F. Supp. 157 (N.D.Ga.1992) (Georgia law).

[22] 831 F.2d at 715.

[23] Bergquist Co. v. Sunroc Corp., 777 F.Supp. 1236 (E.D. Pa. 1991), citing, Dale Horning Co., Inc. v. Falconer Glass Industries, Inc., 730 F.Supp. 962, 966 n.2 (S.D. Ind. 1989).

[24] *See for example* Diskin v. J.P. Stevens & Co., 836 F.2d at 51.

parties expressly agree to them. In the leading case establishing the rule the New York Court of Appeals said:

The reason for this requirement, quite simply, is that by agreeing to arbitrate a party waives in large part many of his normal rights under the procedural and substantive law of the State, and it would be unfair to infer such a significant waiver on the basis of anything less than a clear indication of intent.[25]

Other courts have rejected the idea that arbitration imposes a hardship on commercial parties.[26] In *Trans-Aire*,[27] the Seventh Circuit explained its decision in *Schulze and Burch Biscuit Co.*:

> ...it is clear that the term [providing for arbitration] would impose no substantial hardship upon the nonassenting party. True, the term deprived the party of certain rights. However, for all practical purposes, the term had little effect upon the nonassenting party's economic welfare. That is, the nonassenting party still had an opportunity to prosecute or defend its interests albeit in a different forum.

The court in *Dixie Aluminum Products* held that any argument under state law that arbitration was a hardship compared to a trial had to yield to the policy favoring arbitration set forth in the Federal Arbitration Act.[28]

Most importantly, however, the New York rule entirely confounds the purposes of the Uniform Commercial Code:

(a) To simplify, clarify, and modernize the law governing commercial transactions.

(b) To permit the continued expansion of commercial practice through custom, usage, and agreement of the parties.

(c) To make uniform the law among the various jurisdictions.[29]

This is particularly true when the court fails to consider or even rejects evidence that merchants in general or merchants in that particular

---

[25] In the Matter of Marlene Industries, 45 N.Y.2d at 333-34, 380 N.E.2d at 242.
[26] *See*, Trans-Aire International v. Northern Adhesive Co., 882 F.2d 1254, 1262 (7th Cir. 1989); Dixie Aluminum Products Co., Inc. v. Mitsubishi International Corp., 785 F. Supp. at 160-61.
[27] *Supra*, note 26, at 1262.
[28] *Supra*, note 26, at 161.
[29] Section 1-102.

trade or industry routinely include arbitration provisions in their order or invoice forms. If anything is clear about the Code it is that commercial transactions should be governed by what businesspeople think, not by what judges learned in contracts class.

The Code emphasizes that it is the businessperson's expectations which should predominate when it provides that a "usage of trade" and a "course of dealing" will "give particular meaning to and supplement or qualify terms of an agreement."[30] The Code defines a "usage of trade" as "...any practice or method of dealing having such regularity of observance in a place, vocation, or trade as to justify an expectation."[31] The Code says a course of dealing "is a sequence of previous conduct between the parties to a particular transaction which is fairly to be regarded as establishing a common basis of understanding for interpreting their expressions and other conduct."[32] The Official Comments add "...a sequence of conduct after or under the agreement may have equivalent meaning."[33]

Arbitration in the Business World

There is substantial evidence that many business people consider arbitration the preferred way to litigate commercial disputes. Indeed, in certain industries arbitration appears to be the expected way to litigate these disagreements. For example, a 1997 survey of the general counsel or chief in-house litigators for over 600 of the Fortune 1,000 corporations found significant experience with and appreciation for arbitration, especially in commercial disputes.[34]

Eighty-five percent of the responding corporations had used arbitration in commercial or contract disputes. This was a much higher response rate than for any of the survey's other categories of disputes, e.g., employment (62%), construction (40%), intellectual property (21%) and consumer rights (17%).

There were some variations among the different kinds of industries in their views of arbitration. For example, 100% of the corporations in "mining/construction" had used arbitration. (This was the smallest category among the types of corporations surveyed.) The lowest usage

---

[30] Section 1-205(2) and (3).
[31] Section 1-205(2).
[32] Section 1-205(1).
[33] Comment 2.
[34] David B. Lipsky and Ronald L. Seeber, *The Appropriate Resolution of Corporate Disputes*, CORNELL/PERC INSTITUTE ON CONFLICT RESOLUTION (1998).

was in the "trade" industry, 73%. There were similar variations in how frequently different corporations used arbitration. Ninety percent of the "mining/ construction" corporations used it "occasionally" "frequently" or "very frequently." However, only 44% of "trade" corporations fit into those categories. Even so, the number of corporations in any category who used arbitration "not at all" was small. The largest percentage was 14%, in the "finance" industry. In fact, only in the "trade" sector did a majority of the corporations (56%) state they used arbitration "rarely" or "not at all."

Perhaps, more pertinently, a high percentage in all types of industries reported using arbitration in commercial and contractual disputes. The numbers ranged from a low of 81% in the "insurance" industry to 100% in "mining/construction."

Savings in time and litigation expenses, contractual requirements and management desire are the major reasons why corporations use arbitration. Management desire seems to be the big difference between those corporations which arbitrate very frequently and those which do not. Sixty-nine percent of the former respondents cited it as a reason they arbitrate. Among those corporations which arbitrate rarely or not at all, only 32% and 37%, respectively, said management favored arbitration. Many corporations also believe arbitration allows them increased ability to handle the dispute, particularly because arbitration provides some control over who decides the dispute and scheduling (which may be very important if senior executives must participate).

Some corporations object to arbitration when the subject of the arbitration requires specialized expertise. One respondent told Professors Lipsky and Seeber: "We have a lot of intellectual property disputes, but we don't think arbitrators do a good job with them. There simply aren't any qualified arbitrators in this area."[35] The overwhelming reason given for why the corporations did not use arbitration more frequently was the "unwillingness of opposing party." (Possibly, that "unwillingness" arises only ad hoc and post hoc when one party decides traditional litigation provides a tactically superior forum.)

These statistics naturally raise the question of what distinguishes those corporations which make use of arbitration and other alternative dispute resolution methods from those which do not as a matter of principle. The report's writers found:

---

[35] *Id.* at 29.

...the strongly pro-ADR companies tend to be the very largest ones in the Fortune 1000 and to be known for adopting so-called progressive policies in other areas. For example, many pro-ADR companies were among the first to embrace total quality management and team-based production systems...Most faced significant global competitive pressures and engaged in downsizing in the 1980s. A pro-ADR policy seems closely linked to this array of corporate policies.

The companies in the group that never used ADR tended to be smaller than average (although all corporations listed in the Fortune 1,000 are very large indeed). They also tended to be very profitable and under much less cost pressure than the pro-ADR group. Several have reputations for dealing with unions in a militant fashion.[36]

The writers later comment that the latter group of corporations were "sometimes controlled by one or two families." In sum, even a business "principled" avoidance of arbitration may well be highly subjective, or at least, have little to do with objective surprise or hardship.

A number of judicial decisions acknowledge that in certain industries, especially textiles, arbitration is the trade custom (regardless of the size of the companies involved).[37] Certainly, in those industries a businessperson should not be surprised to find an arbitration provision in an agreement, unless of course, he or she had specifically rejected arbitration in negotiations. However, it seems unlikely that arbitration would come up in the usual course of business negotiations.

Conclusion

In any event, the Cornell study and some of the cases support the position that no major business should be surprised by the appearance of an arbitration clause in a commercial contract or find it a hardship to arbitrate a commercial dispute. Any business which wants to avoid arbitration should include in its standard commercial forms a provision refusing to participate in it.[38] Even so, given the courts' and

---

[36] Lipsky and Seeber, *id.* at 21-22.
[37] *See for example* Lehigh Valley Industries, Inc. v. Armtex, Inc., 19 UCC Rep. 744 (N.Y. App. 1976); Silverstyle Dress Co. v. Aero-Knit Mills, Inc., 11 UCC Rep. 292 (N.Y.Super. 1972).
[38] *See for example* Stanley-Bostitch, Inc. v. Regenerative Environmental Equipment Co., Inc., 697 A.2d 323 (R.I. 1997)(rejecting seller's argument that arbitration provision on

commentators' disagreements over the issues, a party which does not want arbitration should also respond to the other party's standard arbitration provision with a specific objection.

A number of recent studies have found that the largest category of lawsuits is contract and commercial claims. This is particularly true in state courts where the backlogs may be longer. Moreover, state court commercial claims are often smaller and less able to bear the cost of extensive litigation. Greater use and enforcement of arbitration provisions in standardized commercial documents could improve the speed, efficiency and certainty with which those claims are resolved.

---

its invoice was part of the contract where purchaser's form included a provision that any dispute would be determined by the courts in purchaser's state).

II. Careful Use of "Arising" in Drafting Narrow Arbitration Clauses

Ambiguity in "Arising" Phrases: Caution for Drafters of Intended Narrow Arbitration Clauses

by Barry H. Garfinkel and James D. Fry[*]

A lawyer who wishes to draft a narrow arbitration clause should beware of relying too heavily on the term "arising." Usage of this term in arbitration agreements has proven problematic for even the most seasoned practitioners. Over 100 disputes have centered around the construction of "arising," suggesting that the term is vague and judicial interpretations are relatively unpredictable.

Indeed, as the Second Circuit observed in *Louis Dreyfus Negoce S.A. v. Blystad Shipping & Trade Inc.*, "No fixed rules govern the determination of an arbitration clause's scope; while very expansive language will generally suggest a broad arbitration clause...we have also found broad clauses when examining phrasing slightly more limited...."[1] Thus, there are no absolute rules on how to draft a narrow clause, if such is intended.[2]

Nonetheless, some guidance can be derived from the case law. It is well-established that the arbitrability of a dispute is determined on a case-by-case basis. The court will look to the language of the arbitration clause to determine whether the parties intended for all, or only some, of the disputes at issue to be arbitrable. Therefore, parties and their counsel must carefully consider the wording of the clause at the time they enter into their agreement, or else run the risk of incurring an unintended result.

---

[*] Mr. Garfinkel is of counsel to Skadden, Arps, Slate, Meagher & Flom LLP and heads the firm's international arbitration group. Mr. Fry worked as a summer associate at the firm, while attending Georgetown University Law Center. He also worked as a law clerk with the Office of the Assistant Legal Adviser for International Claims and Investment Disputes for the U.S. Department of State.

[1] 252 F.3d 218, 225 (2d Cir. 2001).

[2] ACE Ltd. v. CIGNA Corp., 2001 WL 767015 (S.D.N.Y. July 6, 2001) ("There are no absolute rules for determining whether an arbitration clause is narrow or broad.").

The first step a court takes in determining intent is to classify the clause as "narrow" or "broad."[3] For example, the Third Circuit, in *McDonnell Douglas Financial Corp. v. Pennsylvania Power & Light Co.*, explained that broad clauses purport to refer to arbitration all disputes arising out of a contract while narrow clauses limit arbitration to specific types of disputes.[4] This type of analysis of the arbitration clause enables the court to determine whether the claims are covered by the clause.[5]

Federal courts generally favor arbitration and, hence, they will broadly construe arbitration clauses as they relate to issues of arbitrability, especially when the intent of the parties is ambiguous. As the Supreme Court said in *Mitsubishi Motors Corp. v. Soler Chrysler-Plymouth, Inc.*, "[T]he first task of a court asked to compel arbitration of a dispute is to determine whether the parties agreed to arbitrate that dispute…[A]s with any other contract, the parties' intentions control, but those intentions are generously construed as to issues of arbitrability."[6]

Broad Intent

Courts have often relied on how "arising" is used in an arbitration clause to determine the parties' intent at the time of their agreement. "Arising out of or relating to" and "arising out of or in connection with" have consistently connoted broad intent. In *Prima Paint Corp. v. Flood & Conklin*, the U.S. Supreme Court labeled as broad a clause requiring arbitration of "any controversy or claim arising out of or relating to this agreement."[7] The Fifth Circuit, in *Nauru Phosphate Royalties, Inc. v. Drago Daic Interests*, held that when the parties agreed to an arbitration

---

[3] *Dreyfus*, n. 1, *supra*.

[4] 858 F.2d 825, 832 (3d Cir. 1988). *See also* Certain Underwriters at Lloyd's London v. Colonial Penn Ins. Co., 1997 WL 316459 (S.D.N.Y. June 11, 1997).

[5] *See* Mehler v. Terminiz Int'l Co., 205 F.3d 44, 49 (2d Cir. 2000).

[6] 473 U.S. 614, 626 (1985). *See* AT&T Technologies v. Communications Workers of Am., 475 U.S. 643 (1986) ("[I]n the absence of any express provision excluding a particular grievance from arbitration, we think only the most forceful evidence of a purpose to exclude the claim from arbitration can prevail"). Mehler, n. 5, *supra* ("Once the court has determined the threshold issue of whether an arbitration agreement exists, and that the agreement is a broad one, as here, the court must compel arbitration 'unless it may be said with positive assurance that the arbitration clause is not susceptible of an interpretation that covers the asserted dispute.'")

[7] 388 U.S. 395, 397-98 (1967).

clause governing "any dispute...arising out of or in connection with or relating to this agreement," they "intend[ed] the clause to reach all aspects of the relationship."[8]

Model arbitration clauses that ensure the broadest possible reach, such as those promulgated by the American Arbitration Association, the United Nations Commission on International Trade Law (UNCITRAL), the International Chamber of Commerce (ICC) and the London Court of International Arbitration (LCIA), all suggest this terminology.

Tort Claims

Disputes often arise as to whether tort claims are covered by an arbitration clause. A finding that a clause is broad is more likely to lead a court to hold that such claims are covered. However, it does not preclude a court from examining those claims to determine whether they arise out of or are related to the contract. The Eleventh Circuit, in *Telecom Italia v. Wholesale Telecom Corp.*,[9] predictably determined that an arbitration clause that used the phrase "arising out of or relating to" the contract is broad. But the court went on to establish a test to determine the minimum connection needed between a tort claim and the contract for the clause to apply. That test is whether the tort was an immediate, foreseeable result of the performance of contractual duties.

Narrow Intent?

Some courts have fastened on the phrase "arising from," holding that it indicates an intent to draft a narrow arbitration clause. The Sixth Circuit, in *Vemco, Inc. v. Flakt, Inc.*, found that "arising from" was narrow because it did not purport to have such a wide sweep that would send to arbitration virtually all controversies arising under the agreement.[10]

---

[8] 138 F.3d 160, 164-65 (5th Cir. 1998). *See also* Ferro Corp. v. Garrison Indus., 142 F.3d 926, 938 (6th Cir. 1998) ("all controversies and claims arising out of or relating to this agreement" was broad); Bavaratti v. Joesphal, Lyon & Ross, Inc., 28 F.3d 704, 710 (7th Cir. 1994) ("arising out of or in connection with the business" compelled arbitration of all disputes); Pennzoil Exploration & Prod. Co. v. Ramco Energy Ltd., 139 F.3d 1061 (5th Cir. 1998) ("arising out of " and "in connection with or relating to" was broad); American Recovery Corp. v. Computerized Thermal Imaging, 96 F.3d 88 (4th Cir. 1996) (tribunal to hear all disputes where clause stated "[a]ny disputes arising out of or related to").

[9] 248 F.3d 1109 (11th Cir. 2001).

[10] 96 F.3d 1449 (6th Cir. 1996).

"Arising under" is probably used most often by drafters to signify a narrow clause. The Second Circuit, in *In re Kinoshita & Co.*, said that "arising under" indicates "an intent for the clause to be narrowly applied."[11] Similarly, the Ninth Circuit, in *Mediterranean Enterprises v. Sangyong Corp.*, concluded that "arising hereunder" limited the arbitration to contract performance and interpretation; thus, it excluded from the reach of the arbitration clause claims for contract fraud.[12]

Despite these cases, drafters should be wary of relying on "arising" phrases to restrict the scope of the arbitration agreement.

The reason is that beginning in the early 1980s some courts began to move away from construing "arising" phraseology to indicate narrow intent. In 1983, the Sixth Circuit, in *Cincinnati Gas & Electric Co. v. Benjamin F. Shaw Co.*, concluded that a clause calling for arbitration of disputes "arising out of" this agreement (as distinguished from disputes "arising out of or in connection with" this agreement) indicated a broad clause, rather than a narrow one.[13] In 1984, the Second Circuit, in *Mineracao da Trinidade-Samitri v. Utah International Inc.*, concluded that "aris[ing] or occur[ing] under" the agreement did not indicate a narrow clause.[14] It offered that only the precise language and facts in In re *Kinoshita* would indicate a narrowly drafted clause. The court in *Mineracao* made a useful suggestion; rather than relying on "arising

---

[11] 287 F.2d 951, 953 (2d Cir. 1961).

[12] 708 F.2d 1458, 1463-64 (9th Cir. 1983). See also American Recovery Corp. v. Computerized Thermal Imaging, 96 F.3d 88 (4th Cir. 1996) ("any disputes arising hereunder" would limit arbitration to interpretation and application of the contract, precluding jurisdiction over "related" disputes); Pennzoil, n. 8, *supra* (narrow clauses only require arbitration of disputes "arising out of " the contract); Mineracao Da Trindade-Samitri v. Utah Int'l, 745 F.2d 190, 194 (2d Cir. 1984) ("[T]o ensure that an arbitration clause is narrowly interpreted, contracting parties must use...arising under...or its equivalent..."); Figli v. Fisheries Dev., 499 F. Supp. 1074, 1080 (S.D.N.Y. 1980) ("arising out of " excluded disputes over fraudulent inducement); Sinva v. Merrill Lynch, Pierce, Fenner & Smith, 253 F. Supp. 359, 364 (S.D.N.Y. 1966) ("arising under" characterized as "relatively narrow").

[13] 706 F.2d 155, 160 (6th Cir. 1983). See also Schacht v. Hartford Fire Ins. Co., 1991 WL 171377 (N.D. Ill. Aug. 30, 1991) ("[I]n light of federal policy requiring resolution of all ambiguities in favor of arbitration, and the absence of stronger authority or evidence, we find that a broader interpretation of ['arising out of '] is warranted in this case"); In re Oil Spill by Amoco Cadiz, 659 F.2d 789, 794 (7th Cir. 1981) (clauses covering disputes "arising out of " both the parties' contract and the general relationship).

[14] 745 F.2d at 194, n. 12, *supra*.

under" and like terminology, "the better course, obviously, would be to specify exactly which claims are and are not arbitrable."[15]

Since then, many federal circuit courts appear to have ceased to find differences between "arising out of," "arising under" and similar language.[16] Recent decisions by federal courts in the Second Circuit indicate that this trend is continuing.[17]

Thus, a drafter who wishes to craft a clause that will be construed narrowly, at least in the Second Circuit, should express with specificity those disputes that are to be excluded. Drafters must fully understand the transaction in order to foresee and specify the excluded disputes. Therein lies the challenge of drafting an effective, narrow clause.

This can involve more drafting time. There also may be additional costs associated with negotiating a clause that lists the disputes that are intended to be inarbitrable.

Since this approach may be the only way to reliably withhold certain types of disputes from arbitration, it may be a necessary cost of achieving predictability.[18] Attorneys should not overlook the value of predictability for their clients.

---

[15] *Id. See also* Battaglia v. McKendry, 233 F. 3d 720, 726 (3rd Cir. 2000) ("specify[ing] exactly which claims are and are not arbitrable" is the better course to relying on an "arising" phrase).

[16] *See e.g.,* Gregory v. Electro-Mechanical Corp., 83 F.3d 32, 386 (11th Cir. 1996) (refusing to draw a distinction between "arising under," "arising out of," and traditionally broad phrases); Mar-Len of Louisiana, Inc. v. Parsons-Gilbane, 773 F.2d 633, 636-37 (5th Cir. 1985) (relying on the general presumption of arbitrability to broadly construe "with respect to," a potentially narrow phrase); Sweet Dreams Unlimited, Inc. v. Dial-A-Mattress Int'l, 1 F.3d 639, 642 (7th Cir. 1993) (construing "arising out of " broadly to reach all disputes having an origin or genesis in the contract); Fairchild v. National Home Ins. Co., 2001 WL 985356 (9th Cir. 2001) (finding that "arising...as to," which would have been considered narrow under past decisions, is not unduly narrow, similar to "arising out of or related to" and "in connection with"); Roby v. Corp. of Lloyd's, 996 F.2d 1353, 1361 (2d Cir. 1993) ("relating to," "in connection with" and "arising from" are all the same in broadly construing an arbitration clause); *Battaglia,* n. 15, *supra* (confining Kinoshita, n. 11, *supra,* to its precise facts in determining that there is no distinction between various "arising" phrases.

[17] *See* Radio Computing Serv. v. Cool Partners, Inc., 2001 WL 799579 (S.D.N.Y. July 12, 2001) ("[d]isputes arising out of the License Agreement" was broad); Clarendon Nat'l Ins. Co. v. Lan, 2001 WL 849383 (S.D.N.Y. July 25, 2001) (arbitration of "all disputes arising out of an agreement" is a broad clause).

[18] *See* Weinrott v. Carp, 298 N.E.2d 42, 45-46, 344 N.Y.S.2d 848, 858-54 (1973) ("A demand for specificity as to which particular issues should be submitted to the arbitrators would make the drafting of arbitration agreements burdensome, confusing and often impossible"); Alison Brooke Overby, *Note, Arbitrability of Disputes Under the Federal Arbitration Act,* IOWA L. REV. 1144, 1152-53 (1986) ("requiring parties to specify which

While more work may be required of the drafter of the narrow clause, the work of the attorney wishing to draft a broad arbitration clause is simplified because less specificity is required, although more specificity could foreclose an inquiry such as the one the Eleventh Circuit conducted in the Telecom Italia case. Without clear intent derived from something other than the use of the term "arising," most courts are likely to determine that the parties intended all disputes to be submitted to arbitration.[19]

Model Arbitration Clauses Recommended by Institutional Arbitration Rules and the UNCITRAL

The introduction to the American Arbitration Association's Commercial Dispute Resolution Procedures (effective Sept. 1., 2000) contains this standard arbitration clause: "Any controversy or claim arising out of or relating to this contract, or the breach thereof, shall be settled by arbitration administered by the American Arbitration Association under its Commercial Arbitration Rules."

The model arbitration clause referred to in Article 1 of the UNCITRAL Arbitration Rules (1978) provides: "Any dispute, controversy or claim arising out of or relating to this contract, or the breach, termination or invalidity thereof, shall be settled by arbitration in accordance with the UNCITRAL Arbitration Rules as at present in force." G.A. Res. 31/98, UNCITRAL, 31st Sess., Supp. No. 17, U.N. Doc. A/31/17 (1976).

The International Chamber of Commerce's Rules of Arbitration (1998) provide: "All disputes arising out of or in connection with the present contract shall be finally settled under the Rules of Arbitration of the International Chamber of Commerce by one or more arbitrators appointed in accordance with the said Rules."

The Arbitration Rules of the London Court of International Arbitration (1998) provide: "Any dispute arising out of or in connection with this contract, including any question regarding its existence, validity or termination, shall be referred to and finally resolved by arbitration under the LCIA Rules, which Rules are deemed to be incorporated by reference into this clause.

---

disputes will be arbitrable...is apparently the only means by which parties can unequivocally reserve a future dispute for a court rather than for an arbitrator").

[19] *See AT&T Technologies*, n. 6, *supra*; Schacht v. Beacon Ins. Co., 742 F.2d 386, 390-91 (7th Cir.1984).

III. Arbitration Clauses and the Internet

Arbitration Clauses May Cure Internet Jurisdiction Woes

by Steven C. Bennett[*]

In today's economy most large businesses have, or are in the process of developing, a Web site on the Internet. In some instances courts have held that the operation of a Web site may subject a business to personal jurisdiction in the state or country where the Web-site user is located. For a business interested in controlling litigation costs and exposure, the prospect of being sued anywhere in the world, based on Web-site operation, may be truly worrisome.

The law of personal jurisdiction based on Internet activities is developing rapidly, as the use of the Internet becomes an ever more common part of the commercial world. At present, some courts have distinguished between "passive" and "interactive" Web sites for purposes of determining the existence of personal jurisdiction.[1] A passive Web site is one that essentially provides information to the user (generally, information about the products, services and opportunities of the business). Some courts have concluded that the offering of this kind of

---

[*] The author is a partner in the New York City office of Jones Day where he is chair of the firm's E-Discovery Committee. He co-teaches an arbitration course at Brooklyn Law School. Bennett earned a summa cum laude B.S. from Macalester College and a cum laude J.D. from New York University. He writes a continuing column, "Arbitration" with Professor Samuel Estreicher that has appeared in the NEW YORK LAW JOURNAL since 2004. The views expressed are solely those of the author and should not be attributed to the author's firm or its clients.

[1] Some commentators and courts have suggested that the dichotomy is more of a "sliding scale" between the extremes of passive and interactive Web sites, such that the likelihood of a court exercising jurisdiction is "directly proportionate to the nature and quality of the commercial activity that a nonresident defendant conducts over the internet." Rhoda J. Yen, *Personal Jurisdiction and the Internet: Applying Old Principles to a 'New' Medium*, 76 FLA. B.J. 41 (2002); *see, e.g.*, Cybersell v. Cybersell Inc., 130 F.3d 414 (9th Cir. 1997) (applying sliding-scale approach); Zippo Mfg. Co. v. Zippo Dot Com Inc., 952 F. Supp. 1119 (W.D. Pa. 1997) (same); *see generally* Robert W. Hamilton & Gregory A. Castanias, *Tangled Web: Personal Jurisdiction and the Internet*, 24 LITIGATION 27 (Winter 1998) (summarizing recent case law).

information on a Web site is not sufficient by itself to subject a business to personal jurisdiction in the state or country where the user is located.[2]

An interactive Web site, by contrast, is one that permits a user to become engaged with the business in some significant way. For example, the user may be able to order goods and services from the business. In essence, in such a circumstance, the parties are forming a contract through the Internet. Some courts have held that a business that uses this type of Web site has involved itself enough in the state or country where the user is located that it may be subject to the personal jurisdiction of the courts there.[3]

Because the law in this area is developing so rapidly, there may be substantial variations in treatment of this issue from court to court. But it is fair to say that there is at least a risk that a business operating a Web site (especially, an interactive site) may find itself being sued in jurisdictions where it does not otherwise operate.

Choice of Forum Clause

One way to reduce this risk is for the business to incorporate a choice-of-forum clause in the terms and conditions of use for the Web site. This kind of clause essentially would state that any dispute with a user of the Web site would have to be heard in the courts of a specified jurisdiction (typically, the state or country where the business has its headquarters).

There is one problem with this type of clause: Forum selection clauses are not universally enforced. There is, at present, no multilateral convention among nations on the recognition and enforcement of forum selection clauses. In the United States, moreover, there is no national law that commands that the courts in each state give force and effect to a clause that selects the forum for litigation.

---

[2] *See, e.g.*, Weber v. Jolly Hotels, 977 F. Supp. 327 (D.N.J. 1997) (Italian hotel's Web site, which contained only advertisement, was insufficient to confer jurisdiction in slip and fall suit by New Jersey plaintiff); Black & Decker Inc. v. Pro-Tech Power Inc., 26 F. Supp. 2d 834 (E.D. Va. 1998) (although Taiwanese defendant operated Web site that advertised its potentially infringing products, jurisdiction was not proper because defendant did not actually have any commercial contacts with forum state).

[3] *See, e.g.*, Panavision Int'l L.P. v. Toeppen, 141 F.3d 1316 (9th Cir. 1998) (personal jurisdiction proper where defendant entered into contracts through knowing and repeated electronic transmission of computer files); Millenium Enterprises, Inc. v. Millenium Music, LP, 33 F. Supp. 2d 907 (D. Or. 1999) (personal jurisdiction could be exercised where Web site permitted users to purchase music online).

To be sure, the prevailing law in most jurisdictions throughout the world favors the enforcement of such clauses, but there is no guarantee of enforcement everywhere. The decision whether to enforce a forum selection clause will be made by the individual judge, applying any applicable local laws and treaties and such doctrines as comity, *forum non conveniens*, and local public policy. As a result, even if a forum-selection clause is used, a business may be faced with the same risk (although perhaps reduced) that its Web-site operation may subject the business to personal jurisdiction in courts around this country (and even around the world).

Advantages of Arbitration

The use of an arbitration clause in this circumstance may be a far superior option. Arbitration clauses are generally enforceable as a matter of state, federal and international law. Most states have enacted the Uniform Arbitration Act (or an analog statute), which requires courts to enforce arbitration clauses as they would enforce other contracts.[4] The Federal Arbitration Act has the same effect. The federal act applies when the transaction affects interstate commerce, which is likely to be true of most transactions involving a Web site, and certainly true of an interactive commercial Web site.

In the international arena, the New York Convention on the Recognition and Enforcement of Arbitral Awards, to which more than 100 countries are signatories, binds the courts in each country to enforce arbitration clauses.[5]

Thus, there is a high level of certainty that an arbitration clause will be enforced in both domestic and international transactions. This certainty makes the arbitration clause approach a better approach than the use of an ordinary forum selection clause when it comes to the question of ensuring that the clause will be enforced.

---

[4] The original Uniform Arbitration Act was revised in 2000. At least three states have adopted the revised statute, and bills calling for the implementation of the revised statute have been introduced in the legislatures of at least nine other states.

[5] *See* New York Convention, art. II, sec. 1 ("Each Contracting State shall recognize an agreement in writing under which the parties undertake to submit to arbitration all or any differences which have arisen or which may arise between them in respect of a defined legal relationship, whether contractual or not, concerning a subject matter capable of settlement by arbitration."). The text of the Convention and a list of signatory nations appears after 9 U.S.C.A. §§ 201-208 (implementing the Convention in the United States).

Arbitration also may hold other benefits for a business. The arbitration process typically involves less discovery than ordinary litigation, and it employs less formal procedures, both factors that can make it a less costly means to resolve a dispute.

Arbitration, moreover, is a private process, not generally a matter of public record for all to discover. And there are no juries, which can reduce the randomness of the fact finder's decision. Because the parties select the arbitrator who will decide their dispute, they may choose a true expert as the decision maker, who will likely have a greater level of understanding of the facts and issues in dispute.

Another benefit of arbitration is that the choice of arbitration may avoid the prospect of class actions, which can produce devastating results, and which in some cases may force otherwise unwarranted settlements. Generally, at least in the United States, multiple related arbitration proceedings will not be consolidated absent the consent of the parties.[6] Thus, so long as the arbitration clause and the rules incorporated by reference therein to govern the arbitration do not themselves authorize class or consolidated proceedings, a business may avoid the threat of class actions by choosing arbitration.

Drafting Tips

A business that wishes to incorporate an arbitration clause into the terms of use on its Web site should keep the following considerations in mind in order to maximize the likelihood that a court will enforce an arbitration clause as written.[7]

Express Consent. The user should be required to consent, expressly, to the terms of use of the Web site, as a condition to the purchase or use of any product or service that is made available to the public, and the

---

[6] *See, e.g.,* Connecticut Gen. Life Ins. Co. v. Sun Life Assur. Co. of Canada, 210 F.3d 771 (7th Cir. 2000) (consolidation permissible where parties evidenced agreement to consolidate); Government of United Kingdom of Great Britain v. Boeing Co., 998 F.2d 68 (2d Cir. 1993) (court cannot order consolidation absent agreement, even if the same issues of law and fact are presented in both cases); Baesler v. Continental Grain Co., 900 F.2d 1193 (8th Cir. 1990) (court has no power to order consolidation absent a provision in the arbitration agreement).

[7] For more on drafting enforceable "click-wrap" agreements, *see generally* Steven C. Bennett, *Drafting an Enforceable Click-Wrap Agreement*, N.Y.L.J., JUNE 20, 2000, at 1, col. 1. *See also* Robert Y. Lewis, LIMITING RISK FOR THE INTERNET BUSINESS, N.Y.L.J., MAY 13, 2002, at 5, col. 1.

requirement for such consent should be stated as clearly as possible.[8] Also, a mechanism should be provided for recording the user's consent to the terms. Some Web sites, for example, provide that the user cannot complete a transaction, or visit locations on the Web site, without first clicking on an icon indicating "I consent" or "I agree" to the terms of use.

Prominent Clause. The arbitration clause should be prominently displayed in order to avoid claims of inadvertence or fraud.[9] Especially where the arbitration clause is one of many terms of use, it should be emphasized or highlighted in some way, such as with bold type, solid capital letters, or a label drawing attention to the clause, such as "Important." There is at least some risk that the clause may not be enforced if it is buried in a sea of small type.

Clear Explanation. The meaning of the clause should be clear to the user. For example, the clause could explain that by agreeing to arbitration, the user is giving up the right to proceed in court before a judge or jury. It could also explain that the arbitration award will be final and binding, and that the user will have no right to appeal. If the arbitration clause is written in a deliberately obscure or misleading form, a court might find that it is unenforceable.[10]

---

[8] *Compare* Specht v. NetScape Communications Corp., 150 F. Supp. 2d 1 (S.D.N.Y. 2001) (no contract for arbitration formed where Internet users were not required to read or assent to terms of software license agreement as precondition to downloading software) with *In re* RealNetworks, Inc., Privacy Lit., No. 00 C 1366, 2000 WL 631341 (N.D. Ill. May 8, 2000) (Internet user bound by arbitration clause in license agreement because user was required to accept terms before downloading).

[9] *See, e.g.,* Berger v. Cantor Fitzgerald Sec., 942 F. Supp. 963 (S.D.N.Y. 1996) (factual dispute existed on motion to compel arbitration, where employee claimed that he was given only five minutes to sign agreement, and did not understand the content and scope of the arbitration clause); Jones v. Adams Fin. Serv., 84 Cal. Rptr. 2d 151 (Cal. App. 2d Dist. 1999) (affirming denial of petition to compel arbitration where blind woman suffering from dementia signed loan document as a result of misrepresentation). These cases are quite aberrant. Courts generally hold that there is no obligation to explain or highlight an arbitration provision. *See, e.g.,* Adams v. Merrill Lynch Pierce Fenner & Smith, 888 F.2d 696 (10th Cir. 1989) (no special duty to disclose that written customer agreement contained arbitration clause); Cohen v. Wedbush, Noble, Cooke, Inc., 841 F.2d 282 (9th Cir. 1988) (no duty to explain effects of arbitration clause). Indeed, the Supreme Court has held that a state law requiring prominent notice of arbitration clauses was preempted by the Federal Arbitration Act. *See* Doctors Assocs., Inc. v. Casarotto, 517 U.S. 681 (1996).

[10] *See* Davis v. Blue Cross of Northern Cal., 600 P.2d 1060 (Cal. 1979) (insurer waived right to compel arbitration where arbitration clause was obscurely placed in policies and was ambiguously worded, and insurer failed to bring arbitration procedure to insureds' attention even after learning that insureds did not agree with its determinations).

Procedural Fairness. The arbitration procedures selected should be procedurally fair. The venue for the arbitration, the means of selecting the arbitration, and the costs of the arbitration (among other things) should be considered in this regard. Many parties incorporate by reference the arbitration rules of an alternative dispute resolution sponsoring institution to govern their arbitration proceedings. The choice of arbitration rules promulgated by a prominent organization (such as the American Arbitration Association) should go a long way toward confirming the fairness of the process.

Reasonable Site. To minimize the likelihood of a challenge to the venue for the arbitration, and to enhance the likelihood that the arbitration clause will be enforced if challenged, the site selected for the arbitration should be reasonable.[11] If only one location is selected as the venue for the arbitration, that location may greatly inconvenience and impose an economic hardship on Web-site users who live far away and have only modest means. One option is to offer users a choice of several locations for the arbitration, and the ability to pick the location most convenient for their needs. Another option is to offer an alternative to an in-person hearing, such as arbitration proceedings by teleconference, which would likely reduce the cost and inconvenience involved in resolving the dispute.

Fees and Costs. The filing fees and costs associated with the arbitration should not preclude users from exercising their rights. There has been quite a bit of judicial activity in the area of consumer and employment arbitration, focusing on whether arbitration fees and costs may prevent consumers or employees from vindicating their rights.[12] Courts, however, have not uniformly invalidated arbitration clauses merely because such clauses may impose some expense on the consumer or employee.[13] The Supreme Court, moreover, recently upheld the

---

[11] *See* Martin Bank v. WorldCom, Inc., No. 122484/00, 2002 WL 171629 (N.Y. Sup. Ct. N.Y. Co. Jan. 24, 2002) ("there may be something inherently wrong and unfair in setting the venue for an arbitration in a distant city, when the amount in issue is a relatively small amount").

[12] *See* Brower v. Gateway 2000, Inc., 676 N.Y.S.2d 569 (N.Y. App. Div. 1998) (excessive cost of arbitrating under chosen rules effectively left consumers without forum for disputes); Dobbins v. Hawk's Enter., 198 F.3d 715 (8th Cir. 1999) ("[C]ourts across the country have begun to recognize the potential that arbitration fees will make an arbitration agreement unconscionable....However, whether or not arbitration fees make the agreement to arbitrate unconscionable is something that must be determined on a case-by-case basis in light of the state law governing unconscionability.").

[13] *See, e.g.*, Bradford v. Rockwell Semiconductor Sys., Inc., 238 F.3d 549 (4th Cir. 2001); Brown v. Wheat First Secs., Inc., 2001 WL 855477 (D.C. Cir. 2001).

enforceability of an arbitration agreement in a consumer contract that was silent as to arbitration fees and costs, because the consumer failed to make any showing that the fees and costs were a barrier to vindication of her rights.[14] Despite these developments, the issue continues to produce litigation. Thus, care should be taken in drafting the arbitration provision so that the filing fees and other costs do not appear excessive. If an arbitration sponsoring organization is chosen to supervise arbitration, the Web-site owner should become familiar with the filing fees of the sponsoring institution. The institution may have a special policy or program for consumer disputes under a certain size. Another approach may be to provide in the arbitration clause that the company will pay all or part of the filing and arbitrator fees, or to place reasonable caps on the user's share of the fees.

None of the foregoing points are absolutely essential to have a valid and binding arbitration clause. The point, however, is that if a business chooses to use arbitration as a means to reduce its costs and risks in litigation (including the cost and risk of being sued anywhere in the world), it is important to take steps to ensure that the choice of arbitration will be effective. Businesses with Internet Web sites can take steps to protect themselves from litigation in unwanted locations by opting to arbitrate disputes with users of their Web sites. All they need is a clearly written arbitration clause that is procedurally fair and that clearly obtains the user's consent to arbitration.

The Importance of User Consent

To reduce the potential for litigation, it is vital to secure the user's consent to the arbitration clause, as well as the other terms of use for the Internet Web site. Some courts have not enforced what have been termed "browse wrap agreements," which generally don't require the user to do anything before using the Web site's services. In some cases courts have expressed concern about whether the user had adequate notice of the terms of browse wrap agreements and assented to them.

The enforceability of the arbitration clause can also be enhanced if care is taken in drafting the agreement so that it is procedurally fair, clearly explained and prominently displayed. If consumers are involved in the transaction, however, other considerations, like the cost and venue of the arbitration, should be carefully considered.

---

[14] *See* Green Tree Fin. Corp.-Alabama v. Randolph, 531 U.S. 79 (2000).

IV. Drafting Effective Collective Bargaining Arbitration Agreements

Arbitration Agreements in the Wake of Wright: The Importance of Drafting

by Marshall H. Tanick[*]

The ruling by the U.S. Supreme Court allowing a unionized employee to bypass the grievance-arbitration clause in his union's collective bargaining agreement (CBA) in order to litigate a discrimination claim has focused renewed attention on the drafting of arbitration agreements.

The nuances of negotiation and skillful drafting of agreements to arbitrate have always been important. But they have acquired greater significance in light of the Supreme Court's decision in *Wright v. Universal Maritime Service Corp.*[1] *Wright* held that an arbitration clause in a CBA did not explicitly waive the right to a judicial forum for the assertion of statutory claims, and so did not require the employee to arbitrate an alleged violation of the Americans with Disabilities Act.

The case was brought by Caesar Wright, a South Carolina longshoreman, who allegedly was denied work after he sought and obtained an award of workers' compensation and Social Security disability benefits due to injuries to his right heel and back. At the urging of his union, Wright sued a trade association and six stevedore companies, which he claimed discriminated against him because of his disability. The federal trial and appellate courts dismissed the lawsuit on the ground that Wright failed to exhaust the remedies available under the CBA. The specific remedy the courts referred to was arbitration, because the CBA included a provision calling for "matters under dispute" to be subject to a grievance procedure that included arbitration.[2]

---

[*] The author is a partner in the law firm of Mansfield, Tanick & Cohen, P.A., in Minneapolis, MN. He holds a summa cum laude B.A. from the University of Minnesaota and a summa cum laude J.D. from Stanford Law School. Tanick is a prolific author and has written about arbitration, insurance, and employment, among other topics.

[1] This article is an updated version of Marshall Tanick, *Arbitration Agreements Appropriately Attract Attention*, which appeared in THE HENNEPIN LAWYER (Dec. 1996), at 22.

[2] 119 S. Ct. 391 (1998).

Many observers expected the Supreme Court to use the *Wright* case to address the longstanding tension between the rights of employees under federal discrimination laws on the one hand, and mandatory, binding arbitration clauses on the other.[3] But rather than reconciling those tensions and articulating the respective rights and remedies of employees and employers, the court avoided the issue altogether. Instead, it focused on the specific language of the CBA's arbitration clause, ruling that the clause lacked an "explicit" waiver of statutory rights. Since there was no "clear and unmistakable" language restricting employees from bypassing the grievance mechanism, Wright was entitled to litigate his statutory claim without having to resort to arbitration.

Although the ruling in *Wright* does not resolve the clash between statutory rights and compulsory arbitration, it offers a warning that erstwhile participants in arbitration or other alternative dispute resolution processes should not overlook the terminology of the arbitration agreement. Those who pay insufficient attention to the drafting of this agreement do so at their peril. The initial undertaking to proceed with arbitration forms the fulcrum on which subsequent developments hinge. If it is faulty, the arbitration is likely to flounder and perhaps fail.

Terms of "Endurement"

The arbitration process is completely consensual and, with the exception of boilerplate provisions in some insurance contracts and CBAs, arbitration usually is the product of negotiation and agreement between the parties. Well-documented reasons lead parties to agree to arbitrate. They include a more rapid resolution than in litigation, savings of attorneys' fees and transaction costs, confidentiality and presumed arbitrator expertise.[4]

But how parties agree to arbitrate is more opaque. It is well-known that they are more open to negotiating the ways and means of resolving

---

[3] The CBA also provided that it was intended to cover all matters affecting wages, hours, and other terms and conditions of employment...." Wright was also subject to the Longshore Seniority Plan, which provided that any "dispute concerning or arising out of the terms and/or conditions of this agreement, or...involving the interpretation or application of this agreement, or...arising out of any rule adopted for its implementation" was subject to the grievance procedure.

[4] *Compare* Alexander v. Gardner-Denver Co., 415 U.S. 36 (1974) (employee can pursue racial discrimination lawsuit notwithstanding arbitration clause in CBA), with Gilmer v. Interstate Johnson/Lane Corp., 500 U.S. 20 (1991) (age discrimination claim can be subject of compulsory arbitration).

potential disputes at the outset of a transaction, before a nettlesome problem arises or tempers flare. But when trouble lurks or is already revealed, parties usually are less inclined to agree to arbitration, or to anything else for that matter.

When parties recognize the benefits of arbitration and agree at the formation of their relationship to use the process to resolve any future claim or dispute that may arise, the next critical step is drafting the arbitration agreement in a way that will endure throughout that relationship.

A threshold issue in drafting arbitration agreements concerns the scope of the undertaking to arbitrate. The agreement must be clear in delineating the type of claims that are to be channeled to arbitration. Parties desiring to submit all of their disputes to arbitration should use broad language in order to achieve that objective. A clause providing for arbitration of "all disputes arising under this agreement" may not suffice to cover claims arising under contractual provisions dressed in tort garb.[5]

Prevailing law continues to recognize and encourage arbitration, even when statutory discrimination claims are asserted.[6] As the *Wright* case demonstrates, causes of action arising under statutory discrimination statutes often form the battleground for determining whether arbitration agreements may preclude civil litigation. The courts are split on this issue. Some cases have upheld arbitration of statutory discrimination claims if the parties executed a predispute arbitration agreement.[7] Other cases, however, have held that employees may not waive their statutory rights to a judicial forum.[8] The Supreme Court in the *Wright* case expressly declined to address whether an explicit waiver of the statutory right to litigate would be enforceable.

But *Wright* makes clear that, assuming such a waiver would be enforceable in the particular jurisdiction, the underlying arbitration clause must be sufficiently broad to warrant deprivation of statutory and constitutional safeguards. Phrasing the undertaking as one that covers

---

[5] *It's Good business to Arbitrate—From Labor to Business Disputes*, L.A DAILY J., FEB. 5, 1982, at 56; Fred Herron, *Arbitrate or Litigate*? 25 LAW SOC'Y J. 52 (1987).

[6] *E.g.*, Cenesco v. T. Kakiuchi & Co., 815 F.2d 840 (2d Cir. 1987); Cobler v. Stanley, Barber, Southard, Brown & Assoc., 217 Cal. App. 3d 518, 530 (Cal. Ct. App. 1990); Mansdorf v. California Physicians' Serv., Inc., 87 Cal. App. 3d 412, 417 (Cal. Ct. App. 1978).

[7] *Gilmer, supra,* n. 3.

[8] *E.g.*, Johnson v. Piper Jaffray, Inc., 530 N.W.2d 790 (Minn. 1995); Rosenberg v. Merrill Lynch, Pierce, Fenner & Smith, 170 F.3d 1(1st Cir. 1999).

"all disputes of any kind or character whatsoever between the parties" may suffice.[9]

The standard language prescribed by the American Arbitration Association is even better. It provides for arbitration of "[a]ny controversy or claim arising out of or relating to this contract or the breach thereof...." But *Wright* might even require still broader language to negate statutory lawsuits, such as a clause calling for arbitration of "any and all claims arising under any federal, state or local statutes, laws or regulations."

In some circumstances the parties may wish to narrow the potential scope of arbitration by specifying the relationship or transaction that is subject to arbitration. Doing so would preserve the parties' right to seek redress in a judicial forum for disputes unrelated to the specified relationship or transaction. This could be accomplished by a clause calling for arbitration of "any and all disputes between the parties relating to, or arising out of, the subject matter or transaction."

Tinker Topics

Arbitration agreements also provide the opportunity to tinker with the format of the arbitral process. But arbitration agreements need not focus solely on arbitration as the mechanism for dispute resolution. The parties may wish to provide for one or more nonbinding ADR steps, such as mediation, as a condition precedent to arbitration. If so, they also might wish to empower the arbitrator to preside over the mediation.[10] But if more detachment in the arbitrator is desired, they could provide for a different person to mediate the dispute.

The parties should take advantage of the enormous flexibility of arbitration to tailor the process to their needs. For example, instead of using standard arbitration, they might wish to use "high-low" arbitration, a method in which the parties establish a minimum level of recovery and a maximum ceiling on damages. This type of arbitration eliminates risk as it caps the respondent's damages while ensuring the claimant some recovery. Setting the parameters of the potential outcome is not available to parties to conventional civil litigation. Another type of arbitration the parties might agree to is "last/best offer" arbitration. In this type of

---

[9] *E.g.*, Duffield v. Robertson Stephens & Co., 144 F.3d 1182 (9th Cir. 1998); Paladino v. Avnet Computer Technologies, 134 F.3d 1054 (11th Cir. 1998).

[10] *See* Berman v. Dean, Witter & Co., 44 Cal. App. 3d 999, 1003 (Cal. Ct. App. 1975); Bos Material Handling Inc. v. Crown Controls Corp., 137 Cal. App. 3d 99, 105 (Cal. Ct. App. 1982).

process, each party submits to the arbitrator its final offer. After the hearing the arbitrator will select one of these as the final award.

Regardless of the style of arbitration selected, the parties may want to consider whether the arbitration agreement should provide for some prehearing discovery, and schedule the timing of party exchanges of information. But in making this determination, parties should realize that full blown discovery, as is typical of litigation, is neither desired nor necessary in most arbitral proceedings. Classic discovery is invariably associated with significantly increased transaction costs and attorney time, and thus can defeat the purpose of arbitration in providing a more economical and speedier resolution.

Punitive Damages

Punitive damages are often of great concern to parties. Claimants sometimes want to recover them, while respondents invariably want to avoid them. If the parties wish to allow for an award of punitive damages, they should research the issue under the applicable law. While some jurisdictions, like New York, bar arbitral awards of punitive damages, other states permit such awards.[11] For example, Illinois allows them if the parties have expressly provided for such damages in their arbitration clause.[12] The Supreme Court has upheld the right of parties to recover punitive damages in arbitration proceedings involving agreements subject to the Federal Arbitration Act, notwithstanding state law to the contrary.[13]

Inclusion of a punitive damages clause in an arbitration agreement may be more theoretical than practical. The prospect of a punitive award is likely to be too evocative to yield an agreement between the parties. Rather than stipulating to the prospect of punitive damages, it may be more desirable simply to acknowledge the authority of the arbitrator to award "any and all damages to which a party is entitled," should any disputes proceed to arbitration.

Parties who wish to exclude punitive damages may so provide in the arbitration agreement. Such a provision generally should be respected under the FAA, which calls for arbitration agreements to be enforced in

---

[11] There has been criticism of the med-arb process. Some believe it is unethical for a person who has mediated a dispute to act as an arbitrator in the same case. Some issues relating to med-arb are discussed in Richard P. Flake, *Nuances of Med-Arb: A Neutral's Perspective*, ADR CURRENTS (Vol. 3. No. 2, June 1998), p. 8.

[12] *E.g.*, Kennedy v. Young, 524 N.W.2d 752 (Minn. Ct. App. 1994).

[13] Ryan v. Kontrick, 710 N.E.2d 11 (Ill. Ct. App. 1999).

accordance with their terms. However, the clause may be deemed antithetical to public policy if the underlying dispute is subject to a statute that explicitly authorizes such an award.[14]

The parties may also wish to consider whether to include a "loser-pays" clause with respect to the costs of arbitration, including the prevailing party's attorneys' fees.[15] This would vary the "American rule," under which prevailing parties are unable to recover their attorneys' fees in litigation.

Arbitrators traditionally have had a limited menu of remedies to afford disputing parties. Although they have authority to provide equitable and injunctive relief, they are often reluctant to do so, absent express authorization from the parties.[16] To overcome any such reluctance, the parties may empower the arbitrator in their arbitration agreement to award this form of relief. Or they may provide for arbitration under the AAA's arbitration rules for commercial and employment disputes, both of which grant arbitrators the authority to issue interim relief and injunctive powers, including the ability to provide for the protection of security of property while a dispute is pending.[17]

Appellate Alternatives

Using arbitration severely limits the parties' right to appeal. Under the Uniform Arbitration Act, enacted in most states, awards can be challenged only in narrow circumstances. For example, it must be alleged that there has been either (1) a transparent miscalculation in the calculation of the award, (2) bias, fraud or corruption in the procurement of the award, or (3) an award in excess of the arbitrator's authority.[18] The FAA contains a similarly restrictive standard for appellate review.[19]

---

[14] Mastrobuono v. Shearson, Lehman, Hutton, 513 U.S. 921 (1995); Dean Witter Reynolds v. Trimble, 631 N.Y.S.2d 215 (N.Y. Sup. Ct. 1995).

[15] Graham Oil Co. v. ARCO Prods. Co., 43 F.3d 1244 (9th Cir. 1995).

[16] *See* Metropolitan Waste Control Comm'n v. City of Minnetonka, 242 N.W.2d 830 (Minn. 1976) (scope of arbitrator's power determined by submission); Minn. Stat. § 549.09 (providing for interest on most arbitration awards); Minn. Stat. § 65B.54, subd. 2 (penalty for withholding no-fault payments).

[17] *E.g.*, David Co. v. Jim Miller Construction, 444 N.W.2d 836 (Minn. 1989).

[18] *See* R-36 of the American Arbitration Association Commercial Dispute Resolution Procedures, R-34 of the AAA Construction Industry Dispute Resolution Procedures; and Rule 27 of the AAA National Rules for the Resolution of Employment Disputes.

[19] The UAA has been the subject of a major redrafting effort by the National Conference of Commissioners on Uniform State Laws.

Advocates of arbitration consider the finality of the award to be a strength of the process, while critics see the dilution of appeal rights as a weakness.

Today signatories to an arbitration agreement may not be required to adhere to the "no-appeal" philosophy, since a few courts have held that parties can provide for appellate rights in their arbitration agreement.[20] The parties might even prescribe appellate timetables that diverge from the standard 90-day provision under the UAA.

But agreeing to appellate review of an award would prolong the process, eliminating two of the basic advantages of arbitration—a more rapid resolution and finality. But even if one opts for appellate review, and many lawyers clearly favor it, extending the time limits for appeal may be risky should the 90-day requirement under the UAA or its federal counterpart be viewed as jurisdictional. Exceeding the 90-day period could divest courts of authority to review an arbitration award, notwithstanding an agreement to the contrary by the parties.[21] It is also possible that a court would rule that the parties cannot confer jurisdiction on the appellate court.[22]

Concluding Considerations

One of the undisputed benefits of arbitration is the elasticity it affords the parties in structuring the means of resolving their dispute. This flexibility can be maximized by recognizing the importance of the arbitration agreement as the vehicle for dispute resolution. It is this agreement that gives the parties control over the arbitration process. They can solidify their control in the way they negotiate and draft its provisions. The Supreme Court's ruling in the *Wright* case undermines the use of boilerplate arbitration agreements. To achieve maximum

---

[20] 9 U.S.C. § 10. Courts traditionally have upheld arbitration awards, even when the arbitrators have not followed substantive law. But a few courts have more strictly scrutinized challenged awards. In a recent unusual case a federal appeals court set aside an award because in its view, the award reflected a "manifest disregard of the law or the evidence or both." Halligan, v. Piper Jaffray, Inc. 148 F.3d 197 (2d Cir. 1998). *See* B.H. Garfinkel & R. G. Shamoon, *A Dangerous Expansion of 'Manifest Disregard*, ADR CURRENTS (Vol. 3, No. 4, DEC. 1998), at 1. We are not aware of any other court that has gone so far in broadening the standard of review.

[21] Gateway Technologies v. MCI Telecommunications Corp., 64 F.3d 993 (5th Cir. 1995).

[22] Rothring v. American Bldg. Components, 1987 WL 5818 (Ohio Ct. App. 1987). *But see* Keener v. Gary VonAgency, Inc., 1995 WL 662105 (Ohio Ct. App. 1995) (timeline for filing appeal procedural rather than jurisdictional).

benefit from the arbitral process, parties and their lawyers should concentrate on careful draftsmanship. If they do, they will be reacting in the right way to the *Wright* ruling.[23]

---

[23] *See* Chicago Typographical Union v. Chicago Sun-Times, 935 F.2d 1501 (7th Cir. 1991) (rejecting expansion of the court's jurisdiction); Prof. Andreas Lowenfeld, *Can Arbitration Coexist with Judicial Review?*, ADR CURRENTS, (VOL. 3, NO. 3. SEPT. 1998).

CHAPTER FOUR

SELECTING SERVICE PROVIDERS AND ARBITRATORS

I. Conducting a Successful Arbitration

The Ten Commandments of Arbitration
Some Guidelines for Arbitrators

by Lee M. Finkel and Robert F. Oberstein[*]

How an arbitrator conducts an arbitration is crucial to its success. This article identifies ten behaviors that promote a fair process and preserve the sanctity of arbitration, and are helpful to arbitrators and to parties.

    I.   **Maintain a "judicial" presence.** Parties expect a "judicial" presence at the hearing even though the neutral does not wear a robe. An arbitrator's demeanor establishes that judicial presence by (1) personifying impartiality and fairness in appearance, words and deeds; (2) respecting the parties and the process; (3) demonstrating confidence in her or his abilities; and (4) possessing the management skills to efficiently lead the process.

    II.   **Know the arbitration rules.** Well-prepared parties are familiar with the rules governing arbitration proceedings. Professional arbitrators must be similarly well prepared. One of the many advantages of serving on the American Arbitration Association's roster of neutrals is the guidance provided by its arbitration rules in connection with conducting a fair and impartial hearing.

---

[*] Lee M. Finkel is the associate dean of the College of Graduate Business and Management at the University of Phoenix. Robert F. Oberstein is the Director of the Labor Management Relations Program at Ottawa University, Phoenix. Both authors reside in Arizona and serve on the American Arbitration Association's roster of neutrals.

III. **Control the process.** Arbitrators must control the process from the first contact with the parties until the award is issued. It is easier to lose control than to maintain it. Arbitrators should communicate their guidelines for the conduct of the hearing to all parties. To maintain impartiality, these guidelines must be enforced even-handedly.

IV. **Develop a clear and complete record.** Arbitrators need a clear and complete record to make a reasoned award. When parties fail to establish such a record, arbitrators must decide how much assistance to provide. Offering too much help may create an appearance of bias. Asking obvious but unasked questions may appear to violate the duty of neutrality. These situations require arbitrators to make judgments based on the circumstances at the time. Arbitrators need to be aware of walking this "neutrality tightrope" when actively involved in making a clear and complete record.

V. **Disclose, disclose, disclose.** Parties determine who is fit to serve as the arbitrator, but they cannot make this determination without complete information. Arbitrators should disclose all information regarding a past, present or foreseeable future involvement with any of the parties or their counsel, regardless of how remote, slight or insignificant it may seem to the potential arbitrator. It is preferable to lose an opportunity to serve in a case as a result of full disclosure, rather than lose one's reputation for failing to disclose. Remember, this is an ongoing obligation.

VI. **Demonstrate neutral conduct.** Every arbitrator's enemy is impropriety or the appearance of impropriety. Casual conversations with a party can easily be misperceived by the other side. Socializing with the parties is a luxury arbitrators cannot afford.

VII. **Provide a solution.** Arbitrators are appointed to resolve a dispute, not to create more problems. Their rulings and awards should clearly address and resolve all of the issues raised by the authorized claims and counterclaims in the case filings.

VIII. **Maintain safety.** Disputes usually raise the emotional temperatures of the parties. Certain disputes, particularly where a party has demonstrated violent or threatening behavior, may raise a "red flag" for the arbitrator, who may not wish to become involved. Judicious use of recesses and "time-outs" is helpful when this occurs. An arbitrator's instincts are the best guide in such situations. Ultimately, arbitrators are responsible for their own safety.

IX. **Remain calm.** Arbitrators must control any urge to react in an inappropriate way. Although they feel an urge to scream or laugh during a hearing, they are not permitted the luxury of such emotional outbursts. The process would not survive without this constant restraint by arbitrators, which is essential to maintaining the dignity of the process.

X. **Submit the award promptly.** An arbitrator's responsibilities do not end until the award is submitted. Since the parties look to arbitration for "expedited justice," arbitrators should respond with promptly written awards. It is easier to write the award immediately after the close of the hearing, before memory has time to fade. To minimize the possibility of forgetting, arbitrators should calendar when the award is due.

II. Effective Procedural Management in Arbitration

Administered Vs. Non-Administered Arbitration

by Glen H. Spencer[*]

Whether parties want to use an independent agency to administer their dispute or decide to manage such procedures themselves, the fact remains that all arbitrations need effective procedural management. This article outlines the differences between full administration, limited administration, and non-administration and investigates the advantages, as well as the disadvantages, of each.

Arbitration is a well-established dispute resolution process, which is regularly used to resolve both domestic and international disputes.[1] As such, various arbitral options exist for the users of the process.

Central to the question of "how to arbitrate" is the question of administration. That is, is it necessary or desirable for an administering agency to handle the arbitration as opposed to the parties and the arbitrator directly administering the process themselves.[2] Whatever the choice, it is clear that parties cannot escape the need for procedural management of the arbitration process, and someone, or some organization, has to do it.

For example, someone must ensure that written notice of the arbitration hearing is delivered to all parties in accordance with arbitration statutes. Similarly, someone must ensure that the arbitrator issues the award in a timely manner to ensure its finality. Apart from these legal requirements, there are a host of additional responsibilities that an administrator would regularly perform.

Three possibilities for "administrator" exist: (1) an independent and neutral third-party administrative agency, (2) the arbitrator or chair of a three-person panel, and (3) the parties themselves. So, the question is not whether arbitration should or should not be administered, it is, rather,

---

[*] The author is vice president of educational outreach with the American Arbitration Association, specializing in training legal and human resource professionals in employment-related disputes.

[1] In 1997, the American Arbitration Association alone administered in excess of 77,000 arbitration cases.

[2] FRIEDMAN, *See Is Administered Arbitration Still Needed?*, N.Y. LAW JOURNAL (AUGUST 4, 1994).

who is best situated to perform the administrative functions. Ultimately, the parties will want to achieve the triune purpose of arbitration-speed, economy, and finality.

Proponents of non-administered arbitration, as well as proponents of administered arbitration, will likely assert that each system produces a speedier and more economical process that will result in a final award. Depending on the dispute type, and the participants involved, both assertions are probably true. Which system the user will be most satisfied with depends on a number of factors that are explored herein.

It should also be noted that between the two extremes of full administration and no administration is limited administration. Working definitions of these three options are:

- Full Administration-where some independent administering agency is authorized to handle all procedural aspects of the arbitration from filing to award.

- Limited Administration-where some independent administering agency provides services for selected aspects of procedural arbitration.

- No Administration (Ad Hoc-where no independent administering agency is involved in the procedural aspects of arbitration, and all such matters are handled by the arbitrator or the parties.

Administrative Responsibilities

Filing and Notice

Throughout any arbitration, there should exist explicit definitions and mechanisms for filing claims, counterclaims, motions, and related pleadings. In addition, notice requirements should be clearly spelled out.

Under full administration, all papers are filed with the administrative agency, from the demand for arbitration to final briefs. The administrator would hold any pleading, claim, or motion pending the expiration of an appropriate time for the other side to file a response until the document(s) is forwarded to the arbitrator. Under the American Arbitration Association's Commercial Arbitration Rules, necessary notices may be delivered by regular mail, personal delivery, facsimile, telex, telegram, "or other written forms of electronic communication," to either the named party or their designated representative.[3]

---

[3] Rule 40, Commercial Arbitration Rules, American Arbitration Association.

Under limited or no administration, all papers would likely be filed directly with the arbitrator and opposing side. Rules for responses and replies need to be established by agreement of the parties or the arbitrator. In addition, what constitutes proper notice should probably also be defined to avoid confusion.

Comment: Proponents of administered arbitration argue that having an independent administrator with whom to file motions and pleadings prevents abuses of the process by always affording the other party the opportunity to respond before the pleading or motion is forwarded to the arbitrator. Proponents of non-administered arbitration maintain that the administrator acting as a repository for all papers just adds another layer of communication before the inevitable transmittal of the item to the arbitrator, and encumbers the proceedings with multiple transmittals of documents.

Identification of Claims and Counterclaims

Related to the issues surrounding the definition of notice and how papers are filed, is the official filing and acknowledgment of any claims and counterclaims. There is little worse than an arbitration hearing that begins with confusion over what was properly filed as a claim or counterclaim, and whether the opposing party has had sufficient time to prepare a defense.

Under full administration, the administrator would acknowledge in writing the receipt of a claim or counterclaim and whether it is properly filed (under AAA rules, any claim or counterclaim must conform to certain minimum requirements).[4] Once the other party has had a reasonable amount of time to respond, the claim or counterclaim would be forwarded to the arbitrator. Similarly, any amendments to claims or counterclaims undergo the same procedure, and, "[a]fter the arbitrator is appointed, no new or different claim may be submitted except with the arbitrator's consent."[5]

Under a system of no administration, the arbitrator and the parties are well-advised to ensure a mutual understanding of all claims to be considered at the hearing well before it is scheduled to begin. In addition, some guidance as to deadlines for any new claims and the circumstances under which new claims would be admitted will aid in preventing last-minute claims, and, ultimately, delays.

---

[4] *Id* at 6, 7, and 8.
[5] *Id* at 8.

Selection and Appointment of the Arbitrator

Attorneys experienced in representing parties in arbitration usually contend that there is no more important aspect of arbitration than the selection of the arbitrator. At this stage of the process, there are many administrative options that the parties might want to explore.

Under full administration, parties will likely receive an identical list of proposed arbitrators, with biographical data provided. The proposed arbitrators will be approved members of the agency's panel of neutrals, and will likely be included on the list by virtue of their subject-matter expertise, their reputation as an arbitrator, and their geographic location.

The selection process used by the administering agency may be as simple as "review the list and tell us which arbitrators are acceptable," with the agency hoping for a match. Some mechanism for arbitrator selection will exist, however, where the parties to the arbitration are unable to agree on one individual to serve as arbitrator. The administrative agency may submit additional lists where the parties are unable to agree to any one person on the first list, it may use a strike and rank procedure, and, under certain circumstances, may directly appoint an arbitrator.

Lastly, the agency will handle the official appointment of the arbitrator. Specifically, the arbitrator will be required to execute an oath of office attesting to his or her commitment to faithfully and diligently hearing the dispute, and possibly agreeing to serve in accordance with some set of ethical standards.[6]

This aspect of procedural arbitration is usually used in administration. It is relatively common for parties to access the services of some arbitral agency in the identification of suitable candidates to serve as arbitrator, even if this is the only service requested. Under such a system, the parties would receive a list of proposed arbitrator-just as in full administration-but the exact selection process would be left up to the parties. An alternating strike method is a commonly used selection process under these circumstances.

Under no administration, the parties to the arbitration may employ a host of arbitrator selection mechanisms, and hopefully one that is quick and efficient. The arbitrator selection process may be the one aspect of non-administered arbitration where delays can defeat the purpose of arbitration. Although state arbitration statutes, as well as the U.S. Arbitration Act, authorize the courts to designate an arbitrator where the

---

[6] *See* The Code of Ethics for Arbitrators in Commercial Disputes, (1977).

parties' arbitration agreement has broken down at this step,[7] the time delay associated with a trip to the courthouse will impede a speedy arbitration.

Finally, under a system of no administration, the parties and the arbitrator should make sure that a properly executed oath of office takes place to ensure that the arbitrator is formally authorized to act as arbitrator.

Comment: If selection of the arbitrator is the most important part of procedural arbitration, then serious consideration should be given to the use of limited administration at this important step, even for those who prefer no administration. Depending on the qualifications sought in the arbitrator, parties may benefit from reviewing selected members from arbitral panels. Some organizations can offer arbitrators with special subject-matter expertise, or provide lists of particular types of arbitrators (e.g., practicing attorneys, former judges, business professionals, etc.) if that is desired. One way or the other, the parties should probably attempt to identify as many arbitrators as possible that meet their desired qualifications.

Challenges to the Arbitrator

A challenge to the continuing service of an arbitrator already appointed to hear the case may represent the most troublesome potentiality of non-administered arbitration. Arbitrators are ethically required to make full disclosure to all parties involved in the arbitration of "any interest or relationship likely to affect impartiality or which might create an appearance of partiality or bias."[8] The arbitrator should disclose everything, even if the arbitrator determines that it is not a conflict of interest or will not affect impartiality, because it is up to the parties to make that decision.[9] The parties to the arbitration may then waive any objection based on the disclosure, or either party may object to the continuing service of the arbitrator arguing that the disclosure represents a conflict of interest.

Under full administration, two important features exist that are not available without administration. First, the written comments concerning the arbitrator's disclosure are not shared with the arbitrator, who theoretically may become biased based on a party's argument that the

---

[7] § 3, Uniform Arbitration Act ; 9 U.S.C. Sect. 5; Art. 226 Texas Arbitration Act.
[8] Canon II, Code of Ethics for Arbitrators in Commercial Disputes.
[9] *See* Burlington Northern Railroad Co. v. TUCO, Inc., 960 S.W.2d 629 (Tex. 1997).

arbitrator should remove him-or herself. Second, the administrative agency will determine if the arbitrator should be removed and replaced, not the arbitrator. Almost every arbitrator believes they can be fair and unbiased in deciding a case, and may also be motivated by the potential fees to be collected, and thus unwilling to step down.

In non-administered arbitration, the arbitrator may be required to decide whether self-disclosure requires removal from the case. While judges routinely decide their own ability to act without a conflict of interest, ethical codes for arbitrators and case law do not grant that same authority to private arbitrators. Moreover, under no administration, any party wanting to object to the service of the arbitrator is likely to think twice before doing so in light of the fear of potential prejudice in the arbitrator's substantive decision-making.

Finally, an arbitrator's perspective that he or she will step down if anyone objects for any reason can be equally problematic. Given that one party often has some interest in delaying the arbitration, continual objections to arbitrators who disclose minor relationships provide a very effective delay tactic.

Conduit of Communications

Numerous documents need to be filed in any arbitration process, and telephonic communications will also be necessary. The distinctions between a fully administered arbitration and a non-administered arbitration in the area of communications focus around due process, potential prejudice, and efficiency. Under any system, care must be exercised by all participants to avoid prejudice and *ex parte* communications, while getting information to the arbitrator in a speedy manner.

Under full administration, the administrative agency would act as the conduit for all communications, both written and verbal. Proponents of full administration contend that these procedures help prevent prejudicial information being sent to the arbitrator and *ex parte* communications. Another potential benefit is that the agency would maintain a complete record of the proceeding, which would be made available to either party if needed for any subsequent court proceedings.[10]

Under no administration, the arbitrator will need to exercise care to avoid *ex parte* communications. Under the Code of Ethics for Arbitrators in commercial disputes, an arbitrator is only permitted to have *ex parte*

---

[10] *Supra*, note 3, at 46.

communications on issues of scheduling, and must in turn inform the other party as quickly as possible of the content of their communications.[11] Proponents of no administration contend that the arbitration proceeds more efficiently when the parties are able to submit documents and otherwise contact the arbitrator's office directly without having to go through an administrator.

Scheduler

Scheduling is a constant battle for private arbitration proceedings given the number of schedules that usually need to be accommodated. The difficulty of scheduling is further burdened by the possibility of postponements, requiring that the process occurs multiple times in any given arbitration.

Under full administration, the administrative agency will handle all scheduling details. Under no administration, the arbitrator's assistant would usually handle this responsibility. Regardless of who handles the scheduling, it is a critical function that cannot be overlooked.

Neutral Hearing Location

With very few exceptions, each party will expect a neutral hearing location. Under full administration, the administrative agency will likely have hearing facilities that are made available to the parties. Under limited or no administration, the arbitrator's offices are most commonly used. Sometimes, hotel conference rooms are rented for the hearing when no other option exists.

From time to time, parties complain that the arbitrator conducts too much other business during the hearing day, thus delaying the proceedings. The likelihood of this happening is highest if the arbitrator is hosting the hearing at his or her office.

Finality and the Award

Finality of arbitration is a hallmark of the process, and no matter how fast or economical arbitration is, it is of little value if the award cannot be confirmed as final judgment. The importance of a timely award (which is defined by the parties' agreement to arbitrate or the rules they are arbitrating under) cannot be underestimated, and the entire arbitration

---

[11] *Supra*, note 6.

can be made moot with the issuance of a late award.[12] Awards are also commonly challenged with the argument that the arbitrators exceeded their authority, and a poorly drafted award that appears to award upon an item not submitted to the arbitrators for a decision is susceptible to vacatur for this reason.[13] Finally, excessively wordy awards that attempt to justify every decision made by the arbitrator are inherently problematic by increasing the likelihood of a challenge to the award based on disregard of the law.[14]

The importance of the award document is underscored by the arbitral principle of *functus officio*,[15] which renders the arbitrator without authority once the award is signed. Thus, the impetus to get it right the first time is critically important since the arbitrator is not authorized to change or add to the award in any substantive way once it has been issued. While state arbitration statutes may authorize the arbitrator to act after the award has been issued, it is only to correct typographical or computational errors.[16] The U.S. Arbitration Act does not make any provision for post-award modification or clarification.

Under full administration, the administrative agency is likely to review the arbitrator's award to ensure completeness, accuracy, and finality. Moreover, the administrative agency will encourage arbitrators to decide the case quickly so the award will be timely issued, and obtain an official agreement of the parties if a time extension is necessary.

Under limited or no administration, the arbitrator will be fully responsible to issue a timely award that resolves all issues before him or her, but no others. Hopefully any arbitrator drafting an award without administrative support is well-versed in arbitration law, which should help prevent challenges to the outcome based on a poorly drafted award.

It should also be noted that any time and cost required to effectuate confirmation of a poorly drafted award or one with technical deficiencies is counterproductive to the purposes of arbitration—speed and economy. Ideally, then, any award will be summarily confirmed by the courts if necessary without the need for hearings on the issues involved.

---

[12] If a party in arbitration objects to an award's lateness prior to its issuance, the award may be ruled invalid. *See* Five Keys, Inc. v. Pizza Inn, Inc., 653 P.2d 870 (N.M. 1982); R.E. Bean Construction Co. v. Middlebury Associates, Inc., 428 A.2d 306 (Vt. 1981).

[13] *See, for example*, Valentine Sugars, Inc. v. Donau Corp., 981 F.2d 210, 214 (5th Cir.), *cert. denied*, 113 S. Ct. 3039 (1993).

[14] *See* Wilko v. Swan, 346 U.S. 427 (1953).

[15] See Domke on Commercial Arbitration, §32.01, Wilner Rev.Ed.

[16] § 9, Uniform Arbitration Act; Art. 238 Texas Arbitration Act.

Self-Executing Rules

Everyone will agree that whether the arbitration is administered or not, it should be conducted in accordance with a set of well-drafted rules. Ideally, those rules have also been interpreted at key sections by courts across the country. Regardless, the rules of arbitration should be self-executing.

Self-executing rules will ensure that arbitration will culminate with the expected outcome-an award-no matter what one party might do to delay the proceeding or otherwise prevent the eventual outcome. Given the frequent circumstance that one of the parties to any arbitration has no interest in its conclusion, the use of self-executing rules is very advisable. It should also be noted that a party's reluctance to continue can begin during the arbitration following adverse rulings from the arbitrator. So, two parties and counsel getting along at the beginning of arbitration does not guarantee that this will continue throughout the process.

Clearly, one of the advantages to using full administration is that the agency rules will most certainly be self-executing. Where arbitration rules are not self-executing, and the parties do not have an administrative agency to rely on to make necessary rulings for the matter to go forward, trips to the courthouse will become the only mechanism to keep the arbitration moving.

Under limited or no administration, the parties are well- advised to consider how to continue the arbitration if, for some reason, the other party begins to delay the process. Unless specific authority is granted to some third party or the arbitrator to make necessary decisions for the continuation of the process, the parties should be prepared for a trip to the courthouse.

Pre-Dispute Arbitration Clauses, Institutionalized Arbitration & Mass Claims

The question of whether to access the services of an administrative agency is very different when considering future disputes, or groups of disputes that will always include one entity as a party.[17]

In the case of future disputes clauses included in the various commercial and consumer contracts executed daily across America, reliability is of critical importance. That is, will the arbitration clause as

---

[17] *See* DRAFTING DISPUTE RESOLUTION CLAUSES, American Arbitration Association (1996).

drafted be functional at the time the dispute arises. While some contracts have a relatively short life (e.g., construction contracts) requiring drafters to contemplate only a year or two into the future, others (e.g., real estate leases, limited partnerships, etc.) have terms of decades or an indefinite term.

Many transactional attorneys are likely to feel compelled to include the services of an administering agency in the arbitration clause of a long-term contract. The AAA is the longest existing domestic arbitral institution, having been founded in 1926, and the likelihood that it will still be in existence in the next fifty years is pretty strong. By contracting for the services of an administering agency like the not-for-profit AAA, parties can be confident that the arbitration provisions will be functional at the time of any arbitration.

The use of a non-administered or even limited administration system in a future disputes clause is wrought with potential difficulties, not the least of which is self-execution. Some future disputes clauses attempt to name a specific arbitrator for any future disputes. These clauses suffer from the possibility that the named arbitrator will no longer be practicing at the time the dispute arises or has developed conflicts of interest with one or more of the parties that will prevent service. Executing a non-administered arbitration arising from a future disputes clause is almost sure to include court rulings, ultimately delaying the process and increasing costs.

In cases of institutionalized arbitration (where some company or organization establishes a policy of favoring arbitration for certain types of, or all, disputes) and mass claims, there may exist valid business reasons to use administered arbitration as opposed to non-administered. Companies or organizations that expect to be arbitrating many claims every year may prefer to work with one provider exclusively, because they come to know what to expect, and they also develop a service relationship. Under these circumstances, the provider may offer discounted services based on volume of cases, or may provide additional services in support of the organizational program, such as statistical data on caseload.

In cases of institutionalized arbitration or mass claims, some organizations have chosen a multiple-option arbitration step. In these instances, the company may offer to the employee or consumer or previous client their choice of many arbitral options, one of which might be non-administered arbitration.

Post-Dispute Submission to Arbitration

This category of arbitrations represents the most likely candidates for non-administered arbitration. In fact, when two parties are negotiating an arbitration agreement, the world is their oyster in terms of procedures and how to arbitrate. A host of procedural items can be negotiated once the dispute is identified.

Which process is preferred under this circumstance will likely depend on the attorneys involved and any past arbitration experience of their clients. Attorneys and their clients should consider all of the costs of any process before deciding on full, limited, or no administration. Of course, the various risks of non-administration should be well contemplated.

Besides a perception that administered arbitration can be procedurally burdensome, excessive cost is the other driving force supporting non-administered arbitration. This most likely stems from the fact that fees for arbitration services are sometimes charged up front. Again, it should be noted that parties do not avoid the need for administration if an ad hoc system is selected; it only means that they either pay the arbitrator or the attorneys and their staff to administer the process instead of paying the administrative agency.

Conclusion

Private arbitration is a creature of contract, and, as such, contracting parties are at liberty to structure the process in ways that meet their needs and preferences. As with any contract provision, extreme care should be taken to draft the arbitration to ensure that it will produce the triune purpose of arbitration: speed, economy, and finality.

Administration of the procedural steps of arbitration is a necessary part of any well-managed arbitration. The real question is not whether to have arbitration administered or not, it is who will administer the process-an independent agency, the parties, or the arbitrator.

III. The Benefits of Independent Arbitration Administration

Engalla's Legacy to Arbitration: Why Independent Administration Is Important

*by Edward A. Dauer**

It was like watching a collision in the vacuum of outer space: Something big happened, but it didn't make a sound. On June 30, 1997 the California Supreme Court issued its opinion in *Engalla v. Permanente Medical Group, Inc.*,[1] one of the most closely watched state- court consumer arbitration cases in recent years. The opinion by Justice Mosk reversed the holding of the California Court of Appeals and remanded the case back to the trial court, thereby (for all practical purposes) reinstating the trial court's judgment that the survivors of Wilfredo Engalla need not arbitrate their medical malpractice claim against Kaiser Permanente.[2]

Yet the opinion, a seeming victory for an individual alleging injury from a faulty, self-administered arbitration against a more powerful adversary, makes no substantial change in the role of the courts in consumer arbitrations. That fact, however, does not make the opinion uninteresting. To the contrary, the court's careful hewing to the existing lines adds color to the chiaroscuro of self-administered arbitration.

As binding arbitration comes increasingly to be a condition for consumers doing business with large organizations, and as courts keep their respectful distance while statutes provide a narrow and difficult course for policing and review, the quality of arbitration may depend very significantly upon one single thing-the quality of the administration,

---

* Edward A. Dauer is Dean Emeritus and Professor of Law at the University of Denver. He is an active arbitrator and a student of arbitration with a particular emphasis on health care disputes. Dauer earned an A.B. from Brown University, a cum laude LL.B. from Yale Law School and an MPH form Harvard School of Public Health. His writings include HEALTH CARE DISPUTE RESOLUTION (National Association of Corporate Directors 2003) (with co-authors), *Judicial Policing of Consumer Arbitration,* 1 PEEPERDINE J. DISP. RES. (2000) and *Arbitration Wins; Arbitration Lose,* 10 WORLD ARBITRATION & MEDIATION REPORT (1999).

[1] Cal. 938 P.2d 903 (1997), *reversing* 43 Cal. Rptr.2d 621 (Cal. Ct. App. 1995).

[2] Technically, the cause was remanded for additional factual findings pertinent to Kaiser's motion to compel arbitration and to the Engallas' defense to that motion.

for as the *Engalla* case demonstrates, the quality of arbitration, such as in self-administered systems, will not be assured by the courts.

This is significant. Mandatory pre-dispute arbitration agreements are proliferating rapidly as businesses and others with "market power" come to appreciate the advantages arbitration holds for them. Many of these settings involve "mass" or at least non-negotiable contracts between individuals (consumers, patients, employees) and organizations (banks, health plans, employers).

Abuses of the bargaining process can be policed, of course, through the rules of unconscionability and, as we shall see in *Engalla* itself, by the law of fraud. And where there is a demonstrable abuse of the hearing process, or evident partiality in the arbitrators, statutes and case law in both the federal and state realms allow the courts to set the tainted result aside. Under current federal law, however, these are the only tools available and they are inadequate to deal with aspects of arbitration that are not defects, but that have different consequences for parties differently situated.

For example, take-it-or-leave-it pre-dispute arbitration agreements are not per se unconscionable, fraudulent or otherwise unenforceable.[3] But they nevertheless can be unfair, because their pros and cons fall differently—and systematically—on large organizations and individual consumers. Structural asymmetries in the arbitration process, unless guarded against, almost always favor the corporate party over the individual. For example, arbitration typically constrains or eliminates pre-hearing discovery. That feature applies to everyone alike, but it injures those who need information that the other side has (consumers and employees), more than those who have information the other side needs (large organizations). There is, therefore, a *de facto* unfairness to what is *de jure* quite an even-handed rule.

In addition, there is in arbitration generally no possibility of appeal for even egregious errors of law or misperceptions of facts, and therefore no ready remedy for substantively unjust results. For an organization with a large portfolio of similar claims, an occasional wrong result is a blip in the universe of many cases that are, on the whole, managed more efficiently by arbitration than they would be in the courtroom. For an individual party with just one case, perhaps one case in a lifetime, there

---

[3] The U.S. Supreme Court has held that even in an adhesive context arbitration *per se* is not an inferior process, but only a different one. Gilmer v. Interstate/Johnson Lane Corp., 500 U.S. 20 (1991).

is no statistical pool into which an untoward and unjust result can be drowned.

There may be other disparate impacts, such as the loss of the leverage of publicity and the absence of a jury. These, too, might be more advantageous to corporate interests than to individuals.

Another concern articulated by some is the "repeat player" risk in the modern arbitration market. This is the risk that the neutral will be influenced by the possibility of additional business with the corporate party. Unlike large nonprofit providers, such as the American Arbitration Association, which has thousands of arbitrators on its panels, none of whom own stock in the organization, the most rapidly-growing part of the neutral market is the small firm in which the equity owner is also the arbitrator. It is true that the future business of these entrepreneurial neutrals depends, at least in part, on their observable reputation for fairness. However, on the margins, they simply cannot be completely unaffected by the fact that in a consumer case the organization could be the source of further revenue, while the consumer very likely could not. Rules of law and of arbitrators' ethics require disclosure by an arbitrator-nominee of any facts that "might reasonably create the appearance of partiality or bias." These rules certainly limit the influence of any thoughts of future business. But they may well operate less assuredly in a self-administered system than in one where insistence about disclosure is part of the administrator's job.

The magnitude of the "repeat player" phenomenon has not, to my knowledge, been measured, nor its presence firmly proven. But to whatever extent it does exist, it too yields a subtle and unpoliceable spin uniformly in the direction of the "haves" over the "have nots."

These are among the asymmetries at risk in unguarded arbitration. Because they arise from the structure of the process and not from observable abuses of it, they cannot be policed effectively with existing legal tools.[4] And so, if arbitration favors Kaiser more than it favors Mr. Engalla, and that's why Kaiser chose to require it, even though Mr. Engalla would rather not, then legally speaking, so be it. That, I submit, is a problem.

---

[4] And perhaps not with statutory tools at the state level either. The U.S. Supreme Court in *Allied Bruce-Terminix Cos. Inc. v. Dobson*, 513 U.S. 265 (1995), read the interstate commerce requisite of the Federal Arbitration Act—and therefore its preemptive effect—as broadly as it could, and in *Doctor's Associates Inc. v. Casarotto*, 116 S. Ct. 1652 (1996), confirmed that it meant what it had said: no state may burden contracts to arbitrate with any rule, protective or not, that does not apply to all contracts generally.

These, it must be said, were not the issues explicitly posed in *Engalla*. They do, however, explain why this case and a handful of others like it have been so carefully watched. With contractually mandated arbitration increasingly replacing public adjudication, what should the role of the courts be? Does the risk of process asymmetries call for a sharpened and closer review from the front row seats? Although the court's role in private arbitration was not the legal question before the California Supreme Court, that is, nevertheless, what the case is truly all about.

Case Background

Wilfredo Engalla subscribed, through his employer, to a Kaiser health plan. As a part of the subscription he agreed to arbitrate any future disputes arising from Kaiser's services. In 1991 he was dying of lung cancer, which he alleged Kaiser had negligently failed to diagnose in time. Believing he was required to arbitrate the claim, Engalla attempted to get the arbitration going before he died. It was not to be. Although Kaiser had at the time of Engalla's subscription represented its arbitration process to be expeditious, including the expectation that all three arbitrators could be in place within sixty days of service of the claim, virtually nothing had been done by the 144th day, when Mr. Engalla died. This was not unusual. Delay was vastly more frequent than alacrity in the Kaiser system, the Engallas alleged, and Kaiser itself knew that. Indeed, according to the Engallas, the delays were known in advance and deliberate.

When Mr. Engalla died and Kaiser refused to waive the consequences of the delay,[5] the Engallas refused to arbitrate and repaired to the court to begin discovery. Kaiser then brought a motion to compel and to stay the litigation. The Engallas resisted the motion and the trial court agreed with them—in that court's view, Kaiser had committed fraud in procuring the arbitration agreement (by misrepresenting a speediness it knew would not occur), and had engaged in fraud "in the specific application" (by engaging in dilatory tactics); and in any case the whole arbitration program was "corrupt," oppressive and unconscionable. The trial court was clearly upset with Kaiser.

---

[5] "[U]pon the passing of Engalla, [California case law] required merger of the widow's loss of consortium claim into an indivisible claim for wrongful death, which warrants only a single general damage claim limited to $250,000." 938 P.2d at 914.

Before getting to the appellate courts' analyses, it would be useful to distinguish what Kaiser did from what its program provided, even though it was the program that allowed the problem to happen. Excerpting from the opinion of the Court of Appeals,

> [T]he arbitration program is not only designed, written, and mandated by Kaiser; it is also, as Kaiser concedes, administered by it.... [Kaiser] monitors administrative matters pertinent to the progress of each case including, for example, the identity and dates of appointment of arbitrators. It does not, however, employ or contract with any independent person or entity to provide such administrative services, or any oversight or evaluation of the arbitration program or its performance. Rather, administrative functions are performed by outside counsel retained to defend Kaiser in an adversarial capacity and, as Kaiser further concedes, such counsel are ethically obliged to act zealously and exclusively in the best interests of their client.

Under the Kaiser system as it existed in *Engalla*, everything depended on Kaiser's cooperation in appointing its own arbitrator, and in allowing its arbitrator to participate in appointing the third. Again quoting the Court of Appeals:

> [T]imely appointment of a neutral arbitrator is critical to the progress of the case, inter alia, because the Code of Civil Procedure provides a right to discovery only "after the appointment of the arbitrator or arbitrators"....In fact, in this case, [Kaiser's counsel] asserted that discovery could not commence until the neutral arbitrator was selected, because the neutral arbitrator would have to approve any discovery. Similarly, a hearing date cannot be set until the neutral arbitrator is appointed....In this case, [Kaiser's counsel] refused to discuss disclosure of expert witnesses until the hearing date was set....

Although the arbitration provision specifies that the two party arbitrators "shall" select a neutral arbitrator, in reality the selection is made by defense counsel after consultation with the Kaiser medical-legal department. Kaiser has never relinquished control over this selection decision.

Kaiser's position (for the sake of the litigation) was that it had no duty to design or administer its program as a fiduciary for its subscribers;

that the contractual agreement about arbitration was made at arm's-length; and that it was free to adopt a system that served its own business interests. It was about here that the trial court gagged, while the Court of Appeals saw nothing in which a court should get involved.[6] The critical point-though neither the Court of Appeals nor the California Supreme Court thought it was legally sufficient-is that Kaiser's system was self-administered. There was no independent administrator to run the selection of arbitrators on an equitable basis; there was no administrative machinery for forcing the discovery along; and there was no process for completing the appointments on a timely basis. In short, there was no one there to watch how well this arm's-length process was being run. The parties were running it, and while one side could theoretically inflict the same delays on its adversary, as the other could on it, there was an asymmetry in the process since delays generally favor the defense (particularly when the claimant has terminal lung cancer).

What Kaiser did then, again according to the facts as they were taken for purposes of the appeal, was to delay the appointment of its arbitrator, to delay if not obstruct the appointment of the neutral, and to avoid beginning the discovery aspects of the case.

The Appeals Court Decisions

The Court of Appeals found that "[w]hile some or all of this conduct may have been improper under statutes that regulate lawyers' actions in litigation...and morally reprehensible if undertaken by Kaiser and its attorneys simply to stall the litigation until the claimant died, it is not the stuff of which a claim of fraud is made."

Thus, there was no fraudulent misrepresentation on which Wilfredo Engalla had relied. As to Engalla's claim of "fraud in the specific application" stemming from the obstructions and the delays, the Court of Appeals concluded that even if these allegations would justify a rescission in the first place, they were simply breaches of the contractual

---

[6] The Court of Appeals stated: "[W]hen it "negotiates" and enters into an arbitration agreement, Kaiser's relationship with its subscribers is essentially a standard commercial one, with the parties bargaining at arm's length. Both Kaiser and prospective subscribers are free to act in its or their own business interest and to consult with counsel....Once a claim has been presented for arbitration, the relationship...becomes one of adversaries represented by counsel, with express and implied duties under both the Service Agreement and applicable law. In neither situation is a subscriber justified in claiming that he or she reposed "trust and confidence" in Kaiser, or that Kaiser has obtained control over his or her affairs, such that a fiduciary relationship was created."

duties relating to the arbitration and were, therefore, to be submitted not to the court, but to the arbitrator. With the exception of fraud in the inducement of the arbitration provisions themselves, violation of the covenant of good faith, abuse of process and whatever else, were all arbitrable matters, in which the courts have no role.

The impetus for the Court of Appeals' holding is not hard to understand. If courts were to open their doors generously to mid-process claims of foul, or to challenges to the arbitral process as precursors to submitting to it, the usefulness of arbitration would quickly evaporate. Every matter, or at least some substantial percentage of them, would be the subject of both an arbitration proceeding about the claim and a judicial proceeding about the arbitration proceeding.

While the general rule seems reasonable, the facts before the California Supreme Court apparently seemed otherwise. That court's actual holding began clearly enough: (a) Kaiser's arbitration process did not on its face lack "minimum levels of integrity" and was therefore not in itself unconscionable; (b) a trial court could find that Kaiser had waived its right to compel arbitration if its dilatory conduct was at "such a level of misfeasance as to constitute a waiver"; and (c) what is the central point, Kaiser's knowledge of the delays that almost always attended its arbitration process, combined with its delaying behavior once a claim was brought, was "plain" evidence of promissory fraud in the inducement of the contract. Thus, pending any additional factual findings by the trial court, Engalla could rescind his agreement to arbitrate the malpractice claim.

The Supreme Court viewed the facts before it not as establishing "fraud in the specific application," but as "promissory fraud"-namely, that Kaiser knew that it had no intention of abiding by its contractual promises. Its later behavior evidenced that earlier intention to defraud and established the harm that flowed to the Engallas as a result. Ergo, good old fraud in the inducement.

For critics of the Court of Appeals' decision and for those who believed that a more protective balance should be struck between judicial policing and the needs of arbitral efficiency, the California Supreme Court's opinion doesn't amount to much. It was lightning without thunder, a collision in space without noise. Judicial oversight (in the form of denying a motion to compel) was justified on the old and familiar ground of fraud in the inducement. In contrast to the famous Justice Cardozo, who in his opinions created legal revolutions while insisting that he was doing nothing unusual at all, the California Supreme

Court did nothing unusual at all while (unintentionally perhaps) appearing to be doing something very important indeed.

Not many cases of dilatory or obstructionist arbitration conduct will ever fall within the court's ingeniously applied but still narrow and technically grudging rule. A party aggrieved at being on the receiving end of an unfair proceeding will have to show not only that the adversary was acting unfairly, but that at the time the agreement was made the adversary knew it would later be acting that way and made false and injurious representations to the contrary.

Self-Administration

As to the significance of administration of arbitral systems, Kaiser's administration of its own arbitration program was the crux of the problem for the trial court. Even the Engallas' claim of fraud, the legal category into which all of the facts were packaged, rested on a misrepresentation of the timeliness of the process–a misrepresentation made fraudulent, in the trial court's view, not by the accident of delays, but by Kaiser's knowing involvement in producing them.[7] The Court of Appeals ruled differently. Self-administration and party-arbitration are well-known parts of the arbitral tradition; certainly a process could not be per se unconscionable simply on that account.

In the Supreme Court, the message on administration was mixed. Contrasting Kaiser's process with the AAA's administrative process to illuminate the systematic nature of the delays in Kaiser's system, the court went on to say,

Though Kaiser is not obliged by law to adopt any particular form of arbitration, the record shows that it did not attempt to create within its own organization any office that would neutrally administer the arbitration program, but instead entrusted such administration to outside counsel retained to act as advocates on its behalf. In other words, there is evidence that Kaiser established a self-administered arbitration system in which delay for its own benefit and convenience was an inherent part, despite express and implied contractual representations to the contrary.

Nonetheless, the court found that "none of these features of Kaiser's arbitration program renders the arbitration agreement per se unconscionable." There may have been fraudulent conduct in this one case, but only because Kaiser had made explicit representations contrary to what it knew would be the facts. Thus, while there is agreement that

---

[7] As always, I mean the facts as they were alleged, not as they may actually have been.

self-administration is not evil per se, an important majority seemed to have felt that things would have been much better had Kaiser chosen instead to entrust its system to an independent administrator. The advantages would have been obvious: while a self-administered system can be employed as an asymmetrically useful tool for the benefit of its creator, independent administration from the outset re-establishes the neutral process management that is so much of our tradition of "due process" when it happens in a court.

Engalla's Legacy

Having come this far, what is there to make of all this? Several things, I believe. First, and most obvious, though least important, is the possibility that self-administration can make a finding of fraud in the inducement more likely. Justice Mosk found actionable fraud in the frustration of contractually induced expectations about the process. If Kaiser had not been running the program, the same misrepresentations may or may not have been fraudulent. There was scienter here because Kaiser knew what would happen—because it made the events happen.

A second teaching of the case is that organizations that are truly interested in avoiding the risks of the asymmetries of arbitration would do well to adopt an independently administered model. Likewise, policy-makers who describe in statutes and regulations the fundamentals of fair procedure should consider whether, in whatever setting they are examining, the incremental cost of independent administration is a good—and therefore should be a required—investment in the goal of procedural fairness.

A third point is a suggestion of my own. Self-administered arbitration is not per se unconscionable, and that seems right. Courts cannot police arbitration from a front row seat without destroying many of its core advantages. That seems right too. Yet it seems clear to me (though controverted by some) that in the adhesive settings of employees, consumers, patients and the like, arbitration can offer its advantages unequally and systematically in favor of larger organizations; and that these effects are unpoliceable precisely because they come not from abuses of the process, but from the control of its intrinsic features. To accommodate these several competing ideas, I would suggest a rule of differential judicial scrutiny. Such things are not unknown in the law—courts will often look at factors X, Y and Z in a situation more closely when factor A is present than when it is not. It is a dominant feature of constitutional law, and a frequent feature elsewhere.

So it may be used here. A lower level of scrutiny—the present one, perhaps—applied to all arbitrations generally and to adhesive systems that are independently administered. And a heightened level of scrutiny for those adhesive systems that are, as Kaiser's was, administered by the "stronger" party itself. While independent administration would therefore not be a requisite for "minimal levels of integrity" under the unconscionability concept, its absence would be recognized as a risk that the intrinsic asymmetries could more readily be exploited.

Unconscionability is itself a cluster concept. There is, therefore, no principled reason why a standard such as this could not be an articulated part of its application to arbitration in adhesive settings. Those organizations that benefit from "repeat-player" arbitrations, if any, could continue to do so, being required only to guard against the subtle unfairness self-administration permits. Properly administered systems would keep the courts in the back rows they now occupy, thus not ruining the advantages with busy policeman and busybody rules. At the same time, the untoward risks of arbitration's asymmetries might be better controlled.

There is much to be debated about a proposal such as this one. This essay may not be the place to unfurl all of the arguments and details. It may be enough for now to have raised the issue—to have added some noise, if the metaphor may be given one last breath, to the otherwise noiseless collision of Engalla and Kaiser Permanente. I suspect Wilfredo would be pleased.

IV. The Essential Qualities of an Arbitrator

Striving for Excellence

by Richard Mittenthal[*]

To succeed as an arbitrator, one must grow into the role. No one is born with a judicial temperament, and the difficulty is that there is no true school for arbitrators. Few among us have had the benefit of a full-time mentor to alert us to the practices and pitfalls of the profession. Arbitrators receive little feedback from the parties who alone are in a position to offer constructive criticism regarding their performance. Arbitrators simply learn by doing and perhaps after several hundred cases the true nature of the arbitrator's job begins to take form.

Most arbitrators have the ability to run a hearing, analyze evidence, and write an opinion. But to achieve excellence, each of these skills must be carefully honed. Mere repetition-the number of cases heard and decided-will not guarantee excellence. Something more is necessary. It is my belief, after some 45 years of practice, that the qualities essential to the development of an arbitrator are self-discipline, self-restraint, and self-criticism.

Self-Discipline

At the hearing, the parties' spokesmen explain why they believe there is or is not a contract violation and the witnesses explain the facts of the case. The function of the arbitrator is of course to listen. Typically, arbitrators listen simply to understand what is being said. But if that is their sole object, they seriously limit what can be learned from a hearing. One must also listen to what is left unsaid. And, most important of all, one should listen not just for the purpose of understanding but also for the purpose of deciding. When an arbitrator does that, he or she is far more likely to identify matters not fully developed and to ask questions which elicit information helpful in reaching a decision.

---

[*] The author has been a full-time labor-management arbitrator since 1954. He has worked extensively in the area of postal workers as well as the steel, automotive parts, construction equipment, and beer industries. He was president of the National Academy of Arbitrators in 1997-1998.

This expansive listening takes more concentration, more energy, than most arbitrators are accustomed to. But if an arbitrator can discipline himself to spend this extra energy, he might enhance his ability to find a solution to the problem. No cost-benefit analysis is possible. But from my experience, the benefit is there for those who care to add to their burden.

Before making a decision, arbitrators must immerse themselves in the record. Unless arbitrators are prepared to devote the necessary time and effort to master the case, they cannot grow. This means arbitrators must, at a minimum, know the facts and arguments as well as the parties. And, because of the parties' omissions, they should often know the case better than the parties. That can only be accomplished through unremitting hard work.

Nothing is more dangerous than a sense that the dispute is too minor to warrant a full effort. Nor should one resort to shortcuts as a means of saving time. This may make the work tedious at times. But, once again, self-discipline is essential if you are to achieve the mastery necessary for top-quality work.

Resist the siren call to do something less. Even the best of arbitrators will occasionally produce humdrum opinions far below their capability. The excuses for such work are always the same-the routine nature of the case, the insignificance of the issue, the press of a busy docket, and so on. Such sub-par performance, repeated often enough, is likely to lower one's standards. Self-discipline creates the good habits which will serve you well for a lifetime of arbitration.

Many of us refer to hornbooks, for instance, Elkouri & Elkouri (HOW ARBITRATION WORKS) or Hill & Sinicroppi (MANAGEMENT RIGHTS), for a quick fix to orient ourselves with respect to a given problem. But the general principle and exceptions found in such literature should only be seen as a starting point. One must go further and seek to understand, whenever possible, the basis for a particular theory or principle. Self-discipline demands these extra steps if you are to improve your interpretive powers.

Perhaps the most obvious example of self-discipline is to make sure the award is issued within the appropriate 30- or 60-day time frame. The parties, however dilatory they may be in moving a case to arbitration, appreciate promptness on the arbitrator's part. To be prompt may mean preparing a draft of the facts and arguments before the briefs are received. Or it may mean careful consideration of the decision before the briefs. There is no excuse for the kind of tardiness, occasionally as long as a year, which occurs from time to time. Of course, 50-50 cases do arise and arbitrators can find themselves blocked by indecision. But ultimately, perhaps through self-delusion, such cases are transformed into a 51-49 proposition and decisions can be made. That too can and should be done within the 30- or 60-day period, however painful it may seem. The very act of honoring time limits, conscientiously repeated over a long enough period, is likely to produce the self-discipline necessary to avoid late awards.

Self-Restraint

At the hearing, arbitrators are constantly confronted by the question of self-restraint. Should they intervene? If so, when should they intervene and what should they ask? The principle seems simple: Do not be intrusive; allow the parties to present their case as they wish. That does not preclude the occasional question to ensure that arbitrators understand a witness' answer or a spokesman's argument. Many questions, however, will be answered in time if arbitrators have the patience to allow the spokesman to go about his work unimpeded.

There are circumstances, however, where intervention is unavoidable. When a spokesman is obviously ill-equipped to present a coherent case, the arbitrator must step in. Or when the case is extremely complex and the arbitrator is not absorbing the detail, he or she must seek clarification. How active or passive one should be depends on a variety of such factors. The principal ones are the nature of the dispute, the thoroughness and clarity of the parties' presentations, and the arbitrator's ability to understand.

In decision-making, self-restraint is far more important. The arbitrator is not asked for his completely personalized "sense of justice." Rather, the parties seek the arbitrator's "sense of justice" as filtered through their arguments and the contract language they cite. They certainly do not want the arbitrators to make rulings on the basis of contract language nowhere mentioned in the record. Should arbitrators attempt to do so, they can never be certain how the parties would have construed such contract language. One should not venture into such a vacuum without absolute certainty as to what the language means. That kind of certainty is rarely present. Even if it were, arbitrators could never know why the parties chose to ignore what would otherwise appear to be a controlling contract provision. Self-restraint is the proper course, not just because it is the safer response for the arbitrator, but because it places the responsibility for shaping the nature of the dispute on those closest to it.

None of this should be construed to prevent the arbitrator, in a truly unusual case, from doing exactly what I have said that he should not do. It is possible for self-restraint to produce such an abominable result-for instance, an apparent collusive attempt to deny an employee his contractual rights–that the arbitrator should be free to raise the ignored contract language so as to produce a just result. However, with few exceptions, self-restraint should be a guide in deciding disputes.

In opinion writing, self-restraint is essential. This can be illustrated in many ways. None is more important than the choice of a rationale for the decision. Suppose, for instance, that a grievance can be denied on either factual grounds or contractual grounds. Obviously, the denial on factual grounds will have a lesser impact on the parties. Unless they plainly desire a ruling on the contract as well, self-restraint ordinarily dictates the narrower course does the least possible harm.

Just as arbitrators should seek to limit the rationale for the decision, they should likewise avoid dicta where possible. The arbitrator's charge relates to the case before him, not to other cases not yet filed. Similarly, in choosing one interpretation over another, a value judgment may be critical. The arbitrator may or may not wish to express such value judgments-for instance, the relative weight to be given considerations of flexibility or stability in the workplace-because they may reveal more of himself than he wishes to reveal. There is nothing wrong with omitting any reference to values in this situation so long as the arbitrator otherwise can forcefully support the decision. Just as the parties deliberately keep certain information from us, arbitrators' awards need not express every consideration that led them to their conclusion. Self-restraint is a valuable tool. Although I do not consider myself a minimalist, less is often more in writing opinions. The danger always is that arbitrators will say too much, not too little.

Self-Criticism

Arbitrators cannot do their work well unless they develop a high level of self-criticism. No one else is available to review one's judgment and written opinion. Colleagues may try to help but they are unlikely to invest the time required to be truly helpful. Each arbitrator must simply learn to be his own sternest critic. That requires distancing himself from the work product and later returning to it as if it were someone else's award. As a practical matter, that means putting aside the award for at least a few days after it is written and then examining it again in a thorough review. And that requires conditioning not to be overly impressed with first impressions.

Self-confidence is a highly regarded human trait. But, oddly enough, arbitrators blessed with too high a degree of self-confidence are least likely to develop a high degree of self-criticism. There is no substitute for questioning oneself, for approaching the problem once more from an entirely different angle, for stretching the facts in one direction or another to see whether a chosen theory can withstand the stress.

It can be easy to become self-satisfied too soon. Experimentation with a style of writing, with the form of the opinion, with the limitations of some theory, and so on, is a continuing process. One learns as one struggles.

Conclusion

These remarks are intended to demonstrate what, for me, is a truism. However bright you may be, however extensive your background, however facile your pen, however substantial your caseload, the most important steps toward becoming a better arbitrator involve a better control of oneself through self-discipline, self-restraint, and self-criticism.

V. Counsel's Role in the Selection of an Arbitrator

Selecting the Arbitrator: What Counsel Can Do

by Francis O. Spalding[*]

Skillful participation in the selection of the arbitrator is a hallmark of the skilled advocate in arbitration. Of course, effective advocacy in arbitration demands, at every stage, careful analysis and full understanding both of the similarities and the differences between litigation and arbitration. That which is different is likely to pose the greater challenge to the experienced trial lawyer; and few aspects of arbitration are more different-or, it may be said, more crucial-than selection of the arbitrator.

One deep-seated similarity between litigation and arbitration is the importance that experienced counsel attach to the attributes and characteristics of those who will decide questions of fact and make rulings of law. There is, however, this crucial difference: For all the efforts of trial counsel to seek small, advantageous influence, the law struggles mightily, and generally successfully, to prevent judicial forum-shopping; and limitation on voir dire is an often-discussed reform of civil litigation.

In arbitration, by contrast, something akin to forum-shopping-the search for a panel with the array of experience and skills sought by the parties-is not only permitted but encouraged.

Much rides on the issue of arbitrator selection-not only because the single arbitrator or panel will function both as judge and jury, but also because, absent the kinds of prejudicial misconduct that can justify statutory vacatur of an award, the work of the arbitrator is substantially insulated from judicial supervision or review. This distinctive characteristic of arbitration contributes significantly to the speed, efficiency and cost advantages that this process offers. Careful,

---

[*] Francis O. Spalding is an arbitrator and mediator in Northern California. He serves on the AAA's roster of neutrals and on its Large, Complex Case and Commercial Mediation Panels. He is a member of the Northern California Advisory Council and is Vice Chair of the Mandatory Fee Arbitration Program Executive Committee of the Bar Association of San Francisco. Spalding holds a B.A. from Yale University and a magna cum laude J.D. from Northwestern University School of Law. He has written widely on ADR and serves as a consultant and expert witness on ADR issues.

thoughtful, effective participation in arbitrator selection is an important element keeping the equation in balance.

Opportunities for Party Input

Although counsel has a crucial and subtle role to play in arbitrator selection, counsel can never have full control. (A partial exception might seem to lie in the appointment of the party-selected arbitrator to a tripartite panel-one made up of "party-appointed" arbitrators selected by each side and a "neutral" arbitrator selected by those two-an expensive and cumbersome procedure.)

One effective way to maximize party control of arbitrator selection is by early mutual agreement of the parties, perhaps even before the case is formally submitted to an arbitral forum. The American Arbitration Association has recognized the advantage of early party agreement and has much facilitated such agreement by establishing a roster of neutrals that is both generalized and specialized, made up of well-recognized and experienced practitioners and full-time neutrals.

The AAA's traditional arbitrator-selection process can fairly be viewed as the industry standard, one toward which other forums, such as those maintained by the self-regulatory organizations in the securities industry, appear to be moving. This process involves the assembly by the assigned case administrator, from the entire available pool of qualified panelists, of a list of possible arbitrator candidates of three to five times as many names as there are arbitrator slots to be filled-along with expanded biographical information about the panelists on this list.

It is at this point that counsel has one of the most important opportunities to have appropriate input into the neutral selection process: by advance individual consultation with the case administrator concerning the criteria that counsel hopes to find in the arbitrator. Counsel's articulation of these criteria can provide helpful guidance to the administrator in putting together a list that will please at least one party. It may well turn out that counsel who cannot otherwise agree on the time of day-and who might be unable or unwilling even to agree on the desirable arbitrator criteria-will agree on the suitability of one or more of the names that find their way onto the administrator's list in this way.

If individual consultation between counsel for one party and the administrator on desired arbitrator criteria is good, individual consultation by counsel for all parties is certainly better-and joint consultation by counsel for all parties is probably best of all. The extent to which counsel are willing to consult together about the selection of the arbitrator is necessarily left to them. The arbitrator selection process is likely to benefit from any significant degree of such consultation.

What is the propriety of counsel for one party suggesting particular individuals to the case administrator? This should be problematic only where there exists some prior relationship between the party making the suggestion (including its counsel) and the individual suggested. There should be no basis for objection to a name on the case administrator's list solely on the ground that another party suggested it-particularly since suggestion by one party is often, if not almost always, the starting point for any pre-submission agreement by the parties regarding the individual to serve as arbitrator.

What is absolutely essential is a full exploration–and disclosure to the administrator–by the suggesting party of all pre-existing contacts or relationships between the party proposing the name and the individual named; this is especially the case where the relationship is one that would ultimately be subject to successful challenge for failure to disclose. Failure to meet this standard is equivalent to placing a figurative land mine under this key step in the arbitral process.

Intelligence Gathering

However the name of a candidate may be proposed, counsel's next task is intelligence collection. Whatever the methods used to discover information about potential arbitrators, it is wise to keep in mind this paradox: If a party or counsel begins with too much knowledge about the prospect-particularly knowledge gained in first-hand contact -there may be a strong likelihood that the prospect will be disqualified, for a pre-existing relationship with the prospect may reflect either actual or perceived bias on the neutral's part. Obviously, as noted, such facts require full, forthcoming disclosure. (Current practice puts the entire formal burden of disclosure upon the prospective arbitrator. It may not be apparent, however, why a party with knowledge of a "disclosable" relationship should not be expected to make known the relevant facts, at least to the administrating organization, if not to the opposing parties.)

Although the frequently declaimed dawning of the Information Age certainly offers some new and invaluable means of intelligence gathering about prospective arbitrators, it is important not to forget the best of the traditional methods developed by and relied upon by skilled advocates.

Perhaps the most useful way to analyze the means of intelligence available is not in terms of novelty or venerability, but in terms of functionality. For not every source of information-not even the best sources-is equally good at yielding every kind of information.

Biographical Information. Basic biographical facts amenable to objective determination are the obvious starting point. What profession does the prospect follow? What professional and other experiences does the prospect bring to bear? What is the prospect's age and education? What experience does he or she have as a neutral? And so on.

Under current practice, as previously noted, the AAA's biographies, now much more elaborate in content and much improved in format and readability, are routinely furnished to the parties. An even more important improvement in procedure is this: Every time an arbitrator is appointed by the AAA, the AAA furnishes a copy of the current AAA biography to the arbitrator, who must either certify that it is current or update it.

Sometimes entries in published professional directories contain even more biographical detail than does the AAA biography. Another source of arbitrator résumés is the Internet, where more and more ADR professionals have their own web pages or are included on web pages of ADR providers, law firms or other organizations.

All of this information provides a crucial starting point-and possibly even an end point. The basic biography may show that the prospect in question is an inappropriate candidate. Alternatively, in combination with the candidate's general reputation in the community, it may enable counsel to conclude that the prospect would be acceptable as the arbitrator. If there is doubt, however, further inquiry is likely to be justified; and this will be the case in part because the sources of information in this general category share this common feature (and possible flaw): They have been prepared by, or almost exclusively from, information provided by the arbitrator candidate, and thus may gloss over, or fail to address, concerns of genuine importance.

If more information is needed, counsel might begin by inquiring whether any additional information is available from the case administrator.

Another possible source of facts subject to more or less objective determination is the press. If the candidate has a high enough news profile to have been mentioned in the professional or general press, a search of a computer- accessible database of news reports or an Internet search may be justified. As to the candidate who enjoys less public prominence, such searches, although less likely to turn up numerous entries, still may yield some gem.

Books and Articles. Information of a different character may be revealed by a search for writings by the candidate. The fact that the candidate has written books or articles has some importance as a matter of objective biographical fact, and is likely to be reflected in the sources of information already mentioned. These writings, if related to the arbitration process, may reveal the candidate's understanding of the adjudicative and arbitral processes and his or her approach to, and views upon, such matters as the proper role of the arbitrator, the proper conduct of an arbitration proceeding and the like. At least when the subject matter of a writing appears relevant to the issues in dispute and the writing is reasonably accessible, such a search probably ought to be given high priority. In addition to law library catalogs and the Internet, searches can be made using law-related computer search services to find the full text of recent law review articles. Even today it is probably worth the effort to search computer-accessible sources for written texts, whether or not it is thought worthwhile to visit a remote library in pursuit of such a search.

Anecdotal Information. Beyond objective biographical information and an insight into the views of the candidate, the experienced advocate is likely to place a high premium upon anecdotal information from third parties based on live experience with the candidate in an arbitrator's role. Counsel will be particularly interested in the reactions of other lawyers who have appeared before the candidate in other cases.

Most large law firms and sophisticated advocates skilled in arbitration keep records designed to capture past experience with individual arbitrators in order to inform future choices. Finding the people or firms to ask about prospective arbitrators is the first step in any information search. Home is the first place to start. The everyday experience of lawyers in large firms who receive internal e-mail messages inquiring about a prospective arbitrator confirms how well recognized this methodology is.

If a candidate is someone with long experience in the community, it may be worthwhile to make a "cold call" to acquaintances in other local firms likely to have had some contact with the prospect. In some circumstances–principally in the labor area or if the candidate has appeared as an arbitrator in a securities industry arbitration, a field in which the forums maintained by the National Association of Securities Dealers and other "self-regulatory organizations" make awards available for public inspection–it may be possible to review the prospect's awards and to identify lawyers who represented the parties in those proceedings.

Once such a search is undertaken, each person spoken to ought to be asked to suggest other possible sources.

Not surprisingly, there are potential difficulties in obtaining anecdotal information about arbitrator candidates. Some individuals and firms regard this information as confidential or proprietary; some limit the availability of this type of intelligence to a circle of close, professional friends or colleagues; and in a day when everyone is bombarded by unwanted inquiries, there may be resistance to the effort involved in digging out and forwarding such information, even when there is no other reason to withhold it.

One useful starting point to obtain anecdotal information is the AAA arbitrator résumés furnished to the parties with the list of potential candidates. These résumés may contain the names and telephone numbers of the attorneys for both sides who have appeared before the arbitrator candidate and have agreed to serve as a contact.

Even if anecdotal information can be captured, its value will depend on such variables as who collected it, how long ago and under what circumstances, and how, if at all, it has been memorialized. Old information, or information gathered by someone no longer available to provide a foundation for understanding, may be more misleading than informative. Thus, the worth of the information such a search may reveal needs to be evaluated concurrently with the conduct of the search itself.

Interviews with Prospects. One final method of intelligence-gathering deserves mention, even though its potential cost probably justifies it only in very large or otherwise unusual cases: interviews with prospective arbitrators. One aspect of this tool distinguishes it from the rest: It can be undertaken appropriately only if done jointly by counsel for all parties, and thus depends upon the agreement of the parties. This means, at least in many instances, that the assistance of the administrating organization should be invoked. Even if the parties reach an agreement without the assistance of that organization, they should keep it informed throughout so that it may render needed services promptly.

It is essential to recognize that an agreement to interview arbitrator candidates does not constitute an agreement with respect to arbitrator selection. While counsel for opposing parties may well agree upon a selection based upon the interviews, that outcome is not guaranteed—throwing counsel back upon whatever method for selecting the arbitrator is provided under the parties' agreement or under the applicable rules of the administering organization.

The list of candidates to be interviewed should be winnowed by party agreement. The terms of the arrangement-including whether candidates should be offered a fee for their time in appearing to be interviewed-need to be worked out fully and carefully, lest the process become the seedbed for further disputes between the parties. Presumably an hour or less with each candidate should be sufficient for an appropriate interview. Counsel should agree, insofar as possible, upon questions of common interest, and counsel for individual parties should also be afforded an opportunity to propound questions of particular interest to each. All such questions should be known to all counsel in advance. An agreed order of questions and questioners should make it possible, if the parties so desire, to leave the candidates at least somewhat in doubt as to what party is interested in what question.

In general, questioning should not be addressed to biographical details that may be readily ascertained in the AAA biography or in professional directories. The focus should be on the substantive expertise that has brought the candidate into the pool and, at least in the case of lawyer-candidates, on the candidate's experience in and philosophy of the arbitration process.

It is essential to fully effective advocacy in arbitration that counsel think through and attend carefully to the opportunities, unmatched in litigation, for exercising the influence appropriate to this alternative forum upon the qualifications, the capacities and even the identity of the central figure in the arbitration process-the arbitrator.

What to Look for in an Arbitrator

What qualities are most desirable in an arbitrator? That question is perhaps best answered by considering what it is that arbitrators do.

An arbitrator spends most of the time until the case is submitted listening to the parties and looking at the evidence. Attentive listening and careful observation demand a measured patience—patience enough to hear and observe all that is relevant and appropriate, but also an ability to intercede, politely but firmly, when the bounds of relevance and propriety are exceeded or unnecessary delay is threatened. For while the arbitrator must see and hear attentively that which is properly part of the case, he or she is no less obliged to keep the arbitral process free of distraction and away from detour.

Fairness-the essential touchstone of the arbitral function-demands open-mindedness. The arbitrator must be a master of the "rolling hypothesis," able to assemble whatever has been seen and heard into a cohesive understanding of the case, but always ready, at least until the last submission of the last party has been absorbed, to revise the unfolding story even in fundamental ways, if warranted. Scarcely less important is the perception of fairness. The parties must leave the arbitration process, win or lose, with the sense that they have been heard and understood in full, and that their views of the case have been given thorough, balanced consideration.

The arbitrator conveys this sense of fairness by neutrality, by balance in body language and tone of voice, by evenhandedness in dealing with witnesses for both sides and with evidentiary disputes, and by dealing effectively with obstreperous or provocative counsel or a misbehaving party. The arbitrator must be prepared, however, to put equability to one side when necessary to meet some crisis in the process.

Another quality is the ability and willingness to let the parties' counsel present the case their way. The arbitrator does not sit as a monitor of the advocacy skills and tactics of the parties' attorneys. He or she must be prepared, however, to intervene to keep the proceeding on a coherent track and free of avoidable inefficiency.

Inquisitiveness is a necessary quality in the arbitrator, but this curiosity must be cabined within the limits appropriate to the case. The inquisitive arbitrator will wonder about facts somehow related to the case on which no evidence is submitted. If those facts are relevant to the arbitrator's assigned task, they may be inquired into; if not, no matter how intriguing they may seem, the arbitrator must leave them aside.

In addition, the arbitrator (or panel chair) must know the arbitral process and have the skills to guide and control it in a way that is fair to all parties. Training and, above all, experience, are the sources of these skills. In some cases, special knowledge of the industry or of the business context in which the principal issues arise, is also desirable in the arbitrator.

In sum, the ideal arbitrator will have near-perfect attentiveness and an intellect fully up to the demands of the case; but the other qualities of the ideal-patience, open-mindedness, an equable temperament, restraint, inquisitiveness-each balances on a sort of knife edge; each demands a stable, often near-invisible performance almost all of the time. But always there must be the sense that, upon presentation of a genuine demand, the arbitrator will do something decisive, surgical yet not quite predictable, to put the straying proceeding firmly back upon its proper path.

CHAPTER FIVE

ARBITRATION FOR ARBITRATORS

I. Attorneys Appearing Before Non-Attorney Arbitrators

**Problems and Solutions:
The Attorney and the Non-Attorney Arbitrator**

*by Raoul Drapeau**

Attorneys representing a client in arbitration always want to go all-out to provide their client with the best chance of gaining a favorable judgment. But in hearings before an arbitrator who is not an attorney, special circumstances may arise regarding conduct, technique and presentation of evidence. This article examines the various problems that may arise in such situations and prescribes simple solutions aimed at promoting a smooth interaction between the attorney and the non-attorney arbitrator.

Much has been written about the successes and failures of arbitrators in conducting a fair hearing. Their evaluation, decision-making and meeting-management skills are crucial to producing an equitable award. Because there are winners and losers in such matters, it is not surprising that an arbitrator's performance is called into question from time to time. This is especially true when the arbitrator is not an attorney, because a non-attorney arbitrator can understandably miss legal subtleties or stumble on important points, such as not hearing relevant evidence.

On the other hand, very little has been written about the performance of the attorneys who represent clients in arbitration hearings held before such a non-attorney arbitrator. This is an important issue, because an

---

* The author has 15 years experience as an arbitrator and over 30 years experience in high technology and business, where he heads a technology innovation firm. He is also a member of the American Arbitration Association's panel of arbitrators. He supplies a valuable perspective on the special problems that can arise between attorneys and non-attorney arbitrators. Drapeau holds electrical engineering degrees from Cornell University and Renseleer Polytechnic Institute.

attorney's behavior can certainly have an effect on the outcome of the hearing.

The use of arbitration as an alternative dispute-resolution process has grown strongly in recent years, and many more attorneys are now involved in the process. Unfortunately, their formal classroom education usually does not cover the differences in procedures and customs between the courtroom and the arbitration hearing room. Thus, unless they frequently participate in arbitrations, they either may not know those differences or fully appreciate their importance. Even if they do know them, they may forget them in the heat of the moment, an oversight that can get in the way of the progress of an arbitration hearing, regardless of who the arbitrators are.

However, there is an additional dimension to this situation that can cause trouble for the unmindful attorney, and it is the subject of this article. Commercial arbitration cases can involve a wide and complex range of technical and legal issues. Thus, many disputants select a multiple-member panel. Often, at least one member of these panels is not an attorney, but instead an expert chosen because of technical or business savvy in the issues involved. This person is surrounded in the hearing room by legal experts, some of whom might be panel colleagues, and the disputants' attorneys. All of these people speak a curious and sometimes incomprehensible language that is quite different from that used in the usual technical or business environment. In addition, the litigating attorneys can behave in ways that seem to such arbitrators to confound common sense and work against the avowed objective of getting to the truth. This dichotomy is one of the most troublesome aspects of such hearings, since it can result in avoidable misunderstandings and interruptions.

At the same time, the attorneys may feel uncertain about the technical issues and their own unfamiliar lingo. Clearly, their understanding of these matters can be crucial to making an effective representation of their client's position. In addition, attorneys can worry about how knowledgeable the non-legal panel member(s) are on issues of the law that may arise. This difference in experience can lead to additional misunderstandings and even more serious trouble. But more often it is an avoidable irritant as both sides stumble forward to educate each other in real time in the search for an equitable solution to the dispute.

The issues presented in this article are taken from actual experience and are intended as a guide for attorneys who are participating in an arbitration conducted by a non-attorney arbitrator.

Introductions

This is probably the first time that you will have met the non-attorney arbitrator. Just as in a job interview, a lasting impression—for better or worse—is formed in these first few minutes. But this works both ways. The non-attorney arbitrator will be anxious to display competence in his or her field of expertise, as well the appropriate temperament to manage the hearing and carefully weigh the evidence. Likewise, this is the best opportunity you may get to demonstrate that even though you come from a different business culture and educational background, you respect his or her abilities. In no small regard, the outcome of your case and its effect on your client depends on these mutual perceptions.

Discovery

Some attorneys are used to demanding great amounts of evidence during discovery to buttress their case. However, when carried to extremes this tactic may be seen by a non-attorney arbitrator simply as a means to unnecessarily burden a less-well-heeled opponent. This is because most business people and engineers are used to making decisions from adequate, but not perfect or even complete data. They realize that it is not generally practical or even possible to get every shred of evidence or background data that might apply. So when someone attempts to do just that, it can create a negative impression.

The Non-Attorney Arbitrator and the Panel

Many commercial-arbitration panels are made up solely of attorneys. When the risks are higher or in larger cases, one or more technical members are usually included because of their knowledge of the technical issues. This helps the disputants in that they can have confidence that the technical matters are understood by the panel. But it also helps the arbitrator's non-technical colleagues to do a more effective job, because the technical arbitrator can translate issues into terms that they can better understand.

Naturally, these technical and business professionals rarely know as much about the fine points of law as the protagonists in the hearing. On the other hand, the attorneys may not have had as much experience in arbitration hearings as an experienced non-attorney arbitrator. In fact, because non-attorney arbitrators often serve alone on cases, they may know a lot more than many attorneys do about the practical side of arbitration hearings and their customs. This is particularly so if an attorney's litigation experience has been mostly in the courtroom. Furthermore, a non-attorney arbitrator certainly knows more about his or her technical specialty.

To be sure, attorneys on a panel will naturally be well-equipped to deal with any legal matters that may arise. Technical panel members know their shortcomings in these matters, but are also well aware that they can influence their attorney colleagues on the panel in other, more relevant ways. For example, an attorney member will often turn to a non-attorney arbitrator during or after the hearing for advice, explanation or recommendation. In such situations, a non-attorney arbitrator can tip the balance.

Rules of Evidence

The well-known courtroom rules of evidence are an important aspect of formal legal tribunal procedure. For the most part though, they aren't rigidly adhered to in arbitration hearings. Still, some attorneys try to impose their personal view of what the rules of evidence should be, rather than conform to the arbitrator's presence. In a forum where the preferred emphasis is on substance and equity, rather than on procedure and law, such behavior is sure to be poorly received. An arbitrator possessing only limited legal experience will not appreciate having to continually deal with such unfamiliar matters, or feeling insulted by a lack of intimate knowledge in that area.

Conflicting Evidence

The situation often occurs when opposing attorneys present seemingly irrefutable evidence conclusively proving conflicting points. It can be difficult for even a technically competent panel member to straighten it all out. However, in attempting to do just that, the non-attorney technical panel member will try to focus on what he or she perceives as the matters that were proven technically, not necessarily those that were presented in the most elegant manner or that fit some cited legal precedent.

Expert Witnesses

Even when panel members are experts in the field in question, attorneys should exercise care when deciding to make the testimony of expert witnesses the focal point of their case. For example, when the technical panel member hears from your opponent's expert witness that the bridge collapsed due to your client's egregious design error, he or she knows that you will probably counter with an expert to swear that the fault instead lies in defective materials. These confusing conundrums are stock-in-trade to engineers and business people, who know that real-life situations are commonly filled with seeming contradictions, but that the real truth can usually be rooted out by a careful examination of the right evidence. It is difficult to put yourself in that other person's shoes to determine which piece of evidence they will think is the most important, but you can often get a clue by the questions that they ask.

In any case, contradictory claims and testimonies by experts do not necessarily make the proceedings more interesting or even more helpful to the technical panel member, regardless of the fame or reputation of the witness.

Line of Inquiry

If the arbitrator looks puzzled, it may be due to an uncertainty as to where you are going with your line of inquiry. Remember: In keeping your point obscure so as not to expose your hand to the opposition prematurely, you are also keeping the arbitrator in the dark. So if you are asked to provide some context because the arbitrator is unclear as to why your argument is relevant, giving a vague answer will not provide the expected level of comfort.

Panel Questioning Witnesses

One of the most striking differences between courtroom and hearing-room practice is that your witness may be examined by an arbitrator in a way that a judge rarely would. Arbitrators are generally well aware of the need for the attorneys to bring out their own case, and try not to get ahead of them. But the attorney must recognize that non-attorney arbitrators are searching for the truth, and are not especially concerned with adhering to artificial rules of engagement. If you are finished with a line of questioning and the arbitrator needs to know the answer to a question he or she thinks is logical and important, but one that you have not yet asked, he or she will surely ask it. You may view this as disruptive, but the non-attorney arbitrator is not likely to be dissuaded.

Objections

Litigating attorneys experienced in the adversarial process of the courtroom are used to putting up an aggressive struggle to make sure that every piece of evidence they wish to put before the court is accepted, while vigorously objecting to every shred of evidence that their opponent tries to register. This process is an integral part of the courtroom culture.

On the other hand, non-attorney arbitrators are interested in listening to anything that can help them reach a decision. Thus, they do not see extended discussions about admissibility as helping them in their search for a solution. Consequently, they are inclined to hear all the evidence, because they believe they can decide for themselves what is and is not important. It is also simple human nature for an arbitrator to suspect that an attorney may have something to hide if he or she continually objects to information that seems, on the surface, to be informative.

In the final analysis though, experienced non-attorney arbitrators are likely to rule against excessive objections because they know that one sure ground for overturning an award is if they do not hear evidence that later turns out to be important. Thus, they will usually err on the side of caution.

Jargon

Using complicated technical words and concepts that you believe to be relevant to the case at hand will not impress a technically astute arbitrator who believes that you do not have a clear understanding of their meaning. To avoid this problem it is helpful to define any unusual terms at the outset, or even provide a glossary or graphical presentation to make sure that everyone present has the same understanding.

Remember: Your objective should be the arbitrator's comprehension of your client's position, not merely creating the impression of legal expertise. In fact, it is probably a good idea to go to the opposite extreme and avoid legal jargon whenever possible.

Hearing-Room Style

No matter how many courtroom cases you have successfully prosecuted, and even won, it is no sure claim to success in the hearing room. A style that works in one forum might not go over so well in another, and this is particularly so if your style is aggressive. Whatever their background, arbitrators are used to a more collegiate approach. Aggressive attacks on the opposition and frequent histrionics are likely to work against you in an arbitration hearing before a businessperson who is used to consensus-building, or an engineer used to more thoughtful, analytic probing for the truth. Such panel members will not be amused by these displays, even though they may provide an interesting break in an otherwise dry hearing.

Hearing-Room Humor

By their very nature, arbitration hearings are a serious process with serious consequences. But by intention, arbitration hearings are a less formal setting than a courtroom. As a result, humorous situations occasionally and unexpectedly occur, such as when an exhibit spontaneously crashes to the floor or a weary participant nods off.

Businesspeople, even engineers, are used to injecting humor into a tense situation as a way of defusing tempers, even in serious matters, and so may be the first to laugh. On the other hand, no one likes a humorless sourpuss who glares at every attempt to lighten the mood. So enjoying one of these situations or even laughing at a panel member's attempt at humor is quite acceptable to lighten the mood.

Exhibit Books

Exhibit books can be of great help to any arbitrator in studying the evidence after the hearing. But they are especially useful to the technically oriented arbitrator who may want to delve more deeply into a document than time allows during the hearing. This can occur when the arbitrator discovers an important point deep in the details that neither side brought out during the hearing. However, this examination can be made difficult due to labeling inconsistencies, lack of organization, duplication in the books or torn pages resulting from an overstuffed binder. Since both sides use many of the same documents, often to prove opposite points, there can be considerable overlap in exhibits that could be eliminated by better coordination between the two sides.

It is true that businesspeople and engineers are used to slogging through voluminous reports and analyses on the job. Some are even guilty of preparing them. However, in an arbitration you should not assume that arbitrators with that kind of professional background will also enjoy poring over excessive exhibits, obscure rulings, rambling deposition transcripts and agonizingly detailed technical documents of your documentary evidence, unless they need to for some issue. Technical panel members are not impressed by the poundage of materials they must examine, particularly when they have to carry them back and forth to the hearing each day.

Cumulative Evidence

One might think that the engineer or businessperson would want to hear as much evidence on a particular point as possible. However, that is a luxury that does not often arise in their business. Most of the time, there is a broad range of facts and opinion to evaluate, and not a preponderance of anything. So when they are faced with too much data, it can seem to be "piling on," and can create suspicion as to the true import of that evidence. It can also raise the question as to why other seemingly important points were not equally stressed.

Handling the Unexpected

Unexpectedly, the quiet, unassuming non-attorney arbitrator who hasn't said "boo" to that point, might pipe up with, "Excuse me...," and then call into play the obscure smoking-gun document hidden away in the back of the exhibit book—the one you hoped would not surface. Perhaps the arbitrator might ask the one question that you would rather not be asked. Or in the face of an unanticipated question from the technical panel member, your star witness may inadvertently blurt out the one thing you hoped he would not say.

one of these turns of events is necessarily a crisis, but continuing to barge ahead with your now-irrelevant line of questioning, or worse, putting off the questioner, is not likely to serve your cause well. The engineer or businessperson arbitrator is used to unexpected and unwelcome turns of events, and is not surprised when they happen. What they will look for is to see how you handle it.

Graphical Presentations

Engineers and business executives are trained to think in graphical terms. They will commonly use charts, tables and graphs to express relationships between variables. Thus, when they are sitting on an arbitration panel, it can be less effective if an attorney attempts to make a point purely by exposition, when an engineer would use a graph to express it. So if the sequence of events, the results of a technical evaluation or the visualization of a concept are important in your case, it can be very helpful to the technical panel member if you provide a graphical exhibit.

Post-Hearing Briefs

Post-hearing briefs can be a very useful tool in the hearing process, especially in a complex case. This is especially true if your style does not make your direction clear as you go, but reserves it for the summation and/or closing briefs. However, the utility of briefs to the non-attorney arbitrator is not necessarily in the illumination of fine legal points. They can be very helpful when a point of law is the issue and you were specifically asked to address it. In such a case, the brief provides the opportunity to once again show that you have proven your case legally. However, knowing that the contract is more important than legal precedent in arbitrations, the non-attorney arbitrator is not usually looking for legal proof, but instead a summary of your evidentiary proof. In addition, non-attorney arbitrators are not well-equipped to evaluate purely legal arguments, and may consequently give them less weight.

Most non-attorney arbitrators are also intimately familiar with the mechanical techniques of cutting inter-line spacing, printing in smaller-than-usual type size and putting some of the arguments in tiny footnotes, all to cram as much information in a brief of an agreed-upon length. They have probably done it themselves in technical reports on the job. However, if such legerdemain is seen as violating the rules of fair play, it is counterproductive.

Reconsideration

There are many procedural issues that can be crucial in court-tried cases when it comes to seeking a reversal on technical grounds. As a result, the award of a non-attorney arbitrator may be more likely to come under suspicion than that of a lawyer-arbitrator, who has been trained in the minutiae of the law. Thus in arbitrations, some losing attorneys will immediately leap into action to seek to obtain a reconsideration or even an overturning of the award. They ignore the fact that the governing body of the arbitration—the American Arbitration Association, for example—discourages this activity, and that the courts aren't interested in the merits of the case for that purpose. They file several pounds of additional unsolicited briefs to support their case, even though the arbitrators are now *ex officio*. Their usual argument is that the non-attorney arbitrator obviously ignored the preponderance of evidence that so clearly proved their case. Naturally, the non-attorney arbitrator who persevered in this peculiar and often difficult environment in an attempt to grasp the issues carefully and rule wisely, can easily feel insulted by these actions.

Conclusion

I hope that these examples will show attorneys how to improve their style and, conceivably, their success when presenting before a non-attorney arbitrator. At the very least, they may help keep you from shooting yourself in the foot. See you in the hearing room.

II. Issues Surrounding Party-Appointed Arbitrators

The Role of Party-Appointed Arbitrators

by Richard M. Mosk[*]

The role, responsibilities and obligations of party-appointed arbitrators are often not known or considered by parties and arbitrators and may vary with the type and place of arbitration. Moreover, many issues concerning these arbitrators are still unresolved and views on these issues differ. This article discusses certain law and practice issues that might be of interest to parties and practitioners.

Underlying Purpose

In some arbitrations there are three or more arbitrators. Sometimes all of the arbitrators are selected by an independent institution-often the one administering the proceeding-or by another designated appointing authority. In many instances of multiple arbitrators, each party will appoint an arbitrator, with either those arbitrators or the parties or the appointing authority naming the remaining arbitrator(s).

A multiple arbitrator panel is more expensive and can lead to delays, but it has advantages. Many believe that it reduces the risk that an award might be based on a major misunderstanding. More than one arbitrator can be helpful in resolving complicated cases in the required time. Knowledge by party-appointed arbitrators of the practices and customs of the industry and of the laws of the domicile of the party that appointed them can ensure that the positions and arguments of the appointing parties are considered by the other arbitrators. This is especially so in international arbitrations, in which there may be arbitrators of three different nationalities, and each party may desire that one of the arbitrators be familiar with its domicile's laws and customs. Different viewpoints can be helpful in the deliberation process. Finally, the presence of party-appointed arbitrators may make the award more acceptable to the parties, especially to the one that did not prevail.

---

[*] Richard M. Mosk is an Associate Justice for the California Court of Appeal, Second Appellate District, Division 5, and was formerly judge on the Iran-U.S. Claims Tribunal. He earned an A.B. from Stanford University "With Great Distinction" and a cum laude J.D. from Harvard Law School.

Different Views

There are different perceptions of the duties, obligations and practices of party-appointed arbitrators regarding whether the arbitrators are to be independent of the parties that appointed them; whether they are to be impartial; whether they may have publicly stated views that tend to favor one side of the dispute; whether and to what extent they may engage in *ex parte* communications with the parties that appointed them; the extent to which they must disclose certain relationships and interests; and compensation arrangements.

Opinions on these issues may vary depending on the type of arbitration involved, the location of the arbitration, the subject matter of the dispute, the understanding of the parties, the rules of the administering agency, and any applicable ethical codes. Nevertheless, the law of the jurisdiction governing the arbitration may dictate the practices concerning party-appointed arbitrators.[1] It is also important to recognize that the terms "neutral," "independent" and "impartial" may have different meanings in different locales or situations.

Statutory Regulation

American arbitration statutes do not deal specifically with party-appointed arbitrators. Most statutes simply set forth the grounds on which a court may vacate an award. The Federal Arbitration Act (FAA) provides for vacatur "[w]here the award is procured by corruption, fraud, or undue means" or "[w]here there was evident partiality or corruption in the arbitrators, or either of them."[2] The Uniform Arbitration Act similarly provides for vacatur where the award is procured by corruption, fraud or undue means or in case of "evident partiality by an arbitrator appointed as neutral." This "recognizes that party-designated arbitrators represent their nominators and may act as advocates."[3]

A new California law provides that upon a demand of any party made prior to the conclusion of an arbitration proceeding, an arbitrator must disqualify himself or herself on the statutory grounds provided for

---

[1] *See generally* J. Carter, *Living With the Party-Appointed Arbitrator: Judicial Confusion, Ethical Codes and Practical Advice,* 5 AM. REV. OF INT'L ARB. 97 (1994); M. Smith, *Impartiality of the Party-Appointed Arbitrator,* 6 ARB. INT'L 320 (1990).

[2] 9 U.S.C. § 10(a)(1) and (2).

[3] *Note, Party-Designated Arbitrators and the Duty to Disclose in Tripartite Commercial Arbitration: Barcon Associates, Inc. v. Tri-County Asphalt Corp.,* 4 CARDOZO L. REV. 173, 180 (1982). *See* Pirsig, *The New Uniform Arbitration Act,* 11 BUS. LAW. 44, 48 (1956).

disqualification of a judge.[4] Only arbitrations under a collective bargaining agreement are exempt. This statute would appear to apply to non-neutral arbitrators. The statute is silent as to whether the party's failure to object to a known relationship constitutes a waiver of the right to disqualify an arbitrator.

Another new California statute requires one nominated as a "neutral" arbitrator to make various disclosures concerning past cases involving the parties or attorneys.[5] It is not clear if, under this statute, party-appointed arbitrators would necessarily be considered not neutral.

Court interpretations of the role of party-appointed arbitrators differ widely. Some give wide berth to party autonomy. Others take a restrictive view.

Party Autonomy

As arbitration is, essentially, a contractual process, the parties may generally agree to establish any kind of arbitral mechanism. It has been said, "an interest in the dispute or a relationship with a party, if known to the parties to the agreement when the arbitrator is chosen, will not disqualify the arbitrator from acting."[6] Thus, assuming there is no legal impediment, the parties may establish an arbitral tribunal composed of party-appointed arbitrators who are not independent or impartial.

In some types of arbitrations there is a long-established practice that a party-appointed arbitrator need not be impartial or independent. For example, in so-called tripartite labor arbitrations in the United States, labor and management members of the panel are often considered as partisans and act as advocates for their respective sides.[7] Indeed, the Code of Professional Responsibility for Arbitrators of Labor Management Disputes states in its Preamble that it "does not apply to partisan representatives on tripartite boards."[8]

---

[4] Cal. Code Civ. Proc. § 1282(e).
[5] Cal. Code Civ. Proc. § 1281.9.
[6] In re Cross & Brown Company, 4 A.D.2d 501, 502-3, 576, 167 N.Y.S.2d 573 (1957).
[7] F. ELKOURI & E. ELKOURI, HOW ARBITRATION WORKS 129-31 (4th ed. 1985); O. Fairweather, PRACTICE AND PROCEDURES IN LABOR ARBITRATION 86 (2ND ED. 1983). *See* Lesser, *Tripartite Boards or Single Arbitrators in Voluntary Labor Arbitration*, 5 ARB. J. 276 (1950).
[8] Promulgated by a Committee of the American Arbitration Association, National Academy of Arbitrators and by representatives of the Federal Mediation and Conciliation Service, approved 1975; amended May 29, 1985.

In domestic commercial arbitrations, it has long been assumed that party-appointed arbitrators need not be impartial[9] The New York Court of Appeals stated, "In short, usage and experience indicate that, in the type of tripartite arbitration envisaged by the contract before us, each party's arbitrator 'is not individually expected to be neutral'."[10]

One federal court has described party-appointed arbitrators as "partisans once removed from the actual controversy."[11] In another case, a federal court went so far as to state that it is "commonplace" and "unobjectionable" for a party-appointed arbitrator to help the appointing party prepare for hearings.[12] Other courts have indicated with respect to the arbitration clauses before them that, "[a]n arbitrator selected by one of the contesting parties is effectively an advocate of such party."[13] There are even cases which suggest that a party-appointed arbitrator may be an attorney for the nominating party and need not disclose that relationship.[14]

More recent New York cases seem to recognize that party-appointed arbitrators "allow each party the opportunity to have his side represented on the tribunal."[15] In a recent case, a New York trial judge said that if known in advance, the parties may select an arbitrator with a vested financial interest in the outcome of the arbitration. A provision allowing such a situation does not violate public policy or the right of a party to a fair hearing or due process. The court noted that each of the arbitrators chosen "must swear an oath to faithfully and fairly decide the controversy."[16] An earlier New York Court of Appeals decision said, "Therefore, strange as it may seem to those steeped in the proscriptions

---

[9] *Washington Foreign Law Society Committee on the UNCITRAL Model Law on International Commercial Arbitration,* APP. F. AT 7, reprinted in 2 INT'L ARB. REP. 779, 820 (NOV. 1987).

[10] Astoria Medical Group v. Health Ins. Plan of Greater N.Y., 11 N.Y.2d 128, 134, 182 N.E.2d 85, 87, 227 N.Y.S.2d 401, 404-5 (1962). See also Tipton v. Systron Donner Corp., 99 Cal. App.3d 501, 505, 160 Cal. Rptr. 303, 305 (1979) ("There is no statutory requirement that the arbitrators appointed by the parties must be neutral or impartial").

[11] Stef Shipping Corp. v. Norris Grain Co., 209 F. Supp. 249, 253 (S.D.N.Y. 1962).

[12] Sunkist Soft Drinks Inc. v. Sunkist Growers Inc., 10 F.3d 753, 759 (11th Cir. 1993). *See also* Employers Ins. of Wausau v. National Union Fire Ins. Co. of Pittsburgh, 933 F.2d 1481 (9th Cir. 1991).

[13] Johnson v. Jahncke Service, Inc., 147 So, 2d 247, 248 (La. Ct. App. 1962).

[14] *See* Tipton v. Systron Donner Corp., 99 Cal. App.3d 501, 160 Cal. Rptr. 303 (1979).

[15] Statewide Insurance Company, Inc. v. Klein, 482 N.Y.S.2d 307, 308 (N.Y. App. Div. 1984).

[16] Matter of Selznick, N.Y. Sup. Ct., Westchester Cty., June 12, 1995.

of legal and judicial ethics, a fully known relationship between an arbitrator and a party will not in and of itself disqualify the designee."[17]

However, a New York court cautioned that the law does not sanction overt partiality or corruption in the actual conduct of the arbitration, stating, "Partisan he may be, but not dishonest."[18] In 1972, the U.S. Supreme Court, in a labor context, noted, "Congress has put its blessing on private dispute settlement arrangements..., but it was anticipated we are sure, the contractual machinery would operate within some minimum levels of integrity."[19]

Restrictive Views

Some courts have expressed a more restricted standard for the party-appointed arbitrator. Judge Pound of the New York Court of Appeals long ago stated:

> [T]he practice of arbitrators of conducting themselves as champions of their nominators is to be condemned as contrary to the purpose of arbitrations, and as calculated to bring the system of enforced arbitrations into disrepute. An arbitrator acts in a quasi-judicial capacity, and should possess the judicial qualifications of fairness to both parties, so that he may render a faithful, honest, and disinterested opinion. He is not an advocate whose function is to convince the umpire or third arbitrator....He must lay aside all bias, and approach the cause with a mind open to conviction and without regard to his previously formed opinions as to the merits of the party or the cause. He should sedulously refrain from any conduct which might justify even the inference that either party is the special recipient of his solicitude or favor.[20]

In 1952, the New York Court of Appeals held that an award could be vacated if a party-appointed arbitrator turns out to have been partial or interested.[21] In vacating an award because of the partiality of a party-

---

[17] Siegel v. Lewis, 40 N.Y.2d 687, 689 (N.Y. 1976).

[18] *Astoria Medical Group, supra* n.10, 227 N.Y.S.2d at 407.

[19] Hines v. Anchor Motor Freight, 424 U.S. 554, 571 (1976). *See* Graham v. Scissor-Tail, Inc., 28 Cal.3d 807, 825, 171 Cal. Rptr. 604, 615 (1981).

[20] American Eagle Fire Ins. Co. v. New Jersey Ins. Co., 240 N.Y. 398, 405, 148 N.E. 562, 564 (1925).

[21] Lipshutz v. Outworth, 304 N.Y. 58 (1952).

appointed arbitrator, the Supreme Court of New Jersey, in a 4-3 decision, endorsed Judge Pound's view. Although noting that "standards pertaining to the requisite impartiality of the party-designated arbitrators are not susceptible to precise formulation in the abstract," the court stated that the "parties may agree to any form of dispute resolution that they wish, but they must not seek the backing of the courts for private actions that, while substituting for the judicial function, are fraught with the appearance of bias."[22]

A federal court, in referring to the FAA, noted that the express language of § 10(b), which provides that the court shall vacate the award "[w]here there was evident partiality or corruption in the arbitrators, or either of them," rebuts "the view that Congress contemplated when enacting the FAA that parties would appoint partisan arbitrators...." The court stated, "[t]his underlined language directs that the evident partiality test should apply to every member of the panel."[23]

In another case a federal court required the entire tribunal to be disinterested although two members were party-appointed.[24] More recently a federal court stated that "only scant case law exists on the subject of arbitrator bias in the tripartite context." The court further noted that even if party-appointed arbitrators may be to some extent non-neutral, they still "have a responsibility to be disinterested."[25]

Thus, judicial views of the proper role of party-appointed arbitrators are not consistent.

Domestic Ethical Codes

In 1977, a joint committee consisting of a special committee of the American Arbitration Association (AAA) and a special committee of the American Bar Association (ABA) promulgated a Code of Ethics for Arbitrators in Commercial Disputes (the Code).[26] The preamble to the Code states with respect to three-member arbitral tribunals that include two party-appointed arbitrators: "The sponsors of this code believe that it

---

[22] Barcan Associates v. Tri-County Asphalt Corp., 86 N.J. 179, 190, 196, 430 A.2d 214, 219, 222 (N.J. 1981).
[23] Standard Tankers (Bahamas) Co. v. Motor Tank Vessel, Akti, 438 F. Supp. 153, 159 (E.D.N.C. 1977).
[24] Florasynth Inc. v. Pickholz, 750 F.2d 171, 173 (2d Cir. 1984).
[25] Metropolitan Property and Casualty Ins. Co. v. J.C. Penney Ins. Co., 780 F. Supp. 885, 891, 893 (D. Conn. 1991).
[26] *See* Holtzmann, *The First Code of Ethics for Arbitrators in Commercial Disputes*, 33 BUS. LAW. 309 (1977).

is preferable for parties to agree that all arbitrators shall comply with the same ethical standards"-i.e., act as neutrals. The Code, in Canon VII, recognizes, however, that there are different practices and notes:

In all arbitrations in which there are two or more party-appointed arbitrators, it is important for everyone concerned to know from the start whether the party-appointed arbitrators are expected to be neutrals or non-neutrals. In such arbitrations, the two party-appointed arbitrators should be considered non-neutrals unless both parties inform the arbitrators that all three arbitrators are to be neutral, or unless the contract, the applicable arbitration rules, or any governing law requires that all three arbitrators are to be neutral.

The arbitrators referred to as "non-neutral" arbitrators, according to the Canon, may be "predisposed" toward the party who appointed them, but in all other respects are obligated to act in good faith and with integrity and fairness. They are to disclose all interests and relationships required to be disclosed. They may have *ex parte* communications with the party that appointed them in connection with the appointment of the neutral arbitrator. In addition, they may have *ex parte* communications concerning any other aspect of the case provided they first disclose to the other arbitrators and the parties they intend to do so. If such communications occurred prior to their appointment or meeting of the parties, they must disclose the fact that such communications have taken place. They must not engage in delaying tactics or harass any party or make any untrue statements to the other arbitrators. In adopting this ethical rule, the Joint AAA-ABA Committee embodied the concept expressed by the New York Court of Appeals:

Our decision that an arbitrator may not be disqualified solely because of a relationship to his nominator or to the subject matter of the controversy does not, however, mean that he may be deaf to the testimony or blind to the evidence presented. Partisan he may be, but not dishonest.[27]

International Arbitration

Many assume that party-appointed arbitrators are to be independent and impartial in international commercial arbitration. As the Joint AAA-ABA Committee stated in Canon VII of its Code of Ethics, "It should be noted that in cases conducted outside the United States, the applicable

---

[27] *Astoria Medical Group, supra* n.10, 227 N.Y.S.2d at 407.

law might require that all arbitrators be neutral."[28] One authority has written, in "European practice, failure of the entire tribunal, including the party-appointed arbitrators, to conform to strict standards of independence and impartiality may constitute a professional fault, a serious procedural defect affecting the validity of the award."[29] Another authoritative work stated, "Today there is evidence...of a more general custom requiring independence and impartiality of party-appointed arbitrators in all international commercial arbitrations."[30]

Most institutional international arbitration rules and European arbitration laws make no distinctions between party-appointed and non-party-appointed arbitrators.[31] This is also true of the recent UNCITRAL Model Arbitration Law and the UNCITRAL Rules.

The AAA's International Arbitration Rules provide in Article 7 that "unless the parties agree otherwise, arbitrators acting under these rules shall be impartial and independent." Article 7 requires arbitrators to disclose "any circumstances likely to give rise to justifiable doubts as to [their] impartiality or independence," and Article 8 provides that any party may challenge any arbitrator whenever circumstances exist that give rise to such doubts. This applies to all arbitrators, whether party-appointed or not.

The International Chamber of Commerce (ICC) Arbitration Rules also require every arbitrator to "be and remain independent" of the appointing parties. In addition, before appointment or confirmation by the court, a party-"nominated" arbitrator is required to disclose to the court any interest or fact bearing on the nominee's independence.[32] The ICC has the authority to disapprove a party-appointed arbitrator on the basis of lack of independence, but the parties may agree to waive the requirement of independence of the party-appointed arbitrators. Such

---

[28] AAA-ABA Committee Code of Ethics, Canon VII (emphasis added). The ABA House of Delegates adopted a resolution in 1990 suggesting that the Code of Ethics be amended to provide for neutrality of all arbitrators in international arbitrations. The Code has not yet been amended.

[29] de Vries, *International Commercial Arbitration: A Transnational View*, 1 J. INT'L ARB. 7, 13 (1984).

[30] W. Craig, W. Park & J. Paulsson, International Chamber of Commerce Arbitration, 209 n.6 (2d ed. 1990).

[31] *See* International Chamber of Commerce Arbitration Rules art. 2(4); the Netherlands Arbitration Act of 1986, 4 Code of Civil Procedure arts. 1020-76 (1838), reprinted in 12 Commercial Arbitration Y.B. 370-87. *See generally* M. Smith, *supra* n.1.

[32] ICC Rules of Arbitration, art. 2(7) (Jan. 1, 1988).

express agreements are, however, "rare in ICC practice,"[33] which could reflect the fact that impartiality of party-appointed arbitrators may be required by a local law. Of course, there are instances where, after disclosure, none of the parties chooses to challenge a party-appointed arbitrator who may not be independent.

With respect to international arbitrations, it has been said that a party "is clearly entitled to (and often...choose[s]) an arbitrator having that party's nationality," who "may also come from a similar economic, political and social milieu" and "embrace legal doctrines that the nominating party feels are favorable to its case." This arbitrator "may, therefore, be expected to be sympathetic to positions taken by that party" and "[i]t is in this limited sense that the party-nominated arbitrators need not be 'neutral'."[34]

The Rules of the London Court of International Arbitration, in Article 3.1, specifically provide that "[a]ll arbitrators (whether or not nominated by the parties) conducting an arbitration under these Rules shall be and remain at all times wholly independent and impartial, and shall not act as advocates for any party." This precludes even party agreement on non-neutral party-appointed arbitrators. The rules of other European arbitration institutions generally do not distinguish between the qualifications of arbitrators, no matter how they were selected.

The Code of Ethics for International Arbitrators promulgated by the International Bar Association contains strict rules calling for independence and impartiality of arbitrators, and makes no distinction between party-appointed and non party-appointed arbitrators.[35] Some ethics codes explicitly proscribe certain conduct by arbitrators. For example, the Code of Ethics for Vancouver Maritime Arbitrators (Rule 10) provides, "No arbitrator shall confer with the party or counsel appointing him regarding the selection of a third arbitrator."

Some U.S. courts have not recognized any distinction between domestic and international arbitrations with respect to party-appointed arbitrators-at least in cases subject to United States law. In a case involving an international arbitration the U.S. Court of Appeals for the

---

[33] *Craig, supra* n.30, at 211.

[34] *Id.* at 212.

[35] *IBA Ethics for International Arbitration*, reprinted in 2 INT'L ARB. REP. 287 (April 1987) (*hereinafter* IBA ETHICS). *See* Coulson, *An American Critique of the IBA's Ethics for International Arbitrators*, 4 J. INT'L ARB. NO. 2, 103, 104-5 (1987) (raises question as to whether there is a worldwide "consensus" that party-appointed arbitrators are impartial). It should be noted that the IBA Code of Ethics uses the term "bias" as being equivalent to lack of "impartiality and independence." IBA Ethics, *supra*, rule 3.1

Ninth Circuit stated that "[g]enerally, partisan arbitrators are permissible."[36]

One practitioner of international arbitration has noted, "Many clients assume that the arbitrator they name will favor their case, will be an advocate for them within the tribunal, and will persuade at least the third arbitrator to support their case."[37] The author added, however, "This assumption is seldom correct...particularly in arbitrations under rules requiring the party arbitrator to be as objective as the third arbitrator."[38]

Others are not certain that European practice is different from American practice. They have characterized the idea that party-appointed arbitrators are independent as a "pretense" and perceive European practitioners and arbitrators as clinging to the theory, if not the practice, of "demanding quasi-judicial 'independence,' thus increasing the risk of confusion and hesitation where not only the attorneys but the three arbitrators come from differing legal systems."[39] One difficult problem is what a party-appointed arbitrator who intends to be impartial is to do when the other party-appointed arbitrator acts in a partisan fashion.

Professor Lowenfeld has indicated that such confusion does not generally exist, for he asserts that many international arbitration awards are unanimous. He states, "The suspicion, in other words, that the chairperson decides and the other two arbitrators are simply other kinds of advocates is not borne out in the practice I have seen in the international commercial arena."[40]

In international public arbitrations, when a nation appointed its own arbitrators-sometimes referred to as "national judges" or "national commissioners"-they were often expected to be partisan. Any ambiguity as to their role might be traced to the question of whether a public international arbitration is in reality a diplomatic process.[41] It has been

---

[36] ASTA of California, Inc. v. Continental Ins. Co., 754 F.2d 1394, 1395 (9th Cir. 1985) (modifying and quoting ASTA *of California, Inc. v. Continental Ins. Co.*, 702 F.2d 172, 175 (9th Cir. 1983)).

[37] Geokjian, *ICC Arbitration From a Practitioner's Perspective*, 14 J. INT'L L. & ECON. 407, 410 (1980).

[38] *Id.*

[39] Higgins, Brown & Roach, *Pitfalls in International Commercial Arbitration*, 35 BUS. LAW. 1035, 1043-44 (1980).

[40] A. Lowenfeld, *Book Review*, 42 ARB. J. 53 (Dec. 1987). *See also* A. Lowenfeld, *The Party-Appointed Arbitrator in International Controversies: Some Reflections*, 30 TEX. INT'L L. J. 59 (1995).

[41] Note, *The Use of Tripartite Boards in Labor, Commercial, and International Arbitration*, 68 HARV. L. REV. 293, 325-39 (1954); S. Schwebel, INTERNATIONAL ARBITRATION: THREE SALIENT PROBLEMS 144-54 (1987).

suggested that national commissioners feel bound to vote for the government that appointed them on matters of fundamental national policy or issues not governed by well-established principles of international law.[42]

Judge Schwebel of the International Court of Justice, in discussing the problem of a government-appointed arbitrator resigning-sometimes on instructions of the government-concluded that a withdrawing arbitrator should not be able to frustrate the proceeding. He viewed an arbitration among states as based on a "judicial" model of arbitration rather than on a diplomatic model.[43]

It is difficult to imagine that nationals can be truly independent or unbiased when appointed by the state or an entity of the state. Nevertheless, international arbitral bodies subscribe to the notion of independence and impartiality and maintain that coming from the same "economic, political and social milieu" as the nominating party does not in itself suggest non-neutrality.[44]

To attempt to adhere to and enforce a firm rule of independence and impartiality in international arbitration would, in effect, inhibit international arbitration involving a number of countries. Flexibility appears to be the best policy so long as the parties and the arbitrators are aware of and accept the ground rules.

Practical Considerations

Regardless of the various views, parties, practitioners and arbitrators must take care to comply with the applicable laws, rules and ethical standards. As can be seen, it is essential to check these before contracting to arbitrate in a particular jurisdiction or arbitral institution or under particular arbitral rules. Otherwise, a surprise may await a party at the time of the arbitration or at the time of attempting enforcement of an award. To the extent that there are no controlling laws, rules or ethical standards regarding party-appointed arbitrators, the parties should spell out in advance what is expected of these arbitrators.

If there is no agreement, the parties may have different assumptions as to what the party-appointed arbitrator will or can do. A party can seek

---

[42] *Note, supra* n.41, 68 HARV. L. REV. at 337.
[43] S. Schwebel, *supra* n.41, at 151; Lowenfeld, *supra* n.40, 42 Arb. J. at 53.
[44] *See* R. Mosk, *The Rule of Party-Appointed Arbitrators in International Arbitration: The Experience of the Iran-U.S. Claims Tribunal,* 1 TRANS. LAW. 253 (1988).

judicial intervention or the parties can run the risk that the award will be subject to being vacated.

There are a number of practices that should be considered. Often, the party or its attorney will interview a person before making the determination of party-appointed arbitrator. A federal court held that communications about the issues and reviewing documents with the appointed party and certain other aspects prior to the appointment constituted "overt misconduct."[45] Whether or not the court would apply its ruling to less substantive contacts, it would be safer if the parties made disclosure of pre-arbitration contacts or agreed upon them with the other side.

Clearly, undisclosed *ex parte* communications after appointment are risky in many jurisdictions unless the parties have agreed to such a practice. It is customary that party-appointed arbitrators have *ex parte* contact with the party concerning the selection of a chairperson of the panel. Even as to this, the fact of such communications should be disclosed and agreed to in advance by the parties. Some feel that *ex parte* communications regarding procedures or other non-substantive matters are not inappropriate.

If the party-appointed arbitrator has or has had any relationship with a party or its attorney or has an interest in the subject matter of the arbitration, full disclosure should be made. By making the same type of disclosure as required of a neutral arbitrator, the party-appointed arbitrator in large part protects against an award being vacated if the other party has not made a timely objection. If there is an objection, the problem can be resolved at that time.

As long as the law on the subject of party-appointed arbitrators remains confused and uncertain, full disclosure and agreement of the parties is a prudent course of action.

---

[45] Metropolitan Property and Casualty Co. v. J.C. Penney Casualty Ins. Co., 780 F. Supp. 885, 893 (D. Conn. 1991).

III. Political Correctness— A Barrier to Arbitration Efficiency

The Problem of the "Politically Correct" Arbitrator

by Steven J. Stein[*]

As arbitral, legal and procedural regimes have reached greater maturity, arbitration proceedings in large, complex commercial disputes have tended to become as expensive, complicated and protracted as cases litigated in domestic courts. One factor that has contributed to this undesirable condition is that many arbitrators have adopted a form of "political correctness" to avoid offending the parties that have chosen them.

This manifests itself in a reluctance to manage the process effectively, particularly by failing to impose reasonable limits on the nature and extent of proofs submitted by the parties. Allowing evidentiary matters irrelevant to the issues to be heard delays the final resolution of the case and unnecessarily increases the cost of the process.

Under the rules and practices of the major arbitral agencies, parties are given exceedingly wide latitude in the evidence they can offer in support of their claims and defenses.[1] Offers of proof, however, are subject to the arbitrators' rulings as to relevance, materiality and admissibility of evidence.[2] The major institutional rules also give arbitrators broad discretion to apply law, rules of evidence under

---

[*] Steven J. Stein is counsel to the Geneva law firm of Budin & Partners. He serves on the American Arbitration Association's roster of neutrals for commercial and international cases. He has served on ICC tribunals and as counsel to parties in arbitrated matters for more than 25 years. Stein holds a B.S. from Cornell University and an LL.B. from New York University School of Law. He is the author of *Enforcing Foreign Arbitral Awards*, INTERNATIONAL ARBITRATION CONFERENCE, Cairo, Egypt (March 1995) and *The Drafting of Effective Choice of Law Clauses*, JOURNAL OF INTERNATIONAL ARBITRATION (September 1991).

[1] American Arbitration Association Commercial Arbitration Rule R-33(a) provides: "The parties may offer such evidence as is relevant and material to the dispute...." Art. 19(1) of the AAA International Arbitration Rules provide: "Each party shall have the burden of proving the facts relied on to support its claim or defense."

[2] The AAA's commercial rules state: "The arbitrators shall determine the admissibility, relevance of the evidence offered and may exclude evidence deemed by the arbitrator to be cumulative or irrelevant." R-33(b).

carefully prescribed procedures, or rules governing the conduct of the case.

Furthermore, under some institutional rules, arbitrators are encouraged to conduct the proceedings in the most expeditious manner.[3]

The scope of discretion to admit or exclude evidence does not differ significantly between arbitration and litigation. Judges, for practical reasons, are motivated by congested court dockets and pressure from court administrators to issue rulings that will expedite the closing of cases.

However, arbitrators ordinarily are considerably less zealous in imposing limits on the course of arbitral proceedings. When asked to make a limiting or exclusionary ruling, arbitrators are often heard to say, "We'll take it for whatever it's worth" or words to that effect. This sort of "non-ruling" postpones indefinitely the tough task of weighing the materiality of the offer of proof to a particular issue or the entire case.

There are more than a few possible reasons for such behavior by arbitrators. Many are probably reluctant to cut off a party's proffer of proof out of a "politically correct" but misguided desire not to offend, and remain in the good graces of, the parties. Others may simply come to the hearing unprepared to make difficult judgments excluding proofs, having spent an inadequate amount of time to become familiar with the facts of the case or the applicable law. It is also likely to be the case that arbitrators have their eye on the grounds to vacate an award, particularly the ground that the arbitrator refused to hear evidence pertinent and material to the case.

But the fact is that except in rare cases of arbitrator misconduct, arbitral awards subject to the Federal Arbitration Act are fundamentally unreviewable by the courts.[4] Moreover, even in those cases when the

---

[3] The AAA's commercial rules provide: "The arbitrator, having his or her discretion, shall conduct the proceedings with a view to expediting the resolution of the dispute and may direct the order of proof, bifurcate proceedings and direct the parties to focus their presentations on issues the decision of which could dispose of all or part of the case." R-32(b). The AAA's international rules contain similar provisions in Article 16 (2) and (3). These rules also provide: "The tribunal may conduct the arbitration in whatever manner it considers appropriate, provided that the parties are treated with equality and that each party has the right to be heard and is given a fair opportunity to present its case."

[4] 9 U.S.C. § 10 contains the grounds for vacatur in the Federal Arbitration Act. See cases such as Mitsubishi Motors Corp. v. Soler Chrysler-Plymouth Inc., 473 U.S. 614 (1985). See e.g., Generica Ltd. v. Pharmaceutical Basics Inc., 125 F.3d 1123 (7th Cir. 1997) (arbitrator's refusal to permit continued cross-examination of a nonparty witness that the arbitrator deemed immaterial to the proceeding did not deny a party due process). See also Pegasus Construction Corp. v. Turner Construction Co., 929 P.2d 1200 (Wash. Ct. App.

award has been challenged on the ground that the arbitrator refused to hear pertinent evidence, courts usually uphold awards.[5] This, together with the standard of relevance or materiality in institutional rules, makes arbitrators virtually omnipotent in deciding the probative value of evidence proffered.

Arbitrators should be instructed to exercise their authority to make evidentiary rulings that cut down on hearing time and not allow political correctness to influence their decisions. To this end, arbitrator training programs should emphasize the need to conserve hearing time by imposing reasonable time limitations on the presentation of evidence. They should also teach arbitrators how to apply timesaving methods and techniques that will allow them to make appropriate evidentiary rulings. Arbitrator training programs are the ideal vehicle to teach the desirability of:

- requiring early submissions by the parties to enable the arbitrator to study the case in detail in advance of the hearing;

- discussing the case with other members of the tribunal and identifying together the matters that are relevant to deciding the case and issuing an award;

- using witness statements as a substitute for direct testimony. This technique has proved its utility in many international arbitrations. Witness statements are expressly authorized by the new International Bar Association Rules on the Taking of Evidence in International Commercial Arbitration (Article 4). They are also impliedly authorized by Article 20 of the International Chamber of Commerce Rules, which admonishes the tribunal to "proceed within as short a time as possible to establish the facts...by all appropriate means" (emphasis added), and by R-34 of the Commercial Dispute Resolution Procedures and Rule 16 of the International Arbitration Rules of the

---

1997) (no misconduct found where the arbitrator refused to conduct a full hearing after making the dispositive ruling that neither party complied with the claims procedures required by their contract).

[5] *But see* Halligan v. Piper Jaffray, Inc., 148 F.3d 197 (2d Cir. 1998), where the 2d Circuit, apparently in shock over the injustice of the award, widened the familiar "manifest disregard of law" doctrine to include evidence within the definition of law. Supporters of the finality of arbitration awards may rest a little easier since a different panel of the same court recently upheld an award on the ground that manifest disregard of law was not established. *See* Alberti v. Dean Witter Reynolds Inc., 205 F.3d 1321 (2d Cir. 2000).

American Arbitration Association,[6] which encourage efficiency in conducting the hearings. Use of witness statements could replace the practice of allowing extensive direct examinations of friendly witnesses who are usually coached by counsel to make detailed self-serving recitations;

- limiting cross-examination to matters fundamentally germane to the witness' direct evidence, to prevent counsel from deposing the witness during the hearing.

It is not necessary to amend existing arbitral rules, which are more than adequate, to achieve the goal of efficiency in even the most complex cases. What is required, however, is considerably more prehearing homework on the part of the arbitrators, effective early case management, adequate study of the parties' submissions and evidence, and the courage to make necessary but fair rulings, even those excluding offers of proof that are irrelevant or merely cumulative.

Conclusion

The use of timesaving measures can improve the overall efficiency of the arbitral process. The major administering authorities have improved their arbitration rules and procedures to meet the changing needs of parties. Especially salutary are rules promoting preliminary hearings as an occasion where the parties assist in framing the issues and identifying witnesses and documentary evidence.[7] Other rules make clear that the arbitrator has discretion to make the rulings necessary to conduct efficient, but fair proceedings. The parties and arbitral institutions must encourage arbitrators to exercise their discretion and take steps to shorten arbitrated proceedings without in any way diluting the quality of the process.

---

[6] *See supra*, n. 3.

[7] The ICC's practice of requiring "terms of reference" has played an important role in focusing the tribunal and the parties on the precise issues to be determined. Article 18 of the ICC Rules of Arbitration.

IV. Filling an Arbitrator Vacancy

When Arbitrator Vacancies Arise

by John Wilkinson[*]

An issue that may not have been considered at the time the parties drafted the arbitration clause or agreed to submit their dispute to arbitration is, what happens when an arbitrator dies or has to withdraw after the hearing starts? Will the proceedings continue before the remaining arbitrators? Will a substitute arbitrator be appointed and the proceedings go forward from there? Will the proceedings have to begin anew before a new panel of arbitrators?

The answers to these questions are governed by all or some of the following: (i) the agreement of the parties, which is generally controlling; (ii) the rules of the administering tribunal, which, if applicable, are usually dispositive in the absence of an express agreement on the subject; and (iii) relevant case law, which is normally determinative when there is neither an express agreement nor an applicable tribunal rule.

Agreement of the Parties

The parties can provide for the treatment of arbitrator vacancies in their arbitration clause either directly or by incorporating the arbitration rules of an administering ADR organization, such as the American Arbitration Association, whose rules contain procedures for dealing with arbitrator vacancies. It is important to understand the impact of the arbitration agreement and applicable arbitral rules on arbitrator vacancies to avoid unanticipated consequences if a vacancy should arise.

The agreement of the parties on the subject of arbitrator vacancies almost always governs, regardless of contrary provisions in the rules of

---

[*] The author is of counsel at Fulton, Rowe, Hart & Coon in New York City. He has served on the American Arbitration Association's Large, Complex Case Panel and on its Greater New York Advisory Council for Large Complex Cases. He is the editor co-author of CONOVAN LEISURE ADR PRACTICE BOOK, John Wiley & Sons (1991) is a member of the Board of Editors of the American Arbitration Association's ADR Currents.

The author gratefully acknowledges the assistance of Aimee Nassau in the preparation of this article.

the arbitral institution or case law.[1] For example, in *Szuts v. Dean Witter Reynolds*,[2] the court construed the parties' agreement to require replacement of a removed arbitrator, despite an AAA rule incorporated by reference in the parties' agreement providing for continuation of the hearing before the remaining arbitrators. In this case, after one of the arbitrators was removed in the midst of the hearings, the other two arbitrators finished the hearings and entered an award based on the AAA rule. The court vacated the award, holding that the parties' agreement to proceed before three arbitrators took precedence over the general incorporation of a seemingly contrary rule into the arbitration agreement.[3]

In another case, the court construed an arbitration clause identifying the arbitrator and a substitute in the event of incapacity. In *Backus-Brooks Co. v. Northern Pacific Railway Co.*,[4] the arbitration clause specified a particular arbitrator and in the event of his disability, it specified his replacement. The problem was that at the time of the dispute, both arbitrators were incapacitated. The court held that in these circumstances the parties' agreement evinced an intent to arbitrate only before the two specified arbitrators and, in light of their incapacity, the submission to arbitration was totally revoked.

Tribunal Rules

If the parties agree to administered arbitration under the rules of the administering organization, such as the AAA, those rules typically provide how the proceedings will go forward in the event of a vacancy on the panel, eliminating uncertainty and the possibility of untoward results.

The rules of the various ADR organizations administering arbitration often differ on the subject of arbitrator vacancies. The AAA arbitration rules generally provide that if an arbitrator is unable to perform his or her duties, the AAA may declare the office vacant and the vacancy will be filled in accordance with AAA rules. Many of the AAA rules also contain provisions relating to vacancies in a panel of arbitrators. Under AAA Commercial Arbitration Rule 20, AAA Patent Arbitration Rule 19

---

[1] Szuts v. Dean Witter Reynolds, Inc., 931 F.2d 830, 831-32 (11th Cir. 1991); Cia de Navegacion Omsil, S.A. v. Hugo Neu Corp., 359 F. Supp. 898, 899 (S.D.N.Y. 1973).

[2] *Supra*, n. 1.

[3] *Accord* Wannalancit Textile Co., Inc. v. Prestex, Inc., 439 N.Y.S.2d 15, 17 (N.Y. App. Div., 1981).

[4] 21 F.2d 4, 9 (8th Cir. 1927).

and AAA Employment Arbitration Rule 13, in the event of a vacancy on a panel of neutral arbitrators, the remaining arbitrator or arbitrators may continue with the hearings, unless the parties otherwise agree.[5] By contrast, AAA Securities Arbitration Rule 21 provides that a vacancy on a panel of arbitrators will be filled. Article 10 of the AAA International Arbitration Rules similarly calls for replacement of an arbitrator when an arbitrator dies, withdraws after a challenge or resigns for acceptable reasons. The arbitration rules of the Inter-American Commercial Arbitration Commission (IACAC), the International Chamber of Commerce (ICC) and the United Nations Commission on International Trade Law (UNCITRAL) also provide for filling arbitrator vacancies.[6]

Some arbitration rules, such as Maritime Arbitration Rule 13 of the Society of Maritime Arbitrators, provide for the proceeding to continue on the "existing record" after replacement of an arbitrator, while others provide for the possibility of repeating some of the prior hearings after the vacancy is filled. An example of the latter type is AAA Securities Arbitration Rule 21.[7] However, many arbitral rules applicable to arbitrator vacancies, including some AAA rules and the rules of the New York Stock Exchange, the American Stock Exchange and the National Association of Securities Dealers, say nothing, one way or the other, concerning the repetition of hearings or proceeding on the prior record following the replacement of an arbitrator.[8] This may leave the issue to the discretion of the reconstituted panel members.

Questions that may not be expressly addressed in some tribunal rules include what happens when there is a vacancy in a panel containing party-appointed arbitrators.[9] Another question is whether, in an

---

[5] The following AAA rules contain the same provision: Rule 16 of the AAA Arbitration Rules of the Textile and Apparel Industry; Rule R-10 of the AAA Construction Industry Dispute Resolution Procedures; Rule 19 of the AAA Wireless Industry Arbitration Rules; and Rule 22 of the AAA Arbitration Rules for the Real Estate Industry.

[6] IACAC Rules, Art. 13; ICC Rules, Art. 12 (effective Jan. 1, 1998); UNCITRAL Rules, Art. 13.

[7] *See also* AAA International Arbitration Rules, Art. 11; IACAC Rules, Art. 14; ICC Rules, Article 12; UNCITRAL Rules, Art. 14.

[8] American Stock Exch. Arbitration Rules, No. 602(g); Nat'l Ass'n of Secs. Dealers, Code of Arbitration Procedures, No. 10313; N.Y. Stock Exch. Arbitration Rules, No. 611.

[9] *Compare* Rule 20 of the AAA Rules for Professional Accounting and Related Services Disputes, which specifically provides for the filling of vacancies in both neutral panels and panels with party-appointed arbitrators. Some other AAA rules apply whenever there is a vacancy in a panel, while other AAA rules state that they apply to vacancies in panels of neutral arbitrators. Maritime Rule 13 and CPR Rules, No. 7.8 also specifically provide for replacement of a party-appointed arbitrator.

arbitration with a sole arbitrator, the proceedings must be repeated before the replacement arbitrator. Some rules that expressly provide for this are the AAA Labor Arbitration Rules, the IACAC rules and the UNCITRAL rules.[10] By contrast, the rules of the Center for Public Resources Institute for Dispute Resolution (CPR), give the replacement arbitrator discretion to proceed without repeating prior hearings.[11] Presumably the rules that do not address this directly leave the issue to the discretion of the replacement arbitrator.

Vacancy provisions in the international area have recently undergone some improvement. The problem of the recalcitrant arbitrator is addressed in Article 11 of the AAA International Arbitration Rules. Under this provision, if an arbitrator on a panel fails to participate in the arbitration for reasons that would not constitute acceptable grounds for the declaration of a vacancy under Article 10, the other two arbitrators have the discretion to continue the arbitration and issue the award. In making this decision the remaining arbitrators are guided to consider, among other things, the stage of the arbitration and the reasons given for the third arbitrator's nonparticipation.

An amendment to the ICC arbitration rules, which becomes effective on Jan. 1, 1998, draws a distinction between a vacancy that arises during the hearing and one that occurs after the hearing but before the award. Few, if any, of the rules cited above, draw this distinction—one that has been considered to be crucial in some cases.[12]

Vacancy During the Hearing

The courts have tended to step into the breach to decide vacancy issues where the parties' agreement does not contain provisions for that contingency and tribunal rules are inapplicable.[13] In such circumstances, most courts have held that the disability of an arbitrator requires the hearings to be commenced anew before the new arbitrator or reconstituted panel. As the court acknowledged in *Trade & Transport,*

---

[10] AAA Labor Arbitration Rule 18; AAA Title Insurance Arbitration Rule 18; IACAC Rules, Art. 14; UNCITRAL Rules, Art. 14.

[11] CPR Rules, No. 7.10.

[12] *E.g., American Eagle Fire Ins. Co. v. New Jersey Ins. Co.*, 148 N.E. 562, 565 (N.Y. 1925).

[13] The U.S. Arbitration Act gives U.S. district courts authority to designate arbitrators where the parties disagree as to whether or how such arbitrators should be appointed. 9 U.S.C. § 5. To the same effect, see N.Y. CPLR 7504.

Inc. v. Natural Petroleum Charterers, Inc,[14] "[T]he general rule [is] that where one member of a three-person arbitration panel dies before the rendering of an award and the arbitration agreement does not anticipate that circumstance, the arbitration must commence anew with a full panel."[15]

Judge Frankel followed this rule in *Cia de Navegacion Omsil, S.A. v. Hugo Neu Corp.*, but indicated that he might be reluctant to do so if there was a need for "swift action" or if "the expense [of a new hearing were]...disproportionate to the end in view."[16] This suggests some courts might not rigidly direct a new hearing in the case of an arbitrator vacancy if the new hearing runs counter to strong equitable considerations.

A departure from the rule articulated in *Trade & Transport* is the recent decision in *McMahan & Co. v. Dunn Newfund I, Ltd.*,[17] which held that a new hearing was not required after multiple vacancies in the panel were filled. In this case, three of five arbitrators on an American Stock Exchange panel were replaced at various times during the course of lengthy hearings under the rules of the exchange. In each instance, the new arbitrator read the prior transcripts and the hearings continued from there. With the exception of two recalled witnesses at the final session, there was no repetition of prior testimony. Without citing a single case on the subject of arbitrator vacancies, the New York Appellate Division, First Department, reversed Justice Cahn, who had vacated the award on the ground that the proceeding was fundamentally unfair since a majority of the panel did not hear live testimony. Rejecting that conclusion, the First Department stated that it is not important for arbitrators with expertise in the field in question to observe the demeanor of witnesses and weigh their credibility. The court opined that:

Sint'The demeanor of witnesses may be of enormous importance to a lay jury (or a nisi prius judge), where the trier-of-fact must decide which witness to believe, what portion of their testimony is to be accepted and what weight is to be ascribed thereto....By agreeing to arbitrate a

---

[14] 931 F.2d 191, 194 (2d Cir. 1991).

[15] *Accord* Marine Prods. Export Corp. v. M.T. Globe Galaxy, 977 F.2d 66, 68 (2d Cir. 1992); Mitchell v. Alfred Holmann. Inc., 137 A.2d 569, 574-5 (N.J. Super. Ct. App. Div. 1958).

[16] Statutes of the state whose laws control the arbitration should always be checked, for they may contain provisions on arbitrator vacancies, and the statutes may run counter to generally accepted common law. *See* Board of County Comm'rs ex rel. Board of Trustees, Neosho Mem'l Hosp. v. Central Air Conditioning Co., 683 P.2d 1282, 1287-88 (Kan. 1984).

[17] *Supra*, n. 1, 359 F. Supp. at 899.

controversy, the parties have chosen to rely upon a different standard for weighing credibility— namely, the expertise of the arbitrators in the customs and trade practices of the particular business or industry involved.[18]

McMahan involved a lengthy proceeding, which commenced in March 1989 and did not end until August 1993. While some arbitrators may question the wisdom of the court's reasoning regarding the lack of need for observation of arbitration witnesses, it may be that the prospect of requiring such a lengthy proceeding to be repeated, with the concomitant expense, was the driving force behind this decision.

Vacancy Before the Award

Courts have generally allowed the hearing to continue when a vacancy in a panel containing a party-appointed arbitrator arises after completion of the hearings but before the award is issued. The evolution of this rule began with the *Republic of Colombia v. Cauca Co.*[19] There, a party-appointed arbitrator resigned at a point after the hearing when all issues had been resolved and "when hardly anything remained to be done except to sign the award." When it became clear that the party whose arbitrator resigned was not going to name a replacement before the deadline for terminating the proceedings, the remaining two arbitrators proceeded to execute and enter the award. The U.S. Supreme Court upheld the confirmation of the award, holding that a party may not undermine a submission to arbitration "by withdrawing or adopting the withdrawal of its nominee when the discussions were closed." The court found that what the two remaining arbitrators had done was the "only way of saving the proceedings from coming to naught."[20]

Later this rule was expanded to permit a numerically depleted arbitration panel to issue an award in analogous, but nonetheless different circumstances. In *Amalgamated Association of Street Electric Railway and Motor Coach Employees of America, A.F.L. v. Connecticut Co.*,[21] a party-appointed arbitrator resigned after completion of the

---

[18] 656 N.Y.S.2d 620 (N.Y. App. Div., 1997).
[19] *Id.* at 622.
[20] 190 U.S. 524 (1903).
[21] *See also American Eagle Fire Ins. Co., supra,* n. 12, 148 N.E. at 565 (stating "[otherwise]...no award could be reached in any case if at the eleventh hour one of the three found himself in the minority and sought to serve his own interests or those of the party naming him by resigning"). *See generally* Bullard v. Morgan H. Grace Co., 148 N.E. 559 (N.Y. 1925), which was decided on the same day as *American Eagle Fire Ins. Co.,* and

hearings and after full discussion among arbitrators but before the final award. The arbitration agreement provided that the party whose arbitrator resigned was to name a successor within three days. Rather than waiting the three days, the two remaining arbitrators proceeded to enter an award on the same day their co-arbitrator resigned. The court affirmed the award, holding that the three-day reappointment provision of the arbitration agreement was inapplicable under the circumstances.

Similarly, in *Wannalancit Textile Co.*,[22] one of three arbitrators died after the hearing and before the award. The parties did nothing and the remaining arbitrators proceeded to decide and enter an award. At that point, the losing party moved to set aside the award on the ground that the hearing should have started again before a new panel pursuant to the rules of the General Arbitration Council of the Textile Industry. The court rejected this argument and confirmed the award, stating:

> [A]ll three arbitrators participated in the deliberations and reached a unanimous conclusion [which remained to be put in an award].... Moreover, although notified of the death of the third arbitrator, [the losing party] took no action until the award was handed down. Having elected to play a form of "Russian roulette" it cannot now be heard to complain that it was injured thereby.

The most substantial extension of the Colombia rule was in *Trade & Transport, Inc.*[23] In this case, liability and damages issues had been bifurcated. Subsequent to the liability award and prior to the start of the hearing on damages, the defendant's party-appointed arbitrator died. The defendant appointed a successor and then argued that the party-appointed arbitrators had to select another neutral arbitrator and commence the liability phase anew.

The court rejected this argument, stating:

While there seems to be no case on point relating to death after an award, with damages to be determined later, the courts have held that where one of the arbitrators resigns or withdraws after the arbitrators

---

distinguished the situation where an arbitrator vacancy arises prior to the close of the hearings.

[22] Note that Rule 11 of the AAA's International Arbitration Rules gives the remaining two arbitrators discretion as to how best to proceed when an arbitrator resigns for the purpose of undermining the submission to arbitration. This provision is unique to the AAA's International Rules.

[23] 112 A.2d 501, 502-3 (Conn. 1955).

have heard the evidence, and have had the chance to discuss the issues, the remaining arbitrators maintain their authority to make an award. [citation omitted] By analogy, the death of an arbitrator after an award on liability should not terminate the authority of the remaining arbitrators to issue an award on damages, particularly where a successor nominated by the defendant has been accepted on the panel.[24]

Given this evolution of the law, it may be tempting to conclude that when an arbitrator resigns or becomes disabled after the hearing but before the award, the remaining arbitrators may complete the proceeding, even when there is no manipulation by the third-party arbitrator. But that may not be the case.[25]

In the final analysis, if a vacancy occurring after the hearing and before the award leads to litigation, what will happen will be dictated by the circumstances surrounding the case.[26] If the author can be permitted to predict, the most likely result will be that the remaining arbitrators will be permitted to enter the award.

The law on the subject of arbitrator vacancies is not very extensive, leading to the conclusion that most vacancy situations do not result in serious problems. However, since vacancies, particularly in lengthy arbitration proceedings, can lead to disputes, counsel for the parties should attempt to reach consensus as to what might be the best approach for dealing with this contingency.[27]

---

[24] *Supra*, n. 3.
[25] *Supra*, n. 14, 738 F. Supp. 789 (S.D. N.Y. 1990), *aff'd*, 931 F.2d 191 (2d Cir. 1991).
[26] *Id.* at 791.
[27] See *Cia de Navegacion Omsil, S.A.*, *supra*, n.1, where one of the arbitrators died after the hearing and before the award. In that circumstance, Judge Frankel applied the general rule and directed recommencement of the arbitration.

V. The Arbitrator's Role: Questioning

What Kind of Questions Should Arbitrators Ask?

by Sharon T. Nelson[*]

As an arbitrator, you have been astutely watching the parties put forth their case before you. The witness slowly responds to the party's question. You immediately feel an urge to ask a particular question. What do you do? How do you do it? When do you do it? These are important and universal considerations.

The first step in determining the appropriateness of asking a question as a panelist is to decide the motivation for the question.

Why Do We Ask Questions?

While we may have more than one reason for asking a question, the reasons break down into one of the following eight categories.

1. *Failure to hear.* Probably the most asked category of questions during an arbitration is a variation of "Please repeat that?" Failure to hear is caused either by the sender's voice or the receiver missing it (by being distracted or having a hearing problem). This problem occurs at most hearings.

2. *Confusion.* The second most asked category of question is to alleviate confusion on the part of the arbitrator. A variation of "Please explain what you mean by..." This confusion can be related to the specific matter being discussed (such as a chart or occurrence) or how the testimony fits in with the total picture of the case.

3. *More information.* Arbitrators have also been known to ask for more information with variations of "Please tell me about..." They may believe the information they want is necessary to make a final determination in the case, or just want the information for curiosity's sake.

---

[*] The author is a full-time arbitrator and mediator, and former judge, who is on the mediation/arbitration panels of the American Arbitration Association, the NASD, the IRS, the District of Columbia Superior Court, and the Federal Mediation and Conciliation Service.

4. *Move a matter forward.* The urge to ask questions is often driven by the desire to move a matter forward. Watching a pro se party ask questions of a difficult witness can eat up the most patient person's restraint. The urge to move on may also arise from having heard or litigated many similar cases. They all result in the "Let me just ask..." questions.

5. *Impress others.* We've all watched our patience grow thin when people use a question as an excuse to impress others with their expertise on a subject. This includes variations of the "As I understand it..." questions. This category also includes questions that attempt to trap the witness with the questioner's superior knowledge.

6. *Social questions.* The first thing we usually do when we meet people is to ask them about themselves. Though often formed as a question, these are usually just greetings. However, some are true questions, asked to create or nurture a relationship. Some of these social questions are even asked by lawyers or judges to calm witnesses down when they first take the witness stand, such as questions about one's address or family.

7. *Bored.* Some individuals find the urge to ask questions when they become bored. People differ in their ability to sit passively while others are interrogating.

8. *Manipulation.* This includes the asking of questions for a designed result other than those listed above. While the motivation rarely, if ever, occurs from an arbitrator on the panel, it is often at play by the lawyers or pro se parties.

Having determined the impulse for the question, the next stage is to delve into its appropriateness.

Considerations for Appropriateness

The general rule is that the arbitrators should let the parties, or their lawyers, make their own case. This means the arbitrator should not ask questions. This rule is based on the following theories:

- The parties have designed how they want to present their case. Whether the arbitrator starts interrogating or asking a simple question, it can throw off the organization of the case.

- Asking questions can make the arbitrator look biased.
- Asking questions is the lawyer's payoff for the hard work of preparation.
- If the arbitrator's question makes a lawyer look bad in front of his or her client, he or she will probably never hire the arbitrator again.
- Parties and lawyers often feel the necessity to ask more questions to make sure that the arbitrator's question has been answered or that the answer has the appropriate effect. This results in them spending more time asking for the same information.

At the same time, arbitration is supposed to be an efficient and effective method of resolving disputes quickly, and the arbitrator has an obligation to make a reasoned decision while moving the case forward in the most expeditious manner. The arbitrator, therefore, has a balancing act to perform in determining the appropriateness of panel questions. The following explains some of the considerations with respect to panel questions.

1. "Please repeat that, I didn't hear you." If you didn't hear something, it's hard for the parties to make their case. It's impossible to determine if what was missed was meaningful or not. Parties and lawyers want to know that the arbitrator has heard what is going on. An occasional interruption to get someone (either the witness or his or her lawyer) to repeat what they've said or raise their voice is never unwelcome. Most arbitrators will rely on hand signals after the first reminder.

2. "Please explain what you meant by..." Confusion over what has been said can be similar to not hearing what was said. Yet, on the other hand, asking about it can breach all the theories listed above as to why arbitrators shouldn't ask questions. Questions to resolve confusion that is limited to understanding what the witness is talking about are appropriate. For example, if the witness is discussing a chart, blueprints, or using terms that the arbitrator doesn't understand, then a simple, "Explain what is meant by..." or "What is..." can resolve the mystery.

3. If the confusion is about how the testimony fits into the bigger picture of the case, it should first be discussed with other members of the panel. If one is a sole arbitrator, or if the panel is

confused, the question should be written down and reserved, if asked at all, to the end of the case after the lawyers have made their closing arguments.

4. There are also times when the confusion is minor and doesn't actually interfere with listening to the remainder of the witness' testimony. At the end of the witness' testimony (including cross-examination and re-direct), if the question seems material to understanding what the witness meant, it may be appropriate to ask.

5. "Please tell me about..." This type of question gets arbitrators into the most trouble. Crossing the line to ask for information not provided by the parties is a highly debatable area. Tribunals range in the responsibility and authority granted to the finder of facts and law to seek outcome determinative information. Most administrative law judges are required to create a comprehensive record on the matter at issue. On the other hand, most civil judges rule strictly based on the evidence properly introduced by the parties. Arbitrators are not required to create a record. They are only required to allow in all relevant evidence that is not overly redundant.

6. The rule of thumb is to determine the relevancy of the information that is sought. The first test is whether you can make the decision in the case without the information; not whether the information would be helpful. X-raying your toe to find out if it is broken may provide useful information, but in the final analysis the cure is the same whether it's broken or not.

7. Remember that asking for crucial information which benefits one side's case can give the appearance of bias. If a missing bit of evidence could be used by either side, there is a possibility that both sides have agreed not to use it because it's damaging to both. There may also be other evidence which contains the specific information you are seeking. Always think of the least intrusive means of getting the information (e.g., other documents) before asking.

8. "Let me help move this along by asking..." Arbitration is supposed to be efficient, and the obligation of making it so often rests with the panel chairperson or sole arbitrator. Yet, asking such questions raises all the risks of questioning discussed

above, and assumes that the chairperson has decided the case before it's been heard.

9. As with all the roles of the arbitrator, there is a delicate balance to be reached. Asking such questions would be appropriate in those rare situations where the case is floundering, time is ticking, a pro se party (or lawyer) is just missing the correct way to ask a question, and a simple question or two can put it back on track. There are many ways that a chairperson or sole arbitrator can keep a case moving forward.

10. For example, if an arbitrator truly understands an area, a brief explanation of that understanding to the lawyers will signal to them how to move the case forward. But again, it must be done with great caution and a balancing of all the interests involved.

11. "As I understand it..." So many lawyers use this technique in setting up each question. A good arbitrator will try to limit it since it wastes time and is not evidence. There's really no time when an arbitrator should use this form of questioning of a witness. While it can be tempting, it's the opinion of the panel, and not that of a witness, that's important. Although there may be times when it seems wise to try to get a party to understand what they're missing, it rarely works.

12. "How are you?" While there's no reason to be rude, social questions are generally not asked by an arbitrator. There are clearly exceptions, such as "Do you need a break?" when it appears that a witness is unwell. Generally, it's best to set forth the rules of the proceeding at the beginning of the hearing so that once the case starts, the panel can just observe.

13. Bored. If the impulse to get involved is part of the need to stay awake, it's probably a great time for a break. Otherwise, the impulse just has to be controlled.

Methods of Asking

All the standard rules of communication are as true in the arbitration situation as elsewhere. If you want to appear unbiased, you must sound and look unbiased. That applies to the voice tones used, the words selected, and the body language utilized, in addition to the actual content of the question.

Generally, the best recipe for asking a question is patience. Panel questioning, unless it's based on failure to hear or confusion on what's presently being talked about, should be reserved until both sides have concluded with that witness (direct, cross-examination, re-direct, and re-cross). It's important not to interrupt, because the lawyers may have designated another witness to discuss that information, and waiting will again provide the answers.

Making notes of prospective questions is the perfect first step in controlling one's questions. It affords the questioner the calm opportunity to review the appropriateness of the questions. Experienced arbitrators generally write their questions in such a way as to spot them quickly when it's time to review them. This is done by placing them in the margin of their notes, writing special symbols next to them, or using highlights. At the end of the witness' testimony the questions are reviewed, and, as often as not, most of them are crossed off.

If you determine that an area needs more information, a number of the concerns about asking questions can be resolved if the chairperson notes to the lawyers the area that needs further clarification and allows the lawyers to proceed as they wish.

While asking lawyers to "proffer" how something that appears irrelevant fits into the case is an option, it should be reserved for when the opposing counsel raises the objection. Remember, asking a lawyer (and especially a pro se party) to proffer is the same as asking the lawyer to give away his or her game plan, and is often just an opportunity for the lawyer to waste time making closing arguments ahead of time.

As the chairperson of the panel, one of the best ways to control panelists' questions is to have them filtered through you. This can be done by passing notes during the hearing or through conversation during executive session (including lunch). If a question is inappropriate, make sure the panelist understands why the inquiry is inappropriate so that the panelist doesn't later blurt out the question.

Asking the right question, the right way, at the right time, is a valuable tool. Asking the wrong question or the right question the wrong way, at the wrong time, can be a disaster.

If you follow these guidelines you will be providing the parties with what they really want: someone who lets them put on their case in an efficient manner, while appearing attentive, caring, and unbiased.

VI. Arbitrators Testifying in Court

Must They Be Required to Testify?
Arbitrators in Court

by Norman M. Fera[*]

This article raises the question of when, if ever, it is appropriate to require an arbitrator to give testimony in an appeal of his or her decision. While the practice is not uncommon when an award is up for judicial review, Norman Fera advances a strong argument as to why arbitrators should be accorded the same deference as judges and excused from such proceedings.

It seems inconceivable that a judge of first instance should or would be called as a witness in an appeal or review of his or her own decision. From a practical point of view, the judicial system, already slow and cumbersome, would in short order become gridlocked. Apart, however, from such mundane considerations, there must be sound public policy reasons for refusing to countenance such a practice. If so, then why do arbitrators[1] not enjoy the same deference?[2]

---

[*] The author is a partner in the national law firm of Lang Michener in Ottawa, Ontario, Canada, and is on the roster of court-connected mediators in the Ontario Court (General Division) at Ottawa. Fera holds a B.A. and M.A. from Careleton College and an LL.B. from the University of Ottawa. He has written numerous articles on alternative dispute resolution and is the co-author of two leading legal textbooks.

[1] The better expression is "arbitral tribunal."

[2] The writer acknowledges a certain naiveté in the question. There are differences. These are discussed or alluded to in the jurisprudence. *See, for example*, La Vale Plaza, Inc. v. R.S. Noonan, Inc., 378 F.2d 569, 572, n.13 (3d Cir. 1967), or Glass, Molders, Pottery, Plastics and Allied Workers Int'l Union v. Excelsior Foundry Co., 56 F.3d 844, 847 (7th Cir. 1995). In Commonwealth Coatings Corporation v. Continental Casualty Company, 393 U.S. 145, 150, 89 S. Ct. 337, 340, there are references to the fact that arbitrators are often men of affairs, not part from but of the marketplace and are not subject to the same standards of judicial decorum. On the other hand, the question posed in the text may be answered in part by accepting that there has been (and may still be) judicial hostility toward arbitrators. Recognition of that point appears in *Courier-Citizen Co. v. Boston Electrotypers Union No. 11*, 702 F.2d 273, 278 (1st Cir. 1983).

Case Study

A case[3] in which I was involved as counsel in an application to have the award of the arbitrator judicially reviewed[4] has caused me to seriously reflect on whether it is ever[5] appropriate to require an arbitrator to give testimony after an appeal or review has been commenced in the very matter that is the subject of judicial supervision. In the circumstances of this case, not only did the process leave an aura of impropriety in its wake, it may even be seen to have shaken the foundation of impartiality and neutrality so fundamental to any adjudicative process whether in the private or public sector.

The case concerned a domestic arbitration. The parties agreed to arbitration and signed an agreement which specifically set out a single, identifiable area to be arbitrated. Accordingly, it was patent, and not in dispute, that upon entering the arbitration room, the parties expected and had agreed to have a single matter arbitrated on that date. The arbitration award, however, dealt with other matters.

During the arbitration, the parties had purportedly agreed to have more than one area of dispute arbitrated on that day by the same arbitrator. It was the respondent's position that after the arbitration hearing, a slash (/) and a single word had been added to the arbitration agreement and that the parties had initialed this, although neither party was given a copy of the amended agreement or page where the insertion was made. (Both parties were represented by counsel during the arbitration process.)

---

[3] The case involved the appeal and also an application to set aside the award of a private arbitrator—that is, an arbitrator appointed by the parties involved in private, domestic arbitration which was not the subject of or related to any statutory requirement. The appeal and the setting-aside application were ultimately joined or consolidated and heard together. The court's decision in the Lalonde case is reported in a Canadian topical series: 9 R.F.L (4th) 27. Interlocutory proceedings taken in that case are not, however, reported.

[4] As used in this paper, "judicial review," "judicial supervision," "judicial consideration" or forms of those expressions refer to an appeal and also something which is sometimes less than an appeal and which is variously referred to in different jurisdictions as a remission or setting-aside application or simply as judicial review (as distinct from an appeal). In some jurisdictions, an arbitration award is subject to both an appeal (appellate review) and an application to set aside, vacate, amend, modify, suspend or remit (judicial review). I would reiterate that in this paper, the expression "judicial review" is used in a general sense to encompass all forms of judicial supervision.

[5] The writer acknowledges that there must certainly be some circumstances when it is appropriate and that, in some instances, it would be expedient to do so and blindly foolish not to permit it.

In commencing an appeal and in asking that the award be set aside, the appellant/applicant alleged that:

(a) the award dealt with a dispute that the arbitration agreement did not cover or contained a decision on a matter that was beyond the scope of the agreement, and

(b) the arbitrator erred when, in knowing that the parties had presented themselves to determine only one issue, failed to properly inquire and ascertain of each of the parties that he or she fully appreciated and understood that the hearing would be expanded to deal with an additional significant issue and the ramifications of a final order on such a new issue.

In his affidavit, the applicant/appellant noted that at no time during the entire arbitration proceeding was either party asked directly by the arbitrator whether or not he or she understood that, based on what would happen that day, another area of dispute would also be finally determined by the arbitrator.

No recording of any kind had been made of the arbitration proceedings.

In her arbitration award, the arbitrator stated that at the time of the hearing, the parties and their counsel amended the arbitration agreement. Although the arbitrator conceded that the wording was awkward, she was certain that the parties and their counsel made it clear at the hearing that she had authority to decide both issues. Elsewhere in the award, the arbitrator wrote:

The parties and counsel left in my hands the decision as to whether I would make a final or interim order regarding...[both primary issues]. I...decided that a final order would be more appropriate.

Accordingly, it may be argued that even the text of the award indicated some inconsistency, doubt or ambiguity as to what exactly was to be the jurisdiction of the arbitrator.[6]

The Procedural Maneuverings

A few days before the hearing of the appeal/ review, the solicitor for the respondent corresponded directly with the arbitrator and, among other things, asked for a letter from the arbitrator outlining "recollections" as to the following matters:

---

[6] In the context of labor arbitrations, see *Teamsters Local 312 v. Matlack Inc.*, 118 F.3d 985 (1988), where the court considers the "controversy over the scope of the day's hearing."

(i) When was the issue of whether the hearing would be for a final or interim decision, and what was the discussion that occurred?

(ii) When was the issue raised as to the fact that the arbitration agreement did not specifically call for you determining the second issue, how was that resolved, and when was the amendment made to the arbitration agreement?

The letter to the arbitrator from the solicitor for the respondent was dated October 14 and was supposedly copied to the solicitor for applicant/ appellant on the same date. However, the facsimile identification information at the top of the copy indicated that it was faxed to counsel for the applicant/appellant on October 18. On that same day (October 18), the arbitrator responded to queries posed by the solicitor for the respondent and she said in part:

My recollection is that the question of whether the hearing would be for a final or interim decision was discussed at the outset of the hearing, when I asked for clarification about the issues that were before me. At the beginning of the hearing, I expressed my uncertainty as to the issues that were actually before me; i.e., whether both...[issues] were before me and whether the award I would make would be interim or final. We discussed this, and counsel for the parties agreed that both...[issues] were before me. It is my recollection that at the end of submissions, when we were gathering up the documents, we all acknowledged that the Arbitration Agreement, as originally drafted, only referred to...[one issue] and should also have referred to...[the second issue]....You and...[the other counsel] attended to amending the first clause and you both initialed the change.

Again, the arbitrator was suggesting some confusion as to the scope of her jurisdiction and the agreement reached just prior to commencing the arbitration. (Further, subsequent to her letter of recollections, when giving testimony as a witness, the arbitrator indicated that it was the parties and not their counsel that had initialed the amendment.)

On October 19, after hearing from the solicitor for the applicant/appellant, the arbitrator wrote another letter to the solicitor for the respondent and said in part:

Apparently...[the solicitor for the applicant/ appellant] did not receive a copy of your faxed letter to me of October 14, until October 18. By the time he contacted me on October 18 [objecting to your communication with me], I had already responded in writing to your letter [setting out my recollections] and had sent a copy of that response to him. I called [the solicitor, for the applicant/appellant]...to confirm that he did not feel it was appropriate for me to have responded to your letter without first asking for his comments. In the circumstances, considering there is disagreement between the two of you as to whether or not it is appropriate for me to have written my letter to you or to respond to any questions at an Examination, I think it would be preferable if the two of you tried to come to an agreement as to what, if any, information I should provide to either of you at this point in time regarding my recollection of events at the arbitration. If you cannot come to an agreement, it would be preferable if you had a court determine the extent to which I should provide a response to your questions at this time.

In the jurisdiction where the review/appeal was being heard, a person may be examined as a witness before the hearing of a pending motion or application for the purpose of having a transcript of his or her evidence available for use at the hearing. Further, like in many other jurisdictions,[7]

---

[7] In *Iron Workers Local No. 272 v. Bowen*, 624 F.2d 1255 (5th Cir. 1980), the court permitted testimony from the arbitrator to clarify the status of an award (i.e., the arbitrator was permitted to write post-award letter and testify at trial in order to clarify its decision). Contrast that with the doctrine of *functus officio* (Latin for a task performed) applied strictly at common law to prevent an arbitrator from in any way revising, re-examining or supplementing his award. For discussion in that regard, see *Glass, Molders, Pottery, Plastics* and *Allied Workers Int'l Union v. Excelsior Foundry Co.*, 56 F.3d 844, 846-47 (7th Cir. 1995). In *Colonial Penn Ins. Co. v. Omaha Indem. Co.*, 943 F.2d 327, 329-30 (3d Cir. 1991), the court considered the continued applicability of the *functus officio* doctrine in a non-labor case. In *Teamsters Local 312 v. Matlack Inc.*, 118 F.3d 985 (1988), the United States Court of Appeals, 3rd Circuit, concluded that while under normal circumstances it would not sanction calling an arbitrator to testify, as the written record would suffice, in the circumstances of the case before it, it was not improper for the arbitrator to issue a letter clarifying his misunderstanding concerning the procedure to be followed, prior to a decision resolving the substantive portion of the issue and the basis for disqualifying himself. In the same case, at the lower level, the district court requested that the arbitrator testify at an evidentiary hearing and it rejected the objection of one of the parties to the court's decision to call the arbitrator as a witness. In Britain, Russell on the Law of Arbitration is a leading authority. In the 20th Edition (London Stevens & Sons 1982), the learned authors write at p. 361: "An arbitrator may be called as a witness to give evidence respecting proceedings in the arbitration." Indeed, "an arbitrator who is called as a witness, can... be cross-examined as to the matters he took into consideration in determining the amount of his award." A decision of the Supreme Court of Canada, *Christie v. Toronto Junction* (Town) (1895), 22 O.A.R. 21; *affirmed* 25 S.C.R. 551, is said to stand for the proposition that an arbitrator may be examined as a witness upon a motion to set aside an award. Compare, however, a

there appeared to be no prohibition and few limitations on calling the arbitrator as a witness to give evidence concerning the arbitration.

With the correspondence of the arbitrator already in hand, the solicitor for the respondent proposed that the letter be admitted as evidence or, otherwise, that the arbitrator would be summoned as a witness pursuant to the practice in that jurisdiction. In short order, the solicitor for the respondent issued a summons to witness and this was served on the arbitrator. The solicitor for the respondent enclosed a letter of explanation and indicated that it was proper to examine an arbitrator on certain matters pertaining to the arbitration, especially "procedural issues," and asked that the contents of the arbitrator's letter dated October 18 be accepted so as to dispense with examination of the arbitrator.

The solicitor for the applicant/appellant expressed his views in a letter directed to the other solicitor and said, in part:

(1) Expanding on what we stated earlier [in my letter of yesterday], we believe the continued involvement of the Arbitrator is improper. The Arbitrator rendered [her decision] and reasons for decision as set out in the Arbitration Award. The appeal and review are based on that Award and the record. It is inappropriate to further attempt to involve the Arbitrator as this could lead to the perception that the Arbitrator...is intent on upholding that particular Award or is now part of the respondent's cause as to why...[the] decision should not be appealed and reviewed or that there is an attempt to interfere with the right of the parties to have the matter judicially considered.

(2) The record must stand as is. It cannot be amended, buttressed, further explained or justified after an appeal/review [has been] launched. The procedures followed at the [arbitration] hearing must be ascertained from the record. In procedural matters, the appearance of what was done is as important as what was actually done.

(3) Since your request for the Arbitrator's recollections were forwarded to me on the same day the Arbitrator responded, the

---

Canadian decision of the lower courts in *Agnew v. Assn. of Architects* (Ont.) (1987), 64 O.R. (2d) 8 (Div. Ct.), which has been cited for the proposition that arbitrators are not compellable witnesses on an appeal.

objection not to have been made aware of your contact with the Arbitrator in advance and not to have had an opportunity to respond to your request to the Arbitrator before the Arbitrator responded remains.[8]

Overview

While the language is that of litigation counsel and may seem overstated, the circumstances that led to such assertions and the basic principles they allude to require serious consideration. One wonders whether inherent in the right and process of calling arbitrators as witnesses, there is a tendency to involve the parties or their counsel in sharp practices, to sully those that have acted as third-party neutral arbitrators and to cast doubt on the very fairness of the judicial review process. There is little hyperbole in those suggestions when one considers that, in the case being discussed, the review/appeal process was started based on the written record available to all parties and that at the eleventh hour, just before the award was to be judicially considered, "recollections" of the arbitrator were obtained to challenge the legitimate grounds that had originally presented themselves and which had been put forward in good faith as appropriate to support a judicial review.

Nevertheless, the interlocutory proceeding to suppress the arbitrator's letter as evidence and to excuse or forbid the arbitrator from being a witness failed. That this decision was rendered in the context of a domestic arbitration has little bearing on what the outcome was or should have been and there is no reason to believe that the court was influenced by the relationship of the disputants or the subject matter or nature of the arbitration.

From what has already been suggested and alluded to, there should be significant policy considerations for refusing to permit examination of arbitrators to obtain their testimony to be used in an appeal of their decision before the courts.

A further word about appearances. In the circumstances of the noted case, there was certainly the possibility of the appearance of bias. Equally so, there appeared to be the opportunity for the arbitrator to revisit her award (decision) and, in a sense, to "rewrite it" and "to make it better," and, in so doing to possibly help preserve her reputation, avoid

---

[8] This third point was not phrased exactly in this fashion, but the gist of it has been properly reproduced.

or limit judicial criticism and comment and, obviously, reduce or eliminate certain grounds of appeal.

When looking at the ADR spectrum, next to negotiation, arbitration is, indeed, a venerable process. In our day and age, when ADR is increasingly being looked upon as a true alternative to the more complex and costly procedures in the traditional courts, arbitration and arbitrators cannot and should not be accorded a second-class status. This especially should not be the case where the parties, with the assistance of counsel, have voluntarily selected a private forum, instead of the judicial one, and expressly addressed and limited recourse to the courts in the event of dissatisfaction with the award.

Accordingly, as a general principle, there should be no generally imposed rule that permits one party or the other to summon the arbitrator to explain herself or himself under oath where an appeal and/or review of the arbitration award has been instituted. No such requirement is imposed by the appellate or review courts on their inferior courts and arbitrators should be accorded similar deference, especially in light of the fact that they have been personally selected by the disputants who have specified the forum and directed their minds as to what will and will not be brought before the courts.

Further, as is demonstrated in the case discussed above, once an appeal and/or review is commenced based on the arbitration agreement, the arbitration pleadings and the arbitration award, the other party cannot and should not be permitted to expand upon, clarify or elucidate the "record" or basis upon which the appeal or review has been grounded or based or to attack them. To do so makes a mockery of the grounds specified (by the parties in accordance with their agreement and/or applicable arbitration legislation) for judicial involvement and the limitation period imposed on the appellant/applicant to frame the grounds for such intervention. Also, it may require, among other things, the granting of a reciprocal right. That is, if the responding party may "clarify" the record by examination of the arbitrator (after the appeal is commenced), then the appellant should also be able to do so, but perhaps before applying for judicial supervision, so that it may attempt to garner additional grounds not on the face of the proceedings. In this way, it can be said that each side has been accorded an equal opportunity to "expand" upon what appears on the record. The net result of such a process—whether granted to the respondent and the appellant or just to one of them—is that the arbitration becomes more susceptible to reconsideration (and what that entails) and more open to judicial scrutiny and interference (on interlocutory matters and on the merits) far beyond that which the parties initially contemplated and agreed upon. That, in turn, helps to negate the original intention of the parties to have their dispute finally decided—except to the extent otherwise expressly provided—in a summary fashion by an agreed upon arbitrator in a private forum.

Avoidance Techniques

If the notion of attaching privilege to a person that has acted in a judicial capacity as an arbitrator were to evolve by judicial precedent, then it would likely do so slowly. Especially in those jurisdictions where there has been a tradition of calling arbitrators as witnesses, one cannot expect definitive legislative or judicial intervention in one fell swoop. Accordingly, other effective avenues will have to be considered to help clothe arbitrators with judicial trappings or, at least, to avoid actively involving them in judicial proceedings instituted to review their awards.

Provision and arrangements should be made to have the arbitration proceedings recorded. An electronic back-up, as simple as a tape recorder, should also be available in the event the primary recording system fails. It would seem that before launching an appeal or review, counsel for each party, with the concurrence of the other, should attempt to ascertain the "recollections" of the arbitrator on points that might relate to the very grounds being considered to commence a judicial proceeding to set aside or remit the award.[9]

There are other preemptive measures that should be considered and these may be made part of the arbitration agreement; that is, provisions[10] addressing these points:

1) no matter, issue or dispute, other than those expressly set out in the arbitration agreement shall be heard and decided by the arbitrator;

---

[9] I am not particularly keen about this process, but if the arbitrator is a compellable witness after the judicial review proceedings have been commenced, then it seems prudent that counsel will try to ascertain the full story whether or not it will benefit his client before the judicial proceedings are commenced (rather than after much effort and expense has been incurred). Interestingly, the arbitrator at this stage may refuse to volunteer his or her "recollections."

[10] No attempt has been made to phrase these suggested provisions to encompass a universal usage irrespective of the circumstances, jurisdiction, legislation and contractual considerations. They merely suggest matters to be considered.

2) following the arbitration, no party or its counsel shall in any manner or fashion have contact or communicate with the arbitrator on any matter whatsoever related to the arbitration award or the arbitration process unless the other party and its counsel concurs with the form of contact or communication and its contents or is present at the time of the communication or contact;

3) unless there is mutual consent in writing of the parties and any counsel that assisted the parties at the arbitration, and notwithstanding any statute or rule of agreed-upon procedure, the parties shall not request the arbitral tribunal to explain any matter after the award has been delivered;

4) grounds for appeal or review shall be restricted to the award, documents or exhibits filed or made part of the arbitration proceeding and any record of the proceedings but such record may not be supplemented, once the award has been rendered,[11] by any letters, recollections, notes or testimony of the arbitrator;

5) neither party may call the arbitrator as a witness in any judicial proceeding or requisition, summons or in any way utilize the arbitrator's notes, papers or memorandum, no matter how obtained, in the event the arbitrator's award becomes the subject of an appeal, review or other challenge in the courts.

---

[11] It is arguable whether even this restriction should be inserted.

CHAPTER SIX

PRELIMINARY ARBITRAL PROCEEDINGS

I. Preliminary Conferences: Setting Up the First Meetings

Setting Up the Preliminary Conference: The Tribunal's Initial Communication to Counsel

by Tom Arnold[*]

Arbitrators have shown great interest in the tools they can use to manage the preliminary administrative conference, including letters outlining the topics to be discussed. This article provides a sample of a letter to use to organize the preliminary conference might be of interest to others.

In all arbitrations there must be an initial communication to counsel after the tribunal is constituted. In modest cases that initial communication is usually handled by a telephone conference call from the tribunal to counsel. This first telephone conference call may itself become the preliminary administrative conference. More commonly the initial communication is either a letter or call from the tribunal or the administering agency setting the time and date for an early preliminary administrative conference.

The preliminary conference is most economically conducted by telephone conference in the run-of-the-mill arbitration—indeed in the vast majority of arbitrations. But many major cases are better served with an in-person meeting.

Everybody should prepare for the preliminary conference. In the large case a lot can be done even before the conference takes place.

To facilitate this preparation, an outline of the topics to be discussed should be placed in everyone's hands before the conference call or in-person meeting. I use a form letter as my outline for the first conference

---

[*] The author is of counsel to Howrey, Simon, Arnold & White in Houston, Texas, having founded Arnold White & Durkee. Arnold holds a BSEE and JD from the University of Texas, both with honors. He is the recipient of a Life Membership in the Licensing Executives Society.

call in many arbitrations. In other cases, I send this letter, after appropriate modification for the particular case, to the parties' counsel concurrently with the call setting the date and time for the full preliminary administrative conference. I find that this letter, which has recently been revised to reflect my present thinking on many arbitration issues, sets the tone for a more productive conference and reduces unfair surprise later in the arbitration proceeding.

In ICC cases, where the initial step is preparation of the "terms of reference," the opening communications between the tribunal and counsel are different in detail from those discussed above. But the pursuit of the terms of reference can nevertheless be interleaved with what I coach in this article.

Any letter from the tribunal about the preliminary conference should be designed to serve these purposes:

- render the preliminary administrative conference most productive by giving counsel notice of all the issues the tribunal expects to raise at the conference, and time to prepare;

- reduce surprise all along the way in the arbitration process. There is much variation from arbitration to arbitration, and often counsel are relatively inexperienced (i.e., this is their first or second arbitration) and don't know what to expect or where any of the booby traps are. So they need help in identifying areas of possible surprise;

- get the arbitration process moving by putting counsel in touch with each other about the discovery they think they need and can stipulate to; and

- provide enough background to the tribunal about the issues in the case so that it will be prepared to conduct the preliminary conference efficiently, and cover all the necessary points without any omissions.

The following form letter undertakes to serve these purposes. Commentary appears in brackets.

—— Form Letter ——
Addressee
Re: [case style, number]
Dear Parties:

PRELIMINARY ARBITRAL PROCEEDINGS

This letter is to confirm your participation in a preliminary administrative conference by telephone conference call now planned for ____ 20__ at ___ Eastern Standard time.

Counsel are instructed in the interim before that conference, knowing the limitations on discovery in arbitration, to discuss their views on discovery thoroughly, and seek to reach a stipulation on (1) the exchange of limited information and any required discovery, and (2) a tight discovery schedule. The tribunal is not bound by any such stipulation, but of course it will give favorable consideration to the parties' stipulation and perhaps will be influenced by it.

Please be advised that "litigation" over discovery matters is intensely to be avoided. Intensely to be avoided! The parties and their counsel are each instructed that there shall be no "litigation" and no "sandbagging" over the scope of discovery relating to things within the scope of this directive; the parties and their counsel are each instructed to cooperate in good faith to effectuate completion of the exchanges of documents and information herein directed or otherwise appropriate to the fair and informed resolution of the dispute, in the most cost-effective way. "Sandbagging" and other disingenuous conduct will beget awards of attorneys' fees.

Except insofar as there may be claims of privilege, each party shall produce to the other in the earliest exchange they can arrange, normally within 20 days of this directive, a true and complete, fully legible copy (including legible marginalia) of:

(a) all documents the party is likely to rely upon at any stage of this proceeding,

(b) all documents in the party's control that appear to support the position of any other party, and

(c) all documents in the party's control that are inconsistent with or adverse to any position the party is likely to take at any stage of this proceeding.

The discovery of (b) and (c) is required as a matter of common ethics; of course you would not want to advocate a position inconsistent with documents you know about or have in your control without producing a copy to your adversary. Of course you would not deny a fellow party a fair hearing on the real evidence or facts by withholding a document that would aid its case.

[This has been a part of English practice as a matter of ethics almost forever, and has recently been explicitly adapted into English court rules.]

As to any document subject to a claim of privilege which the parties cannot themselves resolve by prompt attention to the issue, the party asserting the privilege shall timely file with the tribunal (and the arbitration administering agency, if there is one) a list reciting the character of the document (e.g., letter, report, invoice, etc.), the topics/subjects of the document, any and all dates on the documents, the names of all authors and addressees and recipients (including incidental persons receiving copies who are not shown as addressees), and the job or role of all such persons that makes the communication appropriate for a claim of privilege. If this list is too long and burdensome to prepare so as to make the listing highly costly, the tribunal will entertain an application by a party suggesting a potentially more cost- effective procedure.

[Be advised that in many foreign countries, house counsel enjoy no privilege at all; in many countries, patent solicitors enjoy no privilege, etc.]

A number of topics will be discussed at the preliminary administrative conference for which you should be prepared, consistent with the following:

Subject to the practice of any agency administering the arbitration, all official arbitration process papers (motions, applications, briefs, responses, but not including evidentiary papers), shall be timely served upon the administering agency and also upon the tribunal members. Submission by e-mail and/or fax as well as regular mail is deemed acceptable.

Effective at least 10 calendar days prior to the preliminary administrative conference, each party shall have delivered to the tribunal and other parties:

Party positions, contentions. An outline of your contentions and positions and of your adversary's contentions and positions, as you perceive them to be, in not more than two pages total.

Interested parties. A list of the identity of unnamed parties with an interest in this case, and any affiliated, related, predecessor-or-successor-in-interest entities.

Knowledgeable persons. The names and addresses of the persons most knowledgeable about each significant issue in the case, and their relationship to each such issue.

Uncontested facts. In both hard copy and floppy disc forms, a list of facts you perceive to be uncontested or uncontestable. Leave as much space after each fact as the recitation takes plus three lines left blank, so the other party(ies) can fill into the blanks its (their) agreement, perhaps in revised language, or its (their) reasons for not agreeing, and the other party(ies) shall deliver those supplemented documents to the tribunal members and other parties at least two working days prior to the conference.

> *[Getting a stipulated recitation of uncontested facts often takes lots of conference time between lawyers. This mechanism is usually quicker, even though a little duplicitous, and it gets the essential job done without counsel having to find time for coordinated effort and negotiation of language disagreements.]*

Document exchanges. A list of information/documents already exchanged (let's get with it and exchange now what you can); a list of documents agreed to be produced and when; a list of document requests not agreed to, perhaps by category where appropriate; and an agreed schedule, if any, for future exchange of documents or information, including reports from experts.

Stipulated depositions, if really needed. When the parties can agree to take only one or two depositions per side (in a complex case, two or three) that will each take not more than four uninterrupted hours without objections (in a complex case, eight or 10 such hours), they are instructed to file a stipulated deposition schedule 10 days prior to the conference. Absent such a stipulation the parties each shall deliver to their adversary(ies) and the tribunal members, not less than 10 working days prior to the conference, its proposal for a complete all-party deposition program relating at least primarily to witnesses not available to testify at an evidentiary hearing. Witnesses who are available to be called and to testify at the evidentiary hearing shall normally testify only once, at an evidentiary hearing, not in deposition and at a hearing.

> *[Discovery is highly limited in arbitration to achieve cost control. It is rare to depose a witness who can testify at the evidentiary hearing. There is only one argument which if*

credible, is sure to get discovery in arbitration: That the information sought is necessary to ensure the party's due process rights and to guarantee a fair hearing. Other makeweight arguments include: (1) The information sought is very likely, or almost certain, to lead to the discovery of significant, admissible, relevant evidence; (2) Granting the request for discovery will help avoid surprise at the evidentiary hearing; (3) Granting the discovery request will serve to expedite the hearing.

When necessary with respect to a key witness, upon appropriate application by a party, the tribunal may hold evidentiary hearing sessions in a location where the witness may be subpoenaed.]

Expert witness reports. Unless a contrary request is granted, there will be no neutral expert. All party expert witness reports shall include not just an indication of the subjects to be discussed, but the complete sworn direct testimony of the expert, written by that expert, not by counsel. Unless a contrary request is granted, such reports shall be delivered to the other party(ies) and the tribunal members not less than 20 days prior to the relevant evidentiary hearing (or preferably before that time, as agreed by counsel).

Witness lists. Unless a party's contrary request is granted, a list of likely witnesses, together with the subjects of their testimony and their complete resumes showing the background that makes the witnesses relevant, shall be exchanged within 30 days after the preliminary conference. A final list of witnesses and complete biographies indicating the background that makes them relevant as witnesses, shall be exchanged 10 working days before the evidentiary hearing.

Exhibit numbering, submission. Unless a party's contrary request is granted, the complainant's exhibits shall be duplicated for all parties, the tribunal members, and the witness, and, so far as feasible, placed in three-ring loose leaf notebooks of essentially black, brown and/or gray color. The respondent's exhibits shall be similarly duplicated and placed in notebooks of white and/or pastel color. If there should be more respondents, their exhibits shall be similarly duplicated and placed in books of other colors. Photographs of physical exhibits shall be included to the extent feasible. All exhibits shall be exchanged (delivered, not merely mailed) and filed with the tribunal members at least 10 working days before the evidentiary hearing or earlier as the parties may agree.

PRELIMINARY ARBITRAL PROCEEDINGS

[I never complain if counsel does not follow the color-coding suggestion; but when they do, it really is helpful and sometimes saves a lot of arbitrator time.]

Briefing schedule. An agreed briefing schedule, before and after the evidentiary hearing, if any, is welcome. Unless otherwise requested, the parties shall brief the case and deliver their briefs to the tribunal members and the other parties not less than five working days prior to the evidentiary hearing. There shall be no post-hearing briefs—though this point is routinely reconsidered at the close of evidence.

Preparation and hearing time, dates. Each party shall furnish its proposed hearing dates and an estimate of the actual hearing time that will be required, the number of exhibits each party proposes to introduce, and the dates the party is available for the evidentiary hearing. The parties are requested to consider allocating a modestly large amount of hearing time to each party, to be timed on a chess clock, each party to be held to its allotted time.

[Of course in the majority of cases the evidence is concluded roughly within counsel's time estimates so the chess clock's role is mooted. But there was a case in which the hearing was estimated by counsel to take 10 days yet it exploded into 355 hearing days. There have been many other marathon arbitrations that counsel did not anticipate. The chess clock limit to some reasonable, if somewhat long, period of time is very important to cost and time control in such cases, especially if the problem descends from bad faith delay through the volume of evidence offered by a party.]

Other issues to be discussed, or about which counsel should be advised:

Transcript. Whether there shall be a transcript or daily copy; who will pay for it; who will have access to it and when.

Transcript index. Whether there will be a transcript indexed by key word and subject matter. A long transcript that is not indexed ends up helping very little. It costs large amounts of time while the arbitrator hunts for particular testimony. If there is to be a transcript, let it be indexed and timely filed.

Form and limits of award. Whether the award will be supported by reasons. Be advised that unless the parties agree otherwise, a reasoned award shall be constrained to five pages so as to save time and money on an award not normally subject to appellate review.

Interpreters. Whether there shall be interpreters, and who will pay for them.

Mediation. Whether the case is appropriate for mediation. Is this a case in which a "black or white" award is relatively inappropriate, compared with a mediation, for example, of a contract issue that the parties forgot to negotiate at contract drafting time? Mediation is not to be forced, but it should always be favorably considered at the beginning of any dispute resolution discussions.

Witness statements. Whether the direct testimony of any or all witnesses shall be submitted via sworn witness statements, and whether counsel will orally summarize this direct testimony at the evidentiary hearing, followed by cross-examination of the witness. The tribunal will read the entire witness statement in any event.

Evidence order. Is there something in this case to suggest that evidence should be received topic by topic to the degree possible, rather than witness by witness.

Pursuit of bases for informed judgment. While the parties carry the burden of proof with respect to the applicable law, the tribunal may feel, to some degree, a duty itself to elicit facts necessary to make an informed judgment, rather than passively decide that a party did not carry its burden of proof.

Who cross-examines. Unlike the practice in some foreign and international arbitrations, counsel will be afforded an opportunity to cross-examine, as is usual in Anglo-American practice. Members of the tribunal will also be free to cross-examine witnesses.

Authenticity of documents. Subject to a contrary request that is granted, and except for documents that a party has objected to within seven working days of receipt from another party, or in response to live testimony during the evidentiary hearing without prior reason to object, the authenticity of documents will be assumed to be vouched for by the counsel who presents them, and these documents will be received without any further authentication. (Obviously, in large complex cases involving many exhibits, the parties may ask for more than seven days to object.)

Affidavit and hearsay evidence. This evidence is admissible. But do not be deceived into thinking that such evidence is inherently credible. On important disputed issues be sure to provide "cross-examinable" corroborative or nonhearsay evidence so as to improve the credibility of evidence that otherwise might seem incredible to the tribunal even if not controverted.

Evidence exclusion. The tribunal has authority to refuse to hear redundant evidence, evidence whose prejudicial effect outweighs its probative value, and the like. The tribunal will exercise that authority as it deems appropriate.

Cost effectiveness. Cost effectiveness is a guide in evidence rulings and elsewhere in arbitration. For the most part, U.S. trial counsel over-try their cases. Let's work hard to edit this case properly.

Communications with tribunal members. There will be no *ex parte* communications between any arbitrator and any party or counsel except where necessary to the process. For example, when the adversary is unavailable to be joined in a conference call, a call to undertake to schedule a hearing for preliminary relief may, on occasion, be initiated *ex parte*, though, of course, the whole of any *ex parte* communication must be timely reported in detail to the other parties.

Confidentiality. While an arbitration hearing is held in private, the law commanding confidential treatment of evidence or of the existence of the arbitration or of the nature of the process and how the arbitration is being conducted, is highly unreliable, except perhaps in England and Sweden (as of 1999). If the parties want confidential treatment, they should contract for it. Meanwhile, subject to any different contract by the parties, the tribunal directs that information disclosed in this arbitration shall be used by the parties and witnesses only for the purposes of this arbitration and for no other purpose, and all objects, documents and copies thereof, presented by a party shall be returned to that party upon conclusion of the arbitration. Counsel shall ensure that parties, counsel, witnesses, court reporters, and other relevant persons are so advised and agree to be bound by this directive. If anybody does not so agree, the tribunal must be so advised.

Other issues. Any issues which you as a party wish to have discussed or resolved.

The tribunal looks forward to the preliminary conference, in which counsel should be prepared on all the topics mentioned above.

II. Discovery

Discovery in Arbitration: How Much Is Enough?

by Alfred G. Feliu[*]

The use of discovery in arbitration may feel a bit like wearing a well-tailored business suit at the beach—the suit fits, but you are uncomfortable nonetheless. Some might argue that the very concept of discovery in arbitration is an oxymoron, since discovery—that costly, time-consuming pre-trial search for truth—is, in almost all instances, inconsistent with arbitration's well-known goals of resolving disputes expeditiously and inexpensively.

It is no surprise that few well-clad litigators are comfortable on the beach of arbitration. The increased use of arbitration to resolve employment discrimination claims, spurred on by the U.S. Supreme Court's decision in *Gilmer v. Interstate/Johnson Lane Corp.*, 500 U.S. 20 (1991), and progeny, has brought to the forefront the tension between a litigator's expectation of full discovery and arbitration's twin goals of providing for a speedy, cost-effective resolution of disputes. No formal rules have been established to govern discovery in the arbitration context. As expressly stated in Rule 7 of the National Rules for the Resolution of Employment Disputes of the American Arbitration Association, the arbitrator has the authority to order the discovery he or she "considers necessary to a full and fair exploration of the issues in dispute consistent with the expedited nature of arbitration."

As an arbitrator serving on the AAA's employment disputes panel, I have struggled with the question of how an arbitrator is to balance the parties' need—and right—to discover information and documents "necessary to a full and fair exploration of the issues in dispute," against the aims of arbitration. How much discovery is enough in any particular arbitration? Carrying the opening metaphor forward, how do you turn the

---

[*] Mr. Feliu is a partner at Vandenberg & Feliu in New York. He serves on the American Arbitration Association's National Employment Disputes Resolution Panel. He is also a member of the editorial board of ADR Currents. Feliu received a BA and JD from Columbia University. He is editor-in-chief of NEW YORK EMPLOYMENT LAW & PRACTICE, published monthly by American Lawyer Media and has authored or co-authored three books and numerous articles and papers.

litigator's business suit into beachwear suitable for the arbitration setting?

Two basic inquiries must be made by an arbitrator when determining whether discovery is to be ordered in an arbitration. First, should the requested discovery be authorized? Second, if so, what is the proper scope of the discovery order? This article discusses my approach to these important questions.

FRCP as a Frame of Reference

The subject of discovery in arbitration cannot be discussed without reference to the discovery rules (Rules 26 to 37) in the Federal Rules of Civil Procedure (sometimes referred to as the Federal Rules or FRCP). The basic premise underlying federal discovery is offered in Rule 26(b)(1): "Parties may obtain discovery regarding any matter, not privileged, which is relevant to the subject matter involved in the pending action....The information sought need not be admissible at the trial if the information sought appears reasonably calculated to lead to the discovery of admissible evidence."

Rule 26(b)(2) offers grounds upon which a court may limit discovery, such as when the discovery requested is "unreasonably cumulative or duplicative, or is obtainable from some other source that is more convenient, less burdensome, or less expensive," or when "the burden or expense of the proposed discovery outweighs its likely benefit, taking into account the needs of the case, the amount in controversy, the parties' resources, the importance of the issues at stake in the litigation, and the importance of the proposed discovery in resolving the issues." A judge, upon motion by the parties or upon his or her initiative may issue a protective order under Rule 26(c) protecting a "party or person from annoyance, embarrassment, oppression, or undue burden or expense...." Under Rule 26(c), a court may limit the scope or nature of the discovery being demanded, may determine the terms and conditions under which discovery will be had, or may deny a parties' request for discovery in whole or in part.

Most litigators would agree that the Federal Rules work well in the litigation context. Yet few would argue that rules designed for use in a judicial proceeding should strictly apply to the arbitration setting. The AAA's national employment rules confirm the consensus view that the procedures to be followed in arbitration are those best suited to that process and not those employed in the litigation setting. For example,

Rule 22 of these rules expressly provides that with respect to evidentiary issues "conformity to legal rules of evidence shall not be necessary."

But the fact that litigation rules of procedure and evidence are not required to be followed does not compel the conclusion that they must be ignored. The wisdom and experience embodied in these rules have served and will continue to serve both to inform and order arbitration proceedings. The question is—what rules and what settings?

Now, more than ever, arbitrators are deciding statutory claims in which claimants are required to meet statutorily or judicially established burdens of proof. Claimants must be provided with the means to meet their burden, particularly when a pre-dispute mandatory arbitration program compels them to adjudicate their claims in an arbitral—rather than a judicial—forum.

Any attempt to reach the appropriate balance of discovery must first address the key principle underlying the Federal Rules, namely, the notion that anything "relevant" or which may lead to the discovery of admissible evidence is discoverable. Yet this core principle cannot be transplanted intact to the arbitration setting without violating the core arbitration principles of speedy resolution and cost effectiveness. In contrast to litigation, there is no entitlement to discovery in arbitration. A need for the discovery must be shown.

Guiding Principles for Determining Discovery Issues

In determining what is "necessary to a full and fair exploration of the issues in dispute, consistent with the expedited nature of arbitration," I ask the following four questions:

- Is the information sought likely to lead to the discovery of admissible or relevant evidence?
- Will granting the request for discovery help avoid surprise at the hearing?
- Will granting the discovery request serve to expedite the hearing?
- Is the information sought necessary to ensure the parties' due process rights and to guarantee a fair hearing?

In framing the first question—Is the information sought likely to lead to the discovery of admissible or relevant evidence?—I rejected the standard set forth in Rule 26(b)(1) of the Federal Rules as being too broad and unworkable in the arbitration context. That standard calls for the information sought to be "reasonably calculated to lead to the discovery of admissible evidence." Instead, I opted for requiring the information sought to be "reasonably likely" to lead to the discovery of admissible or relevant evidence. This standard does not require to a certitude that admissible evidence will be discovered, but it does require a reasonable likelihood that this will result.

Another way of approaching this inquiry is to ask whether the discovery request is directed at obtaining evidence necessary to establish and support a claim made or defense raised or likely to be raised by the parties. This standard forces the party propounding the discovery request to provide a reasoned basis for believing that information or documents relevant to the arbitration will, in fact, be discovered, and avoids "fishing expeditions" by lazy or unfocused counsel.

The second question—Will granting the request for discovery help avoid surprise at the hearing?—addresses the potential for unfair surprise at the hearing due to the lack of detailed pleadings in arbitration. A demand for arbitration need contain only a brief statement of the nature of the dispute, the amount in controversy, and the remedy sought. Similarly, the respondent need only provide a "brief response to the claim and the issues presented," as well as to any counterclaim raised.

Take the case of a claimant's sexual harassment claim to which the respondent has raised as an affirmative defense that the claimant unreasonably failed to take advantage of any preventative or corrective opportunities provided by the respondent. At the hearing, the claimant reveals for the first time that she did raise her harassment claim with a manager in another department. In this circumstance, the respondent would have cause to claim surprise and could be expected to seek an adjournment of the hearing.

Adequate discovery is necessary to prevent the need to delay or adjourn the hearing due to the belated identification or unearthing of key facts, witnesses, claims or defenses at the hearing itself. Consequently, I am likely to look favorably on any discovery request reasonably aimed at avoiding surprise at the hearing.

The third question—Will the granting of discovery serve to expedite the hearing?—is concerned with moving the arbitration forward. An appropriate dose of discovery could have the following effects, all of which will serve to expedite the hearing; it could (a) eliminate the need to call unnecessary or unhelpful witnesses; (b) focus the testimony of those witnesses who will be called at the hearing; (c) clarify and focus the issues to be addressed at the hearing; (d) dispose of theories, claims, and defenses not supported by the facts; and (e) permit parties to gather facts and information necessary to make and support pre-hearing dispositive motions. Discovery requests with one or more of these goals in mind are more likely to be approved.

The last question—Is the discovery requested necessary to ensure the parties' due process rights and to guarantee a fair hearing?—is concerned with the issue of fairness in the arbitration context. An arbitration hearing, like any adjudicative proceeding in which legal rights are determined, must comport with basic due process principles. Due process principles are embodied in the Due Process Protocol for Mediation and Arbitration of Statutory Disputes Arising Out of the Employment Relationship, which was developed in 1995 by a special task force which included the AAA as well as individuals representing such diverse interests as civil rights organizations, government agencies, and the plaintiffs' and management bars. The AAA has endorsed the Due Process Protocol and will administer only those employment-related arbitrations that comply with it.

The obligation to provide due process rests with the arbitrator throughout the arbitration process. Although reasonable minds may differ on this question, I will authorize, within limits, the discovery necessary to level the playing field to ensure that the claims presented to me are fully and fairly raised and adjudicated. This assures that the parties have the benefit of a fair process.

How Much Discovery Is Enough?

Deciding that a particular discovery request or type of discovery is warranted leads to the question of the proper scope of such discovery.

When a discovery issue is raised by the parties, I generally ask the party making the discovery request to: (a) identify with reasonable particularity the discovery that is being sought; (b) clarify any ambiguous or potentially burdensome discovery request with a focus on how the information or documents being sought will help that party further its case; and (c) refine or narrow the discovery request in question to accomplish that party's goals in the most efficient and cost-effective way possible.

It may be, for example, that although the information being sought is relevant, the discovery method proposed is not the most efficient one available to the parties. Take the case of a claimant in a pay dispute who wants to discover the compensation of comparable employees. To obtain this information the claimant notices the deposition of a member of the respondent's management. The respondent objects. In this situation, the information sought might be obtained more quickly and efficiently by other, less burdensome and less costly means which the arbitrator might explore with the parties. Perhaps, as a result of these discussions, the respondent might decide to provide the relevant information in a computer printout of the payroll, with appropriate redactions, in order to avoid the deposition of its manager.

In general, if requested, I will authorize the deposition of the claimant and at least one of the respondent's key witnesses (e.g., the decision maker in a termination case), and additional depositions where a demonstrable need is shown. I am also likely to authorize the production of documents in response to a reasoned and well-framed document request. I will also generally encourage the parties to stipulate to as many facts as they can. I generally will discourage parties from using interrogatories except to gather very focused information for which testimony will not be required.

I am also receptive to requests to confine the scope of discovery, for example, by limiting: the number of depositions; the time to be spent with each deponent; the number of interrogatories (if any); and the number of document requests. In addition, I will set an early discovery deadline, usually within the 30- to 90-day time frame (depending on the complexity of the issues to be heard), if the parties cannot agree on their own to a reasonable discovery cutoff date.

I generally follow the magistrate judge model of managing discovery by making myself available to address discovery disputes, for example, to render rulings during depositions. I will also conduct additional management or discovery conferences, if needed, after the initial management conference, and will permit the parties to make motions—whether in person, by telephone, or in writing—to compel or for a protective order, if more informal efforts to resolve the dispute have failed.

Conclusion

One principle overrides all others when addressing the question of discovery in arbitration proceedings, particularly where statutory or common law claims are at issue. The parties have selected an alternative, not lesser, forum for the adjudication of their legal dispute. Discovery should be viewed as merely a means to the larger end of providing a just forum for the resolution of the legal issues posed, a forum in which due process is assured and the resolution is fair, efficient and cost effective. The scope of the discovery to be ordered is that necessary to achieve this goal.

III. The Power to Subpoena Third Parties for Prehearing Discovery

Arbitral Subpoena Powers and Prehearing Discovery
by Paul M. Lurie[*]

Whether arbitrators have the power to issue enforceable subpoenas to third parties to obtain prehearing discovery can have enormous practical significance for parties to arbitration.[1] Two recent federal appellate cases discussed below illustrate the difficulty in obtaining this type of discovery under the U.S. Arbitration Act, often referred to as the Federal Arbitration Act.

The authority to issue subpoenas under the FAA is set forth in §7, which states:

> "[A]rbitrators...may summon in writing any person to attend before them as a witness and in a proper case to bring with him or them any book, record, document, or paper which may be deemed material...." In *COMSAT Corp. v. National Science Foundation*,[2] the 4th Circuit recently held that arbitrators do not have the power under §7 to subpoena nonparty witnesses to appear for prehearing depositions.

In *COMSAT*, an arbitrator issued a subpoena requiring the National Science Foundation, a nonparty, to produce documents and employee testimony relating to a construction contract between COMSAT and a project in which NSF was involved. The district court affirmed the issuance of the subpoenas. The Fourth Circuit reversed on the ground that §7 did not authorize arbitral subpoenas for prehearing discovery. However, it also suggested that third-party discovery may be justified if

---

[*] The author is the senior member of the Construction Law Group at Chicago's Schiff Hardin & Waite. He serves on the AAA's National Construction Dispute Resolution Committee and is a Fellow of the American College of Construction Lawyers. Lurie earned a B.A. and J.D. from the University of Michigan. The author wishes to acknowledge the valuable assistance of Annaliese Flynn Fleming in preparing this article.

[1] For a previous treatment of this topic, see Samuel Koda, *Subpoena Issues in Arbitration*, 2 ADR CURRENTS 20 (Spring 1997).

[2] 1999 WL 638609 (4th Cir.) (citations omitted).

the record established a special need or hardship for the subpoenaed materials.[3]

Section 7 might be viewed as the underlying basis for the Second Circuit's similar rejection of subpoena power for prehearing discovery in *National Broadcasting Co. v. Bear Stearns & Co.*[4] This case involved a foreign arbitration in which subpoenas had been issued by a district court prior to the appointment of the arbitrator under International Chamber of Commerce Rules. After the subpoenas were served, the resisting third parties moved to quash. A different district court granted their motion. The Second Circuit affirmed.

In order to avoid the apparent limits of §7, the party seeking to obtain the subpoenas argued that 28 U.S.C. §1782 gave an independent basis for enforcement of the subpoenas. But the 2d Circuit held that an international, but private arbitration was not a "foreign or international tribunal" within the meaning of §1782, leaving the district court without authority to assist discovery in aid of a foreign arbitration, as would otherwise be permitted if §1782 were applicable. The Second Circuit also summarized the limitations of FAA §7 in allowing third-party discovery.

The court stated:

> First, § 7 explicitly confers authority only upon arbitrators; by necessary implication, the parties to an arbitration may not employ this provision to subpoena documents or witnesses. Second, § 7 explicitly confers enforcement authority only upon the "district court for the district in which such arbitrators, or a majority of them, are sitting." Third, the express language of § 7 refers only to testimony before the arbitrators and to material physical evidence, such as books and documents, brought before them by a witness... (citations omitted)

The court acknowledged that "open questions remain as to whether § 7 may be invoked as authority for compelling prehearing depositions and prehearing document discovery, especially where such evidence is sought from nonparties," citing two district court cases that permitted

---

[3] The court said: "[I]n *Burton v. Bush*, 614 F.2d 389, 390 (4th Cir.1980) we contemplated that a party might, under unusual circumstances, petition the district court to compel pre-arbitration discovery upon a showing of special need or hardship.
[4] 165 F.3d 184 (2d Cir. 1999).

this type of discovery and two that opposed it.[5] Although the Second Circuit's holding in the case expressly determines only the reach of § 1782, its denial of the third-party subpoenas for prehearing discovery, after a discussion of the methods for obtaining discovery under § 7, indicates that this section was an unstated basis for its conclusion.[6]

What strategies might a party employ to obtain document discovery from a third party or take its depositions prior to the hearing, in cases governed by the FAA? *COMSAT* provides a possible approach. It left the door open for this type of discovery if "special need or hardship" could be shown. The Fourth Circuit did not define the contours of this exception except to say that, "at a minimum, a party must demonstrate that the information it seeks is otherwise unavailable." If a party believes that it would not be able to satisfy the "special need or hardship" exception or that the court would not recognize that exception, a party could try to persuade the arbitrator to hold a special "hearing" solely for the purpose of receiving documentary evidence from third parties. This approach, however, has never been tested in a reported decision.

State Law Considerations

Section 7(a) of the Uniform Arbitration Act arguably may allow for the production of documents by subpoena without the FAA's requirement that they have to be produced by a witness at a hearing. It provides: "The arbitrators may issue...subpoenas for the attendance of witnesses and for the production of books, records, documents and other evidence...." At least two states have modified their UAA-based arbitration laws to allow prehearing third-party discovery.[7] Thus, parties proceeding under some state arbitration laws may find it easier to obtain prehearing discovery from nonparties.

---

[5] The court cited *Stanton v. Paine Webber Jackson & Curtis, Inc.*, 685 F. Supp. 1241, 1242-43 (S.D. Fla. 1988) (§ 7 permits prehearing document production from nonparties) and *Meadows Indem. Co. v. Nutmeg Ins. Co.*, 157 F.R.D. 42, 45 (M.D. Tenn. 1994) (§ 7 power to compel document production from third parties at hearing encompasses lesser power to compel production prior to hearing). It compared these cases with Integrity Ins. Co. v. American Centennial Ins. Co., 885 F. Supp. 69, 72-73 (S.D.N.Y. 1995) (arbitrator may not rely on § 7 to obtain prehearing depositions from nonparties).

[6] The 2d Circuit concluded: "If the broader evidence gathering mechanisms provided for in § 1782 were applicable to proceedings before...private arbitral panels, we would need to decide whether § 7 is exclusive, in which cases the two statutes would conflict."

[7] *See* KAN. STAT. ANN. § 5-407; Mass. Gen. Laws ch. 251, § 7(e); Cal. Civ. Proc. Code § 1283.05(d); TEX. CIV. PRAC. & REM. CODE ANN. § 171.007(b); UTAH CODE ANN. § 78-31a-8.

One state case allowing an arbitral subpoena of third-party documents prior to the hearing is *State ex rel. South Western Communications v. Board of County Commissioners*,[8] an officially unreported Ohio decision. In this case, the trial court issued a writ of mandamus ordering a government agency to produce public records concerning a construction contract. In affirming the writ, the appellate court found authority for the issuance of subpoenas for the purpose of third-party discovery in the arbitration rules of the American Arbitration Association. The court concluded that under AAA rules, "discovery falls properly within the ambit of the arbitrators' authority and not within the jurisdiction of the courts."

AAA Rules

Parties interested in obtaining third-party discovery should be aware of the provisions governing discovery in the current AAA rules, as revised and in effect on Jan. 1, 1999. There are differences, albeit slight ones, in the language of the various rules, which could possibly affect the ease with which this type of discovery could be obtained.

Rule L-5, applicable to both large commercial cases and large construction cases, provides in relevant part: "The arbitrators upon good cause shown, and consistent with the expedited nature of arbitration, may order the conduct of the deposition of, or the propounding of interrogatories to, such persons who may possess information determined by the arbitrators to be necessary to a determination of a Large, Complex Construction [Commercial] Case."

Rule 10 of the regular construction rules provides: "Consistent with the expedited nature of arbitration, the arbitrator may direct (i) the production of documents and other information, and (ii) the identification of any witnesses to be called...." The last sentence of this rule states: "There shall be no other discovery, except as indicated herein or as ordered by the arbitrator in extraordinary cases when the demands of justice require it."

Rule 23(a) of the regular commercial rules provides: "At the request of any party or at the discretion of the arbitrator, consistent with the expedited nature of arbitration, the arbitrator may direct (i) the

---

[8] 1996 WL 586770 (Ohio Ct. App. 11th Dist.). The Ohio court also cited as authority the *Stanton* case, *supra*, n. 5, and *Mississippi Power Co. v. Peabody Coal Co.*, 69 F.R.D. 558, 565-567 (S.D. Miss. 1976); *Balfour, Guthrie & Co., Ltd. v. Commercial Metals Co.*, 93 Wash. 2d 199 (1980). *See also* Kostakos v. KSN Joint Venture No. 1, 142 Ill. App. 3d 533, 537 (Ill. Ct. App. 1st Dist. 1986).

production of documents and other information, and (ii) the identification of any witnesses to be called." This provision lacks the last sentence of Rule 10, which is quoted above.

Thus, it would seem that when the AAA's large, complex case rules apply, arbitrators have, under L-5, broader power with respect to prehearing and third-party discovery, since the rule expressly authorizes depositions and interrogatories of persons with information that may be necessary to the dispute.[9] This express authority is lacking under the regular commercial and construction rules.

As between the regular construction rules and the regular commercial rules, the differences in language between R-10 and R-23 suggest that it may be easier to obtain third-party discovery under the commercial rules. This is because it may be necessary to show under R-10 of the construction rules that the case is an "extraordinary" one or that "the demands of justice require" such discovery. Such a showing would not appear to be necessary under R-23 of the commercial rules. Thus, a commercial party may have a lower burden to meet in order to obtain a third-party subpoena.

---

[9] The AAA's large, complex case rules can be made applicable by agreement, regardless of the size of the claim.

IV. Procedural and Interim Orders

The Arbitrator's Power to Issue: Procedural and Interim Orders

*by Donald Francis Donovan**

Arbitral procedures, like their court counterparts, are the nuts and bolts of dispute resolution. If in their final deliberations the arbitrators are able to craft a just award based on the law and facts adduced before them, it will only be because the arbitral procedures they and the parties adopted allowed the relevant law and facts to be adequately developed. And, needless to say, the award will be effective only if the arbitrators have been able to enter such orders as might have been necessary to preserve the subject matter of the dispute for their eventual resolution. Out of the twin objectives of fairness and effectiveness arise the powers of an arbitral tribunal to issue procedural orders and orders of interim measures, as well as the corresponding obligation of the parties to abide by them. This article will consider the sources and scope of the arbitrators' authority to issue such orders.

Sources of Authority

There are three sources of authority for arbitrators to issue procedural orders: the parties' agreement, the curial law, and inherent authority.

The Parties' Agreement. The primary source of the authority to issue procedural orders is the parties' agreement to arbitrate. Whether the agreement is between states, between states and private parties, or between private parties, it is fundamental that arbitration is a matter of consent.

---

* The author is a partner in the firm of Debevoise & Plimpton in New York and teaches international arbitration at New York University School of Law. Donovan holds a B.A. from the University of Virginia and a J.D. from Stanford Law School. He is the author of *The Scope and Enforceability of Provisional Measures in International Commercial Arbitration,* INTERNATIONAL COMMERCIAL ARBITRATION: CONTEMPORARY QUESTIONS 82-129 (ICCA Congress Series 2003). Mr. Donovan thanks his colleagues Sally Fitzgerald and John Driscoll for their assistance in preparing this article.

It follows from the consensual character of arbitration that the arbitrators' powers must be determined, in the first instance, by the specific terms of the arbitration agreement. In major international transactions, the parties will generally agree to either institutional or ad hoc arbitration pursuant to an established set of rules, such as those promulgated by the American Arbitration Association, the International Chamber of Commerce, or the International Centre for Settlement of Investment Disputes. They might then adapt their agreement to the specific circumstances by either derogating from—or adding to—the chosen rules.

Each of the principal sets of arbitration rules sets forth the tandem objectives of fairness and effectiveness and then lays down particular rules applicable in the event that the parties do not specify otherwise.[1]

The Curial Law. In many cases, the parties' agreement to arbitrate suffices to govern all aspects of the proceedings. It is also possible, however, that the law of the place of arbitration will act either to override some aspect of that agreement[2] or supplement it.[3] The new English arbitration statute apparently does both, in one sweep, by imposing a nonderogable duty on the arbitrators to "adopt procedures suitable to the circumstances of the particular case, avoiding unnecessary delay or expense, so as to provide a fair means for the resolution of the matters falling to be determined."[4]

The right to designate the place of arbitration (the curial law)—and hence the law governing the proceeding—is a fundamental component of party autonomy. Typically the place of the arbitration for purposes of determining the curial law will be the place the parties choose to physically hold the hearing, though it need not be. Of course, the curial law need not be, and often will not be, the same as the law governing the contract, or even the law governing the arbitration clause itself.

---

[1] AAA Int'l Rules, Art. 16(1); ICC Rules, Art. 15; London Court of International Arbitration Rules, Art. 14.1; ICSID Rules 19, 20(2); World Intellectual Property Organization Rules, Art. 38(a); UNCITRAL Rules, Art. 15(1).

[2] *See, e.g.,* Convention on the Recognition and Enforcement of Foreign Arbitral Awards, done on June 10, 1958, ART. V(2)(A), 21 U.S.T. 2517 (court of Contracting State may refuse to enforce an award if "the subject matter of the difference is not capable of settlement by arbitration under the law of that country").

[3] *See, e.g.,* 9 U.S.C. § 7, providing that arbitrators may "summon in writing any person to attend before them...as a witness and in a proper case to bring with him...any book, record, document, or paper...which may be deemed material as evidence in the case."

[4] English Arbitration Act 1996, § 33(1)(b).

Thus, while the parties generally must subject themselves to some municipal regime of arbitration law that will overlay their own arbitration agreement, the right to choose the place of arbitration, and hence the law governing the proceedings, allows the parties to minimize the restraints placed upon both their procedural choices and the arbitrators' procedural authority, by choosing an arbitral seat whose municipal arbitration law recognizes broad party autonomy.

Inherent Authority. Finally, it is necessary to consider the inherent, or implied, authority of an arbitral tribunal. Even in the face of a detailed agreement to arbitrate, there will always remain the possibility that an issue will arise whose resolution is not dictated by any express or incorporated provision of the agreement. The general statements of the arbitrators' authority included in many sets of arbitration rules will provide guidance, but such statements generally do no more than reiterate the arbitrators' charge to decide cases fairly and effectively.

Thus, even when a detailed clause or chosen set of rules governs, it may be necessary to resort to authority that is not expressly granted either by the agreement to arbitrate or the law governing the proceeding. The question assumes greater importance in the case of a sparer clause—"arbitration in New York," for example, or an ad hoc clause specifying no set of rules or detailed procedures. Considering the question of inherent authority in this context forces us to consider on an empty slate what inherent or implied authority an arbitrator may wield, providing guidance as to the scope of any such authority even in the case of a more detailed clause.

The issue may be considered from the perspective either of the tribunal or of the parties—that is, either as a matter of the authority that inheres in the arbitral function assigned the tribunal by the parties, or of the authority that may be implied from the parties' consent to submit their dispute for impartial resolution by independent decision makers. Surely, certain attributes of authority inhere in an arbitral tribunal's status as an organ charged to impartially resolve a dispute in accordance with law. For example, the International Court of Justice has held that it "possesses an inherent jurisdiction enabling it to take such action as may be required, on the one hand to ensure that the exercise of its jurisdiction over the merits, if and when established, shall not be frustrated, and on the other, to provide for the orderly settlement of all matters in dispute...." The I.C.J. explained that "[s]uch inherent jurisdiction...derives from the mere existence of the Court as a judicial organ established by the consent of States, and is conferred upon it in order that its basic judicial functions may be safeguarded."[5]

So too with respect to an arbitral tribunal. Once constituted, it must be presumed to carry the authority necessary to fulfill its duty to render a fair and effective award. This presumption comports with, or is simply an application of, a more general principle of institutional effectiveness.[6]

Considering the question from the standpoint of the parties' expectations should yield the same result. If inherent powers are necessary to fulfill those expectations, then the parties must be taken to have consented to the exercise of the authority necessary to fairly and effectively resolve the dispute they have submitted to the tribunal. By recognizing the tribunal's inherent authority to make procedural decisions necessary to the conduct of the proceedings, the parties simply perform in good faith their agreement to arbitrate.

The Scope of Authority

As we have seen, the content of the arbitrators' procedural authority may be defined or circumscribed by the parties' agreement or the law of the place. We here want to consider the scope of that authority in the absence of such constraints. A good place to begin is the sets of rules that, after long experience and with the input of arbitration users, have been promulgated by the principal arbitration institutions or, as in the case of the UNCITRAL Arbitration Rules and the ICSID Convention, by international organization or treaty. Identifying the common features of these representative rules may suggest a "customary procedural law" of international arbitration at least as to the scope of the procedural authority of arbitrators. In other words, the survey may suggest a common view that arbitrators must have the authority to control the receipt of evidence, even if there is no consensus on, for example, the proper role of cross-examination in the receipt of witness testimony. Thus, the survey should identify the elements of procedural authority minimally required by a tribunal to carry out its function of resolving the dispute in a fair and effective manner.

Submission of Pleadings. To control a proceeding, the arbitrators must have the authority to determine the scope, number and character of submissions. Hence, each of the representative sets of rules provides a

---

[5] Nuclear Tests (Austrl. v. Fra.) (Judgment), 1974 I.C.J. 253, 259-60 (Dec. 20).

[6] *Cf.* Reparation for Injuries Suffered in the Service of the United Nations (Advisory Op.), 1949 I.C.J. 174, 182 (Apr. 11).

basic structure regarding submissions. The Rules of the London Court of Inter-national Arbitration contain relatively detailed provisions concerning the submission of written statements and documents, which are subject to contrary agreement by the parties or order by the arbitrators.[7]

Time Periods. The arbitrators must also have the authority to determine the sequence of proceedings and their timing. Hence, while the rules generally set out time periods for written submissions aimed at achieving a speedy and effective resolution of the dispute, they also generally permit the arbitrators to extend those periods.

Document Production. For the tribunal to ensure that it is adequately informed of the relevant facts, or that each party has had access to the information necessary to ensure a fair opportunity to present its case, the tribunal must have the authority to define the universe of relevant and available information and provide for equal access to that information. The AAA International Arbitration Rules authorize arbitrators to order the production of documents when "necessary or appropriate" and the LCIA rules when "relevant." The ICC rules provide that "[a]t any time during the proceedings," the tribunal "may summon any party to provide...evidence" additional to that provided in its written submissions, and the UNCITRAL and ICSID rules contain similar provisions.[8]

Conduct of Hearings. If the right to be heard is fundamental to the arbitral process, the arbitral tribunal must have the authority to order that hearings take place; set times, venues and time limits for hearings; determine what evidence or argument should be heard; and make any other orders necessary to conduct the hearing. The representative rules reflect that authority.

Hearings Away from the Seat. The seat of the arbitration will determine the curial law. In some circumstances, however, it will be more convenient to hold some or all of the proceedings in a different location. The representative rules recognize that the hearing may be held in any location for reasons of convenience without altering the juridical seat of the arbitration.

The Language. The language of the proceeding is fundamental to the conduct of the proceeding, as the need to proceed in a disfavored language can pose a great barrier to full participation. The representative rules recognize the tribunal's authority to determine the language or

---

[7] LCIA Rules, Art. 15.
[8] AAA Int'l Rules, Art. 19(3); LCIA Rules, Art. 22.1(e); ICC Rules, Art. 20(5); UNCITRAL Rules, Art. 24(3); ICSID Rule 34(2).

languages in which the arbitration will proceed and, as a corollary, the terms of translation or interpretation.

Evidentiary Matters. The tribunal must have the authority to determine the admissibility and weight of the evidence presented in support of each party's case—an authority intrinsic to the adjudicative or decision-making function. It will be rare when the rules of evidence that might apply to judicial proceedings in a particular municipal system will be appropriate to an arbitral proceeding, but even in that rare case the tribunal would exercise the discretion necessary to apply any such evidentiary code.

Witnesses. The fact-finding function of an arbitral tribunal must encompass the terms on which the tribunal will hear witnesses and the treatment it will give their testimony. The representative rules all make provision for hearing witnesses and making related orders. The LCIA rules make explicit not only that the tribunal may order a witness to attend, but that it may draw adverse inferences from a failure to do so.[9]

Independent Experts. A tribunal may conclude that it requires independent expert advice on particular issues, usually technical or other specialized issues. Each of the representative rules, except the ICSID rules, grants the arbitrators authority to appoint an expert if the tribunal so concludes. The authority to appoint an expert should not be construed as a license to delegate the arbitrators' decision-making authority to the expert.

Absence of a Party. A party may fail to answer the request to arbitrate or the statement of claim, refuse to proceed after losing a jurisdictional challenge or to attend a hearing scheduled over its objection, or at any other point cease its participation. If an agreement to arbitrate is to have any meaning, a party's unilateral refusal to participate cannot disable the tribunal. Hence, each of the representative rules expressly authorizes the arbitrators to proceed with the arbitration, notwithstanding that party's absence, and to render an award.

To sum up, this survey suggests that to fulfill the tribunal's assigned function of rendering a fair and effective resolution of the dispute, the arbitrators must have complete authority over (1) the course and scope of the pleadings and other written submissions; (2) the provision of relevant information to the tribunal and the adverse party, whether such information is in the hands of the parties or otherwise available to the tribunal; and (3) the conduct of the hearing, in the form of both argument

---

[9] LCIA Rules, Art. 20.

and evidence. Hence, regardless of the other terms of the agreement to arbitrate, the arbitrators should have such authority unless it is expressly denied them by that agreement or the law governing the proceeding.

Interim Measures

The final and binding character of arbitration is as fundamental to the process as consent. It follows that, from the inception of the proceeding, the arbitrators must have the authority to enter such orders—conservatory measures, provisional measures, interim measures of protection, or however else characterized—as are necessary to preserve their capacity to render a fair and effective award. By definition, interim measures are provisional, but they partake of the merits in that they necessarily represent a provisional view (or definition) of the claims at issue. If such orders of interim protection are procedural, they are procedural in a different sense than an order, say, directing the production of documents or submission of prehearing briefs.

Underlying General Principle. As the Permanent Court of International Justice explained, the authority to issue provisional measures conferred by its own statute simply reflects the "principle universally accepted by international tribunals...that the parties to a case must abstain from any measure capable of exercising a prejudicial effect in regard to the execution of the decision to be given and, in general, not allow any step of any kind to be taken which might aggravate or extend the dispute."[10] The authority to order interim measures of protection so as to preserve the subject matter of the dispute, and hence the tribunal's capacity to resolve the dispute, is but a necessary component of the tribunal's authority to resolve the dispute in the first place.

This principle applies with equal force to international arbitral tribunals, which have repeatedly held that they have authority to order interim measures of protection. For example, in *E-Systems, Inc. v. Islamic Republic of Iran*, the Iran-U.S. Claims Tribunal held that it had "an inherent power to issue such orders as may be necessary to conserve the respective rights of the parties and to ensure that this tribunal's jurisdiction and authority are made fully effective."[11]

Viewed from the perspective either of the task entrusted to the tribunal or the commitment made by the parties, an agreement to submit

---

[10] Electric Co. of Sofia and Bulgaria (Belg. v. Bulg.) (Interim Measures of Protection), 1939 P.C.I.J. (Ser A/B) No. 79, 194, 199 (Dec. 5).

[11] 2 Iran-U.S. Cl. Trib. Rep. 51, 57 (1983).

a dispute to an arbitral tribunal should be read to confer the requisite authority on the tribunal to preserve the dispute for its resolution.

Rules, Statutes and Conventions. The representative rules considered here generally reflect the arbitrators' authority to order interim measures of protection. For example, the new ICC rules provide: "Unless the parties have otherwise agreed...the arbitral tribunal may, at the request of a party, order any interim or conservatory measure it deems appropriate." The new AAA rules similarly provide: "At the request of any party, the tribunal may take whatever interim measures it deems necessary, including injunctive relief and measures for the protection or conservation of property." Both sets of rules permit the tribunal to require security for the costs of such measures.[12]

The new LCIA rules contain an especially detailed statement of the arbitrators' authority to grant interim measures of protection. They specify that, unless otherwise agreed in writing, the arbitrators may "order any respondent party to a claim or counterclaim to provide security for all or part of the amount in dispute...[or] order the preservation, storage, sale or other disposal of any property or thing under the control of any party and relating to the subject matter of the arbitration; [or] order on a provisional basis...any relief which the [tribunal] would have power to grant in an award; [or] order any claiming or counterclaiming party to provide security for the legal or other costs of any other party by way of deposit or bank guarantee or in any other manner and upon such terms as the [tribunal] considers appropriate."[13]

The municipal law governing the proceedings may also expressly confer the authority to order interim measures. The UNCITRAL Model Law contains such a provision.[14]

The English Arbitration Act 1996 expressly authorizes arbitrators to make orders to provide security for costs, orders relating to the property that is the subject matter of the dispute and is owned by, or in the possession of, a party to the proceedings, and, if so authorized by the agreement, orders awarding on a provisional basis any relief that the tribunal could grant in a final award.[15]

---

[12] ICC Rules, Art. 23(1); AAA Int'l Rules, Art. 21; see UNCITRAL Rules, Art. 26.
[13] LCIA Rules, Art. 25.
[14] UNCITRAL Model Law, Art. 17.
[15] English Arbitration Act 1996, §§ 38, 39.

Finally, the arbitrators' authority to order interim measures may be conferred by an express provision of an international convention.[16]

Derogation from the General Principle. While the authority to order provisional measures plainly qualifies as a general principle, the prevailing view is that parties may derogate from the principle. Arbitral conventions, statutes and rules provide evidence that the parties retain the discretion to override the authority that would otherwise be granted an arbitral tribunal to order interim measures of protection.[17]

Since any derogation from the general principle authorizing interim measures is fundamentally incompatible with the judicial or arbitral function, it should be inferred only on the clearest evidence of the parties' intent, as expressed in the governing instrument. Moreover, to the extent it is argued that a treaty or agreement derogates from the general principle, a tribunal should read the text, if possible, in a manner that conforms the tribunal's authority to that principle.

Judicial Interim Measures. Arbitral tribunals are rarely standing bodies, and they take time to constitute. They also have no direct enforcement power. Hence, if the arbitral mechanism is to be fully effective, a right of recourse to the courts prior to the constitution of the tribunal must be preserved. A contrary rule would preserve the integrity of arbitration at the price of its effectiveness. Each of the representative arbitration rules recognizes such a right, though the ICSID rules require that the parties stipulate a right of judicial recourse in their agreement to arbitrate. The UNCITRAL Model Law is to similar effect.

The extent of court intervention in the form of interim measures of protection should run only so far as the rationale for such intervention. Like interim measures generally, judicially rendered interim measures should be issued when necessary to preserve the capacity of the arbitral tribunal to render an effective award; courts should support, not substitute for, the arbitrators' authority. Hence, as the ICC and LCIA rules expressly recognize, a greater justification will be required for an application to the courts after constitution of the tribunal.[18]

The English Arbitration Act 1996 confirms the authority of a court to order provisional measures in aid of arbitration, while also setting out the

---

[16] *See, e.g.,* U.N. Convention on the Law of the Sea, done on Dec. 10, 1982, Art. 290, 21 I.L.M. 1261 (1982) (vesting International Tribunal on the Law of the Sea with authority to "prescribe any provisional measures which it considers appropriate under the circumstances").

[17] *See, e.g.,* UNCITRAL Model Law, Art. 17.

[18] ICC Rules, Art. 23(2); LCIA Rules, Art. 25.3.

limits to that authority.[19] It provides that the court's power should be exercised only in cases of urgency or, if the case is not urgent, with the permission of the tribunal or the agreement in writing of the parties. It also provides that the court shall act only if or to the extent that the tribunal has no power or is unable to act effectively. It thereby sets forth a rule of restraint that well balances the authority of an arbitral tribunal with its intrinsic limitations.

Institution-Appointed Emergency Arbitrators. Each of the ICC, the AAA, the LCIA, and the World Intellectual Property Organization recently generated proposals to revise their rules to provide for emergency arbitrators who could act urgently on requests for interim measures. Though details differed, each institution considered providing for an institution-appointed "delegate" or "emergency arbitrator" to be available on short notice prior to the constitution of the tribunal to hear and, if appropriate, make orders in respect of a party's urgent application for interim relief. Access to an emergency arbitrator would ensure that the full authority of the arbitral tribunal would be available at all stages of the dispute.

For a variety of reasons, however, including concerns about enforceability, the ICC, the LCIA and the AAA each determined not to include such a provision in the latest revision of its international rules. The WIPO proposal is still under consideration. Hence, at this time, no such proposal has been included in a set of international rules.

A set of "Optional Rules for Emergency Measures of Protection," however, has been included in the latest revision of the AAA Commercial Arbitration Rules, which went into effect Jan. 1, 1999, for use in domestic arbitrations in the United States. These rules, which must be expressly agreed to by the parties or adopted in their arbitration clause, call for the appointment of an emergency arbitrator within one day of receipt of notice by the party seeking emergency relief; they also call for the scheduling of emergency proceedings within two days of the emergency arbitrator's appointment.

The use of these emergency procedures in the domestic context may provide a useful test of their potential in the international sphere, where issues of enforcement, in particular, complicate the picture. For present purposes, they represent a considered attempt to reconcile the possible need for urgent relief prior to the constitution of the tribunal with the principle of arbitral autonomy.

---

[19] English Arbitration Act 1996, § 44

Conclusion

To remind ourselves of the obvious, fairness and effectiveness must remain the objective of any international commercial arbitration. While fair and effective procedures can only provide the start to that objective, there can be no hope of reaching it without them.

CHAPTER SEVEN

EFFECTIVE ARBITRATIONS

I. Preparing Witnesses

Preparing a Witness for Arbitration

by Daniel I. Small[*]

When a person is called as a witness in an arbitration, whether as a party or non-party, it is usually a new and disturbing experience. Few people understand just how completely new and different it is.

The question-and-answer format, whether used in litigation or arbitration, does not produce what we know as "conversation," so the witness should not expect to have a conversational dialogue with the questioner.

In fact, communicating effectively in a question-and-answer format is an extraordinarily unnatural and difficult process, one that requires considerable preparation. A witness must learn a method of communicating that differs considerably from the one we use in our daily lives, one that requires discipline in both listening and speaking.

Yet the relative informality of arbitration can lead to a dangerous relaxation in preparation. The notion that a witness can "just go in and tell my story" is as much an invitation to disaster in an arbitration as it is in the more formal world of litigation. Fortunately, it is possible for anyone to learn how to be an effective witness. However, it takes time, effort, and discipline on the part of both lawyer and witness.

Testimony vs. Conversation

Witnesses who testify in arbitration take an oath to "tell the truth, the whole truth, and nothing but the truth." Most of us learned this oath by

---

[*] Dan Small is a partner with the Miami firm Duane Morris and a former prosecutor for the U.S. Department of Justice. Small graduated cum laude from Harvard University and Harvard School of Law. He is the author of GOING TO TRIAL, DANIEL I. SMALL (ABA 2000) and PREPARING WITNESSES: A PRACTICAL GUIDE FOR LAWYERS AND THEIR CLIENTS, DANIEL I. SMALL (ABA 1998), from which this article was adapted by permission.

rote in childhood. Like many things learned by rote, the words may be known but not understood. Before a witness testifies under oath, he or she needs to understand all three parts of the statement that makes up the oath.

Usually, the hardest part for a witness is to tell "nothing but the truth." That's because the witness has the inclination to converse. But when testifying, much of what is ordinarily said to keep a normal, casual conversation going must be avoided. In friendly conversation we often embellish or shade what we say in innocent and acceptable ways. We guess. We assume. We conceal our memory lapses and lack of knowledge. We gossip. We talk too much, and we speak without thinking carefully. Who among us has not done some or all of these things at one time or another?

In his book SUR L'EAU (ON THE FACE OF THE WATERS), the 19th century French writer Guy de Maupassant described "conversation" as "the art of...knowing how to invest every trifle with interest, to charm no matter what be the subject, and to fascinate with absolutely nothing." Yet, these wonderful qualities of conversation are not appropriate for a witness. If conversing is an art, then testifying is a science. If the goal of a conversationalist is to be interesting, the goal of a witness is to be precise. A witness is not there to entertain, just to tell "nothing but the truth" in a clear, simple way.

Changing ingrained conversational habits for the purposes of testifying is hard work, but it is essential for the witness to testify effectively. This takes a surprising amount of preparation, concentration and discipline. The challenge for the lawyer is to make sure that the preparation is done, and done right. Unfortunately, the reality is that no one teaches lawyers how to prepare a witness, or how to teach a person the difficult process of being an effective witness. The commonly accepted notion that lawyers will pick up these skills as they go along is dangerous nonsense. At best, it is a recipe for a long, trial-and-error learning process, in which real clients are the guinea pigs.

Seven Mistakes Lawyers Make

As a result, many lawyers, even those with considerable experience, may either fail to prepare a witness or do an inadequate job of preparation. A failure in preparation is a failure in representation. You can avoid their mistakes by not resorting to the following excuses for lax preparation.

1. I'm Too Busy.

It's easy for a lawyer to ignore witness preparation. After all, the witness usually doesn't understand the importance of preparing for the arbitration, and the lawyer has other, more immediate demands. Remember, you are not providing proper representation if you allow your client—or even a nonclient —to appear at the arbitration without thorough preparation. You need to find the time to work together with the witness. If you are unwilling to do this, do not take on the representation.

2. Your Client's Too Busy.

Many clients don't comprehend how vital it is to thoroughly prepare for the questioning to come. Many don't want to take the time out of their busy schedule to pay a lawyer to help them prepare for something they believe is unnecessary in the first place. Nevertheless, you must accept the obligation to push hard to overcome your client's reluctance to prepare to testify, however distasteful it may be to push a client in this way.

3. It's Only an Arbitration.

We who believe in ADR promote arbitration as a less formal, less adversarial, less time-consuming, and less expensive means of resolving disputes. The danger comes when you allow your client to take those benefits as a license to "wing it"-and skip witness preparation.

The relative informality of the arbitration hearing may make it easier to forget the need for discipline and preparation of the witness. However, it is important to remember that the challenges and risks of communicating in a closely scrutinized, question-and-answer format are just as serious in an arbitration as in litigation. Opposing counsel can take great advantage of the casual, conversation-prone, loose-cannon witness. You must convince your client--and yourself-of the need to prepare to testify.

4. All Witnesses Are the Same.

Part of the challenge of properly preparing a witness is tailoring the preparation to the individual who will be examined. Witness preparation cannot be conducted in a standardized, "cookie-cutter" way. Witnesses differ enormously, depending on their backgrounds, personality, education, profession, experience as a witness, and their involvement in the issues or events being addressed in the arbitration. What might be appropriate preparation for one witness may be useless gibberish to another. You need to adapt your preparation accordingly.

   5.   *You Never Know What They'll Ask.*

Lawyers sometimes limit their preparation of witnesses because they don't know how to anticipate what a questioner will ask. But the fact that a lawyer rarely knows all of the questions that may be asked should not prevent full preparation, because many of the questions can be anticipated. A lawyer cannot eliminate every surprise that a witness may face, but he or she can certainly help minimize their number and severity. There are a variety of ways to anticipate what a witness will be asked.

Put Yourself in Their Position. I always challenge myself and the attorneys who work with me, as well as my clients, to "put on the other side's hat." How would I view a set of facts if I were the adversary? What questions would I want to ask the witness? Brainstorm these issues with those working with you, in and out of the presence of the client. If resources allow, assign someone to play the role of your adversary and prepare hypothetical questions for cross-examination.

If you are involved in a multi-party dispute, pay attention to the questions asked of other parties to the case. This may give you a good idea of the questions to expect.

You can also research the art of examining and cross-examining witnesses. There are numerous books and manuals, which your law library may have in its collection, that teach this skill. Researching the substantive issues in dispute may also help you formulate questions.

You also have lawyer contacts that are unavailable to your client. From your legal colleagues you may be able to obtain transcripts, file memos, or even oral reports of the type of cross-examination that your adversary's attorney will conduct.

   6.   *Preaching, Not Teaching.*

You cannot tell someone how to be a witness. That has to be taught. You must work with your client to find out what he or she needs to know in this situation. Don't lecture or preach. The key is to listen. Invite questions. Ask for feedback and ask questions yourself. Real learning happens when you have this kind of give-and-take with your witness.

   7.   *Do I Need to Draw You a Road Map?*

Yes, you do! I am constantly amazed to find witnesses who may have been prepared on the facts, but have not been told what's going to happen in the arbitration. These witnesses walk into a strange room in front of strange people, and are intimidated and overwhelmed by the most basic arbitration procedures. They are quickly shaken up and start the questioning at a severe disadvantage. There is nothing condescending about being thorough in your preparation. Tell the witness what will happen in the arbitration. Take the time to explain exactly what the witness can expect. Do it slowly, step-by-step, and leave lots of time to answer the witness' questions.

What Makes for Good Preparation?

Conversations "flow." Learning to be a witness is all about breaking free from that "flow." Flow works in the questioner's favor. An effective witness wants to slow the questioning process down-to break up each question into key parts. The witness needs to learn to listen, think, answer, then stop; then listen, think, answer, and stop again. Witness preparation involves learning a new way of speaking. No one is born with this ability, regardless of age, intelligence, experience, or status. Yet anyone can learn to be a good witness. All it takes is time, hard work, discipline, and the help of an experienced "guide."

II. Expert Testimony

When Experts Testify:
Exploiting the Advantages of Arbitration

by Norman Brand[*]

Experts can be a major cost in litigation, especially when technical or scientific testimony is critical. The Supreme Court's decision in *Kumho Tire Co. v. Carmichael*,[1] requiring judges to rule on the validity of any expert's methodology before permitting opinion testimony, increases the potential cost of using experts in litigation. It also creates new grounds for appeal whenever an expert testifies.

Arbitration can reduce your client's cost of expert testimony, without compromising your ability to argue the case. Arbitration has significant advantages over litigation when expert testimony is critical to your case. First, the parties can choose a decision maker who is an expert in the field (such as a Ph.D. biochemist) or has familiarity with the field (such as an intellectual property lawyer). Second, they can design a process for introducing expert testimony that will ensure its admissibility while reducing its cost. After briefly reviewing the constraints imposed by *Kumho* and its predecessor *Daubert v. Merrell Dow Pharmaceuticals*,[2] we can examine these advantages in greater detail.

The Legal Setting

In *Daubert* the Supreme Court specified the "gatekeeping" role it expected federal judges to perform before admitting an expert opinion based on scientific knowledge. It assigned judges the task of conducting a two-part analysis. First, the court must decide the validity of the methodology the expert used in reaching an opinion. Second, the court must decide whether the opinion testimony is relevant to the argument and would therefore assist the trier of fact.

---

[*] The author is a mediator and arbitrator in San Francisco. He serves on the AAA's Large, Complex Case Panel, is a member of the National Academy of Arbitrators and is a Fellow of the College of Labor and Employment Lawyers. Brand holds a Ph.D. and written and spoken widely on ADR topics.
[1] 119 S. Ct. 1167 (1999).
[2] 509 U.S. 579, 113 S. Ct. 2786 (1993).

Justice Stephen Breyer's opinion in *Kumho* makes clear that judges are to perform this gatekeeping role even when the expert opinion is based on technical or other specialized knowledge. Justice Breyer evaluated specific expert testimony, demonstrating how the trial court should examine the technical expert's methodology. His rigorous methodological analysis sets a high standard.

Kumho also holds that both the trial court's decision on how to review the expert's methodology, and its ultimate conclusion on the admissibility of the evidence, are subject to judicial review.[3] In a concurring opinion, Justice Antonin Scalia warned the lower courts that their discretion to examine the expert's methodology was "not discretion to perform the function inadequately." Why the warning? Perhaps, in light of the deferential standard of review, Justice Scalia feared that some judges might not be inclined to conduct the rigorous examination of an expert's methodology necessary to insure the reliability of opinion testimony.[4]

Choosing the Decision Maker

By arbitrating, rather than litigating, a dispute involving expert opinion, you can choose a decision maker whose education, training, temperament or experience gives you confidence. There are two types of arbitrators you can choose to hear a dispute with critical "expert" issues: (1) the arbitrator who is a professional expert in the field who will decide the central issues in the case and (2) the professional arbitrator who is familiar with the field and can quickly grasp the technical issues and rigorously test the validity of the expert's methodology. The type of arbitrator you choose may be dictated by the nature of the dispute.

Types of Expert Arbitrators

Sensory Experts. When a dispute is about the intangible qualities of a particular product, you may want an arbitrator who is a sensory expert to determine the issue, without the need for party experts. The sensory expert has an inherent skill that has been professionally exercised over time. Perfume blenders, wine makers, and butter testers use their nose

---

[3] In *General Electric Co. v. Joiner*, 522 U.S. 136, 138-9 (1997), the Supreme Court held the standard of review is abuse of discretion.

[4] As Judge Kozinski said in the Daubert remand, judging the validity of a scientific methodology when it is disputed among scientists themselves is a "heady task." Daubert v. Merrell Dow Pharmaceuticals, 43 F.3d 1311, 1316 (9th Cir. 1995).

and palates to offer opinions about the quality of products. These experts rely directly on their senses. Once the expert tastes the butter or smells the perfume, the process of assessing these products is internal; the methodology used to assess them is neither easily explicable, nor subject to close examination or challenge. If a case is about whether a perfume is a "knock off" of a trademarked product, a perfume blender could use his nose to settle whether the allegedly infringing product is likely to fool the consumer.

The textile industry has used sensory experts as arbitrators for many years. These experts are usually textile manufacturers; they use their eyes and hands to judge fabric quality. The criteria for choosing textile experts were developed by an industry group, the General Arbitration Council of the Textile and Apparel Industries. Its rules require arbitrators who "have been active, within the 10-year period prior to appointment, in the textile/apparel business." At the American Arbitration Association, where arbitrations conducted under the council's rules are held, there is a special device used by these arbitrators to examine bolts of cloth. Expert arbitrators have used it to resolve disputes for over sixty years.

The *Kumho* decision suggests that the sensory expert's preparation can be examined by the court, but offers no further insight. It may be that the expertise of a sensory expert is best validated by examining who has relied upon the expert, and for what purpose.[5]

Technical and Scientific Experts. Technical and scientific experts have training and experience in a particular profession, business or industry. The technical expert applies a set of rules from the field to a specific set of facts. For example, an accounting expert may determine that a balance sheet is an accurate representation of the company's financial condition under Generally Accepted Accounting Practices. A materials expert, using principles from metallurgy, may conclude that a ladder failed because certain manufacturing defects reduced its load-bearing ability. The way in which the expert applies these rules constitutes the methodology that can be challenged.

Scientific experts include not only "hard" scientists, but also engineers.[6] These experts apply scientific principles and the "scientific

---

[5] Starbucks may rely upon its chief taster to make decisions about buying millions of pounds of green coffee beans. If a great deal of money is spent by a knowledgeable business based upon the opinions of a sensory expert, that may be an indicator of the expert's reliability.

[6] One headline announcing *Kumho* read: "Court Views Engineers as Scientists," 284 SCIENCE 21 (April 1999).

method" to the known facts. Unlike other experts, the methodology of science experts has often been scrutinized through peer review. Sometimes their methodology represents an accepted way of manipulating data (e.g., SUDAAN, a software program widely used for manipulating large data sets).

When a technical or scientific expert is used as the sole arbitrator in the dispute, the parties must both (1) identify the expert and (2) agree on the methodology the arbitrator will apply to resolve the dispute. This agreed-upon methodology can be embodied in a stipulated submission agreement, which recites that the parties are explicitly limiting how the arbitrator can decide the case. If the arbitrator uses a different methodology, that is a ground to vacate the award, since the arbitrator would have exceeded his powers.[7]

Using an expert arbitrator in this way eliminates the need for costly party experts to testify. It also eliminates the possibility of post-arbitration disputes over whether the methodology was valid. In addition, if the parties memorialize their agreement as to the methodology, that will give them some assurance that the agreed-upon methodology will be followed.

The Arbitrator as Arbiter of Party Experts

You may prefer to have party experts testify before the arbitrator in a highly technical or scientific case. In this case you may choose a professional arbitrator who is knowledgeable in the field, and has demonstrated an ability to quickly comprehend complex problems and make reliable decisions. There are three advantages to choosing this type of arbitrator: (1) the experts who testify will not have to over-simplify their testimony; (2) the arbitrator should be able to more rapidly judge the validity of the methodology used by the party experts; and (3) because the testimony will probably come in more quickly, it will save on expert costs.

Customizing the Process

Unlike litigation, arbitration is a highly malleable process. In a predispute arbitration agreement the parties can create a unique hearing procedure tailored to the technical, scientific or sensory disputes they are likely to encounter. In arbitrations under AAA rules, customizing the

---

[7] 9 U.S.C. § 10(4).

process can be achieved during the prehearing conference. Although the possibilities for customization are almost limitless, I will describe only five approaches: (1) adopting a different standard for expert testimony, (2) "prequalifying" experts, (3) serial decision making, (4) tripartite arbitration, and (5) using expert advisors.

Adopting a Different Standard. Although arbitrators are not legally required to follow technical rules of evidence, professional arbitrators generally use those rules to guide them and to provide predictability for the parties. But the parties can agree to any rules they want, including rules regarding the admissibility of expert testimony.

Thus, even if a professional arbitrator would ordinarily follow the teaching of *Daubert* and *Kumho* when faced with a challenge to an expert's opinion testimony, the parties can stipulate at the prehearing conference to waive any threshold argument about an expert's credentials or methodology. Furthermore, they can agree that (1) the arbitrator will accept relevant expert testimony, and (2) any demonstrated failures in the expert's methodology will go to the weight the arbitrator gives the testimony.

This allows both sides to engage experts knowing they will be permitted to testify. If a party shows flaws in the methodology of the opponent's expert at the hearing, the arbitrator may choose to give little weight to that expert's opinion. This arrangement can only be achieved through arbitration. By changing the standard for admissibility of expert testimony, the parties save the cost of prehearing motions. In addition, since arbitration awards are not reviewable for errors of law, both sides save the potential cost of appeals based on alleged failures to apply *Kumho*. Thus, after the award is issued, they have the certainty necessary for making future business decisions.

"Prequalifying" Experts. The prehearing conference is an ideal place to resolve issues about the expert's methodology. If issues relating to the expert arbitrator's qualifications or an expert witness's credentials or methodology are not waived in this conference, you can propose a cost-effective way of deciding them. For instance, in a case involving sensory experts the arbitrator might require the parties to provide the credentials of their proposed experts. If one party asserts its opponent's proposed expert is unqualified, that could be argued as a motion—well before the hearing on the merits. If the arbitrator agrees with the party challenging the expert's credentials, the party proposing that expert still has adequate time to find another expert, change its approach, or settle the case.

In cases involving technical or scientific experts, the parties can agree at the prehearing conference to submit detailed summaries of how their proposed experts will examine the data and construct an opinion. By a date certain, either side can challenge the methodology to be employed by the other side's expert. If no challenge is timely made, the potential issue is waived. If there are challenges, the arbitrator can hold a preliminary hearing on the proposed methodology. There may be a second hearing to examine a different methodology. Alternatively, a party may simply decide to attack the other party's expert opinion at the hearing, argue that the opinion deserves little weight,[8] or settle the case.

If there is no challenge to a party expert's methodology, or the arbitrator finds a challenged methodology to be valid, the parties could agree that any minor deviations from that methodology will go to the weight the arbitrator accords the expert's opinion, and that a complete failure to adhere to the methodology can result in exclusion of the testimony.

This procedure allows the parties to know before engaging their experts (and paying for their preparation) that they will be permitted, or not permitted, to testify. This can save a significant sum for the client because it occurs early in the process. If the expert's methodology is accepted by the arbitrator, that decision is unreviewable. There is no potential for an appellate court to disagree with the decision and require the entire case to be reheard.

Serial Decision Making. Some-times the issue requiring expert testimony is a threshold issue in the case. Arbitration offers the possibility of serial decision makers. If the narrowest question in a trade secrets case is whether using a particular type of fastener is common knowledge among engineers, it may be most economical to have a jointly chosen, well-respected engineer decide only this point. If the engineer decides it is common knowledge, the issue is eliminated and the parties may be able to negotiate or mediate an overall solution. If the engineer finds it is not common engineering knowledge, the consequences of that determination could be argued and decided in a second arbitration with a non-engineer arbitrator. Alternatively, the hearing could be bifurcated, with the same arbitrator deciding the threshold and underlying issues. If

---

[8] Methodological weaknesses that do not become apparent until the hearing can also reduce the weight the arbitrator gives the expert's opinion.

there is a failure of evidence on the threshold issue, no further hearings need occur.[9]

Tripartite Arbitration. You can also make experts part of a broader decision-making process using "expert tripartite arbitration." Its distinguishing characteristic is that each side's "party-appointed" arbitrator is an expert in the scientific or technical field at issue. These experts, with the advice of counsel, choose a neutral arbitrator who is not an expert in the field, but who has demonstrated an ability to comprehend scientific and technical disputes. All decisions are made by a majority vote. In all the deliberations the experts can advise the neutral arbitrator about what weight to give expert testimony.

If the predispute arbitration agreement does not call for tripartite arbitration, the parties can agree to it after the dispute occurs. The arbitrator may even suggest it in the prehearing conference. The parties would then appoint their partisan expert arbitrators, having already chosen the neutral arbitrator.[10]

Using Expert Advisors. In the pre-hearing conference the parties can agree that the arbitrator will be assisted by an expert advisor. This expert provides advice on scientific or technical issues to the arbitrator, but does not otherwise participate in the decision-making process. The expert advisor can be agreed to by the parties, or chosen by the arbitrator from a group of names submitted by the parties or by some other means. Recently the American Association for the Advancement of Science began a project to help the courts find experts to provide neutral scientific advice. The Court Appointed Scientific Experts Project identifies people who are highly respected in their field to serve as neutral experts.[11] These same experts would undoubtedly be available to act as advisors in arbitration.

The problems that often burden expert testimony—improper extrapolation, anecdotal evidence, too small a sample, false analogies, and the post hoc fallacy—can all be addressed at the prehearing

---

[9] Some would argue that the better practice is to have different arbitrators decide the two issues. That eliminates the possibility of contaminating each decision-making process with knowledge about other aspects of the case, or any financial interest in hearing the entire case.

[10] It is important to distinguish between multiple neutral arbitrators and tripartite arbitration. With multiple neutral arbitrators all of the arbitrators are expected to act as neutrals and all can be challenged and disqualified by either side. In tripartite arbitration the party-appointed arbitrators are not expected to be neutral; they are aligned with the side choosing them. They cannot be disqualified because of that alignment.

[11] *See* 284 SCIENCE 1600 (JULY 1999). This project is only for the courts.

conference before the parties have invested heavily in their experts. Perhaps most important of all, the expert's methodology and conclusions can be carefully scrutinized so that only reliable expert testimony is admitted. In the wake of *Kumho*, when expert testimony is critical to your case, arbitration's advantages are compelling.

III. Tandem Witnesses

Innovations in Arbitration: Using the Tandem Witness Examination When Experts Collide

by Stanley P. Sklar[*]

When an arbitral panel, in a case that requires the testimony of expert witnesses about complex accounting issues, finds time running out before the panel has heard from the experts, the solution may be tandem witness examination, an approach to presenting expert witnesses suggested by James Groton in an article in the Arbitration Journal.

In his article, Groton suggested "that the two opposing expert witnesses be placed on the witness stand at the same time so they could be examined jointly, asked exactly the same questions, and be put in the position of having to directly answer each other's arguments." This procedure was employed in the arbitration referred to above and, as a result, the panel heard two accounting experts testify on complex accounting issues in one hearing day. The experts had been present during the hearings and were anxious to explain to the panel the basis of their opinions. At some point the panel took over the questioning of both witnesses, establishing a reasoned debate between the experts over their respective positions. In short, the panel was able to explore the issues that were critical to its decision-making process. The arbitrators did not have to refer to illegible handwritten notes or search memories for detailed answers to questions asked days or months before.

A Tandem Witness Examination Protocol

- At the initial hearing counsel will submit the expert's curriculum vitae to opposing counsel and to the panel.

---

[*] Stanley P. Sklar is a member of Chicago's Bell, Boyd & Lloyd. Sklar received a B.S. from the University of Illinois and a J.D. from Northwestern School of Law. He is the 2004 recipient of the ABA Forum in the Construction Industry Cornerstone Award and is a member of the International Division Panel of Arbitrators for the American Arbitration Association.

- The witnesses will be accepted as experts by stipulation of the parties. Each party will have the opportunity to challenge the status of the opposing party's expert.

- Both experts will be sworn in at the same time and take the "stand" at the same time. If possible, both experts should be seated side-by-side to facilitate their ability to question each other.

- Claimant's counsel will ask the initial questions, which will be answered by the claimant's witness and then by the respondent's witness. The same question will be asked of each expert witness. This will allow them to answer the question and answer each other's response, thus affording counsel and the panel the opportunity to hear both sides of the issue virtually simultaneously. Alternatively, each side will be allowed to ask questions in five question groups, alternating with each other so as to avoid any perception of undue advantage. The disadvantage of this procedure is that the continuum of questions will be interrupted and the testimony may be disjointed.

- At the conclusion of questioning by claimant's counsel, respondent's counsel may ask questions that have not been asked or that are relevant to its case, using the same procedure set forth in Step 4.

- At this point there will be a break in questioning to permit counsel to consult with their own expert. This will be followed by an additional round of questions in the format of Steps 4 and 5. At the option of counsel, this second round of questions may be asked by the experts of each other, or counsel may continue the questioning, having had input from their respective experts.

- The panel should be able to ask questions of the experts at any time and should encourage the witnesses to ask their counterpart expert questions too.

- The experts should be informed that the flexibility of the arbitration process encourages them to comment on each other's testimony and even engage in direct dialogue with each other, if appropriate and if agreed to in advance by counsel.

The foregoing protocol is a model that works well. It can be modified as needs change. Neutrals should not be afraid to recommend it as an effective means of obtaining this testimony and one that provides cost-saving opportunities as well. It requires the expert to be truly professional, articulate and willing to present the evidence under circumstances far different from the highly-structured court room. It is another way in which the alternative dispute resolution process can provide for creative solutions.

IV. Effective Cross-Examination in Arbitration

Managing Cross-Examination: The Arbitrator's Perspective

by William L.D. Barrett[*]

Cross-examination is as fundamental to arbitration as it is to any adversary process. It is the time-tested means of probing the soundness of assertions made in direct testimony. This article suggests ways in which arbitrators can effectively manage cross-examination and make this vital part of every case more useful in reaching sound decisions.

Purpose of Cross-Examination

Arbitrators know that they cannot accept at face value the assertions of witnesses on direct examination without cross-examination. Witnesses do not often deliberately lie in commercial arbitration, but the tendency to shade the truth, to have selective or faulty recollection, or to omit important facts, happens to some extent in every case. Cross-examination is the tool that exposes these weaknesses. Generally, cross-examination of a witness will reveal that some assertions are believable, some less so and perhaps one or two, not at all. Arbitrators recognize that competently executed cross-examination eases their ultimate job of resolving contradictory claims.

Cross-examination in arbitration has a variety of purposes. One is to use the witness to expose information that will be helpful to the examiner's case. Another is to discredit the witness's direct testimony and thus to diminish the adversary's case. A third objective is to attack the credibility of the witness and, by extension, the entire case of the adversary. Yet, another objective is to show that the witness has made a mistake or was actually unable to observe the event testified about. Cross-examination is controlled by the examiner who sets out to achieve one or more of these objectives.

---

[*] William L. D. Barrett is a partner at Hollyer et al, in New York City. He is a member of the Board of Directors and the Executive Committee of the AAA, Chair of the Greater New York Advisory Council for Large Complex Cases and a member of the AAA's Large, Complex Case Panel.

Unlike direct testimony, which usually takes the form of a narrative, cross-examination typically unfolds as a series of episodes. In each episode, the examiner attempts to achieve one of the objectives described above. It becomes clear sooner or later whether the attempt has been successful. The episodes may seem like rounds in a boxing match, in which either the witness or the examining lawyer prevails.

A crucial element in good cross-examination is solid preparation. The examiner needs to know the goal of the cross-examination of each witness and have planned how to achieve these objectives. In the typical commercial case, a careful review of the documents—particularly those that the witness has authored or which refer to the witness—can usually provide a guide to what the witness will say on direct examination. The examiner then plans how to amplify or challenge the expected assertions by confronting the witness with documents or other testimony that the examiner hopes will reveal errors and inconsistencies.

The Arbitrator's Role in Cross-Examination

In general, the arbitrator's role during cross-examination is simply to listen and rarely to interject. Sometimes there are reasons for reining in cross-examination, but experienced arbitrators are usually reluctant to act unless it is plain that the examination is not getting anywhere or is in some way improper. The arbitrator should assume that the examiner has a plan for the cross-examination and allow that plan to be executed without interference from the arbitrator or others. The arbitrator generally will prevent objections by the witness's lawyer from disrupting the cross-examination. As discussed below, while some objections may be valid, others may be merely disruptive, or be designed to coach the witness.

The arbitrator's most important service in cross-examination generally takes place before the actual examination. It is the elimination of obstacles to a good, well-prepared examination. This includes ensuring that discovery takes place in a timely manner and that both sides know well in advance of each hearing which witnesses will testify, so that their cross-examination can be prepared in advance.

Documentary discovery and the exchange of witness lists are necessary ingredients to proper preparation for cross-examination. If there has been a delay in their production, the resulting cross-examination will not be as effective as it should be. This hurts not only the examining side, but complicates the arbitrator's job of assessing the credibility of the witness's direct testimony. In serious situations of this kind, an adjournment may be required to enable the examiner a reasonable time to review and reflect upon tardily-produced material. It is partly for the arbitrator's own benefit to insist on timely discovery.

Controlling Cross-Examination

Although cross-examination is vital, it can consume a great deal of time. If its objectives are being accomplished, this is time well spent. If little is happening, however, the examination must have some bounds. During cross-examination, the arbitrator should be alert to the objective the examiner is trying to achieve. The purpose of each "round" of cross-examination should become clear after a few questions. If it is not clear within a reasonable amount of time, it is not improper for the arbitrator to ask what the examiner is attempting to accomplish.

It is helpful to keep the witness's direct testimony clearly in mind. Strictly speaking, anything that does not bear on the witness's direct testimony is outside the scope of proper cross-examination. However, in arbitration it is not uncommon for the examiner to try to elicit helpful additional testimony. If this would eliminate the need to have the witness testify at a subsequent hearing, it may be a good use of time. But if cross-examination is being used like a discovery deposition, the examiner can be reminded that the proper time for the examination will be as a part of the examiner's own case. Leading questions, such as "You read the document before you signed it, didn't you?" are proper on cross-examination. If, however, the examination moves beyond direct testimony, the arbitrator should be aware that it is the examiner who is testifying, not the witness.

Lawyers are often not the only participant to create difficulties in cross-examination. Witnesses may be uncooperative and evasive. They sometimes ignore the question and simply answer something else. Unresponsive answers make for a record that is hard to read and to evaluate. In the first instance it is the examiner's job to control the examination and to get answers to the questions asked, even if this requires repetition of the question. A witness who persists in being uncooperative can be admonished that it is the witness' duty to answer the questions posed. It is sometimes necessary for the arbitrator to ask the examiner's question and to insist upon an answer.

A device that the arbitrator can employ to shorten a cross-examination that appears to have strayed is the offer of proof. A request for an offer of proof asks the examiner to explain to the arbitrator what the examiner is trying to accomplish. If the objective is irrelevant or not helpful, the examiner can be asked to move on. After due warning, if the examiner is not able to satisfy the arbitrator that useful and relevant information will be obtained, the examination can be terminated.

Typical Issues Arising on Cross-Examination

All witnesses must be cross-examined, but unfortunately not all examiners are masters of the art. Often, objections to cross-examination are sound and should be sustained.

A common example is the so-called "objection to the form of the question." The objection to form asserts that although there is nothing wrong with the subject matter of the question, there is something missing from the question. For example the question, "When did you arrive at the meeting?" would be objectionable unless the witness had previously testified to attending a meeting. If the witness had not so testified, the objection should be sustained with the instruction to the examining lawyer to "lay a foundation." What constitutes the proper foundation for a question are the matters that must logically have preceded the objectionable question. A proper foundation is important not just to avoid unfairness to the witness, but to make the record clear for the arbitrator's consideration when deciding the case.

Another common "form" objection to questions on cross-examination is that they are compound and have several parts. If such a question is allowed to stand, the answer may be ambiguous and difficult for the arbitrator to interpret. The objection to form can be sustained with the direction to the examiner to break the question into its component parts.

Cross-examination of a party involves some special considerations. Fairness generally suggests allowing reasonably broad cross-examination, going not only into the direct testimony itself, but to the credibility of the party's case. Since there is typically no love lost between a party and the cross-examining lawyer, some elevation of tempers is not uncommon, but this is not always undesirable, as long as it does not get out of hand. It can be useful in assessing credibility to observe a party witness under stress.

However, time can be wasted when the examiner attempts to get concessions or admissions from a party witness. Frequently the thrust of the examination is a request to concede a large part of the party's case. Since that rarely happens, a stand-off ensues. The examiner should be reminded that decision of the ultimate issues is for the arbitrator, not for the parties.

Cross-examination is particularly essential to evaluation of expert testimony. This writer has had the occasion to hear testimony from dozens of expert witnesses. While no statistics are available, experience suggests that a small but significant percentage of experts are completely or largely undone on cross-examination. The examiner may be able to show that an expert's opinion is cursory and based on factual or mathematical errors. It may be that the expert was not given access to all of the facts and may be forced to admit that a different conclusion would have been drawn had these facts been known. Sometimes it develops that an expert has been asked merely to mouth a theory concocted by counsel. In such cases, cross-examination can suggest that the expert's testimony should be given little or no credence.

For these reasons, it is imperative for the arbitrator to ensure that before an expert testifies, the adversary has been furnished with the expert's opinion (or at least a fair summary of it) and, most importantly, the basis for that opinion. This means enough detail about the investigation the expert conducted and the analysis performed that another expert with comparable qualifications could understand and evaluate the soundness of the process leading to the opinion. This material must be available sufficiently in advance of the expert's testimony so that proper cross-examination can be prepared, with the advice of the examiner's expert.

When these steps are followed, the expert's testimony at the hearing can consist primarily of an explanation of the opinion to the arbitrator. Cross-examination can focus on the differences of opinion between the experts on such matters as the thoroughness of the investigation or the existence of alternative methods of analysis that might have yielded other conclusions. This sort of cross-examination is invariably of great assistance to the arbitrator, particularly if a three-person panel and one or more of its members is an expert.

Cross-examination is an essential part of every arbitration case. A well-prepared cross-examination is always helpful to the arbitrator's understanding of the case and the reliability of the witnesses. Understanding the function of cross-examination is the key to making it more focused and useful for the arbitrator's ultimate purpose of reaching a sound award.

V. Improving Presentation to Win at Arbitration

Presentational Skills:
A Quick Reference Guide for Advocates

by Morley R. Gorsky[*]

Written from an arbitrator's perspective, the following article suggests various ways in which advocates and presenters, appearing before arbitrators at arbitral hearings, can improve their presentational skills and thus increase their chances of winning cases for their clients.

The purpose of this article is to present an arbitrator's perspective of what goes on at hearings, to assist those who appear as advocates and presenters for the parties, and to suggest ways in which they can improve their advocacy skills.

The following points represent some matters of advocacy, which while they may appear to be self-evident, can, if they are ignored, have an adverse effect on an advocate's presentation. I expect that many will regard a lot of my "ways" as not being applicable to them. I would only ask that you hear me with an open mind and remember the words of Chuck Barris, the host of the long-canceled "Gong Show": "Denial is not just a river in Egypt."

1. Tell Your Witness It's OK to Tell the Truth

The best guide to good advocacy will be of little value if counsel is unwilling or unable to devote the necessary care and attention to the preparation of a case, including the proper preparation of witnesses. Counsel should tell witnesses they intend to call that they must tell the truth and that they must answer questions put to them.

Some witnesses feel that they should never agree with opposing counsel and regard every question put to them as being of the "trick" variety. In order to avoid doing something that will help the "enemy,"

---

[*] The author is an arbitrator on the Ontario Ministry of Labor list of approved arbitrators, and is a panelist in arbitration seminars conducted by the Law Society of Upper Canada. Gorsky received a B.A. and LL.B. from the University of Manitoba and an LL.M. from New York University. He is the author of EVIDENCE AND PROCEDURE IN CANADIAN LABOUR ARBITRATION, Carswell, (1992), as well as law review articles and government studies.

they refuse to answer questions responsively. Rather than helping their cause, such witnesses undermine their credibility and are of no help (and are frequently an embarrassment) to counsel who called them.

Counsel should not accept nonresponsive answers and should have no compunction about making sure that his or her witness answers appropriately. (After all, why did you ask the question in the first place?) There are many counsel who do so even if this may discomfit the witness. Such counsel are properly more concerned with how the case will appear to the chair than with whether such an approach will offend the witness.

While witnesses should usually be permitted to answer questions "in their own way," they must answer responsively within a reasonable period of time and not engage in lengthy digressions which, when they are completed, leave the arbitrator unsure as to what the answer was. Counsel is responsible for ensuring that the questions put to the witness are answered.

2. *The Role of Common Sense*

In advocating a case, a good presenter has to "teach" the arbitrator about the facts and the law. Based on the assistance of counsel, the chair should know where the case is going and be able to see why evidence being presented is relevant. It is insufficient to tell the arbitrator that what may appear to be muddled and confused will become clear if he or she will just leave counsel alone. Counsel cannot blame the chair when he or she is both frustrated and disappointed because the promise of clarity and relevance is never realized.

There are some occasions when the tactic of seeming to develop a case without a focus is a cleverly constructed stratagem for keeping an opponent (including the opponent's witnesses) off balance. If this is the case and your position is valid, I find no fault with it. Remember, however, although this tactic may have worked for Perry Mason, Perry had certain advantages-he had more control over the script. In real life, I can remember only a few occasions when the strategy worked, and many more times when it "bombed."

Such an approach to presenting a case has the further disadvantage of making it more difficult to follow the evidence at the hearing. If it does not work, it also results in the arbitrator having difficulty in reconstructing the evidence from his or her notes. Sometimes counsel also appear confused while trying to confuse their opponent. Feigning confusion may have worked for Columbo-but will it work for you? Counsel should, in preparing a case, consider the effect of trying the chair's patience while he or she waits for the relevant facts to emerge.

I try to respect the role of counsel and refrain from engaging in second guessing why the case is being presented in a particular way. Counsel should also respect the rights of the arbitrator who is disappointed and frustrated when he or she cannot follow the evidence.

3. *"I Will Come to That Later."*

Be very careful about saying to the chair: "I will come to that later," or "That will become clear later." The chair naturally expects an immediate answer to a question asked of counsel. I am too often disappointed when it doesn't become clear later. There may be good reasons for occasionally finessing an arbitrator's attempts to find out where you are going or what you mean, such as not wishing to alert your opponent or adverse witnesses to your strategy. Unless you are an acknowledged master strategist, however, you should be concerned when this is your too-frequent response to the chair's questions.

Counsel may be perfectly content with the way the evidence is coming out, and it may accord with his or her expectations. However, counsel should try to understand what may be troubling the arbitrator whose concern may be legitimate, and whose request for clarification may be quite proper. Sometimes, when counsel informs the chair that he or she should be patient and that the matter will become clear later if only counsel is left alone to try the case, there is a risk of losing credibility when this does not happen.

4. *Show the Chair That You Welcome Questions Testing Your Arguments*

A frequently expressed concern of counsel is related to intervention from the chair-usually occurring during final argument. Often counsel would prefer to be able to present their argument without having to cope with distracting interruptions from the chair. However, many counsel are pleased (or so they tell me) when a chair asks questions during argument in order to obtain clarification. Although the flow of counsel's argument will not be as smooth as a result of such interventions, this is a small price to pay for the benefit of being in a position to respond to the chair's concerns during rather than after the hearing, when it will be too late.

5. *Engender Trust-the Value of Candor*

It is important that counsel gain the trust of the chair. This will be difficult to accomplish when the chair gets the impression that counsel is so intent on winning that they overlook certain aspects of fairness that arbitrators are entitled to expect. It is natural that counsel will have a bias in favor of the side they represent-but there are limits to the extent the focus on winning can be regarded as acceptable. Effective counsel convey a sense of candor and of not wishing to win at any cost. When counsel develop a reputation for questionable practices, they risk being viewed with suspicion, not only in the instant but in subsequent cases.

Although stated in the context of conventional litigation, the words of the late eminent counsel J.J. Robinette are equally applicable to the field of arbitration: "An advocate's primary duty is to the court, to be fair and frank and honest. His next most important duty is to win his case for his client."

6. Be Cautious in Raising Novel Legal Arguments

Candor includes being scrupulous in your presentation of the law. Although there are usually a number of ways to interpret a legal principle, and it is perfectly proper to make arguments, even novel ones, in favor of a particular interpretation, there are limits as to how far counsel should go in doing so. As is usually the case, it is not possible to state a mechanical rule that will always apply, but at some point counsel should know that an argument is not only far-fetched, but, if pressed, may cause the chair to wonder about his or her ethics, knowledge of the law, or both.

For example, don't try to convince the arbitrator that there is an immediate burden on the party against whom it has been raised, of showing that the doctrine of estoppel doesn't apply.

This is not to suggest that counsel should not argue a novel proposition. However, the effect of raising one should be fully considered before it is pursued. Lawyers are trained to be inventive-they should also be selective. Almost all cases are won or lost on the arbitral jurisprudence as it is generally understood at the time of the hearing.[1]

7. Don't Always Take Advantage of the Lack of Discovery Mechanisms

Many arbitration hearings are conducted without the availability of broad discovery mechanisms, and when they are available in some form, they are often not fully resorted to. As a result, the parties usually are less well-informed about the case they will have to meet (or make for that matter) and are, consequently, less tied down to legal or factual positions

---

[1] P. SEITZ, *The Arbitrator's Lot*, 38 The Arbitration J. 51 (1983).

than they would be in conventional civil litigation. Much evidence, which would have been either agreed to or otherwise established as a result of pleadings, production of documents, or oral discovery (depositions) in a conventional civil case, has to be formally proved unless good sense prevails, and evidence that is not seriously (or realistically) in dispute is agreed to.

Some counsel find the temptation irresistible and agree to very little in the hope that by compelling their opponent to prove everything (even that which counsel has no means of disputing), proof will not be forthcoming. I have observed counsel forcing their opponents to prove facts that are evidently not in dispute, in the hope (almost always a vain one) that they will be unable to do so. What usually happens is that the facts are established, but only after an inordinate amount of time has been expended. In addition, the level of frustration at the hearing is raised.

Where such a tactic is unsuccessful, because the "true" facts eventually tend to come out (often with excruciating slowness), counsel who insists on formal proof may suffer a loss of credibility with the chair.

Arbitrators welcome the professional presentation of a case by counsel. In addition to obtaining agreement on as many facts as possible, it is also a good idea to obtain prior agreement with respect to documents so that the smooth presentation of a case is not impeded unnecessarily.

8. *Counsel's Response to the Nonresponsive Answer*

As an arbitrator, I am puzzled when counsel asks a question of a witness which is not answered responsively, and counsel then continues as if the answer was responsive. This does not mean that the witness remained silent. He or she usually said something by way of an "answer," but the answer was clearly not responsive to the question. I often suspect that counsel actually believe that the question was answered and that the answer was the one that they sought. In such circumstances, the arbitrator could choose to say nothing.

Another option is for the arbitrator to pretend not to have heard the "answer" and repeat counsel's question-and usually get the same non-responsive answer. In this way, counsel should know of the problem and have an opportunity to deal with it.

I am sometimes told that there is a difference between a witness answering a question in a nonresponsive way in cross-examination and doing so in direct. The difference is said to be based on the fact that the cross-examiner will benefit from the nonresponsive answer which demonstrates that the witness is not forthcoming, which will affect his or her credibility. However, the nonresponsive answer, when not immediately objected to, can hurt you. Assuming that the question asked in cross-examination was a serious one and had a serious purpose, why give the witness an opportunity to avoid answering it and, at the same time, undermine your case? The expressed justification for letting a witness, in effect, make a speech on a topic of his or her choosing which is aimed at making some point(s) against your case, overlooks the fact that you may, in the process of showing-up the witness, be letting him or her choose the direction of your cross-examination.

Allowing the witness to direct the cross-examination is no better than allowing the witness to determine the way in which direct evidence will be adduced. In one case, when I concluded, after many questions had been asked in direct, that the presenter had no idea what his witness would say, I asked him where the evidence was going. The answer was: "I'd like to find out, too." When you've lost control of the witness, you've lost control, whether you are engaged in direct or cross-examination.

9. The Limits of Informality

There are some instances when counsel knows that an answer is not responsive and endeavors to convince the chair that it will become so if the witness is only left to "answer in his own way." There are some witnesses who will only answer a question they feel comfortable with-usually one they silently ask themselves as a substitute for the one put by counsel. In my experience, such a witness rarely gets around to answering responsively no matter how much time is given to answer "in his own way."

When, for example, a witness who is asked if he or she saw a door on the north wall of a room, starts to give a short lecture on the history of doors, the witness should be interrupted and the question repeated. If a responsive answer is still not forthcoming, the witness should be directed to answer the question first and add necessary explanatory detail later.

When it is obvious that a witness is not answering a question appropriately, counsel does not gain credibility by insisting that the witness is doing so, but "in his own way." Also, counsel should be aware of the disquieting effect of leaving the chair hanging after a question has been asked but not answered responsively. To joust with the chair, in these circumstances, can only be counterproductive.

10. What to Do When the Chair Is "Wrong" Or Misbehaves

Triers are usually aware of their limitations. They know they sometimes make mistakes in their assessment of the facts or the law. Or they may be having a "bad" day in other ways. Nevertheless, during the course of a hearing, when called upon to make a ruling as to the admissibility of evidence or with respect to other matters, and after having done so, arbitrators expect counsel to go on to something else after the ruling is made. It does not enhance counsel's credibility in the eyes of the chair if he or she refuses to follow directions and continues to reargue the same point (usually in the same way) without any substantial new basis for doing so. Nor does it assist counsel to lose his or her professional "cool" and by words, facial expression, or body language indicate what he or she really thinks of the chair's decision.

This does not mean that counsel should not let the chair know when he or she is wrong. Counsel should defend their position vigorously. The way counsel deal with the situation is all important. It is all a matter of balance.

11. The Intrusive Chair

One of the common complaints expressed by counsel about the conduct of some chairs is that they attempt to take over a case by usurping the role of counsel. Such conduct is, of course, improper-but before concluding that that is what is happening, counsel should consider whether the chair is merely trying to understand the case but is being confused by the manner of presentation. It is one thing for a chair to take over a case by assuming the role of counsel, it is quite another thing for him or her to ask witnesses what they mean by their answers when their answers are unclear, or to ask counsel for clarification of a position.

Above all else, good counsel is clear, and to some extent, responsible for the clarity of their witnesses. I am usually uneasy when counsel and their witness appear to be meeting for the first time at the hearing and/or where the witness seems to have an agenda for the presentation of evidence that is at variance with that of counsel. There are some exceptional counsel who have a genius for getting the evidence they want from their witnesses, even when they have had little opportunity to speak to them prior to the hearing. Most of us lack this gift, and for us there is no substitute for preparation. Your witnesses must know what you expect from them.

12. Don't Let Your Client Usurp Your Role

Sometimes clients will try to influence counsel to advocate their case according to their theory of advocacy. They may strongly suggest that a certain witness be called, that a particular approach to cross-examination be followed, that certain questions be asked or arguments made, or that counsel play "hardball' and be uncooperative with the "enemy."

Some clients do not understand, even after the matter has been fully discussed with them and counsel has explained that their suggestions are inappropriate tactically and/or ethically. Many clients may not understand why you are accommodating the other side by agreeing to facts that are not in dispute or by voluntarily producing documents. The client may not understand why counsel does not resort to the full panoply of cross-examination mechanisms. The client does not understand why counsel is not "tougher," more abrasive, and threatening.

In my experience, good counsel have no difficulty in maintaining their professional integrity while, at the same time, attracting and retaining clients. There is plenty of room for tough advocacy while, at the same time, behaving fairly and ethically. That the forum is arbitration and not the court is no excuse for forgetting the lessons of many of the relevant rules of professional conduct. Nonlawyer presenters should not hide behind the fact that they are not legally trained when it comes to adhering to recognized ethical standards in advocating a case.

There are occasions when counsel, after endeavoring to convince the client of the inappropriateness of a suggestion with respect to the presentation of a case, will fail to do so. Counsel may then attempt to achieve a very precarious balance between proper professional conduct and giving the client what he or she wants. This being an imperfect world, I am used to hearing arguments made or approaches taken which seem to owe more to the wishes of the client to ventilate (which is, up to a point, quite appropriate) than to a professional analysis of the needs of the case. Some counsel, however, are very adept at conveying subliminal signals which say: "I am doing this for the client. Please don't overreact. I'll get to the good stuff soon."

13. Be Assertive, Not Abusive

An advocate is to some extent an actor and must consider what is the best affect or "face" to present to a tribunal. I am not impressed with counsel who is unremittingly abrasive and hostile to his or her opponents, to witnesses, and even to chairs. Such counsel appear to approach a hearing as if anyone associated with the other side is automatically not to be believed and not worthy of respect. It is possible, however, to be tough-minded without being hostile. It is far more effective to reserve for an appropriate time those instances when you may display higher emotion. Demonstrating a milder visage at all other times more often has the beneficial effect of disarming a difficult witness.

Arbitrators are sensitive to the problems of presenters who live in the real world and must avoid unnecessarily antagonizing those they represent (whose view of a case may be unrealistic). In order to move a case along arbitrators will often give messages to counsel that they had better leave a particular approach if they hope to succeed. This can create a difficulty for counsel who realize that their client feels very strongly about the point. Some clients are mightily impressed by counsel who refuse to give up and continue to challenge the arbitrator with increasing vigor. It doesn't take long for vigor to reach a more abrasive level, and there is a temptation to curry favor with the client by becoming increasingly aggressive as the arbitrator continues to reject an argument or evidence. The most successful presenters do not permit themselves to be manipulated by clients.

14.   Taking the Rules of Evidence Seriously

Counsel who more usually appear in court often find the conduct of an arbitration to be "too loose" in its treatment of the rules of evidence.

The fact that arbitrators may not be bound by the conventional rules of evidence in civil cases does not mean that those rules will not be followed or given significant consideration. I believe that for the most part they are honored, but in a different way.

Even in some civil court cases, certain evidence that is objected to will be heard subject to weight. What this usually means is that, except in obvious cases, evidence will be heard and fuller argument, with respect to its weight, given during the course of final argument.

If you have an argument to make with respect to a rule of evidence, it will be listened to and heeded if you take the trouble to present it clearly. There is little difference between the practical impact on a judge and on an arbitrator of a common-sense rule of evidence properly explained. During the course of reviewing the evidence, counsel can explain why a particular rule of evidence ought to be followed and with what result.

15. Leading with Your Chin

Life would be a lot easier for presenters if they could give evidence instead of having their witnesses do so. After all, presenters usually know what their witnesses could testify-if they only would. Unfortunately, some witnesses have difficulty in responding, as anticipated, to the usual prompts, and the presenter has to resort to more pointed prompts, which often result in objections that the questions are leading (usually where the evidence is of a contentious nature). Even where an arbitrator relaxes the rules against leading a witness, advocates should remember the tactical disadvantage of leading. The rule against leading is a common sense one: it is the witness' statement of facts (his or her memory, and statement, of them) and not the presenter's that must be placed before the arbitrator. Where leading is persistent, the arbitrator is likely to apply it in deciding upon the credibility of the evidence. In applying common sense, an arbitrator is not making the hearing unnecessarily technical.

16. The Slippery Slope of Bad Behavior

Most counsel behave civilly towards each other and towards witnesses. When one counsel does not behave civilly towards an opponent, opposing counsel may respond in kind. This is not a smart thing to do. While most chairs accept a certain amount of less-than-perfect conduct, they are appalled by displays of continuing unprofessional behavior, including attempts to gain unfair advantage through such means. As counsel faced with such behavior, it may take a certain amount of self-control to limit your response to raising an objection and not stooping to offending counsel's level, but it is the better course to exercise restraint.

17. The Pitfalls of Re-Examination (Re-Direct)

A frequent dispute that can be encountered by arbitrators at hearings is whether to allow certain questions to be asked in re-examination (re-direct). Sometimes it is difficult to determine if the matter in dispute had been dealt with in cross-examination and is properly the subject of re-examination. I recently was the chair in a case where the cross-examination of a witness took eight days, and it was difficult to make a speedy decision as to whether certain matters had been dealt with in cross-examination. The usual practice, and I believe it is the practice of many chairs, is to allow a question in re-examination even when there is some doubt as to its propriety, as long as counsel for the opposite side is given an opportunity to further examine on the subject. This approach can be frustrating to counsel, but it does not create any serious injustice, as long as counsel has the right to further question the witness on the point.

In my experience as a chair over the last 30 years, counsel asking for such an opportunity has never abused this accommodation by attempting to ask a further series of questions that are of doubtful propriety. Also, I can't remember many occasions when a disputed question had any meaningful impact on the result.

18. Don't Try to Take Advantage of Inconsequential Inconsistencies

As all arguments of law are not equally persuasive, neither is all evidence that might be adduced of equal weight. For this reason, counsel has to decide how much emphasis to place on apparent inconsistencies in the evidence of a witness called by the other side. Counsel, in deciding whether it should be pursued with much vigor, has to be sensitive to the nature of the inconsistency, the reasons for its significance, and its potential for having an important bearing on the outcome. When counsel tries to make too much of an obviously minor matter, they risk trivializing their case, unnecessarily prolonging the hearing, and boring the arbitrator. At worst, such tactics may be seen as a kind of obfuscation intended to confuse the issues rather than a means of seeking a fair and sound disposition of the dispute.

19. Some Lessons from Tolstoy[2]

The problems that I have dealt with are not new, and I have obtained much help from Count Leo Tolstoy's insights. Not his literary ones, but those gained by him as an arbitrator. Like many others who have a day job, Tolstoy moonlighted as an arbitrator, having been appointed by the then equivalent of the Office of Arbitration (in his case the governor of Tula) as an "arbiter of the peace" to settle disputes between landowners and peasants in the fourth precinct of the district of Krapivna, when the serfs were emancipated in 1861.

After his first award, which allowed the serfs' "grievance," there was a storm of protest among the local aristocracy, who regarded him to be pro-serf, and who petitioned the authorities to have him removed from the list of approved arbitrators. Despite the opposition of his peers, he was retained on the list with the support of lieutenant-general Daragan,

---

[2] HENRI TROYAT, WITH THANKS TO TOLSTOY, Penguin Literary Biographies (1987).

the governor of Tula, who spoke of Tolstoy as "a highly educated man, entirely committed to the task at hand...and much respected."[3]

It was said that Tolstoy took every case seriously and that it required great courage and perseverance on his part to perform his duties in the climate of hatred that surrounded him on both sides. "Whatever decision his sense of equity led him to adopt [he] was sure to cause dissatisfaction to both sides."[4]

Conclusion

"Experience is the name everyone gives to their mistakes."[5] This article was written in recognition of the difficulty experienced by counsel who must learn largely by doing, and with a view to highlighting some not infrequently observed problems. For most counsel, the primary teacher of advocacy is experience, under whose tutelage skills are acquired-usually after much pain, suffering, and embarrassment.

Learning to be a competent advocate under existing conditions is difficult because counsel very frequently learn mostly through unsupervised experience. This is not to deny the assistance given to counsel by colleagues and mentors, and sometimes by chairs. Nor does it overlook the knowledge that can be gained from attending lectures and seminars and reading the many fine guides on the art of advocacy.

However, unless a more comprehensive mentoring program is instituted, the progress of counsel towards professional proficiency will continue to be more painful than it ought to be. Perhaps it is time to consider a program where counsel could inexpensively videotape their cases, without the need for an operator or other production assistance. With the cooperation of organizations such as the American Arbitration Association, experienced counsel could serve as ongoing mentors to review portions of the tapes from time to time and offer suggestions that would improve the quality of case presentation. Because the process would be ongoing, good practices could be reinforced and faulty ones discouraged. To see oneself, warts and all, is never pleasant. I believe that the rewards of doing so will make it worthwhile. Those who present cases at arbitration would not be the last ones to benefit from this technology as an aid to reviewing real life performance.[6]

---

[3] *Id.* at 301.
[4] *Id.*
[5] Oscar Wilde, Lady Windemere's Fan, Act 3.
[6] See Gorsky, A Modest Proposal for Videotaping Actual Cases as a Method of Advocacy Training, 23 THE LAW SOCIETY OF UPPER CANADA GAZETTA 82 (1988).

CHAPTER EIGHT

ARBITRATION AND PROFESSIONAL RESPONSIBILITY

I. Arbitration Confidentiality

Confidentiality During and After Arbitration

by Edward Dolido[*]

In contrast to judicial proceedings, where there is a presumption of public access to records and proceedings, arbitration is presumptively confidential.[1] **For many parties, this may be one of the most influential reasons for choosing arbitration. Yet there are no guarantees that the arbitration proceeding will actually remain confidential and the degree of confidentiality the parties obtain in arbitration will, in large measure, be dependent upon their own advance planning and the procedural mechanisms they implement.**

In addition, because arbitration awards frequently become the subject of litigation in a proceeding to confirm or vacate or modify the award, the parties may find that the confidentiality they secured in arbitration evaporates when the dispute reaches the public forum.

Surprisingly, there is no established mechanism for ensuring that the parties receive the benefit of any bargained-for confidentiality when litigating over an arbitration award, and little case law addressing this issue. Nevertheless, there are compelling arguments to be made for

---

[*] The author is a partner in the New York office of Fulbright & Jaworski L.L.P. Dolido holds a B.S. from the Wharton School at the University of Pennsylvanis and a J.D. from Boston University. He is the author of *Overlooked Dangers of the Internet: Some Practical Considerations*, 13 COMPUTER LAW STRATEGIST 1, (February 1997). This article is based on a paper the author presented at a conference on strategies and trends in arbitration and mediation.

[1] The presumption is a practical one rather than a legal one. While most parties elect to conduct their arbitrations in confidence, in the absence of specific agreement (or arbitral rule), the parties generally are free to divulge details of the proceedings. *See, e.g.,* United States. v. Panhandle Eastern Corp., 118 F.R.D. 346 (D. Del. 1988).

protecting the parties' confidentiality when an arbitrated matter ends up in court. This article briefly discusses general confidentiality principles in arbitration and litigation, identifies some mechanisms that might help promote confidentiality in arbitration, and lays out an argument, in reliance on some of the meager precedents that do exist, for maintaining confidentiality when an arbitration award becomes the subject of litigation.[2]

Confidentiality in Arbitration

Since arbitration is a creature of contract, the parties are free to provide for virtually any degree of confidentiality that they wish. Theoretically, confidentiality in arbitration should be easy to achieve; the parties and the arbitrator need only agree to keep the proceedings confidential. The leading arbitration treatise explains succinctly: "Privacy of arbitration is one of the essential factors carefully observed in institutional arbitration where no one other than the parties is allowed to gain any knowledge of the records and files."[3] Thus, the major administrative bodies explicitly recognize that confidentiality in arbitration is to be expected. The American Arbitration Association, for example, has instructed its arbitrators: "One of the reasons that parties resort to arbitration is their desire for privacy. You should therefore maintain the privacy of proceedings, unless both parties agree to open the hearings or unless a statute provides otherwise."[4]

As a practical matter, designating the proceeding as confidential is only half the battle. The proceeding must actually be kept confidential and, in this regard, the degree of confidentiality the parties achieve is a direct function of their decision whether or not to employ arbitration, and if so, the procedures they implement.[5]

Generally, any procedure the parties adopt to increase the confidentiality of their dispute will carry with it increased burdens. For

---

[2] This chapter focuses primarily on the decisions in the federal and state courts of New York. It may be that other jurisdictions offer greater or lesser protections that should be considered in drafting an arbitration clause where confidentiality is important.

[3] M. Domke, Domke on Commercial Arbitration § 24.07 at 387 (3d. ed. 1998).

[4] AMERICAN ARBITRATION ASSOCIATION, A GUIDE FOR COMMERCIAL ARBITRATORS 18 (1995). *See also* R-25 of the AAA Commercial Dispute Resolution Procedures.

[5] As discussed below, the decision to arbitrate provides the parties with the ability to protect the confidentiality of matters that might not be protected in the courts. Conversely, in certain situations, arbitration may provide weaker mechanisms for insuring confidentiality than the judicial system because courts have the power to punish violations as contempt. Arbitrators lack that power.

example, the surest way to maximize confidentiality is to disclose the information to the fewest people. Thus, at one extreme, the parties might provide for an ad hoc arbitration, and they could not only dispense with an administrative body but could eliminate court reporters and third-party witnesses as well. While such procedures would minimize the number of people aware of the dispute, it would impose obvious additional burdens on the parties and the arbitrator. At the same time, it is important to keep in mind the limits of what the parties can control: Even if everyone who participates in the arbitration process vigorously abides by his or her obligations to maintain confidentiality, third parties may nevertheless subpoena information from the parties or even from the arbitrators.[6]

Mechanisms for Increasing Confidentiality

The parties' objectives in seeking confidentiality will differ from case to case and will determine the appropriateness of procedural mechanisms to ensure that confidentiality is maintained. For example, the parties may wish to protect only one piece of evidence (perhaps a single confidential document) or multiple documents on a single subject (e.g., testimony and documents relating to a technology claimed to be a trade secret). In other cases, they may wish to avoid disclosing even the fact that a dispute has arisen between them.

Confidentiality Agreement in Arbitration Agreement. To the extent possible, these objectives should be identified in advance of drafting the arbitration agreement so necessary safeguards can be built into the agreement itself. Once a dispute arises, the benefits of confidentiality often favor one party more than the other. Thus, it can be expected that the party who benefits less will resist steps to impose confidentiality, either because those steps can be onerous, or simply in deference to the time-honored litigation principle that one should refuse to agree to anything that benefits the other party.

---

[6] *See, e.g.*, Grumman Aerospace Corp. v. Titanium Metals Corp., 91 F.R.D. 84, 87-88 (E.D.N.Y. 1981) ("parties [may not] contract privately for the confidentiality of documents, and foreclose others from obtaining, in the course of litigation, materials that are relevant to their efforts to vindicate a legal position"); Kamyr v. Combustion Eng'g, 161 A.D.2d 233, 233, 554 N.Y.S.2d 619, 620 (N.Y. App. Div. 1990) ("Evidentiary material at an arbitration proceeding is not immune from disclosure"). *Cf.* Galleon Syndicate Corp. v. Pan Atlantic Group, 223 A.D.2d 510, 637 N.Y.S.2d 104 (N.Y. App. Div. 1996) (requiring production of documents but implying in dictum that the analysis might be different if there had been a confidentiality agreement).

Dealing with Third Parties. Suppose the parties have agreed to keep not only the entire arbitration proceeding confidential, but also the fact and nature of the dispute. That principle is neutral as between the parties so they might easily agree to incorporate that principle in their arbitration agreement. However, what happens when the arbitration is commenced and one party wishes to interview or call as witnesses third parties who might have knowledge relevant to the dispute? Such questioning will explicitly or implicitly reveal to third parties the existence of the dispute, if not its nature.

An arbitrator is unlikely to preclude a party from interviewing or calling third-party witnesses because the natural inclination is to refuse to suppress evidence and to permit the parties to present whatever evidence they wish. Therefore, unless the arbitration agreement specifically addresses the issue of whether or not there may be third-party witnesses and, if so, what safeguards will be in place, the agreement to not disclose the existence of the dispute may be wholly vitiated once the arbitration proceeds.[7]

If third parties are to testify, there is little that can be done in arbitration to prevent them from disclosing what they learn. Of course, expert witnesses can be required to sign confidentiality agreements before they are retained, and third-party fact witnesses also could be asked to sign such agreements.[8] But if a third-party fact witness refuses to sign a confidentiality agreement, the parties have no recourse. The witness can be compelled by subpoena to testify, but cannot be compelled to remain silent about the proceeding.

Of course, the arbitrators could refuse to hear testimony from third parties who refuse to agree to maintain confidentiality. But they might well refuse to take this step on the ground that it is inherently unfair to deprive a party of relevant evidence as a result of the unilateral actions of a third party over whom it has no control.[9] If, however, the arbitration

---

[7] If the parties do not receive notice that a third-party subpoena has been served on the arbitrator, the arbitrator might quietly comply even if the subpoena otherwise might have been successfully resisted.

[8] One ground for vacating an award in New York is the arbitrator's refusal to hear relevant evidence. Gervant v. New England Fire Ins., 306 N.Y. 393, 400, 118 N.E.2d 574, 577 (N.Y. 1954). However, it would not be misconduct for the arbitrator to refuse to hear evidence that the parties precluded by agreement. In re Civil Service Employees Ass'n v. Soper, 56 N.Y.2d 639, 450 N.Y.S.2d 786, 436 N.E.2d 192 (N.Y. 1982).

[9] Even if third-party witnesses sign confidentiality agreements, the enforceability of these agreements is questionable insofar as there would be no consideration. Nevertheless, such undertakings are likely to have at least some deterrent effect.

agreement specifically states that no witnesses will be permitted to testify absent a signed confidentiality agreement, the arbitrators might be more inclined to preclude such testimony.[10]

Arbitration Clause in Confidentiality Agreement. One mechanism that might further the confidentiality of arbitration is the inclusion of an arbitration clause in the confidentiality agreement itself.[11] The typical confidentiality agreement does not usually contain an arbitration clause. If a party decides to litigate a breach of the confidentiality agreement, the court is unlikely to accept the parties' view of the necessity for confidentiality, as discussed below. This could result in the incongruous situation where a breach of the confidentiality obligation is litigated in an open public proceeding.[12]

Bare Award. Finally, because the arbitration award probably will be confirmed in court so that a judgment can be entered thereon, any findings of fact, conclusions of law, or a detailed discussion of the dispute contained in the award may find its way into the public record. To avoid such disclosure, the parties might specify in their arbitration agreement that the award be limited to a monetary award in favor of the prevailing party. Such a bare award will not disclose confidential information (other than who won the dispute) and has the added benefit (or disadvantage, depending on your point of view) of being more difficult to challenge in court because it does not expose the arbitrators' reasoning to attack.

Judicial Proceedings

Over the past few years, the federal courts have changed their position with respect to the granting of confidentiality orders and sealing the record in civil commercial cases. At one point, such orders were granted routinely by federal courts at the request of the parties. Then the circuit courts admonished that a record should be sealed only in exceptional cases. This position may be softening, but it remains true that federal courts generally will not seal the record simply because the

---

[10] In all likelihood, it would also be reversible error to preclude such testimony. *See supra*, n. 7.

[11] *See supra*, n. 7.

[12] The parties might encounter some resistance in attempting to incorporate an arbitration clause into a confidentiality agreement with an ADR provider because that organization could not ethically administer an arbitration to which it is a party and would find it distasteful to have its arbitration administered by a competitor.

parties might agree that they desire the proceeding to be kept confidential.[13]

The Supreme Court has recognized the existence of a general, common-law right of public access to judicial records.[14] "Thus, while public access to court records and proceedings is not absolute, there has been a long-standing presumption in its favor and against sealing."[15] A similar presumption of openness is embodied in the New York Uniform Rules for Trial Courts which provides, in part: "Except where otherwise provided by statute or rule, a court shall not enter an order in any action or proceeding sealing the court records, whether in whole or in part, except upon a written finding of good cause, which shall specify the grounds therefore.[16] Thus, courts have been instructed that they "must carefully and skeptically review sealing requests to insure that there really is an extraordinary circumstance or compelling need."[17]

Judicial Proceedings Related to Arbitration

When an arbitration award is brought to court to be confirmed or challenged, the presumption of confidentiality that exists in arbitration collides with the presumption of public access that exists in a judicial proceeding. If the parties had agreed to maintain the arbitration in confidence for reasons that do not satisfy a court's view of "extraordinary circumstances," "compelling need," or "good cause," then the possibility exists that the confirmation or vacatur proceedings will be made public. This could lead to the disclosure of hearing transcripts or evidence admitted in the confidential arbitration hearing.[18]

There are surprisingly few reported decisions dealing with this precise issue, perhaps because the orders sealing records are themselves

---

[13] If the breach of a confidentiality agreement is to be arbitrated, a court should still be available to grant a preliminary injunction or other interlocutory relief. The court is less likely to address the broader issue of confidentiality of the arbitration proceedings in this context because it will not reach the merits of the dispute.

[14] A comprehensive discussion of judicial attitudes toward sealing orders, protective orders and secrecy orders is found in Laurie Kratky Dore, *Secrecy By Consent: The Use and Limits of Confidentiality in the Pursuit of Settlement*, 74 NOTRE DAME L. REV. 283 (1999).

[15] Nixon v. Warner Communications, 435 U.S. 589, 597 (1978).

[16] Encyclopedia Brown Prod. v. Home Box Office, 26 F. Supp. 2d 606, 610 (S.D.N.Y. 1998).

[17] 22 N.Y.C.R.R. § 216.1(a). *See also* Aetna Casualty and Surety v. Certain Underwriters at Lloyd's, 176 Misc. 2d 598, 676 N.Y.S.2d 734 (N.Y. Sup. Ct. N.Y. Co. 1998).

[18] *In re* Orion Pictures Corp., 21 F.3d 24, 27 (2d Cir. 1994).

sealed. On the other hand, there are a plethora of cases discussing the general rule (outside the arbitration context) that orders to seal the record can be granted only when certain recognized categories of information (e.g., trade secrets or competitive information) are involved or the potential injury is clearly defined and very serious.[19] Under this rule, neither the existence of a confidentiality agreement nor the consent of all parties to the sealing of the record guarantees that a court will permit documents to be filed under seal.[20]

Worse, the public policy rationale for requiring public access to judicial proceedings is no less compelling when the proceedings involve a confidential arbitration award. That policy emphasizes that public scrutiny is necessary to maintain the accountability and, therefore, the integrity of the judicial system.[21] If courts consistently were to respect the parties' desire to maintain the confidentiality of their arbitration proceedings, then the vast majority of judicial decisions involving arbitral awards effectively would be beyond public scrutiny.

At the same time, when applied to judicial proceedings relating to confidential arbitration awards, this principle of public access wholly undermines the parties' reasonable expectation that arbitration will provide a confidential method of resolving their disputes, and defeats one of the primary advantages of arbitration. The Second Circuit appears to have implicitly endorsed that expectation in *DiRussa v. Dean Witter Reynolds, Inc.*[22] There, it affirmed a district court order sealing the entire record in a proceeding to confirm, modify or vacate an arbitration award (exception for the court's opinions on procedural matters and attorneys'

---

[19] It is not inconceivable that one party, in moving to confirm or vacate a confidential arbitration award, could file the entire record of the arbitration in the district court to show that the award was or was not the end product of a full and fair hearing. Such filing, if public, would wholly vitiate the value of maintaining confidentiality during the arbitration.

[20] *See, e.g.,* Joy v. North, 692 F.2d 880, 894 (2d Cir. 1982), *cert. den.,* 460 U.S. 1051 (1998) ("only the most compelling reasons"); Dept. of Economic Dev. v. Arthur Andersen & Co., 924 F. Supp. 449, 487 (S.D.N.Y. 1996) ("'Good cause' is not established merely by the prospect of negative publicity"). The precise formulation of the standard varies. *See, e.g.,* EEOC v. National Children's Center, 98 F.3d 1406, 1409 (D.C. Cir. 1996) ("strength of any property and privacy interests asserted" must be weighed); Hagestad v. Tragesser, 49 F.3d 1430, 1434 (9th Cir. 1995) ("compelling reason"); Leucadia Inc. v. Applied Extrusion Tech., 998 F.2d 157, 166 (3d Cir. 1993) ("good cause"); SEC v. Van Waeyenberghe, 990 F.2d 845 (5th Cir. 1993) (declining to hold the presumption of public access to be "strong" and requiring a weighing of the respective interests); Brown v. Advantage Eng'g, 960 F.2d 1013, 1016 (11th Cir. 1992) ("extraordinary circumstances").

[21] *See, e.g.,* Vassiliades v. Israely, 714 F. Supp. 604, 606 (D. Conn. 1989).

[22] United States v. Amodeo, 71 F.3d 1044, 1048 (2d Cir. 1995).

fees), without pausing to analyze whether the subject matter was sufficiently "exceptional" to justify such order.

In *DiRussa*, the parties had entered into a confidentiality agreement providing that the documents and information disclosed during the arbitration could be used only for purposes of the arbitration and, if filed in court in connection with the arbitration, would have to be filed under seal. While this agreement was "'narrowly drawn' to protect only information produced by the parties and obtained solely by virtue of their production by an opposing party in the course of the NASD arbitration," it nevertheless appears to have encompassed all information produced during the arbitration, without regard to whether or not the information contained trade secrets or implicated privacy concerns. In other words, under the parties' confidentiality agreement, the criterion for confidential treatment was simple: If the information was obtained during the course of the arbitration, then it would have to be filed under seal in any subsequent court proceeding.

The district court in *DiRussa* sealed the entire record. After the plaintiff objected that the order went beyond the scope of the parties' confidentiality agreement, the court acknowledged that only those portions of the record encompassed by the confidentiality agreement, i.e., only the information obtained during the course of the arbitration, was required to be sealed. Nevertheless, it did not alter the order sealing the entire record because "it [was] not feasible to attempt a partial unsealing within the context of the parties' confidentiality agreement."

The Second Circuit affirmed, holding that "the district court did not abuse its discretion in sealing the file pursuant to the confidentiality agreement." Thus, *DiRussa* stands for the proposition that the parties' agreement to maintain confidentiality in an arbitration proceeding can be respected by the courts through an order sealing the record in a proceeding to confirm or vacate the arbitration award, without regard to the merits of the confidentiality agreement itself. *DiRussa*, therefore, is valuable authority for parties seeking to seal post-arbitration judicial proceedings that do not involve subject matter that courts are more commonly willing to protect.

The sealing of the record when judicial proceedings involve confidential arbitration proceedings may not be irreconcilable with the policy of promoting judicial accountability. An arbitral record that comes before the court in a proceeding to confirm, modify, or vacate, in which the scope of review is extremely limited,[23] may contain documents and testimony that would never have made it into the record in a purely judicial proceeding. The reason is that many of the safeguards inherent in judicial adjudication that are designed to protect parties from scurrilous accusations and unreliable evidence—for example, the rules of evidence that require a foundation for evidence and preclude hearsay—are typically dispensed with in arbitration.[24] This difference, under existing precedents, arguably should be enough to outweigh the policy favoring public access to judicial proceedings.

For example, the Second Circuit has held that documents produced in discovery and "matters that come within a court's purview solely to insure their irrelevance" are not within reach of the presumption of public access precisely because they came before the court without passing through the procedural filters designed to ensure their reliability and truthfulness.[25] Because much of the record of an arbitration will contain similarly unreliable statements due to the lack of strict procedural protections (on the theory that the arbitrators can filter the information themselves without the need to rely on evidentiary rules), the arbitral record should similarly be outside the presumption of public access.

It could also be argued that a confidentiality agreement entered into before or during arbitration is analogous to a protective order entered during litigation. When a confidentiality order in litigation has been challenged, the Second Circuit has reversed the normal presumption requiring the proponent of the order to show good cause for its entry. It stated: "[O]nce a confidentiality order has been entered and relied upon, it can only be modified if an 'extraordinary circumstance' or 'compelling need' warrants the requested modification."[26]

---

[23] 121 F.3d 818 (2d Cir. 1997), *cert. den.*, 522 U.S. 1049 (1998), an age discrimination case in which the former employee arbitrated his claims against his former employer.

[24] *See, e.g.,* 9 U.S.C. § 10 and N.Y. CPLR 7511 (grounds for vacating an award generally limited to fraud, corruption, partiality or misconduct).

[25] For example, AAA Commercial Arbitration Rule R-33(a) provides that "[c]onformity to legal rules of evidence shall not be necessary."

[26] Amodeo, *supra*, n. 21, 71 F.3d at 1048-49. In so holding, the court cited United States v. Charmer Indus., 711 F.2d 1164, 1171 (2d Cir. 1983) and United States v. Corbitt, 879 F.2d 224, 231 (7th Cir. 1989), which noted that pre-sentencing reports in criminal cases generally are kept confidential because, among other reasons, there are no formal limitations on their contents, and they will contain much information which is untrustworthy or simply incorrect. *Cf.* Illinois v. Abott & Assoc., 460 U.S. 557, 567 n.11 (1983) (noting that "grand jury secrecy has traditionally been invoked to justify the limited procedural safeguards available to witnesses and persons under investigation").

This analogy is not perfect, however, because a judicial order presumably would not have been entered initially without a showing of good cause. Nevertheless, the parties' reliance on the confidentiality of the arbitration evokes the same considerations that justify reversing the normal presumption of public access in litigation. Given the policy favoring arbitration and precluding courts from second-guessing arbitral decisions, it would seem reasonable to treat the confidentiality of arbitration as a binding element that is not subject to reconsideration by a court.

Unfortunately, however, under the current state of the law, parties may not safely assume that the judiciary will respect their confidentiality agreement once the arbitrated matter reaches the courts.[27]

Conclusion

While several arguments are suggested here that might persuade a court to seal the record concerning the arbitration proceedings, the significant policy and legal precedents favoring public access might result in public disclosure of those proceedings, despite the parties' assumption that they would remain confidential. To the extent possible, therefore, the parties should chart their arbitral course in advance with an eye towards minimizing the risk of unexpected disclosure when a court is asked to rule on some aspect of the arbitration proceeding.

---

[27] FDIC v. Ernst & Ernst, 677 F.2d 230, 232 (2d Cir. 1982). *See also* Palmieri v. New York, 779 F.2d 861, 864-65 (2d Cir. 1985).

II. The Use of Sanctions in Arbitration

Sanctions & Arbitration Proceedings

by Georgene M. Vairo[*]

Time and again, we hear lawyers and judges complain about frivolous litigation and abusive conduct by counsel. This article discusses the sanctions available to curb abusive behavior during arbitration proceedings.

Since the adoption in 1983 of amended Federal Rule of Civil Procedure 11, lawyers have become increasingly aware of the availability of sanctions. In fact, sanctions awarded under Rule 11 were so numerous that the rule was toned down by amendments adopted in 1993. Nonetheless, Rule 11—together with other federal authority for imposing sanctions, such as 28 U.S.C. § 1927, the court's inherent power, and Federal Rule of Appellate Procedure 38—continues to be a potent tool. Most states have adopted a similar rule to punish those who assert frivolous legal or factual positions or engage in abusive conduct.[1]

Lawyers and arbitrators are not immune from experiencing less than professional behavior in the ADR context. For example, an attorney or party may behave inappropriately in an arbitration or engage in abusive conduct or misuse the judicial system in an action arising out of an arbitration. Often a party to an arbitration agreement will attempt to use the judicial system to avoid or end-run the arbitration.

Whether sanctions are available to punish abusive behavior depends upon the forum where the conduct occurs. If abusive conduct occurs in the judicial arena, the court's sanctioning power may be brought to bear. No agreement among the parties is required. If such behavior occurs in an arbitration proceeding, the arbitrator may sanction the party responsible for such conduct only if the parties' agreement explicitly or

---

[*] Georgene M. Vairo is a professor of law and William M. Rains Fellow at Loyola Law School in Los Angeles. She earned a B.A. from Sweet Briar College, a M.Ed. with Distinction from the University of Virginia and a cum laude J.D. from Fordham University. Vairo is a Member of the Board of Editors of MOORE'S FEDERAL PRACTICE and is the author of *Mass Tort Bankruptcies: The Who, the Why and the How*, 78 AMERICAN BANKRUPTCY LAW JOURNAL 93 (2004).

[1] *See, e.g.*, Cal. C.P. § 177.5; NY Standards and Administrative Policies Chapter C. Rules of the Chief Administrator of the Courts, part 130 (Costs and Sanctions), subpart 130-1.

implicitly authorizes the arbitrator to impose sanctions. It is generally thought that an arbitrator does not have this power absent a contractual provision.[2]

Since the arbitrator's authority to impose sanctions is completely dependent on the arbitration agreement, if the agreement is silent as to sanctions, the arbitrator may not impose them.

The power to impose sanctions may be included in a "sanctions clause" in the parties' agreement. A relatively simple clause might provide: "The arbitrators shall be empowered to impose sanctions and to take other actions with regard to the parties that the arbitrators deem necessary to the same extent that a judge could pursuant to the Federal Rules of Civil Procedure."[3]

The power to sanction also may be incorporated indirectly into an arbitration agreement by adopting the arbitration rules of an ADR provider that includes this power in the arbitrator's authority. For example, Rule 43 of the American Arbitration Association Commercial Arbitration Rules authorizes the arbitrator to award counsel fees and witness expenses to the extent a party asserted a frivolous claim or defense or to a greater extent if the arbitrator deems it just and equitable to do so.

Another example is Article 20 of the Center For Public Resources Model Employment Termination Dispute Resolution Procedures, which provides that the arbitrator may award counsel fees and costs in these circumstances: "upon a finding that the claim or counterclaim was frivolous or brought solely to harass the Employee, the Employer or the Employer's personnel," or "upon a finding that the other Party (a) engaged in unreasonable delay, (b) failed to comply with the Adjudicator's discovery order, or (c) failed to comply with requirements of confidentiality under the Model Procedure."

Of course, parties to arbitration agreements should consider whether it is desirable to give the arbitrator sanction authority for by doing so, they are expanding the arbitrator's arsenal of remedies. If the drafter does not want the arbitrator to have the power to impose sanctions or

---

[2] *See* CALIFORNIA PRACTICE GUIDE — ALTERNATE DISPUTE RESOLUTION 4-103 (Rutter 1995) (unless otherwise agreed, arbitrators have no power to sanction parties for dilatory conduct or for contempt); Luster v. Collins, 15 Cal App. 4th 1338, 1349-50 (1991) (sanctions for violation of arbitrator's order); *cf.* Thompson v. Jesperson, 222 Cal. App. 3d 964, 968 (1990).

[3] Richard Chernick, *Shaping the Arbitration Process by Controlling the Power of the Arbitrator, in Alternative Dispute Resolution; How To Use It To Your Advantage!* (ALI-ABA Course of Study Materials, December 1996).

attorneys' fees or costs, it would be prudent for the drafter to strike any references in the agreement to such matters. To make the point more directly, a clause could also be included stating that the arbitrator shall have no power to impose sanctions or award attorneys' fees and costs.

Contractual Authority

Parties should be aware that the court will closely examine the arbitration agreement to determine whether the arbitrator has the authority to sanction. This is consistent with the analysis in all matters of contractual arbitration—the court will look to see what the parties agreed to.[4]

Most arbitration agreements do not expressly address the question of the arbitrator's power to impose sanctions. If they did, courts would no doubt enforce them. Absent an express provision, the courts will examine the agreement to see if there is a source of sanction authority in a less then explicit provision. Generally, the courts will uphold a remedy selected by an arbitrator so long as it is even arguably authorized in the arbitration agreement.[5]

An example is *David v. Abergel*.[6] In this case the parties' agreement conferred on the arbitrator the power to "grant any remedy or relief to which a party is entitled under California law." The arbitrator found that the claim was frivolous and awarded sanctions against the claimant under California Code of Civil Procedure § 128.5 in the sum of $75,000. The California Court of Appeal upheld the sanction award, finding that the reference in the agreement to "any remedy or relief under California law" was sufficient contractual authority to impose sanctions.

The *David* court said that the clause empowering "any remedy or relief under California law" was critical. It distinguished cases in which the parties simply agreed to submit their dispute to arbitration without any reference to remedies or relief under California law.[7] It also distinguished cases that simply specified that the arbitration would be conducted "as authorized by the Code of Civil Procedure."[8]

---

[4] First Options of Chicago, Inc. v. Kaplan, 115 S. Ct. 1920 (1995) (courts must enforce arbitration agreements as written by the parties just as with other commercial contracts); Moncharsh v. Heily & Blase, 3 Cal 4th 1, 8 (1992).

[5] Advanced Micro Devices v. Intel Corp., 9 Cal. 4th 362, 381, 36 Cal. Rptr. 2d 581, 885 P.2d 994 (1994) (arbitrator's remedy will be upheld so long as arguably based on the arbitration agreement).

[6] 46 Cal. App. 4th 1281 (1996).

[7] Thompson v. Jespersen, *supra*, n. 2.

[8] Luster v. Collins, *supra*, n. 2 ("arbitration as authorized by the Code of Civil Procedure").

There is an important distinction between clauses authorizing any remedy or relief under the law of a particular jurisdiction and clauses simply authorizing "any remedy or relief that the arbitrator deems just and equitable and within the scope of the agreement of the parties." The latter clause is similar to the one invoked by the arbitrator in *Advanced Micro Devices, Inc. v. Intel Corp.*[9] The arbitrator there fashioned a remedy (an imposed license) that a court would not have had the power to impose but which was rationally derived from the contract and the breach. But would such a grant be sufficient to permit sanctions to be imposed against a party for misconduct in an arbitration? Probably not.

In general, grants of authority to devise any remedy or relief the arbitrator believes just and equitable and within the scope of the agreement does not turn the arbitrator into the equivalent of a judge. This language does not adequately convey an intent to give the arbitrator a broad grant of the power to sanction. The sanction power is not necessarily "rationally derived from the contract" and the nature of the arbitrated dispute.

Furthermore, "remedies or relief" generally refers to the remedies a party may be entitled to if it establishes a legal right to recover. Sanctions are different. They generally are not an aspect of the legal right to recover. Indeed, parties usually do not consider the imposition of litigation sanctions when they place the resolution of their dispute in the hands of an arbitrator. What saved the clause in the *David* case, *supra*, was the arguably more explicit clause referencing "any remedy or relief to which a party is entitled under California law."

In order to avoid such fine distinctions, drafters of arbitration agreements who wish to authorize sanctions should include clear provisions regarding the arbitrator's power to impose sanctions or award attorneys' fees and costs. Richard Chernick, an expert on California arbitration law, has suggested the following clause:

> Any controversy, claim or dispute arising out of or relating to this Agreement or the breach, termination, enforcement, interpretation or validity thereof, including the determination of the scope or applicability of this agreement to arbitrate (Dispute), shall be determined by arbitration in Los Angeles, California, before a sole arbitrator, in accordance with the laws of the State of California for agreements made in and to be performed in

---

[9] *Supra*, n.5.

California. The arbitration shall be administered by the American Arbitration Association (AAA) pursuant to its Commercial Arbitration Rules. The arbitrator shall, in the Award, allocate all of the costs of the arbitration, including the fees of the arbitrator and the reasonable attorneys' fees of the prevailing party, against the party who did not prevail. The arbitrator shall also have the power to impose any sanction against any party permitted by California law. Judgment on the Award may be entered in any court having jurisdiction.[10]

As Mr. Chernick advised: "As arbitration of commercial disputes becomes more common, and as parties become more creative in shaping their process to suit their needs, they must be mindful that clear expression of their intent will help them to achieve their objectives and help courts called upon to enforce their clauses to do so consistent with that intent."

Judicial Sanctions

State and federal courts have the power to punish dilatory, frivolous and other inappropriate litigation conduct by imposing monetary and other sanctions.[11] The best known basis for sanctioning parties who use the judicial system to end-run an arbitration proceeding is Rule 11 of the Federal Rules of Civil Procedure. Rule 11 applies to all papers in cases filed in the federal courts that are related to arbitration proceedings. Thus, actions to compel arbitration, stay arbitration, or enforce or challenge an arbitration award are subject to the rule.

It is important to note that Rule 11 does not apply to the papers filed in an underlying arbitration. A seminal case, *Teamsters Local Union No. 430 v. Cement Express*, illustrates the difference. The defendant argued that the plaintiff, who sought enforcement of an arbitration award in federal court, should be sanctioned because the issues were improperly submitted to arbitration. The issue before the court was whether the plaintiff "could reasonably have argued in support of the arbitrator's jurisdiction over the controversy." Because the court found that the plaintiff's position was reasonable, it reversed the sanctions award. It

---

[10] Chernick, *supra*, n.3.
[11] *See, e.g.*, Cal. Code of Civil Procedure §§ 128.5, 128.7, 177.5, 437c(i); Federal Rules of Civil Procedure, Rules 11, 45(c). 9. *See, e.g.*, Sheet Metal Workers, Local No. 162 v. Jason Mfg., 900 F.2d 1392 (9th Cir. 1990) (motion).

reasoned, "Rule 11 was designed to penalize abuse of district court process, not an improper submission to arbitration."[12]

The court set forth the analytical framework for resolving Rule 11 questions in connection with arbitration. Rule 11 does not apply to the arbitration itself. Accordingly, Rule 11 may not be used to punish a party for submitting an issue to arbitration. However, Rule 11 applies to the papers filed in the federal action seeking confirmation of the award.

Typical Scenarios

There are a number of typical scenarios that raise Rule 11 problems. In many cases a party seeking to avoid a contractual duty to arbitrate will file an action seeking to stay or prevent arbitration. Bringing an action in federal court in the face of a clear contractual duty to arbitrate, where no reasonable argument can be made that the action lies outside the scope of the arbitration agreement, may subject the party who filed the suit to sanctions.[13]

For example, in *Confederacion Laborista de Puerto Rico v. Cerveceria India, Inc.*,[14] the union filed a grievance for unjustified discharge pursuant to the administrative procedure provided for in a collective bargaining agreement (CBA). When no agreement could be reached, the union and employer submitted the claim to an arbitrator, as provided in the CBA. While the claim was still before the arbitrator, the union and the discharged employees sued the employer in federal court, and sought to withdraw its grievance before the arbitrator. The district court dismissed the complaint. Relying on Rule 11, the First Circuit affirmed because of well-established precedent requiring exhaustion of procedures under the CBA before bringing a lawsuit. The court stated: "Given the clarity of the precedents of both the Supreme Court and this court on this issue, plaintiffs' claim was entirely unwarranted by existing law or a good faith argument for modification of existing law."

Opposition to a well-grounded action or motion to compel arbitration may also result in a violation of Rule 11. For example, in *Washington*

---

[12] 841 F.2d 66 (3d Cir.), *cert. den.*, 488 U.S. 848 (1988).

[13] *Id.* n. 10. *See also* Local 232, Allied Industrial Workers v. Briggs & Stratton Corp., 837 F.2d 782 (7th Cir. 1988); *In re* Woodcrest Nursing Home, 788 F.2d 894 (2d Cir. 1986); Gelco Corp. v. Baker Indus., 779 F.2d 26 (8th Cir. 1985).

[14] 778 F.2d 65, 66 (1st Cir. 1985). *See also* Mastrobuono v. Shearson Lehman Hutton, 128 F.R.D. 243, 245 (N.D. Ill. 1989).

Hospital Center v. Service Employees International Union, Local 722,[15] since the defendant did not have a reasonable basis in fact or law for opposing arbitration, the court awarded sanctions.

Similarly, when arguments are made that are motivated simply by a desire to forestall complying with an arbitration award, courts may be receptive to motions for sanctions.[16] They will impose a sanction when there is clearly no basis for opposing enforcement of an arbitration award in the federal courts.[17] Courts also may be moved to find a Rule 11 violation when a plaintiff seeks to prevent arbitration.[18]

When there is an obvious jurisdictional bar to arbitration, courts will entertain a sanctions motion. Thus if a party who prefers arbitration responds to an action filed in federal court by moving to compel arbitration, and there is no agreement to arbitrate or other foundation for arbitration, Rule 11 sanctions could be imposed when that party files its opposition papers in the federal court.

Similarly, if the issue of arbitration has already been litigated, sanctions may ensue.[19]

Of course, a party will not be sanctioned for filing papers in connection with arbitration if there has been a reasonable inquiry into the facts and the legal theory espoused is reasonable.[20]

---

[15] *See* Washington Hospital Center v. Serv. Employees Int'l Union, Local 722, 746 F.2d 1503, 1510-13 (D.C. Cir. 1984). *But see* United Food & Commercial Workers Union, Local 1529 v. Delta Catfish Processors, 767 F. Supp. 798, 801 (N.D. Miss. 1991) (denying motion for Rule 11 sanctions against defendant for opposing arbitration).

[16] U.S. Offshore, Inc. v. Seabulk Offshore, Ltd., 753 F. Supp. 86 (S.D.N.Y. 1990).

[17] *See* C. T. Shipping, Ltd. v. DMI (U.S.A.) Ltd., 774 F. Supp. 146, 154-155 (S.D.N.Y. 1991) (sanctioning plaintiffs for seeking to set aside arbitrator's award); Jardine Matheson & Co. v. Saita Shipping, 712 F. Supp. 423, 428-29 (S.D.N.Y. 1989) (sanctions against defendant who tried to prevent enforcement of arbitration award on frivolous ground of arbitrator bias); Quick & Reilly, Inc. v. Jacobson, 126 F.R.D. 24, 26-28 (S.D.N.Y. 1989) (sanctions against plaintiff who sought to prevent enforcement of arbitration award).

[18] Safeco Ins. Co. of America v. Hays, 715 F. Supp. 342, 345 (M.D. Fla. 1989) (on eve of trial. *See also* District No. 8 v. Clearing, 807 F.2d 618 (7th Cir. 1986); Teamsters, Chauffeurs, Local Union No. 330 v. Elgin Eby-Brown Co., 670 F. Supp. 1393 (N.D. Ill. 1987). *Cf.* Cotter v. Shearson Lehman Hutton., 126 F.R.D. 19, 22 n.6 (S.D.N.Y. 1989) (denying defendant's Rule 11 motion without prejudice to renew at the end of proceedings).

[19] *See* Pipe Trades Council U.A., Local 159 v. Underground Contrs. Ass'n, 828 F.2d 609 (9th Cir. 1987) (withdrawn; republished at 835 F.2d 1275).

[20] *See* National Wrecking Co. v. International Bhd of Teamsters, Local 731, 990 F.2d 957, 963 (7th Cir. 1993) (no sanctions for action brought to challenge arbitration award); Schmidt v. Finberg, 942 F.2d 1571, 1575-76 (11th Cir. 1991) (denying sanctions against defendant who moved to vacate arbitration award); York Research Corp. v. Landgarten, 927 F.2d 119 (2d Cir. 1991) (In an arbitration award case, the district court denied Rule 11

sanctions on the ground that one of plaintiff's claims was "colorable." The Second Circuit affirmed.); Automobile Mechanics Local 701 v. Joe Mitchell Buick, 930 F.2d 576 (7th Cir. 1991) (cross motions for sanctions denied because arguments made were not "devoid of arguable merit"); Walters Sheet Metal Corp. v. Sheet Metal Workers, Local 18, 910 F.2d 1565 (7th Cir. 1990) (motion for sanctions against plaintiff who filed action to vacate arbitration award denied); McMahon v. Shearson/American Express, 896 F.2d 17 (2d Cir. 1990) (reversing district court's imposition of sanctions); O'Donnell v. First Investors Corp., 872 F. Supp. 1274 (S.D.N.Y. 1995) (action for breach of contract and misrepresentations not sanctionable even though dispute was within arbitration agreement); Spector v. Torenberg, 852 F. Supp. 201 (S.D.N.Y. 1994) (motion seeking to vacate arbitration award not sanctionable); Complete Auto Transit v. Local 414, IBT, 848 F. Supp. 848 (N.D. Ind. 1994) (same); Complete Auto Transit, Inc. v. Chauffeurs, Local Union No. 414, 848 F. Supp. 848 (N.D. Ind. 1994) (employer's motion to vacate arbitration award reasonable); Trustees of Columbia University v. Local 1199, 805 F. Supp. 216, 221 (S.D.N.Y. 1992) (no sanctions for breach of no-strike claims brought against union where collective bargaining agreement provided for arbitration); Padgett v. Dapelo, 791 F. Supp. 438, 442 (S.D.N.Y. 1992) (no sanctions against party who challenged arbitration award; arguments distinguishing cases and seeking to extend law where made), *aff'd without op.*, 992 F.2d 320 (2d Cir. 1993); Blue Tee Corp. v. Koehring Co., 754 F. Supp. 26 (S.D.N.Y. 1990) ("Respondent made reasonable legal argument for its motion, citing case-law, where it argued that the arbitration was not a final decision."); Southside Internists Group PC Money Purchase Pension Plan v. Janus Capital Corp., 741 F. Supp. 1536 (N.D. Ala. 1990) (plaintiffs who brought action in violation of arbitration agreement not sanctioned because the issues presented were not settled).

III. Attorney-Client Privilege

The Attorney-Client Privilege and Arbitration

by James H. Carter[*]

Is the attorney-client privilege applicable to documents subpoenaed in an arbitration? Contrary to most lawyers' instincts-which would tell them "of course it is"-the answer is not always so clear. And assuming the privilege is applicable, how should arbitrators proceed when confronted with a large volume of material for which a privilege is claimed?

Arbitration rules generally do not say much, if anything, about privileges, and statutes provide even less guidance.[1] Instead, they usually lump references to privileges together—often implicitly—with discussions of evidentiary matters. The American Arbitration Association's (AAA) Commercial Rules merely provide (in Section 31) that "the arbitrator shall be the judge of the relevance and materiality of the evidence offered, and conformity to legal rules of evidence shall not be necessary."

Rules sometimes do reflect a distinction between purely evidentiary matters on the one hand and privileges on the other. Article 22(6) of the 1996 Arbitration Rules of the Commercial Arbitration and Mediation Center for the Americas (CAMCA), for example, provides that in dealing with evidence "the tribunal shall consider applicable principles of legal privilege." Effective April 1, 1997, the AAA will implement proposed changes to its International Arbitration Rules recommended by a task force appointed to study the rules (see page 6 *supra*). The revisions include a provision making clear that a tribunal must give effect to legal privileges.

---

[*] James H. Carter is a partner at New York's Sullivan & Cromwell where he is a coordinator of the firm's International Arbitration Practice. He holds a B.A. from Yale University, studied as a Fulbright Scholar at University of Cambridge and earned an LL.B. from Yale Law School. Carter serves as Chairman of the Executive Committee of the American Arbitration Association's Board of Directors.

[1] One possible exception is § 910 of the California Evidence Code, which states: "The provisions of any statute making rules of evidence inapplicable in particular proceedings...do not make this division [establishing privileges] inapplicable to such proceedings...."

Article 20(6) (formerly Article 22(6)) will state: "The tribunal shall take into account applicable principles of legal privilege, such as those involving the confidentiality of communications between a lawyer and client." In its explanatory commentary concerning this change, the task force stated that it "is aware of several circumstances in which arbitrators have ruled that the attorney-client privilege did not apply in arbitration. The task force felt that such rulings were wrong, and that the rules should be revised in order to make clear that such privileges are to be recognized."[2]

Similarly, Rule 12.2 of the CPR Rules for Non-Administered Arbitration of International Disputes states, "The Tribunal is not required to apply the rules of evidence used in judicial proceedings," but then adds, "The Tribunal shall determine the applicability of any privilege or immunity and the admissibility, relevance, materiality and weight of the evidence offered." Rule 11.2 of the CPR Rules for Non-Administered Arbitration of Business Disputes is more direct; it provides, in pertinent part: "The Tribunal is not required to apply the rules of evidence used in judicial proceedings, provided, however, that the Tribunal shall apply the lawyer-client privilege and the work-product immunity. The Tribunal shall determine the applicability of any privilege or immunity and the admissibility, relevance, materiality and weight of the evidence offered." (emphasis added)

But what if the rules are silent? Arbitration is not litigation, and arbitrators usually need not apply judicial rules of evidence—at least not "strictly." Is the attorney-client privilege that sort of "rule of evidence"? In the absence of rules to the contrary, does an agreement to arbitrate constitute a blanket waiver of privileges, freeing the arbitrators to take any path of convenience they choose? Or are privileges like other substantive legal rights, which are given full effect in the arbitral process?

Tribunal Powers and Legal Privileges

Although arbitration is private dispute resolution, arbitrators act in a quasi-judicial capacity and have obligations and immunities similar to those of judges.[3] The courts have held, in the main, that arbitrators should honor legal privileges as would judges.

---

[2] The author served as a member of the task force.

[3] Allentown Dev. Co. v. Gans, 1995 U.S. Dist. LEXIS 11719 (S.D.N.Y. Aug. 15, 1995) (describing arbitration as a quasi-judicial proceeding); J.P. Stevens & Co. v. Rytex Corp.,

One commentator, noting that there is "relatively little authority" on this subject, nevertheless concludes that, "In general, lower U.S. courts have assumed that privileges are unaffected either by the parties' agreement to arbitrate or the fact that it is the arbitral tribunal (rather than a court) that has ordered discovery."[4]

When the issue has arisen with respect to various types of privileges, courts in New York have recognized explicitly that parties may assert legal privileges whether the forum is judicial or arbitral. *Board of Educ. of Cty. of Buffalo v. Buffalo Council of Sup'rs and Admins.*, 383 N.Y.S.2d 732 (N.Y. App. Div. 1976) (absolute government or executive privilege that bars libel action against Board of Education or its members also bars arbitration of contractual dispute based on same statements); *Local 964, United Bhd. of Carpenters v. Giresi*, 287 N.Y.S.2d 854 (2d Dept. 1968) (appellant could have asserted the privilege against self-incrimination in arbitration had he chosen to participate in the proceeding); *Local 964, United Bhd. of Carpenters v. Langemyr*, 267 N.Y.S.2d 778 (N.Y. App. Div. 1966) (direction by arbitrator to produce records in the face of an assertion of the privilege against self-incrimination is an infringement of constitutional rights).[5]

New York courts also recognize the attorney-client privilege in arbitration. In *Integrity Insurance Co. v. American Centennial Insurance Co.*, 885 F. Supp. 69, 74 (S.D.N.Y. 1995), for example, the district court decided that a client's address was not privileged and that an attorney would have to provide this information if requested "either at the arbitration hearing, or through document discovery...." Although the

---

356 N.Y.S.2d 278 (1974) (arbitrators' quasi-judicial function "demands no less a duty to disclose [bias] than would be expected of a judge"), *aff'd*, 898 F.2d 882 (2d Cir.), *cert. denied*, 498 U.S. 850 (1990); Florasynth v. Pickholz, 750 F.2d 171 (2d Cir. 1984) ("arbitrators act in a quasi-judicial capacity and they, like judges, have an unqualified right to recuse themselves"); Austern v. Chicago Bd. of Options Exch., 716 F. Supp. 121 (S.D.N.Y. 1989) (arbitrators generally protected from suit for their conduct in arbitration proceedings).

[4] Gary B. Born, International Commercial Arbitration in the U.S. 840 (1994) (citing cases).

[5] *See also* Civil Serv. Empls. Assn. v. Soper, 431 N.Y.S.2d 909 (N.Y. Sup. Ct. 1980) (applying New York law to determine that arbitrator could not require the production of physician-patient privileged documents before permitting a mental patient to testify in an arbitration), *rev'd on other grounds*, 447 N.Y.S.2d 62 (N.Y. App. Div. 1981), *aff'd*, 450 N.Y.S.2d 786 (N.Y. 1982); Di Maina v. New York State Dept. of Mental Hygiene, 386 N.Y.S.2d 590 (N.Y. Sup. Ct. 1976) (applying New York law to reverse an arbitrator's decision to forbid discovery of a witness' mental records for use during cross-examination, explaining that the records had been put in issue by the direct testimony).

court did not make an express ruling on the appropriate source of authority, it discussed New York case law on the attorney-client privilege. *See also Civil Serv. Empls. Assn. v. Ontario Cty. Health Facility*, 466 N.Y.S.2d 240 (N.Y. Sup. Ct. 1983) (holding that the decision to testify in an arbitration waives the attorney-client privilege for prior statements given to an attorney under New York law, just as it would in court), *aff'd*, 478 N.Y.S.2d 380 (N.Y. App. Dept. 1984).

Indeed, the failure to apply the law of privilege properly has been raised as a ground for potential vacatur of an arbitral award. *See Fahnestock & Co. v. Waltman*, 1990 U.S. Dist. LEXIS 11024 (S.D.N.Y. Aug. 23, 1990) (holding arbitrators properly applied privilege and did not demonstrate manifest disregard of the law in awarding damages for defamation), *aff'd*, 935 F.2d 512 (2d Cir.), *cert. denied*, 502 U.S. 942 (1991).

Privileges v. Evidentiary Issues

Arbitrators' powers and duties with respect to privileges are quite different from their powers to admit or exclude evidence and generally to deal flexibly with procedural issues. It is entirely proper that arbitral tribunals should have great flexibility in evidentiary matters, just as judges do when sitting without a jury. Many rules of evidence are intended to shield a lay jury from testimony or other evidence deemed to be unreliable; but judges and arbitrators are entitled to draw conclusions regarding reliability of evidence with greater freedom.

Legal privileges, however, are grounded on rights. Privileges such as those protecting attorney-client, doctor-patient, husband-wife, priest-penitent and other types of communications are based on public policies intended to encourage and protect communications in situations where the law deems the freedom to engage in them more important than a party's right to intrude on them for purposes of discovery and use in litigation or arbitration. This is an area of law quite different from evidentiary rules intended to protect jurors. There is no reason why respect for privileges or the scope of privileges should be different in arbitration.

Cases Involving Voluminous Privileged Materials

Most arbitrations do not involve many—or sometimes any—documents for which attorney-client privilege or attorney work-product protection is claimed. When the question does arise, arbitrators, like judges, usually are solicitous of privileges and careful to avoid infringing them, even in the absence of arbitration rules specifying that course. But a few cases present more complicated privilege issues. Under some circumstances, the work of attorneys for one or both parties may be directly at issue,[6] raising privilege questions about a substantial body of documents (and also potentially about testimony, as well).

For example, a party may base a defense on the fact that it sought and followed the advice of counsel—which would put that advice in issue, but would not necessarily waive any privilege attaching to other documents created by or for the attorney in question. Similarly, a case asserting bad faith in the handling of a claim under an insurance policy can put at issue the actions of the insurer's lawyers involved in investigating and advising on the claim and also may raise issues about the insured party's privileges.[7]

Cases of this sort require rulings on how far the privilege extends, and they raise serious practical problems. Assuming an arbitral tribunal is willing in principle to uphold a privilege (to the extent it has not been waived), how should the arbitrators proceed? Should the tribunal review each of the contested documents—which may be voluminous—and thereby effectively see all of the contested legal advice on one side of the dispute (and put itself to quite a bit of detailed document review work in the process)? Can this job be delegated to the tribunal chairman? To someone else?

---

[6] Most courts recognize some version of an "at issue" waiver rule, which prevents a litigant from putting privileged communications "at issue" and then hampering the other party's ability to respond by claiming the privilege. See, e.g., Hearn v. Rhay, 68 F.R.D. 574 (E.D. Wash. 1975). The prototypical example of such a waiver occurs when a party offers reliance on the advice of counsel to prove good faith or reasonableness. Bowne of New York City, Inc. v. Ambase Corp., 150 F.R.D. 465 (S.D.N.Y. 1993).

[7] New York courts, like those of most other jurisdictions, apply a narrow view of when a party puts privileged communications in issue. See Paramount Communications, Inc. v. Donaghy, 858 F. Supp. 391 (S.D.N.Y. 1994); Jakobleff v. Cerrato, Sweeney & Cohn, 468 N.Y.S.2d 895 (N.Y. App. Div. 1983). In New York, the party asserting the privilege must take some affirmative step to place the privileged information "at issue" before the opposing party can claim a waiver. United States v. 281 Syosset Woodbury Road, 862 F. Supp. 847 (E.D.N.Y. 1994); Chase Manhattan Bank N.A. v. Drysdale Sec. Corp., 587 F. Supp. 57 (S.D.N.Y. 1984) (holding that the burden on a party who seeks to pierce the attorney-client privilege is "particularly high"); Hoenig v. Westphal, 52 N.Y.S.2d 605 (N.Y. 1981).

Perhaps no one needs to inspect each document.[8] In *Chiarella v. Viscount Indus. Co.*, 1993 U.S. Dist. LEXIS 16903 (S.D.N.Y. Nov. 24, 1993), the court held that the arbitrators did not exceed their authority or demonstrate manifest disregard of the law by ordering in-camera review of some privileged documents and excluding others from evidence. However, the decision reflects the fact that the arbitrators refrained from actually looking at any privileged materials during the course of that review:

Although the arbitrators initially ordered Chiarella to produce copies of documents for in-camera inspection, upon strong objection from counsel for Chiarella the panel revised its order to require only that Chiarella bring the documents to a hearing for possible in-camera inspection. Ultimately, the arbitrators did not actually inspect any documents but relied on the assertions of Chiarella's counsel during a document-by-document review of the privilege schedule to determine whether any privilege applied to each document. Two such documents were produced to Viscount as a result of that hearing. *Id.* at 3-4.

Sometimes review of a schedule with counsel at a hearing may not suffice.[9] Most arbitral rules and statutes provide no guidance to a tribunal in such circumstances. However, one little-known set of rules does include a general approach to document production that could be helpful in the case of privileged document review: Article 5 of the Standard Rules of Evidence, promulgated in 1987 by the Mediterranean and Middle East Institute of Arbitration. (See sidebar) Using this approach, an arbitrator faced with a large universe of allegedly privileged but potentially relevant documents might appoint an expert to conduct a

---

[8] New York courts require considerably more than the plaintiff's decision to file suit before implying a waiver of the attorney-client privilege in such circumstances. Connell v. Bernstein-Macaulay, 407 F. Supp. 420, 422 (S.D.N.Y. 1976) ("[I]f the mere bringing of a lawsuit waived the privilege, it would have little meaningful existence"); Prudential Ins. Co. of Amer. v. Coca-Cola Enter. Inc., No. 93 Civ. 1456, 1993 WL 276065 (S.D.N.Y. 1993). Some evidence is needed that the party asserting the privilege seeks to rely on it to bolster his or her claims. Arkwright Mut. Ins. Co. v. National Union Fire Ins. Co. of Pittsburgh, No. 90 Civ. 7811, 1994 WL 510043 (S.D.N.Y. Sept. 16, 1994); *see also* North River Ins. Co. v. Philadelphia Reinsurance Corp., 797 F. Supp. 363 (D.N.J. 1992).

[9] Judicial precedents also do not require court review of every allegedly privileged document. Some courts have held that a party seeking to challenge claims of privilege should not expect the court to conduct an in-camera inspection of the documents as a matter of course but first must at least raise some doubt as to the validity of the asserted privilege. *See* Payless Shoesource Inc. v. 174-176 Canal Street L.P., 1996 WL 185712 (S.D.N.Y. Apr. 17, 1996); United States v. American Soc'y of Composers, Authors and Publishers, 1996 WL 633220 (S.D.N.Y. Nov. 1, 1996).

privilege review, either in the first instance or as a final review, and allocate the costs of the exercise on a "loser pays" basis.

Article 5 of the Standard Rules of Evidence

Promulgated by the Mediterranean and Middle East Institute of Arbitration*

1. Each party shall deliver to the Arbitrator, and exchange with the other parties, a list of all the classes of its documents related to the dispute.

2. The other party shall be entitled to request, within 30 days after receipt of such list, a full list of the documents of one or more of such classes (List of Documents) and to inspect one or more of such documents, inspection to take place in such a way as to minimize the inconveniences to the other parties; the applicant shall advance the costs related to discovery, as fixed by the Arbitrator.

3. In case of refusal to provide the List of Documents or to allow inspection within 30 days after receipt of the notice to this effect, the other party shall be entitled to apply to the Arbitrator for an Order of Discovery. The parties are entitled to be heard on such application.

4. Before issuing such an order, the Arbitrator shall satisfy himself that such documents are not irrelevant to the dispute, and that the application does not aim totally or partially to confuse the matter through the production of quantity of unnecessary documents. An application for discovery will have to be examined by the Arbitrator by proceeding to test the relevance of a portion of such documents. On a party's application, before or after his order, the Arbitrator shall conduct a hearing at which the application or his order will be discussed.

5. Whenever the Arbitrator, after such an examination, has the impression that a large number of the documents, production of which is sought, is irrelevant, he shall be entitled to appoint a lawyer as his expert to divide the documents in three classes; those which he considers relevant, the irrelevant ones and those

---

* Reproduced in Gary B. Born, International Arbitration in the U.S. 835–36 (1994).

which might be relevant. The party which seeks production of documents, the relevance of which has been challenged, will have to advance the costs of the expert and to deposit an amount that covers the costs caused to the other party by its inspection (such as the time spent by the other side's staff to attend inspection of the documents which are found irrelevant). All the costs caused by the inspection of the irrelevant documents are to be borne by the party which has applied for their production, even if its claim [on the merits of the case] is eventually successful. Likewise the Arbitrator may, on application, appoint an expert to divide already produced documents into said three categories and to report on them and place the expert and the Arbitrator's costs and the other parties' costs to the charge of the party which has produced irrelevant documents even if the claim of that party succeeds.

6. Apart from general discovery, the production of specific documents may be ordered by the Arbitrator on a party's application at any stage of the proceedings until the hearing for the final addresses of the parties to the Arbitrator.

7. Before deciding on the application, the Arbitrator shall invite the parties to file their written arguments or to be heard if they so wish.

8. The unjustified refusal by a party to discover documents as well as the refusal of a party to testify may be used by the Arbitrator as one of the elements of his decision.

CHAPTER NINE

ARBITRAL AWARDS

I. Writing Arbitration Awards

The Art of Communicating Arbitral Judgments: Write Ya' Heart Out! And Follow the Basic Rules of Arbitration and Clear Writing

by Charles J. Coleman and Gladys Gershenfeld[*]

Arbitrators do three things. They hear cases, make decisions and write them up. Even though they spend more time writing opinions than doing any other part of their job, the literature of arbitration rarely addresses opinion writing. This article provides a set of practical, down-to-earth recommendations on writing better opinions. It examines the audience for the award, provides an alternative to the time-honored structure of the arbitration award, pinpoints a number of stylistic defects, and offers solutions to many conceptual issues and writing problems.

Arbitrators are selected for their judgment and their ability to communicate that judgment. While many books and articles discuss aspects of arbitral judgment, very few address the way that arbitrators communicate those judgments. A recently published bibliography of labor arbitration, for example, contained annotations of 1,336 books, monographs, journal articles and proceedings.[1] Only seven entries addressed decision writing, and the standard bibles such as Elkouri and

---

[*] Charles J. Coleman is Professor Emeritus at the School of Business, Rutgers University in Camden, N.J. He holds a B.S. from St. Joseph's, an M.S. from Cornell, a Ph.D. and an M.B.A. from SUNY Buffalo. He is a member of the National Academy of Arbitrators.

Gladys Gershenfeld is an arbitrator and former Associate Professor of Industrial Relations at Philadelphia University. She holds a B.S. from Boston University and an M.S. from Cornell University.

[1] Charles J. Coleman and Theodora T. Haynes, eds., Labor Arbitration: An Annotated Bibliography (Ithaca, N.Y.: ILR Press, 1994).

Elkouri[2] or Bornstein, Gosline, and Greenbaum[3] do not examine the topic at all.

Richard Mittenthal says that arbitration opinions make "dreary reading," and he wonders whether the parties actually read most of the opinions given to them.[4] Benjamin Aaron says that the landscape of most arbitral awards is bleak. Many of the awards he read indicated that "the writers lacked not only a sense of form, but also a knowledge of the fundamental principles of grammar and syntax. In the wilderness of arbitral rhetoric, one encounters a host of solecisms, misplaced modifiers, dangling participles, and outright misuse of words."[5]

We too have been disappointed in many of the awards that parties have given us to support their cases. Some have been laden with editorial, grammatical or stylistic defects that not only are annoying, but also detract from the arbitrator's reasoning. As a result, we have prepared some practical, down-to-earth approaches to better award writing. We'll examine the award's audience and its structure, the writing, and some do's, don'ts and pitfalls. We'll close with the results of a published survey and a recent one of our own on what advocates liked and did not like in arbitration awards.[6]

Defining the Audience

Everyone wants a clearly written, easily understood analysis that leads to a logical conclusion. While many contend that the writing should be addressed to the advocates,[7] we believe that the arbitration award has at least three audiences, each with different needs. One is the advocates; a second, their clients; and the third, external review agencies such as the courts. The needs of each audience should be a beacon to the arbitrators when they choose words, phrases and sentence construction.

---

[2] Frank and Edna Asper Elkouri, How Arbitration Works (Washington: BNA, 5th Edition, 1997).

[3] Tim Bornstein, Ann Gosline and Marc Greenbaum, eds., Labor and Employment Arbitration (New York: Matthew Bender, 2nd ed., 1997).

[4] Richard Mittenthal, *The Art of Opinion Writing*, Proceedings of the 35th Annual Meeting of the National Academy of Arbitrators (Washington: BNA, 1983) 96.

[5] Benjamin Aaron, *Arbitration Decisions and the Law of the Shop*, 29 LABOR LAW J. 538 (August 1978).

[6] Throughout this article the terms "arbitration award" and "award" are used to represent the entire document and not just the decision at the end.

[7] Donald J. Petersen and Julius Rezler, *Arbitrator Decision Writing: Selected Criteria*, 38 ARBITRATION JOURNAL 18-33 (June 1983).

A. The Advocates. The arbitrator should think first about the losing advocates and their clients, because they are going to examine the award more carefully and more critically. The winning advocates cannot be ignored, but their perceptions of the logic and the writing will be influenced by their victory. Faulty logic, dense writing and clumsy phrases can nevertheless seem the essence of grace and scholarship to the winners.

Losing advocates have lost in two ways: Not only have they lost the case, but their clients may question their judgment in picking the arbitrator. Therefore, losing advocates need awards that they can explain to their clients and that vindicate their judgment. They rely on a fully explained, clearly written analysis to show the client why the case was lost and why the arbitrator's decision, no matter how disappointing, had some justification. The arbitration award should convey this kind of message: "I listened carefully to your argument and I considered it fairly. But I read a particular contract clause or practice differently from you. That reading led me to decide against your position."

B. Their Clients. The clients pose a special communication problem. The arbitrator and the advocate share some common ground: They know the rules, read the same books and use the same expressions. The client rarely participates in this sharing. The arbitrator who keeps the client in mind will avoid esoteric language and unnecessarily complicated sentences filled with subordinate clauses. This approach is basic in all award writing and will be discussed further, but it can be emphasized here. The document is easier to read if major points are highlighted and ideas are expressed in simplified, yet precise writing. The long word or the little-known word should be used if necessary to convey a meaning with precision. But if a shorter, more commonly understood word does the job, that word should be used.

C. Reviewing Agencies. The third audience consists of potential reviewing agencies, usually the courts or government bodies. Poorly crafted awards invite the losing party to contest the outcome in the courts. According to Abrams and Nolan, three conditions should be met to keep an award out of the courts.[8] First, at a bare minimum, the award must be impervious to legal attack. This means that it demonstrably "draws its essence" from the collective-bargaining agreement and the result is consistent with public policy. Second, the opinion must be clear,

---

[8] Roger I. Abrams and Dennis R. Nolan, *Arbitral Craftsmanship and Competence*, 41 NAA 314 (1989).

orderly, reasoned and complete. If the court cannot derive any meaning from the arbitrator's run-on sentences, or if the commission cannot follow the logic, the chance of review probably increases. And third, while it is too much to hope that the arbitrator's arguments will convince the losers that they were wrong, it is not too much to hope to convince them that they have had their day in court. To do this, the arbitrator must show consideration to all of the loser's arguments, fully answer all issues, and write in a comprehensible, forceful and persuasive manner.[9]

Formatting the Award

A. Introduction. Arbitration awards typically begin with administrative detail. This may include how the case reached the arbitrator, where and when the hearing was held, who represented each party, whether transcripts or briefs were filed, and when the hearing was closed. Arbitrators vary about including more than these minimum essentials. Some prefer to complete the record with the names of all the witnesses who appeared for each party, although advocates rarely ask for particular details to be included.

B. Background and Issue. The arbitrator next lays out the background, the issue to be decided, the remedy requested and the contract clauses that are most significant to the decision. We build our model of award writing around an ancient formula: Tell them where they're going, get them there, and tell them where they've been. This section should give the parties a clear idea of your destination and your route. The background should include enough facts to show an understanding of the parties' operations and the grievant's occupation and length of service. It should indicate how the case arose and the decision that is grieved. The issue should be defined with precision, which usually means defined narrowly.

> It is not: The issue is whether or not the employer can deny holiday pay for all absences the day before a holiday.

> It is: Did the employer violate the agreement when Annie Laurie was denied holiday pay for Labor Day in September 1996?

The first definition is too broad; it invites policy decisions beyond the case at hand. The concept of the employer's right to deny holiday pay may underlie the grievance, but in almost every case the arbitrator is

---

[9] *Id.* at 314-316.

called upon to deal with a specific application of such concepts. To build upon another ancient idea, the definition of the issue should answer questions about who, what, when, where, and sometimes, how and why.

If the parties can define a remedy without undue fuss, that's the best course. But sometimes neither the arbitrator nor the parties have the foggiest notion of the difficulties and problems that may be encountered in prescribing a remedy.[10] In these cases it is better to leave the remedy in terms such as, "The Union asks that the grievant be made whole in compensation and seniority." But if a remedy can be stated with precision, that's what should be used. In the situation illustrated above, the remedy sought might be one day's pay at straight time for Labor Day, 1996.

C. *The Contract.* The parties often refer the arbitrator to every contract clause or rule that might conceivably bear upon the grievance. In these days of computer scanners, where any typed material can be inserted into an award electronically, arbitrators are surely tempted to give the parties back everything they offered. Unfortunately, the net result is distracting. By including material that the arbitrator will later ignore, the listing of clauses does not tell the parties where the award is headed. We recommend that this section of the arbitration award quote the essential portions of those contract clauses, employer work rules, laws or regulations that affect the decision and remedy. Some may be paraphrased. For example, in a case where an employee has been terminated for assault:

> Article xyz...This article lists a number of offenses for which employees may be barred from work. One such offense is assaulting a supervisor.

Or, in dealing with standard management-rights and arbitral-powers clauses:

> Article V provides management with broad powers relating to the direction of the work force and scheduling production except as limited by the terms of this Agreement. Article VII prohibits the arbitrator from adding to, subtracting from or modifying the terms of the Agreement.

---

[10] Letter from Peter Seitz to the editor, *Final Comments on Retaining Jurisdiction*, 3-4 STUDY TIME (NEW YORK: AMERICAN ARBITRATION ASSOCIATION, JAN. 1981).

A. Choice of Design

There is a traditional method of constructing arbitration awards. Once the introduction and background are completed, the award goes on to present the positions of each party sequentially, discuss those positions and conclude with the decision. While many arbitrators are comfortable with that approach, we find merit in the alternative of combining the presentation of the parties' positions with the discussion. This approach has two advantages: It eliminates the repetition of each position as it is discussed, to say nothing of the danger of listing positions that are never discussed, and it also assists the arbitrator in analyzing the parties' arguments in a logical sequence of substantive topics.

We outline the two major formats in Exhibit I. We tie the examples into a hypothetical case where an employer assigned overtime to employees, regardless of seniority, because of an emergency, and the parties' arguments centered on contract language, past practice and the claim of an emergency. The traditional format, on the left, goes through the positions of the parties and then the arbitrator's discussion and award. Under the alternative format, there is no separate section on the positions of the parties. The discussion may begin with an overall framework statement and may include the arbitrator's decision. Then the substantive aspects are considered under topical headings. The position of each party is incorporated in the discussion of each aspect, followed by the arbitrator's evaluation on that topic. See Exhibit I.

One other kind of format can be noted. Some arbitrators entering the field from a practice of law follow the design of legal opinions. They list findings of fact by number before the discussion and end with a list of conclusions by number. However, this approach is used less often in labor-management arbitration.

The Discussion Section

Whatever format is chosen, this section should begin with a brief paragraph stating the most important aspects of the case. Consider Roger Abrams' introductory paragraph in the discussion section of a job-combination problem:[11]

> "This is a tale of two jobs—the Senior Toolroom Keeper and a Senior Storeroom Keeper. The Company sought to make them

---

[11] Georgia Power Company and International Brotherhood of Electrical Workers, Local 84, 93-1 Arb (CCH) 4309, 4311 (1993) (Abrams, Arb.).

one, and eventually under the terms of the Agreement they will be combined. In the interim, however, the parties are fighting about who must perform duties previously performed exclusively by the Senior Toolroom Keeper."

In those three sentences, Abrams set the stage for everything that followed. Such a paragraph is a crisp, clear starting point for the body of the discussion. In proceeding with the discussion, arbitrators take one of two approaches. One has been called the "detective story" approach. The arbitrators develop pieces of their reasoning as positions are discussed. Although they know the parties will read the last page first, they withhold their conclusion until the end.[12] This approach probably works best under the Traditional Format. Under the Alternative Format, the arbitrator would more often state the conclusion early and then explain the path to that conclusion.

The discussion is the most important part of the award, whether it is set off in a section by itself under a traditional format, or included with the parties' statements of position. The parties hire arbitrators for their judgment, and here is where they are supposed to shine. The discussion should avoid excessive repetition of the parties' arguments, which is made easier in the Alternative Format. It should be longer than the recital of facts that came earlier and should focus on the key points raised in the testimony and the arguments. There should also be a wrap-up section where the arbitrator indicates which facts, arguments and explanations were most persuasive. Arbitrators who have told the parties that they have taken evidence for "what it is worth" should explain exactly what it was worth. Finally, the arbitrator should write the conclusion in positive, definite terms, even if it is a close decision. The detriment in providing excruciating detail on the difficulty in making the decision is that the arbitrator is likely to communicate a message saying that the case turned on some relatively inconsequential factor or was the result of a coin flipped in the air.[13]

The Statement of the Award

The award to the parties is to be unambiguous and definite. It is designed to provide the parties with a clear understanding of the decision

---

[12] Charlotte Gold, *Critical Observations on Writing Arbitration Opinions*, Unpublished remarks at Continuing Education Conference, National Academy of Arbitrators, 1984.

[13] *Supra*, note 4 at 90-91.

and instructions for implementation. It typically indicates whether the contract was violated and whether the grievance was denied or sustained. In some cases where back pay is awarded, for example, "back pay, less the usual offsets" is sufficient. In other cases, particularly when the arbitrator is on an ad hoc appointment and is a stranger to the parties, more may be needed. The award might have to consider interim earnings, unemployment compensation, workers compensation, seniority and even imputed overtime. Arbitrators may be guided by the parties, but they should not return part of the case to the parties for further negotiation. And although there are different views on this issue, the arbitrator should be reluctant to retain jurisdiction unless requested by the parties or in the instance of an unusually complex award.[14]

Some Ideas on Writing

Having examined the structure of the arbitration award, we turn to style.[15] These are fundamental rules that we believe should govern writing arbitration awards.

A. Write in a way that comes naturally. How many people take on a different character as soon as they pick up their pen or boot up their computer? The short, powerful Anglo-Saxon words that mark everyday speech tend to become longer, more Latinized, when we write. Use becomes utilize, anger becomes hostility and worsen becomes exacerbate. Except in the hands of a master, rich, ornate prose works against the communication intended by the award.

The first draft of an award should be written in the words and phrases that the arbitrator uses in everyday speech. Arbitrators who cannot express their thoughts in their normal language may not have thought the issue through. Perhaps the language is a guise for muddy logic or incomplete thinking. In the second draft, longer words and more formal structures may be brought in if they add precision, clarity, tone or color.

B. Write with nouns and verbs. Adjectives and adverbs cannot carry your thought. They may add shades of meaning and lend grace to a sentence, but the noun or the verb invariably expresses the fundamental thought. If the descriptive word does not add strength or clarity to the

---

[14] John E. Dunsford argues that arbitrators should retain jurisdiction routinely for an indefinite period of time. John E. Dunsford, *The Case for Retention of Remedial Jurisdiction in Labor Arbitration Awards*, 31 GEORGIA LAW REVIEW, 201-279 (FALL 1996).

[15] We acknowledge our debt to William Strunk Jr. and E.B. White, The Elements of Style (New York: Macmillan Publishing Co., Inc., 1979).

thought, it should be cut. Qualifiers such as rather, very, certainly and surely should be pruned wherever possible. They are "the leeches that infest the pond of prose, sucking the blood of words."[16]

C. *Do not construct new words, and spell the ones that you use in the standard way.* The word "impact" is a case in point. Impact has always been a very good noun, but its usage as a verb is often incorrect and could prove to be an annoyance, simply because the award may be read by someone who wants words used in their traditional sense. Words should also be spelled in the orthodox way, because any other form is distracting—for example, "through" rather than "thru," "though" instead of "tho." Once one of the authors had to review a book in which the author consistently used the alternative spelling of "Shakespear" for Shakespeare. As I read the word, I was first distracted and later irritated. I wonder if these feelings influenced my negative review of the book.

D. *Be definite, but do not overstate.* Writing styles differ in terms of directness. The so-called "style of the powerful" consists of direct assertions, little equivocation, few hesitations and brevity. At the other extreme is the "style of the powerless," marked by hedge words ("giving due weight"), meaningless fillers ("in support of its burden") and terms of personal reference ("it grieves me deeply" and "after giving the matter a great deal of thought"). The effect of these stylistic features is reduced assertiveness and a lower level of trust. Studies of jury behavior have shown that those jurors who were exposed to the more powerful styles judged the content to be more credible.[17] However, while the writing style should be definite, the arbitrator should protect against overstatement. When you overstate, you put the reader on guard, making everything else in the document suspect.

E. *Be careful in using hypotheticals to illustrate points, and watch the innocuous aside, the "big picture" and the conjectures.* Examples may often clarify an award, and references to the big picture may create a context, but the further the award strays from the issues, the more likely it treads upon dangerous ground. As awards are broadened, it becomes more likely that arbitrators will be perceived as exceeding their authority. The further we stray into the byways of the relationship, the more likely we move into territory we do not understand, possibly creating some unintended common law.

---

[16] *Id.* at 73.
[17] Bruce Frazier, The Role of Language in Arbitration, 33 NAA 19 (1981).

F. Avoid fancy, particularly foreign words. What do the grievant, the supervisor, the human-resources officer or the business agent think when confronted with res judicata, collateral estoppel, *functus officio*, a fortiori, gravamen, quantum, indicia, sua sponte or conditio sine qua non? If the purpose of the award is communication, should we not eliminate such words or at least provide a translation? "Speech which fails to convey a plain meaning will fail to do the job that speech has to do...clearness is secured by using the words that are current and ordinary."[18] When choosing between the formal and the informal, the regular and the offbeat, the arbitrator should err on the side of established usage. There is simply a better chance of writing a good award if the creativity is addressed to the problem rather than the language.

G. For some of the worst expressions used in arbitration awards,[19] See Exhibit II.

*H. On verbs, sentences, and paragraphs...*Three of the common teachings in treatises on effective writing are to avoid using the passive voice, long sentences and long paragraphs. Our view on verbs is that the active voice (e.g., "I presume") is usually clearer and less cumbersome than the passive voice (e.g., "it is presumed") and should be used where it expresses the thought better. We also think that each paragraph should contain one unit of thought. A different thought warrants a new paragraph.

With regard to sentences, a long sentence filled with subordinate clauses is ordinarily hard to understand. The mind absorbs information in chunks of text. Bigger chunks are difficult to understand and impede communications.[20] But we also think that variety adds spice to the arbitration award. "One can ingest just so many pages filled with simple declarative sentences unvaried by an occasional venturesome independent clause or a single felicitous phrase, before giving up..."[21] The award does not have to be fine literature, but it will read better with some passive verbs and a mixture of short and long sentences that average somewhere between fifteen and twenty-five words. Consider this hopeless sentence from a published arbitration award:

---

[18] *Id.* at 40, quoting Aristotle.
[19] For another list, David Elliot, *When the Hearing is Over: Writing Arbitration Awards in Plain Language*, 46 ARBITRATION JOURNAL 58-59 (December 1991).
[20] *Id.*, at 58.
[21] *Supra* note 5, at 538.

"The Union claims that the Grievant was unaware that he had taken any unearned vacation or that the unearned vacation he had taken would be offset against vacation he earned on subsequent anniversary dates, that the Grievant had no way of knowing of this procedure, and that in the absence of contractual authority, the Grievant cannot be penalized for his use of unearned vacation."

When a sentence becomes a tangled web of commas and clauses, as is the case above, the best recourse is to begin anew, dispersing your ideas into two or more shorter sentences.

I. Some technical details... Typographical errors are insidious, but we must do our best to eliminate them. At a minimum, those arbitrators writing with a computer should employ their spell-check routine. This will catch a number of errors, but will not catch the error when the misspelling is a word in itself (e.g., "affect" and "effect"; "their" and "there"). Some find that reading the award aloud helps to catch these errors (and possibly writing problems and flaws in the logic as well).

To add some variety to the award, refer to Exhibit III for some verbs to express assertions.

One of the most troublesome editorial pitfalls concerns the his/her syndrome. The time is long past when the masculine pronoun was general enough to cover both sexes. Substituting the feminine pronoun does not solve the problem. Nor does the s/he aberration because it distracts the eye and the mind. Some basic alternatives are:[22]

1. Stick to the plural. Instead of saying "Each employee must punch his/her time card," say, "All employees must punch their time cards."

2. Use nouns instead of pronouns. Instead of "If an employee is late, his/her arrival time is noted," say, "If an employee is late, the arrival time is noted."

3. Reword the sentence. Instead of "When a bargaining-unit member files a grievance, he/she must notify the Union," say, "A bargaining-unit member who files a grievance must notify the Union."

---

[22] Gladys Gershenfeld, *The Arbitrator as Writer*, 1985 Proceedings: Thirteenth Annual Conference, Society of Professionals in Dispute Resolution. Washington, D.C., 1986.

4. Substitute "one." Instead of "He/she must be exact," say, "One must be exact."

What Do the Parties Want?

A 1983 survey of parties' pet peeves regarding decision-writing reported on many substantive concerns, such as a resort to a line of argument the parties had not introduced, ignoring arguments introduced by the parties, relying on clauses that one or both parties felt were unjustified, and providing gratuitous advice. Stylistically the critics found, as we have, that the parties deplore Latin phrases, overly long quotes from the contract and statements of position, and criticism of one of the parties or an advocate.[23]

Our informal survey of advocates yielded similar results. One management advocate set the tone for many of the respondents in saying: "When we pick you, we vouch to our clients for you, and we want you to make us proud, even when we lose. We want a fair shot at winning, an intelligent decision that we can explain to our clients, and one that is clearly written." More specifically, some advocates added:

- Set forth the reasons.
- Be sensitive to the ongoing relationship.
- Do not play God.
- Think through the remedy. The remedy in a discharge case should address such issues as seniority, benefits and health care (from a union advocate).
- Proofread carefully and make sure that the document looks professional.
- Do not be overly creative in your reasoning and your award.
- Avoid wit and humor.
- Don't rehash the facts and the arguments for 20 pages and then give a two-page analysis (particularly when charging for four days of study).
- Show some human concern, particularly in a discharge case, but don't tell us how it grieves the arbitrator to…

---

[23] *Supra* note 7, at 28-29.

- Don't tell us how wonderful the losing advocate was or how difficult the decision.

Finally, most of the advocates asked for courtesy. Even if the arbitrator did not believe the grievant, simply state that "questions of credibility were resolved in the employer's favor." Likewise, the arbitrator may point out that a supervisor's actions were improper, but it is cruel to focus attention on the person rather than the act. And the arbitrator may find a brief difficult to follow, but it makes no sense to highlight that for the parties' attention.

Definite, Certain and Concise

Attention to the wishes of the parties and to the standards of effective writing is not only desirable for arbitrators, it is expected under the Code of Professional Responsibility for Arbitrators of Labor-Management Disputes. The Code states a basic principle: "The award should be definite, certain, and as concise as possible." The succinct explanation that follows could serve as a summary of this article:

> When an opinion is required, factors to be considered by an arbitrator include: desirability of brevity, consistent with the nature of the case and any expressed desires of the parties; need to use a style and form that is understandable to responsible representatives of the parties, to the grievant and supervisors, and to others in the collective bargaining relationship; necessity of meeting the significant issues; forthrightness to an extent not harmful to the relationship of the parties; and avoidance of gratuitous advice or discourse not essential to disposition of the issues.[24]

In this article we have tried to help arbitrators write awards that their audiences can understand and might, perhaps, enjoy reading. Clarity is critical, particularly in this litigious age where words that "seem perfectly intelligible to the arbitrator as they are carefully framed in an award become, under the critical and inspired scrutiny of an exigent advocate, a quagmire of uncertainty."[25]

---

[24] NAA, AAA, FMCS, Code of Professional Responsibility for Arbitrators of Labor-Management Disputes, Section 6 (C) (1).

[25] *Supra* note 14, at 222.

Arbitration awards are not supposed to be great literature. However, a good opinion "answers the question put—all of them and no others. It allows its lesson for the future to come from the result, not its pontification." It does not lecture; it does not offer gratuitous advice; it does not denigrate or embarrass.[26] None of us may ever come up with such a wonderful phrase as Thomas Paine did when he wrote: "These are the times that try men's souls." But we can communicate our thoughts clearly and, we hope, with a certain grace. The overall charge was probably stated best by Cervantes, in his introduction to Don Quixote:

> "See to it, rather, that your style flows along smoothly, pleasantly, and sonorously, and that your words are the proper ones, meaningful and well placed, expressive of your intention in setting them down and of what you wish to say, without any intricacy or obscurity."

EXHIBIT I: TWO FORMATTING ALTERNATIVES

A. Traditional Format	B. Alternative Format
The Position of the Union	*Contract Language*
Argument 1: Contract Language	Union and Co. Arguments
Argument 2: Past Practice	Arbitrator's Discussion
Argument 3: Emergency	
The Position of the Company	*Past Practice*
Argument 1: Contract Language	Union and Co. Arguments
Argument 2: Past Practice	Arbitrator's Discussion
Argument 3: Emergency	
Arbitrator's Discussion	*Emergency*
On Argument 1	Union and Co. Arguments
On Argument 2	Arbitrator's Discussion
On Argument 3	
Arbitrator's Conclusions	Arbitrator's Conclusions

---

[26] *Supra* note 4, at 75-76.

EXHIBIT II: THE WORST EXPRESSIONS

"Along the lines of," or "in this vein."
  ⇒ Delete—takes up space and says nothing.

"At this time," or, even worse, "at this point in time."
  ⇒ Use "when."

"Each and every."
  ⇒ Redundant. Use "each," "every" or "any."

"Hereinafter" and "heretofore."
  ⇒ Try "below" or "after"; "above" or "before."

"In lieu of."
  ⇒ Use "instead of" or "in the place of."

"In the course of."
  ⇒ Substitute "during" or "while."

"In the last [or final] analysis."
  ⇒ Delete. What does this add to the award?

"Meaningful" and "meaningless."
  ⇒ Overused, hackneyed and add no meaning.

"On the other hand."
  ⇒ Encourages parties to seek a one-armed arbitrator.

"Personally."
  ⇒ Delete. See text under powerless writing style.

"Pursuant to."
  ⇒ Use "under."

"Sufficient number."
  ⇒ A simpler alternative is "enough."

"The truth is," "the fact is," "the thrust of."
  ⇒ Delete.

EXHIBIT III: VERBS TO EXPRESS ASSERTIONS

A Party:	A Witness:	The Arbitrator:
claims	says	finds
contends	states	notes
argues	reports	points out
agrees	comments	believes
maintains	explains	observes
challenges	relates	doubts
questions	mentions	is convinced
alleges	concurs	is persuaded

II. Arbitrators' Broad Authority to Grant Remedies

Another Look At Remedies in Arbitration

*by Harvey Berman**

It is widely recognized that arbitrators have broad authority to order any type of relief, even if the relief could not be awarded by a court.[1] This flexibility can be understood to result, in part, from expansive arbitration clauses that often expressly or impliedly provide the arbitrator with a broad power to design remedies, and from the limited appealability of arbitration awards.[2] Yet many attorneys and arbitrators don't realize how much flexibility arbitrators have in crafting awards.

While monetary damages are most often awarded in commercial cases, arbitrators have frequently awarded equitable and other forms of relief, including specific performance, injunctive relief, consequential damages, liquidated damages, attorneys' fees and punitive damages.[3]

Because of the confidentiality of arbitration, the only opportunity to examine commercial arbitral remedies occurs when an award is in court. In this article we will examine some cases in which arbitral remedies have been specifically challenged for the purpose of seeing how

---

[*] The author is a partner in Bodman LLP in Ann Arbor, Michigan, where he concentrates in commercial, construction and real estate law. He holds a B.A. from Case Wester Reserve University and a J.D from Clevelan-Marshall College of Law. Thomas Breutsch assisted in researching this article.

[1] Uniform Arbitration Act §12. The fact that the arbitration agreement may have given the arbitrator great flexibility to afford remedies that a court could not, has not stopped litigants from arguing, on a motion to vacate the award, that the arbitrator exceeded his or her authority by granting a particular form of relief.

[2] 9 U.S.C. §10; U.A.A. §12.

[3] *For example*, arbitrators have required construction contractors to repair damage to the owner's property, complete punch list items, and obtain insurance for the remainder of the construction project. Wright v. Land Developers Constr. Co., 554 So. 2d 1000 (Ala. 1989). They have enforced commercial agreements by requiring a breaching party to fulfill its contractual obligations. Morris v. Zuckerman, 69 Cal. 2d 686, 446 P.2d 1000 (Cal. 1968). They have even required a company to change its corporate name. Engis Corp. v. Engis Ltd., 800 F. Supp. 627 (N.D. Ill. 1992). And they have ordered two corporations to exchange their stock. *See* Executone Information Sys., v. Davis, 26 F.3d 1314, 1332-33 (5th Cir. 1994), discussed *infra*.

arbitrators craft remedies they believe are appropriate, and how the courts have responded to these challenges.[4]

The Arbitration Agreement

We begin with a brief look at the arbitration agreement, an important source of the arbitrator's authority in the arbitration. It goes without saying that because arbitration is almost always a contractual matter, the agreement to arbitrate usually determines the scope of the arbitrator's authority, including the authority to grant remedies. The authorized remedies may be expressly provided in the arbitration agreement or incorporated by reference. Other remedies may be implied from the specific or general terms of the arbitration agreement or any contract relating to the arbitration. If the arbitration agreement provides for broad remedial powers, courts generally interpret the agreement to allow the arbitrator great latitude in selecting an appropriate remedy.

If the arbitration clause calls for arbitration pursuant to the Commercial Arbitration Rules of the American Arbitration Association, Rules R-45 and R-36 will determine the scope of the arbitrator's remedial authority. AAA R-45(a) allows an arbitrator to award any remedy or relief that the arbitrator deems just and equitable and within the scope of the parties' agreement, including, for example, specific performance of a contract.

Most courts have interpreted this language to provide the arbitrator with very broad authority to award remedies.[5]

---

[4] This article deals with permanent relief, not interim remedies. Also, it does not deal with punitive damages or attorneys' fees, which have been the subject of prior articles in ADR Currents. See David Rivkin, *Courts Differ on Arbitrability of Time Limitations*, 1 NO. 2 ADR CURRENTS 21 (Fall 1996)(punitive damages), and Mary A. Bedikian, *Attorneys' Fees in Arbitration*, 2 NO. 3 ADR CURRENTS 20 (Summer 1997). *See also* Alan Rau, *Does State Arbitration Law Matter At All? Part I: Federal Preemption*, 3: 2 ADR CURRENTS 19 (June 1998)(discussing the extent to which the Federal Arbitration Act preempts state law restrictions on arbitral awards of punitive damages).

[5] *For example*, in Advanced Micro Devices v. Intel, 885 P.2d 994 (Cal. 1994), discussed *infra*, the court upheld an award providing for an innovative equitable remedy, although the relief provided was not specifically authorized by law or by express agreement. The arbitration clause employed language identical to the AAA's R-45, which the court observed provided a "broad grant of authority" with respect to remedies. *See also In re Astey*, 19 Misc. 2d 1059, 189 N.Y.S.2d 2 (N.Y. Sup. Ct. 1959)(arbitrator did not exceed his power by granting equitable relief though the relief could not be awarded in a judicial proceeding); Engis Corp. v. Engis Ltd., n. 3, *supra*. *See also* Daniewicz v. Thermo Instrument Sys., 992 S.W.2d 713 (Tex. Ct. App. 1999), discussed *infra*.

Rule R-45 also specifically authorizes the arbitrator to issue interim and interlocutory awards, and to assess fees, expenses, compensation, interest and attorneys' fees (the latter only if (1) the parties have requested such an award, and (2) they are authorized by law or in the arbitration agreement).

AAA Rule R-36 provides an additional grant of authority to take necessary interim measures, including injunctive relief and measures to protect or conserve property, and to require security for costs.

The AAA's commercial rules now also contain "Optional Rules for Emergency Measures of Protection," which enable the parties to obtain emergency relief before the tribunal is constituted. These rules empower the AAA to quickly select an emergency arbitrator who can award interim emergency relief.[6] To be applicable, however, the parties must provide for these rule to apply in their agreement to arbitrate.

An arbitration agreement (or another applicable agreement) may delineate or otherwise limit the remedies that an arbitrator may award. Courts generally find that arbitrators lack authority to award excluded forms of relief.[7] It should be remembered, however, that an apparent limit on the arbitrator's remedies is first subject to construction by the arbitrator, and thus could be deemed inapplicable in the circumstances of the case. For example an express exclusion of consequential damages could be ineffective if the arbitrator determines that the claimant's economic loss was a direct damage, not a consequential loss.[8]

---

[6] An emergency arbitrator who is satisfied that the party seeking emergency relief has shown an entitlement to such relief and that immediate and irreparable loss or damage will result in its absence, may grant the relief in an interim award that states the reasons in support of the decision.

[7] *For example*, in *In re* Farkar Co., 583 F.2d 68 (2d Cir. 1978), the 2d Circuit held that when an agreement stated that "in no event shall RAHCO be liable for special or consequential damages," the arbitrator lacked power to include consequential damages in the award, even through the agreement also referenced AAA rules.

[8] *See* Team Scandia, Inc. v. Greco, 6 F. Supp. 2d 795 (S.D. Ind. 1998). Here the arbitration agreement stated that any award of damages "shall be limited to actual damages as derived from the terms and conditions of this Agreement...[T]here shall be no award of punitive damages, consequential damages...and/or the like." In a dispute involving allegations by a race car driver that the race team breached their agreement, causing him to lose sponsorships, the arbitrator awarded him damages for loss of sponsorship and economic loss. The arbitrator reasoned that these forms of damages were direct losses, not consequential losses. A federal district court concluded that the award did not exceed the arbitrator's authority because his decision, rightly or wrongly, was based upon a legal determination that the loss of sponsorship was not a consequential damage. The court explained that arbitrators do not exceed their powers by misconstruing a contract. The court also emphasized that "courts must not visit the merits of the arbitrator's decision and thus

Other Sources of Authority

The parties' submissions to the arbitrator are another source of authority for arbitral remedies. If the issues submitted to arbitration are limited in a way that could restrict the range of remedies that the arbitrator could award, a court could find that the arbitrator lacked authority to award a particular remedy.

For some types of remedies, statutory authority may be required. In some jurisdictions, unless a statute specifically authorizes the award of attorneys' fees or punitive damages, these remedies must be expressly authorized in the parties' arbitration agreement. Remedies involving attorneys' fees and punitive damages are beyond the scope of this article.

Judicial Approaches

It is against this backdrop that arbitrators must devise a remedy appropriate to the facts of the dispute before them. When a party is unhappy with the arbitrator's choice of award, it may seek vacatur, contending that the arbitrator exceeded his authority. Some courts have expressed frustration at parties who take this tack.[9] Nevertheless, as the cases below illustrate, the court will review the sources of the arbitrator's authority to determine whether the arbitrator acted properly in issuing the award.

Partnership disputes. In *EEC Property Co. v. Dr. Martin Kaplan*, which involved a partnership formed to own and operate a medical office building, the arbitrator ordered payment of money damages to two of the six partners and gave them the right to withdraw from the partnership and receive the value of their respective partnership interests according to the method specified in the partnership agreement.[10] The arbitrator also accelerated the payment schedule for the buyout so that it coincided with the completion of the office building's mortgage payment.

The partnership claimed that the arbitrator exceeded his authority because the buyout was not authorized in the partnership agreement, and

---

allow the disappointed party to bring his dispute into court by the back door, arguing that he is entitled to appellate review of the arbitrator's decision."

[9] *See* Chandra v. Bradstreet, 727 So. 2d 372 (Fla. Ct. App. 1999). ("[T]he promise of arbitration is spoiled if parties disappointed by its results can delay the conclusion of the proceeding by groundless litigation in the district court followed by groundless appeal to this court; we have said repeatedly that we would punish such tactics and we mean it.") Team Scandia, n. 8, *supra*.

[10] 578 N.W.2d 381 (Minn. Ct. App. 1998). *See also* Sharpe v. Lytal & Reiter, 702 So. 2d 622 (Fla. 1997) (partnership dissolution).

because it was not specifically raised in the parties' submissions. The Minnesota Court of Appeals acknowledged that the award varied from the partnership agreement. Nevertheless, it found support for the award in the arbitration clause, the partnership agreement, and the parties' submissions. It cited the broad powers given to the arbitrator in the arbitration clause and the absence of any limitations on remedies. It noted that the partnership agreement provided a method of valuation for withdrawing partners; and that the parties' submissions indicated a desire to preserve the partnership through the buyout remedy. An important fact in this case was that before the award was issued the arbitrator informed the parties that he was considering the buyout. Since the partnership failed to object to that remedy prior to the hearing, the court found that the partnership had waived its objection to the remedy.

Buyer/seller disputes. In *Danie-wicz v. Thermo Instrument Systems*, the arbitrator not only awarded monetary relief for breach of a contract to sell a manufacturing business, he incorporated some of the terms of the contract in the remedy.[11] The award required the buyer to make a $4 million lump sum payment for breach of the clause requiring the buyer to use its "best efforts" to promote the seller's products. The award also required the buyer to continue to pay royalties to the seller for the balance of the contract.

The buyer argued that the panel abused its authority because the remedies were not requested by either party. The Texas Court of Appeals rejected the contention that the remedy must be specifically requested by a party. The court found that since the arbitrators were asked to find a breach of contract and to award damages commensurate with the breach, the award did not exceed their authority. The court explained, "[T]he award remedied those wrongs that could no longer be reasonably governed by the original contract and incorporated the contractual terms for those areas that still fit."

In *Executone Information Systems v. Davis*, in which the buyer of a company challenged the accuracy of financial information given to determine the purchase price, the Fifth Circuit upheld an award that included money damages, the issuance, exchange and surrender of corporate stock, and the filing of a registration statement with the Securities and Exchange Commission registering all shares of stock issued to the defendants. In confirming these remedies, the court applied the "essence" test, concluding that the arbitrator's award "drew its

---

[11] *See* n. 5, *supra.*

essence" from the purchase agreement.[12] The court reasoned that the award was not contrary to the express terms of the parties' agreement. Moreover, it was rationally inferable from the parties' central purpose in reaching a purchase price based on a fair calculation of the adjusted pretax profits of the company being sold.

Shareholder disputes. The award in *Hayob v. Osborne* held one 50% shareholder personally liable for the corporation's debt to the other 50% shareholder, even though under Missouri law, shareholders are not liable for the debts of their corporations.[13] The plaintiff sued his co-shareholder, seeking reimbursement of expenses paid on the corporation's behalf and damages for the defendant's failure to produce certain corporate records. Subsequently, the plaintiff filed an amended petition seeking to hold the defendant liable individually. The parties agreed to submit the dispute to arbitration in accordance with Missouri law under the rules of the AAA. Their agreement provided that the arbitration shall determine the controversy and claims in the amended petition and answer, which were incorporated into the agreement. The arbitrator found the defendant was personally liable for the corporation's debt to the plaintiff.

The defendant claimed that the award violated Missouri law, which governed the arbitration. The Missouri Court of Appeals upheld the award because the issue of the plaintiff's personal liability was raised in the amended petition. The court cited in support the Missouri vacatur statute, which states that "the fact that the relief was such that it could or would not be granted by a court of law or equity is not a ground for vacating or refusing to confirm the award." It also noted that in Missouri, manifest disregard of the law is not a statutory basis to vacate an award. The court said:

> Arbitrators exceed their jurisdiction only when they decide matters beyond the scope of the arbitration agreement or which clearly were not submitted to them for arbitration. Since the issue of personal liability was submitted to the arbitrator in this case, the arbitrator did not exceed his authority even though the award was repugnant to state law.

---

[12] 26 F.3d 1314 (5th Cir. 1994). The "essence" test is commonly used in labor cases, i.e., does the award draw its essence from the collective bargaining agreement or was the arbitrator's award drawn from the letter or the purpose of the underlying contract, in this case, the purchase agreement. The court indicated that it had applied the essence test in other non-labor cases.

[13] 992 S.W.2d 265 (Mo. Ct. App. W.D. 1999).

In *Chandra v. Bradstreet*, the award combined treble damages for embezzlement with an order stopping those who benefited from the embezzlement from benefiting further.[14] The case arose out of two lawsuits involving a company providing medical services, and the professional associations that were its shareholders. Each side claimed the other owed it large sums of money. The company's operating agreement called for all disputes between members and/or the company to be submitted to binding arbitration. In the arbitration, a shareholder who was a defendant in the lawsuit alleged that one of the plaintiff shareholders had embezzled money from it. The defendant also alleged that two other plaintiff shareholders had misappropriated money from the company. Among other relief, the defendant sought dissolution of the company.

The arbitrator found that one plaintiff had embezzled funds and awarded treble damages against him for civil theft. The award also estopped this plaintiff from receiving any distributions from the dissolved company. The arbitrator also found that two other plaintiffs had benefited from the theft and the award estopped them from receiving a distribution of funds from the company to the extent of the first $75,000 recovered.

The plaintiffs argued that the arbitrator exceeded his authority because the company never made any affirmative claims for relief and because the estoppel award was contrary to the operating agreement. But the Florida Court of Appeals found the award was valid in all respects because the issues to which the remedies related were within the scope of the submissions to the arbitrator. In upholding the award, the court noted that its review of awards is very limited, and that it must avoid "judicialization" of the arbitration process. The court also stated:

> A high degree of conclusiveness attaches to the arbitration award. Such conclusiveness is required because the parties have, by agreement substituted a tribunal of their own choosing for the forum provided by law. To permit a dissatisfied party to set aside the arbitration award and invoke the judgment of the court on the merits would destroy the purpose of arbitration.

Intellectual property disputes. The current climate of judicial respect for arbitral remedies has enabled arbitrators to sometimes award

---

[14] *See* n. 9, *supra*. The court reinstated the award that had been vacated by the trial court.

extraordinary forms of relief. A good example is the award in *Advanced Micro Devices (AMD) v. Intel Corp.*[15] Here the arbitrator determined that it was appropriate to award one of the parties a permanent, royalty-free license over certain intellectual property for the other party's breach of a software licensing agreement and for bad faith.

The dispute arose out of a 1982 agreement between computer chip makers AMD and Intel, which provided that either party could elect to be a "second source" for products offered to it by the other. Under this agreement, the non-developing company would receive technical information and licenses needed to make and sell the product, while the company that developed the product would receive a royalty and the right to be a second source for products developed by the other company. In the period before the contract was entered into, AMD was attempting to secure entry into the 16-bit microprocessor market, while Intel had already developed its own 16-bit microprocessor, the 8086, and needed another producer to second source that chip and its expected progeny.

Disagreements over product exchanges led AMD to seek arbitration pursuant to the parties' agreement. The parties agreed that "the arbitrator may grant any remedy or relief which the arbitrator deems just and equitable and within the scope of the agreement of the parties, including, but not limited to specific performance of a contract." The agreement also instructed the arbitrator to "interpret and apply" these rules insofar as they relate to his power and duties. A temporary judge who was also then chosen the arbitrator included in his order of submission the following with respect to each issue submitted: "[T]he arbitrator is authorized to fashion such remedy as he may in his discretion determine to be fair and reasonable but not in excess of his jurisdiction."

After lengthy arbitration proceedings, the arbitrator found that Intel had breached the implied covenant of good faith and fair dealing, as well as an implied covenant requiring the parties to negotiate reasonably to make their relationship work. The arbitrator found that Intel breached these covenants when it decided to frustrate the operation of the contract by taking no more products from AMD and by keeping this decision from AMD and the public.

The arbitrator also found that AMD was partially responsible for its own damages because it had unnecessarily delayed seeking alternative ways to enter the 32-bit chip market. The arbitrator said that AMD should have sought arbitration or begun reverse engineering the 32-bit

---

[15] *See* n. 5, *supra*.

chip much sooner. Since AMD did not produce its own 32-bit chip until 1991, the arbitrator declined to award the company the hundreds of millions of dollars it sought from Intel in lost 32-bit chip profits.

The arbitrator nevertheless ruled that AMD had lost profits and goodwill as a result of Intel's conduct, that actual damages were immeasurable, and that nominal damages were inequitable. Accordingly, the arbitrator decided that the proper remedy was to relieve AMD from legal harassment by Intel over AMD's alleged use of Intel intellectual property in the reverse engineered AMD 32-bit chip. Therefore, in addition to other relief that was not in dispute, the arbitrator awarded AMD a permanent, nonexclusive, royalty-free license to any Intel intellectual property embodied in AMD's 32-bit chip, and a further two-year extension of certain patent and copyright licenses previously provided by Intel to AMD to the extent they related to the AMD 386.

Before ruling on Intel's challenge to the award, the California Supreme Court, in a scholarly opinion, devised a specific standard of review for arbitral remedies. This standard calls for a court to determine whether the arbitrator's choice of remedy bears some rational relationship to both the contract and the breach. The court explained that unless expressly restricted by the agreement, arbitrators "enjoy the authority to fashion relief they consider just and fair under the circumstances existing at the time of the arbitration, so long as the remedy may be rationally derived from the contract and the breach." In the words of the court:

> [A]n award may not be vacated merely because the court is unable to find the relief granted as authorized by a specific term of the contract. The required link may be to the contractual terms as actually interpreted by the arbitrator (if the arbitrator has made the interpretation known), to an interpretation implied in the award itself, or to a plausible theory of the contract's general subject matter, framework, or intent....Where the damage is difficult to determine or measure, the arbitrator enjoys the correspondingly broader discretion to fashion a remedy. The award will be upheld so long as it was even arguably based on the contract; it may be vacated only if the reviewing court is compelled to infer the award was based on an extrinsic source. In close cases the arbitrator's decision must stand.

Applying this standard of review, the California Supreme Court found that the challenged remedies were "rationally drawn from the arbitrator's conception of the contract's subject matter and the effect on AMD of Intel's breach." Thus, the award did not exceed the arbitrator's powers. There was nothing to indicate that the arbitrator resorted to an extrinsic source in fashioning the remedy.

Helpful to the court's decision was the fact that the arbitrator gave a lengthy explanation of his understanding of the contract and the breach and his reasons for making the award. The court made a detailed comparison of the award and the breach but cautioned that this will not be required in all cases. "[I]n many cases the required rational relationship between the breach and the award may be found in the fact that the arbitrator has awarded the injured party relief or the same general type as that a jury or court could have provided had the claim been litigated, even if the quantity, extent or parameters of the award differ in some respects from that to which the party was legally entitled."[16]

Conclusion

Arbitrators should study the arbitration agreement for any limits on their remedial authority, as well as the parties' submissions. Given a broadly worded arbitration clause, and the absence of any limitations affecting remedies, arbitrators have the flexibility to award even unusual relief if appropriate to resolve the dispute. Parties who wish to circumscribe the arbitrator's authority with respect to remedies may, of course, address that issue in the drafting of the arbitration agreement.[17] However, limiting arbitral remedies through drafting may create problems of interpretation.[18]

---

[16] One judge dissented, preferring the rule than an award must fall within the range of remedies a court could award and bear a rational relationship to the contract. The dissenter found that the award failed both prongs of this test.

[17] See Marshall H. Tanick, Arbitration Agreements After Wright: The Importance of Drafting, 4 NO. 3 ADR CURRENTS 5 (Sept. 1999).

[18] *Cf.* Green v. Ameritech Corp, 2000 WL 10606 (6th Cir. Jan. 6, 2000) (if a party wants a more detailed opinion from the arbitrator, the parties must be more specific in their arbitration agreement, and may be better off using familiar legal terms).

III. Punitive Damages

Punitive Damages in Arbitration: The Debate Continues

by Lorenzo Marinuzzi[*]

The debate as to whether arbitrators are empowered to authorize punitive damages is ongoing. Court decisions have done little to clear the air, other than to make it even more apparent that there is a greater need for the parties to make their intentions clear as to the parameters of arbitral authority when agreeing to the language of the arbitration clause. "One thing is clear," says Lorenzo Marinuzzi. "The standard boilerplate arbitration agreement is changing this very day." In this article, Marinuzzi takes a close look at the relevant case law.

When parties submit a disputed matter to arbitration, they seek a resolution independent of the judicial authority of the state. The promise of an often faster, less expensive, less formal and more convenient process makes arbitration a reasonable alternative to ordinary court proceedings.[1] Punitive damages are generally awarded for the public benefit and in the interest of society as a whole. Punitive damages, unlike compensatory damages, do not seek to compensate a wronged party, but rather are in addition to compensatory damages. When a party is ordered to pay punitive damages, that party is punished so that they and others may be deterred from engaging in the same course of conduct in the future.[2]

Although it is well-established that courts may award punitive damages when the circumstances so permit, there is a dispute as to whether arbitrators are empowered to make such an award. The implications and ramifications are obvious. A contract that forces parties to arbitrate all disputes may shield a wrongful party from the penalty it might have been subject to in a court proceeding while, at the same time, the aggrieved party may be denied the reward he or she truly desires.

---

[*] The author is a graduate of the Fordham University School of Law and is an associate member of the law firm of Otterbourg, Steindler, Houston & Rosen in New York City.

[1] 5 Am Jur 2d, Arbitration and Award § 1 (1994).

[2] 22 Am Jur 2d, Damages § 237 (1994). *See also* Pacific Mutual Life Ins. Co. v. Haslip, 499 U.S. 1, 19 (1991) ("Punitive damages are imposed for purposes of retribution and deterrence.")

In an era where most employment contracts and securities agreements contain boilerplate language that requires both parties to submit all disputes to arbitration, the issue of whether an arbitrator is authorized to award punitive damages is of key importance.[3] Not surprisingly, many factors contribute to the debate. When parties include a pre-dispute agreement to arbitrate in their form of contract, they often do not anticipate that the mere inclusion of this language can mean the difference between a small award and a much greater award.[4]

Consider a typical pre-dispute arbitration agreement contained in a contract. It might read as follows:

> "This agreement and its enforcement shall be governed by the laws of the State of New York. Any controversy arising out of or relating to [client's accounts, employment, etc.] shall be settled by arbitration in accordance with the rules, then in effect, of the American Arbitration Association."[5]

Whether under this or similar language an arbitrator is empowered by law or otherwise to award punitive damages depends on a number of factors that courts have considered and will continue to consider for some time.

Because contract interpretation is a matter of state law, the state where the agreement is made and enforced is important, as is the choice-of-law state and the applicable federal district where litigation may be brought. Another factor is the particular language of the pre-dispute agreement itself. Often, the technical phrasing of the agreement is the determining factor. As a result of *Mastrobuono v. Shearson Lehman Hutton, Inc.*,[6] the wording of the pre-dispute arbitration clause is of great

---

[3] Most of the litigation revealed in my research revolves around brokerage agreements and employment disputes.

[4] This article will focus on pre-dispute arbitration agreements because they dominate the case law on the subject. The reason is simple; when parties agree to arbitrate after the nature of the claim is known, they are usually fully aware of all of the implications of arbitration, including the availability or lack of punitive damages. See Jordan L. Resnick, Note, *Beyond Mastrobuono: A Practitioners' Guide to Arbitration, Employment Disputes, Punitive Damages, and the Implications of the Civil Rights Act of 1991*, 23 HOFSTRA L. REV. 913, 915 n.5 (1995).

[5] Although this language is typical, many agreements are governed by the rules of the National Association of Securities Dealers, Inc. or the Board of Directors of the New York Stock Exchange, Inc. and/or the American Stock Exchange. This is especially true in most brokerage agreements. *See, for example*, Mastrobuono v. Shearson Lehman Hutton, 115 S. Ct. 1212, 1995 LEXIS 1820 (1995).

[6] 115 S. Ct. 1212, 1995 LEXIS 1820 (1995).

importance. Courts may also consider the specific procedural rules of the arbitral body chosen by contract to arbitrate the disputes. Congressional enactments like the Federal Arbitration Act (FAA)[7] and Title VII of the Civil Rights Law of 1991[8] may play particularly important roles in the determination as well.

Although the current status of the law is still not clear, it would appear that punitive damages are now an available remedy for arbitrators to award, depending mostly on the interpretation and wording of the agreement to arbitrate. This article maps out the various factors affecting the authority of arbitrators to award punitive damages. Because an explanation of the current law is incomplete without a historical discussion, the article begins with a discussion of the FAA and its effect on arbitration. Next, it discusses the Garrity rule, which prohibited arbitrators, as a matter of law, from awarding punitive damages.[9] The article then discusses the inherent conflict between prohibiting punitive damage awards in arbitration and other legislative enactments like the FAA and the statutory grant of punitive damages in employment discrimination cases under the Civil Rights Law of 1991.[10] It then briefly describes the circuit split revolving around Garrity and the reasoning behind courts' unwillingness to adhere to the New York State Court of Appeals' decision. Finally, the article discusses the *Mastrobuono* case, the Supreme Court's attempt to resolve both the issue at hand and the circuit split, and its ramifications on the arbitration process.

The Federal Arbitration Act

In 1925, Congress enacted the Federal Arbitration Act and "formally recognized arbitration as a valid alternative to judicial dispute resolution."[11] The FAA established a federal policy favoring arbitration and required courts to rigorously enforce arbitration agreements.[12] The purpose of the FAA was to reverse the longstanding judicial hostility to arbitration that existed at English common law and was subsequently

---

[7] The Federal Arbitration Act, Pub. L. No. 68-401, 43 Stat. 883 (1925), *codified as amended* at 9 U.S.C. §§ 1-16 (1988 & Supp. V 1993).

[8] 42 U.S.C. § 1981 (a)(Supp. 1993).

[9] Garrity v. Lyle Stuart, Inc., 353 N.E.2d 793 (N.Y. 1976).

[10] *See supra*, note 8.

[11] See Beth H. Friedman, Note, The Preclusive Effect of Arbitral Determinations in Subsequent Federal Securities Litigation, 55 FORDHAM L. REV. 655, 659 (1987).

[12] *See* Julie A. Friedlander, Note, *Punitive Damages as a Remedy for Discrimination Claim Arbitrations in the Securities Industry*, 23 HOFSTRA L. REV. 225, 229 (1994). *See also* Shearson/ American Express Inc. v. McMahon, 492 U.S. 220, 224 (1991).

adopted by American courts, and to place arbitration agreements on equal footing with other contracts.[13]

The FAA provides that if parties have agreed to arbitrate their disputes, courts would enforce the agreement. Virtually all types of claims have been compelled to arbitration.[14] The courts have heard contract claims,[15] copyright claims,[16] ERISA claims,[17] RICO claims,[18] Civil Rights claims,[19] antitrust claims[20] and securities claims,[21] to name a few.[22]

The FAA has been called something of an "anomaly"[23] in the area of federal court jurisdiction.[24] Without providing an independent ground for federal jurisdiction, it created a body of substantive law establishing the courts' duty to honor arbitration agreements. Despite the FAA, there must exist some other independent basis for federal court jurisdiction.

The chief case that shows the might of the FAA is *Moses H. Cone Memorial Hospital v. Mercury Construction Corp.*,[25] decided in 1983.

---

[13] *See* Friedlander, *id.*, at 229-230. *See also* Gilmer v. Interstate/Johnson Lane Corp., 500 U.S. 20, 24 (1991).

[14] § 2 of the FAA states that agreements to arbitrate are only enforceable when they "evidence a transaction involving interstate commerce." 9 U.S.C. § 2 (1992). Because interstate commerce is so broadly defined, virtually all business and employment disputes are covered by the FAA. See Resnick, *supra*, note 4, at 920.

[15] *See generally* Moses H. Cone Memorial Hospital v. Mercury Construction Corp., 460 U.S. 1 (1983).

[16] Claims under the Copyright Act of 1976, 17 U.S.C. §§ 101-1010 (1988 & Supp. V 1993), *e.g.*, McMahan Sec. Co. v. Forum Capital Markets, L.P., 35 F.3d 82, 89 (2d Cir. 1994).

[17] Employee Retirement and Income Security Act, 29 U.S.C. §§ 1001-1461 (1988 & Supp. V 1993). *See, for example*, Pritzker v. Merrill Lynch, Pierce, Fenner & Smith, Inc., 7 F.3d 1110 (3d Cir. 1993).

[18] Racketeer Influenced and Corrupt Organizations Act, 18 U.S.C. §§ 1961-1968 (1988 & Supp. V 1993). *See, for example*, Shearson American Express Inc. v. McMahon, 492 U.S. 220 (1987).

[19] Age Discrimination in Employment Act claims, 29 U.S.C. §§ 621-634 (1988 & Supp. V 1993). *See, for example*, Gilmer v. Interstate/Johnson Lane Corp., 500 U.S. 20, 26 (1991) (compelled arbitration of age discrimination claim).

[20] The Sherman Act, 15 U.S.C. §§ 1-36 (1988 & Supp. V 1993). *See, for example*, Mitsubishi Motors Corp. v. Soler Chrysler-Plymouth, Inc., 473 U.S. 614 (1985).

[21] The Securities Act of 1933, 15 U.S.C. §§ 77a-77aa (1988). *See, for example*, Shearson American Express v. McMahon, *supra*, n. 16.

[22] *See* Resnick, *supra*, note 4, at 919-920.

[23] *See Moses H. Cone*, 460 U.S. at 26 nn.34-35.

[24] *See* David J. Efron, Note, *Muddied Waters: Awards of Punitive Damages in Disputes Arbitrated Pursuant to Brokerage Firm Customer Agreements*, 7 DE PAUL L.J. 333, 335 (1995).

[25] *See supra*, note 15.

Moses H. Cone involved a contract dispute between a hospital and a construction company.[26] The parties had an agreement that all disputes would be resolved through arbitration.[27] The hospital brought suit in state court and the construction company brought suit in federal court, seeking an order compelling arbitration under the FAA.[28] The federal district court granted the hospital's motion to stay the federal court proceeding pending resolution of the state court matter.[29]

The Supreme Court reversed the district court's order. The court held that §2 of the FAA "created a body of federal substantive law of arbitrability, applicable to any arbitration agreement within coverage of the Act.'"[30] The court further held that §2 of the Act "is a congressional declaration of a liberal federal policy favoring arbitration agreements, notwithstanding any state substantive or procedural policies to the contrary."[31] Most important is that the court concluded that "any doubts concerning the scope of arbitrable issues should be resolved in favor of arbitration, whether the problem at hand is in the construction of the contract language itself or an allegation of waiver.'"[32]

As impressive as this language may seem, it, in and of itself, was not enough to ensure that arbitrators had authority to award punitive damages even when the dispute was covered by the FAA. The reason was usually that the parties had chosen to be bound by other rules or the laws of a state that did not directly conflict with the FAA's goal of fostering arbitration.[33] In certain pure state claims, the FAA did not have any effect.

Garrity v. Lyle Stuart, Inc.[34] *–"The New York Rule"*

In this landmark case, which has been the epicenter of the entire debate, the New York Court of Appeals held that an arbitrator had no

---

[26] *Id.* at 4, 5.
[27] *Id.*
[28] *Id.* at 6-7.
[29] *Id.* at 7.
[30] *Id.* at 24.
[31] *Id.* (Italics added).
[32] *Id.* at 24-25.
[33] For most courts, the question is what the parties intended by their choice of language. It seems that, at least before *Mastrobuono*, courts would read the identical boilerplate arbitration agreement provisions and choice-of-law provisions and decide them according to whether that particular court adhered to the *Garrity* principle. See discussion of *Garrity*, *infra* note 34 and accompanying text.
[34] 353 N.E2d 793 (N.Y. 1976).

authority to award punitive damages. In *Garrity*, an author sued her publisher in two separate actions for breach of contract and various intentional torts. On the publisher's motion, the court stayed the actions because, as the publisher asserted, the parties had agreed to arbitrate all disputes.[35]

Garrity filed an arbitration demand requesting withheld royalties and seeking punitive damages, alleging that the royalties had been intentionally and maliciously withheld to force settlement of earlier claims.[36] The arbitration panel awarded Garrity full compensatory damages and $7,500 in punitive damages, plus interest and attorneys' fees. The award was confirmed by both the Court of Special Term and the Appellate Division.[37] The issue on appeal was whether the arbitrator had the power to award punitive damages.[38]

A 4-3 court of appeals held that "an arbitrator has no power to award punitive damages, even if agreed upon by the parties."[39] In reaching this somewhat disturbing[40] conclusion, Chief Judge Breitel, writing for the majority, reasoned that although arbitrators are free to fashion appropriate remedies, such remedies must be compensatory.[41] Because punitive damages are used to punish wrongdoers, allowing an arbitrator to award them would allow the arbitrator to usurp a function reserved for the state and its judicial system.[42] Pointing out that jury awards of punitive damages are subject to the scrutiny of the trial judge and appellate review, Judge Breitel wrote, "if arbitrators were allowed to impose punitive damages, the usefulness of arbitration would be destroyed. It would become a trap for the unwary given the eminently desirable freedom from judicial overview of law and facts."[43]

---

[35] *Id.* at 794.
[36] *Id.*
[37] *Id.*
[38] *Id.*
[39] *Id.* (*citing* Publishers' Association v. Newspaper & Mail Deliverers' Union, 114 N.Y.S.2d 401, 404-06 (1952)) (italics added).
[40] It is particularly disturbing because freedom of contract is all but rejected by the highest court in New York, at least with regards to the issue at hand.
[41] *Supra* n.2, at 794-795.
[42] *Id.* at 796.
[43] *Id.* at 797. This is rather ironic. How about the countless others who have been denied the opportunity to pursue punitive damage claims because they have been compelled to arbitrate in a judicial forum that adhered to the belief that a New York choice-of-law provision made Garrity controlling? *See also* Thomas J. Stipanowich, *Punitive Damages in Arbitration Garrity v. Lyle Stuart, Inc. Reconsidered*, 66 B.U.L. REV. 953, 961-62 (1986).

Statutory Conflicts

There is an inherent conflict between federal and state authority when a claim for punitive damages is brought under a federal statute but is prohibited by an arbitration agreement read to prohibit punitive damage claims. Such is the case with claims brought under Title VII. With regards to such employment claims, Congress has specifically legislated that "the complaining party may recover compensatory and punitive damages."[44] At the same time, the underlying employment agreement may contain a New York choice-of-law provision and require that all disputes be submitted to arbitration.

Because courts have held that Title VII claims are arbitrable, and because Congress has expressly provided for the availability of punitive damages, it seems logical that courts would infer that Congress must have intended that arbitrators have the authority to award punitive damages, at least when the claim revolves around a federal statute.[45] Although this reasoning has been adopted by most federal circuits and states, it is clearly at odds with the Garrity rule.[46] This rule has frustrated the Congressional reasoning behind making punitive damages available.[47] Such a rule, which enforces an arbitration clause while prohibiting arbitrators from considering punitive damage claims, insulates those guilty of the very behavior Congress sought to curtail.

There is no easy solution to this conundrum. Some have suggested that courts should allow an aggrieved party to "opt out" of an arbitration agreement if arbitration would deny him or her the punitive damages the party may be entitled to.[48] However, if a plaintiff is allowed to remove all arbitrable claims by raising a single claim for punitive damages, forum shopping would become prevalent, as punitive damage claims would be included in complaints solely to avoid arbitration.[49] Were a court to allow a plaintiff to opt out, the court would, in effect, be subverting one federal policy in an effort to uphold another. It would be quite odd for a court to ignore the FAA's mandate in favor of arbitration so that a party

---

[44] 42 U.S.C. § 1981 (a)(1) (Supp. 1993) (Italics added).

[45] *See* Todd Shipyards Corp v. Cunard Line, Ltd., 943 F.2d 1056 (9th Cir. 1991) (finding that arbitration panel had authority to award punitive damages in case involving maritime breach of contract). *See also* Friedlander, *supra*, note 12, at 235.

[46] This will be explored in the discussion of the circuit split below.

[47] *See* Friedlander, *supra*, note 12, at 235-236.

[48] *See generally*, C. Evan Stewart, *Punitive Damages in Arbitration*, N.Y.L.J., JULY 21, 1994, at 1, 4. *See also* Resnick, *supra*, note 4, at 948.

[49] Resnick, *supra*, note 4, at 948.

guilty of practicing employment discrimination might be liable for punitive damages.[50]

The Circuit Split

With the strong language of *Garrity*, it is not surprising that most employment and brokerage contracts have a New York choice-of-law clause. Since most of these contracts are drawn up by the deep pockets on a "take it or leave it basis," isolating oneself from punitive damages is a rather desirable goal. For other parties that did not intend to foreclose punitive damage claims, a New York choice-of-law clause nonetheless has the same effect.

Or does it? That depends on where you are. In the face of identical language incorporating a New York choice-of-law clause in an agreement to arbitrate, courts have come out on opposite ends; some rejecting *Garrity* while others have upheld it. The reasoning has usually been the particular language of the agreement itself. Under the guise of the FAA,[51] courts have sought to discern what the parties to a contract intended by including a New York choice-of-law clause while specifying an arbitration body and its rules to conduct the arbitration. The results are not uniform.

In *Barbier v. Shearson Lehman Hutton, Inc.*,[52] decided by the Second Circuit,[53] an arbitration panel awarded customers of Shearson compensatory and punitive damages against Shearson in the total amount of $155,645 for claims of breaches of fiduciary duty and contract and for conversion.[54] Not surprisingly, the firm's customer agreement contained a New York choice-of-law provision and called for arbitration of any dispute according to the rules of the NASD or the NYSE.[55] Searching for the intent of the parties, the court found that it was "apparent from the inclusion of the choice-of-law provision [in the customer agreement] that the parties intended to be bound by *Garrity*."[56] Accordingly, the court vacated the award of punitive damages.[57]

---

[50] *See generally, Id.* See also *Friedlander, supra,* note 12, at 236; Thomas J. Kenny, Comment, *Punitive Damages In Securities Arbitration: The Unresolved Question of Pendent State Claims,* 37 CATH. U.L. REV. 1113, 1115 (1988).

[51] *See supra,* note 7.

[52] 948 F.2d 117 (2d Cir. 1991).

[53] The geographical home of Garrity.

[54] *Id.* at 117, 118.

[55] *Id.* at 119.

[56] *Id.* at 122.

[57] *Id.* at 123.

Interestingly, the Second Circuit Court in *Barbier* did not, in establishing the parties' intent, analyze whether the applicable arbitration rules specified in the customer agreement permitted punitive damages. Was it fair for the court to establish the parties' intent from the choice-of-law provision alone?[58]

Often, the procedural rules of the arbitrating agency can be read to allow an arbitrator to make an award of punitive damages. The American Arbitration Association (AAA) is a not-for-profit organization offering a broad range of dispute resolution services. The AAA has adopted a set of Commercial Arbitration Rules to establish uniform procedures.[59] Although no AAA rule expressly empowers arbitrators to award punitive damages, rule 43 ("Scope of Award") provides, in pertinent part, that "the arbitrator may grant any remedy or relief that the arbitrator deems just and equitable and within the scope of the agreement of the parties, including, but not limited to, specific performance of the contract."[60]

Using this broad provision, the Eighth Circuit Court of Appeals in *Lee v. Chica*[61] allowed an arbitrator to award punitive damages. In *Lee*, an arbitration panel awarded $31,800 in punitive damages to the customer of a brokerage house based on claims of fraud and breach of fiduciary duty. The firm's customer agreement called for submission of all disputes to arbitration according to the rules of the AAA and contained a Minnesota choice-of-law provision.[62] The court held that "when the choice-of-law provision in an arbitral clause incorporates the rules of the AAA…AAA arbitrators may grant any remedy or relief including punitive damages."[63] The court further held that even if Minnesota law prohibits an arbitrator from awarding punitive damages, like New York law, "when the parties…agree to arbitration under the rules of the AAA and the arbitration issues involve interstate commerce, the FAA[64] gives force to the rules of the AAA."[65]

---

[58] *See* Efron, *supra*, note 24 at 341. ("Clearly,…discernment of intent based on this agreement is highly speculative.")

[59] Commercial Arbitration Rules, AAA (as amended and effective on July 1, 1996).

[60] *Id.* at Rule 43.

[61] 983 F.2d 883 (8th Cir. 1993), *cert. denied*, 114 S. Ct. 287 (1993).

[62] *Id.* at 884.

[63] *Id.* at 887.

[64] The FAA mandates that any doubts concerning the scope of arbitrable issues should be resolved in favor of arbitration. *See supra*, note 32, and accompanying text.

[65] *Supra*, note 61, at 888. As David J. Efron points out, the court's analysis is unclear. How does the FAA give force to the AAA rules? Was it based on the conflict between state

An interesting approach taken by the California Court of Appeals in *J. Alexander Securities, Inc. v. Mendez*,[66] was to confine the choice-of-law provision to substantive matters, giving arbitrators free reign in procedural and remedial matters. In *J. Alexander*, the brokerage firm's customer agreement provided that it was to be governed by New York law, and also contained a provision requiring the parties to submit disputes to arbitration under the rules of the NASD or the NYSE.[67] Alleging claims of account churning and deceptive practices, the client demanded arbitration, where she was awarded $27,000 in punitive damages by the arbitration panel.[68]

The firm sought to have the award vacated by the California appellate court on the ground that New York law prohibited such awards.[69] The motion was denied and the award affirmed by the court.[70] Also citing to the FAA's guiding principle that all doubts concerning the scope of arbitrable issues should be resolved in favor of arbitration,[71] the court held that the New York choice-of-law provision "merely designated the substantive law that the arbitrators must apply in determining whether...punitive damages [are warranted], and did not deprive the arbitrators of their authority to award [punitive damages]."[72] The court was not persuaded by *Garrity*. The court concluded that, absent a clause in the contract or in the AAA rules prohibiting punitive damages, the arbitrators did not exceed their powers in making the award.[73]

It is clear that the status of punitive damages in arbitration was not uniform from court to court, jurisdiction to jurisdiction. While the courts in the First, Eighth, Ninth and Eleventh Circuits, and California's appellate courts, rejected the notion that a particular choice-of-law requires that they deny enforcement of an award of punitive damages by

---

law and the arbitration rules that the FAA helped resolve in favor of arbitration? *See* Efron, *supra*, note 24, at 344.

[66] 21 Cal. Rptr. 2d 826 (Cal. Ct. App. 1993), *rev. denied*, 1993 Cal. LEXIS 6354 (1993), *cert. denied*, 114 S. Ct. 2182 (1994).
[67] *Id.* at 827-828.
[68] *Id.* at 828.
[69] *Id.*
[70] *Supra*, note 66, at 828.
[71] *See supra*, note 32, and accompanying text.
[72] *Supra*, note 66, at 830.
[73] *Id.* at 832. Implicit in the analysis is the assumption that the Garrity rule is not substantive law. *See supra*, note 24, at 345. *But see* Fahnestock & Co. v. Waltman, 953 F.2d 512, 518 (2d Cir. 1991) (holding "that [because] the *Garrity* rule is grounded in state policy concerns renders it no less a rule of substantive law.").

an arbitrator, the Second and Seventh circuits followed the New York choice-of-law by refusing to uphold the awards.[74]

Mastrobuono to the Rescue—Sort of

Once and for all, the U.S. Supreme Court was given the opportunity to resolve the circuit split and settle the matter. On March 6, 1995, the Supreme Court, in a landmark decision, reversed the Seventh Circuit Court of Appeals in *Mastrobuono v. Shearson Lehman Hutton Inc.*[75] The issue in the case, according to the court, was to determine "what the contract has to say about the arbitrability of petitioners' claim for punitive damages."[76]

In *Mastrobuono*, the customer agreement contained a New York choice-of-law provision and called for arbitration of any dispute according to the rules of the NASD, the NYSE or the AMEX.[77] The Seventh Circuit found that by choosing New York law without excluding its arbitration rules, the parties chose to be bound by *Garrity*.[78] The circuit court concluded that "the more sensible construction of the agreement is that the *Garrity* rule always controls, whether the parties choose the NASD, NYSE or American Stock Exchange rules."[79]

The Supreme Court expressed the same view as the California Appellate Court, namely, that the choice-of-law provision "might include only New York's substantive rights and obligations, and not the State's allocation of power between alternative tribunals."[80] The court concluded that the New York choice-of-law provision is not, "in itself, an unequivocal exclusion of punitive damages."[81] Instead, the court ruled that the arbitration agreement, standing alone, strongly implies that an award of punitive damages is "appropriate."[82] The court noted that the arbitration clause authorized arbitration in accordance with the rules of the NASD and that the NASD manual cautioned that arbitrators could consider punitive damages as a remedy.[83]

---

[74] *See* Resnick, *supra*, note 4, at 933.
[75] 15 S. Ct. 1212, 1995 U.S. LEXIS 1820 (1995).
[76] *Id.* at *4.
[77] *Id.* at *12.
[78] Mastrobuono v. Shearson Lehman Hutton, Inc., 20 F.3d 713, 717 (7th Cir. 1994), *rev'd*, 115 S. Ct. 1212, 1995 U.S. LEXIS 1820 (1995).
[79] *Id.* at 718.
[80] *Mastrobuono*, 115 S. Ct. 1212, 1995 LEXIS 1820 at *14.
[81] *Id.*
[82] *Id.* at *15.
[83] *Id.* Although the court noted that the language was not a clear authorization of punitive damages, it held that it was "broad enough to contemplate such a remedy."

The court found that "at most, the choice-of-law clause introduces an ambiguity into an arbitration agreement that would otherwise allow punitive damage awards."[84] The court reasoned that the best way to harmonize the two provisions is to read the "laws of the State of New York" to encompass substantive principles that New York courts would apply, but not to include rules limiting the authority of arbitrators.[85] Thus, the Court held that the "choice-of-law provision covers the rights and duties of the parties, while the arbitration clause covers arbitration."[86] Neither clause, the court noted, conflicted with one another.[87]

Although the Supreme Court's decision may seem, at first blush, to direct the courts on how to resolve conflicts between state law and the policies of the FAA, such a conclusion would overstate the breadth of the court's decision.[88] Only three limited conclusions can be gleaned from the court's decision.[89] The court held that punitive damages would be available in an arbitration if:

1. the contract at issue is the same as the Shearson Lehman Hutton client agreement in *Mastrobuono*;[90]

2. the contract merely makes "reference to 'the laws of the State of New York'" without more explicit language to explain the implications of the choice-of-law with regard to the availability of punitive damages;[91] or

3. the contract does not specify which provisions will take priority while incorporating state law that restricts punitive damage awards and arbitration procedures that award punitive damages.[92]

---

[84] *Id.* at *17.
[85] *Mastrobuono*, 115 S. Ct. 1212, 1995 LEXIS 1820 at *20.
[86] *Id.*
[87] *Id.*
[88] *See* Resnick, *supra*, note 4, at 935. Resnick notes that the ruling of the New York Court of Appeals absolutely barring an award of punitive damages by an arbitrator is now a nullity, inasmuch as the Supreme Court held that "if contracting parties agree to include claims for punitive damages within the issues to be arbitrated, the FAA ensures that their agreement will be enforced according to its terms even if a rule of state law would otherwise exclude such claims from arbitration." (*quoting Mastrobuono*, 115 S. Ct. 1212, 1995 LEXIS 1820 at *11.)
[89] Resnick, *supra*, note 4, at 935.
[90] *Id.* at 935-936.
[91] *Id.* at 936. (*quoting Mastrobuono*, *supra*, note 85, at *13.)
[92] *Id.*

As Resnick points out, *Mastrobuono* does not unequivocally resolve the dispute. It leaves open to debate whether a state court would have to interpret a customer agreement the same way as the Supreme Court did. Even the Supreme Court acknowledged that contract interpretation is a matter of state law,[93] although the Supreme Court would review an interpretation if the interpretation by the state court denies a federal right.[94] While this caveat may mean that claims brought under the various securities or federal employment statutes will allow arbitrators to award punitive damages, it does not guarantee that pure state claim arbitrations may include claims for punitive damages.

In fact, New York courts have been somewhat unwilling to embrace *Mastrobuono*. In *Dean Witter Reynolds, Inc. v. Trimble*,[95] Trimble filed a claim for punitive damages in an American Stock Exchange arbitration pursuant to the "AMEX Window" because the parties did not have an arbitration agreement. Distinguishing this case from *Mastrobuono*, the court dismissed the punitive damages claim and, despite the Supreme Court's ruling, held that, in New York, arbitrators are not empowered to award punitive damages.[96] The court further added in dicta that even if the case involved a contract with the identical New York choice-of-law clause, the court would not be bound to interpret it in the same way the Supreme Court did in *Mastrobuono*, since the interpretation of contracts is a matter of state law.[97]

Although the New York Court of Appeals may be willing and ready to overturn *Garrity*, the opportunities are rare. With respect to awards, an arbitrator's decision is only reviewable when the arbitrator has exceeded his or her authority.[98] If an arbitrator does not award punitive damages because he or she feels that making such an award will exceed arbitral authority, then review is unavailable.[99]

---

[93] *Supra*, note 85, at *14 n.4.
[94] *See* Volt Information Sciences, Inc. v. Board of Trustees of Leland Stanford Junior University, 489 U.S. 468, 482 (1989).
[95] No. 119930/94, 1995 N.Y. Misc. LEXIS 401 (Sup. Ct. June 13, 1995).
[96] *Id.* at *5-7. *See also* Resnick, *supra*, note 4, at 944-945.
[97] *Id.* at *7 n.4. *See also* N.Y.L.J., July 5, 1995, at 26 (N.Y. Sup. Ct.) (discussing Merrill Lynch, Pierce, Fenner & Smith, Inc. v. Levine)(citation omitted). The court dismissed the causes of action because the statute of limitations had run, but stated that the claim for punitive damages was barred by New York law, applicable by virtue of the choice-of-law clause, and because the client resided in New York.
[98] Of course, the decision is also reviewable in other situations, such as when the integrity of the proceeding is in question.
[99] *See* Resnick, *supra*, note 4, at 967-968.

Although many hoped that *Mastrobuono* would finally resolve the debate, the lack of certainty that followed and still exists can only mean that the public at large must take steps to answer the question for itself. The principal response by contracting parties has been to explicitly provide for or prohibit the possibility for arbitrators to make such an award. There are currently proposals in the securities industry to rewrite the standard customer agreements. In fact, Smith Barney has already changed its client agreement in an effort to give more force to New York law.[100] This, however, is not the same as specifically prohibiting an arbitrator from making a punitive damage award, especially if the FAA is applicable. Other firms have included language that specifically precludes arbitrators from making punitive damage awards.[101]

One thing is clear: The standard boilerplate arbitration agreement is changing this very day. Because the particular language of the agreement provides the key evidence of the parties' intent, most parties should be as specific as possible with regards to the arbitrators' authority. Although an exclusionary provision may not stand up against claims that guarantee the availability of punitive damages by statute, parties are strongly encouraged to make their intentions clear.

---

[100] The new agreement is now "governed and construed in accordance with the laws of the State of New York, including, but not limited to, the law of New York regarding...damages recoverable in arbitration...." Smith Barney Client Agreement, paragraph 7 (1995). Resnick, *supra*, note 4, at 940.

[101] "The arbitrator shall not have the authority to award punitive damages to either party...." *See* Resnick, *supra*, note 4, at 939 n.153.

IV. Clarifying an Award: The Third Circuit's View

Remanding an Award for Clarification
A Common Sense Approach to Functus Officio

by Richard H. Porter[*]

Under what circumstances may a federal court remand an arbitration award to an arbitrator for "clarification"? Although the question, addressed by the Third Circuit in a 1999 case[1], seems simple enough, the answer is not always clear.

The answer frequently depends on a number of variables, including the nature of the clarification sought, the jurisdiction in which the issue is raised, and whether the award allegedly in need of clarification was issued in a proceeding governed by the Labor Management Relations Act,[2] or in a reinsurance or other commercial dispute. For example, in labor arbitrations there is a bias favoring remands for clarification. The general rule is that a district court should not itself clarify an ambiguous arbitration award, but should remand the award to the arbitrator for clarification.[3]

---

[*] Richard H. Porter is a partner, focusing on reinsurance issues, at Steptoe & Johnson LLP in Washington, D.C. Mr. Porter is a former vice chair of the firm's litigation practice group. He received his J.D. with honors from Georgetown University. Porter currently serves on the Ethics Committee of ARIAS U.S. and is the former chairman of the Insurance Law Committee of Lex Mundi, an international organization of 151 independent law firms.

[1] Official & Prof'l Employees Int'l Union, Local No. 471 v. Brownsville Gen. Hosp., 1999 WL 562678 (3d Cir. Aug. 3, 1999). It is well settled that "the grounds for vacating arbitration awards are very narrow." See Federal Arbitration Act, 9 U.S.C. § 10. Courts have consistently held that "arbitration awards are subject to very limited review in order to avoid undermining the twin goals of arbitration, namely, settling disputes efficiently and avoiding long and expensive litigation." DiRussa v. Dean Whitter Reynolds, Inc., 121 F.3d 818, 821 (2d Cir. 1997) (citation omitted), *cert. den.*, 118 S. Ct. 695 (1998); Clarendon Nat'l Ins. Co. v. TIG Reinsurance Co., 183 F.R.D. 112, 115 (S.D.N.Y. 1998). A party seeking to overturn an arbitration award is under a heavy burden to prove that the standards for such relief have been met. Blue Bell, Inc. v. Western Glove Works, Ltd., 816 F. Supp. 236, 240 (S.D.N.Y. 1993); Kennecott Utah Copper Corp. v. Becker, 1999 WL 586970 (10th Cir. Aug. 5, 1999).

[2] 29 U.S.C. § 185.

[3] *See, e.g.,* San Antonio Newspaper Guild Local No. 25 v. San Antonio Light Div., 481 F.2d 821, 825 (5th Cir. 1973); United Steelworkers of Am., AFL-CIO-CLC v. Danly Mach. Corp., 852 F.2d 1024, 1027 (7th Cir. 1988); Oil, Chem. & Atomic Workers Int'l Union, Local 4-367 v. Rohm & Hass, Texas, Inc., 677 F.2d 492, 493-94 (5th Cir. 1982); United

The Brownsville Case

In *Official & Professional Employees Int'l Union, Local No. 471 v. Brownsville General Hospital*, a union employee of the hospital was suspended because of allegations of sexual harassment. The employee filed a grievance, but agreed to undergo counseling. The hospital arranged to have the employee counseled by a particular therapist. After eight therapy sessions, the counseling relationship broke down and the employee ceased seeing the designated therapist. The hospital then sought to terminate the employee, who filed a formal grievance. The arbitrator held that, although the hospital did not have a right to terminate the employee, it did have a right to suspend him pending completion of the previously agreed-to course of counseling. Specifically, the arbitrator's award stated: "The grievant will be reinstated, without back pay, but only after he completes the course of counseling as prescribed by Dr. Crabtree, and after Dr. Crabtree advises the Hospital that the grievant has completed the required course of counseling."

When Dr. Crabtree refused to continue to work with the employee, the employee continued counseling, but with another therapist. The hospital again sought to terminate the employee and the union filed suit seeking enforcement of the award on the ground that the employee was in substantial compliance with its terms. In the alternative, the union requested that the award be remanded to the arbitrator for clarification in view of the refusal of the original therapist to continue to work with the employee. The district court remanded the issue to the arbitrator because it recognized that the arbitrator had "mistakenly assumed that Dr. Crabtree would agree to further sessions with [the employee]." Relying on the doctrine of *functus officio*, the hospital appealed the remand, contending that the arbitrator lacked authority to reconsider his award.

Traditionalists and commentators who favor the continued application of common-law doctrines, particularly those with Latin roots, may be troubled by the Third Circuit's decision, but I believe the court got it right. The arbitrator's award obviously assumed that the therapist named in the original award would continue to be available to counsel the union employee. The district court was placed in a difficult position when the therapist refused to continue working with the employee. Essentially, the court was left to guess how the arbitrator would have

---

Food & Commercial Workers Local 100A v. John Hofmeister & Son, Inc., 950 F.2d 1340, 1345 (7th Cir. 1991).

decided had he known of Dr. Crabtree's unwillingness to continue the counseling.

The district court took a common sense approach-it remanded the award to the arbitrator for clarification. The fact that the Third Circuit's decision affirming the district court is likely to be somewhat controversial is testimony to the fact that *functus officio*, although sometimes ridiculed,[4] retains considerable vitality. The Third Circuit's lengthy discussion of the doctrine is a clear indication that *functus officio* is not an easy obstacle to overcome when lawyer and client face a situation in which they must ask a federal court to remand what purports to be a final arbitration award.

Functus officio, which in Latin refers to "[a] task performed," is a shorthand term for the common-law doctrine that bars an arbitrator from revisiting the merits of an award once it has been issued.[5] The doctrine has its origins in the perception that arbitrators, "not being professional judges or subject to the constraints of judicial ethics" may yield to *ex parte* pressures aimed at getting them to change their minds.[6] The doctrine has been criticized frequently. Chief Judge Richard Posner of the Seventh Circuit has questioned the underlying rationale given the fact that "[a]rbitrators are no more infallible than judges. They make mistakes and overlook contingencies and leave much to implication and assumption...." If the opportunities for judicial remand are severely limited, "the result is a significant gap in the system of arbitral justice." The practical effect of the doctrine, as Posner has observed, is that "there

---

[4] Glass, Molders, Pottery, Plastics & Allied Workers Int'l Union Local 182B v. Excelsior Foundry Co., 56 F.3d 844, 846 (7th Cir. 1995) (*citing* Newman v. Corado, 897 F.2d 1579, 1583 (Fed. Cir. 1990)); Red Star Express Lines v. International Bhd. of Teamsters Local 170, 809 F.2d 103, 106 (1st Cir. 1987); Local P-9 United Food & Commercial Workers v. George A. Hormell & Co., 776 F.2d 1393, 1394 n.1 (8th Cir. 1985); United Steelworkers of Am. v. Ideal Cement Co., 762 F.2d 837, 841 n. 3 (10th Cir. 1985); Industrial Mut. Ass'n, Inc. v. Amalgamated Workers Local 383, 725 F.2d 406, 412 n. 3 (6th Cir. 1984).

[5] *See* BLACK'S LAW DICTIONARY 673 (6th ed. 1990); Teamsters Local 312 v. Matlack, Inc., 118 F.3d 985, 991 (3d Cir. 1997).

[6] *Glass, Molders, supra*, n. 4, 56 F.3d at 847. Or, as another court explained: "The policy which lies behind this is an unwillingness to permit one who is not a judicial officer and who acts informally and sporadically, to re-examine a final decision which he has already rendered, because of the potential evil of outside communication and unilateral influence which might affect a new conclusion. The continuity of judicial office and the tradition which surrounds judicial conduct is lacking in the isolated activity of an arbitrator...." *See* La Vale Plaza, Inc. v. R.S. Noonan, Inc., 378 F.2d 569, 572 (3d Cir. 1967).

is nobody to whom the parties can turn" if an arbitrator is unable to consider a motion for reconsideration, clarification, amendment or other modification.[7]

Exceptions

With the passage of time, the rigidity with which *functus officio* was originally applied has eased somewhat. A number of exceptions to the doctrine have been crafted and the Third Circuit has been at the forefront of that movement.[8]

The case law suggests that there are now three well-accepted exceptions.[9] First, a court may remand an award to an arbitrator to allow the correction of a mistake that is apparent on the face of the award. Second, a remand is permitted when the award fails to adjudicate an issue that was submitted to the panel. Third, a remand may be appropriate if the arbitrator's award, although seemingly complete, raises a doubt as to whether the submission to the arbitrator was fully executed.[10]

Most frequently, courts will permit a remand if the award can fairly be characterized as "ambiguous."[11] Ambiguity frequently lies in the eyes of the beholder, but it is generally accepted that ambiguity may be apparent on the face of the award or demonstrated by extraneous, but objectively ascertainable facts.[12] However, "new evidence" discovered after an award has been issued is not sufficient to warrant a remand.[13]

Although there is certainly room for debate as to the continuing need for *functus officio*, a rigid application of the doctrine is at odds with both the increasing use of arbitration and the respect that arbitration has

---

[7] *Glass, Molders, supra*, n. 4, 56 F.3d at 847; *Clarendon Nat'l Inc., supra*, n. 1, 183 F.R.D. at 117.

[8] *See, e.g.*, Colonial Penn Ins. Co. v. Omaha Indem. Co., 943 F.2d 327, 334 (3d Cir. 1991).

[9] At least one circuit, the 8th, purports to recognize only two exceptions to the *functus officio* doctrine—"for mistakes evident on the face of the award and for changes when the parties consent." *See* Legion Ins. Co. v. VCW, Inc., No 99-1009 (8th Cir. Oct. 21, 1999).

[10] *Colonial Penn., supra*, n. 8, 943 F.2d at 332.

[11] *See, e.g.*, Mutual Fire, Marine & Inland Ins. Co. v. Norad Reinsurance Co., 868 F.2d 52, 58 (3d Cir. 1989); La Vale Plaza, *supra*, n. 6; Americas Ins. Co. v. Seagull Compania Naviera, S.A., 774 F.2d 64, 67 (2d Cir. 1985); Island Creek Coal Sales Co. v. City of Gainesville, 764 F.2d 437, 440 (6th Cir.), *cert. den.*, 474 U.S. 948 (1985); Lanier v. Old Republic Ins. Co., 936 F. Supp. 839, 848 (M.D. Ala. 1996).

[12] Colonial Penn, *supra*, n. 8, 943 F.2d at 334.

[13] *See, e.g.,* McClatchy Newspapers v. Central Valley Typographical Union No. 46, 686 F.2d 731, 733 (9th Cir.), *cert. den.*, 459 U.S. 1071 (1982).

garnered as a preferred and efficient means of resolving civil disputes.[14] Clearly, parties that have agreed to arbitrate their dispute should receive what they bargained for-an award from the arbitrator that addresses and resolves all aspects of the dispute. If an award is at all ambiguous-either because it is unclear on its face or, because, as in *Brownsville*, it is premised on a condition subsequent that never occurred, thus rendering performance impossible, then it makes sense to ask the arbitrator to clarify the decision in light of the changed circumstances.[15] If a federal court lacks the power to remand the award to the arbitrator in such circumstances, it would have to guess what the arbitrator would have done with a more accurate view of the future. The principal benefit of a remand is that it is "more likely to give the parties the award [they bargained for]."[16]

The concerns that proponents of *functus officio* have raised with respect to the susceptibility of arbitrators to extraneous pressures are not frivolous. However, courts are fully capable of addressing these concerns directly. As Judge Posner suggested: "Concern about *ex parte* communications with arbitrators strikes us as a better reason for barring such communications than for denying arbitrators all power to revisit their awards."[17] The possibility of mischief can be avoided by a remand that instructs the arbitrator to avoid *ex parte* communications and to limit reconsideration to clarification of the award.

Returning to *Brownsville*, it seems clear that the district court discharged its responsibility with appropriate deference for the doctrine

---

[14] *See, e.g.,* Moses H. Cone Mem. Hosp. v. Mercury Constr. Corp., 460 U.S. 1, 24-25 (1983); AT&T Technologies, Inc. v. Communication Workers of Am., 475 U.S. 643, 650 (1986); Ziegler v. Whale Secs. Co., 786 F. Supp. 739, 741 (N.D. Ind. 1992).

[15] Although *Brownsville* does not fit neatly within the "completion" exception to *functus officio,* some courts have commingled the "completion" and "ambiguity" exceptions. Thus, for example, in *Glass, Molders, supra,* n. 4, the court held that the remand of an award to address a "contingency" that arose after the award "is within an exception to the doctrine." *Accord,* International Bhd. of Teamsters v. Silver State Disposal Serv., 109 F.3d 1409, 1411 (9th Cir. 1997). Other courts, without a great deal of critical analysis, simply speak in terms of a "clarification exception" to the *functus officio* doctrine. *See, e.g., Kennecott Utah Copper Corp., supra,* n. 1. *Brownsville* seems to be more in the first category of cases that find an "ambiguity" when an unanticipated contingency or event subsequent to the award raises significant questions as to how the arbitrator might have ruled had he taken the contingency or future event into consideration.

[16] *Colonial Penn, supra,* n. 8, 943 F.2d at 334; *see also* Galt v. Libbey-Owens-Ford Glass Co., 397 F.2d 442 (7th Cir.), *cert. den.,* 393 U.S. 925 (1968). District courts should not try to interpret ambiguous awards. Flender Corp. v. Techna-Quip Co., 953 F.2d 273, 279 (7th Cir. 1992).

[17] *Glass, Molders, supra,* n. 4, 56 F.3d at 847.

and yet with a high degree of common sense. The Third Circuit noted with approval the limitations that the district court imposed on the arbitrator: "[T]he district court was entirely correct in stating that the arbitrator is not free upon remand to revisit the merits of the arbitration." It also noted that the district court limited the arbitrator to clarifying the remedy in view of the therapist's post-award refusal to continue the counseling relationship. The salutary effect of the Third Circuit's affirmance of the lower court's decision is likely to be a "clarified award" that affords the parties arbitral justice. This, it seems to me, is preferable to requiring the district court to enforce the original award as written, which, in this case, would have necessitated immediate termination of the employee because of his failure—perhaps for reasons not of his own making—to complete the course of counseling specified in the original award.[18]

---

[18] The court even went so far as to make it clear that the arbitrator, in clarifying the award, could take into consideration the reasons why the therapist declined to continue the counseling process. Presumably, this would leave the arbitrator free to modify the award, if he were to find, on remand, that the employee, without good cause, abandoned the counseling program that was prescribed in the original award.

V. "Final" Interim Awards for Liability

The "Finality" Principle and Partial Awards

by John Wilkinson[*]

The recent trend is for courts to rule that an interim award that decides only the issue of liability is final for purposes of judicial review under the FAA. This article explains the impact of this trend on the efficiency of arbitration.

The law concerning the finality of partial arbitration awards has been highly volatile. The U.S. Court of Appeals for the Second Circuit is primarily responsible for the checkered history of these cases, which have not always been notable for clarity in reasoning or for concern for the well-being of the arbitration process. The momentum in this area has recently been assumed by the First Circuit with a decision[1] that a partial award is final if the award completely disposes of a separate, independent claim, or finally determines liability under circumstances where the parties have agreed to bifurcate the liability issues from the damages issues. The policy concerns raised by this and earlier decisions are discussed below. Moreover, practitioners should be warned that the "firmness" of this holding may last only as long as the next case.

Judicial Review

Prior to the 1980s, there was little controversy over what rendered an arbitration award final for purposes of a motion to confirm or vacate under the Federal Arbitration Act (FAA).[2] An award was not final until all the issues in the arbitration were decided.

The early law on this subject was well described in the leading case *Michaels v. Mariforum Shipping, S.A.*,[3] which involved a dispute between the owner and a charterer of a commercial vessel. In an interim award the arbitrators decided the liability issues on five of the owner's six counterclaims and reserved decision on all issues related to the

---

[*] John Wilkinson serves on the American Arbitration Association's Large, Complex Case Panel and on its Greater New York Advisory Council for Large, Complex Cases. In addition, he serves on the editorial board of this newsletter.
[1] Hart Surgical, Inc. v. Ultracision, Inc., 244 F.3d 231 (1st Cir. 2001).
[2] 9 U.S.C. §§ 9, 10.
[3] 624 F.2d 411 (2d Cir. 1980).

owner's claim for damages and the charterer's claims against the owner. The charterer petitioned to vacate the award under § 10 of the FAA.

The Second Circuit held that the petition was premature since the award was not yet final. In reaching this conclusion, the court enunciated the rule concerning finality of arbitration awards. It observed that "the award under review here does not purport to be final but is merely a first step in deciding all claims submitted to arbitration." It explained that "[i]n order to be 'final,' an arbitration award must be intended by the arbitrators to be their complete determination of all claims submitted to them." In this case the court concluded: "Since the interim award here did not decide any of Charterer's claims, it obviously was not a final determination of all issues submitted. Moreover...the award did not finally dispose of any of the claims submitted, since it left open the question of damages on the four counterclaims of Owner that it sustained and reserved decision on the fifth."[4]

The foregoing rule was intended to further the policy of encouraging arbitration and its goals of efficiency and cost effectiveness. It would not be desirable for an arbitration to have to periodically grind to a halt to accommodate piecemeal applications or appeals to the court. This rationale was expressed by the New York Court of Appeals in *Mobil Oil Indonesia v. Asamera Oil (Indonesia) Ltd.*: "There can be no doubt that the State favors and encourages arbitration 'as a means of conserving the time and resources of the courts and the contracting parties' ...; and for the court to entertain review of intermediary arbitration decisions involving procedure or any other interlocutory matter, would disjoint and unduly delay the proceedings, thereby thwarting the very purpose of conservation. Not only the limitations of the statute, but policy considerations as well, dictate that the courts refrain from entertaining such interlocutory determinations made by arbitrators."[5]

---

[4] *Id.* at 413-14. See Puerto Rico Maritime Shipping Auth. v. Star Lines Ltd., 454 F. Supp. 368, 372 (S.D.N.Y. 1978) ("It is the general rule with regard to the confirmability of arbitration awards that, in order to be 'final' and 'definite,' the award must both resolve all the issues submitted to arbitration, and determine each issue fully so that no further litigation is necessary to finalize the obligations of the parties under the award.").

[5] 43 N.Y.2d 276, 281-82, 372 N.E.2d 21, 401 N.Y.S.2d 186, 188 (N.Y. 1977). The court noted similar concerns in a much earlier decision in *American Express Warehousing v. Transamerica Ins. Co.*, 380 F.2d 277, 280 (2d Cir. 1967) (court favored a strict requirement of finality prior to appeal and, in support, mentioned "the elimination of unnecessary appeals, since the complaining party may win the case or settle it;...the potential for harassment of litigants by nuisance appeals, and the fact that any appeal tends to delay or deter trial or settlement of a lawsuit...").

In 1986 the Second Circuit departed from the longstanding requirement that an arbitration award must be "a final determination of all issues submitted" in order for a district court to confirm or vacate the award under the FAA. In *Metallgesellschaft A.G. v. M/V Capitan Constante*,[6] the court held that it was proper to confirm an interim award that finally and definitely determined a separate independent claim.

The plaintiff in *Metallgesellschaft* sought damages for an alleged short shipment of oil, while the defendant counterclaimed for unpaid freight charges in connection with the same shipment. The arbitrators rendered a partial award on the counterclaim in favor of the defendant, which award the district court confirmed. On appeal, the plaintiff argued that the award was not final because the arbitration panel had not yet resolved all of the issues submitted to it.

A divided Second Circuit upheld the order confirming the award. It stated that "an award which finally and definitely disposes of a separate independent claim may be confirmed although it does not dispose of all the claims that were submitted to arbitration."[7] Interestingly, the court never mentioned its earlier contrary holding in *Michaels*. The court simply pointed to the portion of Rule 54(b) of the Federal Rules of Civil Procedure that states that a trial court "may direct the entry of a final judgment as to one or more but fewer than all of the claims...upon an express determination that there is no just reason for delay...." Using Rule 54(b) as its cornerstone, the court noted that "[i]f this action had remained in the district court rather than proceeding to arbitration, [defendant] undoubtedly would have been entitled to summary judgment in its favor for the amount of the unpaid freight."

The court further explained that "[t]he purpose of arbitration is to permit a relatively quick and inexpensive resolution of contractual disputes'....It would be a perversion of this salutary design for a ship owner to be denied the same prompt and commercially important relief from an arbitration panel that it could have received from a court."[8]

---

[6] 790 F.2d 280 (2d Cir. 1986).
[7] *Id.* at 283. *For similar holdings, see Zephyros Maritime Agencies v. Mexicana De Cobre*, S.A., 662 F. Supp. 892 (S.D.N.Y. 1987); *Compania Chilena De Navigacion Interoceanica, S.A. v. Norton, Lilly & Co.*, 652 F. Supp. 1512 (S.D.N.Y. 1987); *Bull H/N Info. Sys., v. Hutson*, 983 F. Supp. 284, 289 (D. Mass. 1997), *aff'd*, 229 F.3d 321 (1st Cir. 2000).
[8] *See* n. 6, *supra*, 790 F.2d at 282. In 1980, six years before *Metallgesellschaft*, a trial court in the 2nd Circuit had similarly decided in Eurolines Shipping Co. v. Metal Transport Corp., 491 F. Supp. 590 (S.D.N.Y. 1980), that "an interim award that finally and definitively disposes of a separate, independent claim may be confirmed...." *Eurolines* was

In a vigorous dissent, Judge Wilfred Feinberg emphasized that Rule 54(b) was limited to litigation and had no application to the very different world of arbitration. More importantly, he expressed concern about the implications of the majority's decision on the arbitration process: "[I]n the long run, I fear that confirmation of such separate and independent claims will make arbitration more complicated, time consuming and expensive....Just as piecemeal review disrupts and delays ongoing litigation in the courts, confirmation of partial awards will inevitably interrupt and extend arbitration proceedings....It will make arbitration more like litigation, a result not to be desired. It would be better to minimize the number of occasions the parties to arbitration can come to court; on the whole, this benefits the parties, the arbitration process and the courts."[9]

Statute of Limitations Issues

The next key decision on finality of partial awards, *Kerr-McGee Refining Corp. v. M/T Triumph*,[10] held that a partial award on liability was not final for purposes of activating the FAA's time limitations. In this case, the arbitration panel issued a "partial final award" in September 1988 in favor of Kerr-McGee on its claim that the delivery of certain cargo was short and that it thus had paid too much for the cargo. In March 1990 the arbitrators issued a "decision and final award" that additionally decided that the short delivery of cargo to Kerr-McGee was part of a violation of the Racketeer Influenced and Corrupt Organizations Act. Kerr-McGee moved to confirm both awards. M/T Triumph argued that the application to confirm the interim award was not timely since it was not made within one year of the award, as required by § 9 of the FAA.[11]

The Second Circuit, however, rejected that position, holding that the one-year limitations period did not begin to run in 1988, as M/T Triumph had argued, because the partial award was not final at that time.

In reaching this conclusion the court seemed to limit *Metallgesellschaft* to its facts, while adhering to the portion of *Michaels*

---

decided on June 26, 1980; the 2nd Circuit's opinion in Michaels, supra, which is seemingly at odds with *Eurolines*, was decided June 27, 1980.

[9] *See* n. 6, *supra*, 790 F.2d at 285.

[10] 924 F.2d 467 (2d Cir. 1991).

[11] FAA § 9 requires a motion to confirm an arbitration award to be made within one year after the award is made, and § 12 requires a motion to vacate to be made within three months after the award is filed or delivered.

that held that a partial award that decides liability but not damages is not final for purposes of review under the FAA.

The court acknowledged the principle that "[a]n award that finally and conclusively disposes of a separate independent claim" may be confirmed even if it does not dispose of all the claims that were submitted to arbitration (citing *Metallgesellschaft*). But then it concluded: "When it issued the Partial Final Award, the arbitration panel expressly left open whether, as a result of Triumph's breach, Kerr-McGee was also entitled to punitive or RICO damages, costs and attorneys' fees. It is thus apparent, as the district court found, that this award merely decided the issue of liability and partial damages on the shortage claim, which was a predicate act to the RICO claim, and did not finally dispose of an independent claim because it left open the question of damages."

Functus Officio

If it seemed that a relatively clear (if imperfect) rule had emerged in *Kerr-McGee*, the clarity was soon clouded by the Second Circuit's decision three months later in *Trade & Transport v. Natural Petroleum Charterers*.[12] There, the court held, on the basis of the particular facts and circumstances, that an arbitration award on liability alone but not damages was final.

Natural Petroleum had chartered a vessel from Trade & Transport to make five voyages transporting petroleum products. A dispute arose concerning the amount owed to Trade & Transport (demurrage) for the first three voyages, and the availability of the vessel for the fourth voyage. As a result of the timing controversy Natural Petroleum cancelled the fourth voyage. At the arbitration hearing, the parties asked the arbitrators to make an immediate determination as to liability for cancellation of the fourth voyage, leaving for later, decisions on both the calculation of damages, if any, for that voyage, and the issue of demurrage for the first three voyages.

The arbitrators acceded to this request and issued a "partial final award" finding that Natural Petroleum was liable on the cancellation issue. Thereafter, Natural Petroleum asked the arbitrators to reopen the partial award to consider additional evidence on liability, but the arbitrators rejected this application on the ground that the award was final and thus they lacked power to reopen or modify it.

---

[12] 931 F.2d 191 (2d Cir. 1991).

The district court confirmed the award and Natural Petroleum appealed, contending that the arbitrators erred in refusing to reopen the partial award in order to take further evidence. Its point was that because the award determined liability but not damages, it was not final and thus not immune from reconsideration within the meaning of the FAA. The Second Circuit rejected this position, finding that the partial award was *functus officio* and could not be revisited by the arbitrators: "[T]he submission by the parties determines the scope of the arbitrators' authority....Thus, if the parties agree that the panel is to make a final decision as to part of the dispute, the arbitrators have the authority and responsibility to do so....[O]nce arbitrators have finally decided the submitted issues, they are, in common-law parlance, '*functus officio*,' meaning that their authority over those questions is ended....Thus, if the parties have asked the arbitrators to make a final partial award as to a particular issue and the arbitrators have done so, the arbitrators have no further authority, absent agreement by the parties, to redetermine that issue."[13]

While *Trade & Transport* held that an award on liability was final within the limited facts of that case, it is unlikely that the Second Circuit intended that decision to overrule its holdings in *Kerr-McGee* and *Michaels* that such partial awards are not final. First, the Second Circuit did not mention either of these cases (even though *Trade & Transport* was decided shortly after *Kerr-McGee*). Second, *Trade & Transport* is distinguishable because the earlier cases were concerned with finality for purposes of judicial review while *Trade & Transport* addressed when an award is sufficiently final that it can no longer be reconsidered by the arbitrators.

While the intended scope of *Trade & Transport* appears to be narrow, it has nonetheless been broadly interpreted in a manner that seriously erodes the rule that awards limited to liability are not final for purposes of review under the FAA. In *McGregor Van De Moere, Inc. v. Paychex, Inc.*,[14] the arbitrators, at the request of the parties, entered an interim award on liability, which the district court confirmed. When one party thereafter petitioned the court to confirm the interim award on liability, the other party objected on the ground that the award was not final. The court overruled that objection in reliance on *Trade & Transport*, stating: "As in *Trade & Transport*, the panel here

---

[13] *Id.* at 195.
[14] 927 F. Supp. 616 (W.D.N.Y. 1996).

conclusively decided every point required by and included in the parties' submissions concerning liability, [the award] was therefore final as to that issue."

Further, the court evinced what might best be termed "indifference" to whether the effect of its decision might run counter to the goals and purposes of arbitration. Responding to Paychex's argument that the petition should be dismissed because to allow a party to seek confirmation of an award under these circumstances would promote piecemeal litigation and would waste judicial time and resources, the court said: "Where it is clear that an award is final for purposes of the FAA, however, I do not believe that the interests of judicial economy are themselves sufficient to justify dismissing a properly brought petition."[15]

Further Developments

The First Circuit has followed the lead of *McGregor Van De Moere* in the recently decided case of *Hart Surgical v. Ultracision*.[16] There, the parties had agreed to bifurcate the arbitration into liability and damages phases and the arbitrators had accordingly entered a partial award on liability alone. The losing party moved to vacate the award under § 10 of the FAA, but the district court dismissed that motion on the ground that the award was not final. The First Circuit reversed, primarily on the basis of *Trade & Transport*, finding that the partial award on liability was final for purposes of judicial review.[17]

The court concluded that *Kerr-McGee* was irrelevant to the issue before it. It stated (or at least implied) that the sole reason the court in *Kerr- McGee* declined to rule that a partial award on liability was final was that a holding that the award was final "would have barred Kerr-McGee from confirming the partial award which had been decided more than one year prior."[18]

In fact, the *Kerr-McGee* court stated that it was unnecessary to consider the limitations issue but "question[ed] whether the one-year

---

[15] *Id.* at 618. In other less controversial decisions it has recently been held that an arbitration award is final even though: (i) there are subsequent, minor modifications which do not change the substance of the award or the relief granted, *Fradella v. Petricca*, 183 F.3d 17 (1st Cir. 1999); or (ii) the award leaves for the future a purely ministerial calculation of damages, *Flender Corp. v. Techna-Quip Co.*, 953 F.2d 273 (7th Cir. 1992).

[16] *See* n. 1, *supra*.

[17] A similar result was reached in *Corporate Printing Co. v. N.Y Typographical Union No. 6*, 1944 WL 376093 (S.D.N.Y. July 18, 1994).

[18] *See* n. 11, *supra*.

limitation should apply to a party seeking confirmation of an award that does not end the arbitration, since such a rule will make arbitration more complicated, time consuming and expensive."[19]

The First Circuit in *Ultracision* stated that the primary concern with holding certain interim arbitration awards final for purposes of review is that a party who, in good faith, waits until the conclusion of the entire case to move to vacate or confirm an interim award might face dismissal of the petition as a result of the limitations periods, which begin to run when the award becomes final. But the court's discussion of the statute of limitations never mentioned the *Kerr-McGee* court's observation, quoted above, that so unfair a result was highly unlikely.

Instead, the First Circuit simply concluded that there was no danger of a "limitations" injustice in the case before it since the parties had stipulated to the bifurcation of liability from damages, and had thus agreed that the partial award on liability was final for limitations and other purposes.

This reasoning, although adopted by some other courts,[20] strikes this author as flawed since an agreement to have the arbitrators issue a preliminary, partial award on liability is a far cry from an agreement that the partial award will be considered final for purposes of judicial review and the limitations provisions in the FAA.

There is also a logical inconsistency with holding a partial award on liability to be final within the meaning of the FAA. The court in *Metallgesellschaft* reasoned that a court's judgment on one of several claims can be final for purposes of FRCP Rule 54(b), and that it would be wrong for an arbitration claimant "to be denied the same prompt and commercially important relief from an arbitration panel that it could have received from a court." But the fact is that a judgment on liability (but not damages) in a federal court litigation is not final for any purpose.[21] If the federal court rules on finality are to be applied to arbitration (as in *Metallgesellschaft*), one would think that the rule that judgments on liability alone are not final should similarly be incorporated into the arbitration process. The more recent decisions discussed here, however, pay little if any heed to this point.

---

[19] *See* n. 10, *supra*, 924 F.2d at 471.

[20] *See* cases at ns. 12 & 14, *supra*.

[21] *In re* Martin-Trigona, 763 F.2d 135 (2d Cir. 1985); Sun Shipbuilding & Dry Dock Co. v. Benefits Review Bd., 535 F.2d 758 (3rd Cir. 1976); Forschner Group v. Arrow Trading Co., 124 F.3d 402, 410 (2d Cir. 1997); ("where liability has been decided but the extent of damages remains undetermined, there is no final order").

Impact on Arbitration

The view that a partial arbitration award is final for most (if not all) purposes if it completely determines a separate independent claim, or finally determines liability under circumstances where the parties agreed to segregate liability from damages, has significant adverse consequences for arbitration.

Under this rule, parties have no choice but to file a time-consuming petition to the district court following a partial award since, otherwise, the limitations periods for confirming or vacating the award could well expire. By encouraging this piecemeal review of arbitration awards, it substantially lengthens and complicates arbitration, which is dependent on efficiency and cost effectiveness.

Furthermore, bifurcating the arbitration in an appropriate case has been an effective cost-saving tool. In complex cases, parties often agree to postpone determination of the calculation of damages until after there has been a finding on liability. Thus, during the liability phase there is no need to introduce evidence on the damages issues. And if no liability is found, there is no reason to have a damages phase. This procedure has been used successfully in numerous arbitration proceedings. Holding a partial award on liability to be final, however, will necessarily discourage parties from agreeing to use the bifurcation procedure.

Under the circumstances, it would be welcome indeed if a federal appeals court would reconsider the issue from the perspective of what is good for arbitration and, hence, for dispute resolution in general.

VI. Post-Decision Debriefing- Point and Counter-Point

POINT

The Case for Post-Decision Debriefing in Arbitration

by David J. Hickton and Kelly B. Bakayza[*]

In this article, the author advocates offering parties the opportunity to meet with the arbitrator after the award is issued to discuss the reasons underlying the award, provided certain conditions are met. Following is the opposing view.

Alternative dispute resolution (ADR) processes are increasingly being used to resolve disputes because they are more efficient and economical than litigation. The move to various methods of ADR has revolutionized civil litigation in the United States. As one commentator has said, "Twenty years ago alternative dispute resolution was primarily the concern of a few 'ivory tower' academics; ten years ago it was part of the practice of a few idealistic practitioners; today it is an integral part of the practice of law."[1]

Despite the growth of arbitration, it is still an under-utilized option. One possible reason is that a poor experience in arbitration may be enough to taint a practitioner's desire to use and recommend it. Another is that the limited ability to appeal an award—which many proponents view as one of its prime benefits—is a feature of arbitration that many attorneys find disquieting.

The question then becomes: What can be done to increase the likelihood that practitioners will choose arbitration? One answer is to augment the process so that it provides not only a just result, but also an understanding of the result. This is easily accomplished by post-decision debriefing.

Post-decision debriefing provides practitioners and their clients with insight into the rationale for the award. Furthermore, this procedure

---

[*] Mr. Hickton is a founding partner of Burns, White & Hickton LLC in Pittsburgh, specializing in civil and commercial law. He holds a B.A. from Pennsylvania State University and a J.D. from University of Pittsburgh School of Law.

Ms. Bakayza is the Attorney/Advisor at the Office of the Solicitor for the U.S. Department of the Interior.

[1] Robert F. Cochran Jr., *Must Clients Tell Lawyers about ADR?* ARBITRATION J. 8 (June 1993).

provides feedback to practitioners to help them improve their advocacy and case-presentation skills. The arbitration process itself becomes more palatable when the practitioners and their clients understand the reason for an adverse award.

Secrecy of Jury Deliberations

The concept of debriefing emanates from the post-verdict debriefing procedure in litigation. Although criticisms of the civil jury system exist,[2] the fact remains that the system has sustained us well. The jury performs a vital function in the American system of justice and, accordingly, our legal system zealously defends the secrecy of jury deliberations.[3]

There are substantial policy reasons to justify this protection, including the desire to encourage frank discussion among jurors; promote the stability of verdicts; and maintain the privacy of jurors.[4] To protect the sanctity of jury deliberations, a complex set of rules evolved limiting the amount of information a court will review upon appeal.[5] Parties may not base an appeal on post-verdict reports of jury deliberations absent a showing of undue influence.[6] Undue influence was discussed in detail in *Tanner v. United States*, where the Supreme Court agreed that Federal Rule of Evidence 606(b) prevented jurors from testifying against their own verdicts, even though one juror had alleged that the entire jury deliberation had been "one big party." The court reasoned that juror intoxication was not an "outside influence" about which jurors may testify.[7]

Although internal influences are generally not admissible to impeach a jury verdict, evidence of "extraneous influence" may be admitted. Extraneous juror influence can occur in a myriad of situations. The Supreme Court permits post-trial inquiry into allegations of external influences that may have improperly impacted a jury verdict. In *Mattox*

---

[2] *See* ROBERT J. MACCOUN, GETTING INSIDE THE BLACK BOX: TOWARD A BETTER UNDERSTANDING OF JUROR BEHAVIOR (RAND, DECEMBER 1987) ("Critics claim that civil juries are unpredictable, inequitable and incapable of coping with complex litigation").

[3] Tanner v. United States, 483 U.S. 107, 126, 107 S. Ct. 2739, 2751 (1987) (reaffirming that jury deliberations are protected).

[4] Clifford Holt Rupert, *Are Verdicts, Too, Like Sausages: Lifting the Cloak of Jury Secrecy*, 146 U. PA. L. REV. 217, 226 (1997).

[5] The "no impeachment rule" is an outgrowth of this evolution. *See* Elizabeth Schlaff, *Impeachment of Verdicts by Juror Testimony*, 61 CONN. B.J. 215 (1987).

[6] Fed. R. Evid. 606(b).

[7] *Tanner*, n. 3, *supra*, 483 U.S. at 107, 107 S. Ct. at 2739, 2749.

v. United States, the Court held that prejudicial evidence overheard by the jurors was admissible to impeach a jury verdict.[8] Similarly, the Court has allowed testimony regarding a bailiff's comments to a juror concerning the defendant.[9] Finally, the Court admitted post-verdict testimony that a juror in a criminal case had submitted an application for employment to the district attorney's office.[10]

The distinction between internal and external influences is important. The distinction was designed to minimize harassment of jurors by a defeated party who hopes that evidence of misconduct might be established to set aside a verdict.[11] Clearly, full and frank discussion in the jury room, the jury's willingness to return an unpopular verdict, and the community's trust in the jury system would be undermined by extensive post-verdict scrutiny.[12] Also, if evidence could easily be secured through inquiry into the jury's deliberation, a private process could become a subject of public investigation and public discourse.

Post-Verdict Juror Contact

Whereas the jury process is closely guarded during deliberations, most courts permit post-verdict contact with the jury.[13] In *Martinez v. Food City Inc.*, the district judge commented that the discharged jurors were "relieved of the prohibition against discussing the case with anyone, and were free to talk with the attorneys or anyone else if they desired."[14] Other courts, however, have attempted to insulate jurors from unwanted scrutiny[15] and harassment[16] by supervising post-trial communications with jurors.

---

[8] *See* Mattox v. United States, 146 U.S. 140, 149, 13 S. Ct. 50 (1892).

[9] *See* Parker v. Gladden, 385 U.S. 363, 365, 87 S. Ct. 468, 470, 17 L. Ed. 2d 420 (1966).

[10] *See* Smith v. Phillips, 455 U.S. 209, 102 S. Ct. 940, 71 L. Ed. 2d 78 (1982).

[11] *Id.*

[12] *See* Note, *Public Disclosure of Jury Deliberations*, 96 HARV. L. REV. 886, 888-92 (1983).

[13] *See* Susan Crump, *Jury Misconduct, Jury Interviews, and the Federal Rules of Evidence*: Is the Broad Exclusionary Principal of Rule 606(b) Justified? 66 N.C. L. REV. 509, 526 (1988) (noting that some courts prohibit post-trial interviews or have restrictions on the scope of questions that can be asked. However, most courts grant the request of counsel to conduct post-trial interviews).

[14] 658 F. 2d 369, 371 (5th Cir. 1981).

[15] *Note*, n. 12, *supra*, at 901.

[16] United States v. Hall, 424 F. Supp. 508, 538 (W.D. Okla. 1975), *aff'd*, 536 F.2d 313 (10th Cir.), *cert. den.*, 429 U.S. 919 (1976).

Legitimate reasons exist for post-trial communications with jurors, as long as they are not harassed. Post-trial interviews open the window on the deliberative process.[17] One commentator noted, "The members of the jury have usually watched the attorneys for several weeks and the information they can provide is invaluable in understanding which witness, exhibit, event or other piece of evidence was important and which was ignored."[18] This information can provide insight on how to present future cases. What the attorney viewed as the best evidence may have been confusing or the person that the attorney positioned as the best witness may have actually alienated some or all of the jurors.[19]

Most trial lawyers who have participated in post-verdict discussions report that even after a disappointing result, the collective view of the jury is usually a logical and fair assessment of the case. The explanation learned from these discussions leaves all involved with a respect for the fact finder, the jury and the trial process.

Comparison with Arbitration

In arbitration, the parties seek the wisdom of one or three arbitrators, rather than the collective wisdom of the jury. Arbitration offers a final disposition of differences between the parties in a faster, less costly, more expeditious and informal manner than a traditional court proceeding.[20]

Arbitration addresses some, but not all, criticisms of the judicial system. Jurors are selected from a cross-section of the community and symbolically represent the collective opinion of society.[21] Critics of the jury system contend that it is full of examples of alleged jury deterioration.[22] Arbitrators are chosen for their expertise and judgment.[23]

---

[17] MACCOUN, n. 2, *supra* (discussing the methodology in which post-trial interviews should be conducted in order to maximize the benefits derived from interviewing the jurors).

[18] John Kidd, *Jury Trials and Mock Jury Trials*, 321 PLI/PAT 137, 174 (1991) (discussing the impact post-trial interviews can have on future patent law cases).

[19] *Id.*

[20] George L. Blum, *Annotation, Setting Aside Arbitration Award on Ground of Interest or Bias of Arbitrators-Torts*, 64 A.L.R.5TH 475 (1998) Kenneth J. Rigby, *Alternative Dispute Resolution*, 44 LA. L. REV. 1725 (1984) (an arbitrator may not be restricted to the rules of evidence, may conduct the proceeding in an informal setting conducive to negotiation and settlement, may be less expensive, and consume less time).

[21] Nancy S. Marder, *Deliberations and Disclosures: A Study of Post-Verdict Interviews of Jurors*, 82 IOWA L. REV. 465, 468 (1997).

[22] Some contend that jurors are a disinterested lot, which does not generally represent a cross section of society.

Perhaps, then, arbitration capitalizes on the expertise of the arbitrators to render an impartial, educated decision without the disadvantages of the jury system.[24]

An arbitrator occupies a unique position in the resolution of disputes. The long-standing rule regarding the separation of the functions of the jury and trial judge is reinvented in arbitration. Whereas, in traditional jurisprudence, the jury decides issues of fact and the trial judge decides issues of law[25]; in arbitration, the arbitrator performs both functions, serving as fact finder and judge.

Generally, participants have the opportunity to select an arbitrator of their choice. It has been said that arbitrators are chosen for their judgment and ability to communicate that judgment.[26] If the participants have agreed upon the selection of an arbitrator, they are more likely to be satisfied with the arbitrator's conclusions.[27] The irony, however, is that most arbitrators' awards are not explained. The Commercial Arbitration Rules of the American Arbitration Association (AAA) do not require arbitrators to explain the reasons behind their opinions unless the parties have requested a reasoned award in writing prior to appointment of the arbitrator, or unless the arbitrator determines that a reasoned award is appropriate.[28] Commentators have noted that arbitration awards are rarely accompanied by written opinions.[29]

The U.S. Supreme Court has held that "arbitrators need not disclose the facts or reasons behind their awards"[30] and that "arbitrators owe no obligation to the courts to give reasons behind their awards."[31] Thus, as a

---

[23] Charles J. Coleman & Gladys Gershenfeld, *The Art of Communicating Arbitral Judgments: Write Ya' Heart Out*, 52 DISP. RESOL. J. 46 (1997).

[24] Critics contend that jury awards are often excessive and unpredictable.

[25] Sandella v. Dick Corp., 729 A.2d 813 (Conn. App. Ct. 1999).

[26] Coleman & Gershenfeld, n. 23, *supra*, (recommending that arbitrators communicate more effectively with the parties to the dispute through decision writing).

[27] Rigby, n. 20, *supra*, at 1734.

[28] *See* AAA Commercial Arbitration Rule R-44. See AAA Construction Industry Arbitration Rule R-42. See also, A Guide for Commercial Arbitrators (American Arbitration Association 2000) (*hereafter* Guide) (explaining that a reasoned opinion generally is not required).

[29] Overton A. Currie & Charles W. Surasky, *Arbitration Awards, in* HARRIS, SINK & WULFF, eds., ADR: A PRACTICAL GUIDE TO RESOLVE CONSTRUCTION DISPUTES 177 (American Arbitration Association 1994).

[30] Bernhardt v. Polygraphic Co. of Am. 350 U.S. 198, 203, 76 S. Ct. 273, 100 L. Ed. 109 (1956).

[31] United Steelworkers of Am. v. Enterprise Wheel & Car Corp., 363 U.S. 593, 598, 80 S. Ct. 1358, 4 L. Ed. 2d 1424 (1960).

general rule, the award usually consists of a brief direction to the parties on a single sheet of paper. It contains no instructions for the parties.[32]

Many arbitrators mistakenly believe that the single most important part of an arbitration proceeding is the award itself.[33] The award represents the peak of the process.[34] This may be true for the winning party. But because an award, in most cases, merely dictates the result, it rarely provides either party with the reasoning behind the decision.

The asserted reason for this brevity is that "written opinions might open avenues for attack on the award by the losing party"[35] who may demand that the court schedule a full-blown traditional trial.[36] This would jeopardize the speed and finality of arbitration.[37]

In the context of labor arbitration, where reasoned awards are the practice, parties appreciate a clearly written, easily understood analysis of the decision. Commentators say this helps to prevent future disputes before they become the basis of adjudication.[38] But in cases where reasoned awards are not used, the policy considerations and lessons of the traditional jury system described above support offering post-decision arbitration debriefing. Effective dispute resolution involves not only a just result, but a process that promotes understanding, a procedure in which the parties can learn how the arbitrators reached the result.

Post-decision debriefings would increase the satisfaction of the parties and attract more participants to the arbitration process. Since arbitrators typically are chosen for their ability to communicate and their expertise in a particular field, they should be up to this task. How readily defeat is tolerated and further litigation is avoided may depend upon how the arbitration award is explained.

Experience with Debriefing

I have adopted the practice as an arbitrator of advising the parties of the opportunity for post-decision debriefing. The parties are given the chance to meet together or separately with the arbitrator provided two

---

[32] GUIDE, n. 28, *supra* ("As a general rule, the award consists of a brief direction to the parties on a single sheet of paper").

[33] *See generally*, Currie & Surasky, n. 29, *supra*, at 177 (claiming that the arbitration award is the pinnacle of the process).

[34] *Id.*

[35] GUIDE, n. 28, *supra*.

[36] Robert M. Parker & Leslie J. Hagin, *ADR Techniques in the Reformation Model of Civil Dispute Resolution*, 46 SMU L. REV. 1905, 1910 (1993).

[37] Gabriel M. Wilner, Domke on Commercial Arbitration §29:06 (West 1998).

[38] Coleman & Gershenfeld, n. 23, *supra*.

conditions are met. First, they must agree that either party may avail itself of a session with the arbitrator. If one party does not agree, the arbitrator will not discuss the case after the decision. Second, if post-decision briefing is to occur, the parties must agree to abide by the same rules with respect to jury deliberations. Thus, nothing from the post-decision briefing may be used as a basis to appeal the arbitration result. The post-decision briefing sessions are free and last as long as the parties desire.

This procedure has been used in twelve arbitrations and has been favorably received. Disappointed parties who did not prevail saw more clearly what was not so apparent from their position as litigants. In every instance where this procedure has been employed, my sense is that the process has worked and that a fair and just result was obtained.

Some arbitrators may have concerns about this procedure. The AAA discourages arbitrators from communicating with parties about the award after it has been issued. This should not be a real problem if the procedures suggested here for conducting a post-decision debriefing are followed.

Frequently, as arbitrators, we do only half our job. We have a responsibility to render a just result as well as a responsibility to ensure that the result is understood. Arbitrators should leave the parties satisfied that they were involved in a fair and worthwhile process. A post-decision investment of time to brief the parties is an invaluable tool with which to accomplish this goal.

COUNTERPOINT

The Case Against Post-Decision Debriefing in Arbitration

by Steven A. Arbittier

Mr. Arbittier is a partner in Ballard Spahr Andrews & Ingersoll Ballard Spahr Andrews & Ingersoll LLP in Philadelphia. Arbittier is chairman of the Procedural Rules Committee of the National Construction Dispute Resolution Committee of the American Arbitration Association. He received a B.A. from the University of Pennsylvania and a J.D. from the University of Pennsylvania School of Law. Since 1982, he has edited the Philadelphia Court of Common Pleas Civil Practice Manual.

Here, the author contends that debriefing sessions have the potential to become acrimonious. He questions why an arbitrator would want to be called upon to justify the award.

For many years the mantra of seasoned arbitrators has been: "When rendering an award, the less said the better." Not any more.

One of the consequences of the ADR revolution has been a growing awareness that the parties control the process and are free to tailor it to meet their needs. Nothing is more frustrating after a hard-fought arbitration (particularly to the losing party) than not having the foggiest idea how or why the arbitrators did what they did. That is why the American Arbitration Association's arbitration rules give the parties the power to require arbitrators to explain themselves. Rule R-42 of the AAA Construction Industry Arbitration Rules states: "The arbitrator shall provide a concise, written breakdown of the award. If requested in writing by all parties prior to the appointment of the arbitrator, or if the arbitrator believes it is appropriate to do so, the arbitrator shall provide a written explanation of the award."

Similarly, Rule R-44(b) of the AAA Commercial Arbitration Rules states: "The arbitrator need not render a reasoned award unless the parties request such an award in writing prior to appointment of the arbitrator or unless the arbitrator determines that a reasoned award is appropriate."

The need for a "written explanation" or a "reasoned award" is often more than just psychological. Communicating the elements of the award may have a direct impact on disputes with third parties. For example, in a typical construction case involving an owner and contractor, non-parties (such as design professionals on the owner's side of the transaction, or subcontractors on the contractor's side) may face future litigation or arbitration if their performance is implicated in the award. For this reason, the AAA construction rules require the arbitrators to provide a "concise, written breakdown of the award" even if it has not been requested by the parties.

Benefits of a Written Award

Thus, by requiring the arbitrators to provide a written explanation of the award when requested by the parties prior to the arbitrator's appointment, the rules assure that the parties and any non-parties who are monitoring the proceedings will learn when the battle is over—not only what happened—but why it happened. It is hard to quarrel with a process that promotes this kind of open communication.

But communication is not the only point of this rule. It allows the parties to make sure that decisions by arbitrators are informed and correct.

Permit me to reveal one of the "secrets of the temple": knowing that the parties are expecting a "written explanation" or a "reasoned award" can have a significant impact on the arbitrator's performance at the hearings and during deliberations. An arbitrator who has to explain the basis for the award in writing is likely to work harder to stay on top of the evidence. This arbitrator will insist that the parties clearly explain their positions before closing the record.

This is not to say that an arbitrator who is required to render only a "bottom line" award pays less attention to the evidence. But, human nature being what it is, I posit that there is a heightened attentiveness to details when the arbitrator has the obligation to write an explanation of the award.

The writing of a reasoned decision can significantly impact the award itself. Ask experienced judges about what happens during the opinion-writing process. Most admit that their decisions sometimes change. Connections that seemed logical at first blush may evaporate when we think hard about them in an effort to explain our reasoning—in the same way that brilliant ideas that come in the middle of the night seem to lose their brilliance in the cold light of day.

In short, the requirement that an arbitrator render a reasoned award enhances not only the quality of communications but also the quality of justice.

Disadvantages of Debriefings

It is possible that arbitrators who know they will be "debriefed" after the award will work harder and do a better job. But there is a big difference between being called upon to explain a decision and being called "on the carpet" to explain it.

Debriefing sessions clearly have the potential to become hostile and acrimonious, a forum for recriminations and accusations. Do arbitrators really need this aggravation?

There are probably some arbitrators who would refuse a case in which they knew in advance that a reasoned award was required. In my view, the ADR movement is better off without them. But I would not say the same thing about an arbitrator who shies away from a case simply to avoid the hostility and second guessing in a debriefing session.

When I sit as an arbitrator and the parties tell me that they want a written opinion explaining the award, I am happy to oblige. However, I would probably be less forthcoming with an explanation in a written opinion if I knew that it might be used in a debriefing session to cross examine me about the award. And that is true even if the parties agreed that what the arbitrator said in the debriefing session could not be used to impeach the award.

Trying to imagine what a debriefing session would be like after a hotly contested arbitration, I thought of some "debriefing sessions" held at our family dinner table after a parental decision that was less than popular with the younger family members. After a lot of hemming and hawing, I would "explain" myself in the following words: "Because I'm the father, that's why." Perhaps I could be convinced to give post-award debriefings a try if I were given the power to terminate all further discussion simply by saying, "Because I'm the arbitrator, that's why."

CHAPTER TEN

ARBITRATION AND COURT PROCEEDINGS

I. Venue Under the FAA

Lessons from the High Court's Broad Reading of FAA Venue

by Cary R. Singletary[*]

The U. S. Supreme Court arbitration ruling in *Cortez Byrd Chips, Inc., v. Bill Harbert Construction Co.* 529 U.S. 193 (2000) may cause lawyers to rewrite their future arbitration agreements to specify the venue for court actions to confirm, vacate or modify an arbitration award as the Court held that the Federal Arbitration Act's venue provisions permit parties to bring a motion to vacate or modify an award either in the district where the award was made or in any district proper under the general venue statute.

This case arose from a dispute between Cortez Byrd Chips Inc. and Bill Harbert Construction Co. over payment for charges made in a construction project. Cortez Byrd had contracted with Harbert to construct a wood chip mill in Brookhaven, Miss., for approximately $1.3 million. The parties stipulated that the price could only be increased or decreased by a written change order. Harbert sought a payment increase when no written change order had been provided. When the parties were unable to mutually resolve the dispute, Harbert sought arbitration pursuant to the construction contract's agreement to arbitrate. That agreement called for arbitration in accordance with the Construction Industry Rules of the American Arbitration Association. But it did not name the court where any future action to confirm the award should be

---

[*] Cary R. Singletary is a full-time mediator and arbitrator in Tampa, Florida. He is a member of the Commercial and Employment Arbitration panels of the American Arbitration Association. Singletary received a B.A. from the University of Tampa, an M.A. from Rollins College and a J.D. cum laude from Stetson Universtiy College of Law. Singletary is the author of *Voluntary Trial Resolution—A New Dispute Resolution Process in Florida,* THE CHECKOFF, VOLUME XXX, NO. 4, July 2000, The Florida Bar.

brought. Instead, it provided that "the award...shall be final, and a judgment may be entered upon it in accordance with applicable law in any court having jurisdiction thereof." It also provided "that the agreement...shall be specifically enforceable under applicable law in any court having jurisdiction thereof," and that the law of the place where the project was located governed.

The arbitration hearing took place in Birmingham, Ala., Harbert's principal place of business. The arbitrators made an award in Harbert's favor, granting a price increase. Three weeks later, Cortez Byrd sought to vacate or modify the award in federal court in Mississippi, where the contract had been performed. Jurisdiction was based upon diversity of citizenship under the general venue statute, 28 U.S.C. § 1391(a)(2). Seven days later, Harbert sought to confirm the award in the Northern District of Alabama, where the arbitration took place. However, the Alabama court refused to dismiss, transfer or stay its proceedings. The 11th Circuit affirmed.

The precise issue presented to the Supreme Court was whether the venue provisions in §§ 10 and 11 of the FAA should be interpreted restrictively or permissively. That is, do they allow a motion to vacate or modify an award to be brought only in the district in which the award was made, or also in any district proper under the general revenue statute?

The FAA's § 9 permits parties to specify in an arbitration agreement the court where a judgment may be sought to confirm an award. Absent such a provision, "such application may be made to the United States court in and for the district within which such award was made." By contrast, § 10(a), which governs venue for motions to vacate, provides that "the United States court in and for the district wherein the [arbitration] award was made may make an order vacating the award...." Section 11 contains a like provision with respect to motions for modification or correction of an award.

The Supreme Court held that the FAA's venue provisions are permissive, even though there is language in the law supporting a restrictive view. It reasoned that if the provisions were restrictive, they would supplant, rather than supplement the general venue statute.

The Court analyzed the circumstances existing in 1925 when the FAA was enacted. Since a considerably more restrictive general venue statute was then in effect, the FAA's venue provisions had a liberalizing effect on venue. The Court hypothesized that if §§ 10-11 limited venue to the district where the award was made, then an action to confirm an award in the place selected in the parties' arbitration agreement would have to be held in abeyance while an objecting party returned to the district of the arbitration to modify or vacate the award. And if that motion failed, the parties would then return to the forum selected in their agreement for the confirmation order. The Court concluded that this was clearly at odds with the FAA's policy of rapid and unobstructed enforcement of arbitration agreements, and with the desired flexibility of parties in choosing an arbitration site.

The Court further reasoned that a restrictive interpretation would place § 3 of the FAA in needless tension with §§ 9-11 due to its decision in *Marine Transit Corp. v. Dreyfus*, which held that a court with power to stay an action under § 3 also has the power to confirm any ensuing arbitration award.

Effect on Practitioners

The Court's decision fosters the use of arbitration as a process amenable to the needs of the parties. It enables parties to conduct the hearing at a practical location without sacrificing venue for confirmation of the award. They can now contract where they wish to file a civil action to confirm the award, without concern that §§ 10 and 11 will force them to go to that court for a motion to vacate or confirm the award. This flexibility creates an environment that promotes the future use of arbitration.

This decision may prompt attorneys who draft arbitration clauses to consider placing a venue provision into the agreement, specifying where motions to confirm, vacate or modify must be filed. Without such a provision the potential exists for a "rush to the courthouse" after the award to obtain the most favored permissible venue.

Further, a venue provision could reduce litigation because the prevailing party could wait three months after the award was issued before determining to seek confirmation under § 9. Section 9 permits the winner up to one year to seek confirmation, while § 12 requires the loser to move to vacate or modify the award within three months after the award was filed. Thus, if no motion to vacate or modify is filed within the three-month period, it probably means the award will be paid without confirmation being necessary.

II. Waivers

Waiver of the Contractual Right to Arbitrate

by Terry L. Trantina[*]

When faced with a failure to arbitrate a dispute covered by a written agreement requiring binding arbitration, you have choices. A contractual obligation to arbitrate a dispute will, under either applicable federal or state arbitration law, be rigorously enforced at the request of any party[1] and even by third-party beneficiaries of that contract[2] with a very limited inquiry.[3] However, the right to arbitrate is not absolute and both state and federal courts have held that the contractual right to arbitrate disputes can be waived like any other contractual right.[4]

Unlike many other obligations in a contract, a provision requiring arbitration of a dispute is by statute specifically enforceable and an agreement to arbitrate disputes carries a presumption of validity not

---

[*] Terry Trantina is a partner in Blank Rome Tenzer Greenblatt, in the New York office and is an adjunct professor of ADR at Seton Hall University Law School. He also serves as vice chair of the ABA Dispute Resolution Section Arbitration Committee and is also vice chair of the Dispute Resolution Committee of the ABA Business Law Section. He holds a B.A. from Notre Dame and a J.D. from the University of Santa Clara School of Law. Trantina is the author of *Consumer Arbitration in the U.S.*, LONDON COURT OF INTERNATIONAL ARBITRATION (London, March 1999).

[1] *See* Dean Witter Reynolds Inc. v. Byrd, 4790 U.S. 213, 221 (1985); Mitsubishi Motors Corp. v. Soler Chrysler-Plymouth, Inc., 473 U.S. 614, 625 (1985).

[2] *See* Collins v. International Dairy Queen, 2 F. Supp. 2d 1465 (M.D. Ga. 1998); American Bureau of Shipping v. Tenacara Shipyard S.P.A., 170 F.3d 349 (2d Cir. 1999); Nesslage v. York Sec., 823 F.2d 231, 233-234 (8th Cir. 1987); Letzia v. Prudential Bache Sec., 802 F.2d 1185, 1187 (9th Cir. 1986); Mowbray v. Moseley, Hallgarten, Estabrook & Weeden, Inc., 795 F.2d 1111, 1116-1117 (1st Cir. 1986).

[3] *See* Sedo, Inc. v. Petroleos Mexicanos Mexican Nat'l Oil, 767 F.2d 1140, 1144 (5th Cir. 1983); Moses H. Cone Mem. Hosp. v. Mercury Constr. Corp., 460 U.S. 1, 24-25 (1983).

[4] *See* Southern Sys. v. Torrid Oven Ltd., 105 F. Supp. 848, 852 (W.D. Tenn. 2000); Sedillo v. Campbell, 5 S.W.3d 824, 826 (Tex. App. 1999); Waldman v. Old Republic National Title Ins. Co., 12 P.3d 835, (Colo. App. 2000); Guess? Inc. v. Superior Court of L.A., 79 Cal. App. 4th 553, 94 Cal. Rptr. 2d 201 (Cal. App. 2000); Metz v. Merrill, Lynch, Pierce, Fenner & Smith, 39 F.3d 1482, 1489 (10th Cir. 1994); Miller Brewing Co. v. Fort Worth Distributing Co., 781 F.2d 494, 497 (5th Cir. 1986).

extended to any other contractual provision.[5] This statutory right to enforce agreements to arbitrate and the presumptive validity of such provisions creates a corollary burden for the party seeking to enforce a waiver of that obligation.[6] As a result, the courts have uniformly held that there is a very strong presumption against the waiver of the right to arbitrate a dispute.[7]

Although state and federal courts have no litmus test for determining when there has been a waiver, they have held that a contractual right to arbitrate may be waived either by (1) a significant delay or failure to invoke that right, or (2) taking steps in another forum in connection with the dispute that are inconsistent with the intent and right to arbitrate that dispute.[8]

In addition, the majority of courts have held that delay or action inconsistent with the obligation to arbitrate must also cause demonstrable and significant prejudice to the party asserting that the right to arbitrate has been waived. Some of these courts have held that prejudice is the determining factor and that waiver may not be based on delay or inconsistent action alone.[9] Others have held that prejudice is simply one

---

[5] *See Moses H. Cone*, n. 3, supra, 460 U.S. at 24-25. *See also* PaineWebber Inc. v. Hartmann, 921 F.2d 507, 512-13 (3d Cir. 1990) (genuine ambiguities weighed against the resisting party); Harris v. Green Tree Financial Corp., 183 F.3d 173 (3d Cir. 1999).

[6] *See* Upstate Shredding, LLC v. Carloss Well Supply Co., 84 F. Supp. 2d 357 (N.D.N.Y. 2000) (principle that doubts concerning arbitrability should be resolved in favor of arbitrating dispute applies to issue of waiver); Leadertex v. Morganton Dyeing & Finishing Corp., 67 F.3d 20, 25 (2d Cir. 1995).

[7] *See* Enviro Petroleum, Inc. v. Kondur Petroleum, 91 F. Supp. 2d 1031 (S.D. Tex. 2000); Chappel v. Laboratory Corp. of America, 232 F.3d 494 (9th Cir. 2000); *In re* Bruce Terminix Co., 988 S.W.2d 702, 704 (Tex. 1998); Van Ness Townhouses v. Mar Indus. Corp., 862 F.2d 754 (9th Cir. 1988); Britton v. Co-op Banking Corp., 916 F.2d 1405 (9th Cir. 1990).

[8] *See* Doctor's Assoc. v. Distajo, 107 F.3d 120, 130-134 (2d Cir. 1997); Great W. Mortgage Corp. v. Peacock, 110 F.3d 222, 233 n. 51-52 (3d Cir. 1997); AT&T Corp. v. Vision One Sec. Sys., 914 F. Supp. 392, 395-396 (S.D. Cal. 1995); Municipal Energy Agency of Miss. v. Big Rivers Elec. Corp., 804 F.2d 338, 345 (5th Cir. 1986); Germany v. River Terminal Ry. Co., 477 F.2d 546, 547 (6th Cir. 1973); Martin Marietta Aluminum v. General Elec. Co., 586 F.2d 143, 146 (9th Cir. 1978); Cabintree of Wisconsin, Inc. v. Kraftmaid Cabinetry, 50 F.3d 388 (7th Cir. 1995); Morrison Restaurants v. Homestead Village of Fairhope, 1998 WL 97556 (Ala. 1998) (filing motion for summary judgment constitutes waiver of right to mediate and arbitrate).

[9] *See* Rush v. Oppenheimer, 779 F.2d 885, 887 (2d Cir. 1985) (waiver of right to compel arbitration may be found only where prejudice to the other party is demonstrated); *accord Leadertex*, n. 6, supra, 67 F.3d at 26; Gavlik Constr. Co. v. H. F. Campbell Co., 526 F.2d 777, 782 (3d Cir. 1975); Walker v. J. C. Bradford & Co., 938 F.2d 575, 577 (5th Cir. 1991); *Miller Brewing*, n. 4, *supra*, 781 F.2d at 497.

of the factors to be considered and place the primary focus on the extent to which a party has taken inconsistent action (for example, whether the party has pursued litigation processes, including discovery, that might not be available in arbitration, or has failed to assert the right to arbitrate the dispute in its answer and has attempted instead to have the suit dismissed on the merits).[10]

The application of either state or federal waiver law by the court depends on whether state arbitration law or the Federal Arbitration Act (FAA), 9 U.S.C. §§1-16, applies,[11] not on whether the waiver claim is raised in state or federal court.[12] Both state and federal courts are required to apply the FAA when the agreement evidences a transaction involving interstate commerce.[13]

Whether state or federal law is applied and whether prejudice is the determining factor or not, all courts typically look for the following indicia of a waiver:

---

[10] *See Southern Sys.*, n. 4, supra (prejudice is one factor to consider); A.G. Edwards & Sons v. National Found. for Cancer Research, 821 F.2d 772, 777 (D.C. Cir. 1987) (inconsistency is the determinative factor; prejudice is merely a relevant factor among others); *Cabinetree*, n. 8, *supra*, 50 F.3d 388, 390 (prejudice is just one factor, but not an essential one); *Metz*, n. 4, *supra*, (one of six factors); *Guess*, n. 4, *supra*, 94 Cal. Rptr. 2d at 203; First Community Insurance v. F-Con Contractors, 2000 WL 274001 (Tex. App.-Dallas 2000).

[11] *See Distajo*, n. 8, *supra*, 107 F.3d at 130-131 (citing Merrill, Lynch, Fenner & Smith, Inc. v. Lecopulos, 553 F.2d 842, 845 (2d Cir. 1977)). The FAA applies very broadly to any written contract requiring arbitration of a dispute which evidences a transaction involving interstate commerce, whether or not the contract specifically states that the FAA applies. If interstate commerce is not involved or if the parties' arbitration provision expressly provides that a particular state's arbitration law governs, the arbitration obligation and the waiver test, notwithstanding the FAA, will be governed by state law. *See* Volt Information Sciences v. Board of Trustees, 489 U.S. 468 (1989). Note that a contract's general state choice-of-law provision is usually insufficient evidence of an intent to trump the application of the FAA to make that state's substantive state law govern the arbitration obligation. *See* Chiron Corp. Ortho Diagnostic Sys., 207 F.3d 1126 (9th Cir. 2000) (standard choice-of-law provision does not invoke state arbitration or procedural law, only substantive law governs claims and only FAA governs arbitration); National Union Fire Ins. Co. of Pittsburgh v. Belco Petroleum, 88 F.3d 129, 134-135 (2d Cir. 1996) (same); Wolsey, Ltd. v. Foodmaker, Inc., 144 F.3d 1205 (9th Cir. 1998).

[12] *See Moses H. Cone*, n. 3, *supra*, 460 U.S. at 26-27 (the FAA's requirements apply equally to state and federal courts). Although a state court must follow federal law and must look to the federal courts for interpretation of the FAA, it need not necessarily follow the interpretations of the federal courts for the district or circuit in which the state court is located. It is free to follow the interpretation of other federal courts that appear more persuasive if the federal courts are split on an issue. *See also* Harris, n. 5, *supra*.

[13] Allied-Bruce Terminix Cos. v. Dobson, 513 U.S. 265, 274-78 (1995).

- whether a party's actions are inconsistent with the right to arbitrate;
- whether litigation machinery has been substantially invoked and the parties were well into preparation of a lawsuit before one party notified the opposing party of its intent to arbitrate;
- whether a party either requested enforcement of the arbitration clause close to the trial date or delayed for a long period before seeking a stay;
- whether a defendant seeking arbitration filed counterclaims without asking for a stay of proceedings;
- whether important intervening steps, such as taking advantage of judicial discovery procedures not available in arbitration, had taken place; and
- whether the delay has affected, misled or prejudiced the opposing party.[14]

The criteria for a legal waiver under state or federal law are always applied on a case-by-case basis[15] and normally have been found to be a threshold question of law for a court rather than for an arbitrator.[16] The party asserting that there has been a waiver carries a very heavy burden of proving the criteria for a waiver are met.[17] Finally, the scope of the waiver that may be asserted is limited to disputes that are both arbitrable under the parties' agreement[18] and involve claims raising the same legal and factual issues that were put at issue in the inconsistent litigation.[19]

---

[14] *Metz*, n. 4, *supra* 39 F.3d at 1489; *Leadertex*, n. 6, *supra*, 67 F.3d at 25.

[15] *See Distajo*, n. 8, *supra*, 107 F.3d at 130-131 (citing cases); St. Mary's Med. Ctr. v. Disco Aluminum Prod. Co., 969 F.2d 585, 588 (7th Cir. 1992); Stifel, Nicolaus & Co. v. Freeman, 924 F.2d 157, 159 (8th Cir. 1991); Morewitz v. West of England Ship Owners, 62 F.3d 1356, 1365 n. 16 (11th Cir. 1995).

[16] S & R Co. of Kingston v. Latona Trucking., 159 F.3d 80 (2d Cir. 1998). *But see* Grumhaus v. Comerica Sec., 223 F.3d 648 (7th Cir. 2000).

[17] *See* Goldsmith v. Pinez, 84 F. Supp. 2d 228 (D. Mass. 2000). Microsystems Corp. v. Dahod, 84 F. Supp. 2d 396 (E.D.N.Y. 2000).

[18] *See* Sweater Bee by Banff v. Manhattan Indus., 754 F.2d 457, 463 (2d Cir.) *cert. den.*, 474 U.S. 819 (1985); *AT&T.*, n. 8, *supra*, 914 F. Supp. at 396.

[19] *See Distajo*, 107 F.3d at 132-133 (*citing* Shearson Lehman Hutton, Inc. v. Wagoner, 944 F.2d 114, 122 (2d Cir. 1991)); *Graumhaus*, n. 16, *supra*, 223 F.3d at 652-53 (citing another case).

When Waiver Issues Arise

Waiver of the right to arbitrate a dispute commonly arises in two ways. It may arise when a dispute is subject to a mandatory arbitration provision but the injured party does not pursue a remedy in any forum.[20] The waiver argument is made much later when the injured party seeks redress for the dispute, either in arbitration or in court. Assuming the applicable statute of limitations has not yet run, the party seeking to invoke the waiver doctrine may do so in a motion made to a court with jurisdiction over the parties' agreement. The application of the contractual waiver doctrine in such cases resembles in many respects the equitable limitation defenses of laches or estoppel and would involve sleeping on one's known rights and, in most cases, the existence of some identifiable prejudice to the moving party (for example, destruction of documents or unavailability of material witnesses).

More commonly, the waiver issue arises in the context of a lawsuit by one party to an arbitration agreement. The waiver doctrine may be asserted against the party that files a lawsuit or counterclaims going to the merits of the arbitrable dispute, rather than pursuing arbitration of that dispute as required by the contract.[21] Some courts hold that filing suit knowing that an obligation to arbitrate exists raises an implicit, rebuttable presumption that the right to arbitrate the dispute has been waived.[22]

Waiver also may be asserted against the other party to the lawsuit if that party does not act promptly to preserve and enforce the arbitration obligation. An agreement to arbitrate is an affirmative defense and affirmative defenses may be waived if not affirmatively pled. Although the federal circuits are split on whether a failure to assert the defense is by itself sufficient to constitute a waiver, it is an act inconsistent with a later assertion of the right to arbitrate which may ripen into a waiver.[23]

---

[20] When waiver is asserted on the basis that no action has been taken in any forum, only the party that has been injured (i.e., the one who possesses the claim) must go forward with arbitration to avoid a waiver. The other party need not sue in order to avoid a waiver. *See In re Bruce Terminix* Co., n. 7, *supra*, 988 S.W.2d at 705-706.

[21] *See* WorldSource Coil Coating v. McGraw Constr., 946 F.2d 473, 479 (6th Cir. 1991) (submission of arbitrable issues in court constitutes a waiver, regardless of prejudice); PPG Indus. v. Webster Auto Parts, 128 F.3d 103, 107-09 (2d Cir. 1997) (five-month delay in asserting right to arbitrate counterclaims, failing to file motion to stay, filing substantive motions and taking pre-trial discovery of arbitrable claims creates waiver).

[22] *See Grumhaus*, n. 16, *supra*, 223 F.3d at 650-653 (the election to proceed in a non-arbitral forum was presumptive waiver, but other factors may absolve defaulting party); *Cabintree*, n. 8, *supra*, 50 F.3d at 390-391.

[23] *See Guess*, n. 4, *supra*, 94 Cal. Rptr. 2d at 204; Central Trust Co. v. Anemostat Products Div., 621 F. Supp. 44, 46 (S.D. Ohio 1985) (filing action serves notice to

Many times lawsuits are filed because counsel does not recognize that the language of the arbitration provision sweeps in almost all disputes if the magic words "arising out of or relating to" are used in the arbitration provision,[24] or because counsel believes, incorrectly, that the contractual obligation can be avoided by, for example, a fraudulent inducement claim.[25] In any case, the mere filing of an action in court is rarely enough to trigger the waiver doctrine.[26]

If the defendant promptly moves to enforce the arbitration obligation, such suits are simply treated, at worst, as a separate breach of the parties' contract for which damages may be sought in arbitration. The courts have also held that seeking relief for a dispute by participating in any of the following is not inconsistent with the obligation to arbitrate: related collective-bargaining contract proceedings,[27] court-mandated mediation proceedings,[28] or administrative proceedings conducted by government agencies[29] participating in settlement discussions.[30]

---

defendant that the plaintiff is refusing to arbitrate; within reasonable time defendant must determine whether to insist on arbitration); Kramer v. Hammond, 943 F.2d 176, 179 (2d Cir. 1991) (failure to raise arbitration as affirmative defense and asserting counterclaims); *Leadertex*, n. 6, *supra*, 67 F.3d at 26 (filing responsive pleading without raising arbitration, engaging in discovery, eight-month delay in asserting arbitration resulting in economic harm); Cotton v. Stone, 4 F.3d 176, 179-80 (2d Cir. 1993) (waiver found because defendant did not file an interlocutory appeal); *contra Metz*, n. 4, *supra*, 39 F.3d at 1489 (failure to take interlocutory appeal does not preclude raising the issue on appeal from the final judgment); S & H Contractors v. A.J. Taft Coal Co., 906 F.2d 1507, 1513 (11th Cir. 1990) (inconsistent actions); *Southern Sys.*, n. 4, *supra*, 105 F. Supp. 2d at 855-56 (waiver found despite claim that obligation to arbitrate was only recently discovered); RTKL Assoc. v. Four Villages Ltd. Partnership, 620 A.2d 351, 354-56 (Md. Ct. App. 1993) (waiver found; not necessary to decide whether prejudice must be shown).

[24] *See* Simula, Inc. v. Autoliv, Inc., 1999 WL 253191 (9th Cir. Apr. 30, 1999); Keifer Specialty Flooring v. Tarkett, Inc., 1999 WL 232041 (7th Cir. Apr. 21, 1999).

[25] Prima Paint Corp. v. Flood & Conklin Mfg., 388 U.S. 395, 402 (1967); *Upstate Shredding*, n. 6, *supra. See also* Acevedo Maldanado v. PPG Indus., 514 F.2d 614, 616 (1st Cir. 1975) (may not avoid arbitration by casting contract claims as torts).

[26] *See* Pennzoil v. Arnold Oil Co., 30 S.W.3d 494 (Tex. Ct. App. 2000) (seeking discovery did not waive arbitration right).

[27] *See* Kennedy v. Superior Printing, 215 F.3d 650 (6th Cir. 2000) (collective bargaining agreement); *Microsystems*, n. 17, *supra* (same).

[28] *See* Ahing v. Lehman Bros., 1997 U.S. Dist. LEXIS 15937 (S. D. N.Y. 1997) (participation in court-ordered mediation).

[29] *See* Dexter v. Prudential Ins. Co., 213 F.3d 1336 (10th Cir. 2000) (participation in agency proceedings).

[30] *See* Southwest Indus. Import & Export v. Wilmond Co., 524 F.2d 468, 470 (5th Cir. 1975) (participation in protracted settlement negotiations).

They have also found that the filing of an action that merely seeks to preserve assets or maintain the status quo until arbitration may be pursued is not an act inconsistent with the duty to arbitrate. At least one ADR provider's arbitration rules expressly state that the filing of such court actions will not constitute a waiver.[31]

Nevertheless, there are occasions when lawsuits are knowingly filed in an attempt to escape a clear and obvious arbitration obligation, or to test whether the other party will enforce that obligation. Faced with the filing of a suit that is inconsistent with the obligation to seek a remedy through arbitration, the defendant has two basic options. If it is strategically beneficial, the defendant may join voluntarily in the suit and by participating actively seek an explicit (or achieve an implicit) mutual waiver of the arbitration obligation.[32] Alternatively, the defendant may answer the complaint and plead the mandatory, exclusive remedy of arbitration as a defense or move the court in which the suit is pending (or another court with jurisdiction over the obligation to arbitrate) to enforce the arbitration clause. If the motion is denied, it may preserve the obligation to arbitrate through timely interlocutory appeal.

It is never advisable for a party seeking to enforce an arbitration clause to assert counterclaims in the court proceeding. The better course is to file a proper demand for arbitration, as specified by the arbitration agreement. A failure to plead the mandatory obligation to arbitrate as a defense, combined with the pleading of counterclaims, either through inadvertence or in the mistaken belief that there may be two bites at the apple, may lead to a loss of the right to subsequently assert that defense.

Waiver may arise in still another manner. If the defendant in a suit is successful in getting the court to order the case to arbitration, the plaintiff may still attempt to thwart the arbitration proceeding by engaging in delaying tactics (such as refusing to appoint an arbitrator, pay the required fees or provide discovery). Although it may be possible to seek redress for delay once an arbitrator is appointed, it is also possible in extreme circumstances to seek relief from the court that referred the matter to arbitration. In extreme cases, the court may order withdrawal of the matter from arbitration and order the claims dismissed.[33]

---

[31] American Arbitration Association Commercial Arbitration Rules, R-50(a). *See AT&T*, n. 8, *supra*, 914 F. Supp. at 397 n. 7. *But see S & R Co.*, n. 16, *supra* (15-month participation in discovery; waiver found despite no waiver clause and no waiver rule incorporated in agreement).

[32] *See Goldsmith*, n. 17, *supra* (party may implicitly waive arbitration by engaging in litigation).

[33] *See* Morris v. Morgan Stanley & Co., 942 F.2d 648, 653 (9th Cir. 1991); RoadTech, Inc. v. M J Highway Tech. Ltd., 83 F. Supp. 2d 677 (E. D. Va. 2000).

One final point on waiver and the practitioner's alternatives. The courts uniformly enforce arbitration clauses as written by the parties and give effect to the procedures they crafted even though such procedures vary rules or practice that would ordinarily apply.[34] The issue of waiver, like almost any other matter, may be addressed proactively by the practitioner before the issue arises.

Minimizing Waiver Issues

When drafting the parties' arbitration provision, the practitioner may expressly establish the specific waiver criteria that will govern if one party elects not to honor the obligation to arbitrate when a dispute covered by the agreement arises. It may be advisable, at a minimum, to expressly state that taking a dispute to court rather than following the prescribed arbitration process will constitute a separate breach of the parties' agreement for which damages, including attorneys' fees, are recoverable.

It also may be possible to specify in the arbitration provision that a refusal to voluntarily drop an inappropriately filed suit in the face of a request or motion to do so will constitute a complete waiver of that party's right to pursue any remedy for the alleged dispute, whether in court or in arbitration.

The arbitration clause also may cover other attempts to frustrate arbitration of disputes, such as the failure to pay arbitrator fees when required or to comply with discovery orders by the arbitrator. As long as the provision establishing the criteria for finding a waiver of the right to arbitrate is reasonable-that is, it must contain due process notions of notice and opportunity to promptly cure the breach, and must apply even-handedly to both parties-there is no reason why it should not be upheld under current statutory and decisional law.

---

[34] *See* First Options of Chicago v. Kaplan, 131 L. Ed. 2d 992-94; Green Tree Fin. Corp. v. Randolph, 531 U.S.79, (2000); Syncor Int'l Corp. v. McLeland, 120 F.3d 262 (4th Cir. 1997), *cert. den.*, 118 S. Ct. 1039 (1998); Lapine Tech. Corp. v. Kycocera Corp., 130 F.3d 884 (9th Cir. 1997); *Great W. Mortgage*, n. 8, *supra*, 110 F.3d at 230-232; Armendariz v. Found. Health Pyschcare Serv., 24 Cal. 4th 83, 6 P.3d 669, 99 Cal. Rptr. 2d 745 (2000).

III. State Arbitration Law

Does State Arbitration Law Matter At All?
PART I: FEDERAL PREEMPTION
by Alan Scott Rau[*]

This is the first part of a two-part article. Part one provides an overview of current law on preemption; Part two addresses continuing problems that have not been laid to rest by existing precedent.

For many years after the passage of the Federal Arbitration Act in 1925, state and federal arbitration law seemed to coexist peacefully—developing along parallel lines without anyone being much concerned about the disparities between them. Arbitration is already esoteric enough as a subject of inquiry; it seems fair to say that for most attorneys, the FAA was safely cabined in the more sophisticated forms of practice centering around litigation in the federal courts.

But over the past decade or two, and particularly since the "litigation explosion" and concerns about crowded dockets have begun to loom so large in the judicial consciousness, federal courts have managed to create out of the rudimentary and skeletal statute a highly-developed structure, one that now above all facilitates and supports the arbitration process. A newly-discovered, but relentless, "pro-arbitration" policy has given rise to a federal imperialism that inevitably calls into question the legitimacy of all sorts of state laws dealing with dispute resolution. The lion is no longer lying down with the lamb; it has, instead, eagerly been passing around the mint jelly.

Virtually all states have enacted so-called "modern"[1] arbitration statutes similar in concept to the FAA, which ensure the enforceability of

---

[*] Alan Rau is the Robert F. Windfohr & Anne Burnett Windfohr Professor of Law at the University of Texas at Austin School of Law. He holds an LL.B. from Harvard School of Law. Rau serves on the Commercial and International Panels of the American Arbitration Association. He is co-author of PROCESS OF DISPUTE RESOLUTION: THE ROLE OF LAWYERS (3rd ed. 2002); ADR AND ARBITRATION: STATUTES AND COMMENTARY (West 1998) and CASES AND MATERIALS ON CONTRACTS (West 1992).

[1] The distinguishing characteristic of a "modern" arbitration statute is that it provides for specific performance of an executory agreement to arbitrate future disputes, thereby preventing a party from "revoking" the agreement before an award has been rendered.

agreements to arbitrate future disputes. But even in states where the overall climate is benign, rear-guard actions are regularly found on behalf of local businesses, franchisees, consumers or employees-groups for whom state legislatures can be expected to show particular tenderness. In such cases, the recalcitrance or obtuseness of state judges has occasionally made necessary intervention by federal courts.

When disparities between state statutes and the FAA cannot safely be ignored, how is the practitioner to react? Can the entire corpus of state arbitration legislation simply be treated as an irrelevant relic of a simpler age? Or is there still a place for state arbitration law in the face of the federal statute? In a little more than a decade, the U.S. Supreme Court has taken up this subject of state-federal relations perhaps half a dozen times-and still we do not have an adequate answer to the question.

Dominance of the FAA

The historical background is sufficiently well-known so that a detailed treatment should be unnecessary. In cases like *Prima Paint* and *Moses Cone*, the Supreme Court, in a tour de force, transformed what was originally conceived as a "procedural" statute—intended merely to govern the conduct of litigation in federal courts—into a "substantive" exercise of Congress' power to regulate interstate and foreign commerce.[2] After such cases, the inference was inevitable that state courts too are required to enforce arbitration agreements coming within the scope of the FAA. The Supreme Court so held in *Southland Corp. v. Keating*: "[S]ince the overwhelming proportion of all civil litigation in this country is in the state courts, we cannot believe Congress intended to limit the Arbitration Act to disputes subject only to federal-court jurisdiction."[3] In *Southland*, the Court was faced with a statute enacted for the protection of franchisees, which the California courts interpreted to grant franchisees the inalienable right to judicial consideration of any claims, despite the presence of an arbitration clause in the franchise agreement. The Court held that the statute, as interpreted by the state courts, violated the Supremacy Clause, since in § 2 of the FAA Congress had "declared a national policy favoring arbitration and withdrew the power of the states to require a judicial forum for the resolution of claims which the contracting parties agreed to resolve by arbitration." Federal

---

[2] Prima Paint Corp. v. Flood & Conklin Mfg. Co., 388 U.S. 395 (1967); Moses H. Cone Memorial Hosp. v. Mercury Constr. Co., 460 U.S. 1 (1983).

[3] 465 U.S. 1, 15 (1984). *See also* Perry v. Thomas, 482 U.S. 483, 491 (1987).

policy therefore required that arbitration agreements be placed "upon the same footing as other contracts."

Out of the bare command of § 2 that agreements to arbitrate shall be "valid, irrevocable, and enforceable," the courts have spun out an obligation to enforce such agreements with draconian rigor. States may not for any perceived policy "single out" or be "hostile" or "inhospitable" to arbitration agreements, "undermine" them or discriminate against them by treating them "more harshly than other contractual terms.[4] Under this view, arbitration is simply and entirely about agreement. If enforcing an arbitration clause necessitates inefficient, piecemeal, duplicative proceedings-either because not all the parties to the dispute are signatories, or because not all the claims asserted are arbitrable–why, so be it.[5]

The preemptive effect of the FAA, of course, only comes into play when an arbitration agreement comes within its scope. If the statute is not applicable, Erie considerations would obligate federal courts to follow the state law of arbitration.[6] But the Supreme Court—sweeping away any possible limitations grounded in statutory ambiguity—has recently made it clear that the FAA is henceforth to embrace all forms of commercial activity in a modern economy.

In *Allied-Bruce Terminix Cos., Inc. v. Dobson*,[7] the Court held that the FAA "signals a congressional intent to exercise its Commerce Clause powers to the full." So interpreted, the FAA was held to apply to a contract in which home owners obtained a lifetime "termite protection plan" from the local office of a Terminix franchisee. Therefore, the state courts were obligated to enforce the arbitration clause in the termite contract even though the clause was unenforceable under state law.

If Congress has legislated in the FAA to the outer limit of its constitutional authority -reaching any transaction that merely "affects"

---

[4] *See* Securities Indus. Ass'n v. Connolly, 883 F.2d 1114 (1st Cir. 1989)(securities dealer-customer agreement); Saturn Distrib. Corp. v. Williams. 905 F.2d 719 (4th Cir. 1990) (contracts between automobile manufacturer and local dealers); Seymour v. Gloria Jean's Coffee Bean Franchising Corp., 732 F. Supp. 988 (D. Minn.1990). *See also* Progressive Casualty Ins. Co. v. C.A. Reaseguradora Nacional de Venezuela, 991 F.2d 42 (2d Cir. 1993); Baravati v. Josephthal, Lyon & Ross, Inc., 28 F.3d 704, 711 (7th Cir. 1994).

[5] *See Moses H. Cone*, n. 2 *supra*, 460 U.S. at 20 ("the relevant federal law requires piecemeal resolution when necessary to give effect to an arbitration agreement"). *See also* Dean Witter Reynolds Inc. v. Byrd, 470 U.S. 213, 217, 221 (1985).

[6] *See* Bernhardt v. Polygraphic Co. of America, Inc., 350 U.S. 198 (1956).

[7] 513 U.S. 265 (1995).

commerce[8]-then any deviations from the FAA are likely to be peripheral and short-lived.[9]

Volt and the Fiction of "Choice of State Law"

Whatever received wisdom had developed in this area was thrown into disarray by the *Volt* case, in which the Supreme Court seemed to leave open at least some room for the application of restrictive state arbitration laws.[10] In *Volt*, the California courts gave effect to a state statute that permitted a court to stay arbitration, or refuse enforcement of an arbitration agreement, if a party to the agreement is also a party to pending litigation with a third party "arising out of the same transaction or series of related transactions and there is a possibility of conflicting rulings on a common issue of law or fact."[11] The Supreme Court agreed that application of this statute did not violate federal law, since the FAA does not "reflect a congressional intent to occupy the entire field of arbitration."

Volt has been severely criticized for erecting an entire legal framework on a fiction—and an implausible one at that: The construction contract in *Volt* provided that "[t]he contract shall be governed by the law of the place where the project is located." In denying the contractor's petition to compel arbitration, the California courts took this boilerplate choice-of-law clause, "piggy-backed" it onto the state statute restricting arbitration—and somehow turned the combination into a contractual limitation on arbitration! In the eyes of the California Court of Appeal, the parties had simply chosen to "incorporate the California rules of arbitration...into their arbitration agreement." Deferring to that finding, the Supreme Court agreed that the party seeking to compel arbitration "had no such right in the first place, because the parties' agreement did

---

[8] *See id.* at 273-75 (statutory phrase "involving commerce" should be read as "broader than the often-found words of art 'in commerce'"; it is instead the "functional equivalent" of the term "affecting" commerce). *See also* Hurst v. Tony Moore Imports Inc., 699 So. 2d 1249 (Ala. 1997).

[9] *But cf.* Porter & Clements, L.L.P. v. Stone, 935 S.W.2d 217 (Tex. Ct. App. 1996) (holding that a suit by two Texas residents against the Texas law firm that represented them in a federal court suit against a nonresident corporation, was not covered by the FAA, even though the fee agreement contained an arbitration clause).

[10] Volt Information Sciences, Inc. v. Board of Trustees of Leland Stanford Jr. Univ., 489 U.S. 468, 476 (1989). I have discussed *Volt* and its aftermath in considerably more detail in A.S. Rau, *The UNCITRAL Model Law in State and Federal Courts: The Case of 'Waiver*, 6 AMER. REV. INT'L ARB. 223, 241-261 (1995).

[11] Cal. Code Civ. Proc. § 1281.2(c).

not require arbitration to proceed in this situation." The FAA did "not require parties to arbitrate when they have not agreed to do so."

For the Supreme Court, the case was one in which the parties had, in effect, chosen to opt out of a portion of the federal statute, by preferring to arbitrate under a particular and more efficient "set of procedural rules." This seems a curious and tendentious way of characterizing what was in fact the state's arbitration law.

The *Volt* case was responsible for a considerable amount of confusion—and it has inspired some astonishingly wooden reactions. One Texas statute, for example (happily now repealed), required a contract to contain a prominent notice that it was subject to arbitration- "typed in underlined capital letters, or...rubber-stamped prominently, on the first page of the contract."[12] Such state statutes historically have been quite common. Presumably designed to guard against "surprise" and ensure that consent to arbitration has been knowing and informed, they also must be perceived as lingering remnants of the common law's distrust of or hostility to arbitration. As applied to contracts within the coverage of the FAA, such requirements have long been of doubtful validity.[13] At least in the absence of any contractual choice of law, the invalidity of such statutes is now beyond question as a result of *Doctor's Associates, Inc. v. Casarotto.*[14]

Nevertheless, a number of recent decisions have upheld the notice requirement in the Texas statute against challenges on the ground of federal preemption. In one such case, the parties had provided in their contract that arbitration was to take place "pursuant to the laws of the state of Texas." The court reasoned that, on the authority of *Volt*, this choice-of-law provision allowed the statutory notice requirement to escape preemption. Since the parties had chosen to arbitrate under Texas law, the court held the Texas Act prevailed over the FAA and the arbitration agreement was unenforceable because it did "not conform to the Texas Act."[15]

---

[12] *See* A.S. Rau & E. Sherman, Rau & Sherman's Texas ADR and Arbitration: Statutes and Commentary 274-277 (1997 ed.).

[13] *See* Collins Radio Co. v. Ex-Cell-O Corp., 467 F.2d 995, 998 (8th Cir. 1972)(FAA "plainly voids all doctrines of invalidity, unenforceability and revocability which apply only to arbitration agreements"); Woermann Constr. Co. v. Southwestern Bell Tel. Co., 846 S.W.2d 790, 793 (Mo. Ct. App. 1993)(10-point arbitration notice requirement invalid).

[14] 116 S.Ct. 1652 (1996).

[15] American Physicians Serv. Group, Inc. v. Port Lavaca Clinic Assocs., 843 S.W.2d 675, 678 (Tex. Ct. App. 1992). *Accord*, Al's Formal Wear of Houston Inc. v. Sun, 869 S.W.2d 442, 444 n.3 (Tex. Ct. App. 1993).

Are we to suppose that the parties to this contract agreed to arbitration, while at the same time intending to adopt a body of state law that would in all possible circumstances make their agreement to arbitrate invalid? One who believes that is capable of believing anything.

Now the *Volt* Court did stress that "the California rules of arbitration...generally foster the federal policy favoring arbitration," and are "manifestly designed to encourage resort to the arbitral process." In its view, giving effect to the parties' choice of law did not conflict with any federal policy, since the FAA itself "contains no provision designed to deal with" the complex practical problems that can arise in multiparty disputes, as the California statute does. All this suggests that the reach of the holding in *Volt* may be quite modest.

Perhaps, where a state court reads a contract's choice-of-law clause to incorporate restrictions on arbitration, this may be permissible in the case of seemingly "efficient" limits on arbitration, in the overall context of a nurturing statutory scheme—limits that the parties themselves might rationally have chosen without lessening their commitment to the process. In such circumstances, deference to the interpretational competence of a state court may well be justified.

For example, consider an agreement that purports to be governed by Connecticut law. Connecticut law requires that motions to vacate arbitration awards be made within thirty days. The choice-of-law clause may well be considered effective to impose this time limit, even in a case otherwise governed by the FAA—and even though, in the absence of a choice-of-law clause, the FAA's 90-day limit would most likely override inconsistent state law.

This is a plausible result under the above analysis, given that the enforceability and general currency of arbitration awards can only be heightened by imposing on the losing party a shorter time limit in which to challenge the award.[16] But such deference to state interpretations would presumably stop at the point where a choice-of-law clause is read

---

[16] In these circumstances one federal court has given effect to the Connecticut law; however, it made no inquiry into the effect on the FAA's statutory scheme of a shorter limitations period, contenting itself with a citation to *Volt* and the perfunctory remark that "applying Connecticut law here actually promotes the FAA's primary goal by enforcing the parties' contract to arbitrate according to its terms." Ekstrom v. Value Health, Inc., 68 F.3d 1391, 1396 (D.C. Cir. 1995). State statutes that extend the period for challenges may be more difficult to uphold. Cf Florasynth, Inc. v. Pickholz, 750 F.2d 171, 177 (2d Cir. 1984).

in such a way as to capture a body of state law that operates in a way truly inimical to the arbitral process.[17]

Now it is certainly true-as the Supreme Court seemed to suggest-that the problem of multiparty disputes has proven over the years to be particularly intractable for the arbitral process, and that the California legislation at issue in *Volt* was an attempt to solve it. But there still remains a considerable paradox—that the effect of applying that statute was to deny a motion to compel arbitration in precisely those circumstances that earlier cases applying the FAA had found to require the granting of such a motion.[18] Perhaps the *Volt* Court was looking beyond the particular provision of state law in question in that case-envisaging an inquiry into whether the state's overall legislation on the subject of arbitration was "generally" favorable to the arbitral process. But surely it is both unlikely and undesirable that we should be expected to characterize in such neat terms an entire complex regulatory scheme.

Punitive Damages

A few years later, the door that was so carelessly left ajar in *Volt* for state regulation of arbitration seemed to slam shut. In a number of states (most notably New York), it has long been held that arbitrators are prohibited from awarding punitive damages, even when the agreement can be read to give them that power. Under *Volt*, what would be the effect of a clause providing that the agreement "shall be governed by the laws of the state of New York"? Would this boilerplate choice-of-law clause constitute an "exclusion" of punitive damages? Faced with such a clause in the Mastrobuono case,[19] the Supreme Court answered "no," choosing to read the choice-of-law clause as referring only to the "substantive principles" that state courts would apply—i.e., the rules of

---

[17] *See Connolly*, 883 F.2d at 1120 n. 3, and *Gloria Jean's Coffee Bean Franchising*, 732 F. Supp. at 995, both cited in n. 4 *supra; see also* Weatherly Cellaphonics Partners v. Hueber, 726 F. Supp. 319 (D.D.C. 1989).

[18] *See Moses H. Cone.*, n. 2 *supra*, 460 U.S. at 19-21. In *Woermann Constr. Co.*, n.13 *supra*, 846 S.W.2d at 793, the court said: "[I]n *Volt*, state procedures were not applied in such a manner as to deny arbitration, but simply to deny arbitration until related litigation had been decided." But this is a distinction without a difference; any state court litigation among the contractor, the owner, and related companies in *Volt* would have obvious res judicata or collateral estoppel effect in any subsequent arbitration among the same parties. This is, however, rapidly becoming a standard rhetorical move, used when it is thought desirable to explain or distinguish *Volt*. See *Casarotto*, n. 14 *supra*, 116 S.Ct. at 1656-57.

[19] Mastrobuono v. Shearson Lehman Hutton, Inc., 514 U.S. 52 (1995).

decision governing the merits of the dispute.[20] Once the choice-of-law clause was out of the way, there was nothing left that could be pointed to as an attempt by the parties to contract around the usual understanding in FAA cases-that arbitrators have virtually unlimited discretion in choosing appropriate remedies. In the Supreme Court's view, "in the absence of contractual intent to the contrary, the FAA would preempt the [New York] rule."

Squaring *Volt* and *Mastrobuono*, as Professor Park has written, is "difficult to say the least."[21] There is at least one distinction that the Supreme Court itself put forward: It was the California state courts in *Volt* which interpreted the parties' choice-of-law clause as a reference to the California law of arbitration; the Supreme Court simply deferred to their reading. In *Mastrobuono*, by contrast, the case arose in the federal system, and the Supreme Court appeared to construe the contract *de novo*, finding that its conclusion accorded with "the only decision-maker arguably entitled to deference-the arbitrator." So no state court was involved at any time.[22]

For a while after *Mastrobuono*, New York courts were ready to indulge in the grossest forms of wishful thinking-believing that they remained free to construe choice-of-law clauses differently from the Supreme Court in *Mastrobuono*, and that federal courts would have to defer to their reading even if the result would be to exclude punitive damage awards.[23]

---

[20] This is, after all, the usual function of a choice-of-law clause, which is not generally thought to reach such matters as the enforceability of the arbitration agreement itself, the powers of the arbitrators, "the state's allocation of power between alternative tribunals," or "the regimen or scheme of arbitral procedural law under which the arbitration was conducted"—i.e., the *lex arbitri*. In addition, a choice-of-law clause is usually not intended to say much about the respective spheres of state and federal law (as opposed to a choice among state laws). The FAA too is, after all, "the law of New York."

[21] William Park, *When and Why Arbitration Matters*, in G.M. BERESFORD HARTWELL (ed.), THE COMMERCIAL WAY TO JUSTICE (1997).

[22] There is an alternative distinction. Unlike the statute in *Volt*, which attempted to craft a more efficient solution to the problem of multiparty disputes, the New York rule barring punitive damages awards seems an historical throwback-a relic of a time when distrust of the arbitral process was much more common. But if *Volt* really requires such a case-by-case assessment of the reading of contracts by state courts—a determination on an individualized basis of the extent to which such interpretation is permitted to diverge from federal arbitration policy-then the decision is "simply unworkable," and Mastrobuono may indicate that the Court is on the verge of understanding this. *See* Rau, n.10 *supra*, at 257-58, 279-80.

[23] *See* Dean Witter Reynolds, Inc. v. Trimble, 631 N.Y.S.2d 215, 217 n.4 (N.Y. Sup. Ct. 1995); Merrill Lynch, Pierce Fenner & Smith, Inc. v. Levine, N.Y.L.J., July 5, 1995, at p. 26 (N.Y. Sup. Ct.).

This, however, was clearly a non-starter. It failed to take seriously the "liberal federal policy favoring arbitration agreements," which has been the subject of a relentless Supreme Court jurisprudence. Whoever is doing the work of interpretation, the reading of ordinary contracts must still be informed to some extent by a "healthy regard" for this federal policy and the federal rights it confers. In recent cases the New York courts seem, at last, to have sensibly capitulated—and they now appear to consider themselves bound by the *Mastrobuono* reading of choice-of-law clauses to permit arbitral awards of punitive damages.[24]

On a related front, the New York courts also will construe choice-of-law clauses so as not to capture the state's rule granting to the courts-rather than to the arbitrators themselves -the power to decide whether a particular claim is time-barred. Here too the state rule may not trump the federal understanding that the eligibility of a claim for arbitration is a question for the arbitral panel.[25]

The notion that state arbitration law at odds with the dictates of the FAA can be reintroduced through the device of a choice-of-law clause has been steadily eroding, and is being increasingly ignored. *Volt* has become peripheral to the point where it is now often said that the case can be "limited to its own facts."[26] The bottom line is that courts are increasingly recognizing that this case "has proven to be simply unworkable" and is awaiting "a decent burial."[27]

---

[24] *See* Americorp Sec., Inc. v. Sager, 656 N.Y.S.2d 762 (N.Y. App. Div. 1997); Prudential Secs. Inc. v. Pesce, 642 N.Y.S.2d 466 (N.Y. Sup. Ct. 1996); Olde Discount Corp. v. Dartley, N.Y.L.J., Dec. 12, 1997, at pp. 26-27 (N.Y. Sup. Ct.).

[25] "A boilerplate choice-of-law clause does not necessarily signify the parties' acceptance of limitations imposed by New York law with respect to the contractually conferred power of an arbitrator to determine all issues, including arbitrability." Smith Barney Shearson Inc. v. Sacharow, 666 N.Y.S.2d 990 (N.Y. 1997). One might think that the acceptability of state law in all these cases would be enhanced by the fact that even federal law on the subject remains murky. There appears to be no consensus as to how such contractual time limits should be viewed: Seeing them as mere procedural hurdles would evoke the Wiley line of "procedural arbitrability" cases. John Wiley & Sons, Inc. v. Livingson, 376 U.S. 543 (1964). Seeing them, on the other hand, as substantive limitations on arbitrable claims would instead evoke the First Options presumption—that it is for courts to decide "arbitrability" issues unless the parties clearly say otherwise. First Options of Chicago, Inc. v. Kaplan, 514 U.S. 938 (1995).

[26] *See* Dean Witter Reynolds, Inc. v. Sanchez Espada, 959 F. Supp. 73, 83 (D.P.R. 1997); NOS Communications, Inc. v. Robertson, 936 F. Supp. 761, 765 n.1 (D. Colo. 1996). But can we ever conceive of a case thought to be properly decided which nevertheless has no resonance at all beyond its "own facts"? Surely, in our common law system, no such animal can exist.

[27] RAU, n. 10 *supra*, at 257, 285.

Most recently, in *Casarotto*, a weary Supreme Court emphasized once again-in the face of some studied obtuseness on the part of the Montana courts-that state laws "singling out arbitration provisions for suspect status" will not be permitted.[28] The Court struck down a Montana law conditioning validity of an arbitration agreement on notice "typed in underlined capital letters on the front page of the contract." Since then, state courts seem to have fallen into a dutiful, if sometimes sullen compliance; a large number of state statutes which declared whole categories of disputes inarbitrable, or which had placed special burdens on the arbitral process, have been swept away.[29]

Some Parting Thoughts

What, then, are we left with? What is the role of state law in governing arbitration proceedings? Part two of this article will examine a number of areas in which we can expect preemption issues to continue to arise-and to be critical to the outcome of litigation. For example, just as federal courts in diversity cases are not required to turn themselves into pale copies of the nearby state courthouse, so state courts too are not required to abandon their procedures in favor of federal ones; indeed they are expected to control their proceedings in what might be viewed as mere "procedural" matters, without infringing unduly on federally guaranteed rights. (Here, as with *Erie* itself, we have a line that can be policed only with considerable difficulty.) And if "arbitration is contract,"[30] then the backdrop against which contracting parties write their agreements—that body of "general contract law principles" governing the formation and validity of private agreements-will retain considerable vitality. These and other subjects will be treated in some detail in part two.

---

[28] *Casarotto*, n. 14 *supra*, 116 S.Ct. at 1656.
[29] *E.g.*, Primerica Fin. Servs., Inc. v. Wise, 456 S.E.2d 631 (Ga. Ct. App. 1995)(employment); Palm Harbor Homes, Inc. v. McCoy, 944 S.W.2d 716 (Tex. Ct. App. 1997)(consumer contracts); Soil Remediation Co. v. Nu-Way Environmental, Inc., 476 S.E.2d 149 (S.C. 1996); Duggan v. Zip Mail Servs., Inc., 920 S.W.2d 200 (Mo. Ct. App. 1996); *see also* Hoffman v. Cargill, Inc., 968 F. Supp. 465 (N.D. Iowa 1997); Morrison v. Colorado Permanente Medical Group, 983 F. Supp. 937 (D. Colo. 1997); Central Jersey Freightliner, Inc. v. Freightliner Corp., 1997 WL 754978 (D.N.J.); Schooley v. Merrill Lynch, Pierce, Fenner & Smith, Inc., 1997 WL 45271 (10th Cir.).
[30] Cf. A.S. Rau, Arbitration as Contract: One More Word About First Options v. Kaplan, MEALEY'S INT'L ARB. REP., Mar. 1997 at p. 21.

Does State Arbitration Law Matter At All?
PART II: A CONTINUING ROLE FOR STATE LAW

by Alan Scott Rau

This is the second part of a two-part article that deals with a continuing issue in arbitration law-disparities between federal and state arbitration statutes.

In the first part of this article I traced the line of cases-beginning with *Southland Corp. v. Keating*—in which the Supreme Court appeared to impose on the states an absolute obligation to apply the Federal Arbitration Act, and, at the same time, extended the reach of this federal statute to embrace virtually every sphere of commercial activity. As a result of all these cases, it should be clear enough now that state law, common-law or statutory, "hostile to arbitration" is preempted by federal law "friendly to it."[31]

Of course, just what constitutes this forbidden hostility to arbitration may not always be self-evident. It has been held, for example, that a state may not attempt to give customers of brokerage houses the option of arbitration before the American Arbitration Association or other independent nonindustry forum, as well as before the usual industry forum.[32] One might think that a state statute to that effect would simply be a form of regulation aimed at expanding consumer choice, in the interest of process fairness. Yet—since the customer's option in favor of the AAA could presumably be exercised at the time that a dispute arose-the effect of the state law was to override any forum-selection terms that might have been contained in the arbitration agreement itself. What is apparently impermissible about the state's action is that it prevents the stronger party in a contract of adhesion from imposing in advance a certain term (industry-forum arbitration) on the weaker party—although the power to do this in other, non-arbitration agreements remains generally unconstrained! This is, then, just that type of legislative encroachment, directed specifically to arbitration agreements, that will violate the FAA. Precisely the same rationale explains why states may not attempt to ensure that arbitration take place locally rather than in some distant forum.[33]

---

[31] Baravati v. Josephthal, Lyon & Ross, Inc., 28 F.3d 704, 711 (7th Cir. 1994).
[32] Securities Industry Ass'n v. Lewis, 751 F. Supp. 205 (S.D. Fla. 1990).
[33] *See* Management Recruiters Int'l, Inc. v. Bloor, 129 F.3d 851, 856 (6th Cir. 1997) (dictum).

The fact that state regulation is not strictly confined to arbitration agreements-but may sweep more broadly, invalidating other suspect clauses as well—will not necessarily save state legislation from a preemption challenge.[34] And, for that matter, a state's failure to affirmatively advantage arbitration agreements in accordance with federal policy might also be a form of proscribed hostility. For example, state courts are apparently expected to construe arbitration clauses in such a way as to presume the arbitrability of the dispute.[35] They are also expected to refer to arbitration even the question of the validity of the container contract itself on the ground that the arbitration agreement is "separable."[36] State courts also may not ignore the strong presumption against waiver found in the federal common law of arbitration and, in all likelihood, may not invoke their usual bright-line rule to deny arbitration to a litigant who—after considerable vacillation—attempts only belatedly to initiate the arbitral process.[37]

It may well be asked, then, what are we left with? What, if anything, is the role of state law in governing arbitration proceedings? That question is the subject of the remaining discussion in this installment-which examines a number of problem areas where state-law issues can be expected regularly to arise in the conduct of litigation.

"Reverse Erie": Effects on Procedure in State Courts

As I pointed out in Part I, we can expect that state courts will continue to control the conduct of their own proceedings in what might be viewed as mere "procedural" matters, as long as this does not infringe unduly on federally guaranteed rights. It is, after all, "a general and

---

[34] *See* RAU & SHERMAN, RAU & SHERMAN'S TEXAS ADR AND ARBITRATION: STATUTES AND COMMENTARY 526-27 (1997 ed.) (discussing a state statute requiring conspicuous notice of a provision in a consumer contract that makes the contract "subject to the laws of another state, to litigation in the courts of another state, or to arbitration in another state"); *see also* Doctor's Assocs., Inc. v. Hamilton, 150 F.3d 157, 162-63 (2d Cir. 1998); Saturn Distrib. Corp. v. Williams, 905 F.2d 719, 724-26 (4th Cir. 1990).

[35] *See* Prudential-Bache Securities, Inc. v. Garza, 848 S.W.2d 803 (Tex. App. 1993); Brennan v. King, 139 F.3d 258 (1st Cir. 1998) (presumption of arbitrability "is a weighty additive to state-law principles of contract construction").

[36] *See* Ferro Corp. v. Garrison Industries Inc., 142 F.3d 926 (6th Cir. 1998) ("join[ing] the long line of cases distinguishing Volt" out of existence). *But see* Allstar Homes, Inc. v. Waters, 711 So. 2d 924 (Ala. 1997) (missing the point).

[37] *See* RAU, *The UNCITRAL Model Law in State and Federal Courts: The Case of Waiver*, 6 AMER. REV. OF INT'l. ARB. 223, 228 & n.18, 261-279 (1995); NOS Communications, Inc. v. Robertson, 936 F. Supp. 761 (D. Colo. 1996).

unassailable proposition" that states "may establish the rules of procedure governing litigation in their own courts," even where the controversy is governed by substantive federal law.[38] This is of course the familiar "reverse-Erie" question: To what extent must a state abandon or adapt what would otherwise be considered its normal rules of "procedure" in order to give full effect to a federal right?[39]

The starting point is that the Supreme Court has not actually held that the Federal Arbitration Act is now in its entirety part of the law of the several states. The purported holding of the *Southland* line of cases is rather narrower—merely that states must respect the mandate of § 2 of the FAA, which makes agreements to arbitrate "valid, irrevocable, and enforceable." This is the core of what the Court has termed the "federal substantive law of arbitrability." By contrast, §§ 3 and 4 of the Act appear to speak only in terms of proceedings in federal district court. They are, in that respect, relics of the original conception of the FAA as a merely "procedural" statute.

While the Supreme Court has been curiously and consistently coy on the question of whether state courts are bound by §§ 3 and 4,[40] it seems obvious enough that these provisions exist to supply the remedial mechanisms necessary to make the core substantive mandate of § 2 effective. Once it is held that the states are bound by § 2 to treat arbitration agreements as enforceable, the suggestion that the remedy of specific performance is not necessary to vindicate the federal interest simply flies in the face of history—returning us to the era before modern arbitration statutes, when predispute arbitration clauses were enforceable only through the dubious means of actions for damages. In addition to the obligation to grant stays or compel arbitration, other provisions of §§ 3 and 4 may also call on states to align their procedures to some extent with the demands of federal arbitration policy. To say, for example, that courts "shall proceed summarily to the trial" of any issue concerning the making of the arbitration agreement may require applications to be heard under a state's local version of motion practice, or at least in some expeditious and summary hearing rather than in a plenary action.

---

[38] Felder v. Casey, 487 U.S. 131 (1988).

[39] *See id.* at 150-52 ("[f]ederal law takes state courts as it finds them only insofar as those courts employ rules that do not impose unnecessary burdens upon rights of recovery authorized by federal laws").

[40] RAU, *supra*, n. 7 at 245-46 & n.85.

Other aspects of §§ 3 and 4 may not, however, "dig into"[41] substantive rights in quite the same way. Section 4 provides for a jury determination of contested issues concerning the "making of the arbitration agreement." But a state may prefer that these issues be decided by the court.[42] To have a court rather than a jury pass on the existence of an arbitration agreement hardly appears to undermine or frustrate the arbitration process; moreover, a bench trial of the issue should not be expected to "frequently and predictably"[43] lead to different outcomes.[44] State rules denying a jury trial are certainly consistent both with the summary nature of the proceeding, and with the traditional treatment of these specific performance actions as equitable-and they can only result in making arbitration a speedier and more efficient process. After such an analysis it might be concluded that state law ought to govern on such matters, even where the parties themselves have not expressly chosen to adopt such law.

Other provisions of the FAA are also closely intertwined with the conduct of judicial proceedings, giving rise to similar "reverse-*Erie*" questions. Consider § 16, for example, which governs the appealability of trial-court orders dealing with arbitration. Some commentators take the position that § 16 "requires state courts to follow its dictates rather than their own interlocutory appeal rules."[45] This makes eminent sense in light of the pro-arbitration policies underlying the section-and in particular its apparent commitment to getting the parties into arbitration as expeditiously as possible. As a general matter, § 16 makes it clear that "orders favoring litigation over arbitration are immediately appealable whereas those which favor arbitration at the expense of litigation are not."[46]

---

[41] *See* Brown v. Western Ry. of Ala., 338 U.S. 294, 296 (1949).

[42] *See, e.g.*, Rosenthal v. Great Western Fin. Securities Corp., 58 Cal. Rptr. 2d 875 (Cal. 1996).

[43] Felder v. Casey, *supra*, n. 8 at 138.

[44] It is not particularly clear in any event what role the choice of a jury in § 4 was intended to play in the overall statutory scheme. For some reason it is only "the party alleged to be in default"—presumably the party who has "failed, neglected, or refused" to proceed with arbitration—who under § 4 is entitled to ask for a jury trial; the party "aggrieved" by such "failure, neglect, or refusal" has no equivalent right.

[45] MACNEIL, SPEIDEL, & STIPANOWICH, FEDERAL ARBITRATION LAW 10:49-50, 43.1.3.2 (1994); Berger Farms v. First Interstate Bank of Oregon, N.A., 939 P.2d 64 (Ore. App. 1997).

[46] United Offshore Co. v. Southern Deepwater Pipeline Co., 899 F.2d 405, 407 (5th Cir. 1990).

Unfortunately, the current case law in the states is not entirely in accord. Under the FAA, for example, trial court orders denying a stay of litigation in favor of arbitration are expressly made appealable. State law, however, may make no provision for the appeal of such orders. Must state courts nevertheless permit an interlocutory appeal in cases governed by the FAA? Some state courts have said no. One court, questioning whether Congress "can grant to this state appellate court jurisdiction over appeals which the [state] Legislature has not," found that it would "boggle the mind" if the substantive rights created by the FAA could become, in turn, a right "to obtain rewriting of procedural rules and statutes pertaining to the manner" in which a litigant proceeds through state courts.[47]

In the converse situation, we can find cases where state appellate courts will interfere immediately with a trial court's order "favorable" to arbitration—and not only in those rare circumstances where §16 would have permitted an appeal,[48] but also in the classic "embedded" proceedings where § 16 is quite clear that no interlocutory appeal would have been available.[49]

Teaching Old Dogmas New Tricks

Parties write their arbitration agreements against a well-established backdrop of private law-including contract law as well as agency and property law—to define their rights. Arbitration must be understood primarily through the lens of contract rather than of adjudication. It not only benefits from the same tolerance we extend to private contractual arrangements, but it is subject to the same limitations we commonly impose on such arrangements. And contract law, of course, is essentially state law; federal courts are rarely, if ever, called upon to develop a federal common law of private agreement.[50]

---

[47] Batton v. Green, 801 S.W.2d 923, 927, 930 (Tex. App. 1990); *see also* Jack B. Anglin Co., Inc. v. Tipps, 842 S.W.2d 266 (Tex. 1992).

[48] The extent of deviation from the FAA is minimized, however, where remedies alternative to appeal are provided—where, for example, a writ of mandamus is available to correct a trial court's "abuse of discretion" in refusing to compel arbitration or to stay litigation. Such writs are often granted despite the frequent warning that mandamus "is an extraordinary remedy and, obviously, should not be used to substitute for an interlocutory appeal where an interlocutory appeal is proscribed." *See generally* RAU & SHERMAN, *supra*, n. 4 at 345-49.

[49] *E.g.,* Freis v. Canales, 877 S.W.2d 283 (Tex. 1994).

[50] *E.g.,* Solis v. Evins, 951 S.W.2d 44 (Tex. App. 1997) (mandamus granted in defamation suit in which defendant successfully moved for a stay and for an order to

The Supreme Court has conceded that states may regulate arbitration clauses "under general contract law principles"[51]—that is, state law governing "issues concerning the validity, revocability, and enforceability of contracts generally."[52] So, for example, in deciding whether an arbitration agreement is binding on a nonsignatory,[53] or on a signatory who did not bother to read it,[54] or on one who alleges that it was a mere "preliminary agreement" not yet intended to be binding,[55] we would necessarily look to the ordinary contract law of the state whose law otherwise governs the transaction.

Even this enclave of state contract law, however, must be subject to continual policing to ensure that the federal interest in arbitration is not disserved. *Southland* can continue to have bite in all sorts of unexpected ways. For example, when a court attempts to determine whether a contract has been formed, it may well deem an arbitration clause to be a "material alteration" of an offer for the purposes of the Uniform Commercial Code's "battle of the forms" provisions-at least in industries where arbitration has not yet become a customary and expected means of dispute resolution.[56] But were a court to hold that arbitration is necessarily a per se "material alteration"-thereby preventing the arbitration clause from becoming part of the contract-that would be an impermissible presumption having the effect of undermining federal policy.[57]

The problem is that where contract doctrine calls for courts to engage in intensive, fact-oriented application of broad, unexceptional standards, it will be particularly hard to monitor state cases to ensure conformity

---

compel arbitration; the trial court's abuse of discretion "cannot be remedied on appeal, as the order compelling arbitration effectively foreclosed relator's right to appeal").

[51] One court has suggested that in cases governed by the New York Convention, a "federal law of contracts" applies. Kahn Lucas Lancaster, Inc. v. Lark Int'l Ltd., 1997 WL 458785 (S.D.N.Y.). This may reflect some confusion between the New York Convention and the Vienna Sales Convention—or a simple misunderstanding of the effect of 9 U.S.C. § 203.

[52] Allied-Bruce Terminix Cos., Inc. v. Dobson, 513 U.S. 265, 281 (1995).

[53] Perry v. Thomas, 482 U.S. 483, 492 n.9 (1987); *see also* First Options of Chicago, Inc. v. Kaplan, 514 U.S. 938, 944 (1995).

[54] *See, e.g.*, Thomson-CSF, S.A. v. American Arbitration Ass'n, 64 F.3d 773 (2d Cir. 1995) (surveying theories under which nonsignatories may be bound to arbitrate).

[55] *See, e.g.,* Randolph v. Green Tree Fin. Corp., 991 F. Supp. 1410 (M.D. Ala. 1997).

[56] *See, e.g.*, Banner Entertainment, Inc. v. Superior Court, 72 Cal. Rptr.2d 598 (Cal. App. 1998).

[57] UCC art. 2-207; Helen Whiting, Inc. v. Trojan Textile Corp., 121 N.E.2d 367 (N.Y. 1954) (taking judicial notice of the common practice of arbitration in the textile industry).

with federal law. State courts that have historically shown some animosity towards the enforcement of arbitration agreements may read the law of equitable estoppel narrowly so as to allow a party to avoid having to arbitrate with nonsignatories.[58] And courts that are uneasy about the use of arbitration in contracts of adhesion may manage to find that an agreement to arbitrate is not supported by consideration-even though an alternative analysis would readily be available.[59]

"Unconscionability" is another familiar doctrinal construct whose virtue lies precisely in its vagueness; it provides abundant opportunity for covert manipulation by a state court inclined not to enforce an arbitration agreement and ingenious enough to conjure up some ill-defined mixture of lack of sophistication, surprise, gross disparity in bargaining power, and "harsh or oppressive terms" lacking any "commercial justification."[60] Even so, it is astonishing that in this post-*Southland* era, one can still find an occasional state court obtuse (or ingenuous) enough to tip its hand and tell us that one element of unconscionability, justifying a refusal to order arbitration, is precisely that by agreeing to arbitrate a party waives his constitutionally-guaranteed rights to due process of law and trial by jury![61]

State Law as "Gap Filler"

One often hears it said that state arbitration law-despite *Southland* and its progeny—can still be utilized to "fill gaps" that are not addressed in what is after all a 73-year-old skeletal federal statute. This way of putting things is not really very satisfactory, for conceptually there can be no "gap" in a common-law system. A rich federal common law—

---

[58] Progressive Casualty Ins. Co. v. C.A. Reaseguradora Nacional de Venezuela, 991 F.2d 42 (2d Cir. 1993); *contra*, Avedon Engr'g, Inc. v. Seatex, 126 F.3d 1279 (10th Cir. 1997).

[59] *E.g.*, Isbell v. Southern Energy Homes, Inc., 708 So. 2d 571 (Ala. 1997); Stewart Title of Mobile, Inc. v. Montalvo, 709 So. 2d 1194 (Ala. 1998).

[60] *E.g.*, Gibson v. Neighborhood Health Clinics, Inc., 121 F.3d 1126 (7th Cir. 1997); Tenet Healthcare v. Cooper, 960 S.W.2d 286 (Tex. App. 1997). However, consideration for a promise to arbitrate might, on time-honored grounds, be found (a) in the stronger party's promise to be bound by the results of any arbitration (see Johnson v. Circuit City Stores Inc., 148 F.3d 373 (4th Cir. 1998)); (b) in the stronger party's promise to submit its own future claims to arbitration; (c) in other promises exchanged in the overall agreement between the parties; or (d) in employment cases, by the fact of continued employment made available to an at-will employee who agrees to an arbitration clause.

[61] *See* Stirlen v. Supercuts, Inc., 60 Cal. Rptr. 2d 138, 145, 152 (Cal. App. 1997); *see generally* MURRAY, RAU, & SHERMAN, PROCESSES OF DISPUTE RESOLUTION: THE ROLE OF LAWYERS 596-606 (2d ed. 1996).

what the Supreme Court prefers to call the federal substantive law of arbitrability-is being generated every day, by federal and state courts alike, as a means of spinning out all the implications of the 1925 federal statute. This is a task that is inextricably linked to the question of the proper interpretation of the statute itself. And the dimensions of the federally granted right to arbitrate must continue to be a matter of national concern, leading to a common law binding in state as well as federal courts.

So the notion of having recourse to state law to fill gaps in the federal scheme really amounts to just this: State law may occasionally be used to supply some background rules as to what the parties to the arbitration agreement are presumed to have intended. Default rules are always necessary in contracts, if only as a starting point for pre-dispute planning and drafting. But state default rules can hardly come into play of their own force, as regulatory law. Courts may resort to them, first, only by virtue of the parties' silence. Thus, in the frequent case where matters are already addressed by institutional rules, or by arbitral practice, the content of state law is simply irrelevant. Second, courts may look to state law only with the permission of federal law. Even if a uniform federal rule has not yet developed, the courts must still ask whether the state's background rule will "effectuate federal policy"[62] and whether it is a plausible candidate for incorporation into federal common law.[63]

In other words, as an alternative to fashioning a newly-minted uniform federal rule, federal courts may instead choose to borrow rules of state arbitration law—but only, in Justice Holmes' typically quotable phrase, as a "benevolent gratuity."[64] Presumably the Supreme Court meant nothing more than this when it said in the *Volt* case that the FAA cannot "reflect a congressional intent to occupy the entire field of arbitration."[65]

Here is an obvious example: A state may choose to assume that-in the absence of some agreement to the contrary—arbitrators in international cases routinely have the power to award attorneys' fees to the prevailing party. This choice diverges from the usual domestic

---

[62] Northcom, Ltd. v. James, 694 So. 2d 1329, 1338-39 (Ala. 1997).

[63] Textile Workers Union of Amer. v. Lincoln Mills of Ala., 353 U.S. 448, 457 (1957) (substantive law under the Taft-Hartley Act is federal law, "[b]ut state law, if compatible with the purpose of [the Act,] may be resorted to in order to find the rule that will best effectuate the federal policy").

[64] For an example of this analysis, in the context of a discussion of state rules on waiver, *see* Rau, *supra*, n. 7 at 268-79.

[65] Southern Pacific Co. v. Jensen, 244 U.S. 205, 220 (1917).

understanding-that is, the "American rule" on fees-but it would align the state with the general consensus in the practice of international commercial arbitration, and so should certainly be tolerated. Such a default rule increases the efficacy of arbitration awards by extending to claims for attorneys' fees the same presumption of arbitrability that is routinely applied in assessing arbitral competence to hear any other type of claim, including a claim for punitive damages.[66]

Occasionally the silence of the FAA may permit state law to supply other presumptions as well-for example, an inference that the parties were willing to consolidate related arbitrations-although the well-established federal common law to the contrary makes this seem much more doubtful.[67]

Conclusion

It is increasingly common these days to find cases in which courts indulge in lengthy, solemn, ritual inquiries into whether federal or state law is to govern, and then belatedly concede—often in a footnote—that after all, the question makes "no perceptible difference" to the result.[68] In view of the developments sketched here, it may well be asked whether attention to the reform of state arbitration law—which was indeed an important concern before the imperialist expansion of federal substantive law—is really worth the candle. Certain well-recognized areas of traditionally intense state interest of course remain. For example, in the McCarran-Ferguson Act, Congress immunized state regulation of the insurance industry from the effects of FAA preemption.[69] But in the run-of-the-mill case, the role of state law in arbitration practice can only be termed marginal[70]—and, as federal common law is spun out still further, that role can only diminish.

---

[66] Volt Information Sciences, Inc. v. Board of Trustees of Leland Stanford Jr. Univ., 489 U.S. 468, 477 (1989).

[67] Seeing this as an application of the obligatory "presumption of arbitrability" explains why cases like *PaineWebber Inc. v. Bybyk*, 81 F.3d 1193 (2d Cir. 1996) are correct—and why cases like *Walker v. Warren*, 1997 WL 572936 (Mass. Super.) are wrong.

[68] *See, e.g.*, New England Energy Inc. v. Keystone Shipping Co., 855 F.2d 1 (1st Cir. 1988); *see generally* RAU & SHERMAN, *Tradition and Innovation in International Arbitration Procedure*, 30 TEX. INT'L L.J. 89, 112-18 (1995).

[69] *E.g.*, Ford v. NYLCare Health Plans of the Gulf Coast, Inc., 141 F.3d 243, 250 n.7 (5th Cir. 1998).

[70] *Compare* Friday v. Trinity Universal of Kan., 939 P.2d 869 (Kan. 1997) (exclusion of "contracts of insurance" from state arbitration statute is not preempted thanks to the McCarran-Ferguson Act), *with* Little v. Allstate Ins. Co., 705 A.2d 538 (Vt. 1997) (similar statute preempted by FAA).

CHAPTER ELEVEN

JUDICIAL REVIEW OF ARBITRATION

I. A Discussion in Two-Parts of Judicial Review of Arbitration

PART I

Contractual Expansion & Limitation of Judicial Review of Arbitral Awards

by Kenneth M. Curtin[*]

If arbitration is indeed a creature of contract, does it mean that parties should be able to provide for either an expansion or a limitation of judicial review of arbitration awards in their contracts? The following article is a two-part discussion by Kenneth Curtin of cases which show how some parties have tried to do just that, sometimes directly contradicting the goals of the Federal Arbitration Act and the New York Convention, both of which limit judicial review of arbitral awards.

As the cost and delay of litigation in national courts continue to rise, parties contemplating a contractual relationship have sought alternative methods of dispute resolution. One of the most prevalent techniques of alternative dispute resolution is arbitration. In fact, in recent decades, a profusion of organizations have sprung into being specializing in both national and international arbitration.[1] Different countries have also encouraged the use of arbitration by passing legislation recognizing, both

---

[*] The author is a partner at Ruden, McCloskey, Smith, Schuster & Russell, P.A. in West Palm Beach, Florida. He specializes in complex commercial and construction litigation in state and federal courts and in arbitration and other ADR proceedings. Curtin received a B.A. magna cum laude from University of South Florida, a J.D. from University of Florida College of Law, and an M.B.A. from Florida Atlantic University. This article was originally published in the Ohio State Journal on Dispute Resolution, vol. 15 (2000).

[1] Many of these arbitral organizations, such as the International Chamber of Commerce and the American Arbitration Association, located in Paris and New York respectively, were formed many decades ago.

nationally and internationally, the enforceability of agreements to arbitrate and any corresponding arbitral awards. Furthermore, national courts have encouraged the use of arbitration by liberally interpreting these national and international accords in favor of arbitration.

Judicial Review of Arbitral Awards

Traditionally, national courts have intervened in arbitral proceedings in two situations. First, at the onset of arbitration to determine whether the agreement to arbitrate is valid and enforceable, or, in other words, whether the issue itself is arbitrable or whether it concerns an area where public policy dictates that all such disputes be resolved by the courts. Second, at the end of an arbitration, when a court is asked to enforce an arbitral award and where the court reviews the award to assure that the award's enforcement will not violate any procedural due process or other public policy concerns. As arbitration has gained acceptance, both nationally and internationally, the United States and other countries have passed legislation to enforce both agreements to arbitrate and arbitral awards.

In the U.S., the Congress enacted the Federal Arbitration Act (FAA) in 1925.[2] The expressed intention of the FAA was to reverse past judicial animosity towards arbitration and "place arbitration agreements upon the same footing as other contracts."[3] On an international scale, most of the world's leading trading nations, including the U.S., have acceded to the New York Convention on the Recognition and Enforcement of Foreign Arbitral Awards (New York Convention).[4] The FAA and the New York Convention reversed the traditional judicial hostility towards arbitration, and succeeded in transforming the U.S. into an arbitration-friendly jurisdiction. Today, American courts routinely validate and enforce arbitral agreements, even though they may implicate fundamental issues of deeply held public policy, such as securities violations,[5] RICO

---

[2] Federal Arbitration Act. 9 U.S.C. § 1 et seq. (1995).

[3] H.R. Rep. No. 96, 68th Cong., 1st Sess., pt. 1, at 2 (1924). *See* United States Asphalt Refining Co. v. Trinidad lake Petroleum Co., 229 F. 1006, 1010-11 (S.D.N.Y. 1915) for an example of the early American judicial hostility towards arbitration.

[4] The United Nations Convention on the Recognition and Enforcement of Foreign Arbitral Awards, June 10, 1958, 21 U.S.T. 2517 (codified as amended at 9 U.S.C. § 201-08 (1995)).

[5] Scherk v. Alberto-Culver Co., 417 U.S. 506 (1974); Rodriguez de Quijas v. Shearson American Express, 490 U.S. 477 (1989), *overruling,* Wilko v. Swan, 346 U.S. 497 (1953).

claims,[6] anti-trust causes of action,[7] employment discrimination,[8] and civil rights cases,[9] to name just a few.[10]

However, judicial recognition of arbitral agreements is only the first step; courts still need to recognize and enforce corresponding awards by arbitrators. Long before the enactment of either the FAA or the New York Convention, the U.S. Supreme Court held that arbitral awards should be enforced to assure the quick settlement of disputes and encourage the use of arbitration as an alternative dispute resolution technique.[11] In keeping with this tradition, both the FAA and the New York Convention specifically hold that enforcement of arbitral awards should be routinely granted and upheld.[12] Nonetheless, the FAA and the New York Convention both contain similar "laundry lists" of exceptions by which a court may vacate an arbitral award.[13] These exceptions include various safeguards to assure that minimum levels of procedural and substantive due process are observed in arbitral proceedings,[14] a public policy exception to enforcement,[15] and, in the U.S., a judicially created exception to enforcement where an award is rendered in "manifest disregard" of the law.[16]

---

[6] Shearson American Express, Inc. v. McMahon, 482 U.S. 220 (1987).

[7] Mitsubishi Motors Corp. v. Soler Chrysler-Plymouth, Inc., 471 U.S. 614 (1985), *reversing* American Safety Equipment Corp. v. J.P. Maguire & Co., 391 F.2d 821 (9th Cir. 1968).

[8] Gilmer v. Interstate/Johnson Lane Corp., 500 U.S. 20 (1991).

[9] Feinberg v. Bear, Stearns & Co., 1991 WL 79309 (S.D.N.Y. 1991). See G. Richard Shell, ERISA and Other Federal Employment Statutes: When is Commercial Arbitration an 'Adequate Substitute' for the Courts? 68 TEX. L. REV. 509, 569-70 (1990).

[10] *See* Bird v. Shearson Lehman American Express, Inc., 926 F.2d 116 (2d Cir. 1991); and Pritzker v. Merrill Lynch, Pierce, Fenner & Smith, Inc., 7 F.3d 1110 (3d Cir. 1993); Genesco, Inc. v. Kakiuchi & Co., 815 F.2d 840 (2d Cir. 1987).

[11] In *Burchell v. Marsh*, 58 U.S. 144, 349 (1854), the U.S. Supreme Court stated:
If the award is within the submission and contains the honest decision of the arbitrators, after a full and fair hearing of the parties, a court of equity will not set it aside for error, either in law or fact. A contrary course would be a substitution of the judgment of the chancellor in place of the judges chosen by the parties and would make an award the commencement, not the end, of litigation.

[12] Federal Arbitration Act, § 2 & § 9: New York Convention art. 11 & 111.

[13] The grounds for vacating an arbitral award under the FAA are located in Article 10 and include: where the award was procured by corruption, fraud or undue means (Article 10(a)); evidence of arbitrator impartiality or corruption (Article 10(b)); arbitrator misconduct which prejudices the rights of the parties (Article 10(c)); and, where the arbitrators exceeded their powers (Article 10(d)).

[14] *See infra* part A.

[15] *See infra* part B.

[16] *See infra* part C.

A. Procedural and Substantive Exceptions to Award Enforcement

The FAA and the New York Convention both contain exceptions to an arbitral award's enforcement to assure that a certain level of procedural and substantive due process is observed in the arbitral proceedings. A commonly asserted exception by a party attempting to annul an arbitral award is that the arbitrators "exceeded their powers,"[17] or, phrased differently, that the award dealt with issues beyond the scope of the agreement to arbitrate.[18] This exception is rarely successfully employed for several reasons. First, the use of standardized arbitration clauses in commercial contracts provides assurance that the scope of an arbitral clause will encompass almost every conceivable issue.[19] Second, courts rarely second-guess and overrule an arbitrator's construction of an agreement to arbitrate, due to the fact that there exists a judicially created "powerful presumption" that the arbitrators acted within their powers.[20] Third, courts liberally construe agreements to arbitrate to include most issues within their scope, even when the scope of an agreement is questionable.[21]

Other due process concerns focus on the inability or difficulty of the arbitral process to subpoena witnesses or conduct discovery on the same level as that of a national court. Nonetheless, American courts have stated that a party, by agreeing to arbitrate, relinquishes its right to subpoena witnesses and other rights that it may have had in court in favor of arbitration with all of its "advantages and drawbacks."[22] Therefore, the mere inability to produce witnesses is not sufficiently violative of a party's due process rights to avoid enforcement of a corresponding arbitral award. Courts are likewise reluctant to enjoin the

---

[17] FAA, § 10(a)(4).

[18] New York Convention, art. V(1)(c).

[19] Various international arbitration organizations have promulgated standard arbitration clauses that are internationally recognized as enveloping most, if not all, issues of litigation within their scope. See ICC Rules of Conciliation and Arbitration, Standard ICC arbitration Clause (1988); American Arbitration Association International Arbitration Rules, Model Arbitration Clauses (1993); UNCITRAL Arbitration Rules, Model Arbitration Clauses (1977).

[20] Parsons & Whittemore Overseas Co. v. Societe Generale de l'Industrie du Papier, 508 F.2d 969, (2d Cir. 1974); Abraham v. Shigur Express Ltd., No. 91 Civ. 1238 (SWK), 1991 US Dist. Lexis 12267, at * 13-14 (S.D.N.Y. Sept. 3, 1991).

[21] In the U.S., see Moses H. Cone Hospital v. Mercury Construction Corp., 460 U.S. 1, 24-25 (1983). In England, see Ulysses Compania Naviera SA v. Huntingdon Petroleum Services Ltd., 1 Lloyd's Rep. 160 (Q.B. Com. Ct. 1990).

[22] *Parsons*, 508 F.2d at 975; Gilmer v. Interstate/Johnson Lane Corp., 500 U.S. 20, 31 (1991).

enforcement of an arbitral award even on the grounds of fraud, holding that the fraud must not have been discoverable upon the exercise of due diligence prior to the arbitration and must relate to a material issue.[23] Moreover, a party contending that an award should not be enforced due to a procedural deficiency, must first demonstrate that the right to contest the procedural deficiency was preserved during the arbitral proceeding. In other words, the party must show that the procedural deficiency was presented to the arbitral tribunal and ignored in order to employ the deficiency as an argument for avoiding enforcement of the award.[24]

The FAA and the New York Convention also provide exceptions to the enforcement of an award on the basis of party incapacity, illegality of the arbitral agreement, and arbitrator corruption or fraud.[25] These exceptions would prevent even the enforcement of a judicial award. However, courts seldom deny the enforcement of an award on these bases. This is mainly due to the fact that these exceptions deal with extreme situations that rarely manifest themselves. Nevertheless, even when arbitrator corruption or fraud is suspected, the party opposing the award must corroborate evident partiality by focusing on the relationship between the arbitrators and the other party, such as economic or personal ties between the two.[26] Arbitrator corruption or fraud cannot be simply inferred from the fact that the arbitrator's findings were unsupported by the weight of the evidence.[27]

Parties opposing an arbitral award have attempted to annul enforcement on the basis that the arbitration agreement constituted a contract of adhesion. Courts have affirmatively and categorically denied these attempts to describe arbitral agreements as contracts of adhesion.[28] Finally, parties opposing an arbitral award have attempted to re-employ the non-arbitrability defense by reasserting at the award enforcement

---

[23] National Oil Corp. v. Libyan Sun Oil Co., 733 F. Supp. 800, 814 (D. Del. 1990); see LaFarge Conseils et Etudes v. Kaiser Cement & Gypsum Corp., 791 F.2d 1334, 1338 (9th Cir. 1986).

[24] International Std. Elec. Corp. v. Bridas Sociedad Anonima Petrolera, 745 F. Supp. 172, 180 (S.D.N.Y.1990).

[25] Federal Arbitration Act, §10(a)(1)(2); New York Convention, art. V(l)(a).

[26] Sidarma Societa Italiana Di Armamento Spa, Venice v. Holt Marine Industries, Inc., 515 F. Supp. 1302, 1306 (S.D.N.Y. 1981), aff'd, 681 F.2d 802 (2d Cir. 1981).

[27] Southwind Shipping Co. v. S/T STOIC. 709 F. Supp. 9. 83 (S.D.N.Y. 1989).

[28] Mitsubishi Motors Corp. v. Soler Chrysler-Plymouth, Inc., 473 U.S. 614, 632-33 (1985); David L. Threlkeld & Co. v. Metallgesellschaft Ltd., 923 F.2d 745, 249 (2d Cir. 1991); Vimar Seguros y Reaseguros v. M/V Sky Reefer, No. 91-13345 WF, 1993 U.S. Dist. Lexis 5672, at *8-13 (D. Mass. Apr. 19, 1993); see also Vimar Seguros Y Reaseguros v. M/V Sky Reefer, 115 S. Ct. 2322, 2325 (1995).

stage that a court should refuse enforcement because the underlying issue was non-arbitrable at the outset.[29] In reality, the non-arbitrability exception is rarely asserted.[30] Moreover, recent case law in the U.S. Supreme Court in the last few decades has further regulated the non-arbitrability exception to a mere academic oddity.[31] In fact, some commentators suggest that American courts should cease altogether to recognize the non-arbitrability defense in award enforcement proceedings.[32]

The procedural and substantive due process exceptions to award enforcement, while frequently pled, are rarely successful. The non-arbitrability of subject matter exception is merely an attempt to relitigate the arbitrability question, which should properly be litigated, if at all, before the arbitration begins and in which the U.S. Supreme Court has consistently found in favor of arbitration. The other due process exceptions, such as scope of the arbitral clause, discovery deficiencies, and arbitrator corruption or fraud arise either from poorly worded arbitration agreements or from problems in the arbitral process. As arbitration has become more accepted and employed, both arbitral clauses and the arbitral process have improved, limiting the need of these exceptions. However, the due process exceptions are not the only exceptions to enforcement. On the contrary, the most frequently employed and litigated enforcement exception is the public policy exception, which is complicated by the various choices of law open to parties.

B. *The Public Policy Exception to Award Enforcement*

The New York Convention and the FAA both dictate that an enforcing court may [33] refuse to recognize or enforce an arbitral award if enforcement of such an award would be contrary to the public policy of the enforcing nation.[34] The public policy exception to award enforcement is the most widely asserted exception to award enforcement, especially in respect to foreign arbitral awards or awards based on foreign law. In fact,

---

[29] New York Convention, art. V(2)(a).
[30] *Parsons*, 508 F.2d at 975.
[31] *Supra*, notes 5-10, and accompanying text.
[32] Heather R. Evans, *The Nonarbitrability of Subject Matter Defense to Enforcement of Foreign Judicial Arbitral Awards in the United States Federal Courts*, 21 N.Y.U.J. INT'L. L. & POL. 329, 352 (1989).
[33] It should be noted that even the public policy exception to enforcement is discretionary in nature.
[34] FAA, § 10; New York Convention, art. V(2)(b).

the U.S. Supreme Court, on numerous occasions, has specifically reserved the right at the award-enforcement stage to review an award to assure that the combination of a choice-of-forum and choice-of-law clauses in an arbitration agreement did not serve to defeat statutorily protected rights in violation of public policy.[35]

The public policy exception is only to be employed where enforcement would violate a forum State's "most basic notions of morality and justice."[36] This restricted interpretation of the public policy exception is warranted in order to safeguard the pro-arbitration policies of the New York Convention and the FAA and to prevent the creation of a public policy loophole encompassing not only foreign awards being enforced in the U.S., but also American awards being enforced abroad.[37] The public policy exception is further limited by the nature of the dispute and the type of public policy involved. The nature of the transaction and the nationality of the parties involved determine which one of three types of public policy are relevant: domestic, international, or transnational public policy. The standard of review for annulling an arbitral award differs depending on which type of public policy is applicable.

1. Domestic Public Policy

In a domestic arbitration, i.e., an arbitration involving only one nation and citizens of only that one nation, an enforcing court needs only to take cognizance of national public policy notions. The standard of review is whether the arbitral award would violate local standards of morality and justice. Since the underlying transaction only concerns one nation, the enforcing court only needs to consider that nation's public policy, which is usually its own notions of public policy. In the U.S., domestic public policy are those notions that would vitiate any contractual relationship whether or not the contract contained an agreement to arbitrate. In other words, the outside limit of domestic public policy is the parties' freedom of contract under the interested nation's laws.[38]

---

[35] Mitsubishi Motors Corp. v. Soler Chrysler-Plymouth, Inc., 473 U.S. 614, 637 n.19 (1985); Vimar Seguros Y Reaseguros v. M/V Sky Reefer, 115 S. Ct. 2322, 2330 (1995).

[36] Parsons & Whittemore Overseas Co. v. Societe Generale de l'Industrie du Papier, 508 F.2d 969, 974 (2d Cir. 1974).

[37] *Id.* at 973-74; see also Brandeis Intsel Ltd. v. Calabrian Chems. Corp., 656 F. Supp. 160, 167 (S.D.N.Y. 1987).

[38] Mark A. Buchanan, *Public Policy and International Commercial Arbitration*, 26 ANT. BUS. L.J. 511, 513 (1988).

2. International Public Policy

In an international arbitration, i.e., an arbitration involving two or more nations and citizens of two or more nations, an enforcing court needs to take cognizance not only of its own public policy, but also the public policy of other interested nations and the special needs of international commerce. Consequently, international public policy is those national public policy concerns that should also be applied in an international context.[39] One nation's public policy should only prevail if warranted by the nature of the dispute, statute, or public policy objective involved, which should be determined by comparing the connections existing between the case at hand and each of the nations involved in the dispute.[40] In other words, international public policy is a balancing of the interests between the various nations involved and the needs of international commerce for an equitable resolution of international disputes.

Almost every major trading nation, either explicitly or by implication, considers and employs international public policy when deciding whether to enforce a foreign arbitral award. For example, French jurisprudence specifically delineates between domestic and international public policy.[41] On the other hand, American jurisprudence views the international aspect of an arbitration as a mitigating factor in deciding whether an award is enforceable.[42] No matter whether a court specifically differentiates between national and international public policy, it is clear that annulling an international arbitral award on public policy grounds is extremely difficult. Only where a foreign arbitral forum and foreign choice-of-law clause "operated in tandem as a prospective waiver of a party's right to pursue statutory remedies" will a court condemn the award as against public policy.[43]

---

[39] *Id.* at 514.

[40] Andreas Bucher, International Arbitration in Switzerland 105 (1989).

[41] *See* Societe Labinal v. Societes Mors et Westland Aerospace, 4 REVUE DE L'ARBITRAGE 645, 650 (1993); Societe Almira Films v. Pierrel es Quai, 4 *Revue de l'Arbitrage* 711, 714-15 (1989).

[42] *See* Mitsubishi Motors Corp. v. Soler Chrysler-Plymouth, Inc., 473 U.S. 614, 629 (1985); Parsons & Whittemore Overseas Co. v. Société Générale de l'Industrie du Papier, 508 F.2d 969, 974 (2d Cir. 1974); Antco Shipping Co. v. Siderrnar, 417 F. Supp. 207, 216-17 (S.D.N.Y. 1976); National Oil Corp. v. Libyan Sun Oil Co., 733 F. Supp. 800, 819-20 (D. Del. 1990).

[43] It should be noted that while this black letter law is frequently quoted, rarely do courts ever find that the combination of a foreign choice-of-forum and choice-of-law

3. Transnational Public Policy

The third type of public policy considered by national courts in the recognition and enforcement of arbitral awards is transnational public policy. Transnational public policy represents the "international consensus as to universal standards of accepted norms of conduct that must always apply and provide limitations to public as well as private international relationships and transactions."[44] A national court need only consider transnational public policy when the arbitration is both international in scope and subject to the lex mercatoria.

The *lex mercatoria*, or "law merchant," is a governing law that has no direct connection to any national law, but rather represents a combination of "rules of law which are common to all or most of the States engaged in international trade."[45] The *lex mercatoria* is often selected as a governing law by parties to an international agreement as a method to avoid being subjected to an undesirable foreign law when the parties cannot mutually decide upon another governing law. This situation often arises where one of the parties is a state or state-dominated enterprise, but is not necessarily limited to those circumstances.[46] The use of the *lex mercatoria* is highly controversial and many have even questioned its very existence.[47] However, for every detractor, there are those who steadfastly believe in the existence of the *lex mercatoria*,[48] and, in fact, it has been employed as the governing law in various international contracts.[49] The major problem hampering the use of the *lex mercatoria* in international arbitration is the uncertainty

---

clauses have operated to waive a party's statutory rights to the extent warranting denial of enforcement of an arbitral award.

[44] Buchanan *supra* note 38, at 511.

[45] Ole Lando, *The Lex Mercatoria in International Commercial Arbitration*, 34 INT'L & COMP. L.Q. 747 747 (1985); Andreas F. Lowenfeld, *Lex Mercatoria: An Arbitrator's View*, 6 ARB. INT'L 133 (1990); Buchanan, *supra* note 38, at 511.

[46] Bucher, *supra* note 40, at 106.

[47] F.A. Mann, *England Rejects Delocalized Contracts and Arbitration*, 33 INT'L & COMP. L.Q. 193, 196-97 (1984); Georges R. Delaume, *Comparative Analysis as a Basis of Law in State Contracts. The Myth of the Lex Mercatoria*, 63 TUL. L. REV. 575 (1989); Keith Highet, *The Enigma of the Lex Mercatoria*, 63 TUL. L. REV. 613 (1989).

[48] Berthold Goldman, *The Applicable Law: General Princples of Law-The Lex Mercatoria*, in CONTEMPORARY PROBLEMS IN INTERNATIONAL ARBITRATION 113 (Julian D.N. Lew ed., 1987).

[49] *See* Eagle Star Insurance Co. v. Yuval Insurance Co., 1 Llyod's Rep. 357 (C.A. 1978); Deutsche Schachtbau- und Tiefbohrgesellschaft v. Ras Al Khaimah National Oil Co., 2 All E.R. 769 (C.A. 1987); Channel Tunnel Group Ltd. v. Balfour Beatty Construction Ltd., 1 All E.R. 664 (H.L. 1993).

over its exact definition and parameters. Notwithstanding this uncertainty, it is clear that the lex mercatoria does exist, and increasingly international treaties, model laws, and private organizations specializing in codifying international trade norms are continuing to diminish this uncertainty by formulating and elucidating generally accepted norms of commercial trade.

A court reviewing an international arbitral award based on the lex mercatoria should apply fundamental general principles of law without inquiring whether the dispute has any relationship to a particular State.[50] In this way, transnational public policy is differentiated from international public policy, where a reviewing court must consider the public policy of all interested States. Those transnational principles comprising the *lex mercatoria* originate from the "international community of States," and, therefore, must be respected as international obligations and remain independent from any relationship the particular case might have to one State or another.[51]

C. The "Manifest Disregard of the Law" Exception to Award Enforcement

The statutory exceptions to award enforcement enunciated in the FAA and the New York Convention, while frequently asserted by parties attempting to avoid enforcement of an arbitral award, are not the only exceptions to award enforcement. In American jurisprudence, there exists a nonstatutory exception to an arbitrator's award for those situations in which an award is deemed in "manifest disregard of the law."

As a general rule, an arbitral award cannot be set aside for errors in law or fact by the arbitrators. The Supreme Court of the United States, long before the drafting of either the FAA or the New York Convention, held that if an arbitral award is within the submission of the arbitrators, a court "will not set it aside for error, either in law or fact."[52] Despite this steadfast refusal to recognize errors of law or fact as a basis for denying enforcement of an award, parties have attempted to circumvent the Supreme Court and argue that awards in "manifest disregard of the law" should not be enforced. The "manifest disregard" exception stems from

---

[50] Bucher, *supra*, note 40, at 120.
[51] *Id.* at 121.
[52] Burchell v. Marsh, 58 U.S. 344, 349 (1854); *supra*, note 11; United States Paperworkers Int'l Union, AFL-CIO v. Misco, Inc., 484 U.S. 29 36 (1987).

the Supreme Court case of *Wilko v. Swan*,[53] in which the Supreme Court held a domestic dispute involving the Securities Act of 1933 was not arbitrable.

In *Wilko*, the Court stated that "interpretations of the law by the arbitrators in contrast to manifest disregard are not subject, in the federal courts, to judicial review for error...."[54] In spite of the fact that the Supreme Court subsequently overruled the *Wilko* Court,[55] parties alleging that an arbitrator erred in a matter of law have expanded the language of *Wilko* into a non-statutory exception to award enforcement.[56]

The "manifest disregard" exception is conservatively construed and rarely employed. An arbitrator must not only appreciate the existence of a clearly governing and understandable legal principle, but also decide to ignore it in order for a corresponding award to be in manifest disregard of the law.[57] This conservative application of the "manifest disregard" exception has been consistently followed by American courts.[58] In fact, many courts seriously question whether the "manifest disregard" exception really exists, and others specifically limit this judicial exception to domestic arbitrations, holding that in international arbitrations under the New York Convention, no such exception exists.[59] Therefore, while courts may cite and consider the "manifest disregard" exception to award enforcement, in reality, the exception is little more than an historical oddity which is rarely, if ever, successfully asserted.[60] Finally, the American viewpoint that arbitrators need not explain their reasoning further limits the "manifest disregard" exception, because

---

[53] 346 U.S. 497 (1953).

[54] *Id.* at 436.

[55] At first, the Supreme Court merely distinguished *Wilko*, a domestic case, from international cases, holding that international arbitrations involving securities disputes were arbitral, while domestic cases were non-arbitral.

[56] *See* Merrill Lynch Pierce & Smith, Inc. v. Bobker, 808 F.2d 930, 933 (2d Cir. 1986).

[57] Siegel v. Titan Industrial Corp., 779 F.2d 891, 893 (2d Cir. 1985).

[58] Parsons & Whittemore Overseas Co. v. Societe Generale de l'Industrie du Papier, 508 F.2d 969, 977 (2d Cir. 1964); Southwind Shipping Co. v. S/T STOIC, 709 F. Supp. 79, 83 (S.D.N.Y. 1989); ExportEhleb v. Maistros Corp., 790 F. Supp. 70, 74 (S.D.N.Y. 1992).

[59] Parsons, 508 F.2d at 977; Brandeis Intsel Ltd. v. Calabrian Chems. Corp., 656 F. Supp. 160, 167 (S.D.N.Y. 1987); Abraham v. Shigur Express Ltd., No. 91 Civ. 123g (SWK), 1991 US Dist. Lexis 12267, at *10 (S.D.N.Y. Sept. 3, 1991); Barvati v. Josephthal, Lyon & Ross, Incorp., 28 F.3d 704, 706 (7th Cir. 1994).

[60] *See* Montes v. Shearson Lehman Brothers, Inc., 128 F.3d 1456 (11th Cir. 1997); see also Daniel Blonsky, *The 11th Circuit Puts a Major New Dent in the Armor Surrounding Arbitration Awards*, 72 FL. BAR J. 74 (1988).

without a written opinion it is almost impossible to determine whether an arbitrator understood a legal principle, but ignored it.[61]

The passage of the FAA and the New York Convention and corresponding strict judicial interpretation of their provisions has helped to advance the use of international arbitration by assuring that arbitral awards are recognized and enforced by national courts. Despite the success, or perhaps because of the success, of the FAA and the New York Convention, parties have attempted to both contractually limit and expand judicial review of arbitral awards. Such attempts have met with mixed success for a variety of reasons.

PART II

Contractual Expansion & Limitation of Judicial Review of Arbitral Awards

by Kenneth M. Curtin

The conclusion of this two-part discussion examines various court decisions and their implications lead the author to propose that a "strict, unguided adherence to the principle of freedom of contract needs to be tempered with a respect for the arbitration process."

Contractual Expansion and Limitation of Judicial Review

Parties agree to arbitrate disputes for several reasons. For instance, in international agreements, arbitration is considered a neutral forum when parties cannot agree on which nation's courts should have jurisdiction over a dispute. Arbitration is also generally considered less time consuming and expensive than litigation. Further, in arbitral proceedings, parties, to a certain extent, can control the makeup of the arbitral panel, thereby employing arbitrators who possess knowledge and expertise in certain areas of the law or business community.[62] The advantages of arbitration are united in a common thread, namely, in order to benefit from these advantages, any corresponding arbitral award needs to be recognized and enforced by national courts. The FAA, on a national

---

[61] Advest, Inc. v. McCarthy, 914 F.2d 6, 10 (lst Cir. 1990); Sobel v. Hertz, Warner & Co., 469 F.2d 1211, 1214 (2d Cir. 1992).

[62] *See* Robert Donald Fischer & Roger S. Haydock, *International Commercial Disputes: Drafting an Enforceable Arbitration Agreement*, 21 WM. MITCHELL L. REV. 941, 947-56 (1996).

scale, and the New York Convention, on an international scale, have gone a long way toward unifying arbitration law and assuring the enforceability of awards. However, in some instances, parties have attempted to contractually alter the effect of the FAA and the New York Convention by either expanding or limiting judicial review of arbitral awards.

A. *Contractual Expansion of Judicial Review*

The standard of judicial review under the FAA and the New York Convention, as discussed above, is extremely limited. The effect of this limited judicial review is that the vast majority of arbitral awards are recognized and enforced as a matter of course not only in American courts, but also around the world. In this regard, parties have attempted to contractually enlarge the judicial role in reviewing arbitral awards beyond that contemplated by the FAA and the New York Convention. These attempts have met with mixed results—some being enforced on the theory of freedom of contract and others being denied on the basis of preserving the integrity of the arbitral process.

1. *The Freedom of Contract Viewpoint*

In *Gateway Technologies Inc. v. MCI Telecommunications Corp.*,[63] the Fifth Circuit held that the FAA does not prohibit parties who voluntarily agree to arbitration from providing contractually for a more expansive judicial review of an award than the default standard provided in the FAA. In *Gateway*, MCI, after successfully bidding on a government contract to supply telephone service to state inmates, subcontracted with Gateway to furnish, install, and maintain all the equipment necessary to provide automated collect calls.[64] The subcontract agreement contained an arbitration clause providing that in the event of any disputes, the parties agree to binding arbitration, "except that errors of law shall be subject to appeal."[65]

A dispute arose between the parties with MCI contending that the Gateway automated system design was improperly completing many collect calls and Gateway responded by alleging that MCI merely wished to integrate the Gateway system into its own, thereby realizing a significant profit.[66] Eventually, MCI integrated the two systems and

---

[63] 64 F.3d 933 (5th Cir. 1995).
[64] *Id.* at 995.
[65] *Id.*
[66] *Id.* at 995 n.2.

terminated its contract with Gateway. The dispute was submitted to arbitration and the arbitrator found that MCI had breached its contractual duty to negotiate in good faith and awarded actual as well as punitive damages to Gateway.[67] The United States District Court for the Northern District of Texas confirmed the arbitral award, refusing to review the award under a strict "errors of law" analysis in deference to the federal policy favoring arbitration.[68] MCI appealed arguing that the court erred in not reviewing the award for "errors of law" in accordance with the parties' agreement to arbitrate disputes.

The Fifth Circuit held that such a contractual modification expanding the court's power to review an arbitral award was acceptable, because arbitration is a creature of contract.[69] The Appeals Court reasoned that the public policy purpose of the FAA was to ensure that private agreements to arbitrate are enforced according to their terms, and that the FAA's pro-arbitration policy does not operate without regard to the wishes of the contracting parties.[70] The Appeals Court rejected the District Court's unwillingness to enforce the contract because "the parties have sacrificed the simplicity, informality, and expedition of arbitration on the altar of appellate review."[71] While conceding that the parties' agreement to expand judicial review may not have been "prudent," the Appeals Court reasoned that federal arbitration policy demanded that the court conduct its review according to the terms of the arbitration contract.[72]

The Fifth Circuit in *Gateway* relied upon several U.S. Supreme Court decisions in which the Court upheld a party's right to select the procedural rules that will govern an arbitration.[73] However, Gateway did not concern the selection of procedural rules governing the arbitral process, but rather concerned the judicial enforcement of a corresponding award. Nonetheless, the decision in *Gateway* is not without precedent. Other federal and state courts have upheld the contractual expansion of judicial review over arbitral awards in substantially the same

---

[67] *Id.* at 996.
[68] *Id.*
[69] *Id.*
[70] *Id.* at 996-97.
[71] *Id.* at 997.
[72] *Id.*
[73] *See* Volt Information Sciences, Inc. v. Board of Trustees of Leland Stanford Junior Univ., 489 U.S. 468, 469 (1989); Allied-Bruce Terminix Companies. Inc. v. Dobson, 115 S. Ct. 834 (1995).

circumstances.[74] On the other hand, the Fifth Circuit decision in *Gateway* was not the end of the debate.

2. Preserving the Integrity of the Arbitral Process

In *LaPine Technology Corp. v. Kyocera Corp.*,[75] the District Court for the Northern District of California held that while parties may contract freely with respect to the manner in which they arbitrate their disputes, they may not by agreement expand the provisions for judicial review contained in the FAA. *LaPine* concerned the enforceability of an arbitral award conducted before a panel of the International Court of Arbitration of the International Chamber of Commerce.[76] The underlying dispute concerned an agreement between LaPine Technology Corporation (LaPine), Kyocera Corporation (Kyocera), and Prudential Capital and Investment Services, Inc. (Prudential). The agreement provided for the design, manufacture, and marketing of a computer disk drive, whereby LaPine was to design and market the product, Prudential was to finance the product, and Kyocera was to actually manufacture the disk drive.[77]

The project ran into immediate financial problems and a complicated reorganization of the parties' agreement commenced.[78] Eventually, the parties entered into a definitive agreement that contained an arbitration agreement in the event of disputes. The arbitration agreement provided for arbitration in accordance with the Rules of Conciliation and Arbitration of the International Chamber of Commerce (ICC). The arbitration agreement also stated that any corresponding award would be vacated or modified not only on the basis of the FAA, but also where an enforcing court found the award was based on errors of fact or law.[79] The ICC arbitral panel rendered an award in LaPine's favor and, thereafter, LaPine moved the court to confirm the arbitral award while Kyocera moved to vacate the award.[80] Kyocera's main contention was that the arbitrators had made errors of fact and law.

---

[74] Collins v. Blue Cross Blue Shield of Michigan, 638 F. Supp. 638, 541-42. (E.D. Mich. 1995); Primerica Financial Services, Inc. v. Wise, 456 S.E.2d 631, 633-34 (Ga. Ct. App. 1995).
[75] 909 F. Supp. 697 (N.D. Cal. 1995).
[76] *Id.* at 698-99.
[77] *Id.* at 699.
[78] *Id.* at 700-01.
[79] *Id.* at 702.
[80] *Id.* at 701.

The District Court held that while parties may contract freely with respect to the manner in which they arbitrate their disputes, they may not by agreement expand the provisions for judicial review contained in the FAA.[81] The Court specifically cited and took judicial notice of the *Gateway* and other decisions upholding contractual provisions expanding a court's review of awards, but declined to follow those decisions.[82] The Court's reasoning was twofold.

First, the Court reasoned that federal jurisdiction cannot be created by contract and the role of the federal courts cannot be subverted to serve the private interest at the whim of the contracting parties. In other words, while parties may fully regulate by agreement the conduct of arbitration proceedings, they may not enlarge the adjudicatory process by enlarging the limits upon it set by statute.[83] Second, the Court reasoned that allowing parties to contractually expand the scope of judicial review was repugnant to public policy. Arbitration, reasoned the court, is motivated by a desire to avoid the delay and costs of a judicial trial, and, in this regard, a court should refrain from substituting its judgment for that of the arbitrator's in order to assure the finality of an award.[84] Therefore, the Court held that a more serious obstacle to the contractual expansion of judicial review was grounded in public policy—the public policy which supports arbitration and those aspects of arbitration which are beneficial to the parties as well as to the courts whose responsibilities are eased by alternative forms of dispute resolution.[85]

The District Court decision in *LaPine* is not without judicial authority and persuasive precedent. In *Chicago Typographical Union No. 16 v. Chicago Sun-Times*,[86] Judge Posner of the Seventh Circuit held parties could not contract for judicial review of an award since a court's jurisdiction cannot be created by contract. Furthermore, the Court's deference to the public policy behind arbitration, especially in light of the FAA and the New York Convention,[87] demonstrates an attempt to protect the integrity of the arbitral process, because allowing parties to contractually expand judicial review, in contrast to the limited review offered by statute, would serve to diminish the reputation of commercial

---

[81] *Id.* at 703.
[82] *Id.* at 702-704.
[83] *Id.* at 703.
[84] *Id.* at 705.
[85] *Id.* at 705-06.
[86] 935 F.9d 1501, 1505 (7th Cir. 1991).
[87] *Supra*, notes 2-10.

arbitration as an effective form of ADR.[88] However, such public policy concerns are not implicated when parties to an arbitral agreement contract for limited judicial review.

Nevertheless, the Ninth Circuit reversed the District Court's decision in *LaPine*. The Ninth Circuit sided with the Fifth Circuit's reasoning in the *Gateway* decision and held that the parties' agreement to expand judicial review must be honored.[89] The Ninth Circuit cited the same Supreme Court cases cited by the Fifth Circuit on the freedom of contract and held that the purpose behind the FAA was not to relieve overburdened court dockets, but merely to avert judicial interference with the contractual rights of parties.[90] However, the Ninth Circuit, as with the Fifth Circuit, failed to consider the difference between freedom of contract in regards to procedural rules rather than substantive rules and failed to consider at all the interplay between the FAA and the New York Convention. These considerations indicate that contractual expansion of judicial review is not appropriate, especially in international arbitrations, and that the District Court in *LaPine* came to the proper conclusion.

B. Contractual Limitation of Judicial Review

Despite the limited standard of judicial review offered by the FAA and the New York Convention, parties may wish to further limit the possibility and purview of judicial review. The intent behind further limitation of judicial review at the award enforcement stage is obvious—parties enter into arbitral agreements to avoid the necessity and cost of litigating a controversy; therefore, protracted litigation at the award enforcement stage would serve to counter any benefits bestowed by the initial choice of arbitration as an ADR technique. This overriding policy objective is only enhanced when the arbitration is international. In an international arbitration, the parties hail from nations which may have vastly different legal systems; consequently, arbitration may be the only effective compromise in the event of a dispute. If, after a successful arbitration, such parties are still faced with prolonged and costly award enforcement litigation in a foreign court, all the benefits of arbitration would be destroyed, especially the neutral forum so cherished by participants in international trade. As a result, some parties find it prudent to foreclose the possibility of disputing an arbitral award in a

---

[88] *Supra*, notes 12-13.
[89] LaPine Technology Corp. v. Kyocera Corp., 130 F.3d 884 (9th Cir. 1997).
[90] *Id.* at 890-91.

national court. Such a foreclosure may either be expressed directly in an agreement to arbitrate, or may be implied through the selection of certain rules governing the arbitral process.

1. Express Limitation of Judicial Review: Exclusion Agreements

Other than the New York Convention, English law on arbitration is basically combined in three national Acts on arbitration, each of which adds a facet to English arbitration law. These Acts include the Arbitration Act of 1950,[91] the Arbitration Act of 1975,[92] and the Arbitration Act of 1979.[93] According to the Arbitration Act of 1979, parties may, before or after a dispute arises, agree in writing to waive the right to bring questions of law before the courts. The effect of such an agreement is to eliminate most judicial review of arbitral awards rendered in England. These "exclusion agreements," as they are commonly called, are only valid in international arbitrations, and are not recognized where all the parties involved are British, unless the exclusion agreement is entered into after the commencement of arbitral proceedings.[94]

However, an arbitral award can still be set aside for arbitrator "misconduct," regardless of an exclusion agreement.[95] An exclusion agreement under English law must be in writing, but need not be expressly labeled an exclusion agreement. In fact, the text of the Act specifically states that an agreement may be an exclusion agreement "whether or not it forms part of an arbitration agreement."[96] Consequently, an exclusion agreement may even exist outside the context of the arbitral agreement. In this regard, courts have found the use of exclusion agreements by the mere implied reference to the binding nature of arbitral awards located in the procedural rules chosen by the parties to governing the arbitral process.

2. Implied Limitation of Judicial Review

English courts have liberally interpreted the definition of "exclusion agreement." For example, in *Marine Contractors Inc. v. Shell Petroleum*

---

[91] Arbitration Act of 1950, ch. 27, §§ 1-44.
[92] Arbitration Act of 1975, ch. 3, §§ 1-8.
[93] Arbitration Act of 1979, ch. 42, §§ 1-5.
[94] Arbitration Act of 1979, §3(6).
[95] Arbitration Act of 1950, §23; see also William W. Park, National Law and Commercial Justice: Safeguarding Procedural Integrity in International Arbitration, 63 TUL. L. REV. 647, 693 (1989).
[96] Arbitration Act of 1979, § 3(1)(2).

Development of Nigeria Ltd.,[97] the English Court of Appeals held that a valid exclusion agreement was incorporated by the parties by their selection of the ICC Rules of Conciliation and Arbitration as governing the procedure of the arbitral process. In *Marine Contractors*, Marine contracted with Shell to lay oil pipeline in Nigeria; the contract contained an arbitral clause providing for the arbitration of any disputes in London under the auspices of the ICC.[98] The arbitrator made an interim award and Marine applied for leave to appeal which the court denied, holding that a valid exclusion agreement existed.[99]

The court interpreted Article 24 of the ICC Rules[100] which reads that a corresponding "arbitral award shall be final" and by submitting the dispute to arbitration by the ICC the parties shall be deemed ... to have waived their right to any form of appeal insofar as such waiver can validly be made" as by implication forming an exclusion agreement.[101] Therefore, in England, a valid exclusion agreement need not be specially expressed by the parties, but may be implied through the selection of a set of procedural rules waiving the right to appeal.[102]

The implied formation of an exclusion agreement is not necessarily a phenomenon limited to English courts. In *CBI NZ Ltd. v. Badger Chiyoda*,[103] the New Zealand Court of Appeal upheld the implied incorporation of an exclusion agreement through the use of the ICC Rules even in the face of a public policy challenge. The New Zealand court reasoned that the implied exclusion agreement was valid and not contrary to public policy because "modern public policy points strongly towards non-interference with arbitral decision if the parties clearly intended them to be final."[104] Nevertheless, the court did place two restrictions on the use of implied exclusion agreements. First, the court held that arbitrator misconduct and an arbitration in excess of the terms of reference remained open to appeal, notwithstanding the implied use of an exclusion agreement. Second, the court held that it may still intervene if unequal bargaining power or exploitation of a monopoly position forced a party to submit to an exclusion agreement.[105]

---

[97] 2 Lloyd's Rep. 77 (C.A. 1984).
[98] *Id.* at 78-79.
[99] *Id.* at 78.
[100] ICC Rules of Conciliation and Arbitration, art. 24(1)(2) (1988).
[101] *Id.* at 79.
[102] *See also* Arab African Energy Corp. v. Olieproduken Nederland, B.V., 2 Lloyd's Rep. 419 (Q.B. Com. Ct. 1983).
[103] 2 NZLR 669 (C.A. 1989).
[104] *Id.* at 680.
[105] *Id.* at 679.

The use of exclusion agreements in Commonwealth and Continental European nations has gained popularity in the last few decades, although this trend has yet to cross the Atlantic into the U.S.[106] The increased use of exclusion agreements demonstrates the integrity of the arbitral process and the trust that parties have in such a process. The use of exclusion agreements will not only ensure the uninterrupted enforcement of arbitral awards, but will also promote the intentions of the parties in agreeing to arbitrate disputes. However, concerns over the lack of any judicial review in the event that the integrity of the arbitral process erodes is still a major concern. Furthermore, how courts should reconcile the increased use of the contractual expansion of judicial review versus the increased use of contractual limitation of judicial review presents a public policy quagmire which warrants further discussion.

Reconciling Contractual Expansion and Limitation of Judicial Review

As parties to both national and international agreements continue to experiment with contractual clauses that either expand or limit judicial review of arbitral awards, the dichotomy between the seemingly competing public policy forces of contractual freedom and award enforcement will become further pronounced. However, the seemingly irreconcilable conflict between freedom to contract and strict award enforcement can best be resolved by evaluating these two public policy viewpoints in connection with the two major goals of the FAA and the New York Convention.

The drafters of the FAA and the New York Convention envisioned an arbitration system whereby national tribunals would not only recognize and enforce agreements to arbitrate, but also would strictly recognize and enforce corresponding arbitral awards. Only if these two goals are met will arbitration become a viable ADR technique. By evaluating contractual expansion and limitation of judicial review in the context of these two goals, contractual freedom can be expanded, while still maintaining the overall integrity of the arbitral process.

A. *Procedural Versus Substantive Freedom of Contract*

The Fifth and Ninth Circuits in the *Gateway* and *LaPine* decisions relied heavily upon the notion of freedom of contract in upholding

---

[106] There appears to be no real mention of exclusion agreements in American law, although some cases tend to hint at the acceptance of contractual limitation of judicial review.

contractual expansion of judicial review.[107] However, both courts failed to realize the difference between procedural and substantive freedom of contract. The District Court in the *LaPine* decision touched upon this concern, but did not elaborate, preferring to merely state that enlargement of judicial review was outside of the permissible range of a party's freedom of contract.[108] Nevertheless, the District Court made the right decision even though its reasoning was not fully developed.

The decisions in *Gateway* and *LaPine* both relied upon a multitude of rulings enforcing parties' freedom of contract in regards to various aspects of the arbitral process. However, all of these decisions concerned the scope and procedural regulations of the arbitral process, not the substantive enforcement of awards or of the arbitration agreement itself. For instance, in *Volt Information Sciences, Inc. v. Board of Trustees of Leland Stanford Junior University*[109] the Supreme Court upheld a California Appellate Court's decision holding that parties may contract for the California rules of arbitration, rather than the FAA, to govern the procedural regulations of their arbitration.

Moreover, the Supreme Court has upheld parties contractual freedom as to the scope of the arbitration and the issues an arbitrator is empowered to decide. For instance, parties are free to contract whether arbitrators will have the authority to award punitive damages[110] and are even free to grant the arbitrators the power to decide the arbitrability issue itself.[111] Finally, parties are even free to contract as to the forum in which any judicial dispute concerning the arbitration agreement or award may be commenced.[112] Consequently, it is undisputed that the powers of an arbitrator derive from, and are limited by, the agreement to arbitrate.[113]

Nevertheless, while parties are free to contract as to the procedure, scope, and forum of an arbitration, parties are not necessarily free to contract as to the extent of judicial review of an arbitral award. An expansion of judicial review would go beyond merely contracting as to

---

[107] *Supra*, notes 63-74 and 89-90.

[108] *LaPine*, 909 F. Supp. at 705. The District Court relied heavily upon the 7th Circuit decision of *Chicago Typographical Union v. Chicago Sun-Times*, 935 F.2d 1501 (7th Cir. 1991).

[109] 489 U.S. 468 (1989).

[110] Mastrobuono v. Shearson Lehman Hutton, 115 S. Ct. 1212, 1216 (1995).

[111] First Options of Chicago, Inc. v. Kaplan, 115 S. Ct. 1923-24 (1995).

[112] McDermott Int'l. Inc. v. Lloyds Underwriters of London, 944 F.2d 1199, 1208-09 (5th Cir. 1991).

[113] *See* Advanced Micro Devices, Inc. v. Intel Corp., 885 F.2d 994, 1002 (Cal. 1994).

the scope or procedure of the arbitration and would be contracting as to the substantive enforcement of the award. Such a process would contradict the limited judicial review standards enunciated in the FAA and the New York Convention. In fact, the majority of exceptions in the FAA and the New York Convention deal with procedural irregularities to ensure that the parties' freedom to contract for arbitration does not impermissibly overstep all bounds of fairness and justice. Only the public policy exception encompasses a substantive review of the arbitral award, and even this exception is narrowly interpreted to protect the integrity of the arbitral process.

In short, parties should be allowed to contractually negotiate as to the scope and procedure of arbitration, but not as to the substantive enforcement of arbitral agreements or awards. Such appears to have been the case in the Supreme Court decision in *Volt Information Sciences, Inc. v. Board of Trustees.*[114] In *Volt*, the parties agreed to not only arbitrate all disputes between them, but also included a provision in the contract that the law of the State of California would govern all disputes.[115] However, the California Arbitration Act contained a provision allowing a court to stay arbitration pending the resolution of a related litigation, while the FAA contained no such provision. As a result, the party opposing arbitration argued that the choice of the law of California violated the provisions of the FAA.[116]

The Supreme Court realized that Section 4 of the FAA on enforcement of arbitral agreements does not confer a right to compel arbitration of any dispute at any time, but merely confers the right to obtain an order directing that arbitration proceed in the manner provided for in [the parties'] agreement.[117] The Court went on to reason that the California Arbitration Act did not offend the federal policy favoring arbitration since there is no federal policy favoring arbitration under a certain set of procedural rules.[118] Consequently, the Court held that by permitting courts to rigorously enforce such arbitration agreements according to their terms, the Court would give effect to the contractual rights and expectations of the parties, without violating the policies behind the FAA.[119]

---

[114] 89 U.S. 468 (1989).
[115] *Id.* at 470
[116] *Id.* at 471-72.
[117] *Id.* at 474-75; 9 U.S.C. § 4.
[118] *Volt*, 489 at 476.
[119] *Id.* at 479.

In conclusion, the Supreme Court in *Volt* reaffirmed the right of parties to contract as to the procedural rules of an arbitration since such freedom of contract would not interfere with the policies of the FAA. However, to allow parties to contract as to substantive enforcement would endanger the integrity of the arbitral process and hamper the effectiveness of arbitration as an ADR technique, thereby "doing violence" to the policies behind the FAA. These concerns are further highlighted when the arbitration and the parties are international in nature.

B. The FAA Versus the New York Convention

The U.S. enacted the FAA on Feb. 12, 1925. As stated before, the goal of the FAA was to "place arbitration agreements upon the same footing as other contracts."[120] On the other hand, Congress in passing the FAA also recognized the benefits offered by arbitration, especially the fact that it is usually less costly and time consuming than litigation.[121] However, in *Dean Witter Reynolds, Inc. v. Byrd*,[122] the Supreme Court held that the overriding concern of Congress in passing the FAA was to ensure enforcement of agreements into which parties had entered, not to realize and promote the benefits of arbitration.

Therefore, federal courts have consistently held that the FAA preempts state laws that tend to interfere with parties' contractual right to enter into arbitration agreements. For instance, in *Southland Corp v. Keating*,[123] the Supreme Court ruled that a provision of the California Franchise Investment Law requiring judicial interpretation of claims arising under that law violated the federal provisions or the FAA and, as a result, allowed the arbitration of various claims under the law. Similarly, three years later, the Supreme Court held that the FAA preempted a provision of the California Labor Code which purportedly authorized employees access to the courts in an action for wages despite the existence of an agreement to arbitrate such controversies.[124] Since

---

[120] *See supra* notes 2-3.

[121] The House Report accompanying the FAA stated the following:

It is practically appropriate that the action should be taken at this time when there is so much arbitration against the costliness and delays of litigation. These matters can be largely eliminated by agreements for arbitration, if arbitration agreements are made valid and enforceable.

H.R. Rep. No. 96, 68th Cong., 1st Sess., 2 (1924)

[122] 470 U.S. 213 (1984).

[123] 465 U.S. 1 (1984).

[124] Perry v. Thomas, 482 U.S. 483 (1987).

such rulings, federal courts have consistently held that the FAA preempts state laws that limit the parties' ability to enter into arbitration agreements.[125]

The U.S. acceded to and enacted the New York Convention on July 31, 1970.[126] The underlying goals of the New York Convention differ from those of the FAA. The primary goal underlying the adoption and implementation of the Convention by the U.S. was to "unify the standards by which agreements to arbitrate are observed and arbitral awards are enforced in signatory countries."[127] The rationale behind unifying standards in regards to the recognition and enforcement of arbitral agreements is rooted in the very nature of international transactions. At times, parties to an international transaction desire an independent and neutral forum in the event any disputes arise. For instance, a foreign corporation may, rightly or wrongly, be apprehensive over litigating a dispute in the courts of its adversaries' nation. This is particularly true when one of the parties is a state-owned or state-supported entity.[128] Consequently, the New York Convention presented an opportunity to unify international standards of arbitration in order to promote arbitration as an alternative method of dispute resolution.

In fact, just as the FAA preempts any contradictory state laws, the New York Convention preempts any contradictory provisions of the FAA whenever an arbitration agreement is international in nature. For example, in *McDermott International v. Lloyds Underwriters of London*,[129] the Fifth Circuit held that the FAA's requirement that both parties consent before an arbitral award could be affirmed was preempted by the New York Convention which did not require consent for confirmation. The Fifth Circuit reasoned that the FAA is the approximate domestic equivalent of the New York Convention such that it incorporates the FAA except where the FAA conflicts with the Convention's specific provisions.[130]

---

[125] S+L+H S.p.A. v. Miller-St. Nazianz, Inc., 988 F.2d 1518 (7th Cir. 1992); Baravati v. Josephtahl. Lyon & Ross, Inc., 28 F.2d 7W, 711 (7th Cir. 1994); Allied-Bruce Terminix Companies. Inc. v. Dobson, 115 S. Ct. 834, 843 (1995).

[126] *Supra*, note 4.

[127] Scherk v. Alberto-Culver Co., 417 U.S. 506, 520 n.15 (1974).

[128] DeVries, *International Commercial Arbitration: A Contractual Substitute for National Courts*, 57 TUL. L. REV. 42, 64-67 (1982); Allison, John R., *Arbitration of Private Antitrust Claims in International Trade: A Study, in the Subordination of National Interests to the Demands of a World Market*, 18 N.Y.U. J. INT'L L. & POL. 361, 379 (1986).

[129] 120 F.3d 583 (5th Cir. 1997).

[130] *Id.* at 588.

The differing goals of the FAA and the New York Convention and the difference between substantive and procedural freedom of contract may shed light upon whether parties should be allowed to expand or limit judicial review over arbitral awards. The goals of the FAA and the New York Convention can be reconciled and promoted by allowing contractual limitation of judicial review and disallowing contractual expansion.

C. *Contractual Expansion Versus Contractual Limitation*

As discussed above, national tribunals have not only recognized the ability of parties to contractually expand judicial review of arbitral awards, but have also recognized the right to contractually limit judicial review. However, while the contractual limitation of judicial review tends to promote the overall goals of both the FAA and the New York Convention, contractual expansion tends to contradict at least in part some of the goals of the FAA and the New York Convention. Nevertheless, the seemingly irreconcilable conflict between the twin goals of promoting freedom of contract in regard to arbitral agreements and the strict enforcement of arbitral awards is not as irreconcilable as it appears to be.

The first step to reconciling contractual expansion and limitation of the judicial review of arbitral awards is to recognize the difference in the types of contractual expansion and limitation. Arbitration is not a judicial process, but rather an alternative method of dispute resolution with differing rules, regulations, and procedures. In fact, there are literally hundreds of procedural rules and regulations promulgated not only by national and state legislatures, but also by private institutions such as the American Arbitration Association and the International Chamber of Commerce. As a result, parties have no dearth of arbitration rules from which to choose. Moreover, parties commonly contractually choose a particular set of rules to apply to any dispute and may even modify portions of those rules. Therefore, allowing parties to freely contract as to procedural rules and the scope of any arbitration not only promotes freedom of contract, but also promotes arbitration as an ADR technique.

On the other hand, the substantive review and enforcement of arbitral awards by national courts is severely restricted in the U.S. by the FAA and internationally by the New York Convention. Allowing parties to contractually expand such review certainly would expand the parties' freedom of contract, but would also endanger the goals of the FAA and the New York Convention to assure certainty and predictability in the enforcement of arbitral awards. However, allowing parties to contractually limit the already stringent standards of judicial review would not only expand freedom of contract, but would also increase the certainty and predictability of award enforcement.

The desire for certainty and predictability in award enforcement is self-evident in an international arbitration, but is also applicable in a domestic arbitration. For example, if an Alaskan corporation enters into a contract with a Florida corporation to provide raw materials, the two corporations may decide to arbitrate any disputes in Los Angeles County, California—a neutral forum and a relatively halfway point between the home bases of the two corporations. If the Florida corporation is successful, any corresponding arbitral award would have to be recognized by the Alaskan courts in order for the Florida corporation to seize any assets of the Alaskan corporation to satisfy the arbitral award. The award enforcement procedure may be jeopardized if the Alaskan courts can review the arbitral award *de novo* and the Florida corporation may find itself relitigating the dispute in the Alaskan courts which is exactly what the Florida corporation sought to avoid in entering into an arbitration agreement.

The District Court in *LaPine* appeared to recognize to an extent the difference between procedural and substantive freedom of contract. However, the District Court failed to further elaborate on the public policy considerations of the same, but rather merely held that parties could not upset the judicial review limits set by statute—presumably neither enlarging nor limiting such review.[131] On review, the Ninth Circuit failed to recognize the public policy differences in procedural versus substantive contractual expansion and limitation. The Ninth Circuit merely held that the FAA was not designed to "avert overburdened court dockets."[132] The court failed to grasp that contractual expansion of judicial review interferes with one of the main reasons parties enter into arbitral agreements, i.e., to avoid the judicial process and being subjected to the courts of an adversary. Strict adherence to the notion of freedom of contract in allowing expansion of judicial review is perhaps merely a revival of the old judicial hostility towards arbitration that the FAA sought to remedy.[133]

The second step to reconciling contractual expansion and limitation is to recognize the difference between national and international

---

[131] *LaPine*, 909 F. Supp. at 803 (N.D. Cal. 1995).
[132] *LaPine*, 130 F.3d at 890-91 (9th Cir. 1997).
[133] *Supra*, note 3.

arbitration. As discussed above, the underlying goal of the FAA and the New York Convention differ in that the FAA sought to reverse past judicial hostility towards arbitration, while the New York Convention sought to unify international standards by which agreements to arbitrate and arbitral awards are enforced. The rationale behind the New York Convention is self-evident—the primary reason why parties to an international transaction desire arbitration is to ensure that any disputes are resolved in a neutral forum. The desire for a neutral forum is even more pronounced where one of the parties is a state-owned or supported enterprise. To relieve these concerns, the New York Convention dictates that arbitral awards will be recognized in the court of a signatory nation except in a few limited circumstances.[134]

In the international context, contractual limitation of judicial review enhances both the parties' freedom of contract and their desire to ensure the enforceability of any corresponding arbitral award. On the other hand, contractual expansion of judicial review could serve as a mechanism to circumvent the goal of the New York Convention to unify national laws on arbitration in order to promote international trade and commerce. The District Court and the Ninth Circuit in the *LaPine* case both failed to recognize this critical difference. The *LaPine* case involved the quintessential international transaction: a sale of goods between an American and a Japanese corporation. As a result, the New York Convention should have applied to the transaction, not the FAA.[135] Nevertheless, the Ninth Circuit in *LaPine* only discussed the FAA and not the New York Convention, even though the goals and provisions of the Convention should have taken precedence over those of the FAA. In short, if the U.S. is to be able to gain the benefits of international accords, such as the New York Convention, and have a role as a trusted partner in multilateral endeavors, its courts should be cautious in applying goals from domestic laws, such as the FAA.[136]

Reconciling the goals of the FAA and the New York Convention when considering the validity of contractual expansion or limitation of judicial review is relatively simple. First, one must determine if the contractual provision affects a procedural or substantive rule of

---

[134] *Infra*, part II.

[135] One can contrast the *LaPine* case with the 5th Circuit *Gateway* case which was essentially a sales and service contract between two domestic corporations. *Compare Gateway*, 64 F.3d at 995-96 (5th Cir. 1995) with *LaPine*, 909 F. Supp at 697 (N.D. Cal. 1995).

[136] *See* Vimar Seguros y Reaseguros v. M/V Sky Reefer, 115 S. Ct. 2322. 2329 (1995).

arbitration. Procedural rules can always be revised by contract, but substantive rules should only be allowed to be revised when they promote not only freedom of contract, but also underlying desire to have certainty and predictability in the enforcement of an arbitral decision. Second, one must determine if the arbitration is domestic or international. In an international arbitration, the goals of uniformity, certainty, and predictability should take precedence over freedom of contract or else the use of international arbitration would be jeopardized. Therefore, in almost all situations, contractual limitation of judicial review should be allowed, while contractual expansion beyond that offered by the FAA and the New York Convention as to the substantive review of an award should be disallowed. A stringent adherence to the freedom of contract notion in all situations, including contractual expansion of judicial review, would only serve to damage the integrity of the arbitral process and serve to reincarnate the old judicial hostility towards arbitration.

Conclusion

In recent decades arbitration has increasingly become a desirable alternative to litigation—especially between parties of differing nationalities. In order to promote arbitration, the U.S. enacted both the FAA and the New York Convention. Both these legislative enactments severely limit judicial review of the arbitral process and any corresponding award. In recent years, parties have attempted to either contractually expand or limit judicial review of arbitral awards. Provisions expanding or limiting judicial review have been held enforceable under the doctrine of freedom of contract. However, contractual expansion of judicial review can have adverse effects on the integrity of the arbitral process. This is especially true in an international context. Consequently, a strict, unguided adherence to the principle of freedom of contract needs to be tempered with a respect for the arbitration process and the goals of both the FAA and the New York Convention.

II. Judicial Review and Arbitration

Can Arbitration Coexist with Judicial Review?
A Critique of LaPine v. Kyocera

by Andreas F. Lowenfeld[*]

Once parties to a commercial relationship agree to submit their differences to arbitration, the understanding in the United States has been that they commit themselves to abide by the decision of the arbitrators, subject to very limited review by the courts. Under the Federal Arbitration Act, as well as the Uniform Arbitration Act and the arbitration law of most states, a court may set aside an award if it finds gross misbehavior by the arbitrators, such as corruption, fraud, undisclosed conflict of interest, or refusal to hear pertinent evidence.[1]

Some courts-and a good many losing counsel-have sought to build on the suggestion by the U.S. Supreme Court in *Wilko v. Swan* that arbitral awards may be set aside for "manifest disregard of the law."[2] But even if that standard is valid, it can hardly ever be shown, except in association with corruption or comparable misconduct. Honest arbitrators do not manifestly disregard the law. But they may well misconstrue the law, or misapply it, or get the facts wrong. So, of course, may judges, administrative agencies, tax assessors, and other decision-makers. But whereas in virtually every judicial system a losing party has at least one chance to challenge the outcome of a legal proceeding, arbitration is different.

Why is this so? The proposition may be formulated in different ways, but it comes down to saying that by agreeing to arbitration, the parties have agreed to abide by the decision of their chosen tribunal, and how a court might have decided the same controversy is not significant. Looked at from the other side, arbitration relieves overburdened courts of

---

[*] Mr. Lowenfeld is the Herbert and Rose Rubin Professor of International Law at New York University School of Law, and an active arbitrator. He holds an A.B. from Harvard College and and LL.B. from the Harvard School of Law. He serves on the roster of neutrals of the American Arbitration Association.

[1] 9 U.S.C. § 10; 7 U.L.A. § 12; *See, e.g.* N.Y. C.P.L.R. §§ 7510, 7511; Cal. CCP § 1286.2.

[2] 346 U.S. 427 (1953), *discussed* on p. 12. See I.R. MACNEIL et al, 4 FEDERAL ARBITRATION LAW § 40.07 (1995 and Supp).

a substantial workload; if they are brought back in to oversee the results of an arbitration, much of this advantage is lost.

Putting aside the burden on the courts, the question comes up whether parties can opt for a hybrid regime. Can they enjoy the benefits of arbitration—quicker resolution, avoidance of juries, participation in the selection of the decision-maker, less formality and more confidentiality—and still provide in their agreement to arbitrate for substantive control by the courts?

A recent decision of the Court of Appeals for the Ninth Circuit, *LaPine Technology Corp. v. Kyocera Corp.*,[3] says yes, though with a doubting concurrence and a dissent. Essentially, the principal opinion by Judge Fernandez concludes that if the parties' agreement was different from the standard agreement to arbitrate, so be it. The agreement to arbitrate, though unusual, was not unlawful, and the duty of courts is to enforce lawful agreements. Judge Kozinski, in his concurrence, worried about a new function of the courts not authorized by statute. But he concluded:

> Given the strong policy of party empowerment embodied in the [FAA], I see no reason why Congress would object to enforcement of this agreement. This is not quite an express congressional authorization but, given the Arbitration Act's policy, it's probably enough.[4]

Had I sat on the panel of the Ninth Circuit in *LaPine*, I think I would have dissented, though I am not sure. I have used this article to try to think through some of the ramifications of the *LaPine* case. Before doing so, a little comparative law and a little history are in order.

The Changing English Approach

Excluding judicial review of arbitral awards is by no means inevitable. In England, for instance, the practice until 1979 was that questions of law could be, and in many instances must be, submitted to the High Court for review, by way of a so-called special case or case stated.[5] The decision of the High Court, in turn, could be appealed to the Court of Appeal, and with leave further to the House of Lords. The result

---

[3] 130 F.3d 884 (9th Cir. 1997).
[4] *Id.* at 891 (concurring opinion).
[5] The practice was codified in the Arbitration Act 1950, § 21, 14 Geo. 6 ch. 17, and later repealed as described below.

was a relatively stable and well-articulated body of commercial law, often originating in controversies having no connection with England other than the fact that the parties had provided for arbitration in London. On the other hand, the practice contradicted the claim that arbitration was quick and inexpensive as compared to litigation in court.[6]

The case stated was abolished in 1979, and the role of courts in reviewing arbitral awards was cut down considerably.[7] But the 1979 Arbitration Act, in section 1, still gave parties the right to appeal questions of law arising out of an arbitral award, subject to obtaining leave of the High Court. In recognition of the fact that the appeal procedure of London arbitration had induced many consumers of arbitration to provide for arbitration in Paris, New York, Geneva, etc., rather than in London, section 3 of the Act permitted parties to enter into so-called exclusion agreements, by which they renounced the right of appeal from arbitral awards. But the reluctance of the English legal community to give up, or even permit giving up, appeals from arbitral awards came through in section 4, which said section 3 did not apply to domestic arbitrations, nor to three common types of controversies heard in London arbitrations—claims in admiralty and claims arising out of insurance or commodity contracts.[8]

---

[6] *See, e.g.*, the following excerpt from the speech by Lord Wilberforce in the *House of Lords in Cie. Tunisienne de Navigation S.S. v. Cie. d'Armement Maritime S.A.*, [1971] A.C. 572 at 600: "It is surely regrettable that, after a choice of English arbitrators, these foreign parties should have been subjected to litigation in three courts on top of the arbitration and that on a preliminary point. I venture to think that a question of the proper law of a commercial contract ought to be regarded as primarily a matter to be found by arbitrators: for after all, the question is one of estimating competing factors in the light of commercial intention....

"The expertise of City of London arbitrators (which motivates the use of London arbitration clauses) suggests that these considerations are best left to them and the proposition that this being a "matter of law" is something better left to the courts is one the correctness of which is open on the record. If, for uniformity or otherwise, supervision by the courts is sometimes required, I cannot but think that, otherwise than in exceptional cases by leave, decision by the commercial judge should end the matter."

[7] Arbitration Act 1979, L. 1979 ch. 42.

[8] The question arose under the 1979 Act whether an agreement to arbitrate under ICC rules, which stated that by submitting their dispute to those rules "the parties shall be deemed to have undertaken to carry out the resulting award without delay and to have waived their right to any form of appeal insofar as such waiver can validly be made," constituted an exclusion agreement. After some uncertainty, it was held that such an agreement—i.e., London arbitration, ICC rules—qualified as an exclusion agreement. Arab African Corp. Ltd. v. Olieprodukten Nederland B.V., [1983] 2 Lloyd's Rep. 419 (Q.B.);

In 1996, after several years of study and debate within the legal and arbitration communities, Parliament adopted a comprehensive Arbitration Act, bringing together in one user-friendly piece of legislation a body of law previously scattered in at least four prior statutes plus numerous judicial decisions.[9] The Act set out in section 1 the general principles governing arbitration in England:

> (a) the object of arbitration is to obtain the fair resolution of disputes by an impartial tribunal without unnecessary delay or expense; (b) the parties should be free to agree how their disputes are resolved, subject only to such safeguards as are necessary in the public interest; (c) in matters governed by this part the court should not intervene except as provided by this part.

Having said this and clarified many previously unclear provisions of the law of arbitration, the Act essentially retains the provisions for appeal adopted in 1979, except that parties to admiralty, insurance, and commodity contracts may now enter into exclusion agreements,[10] and so may parties to domestic contracts calling for arbitration.[11] Unless all parties to the arbitration agree that the High Court should review the award, appeal is always discretionary. The Act sets out guidelines for the High Court on whether to grant leave, adapted from a decision of the House of Lords under the 1979 Act.[12]

> Leave to appeal shall be given only if the court is satisfied-(a) that the determination of the question will substantially affect the

---

Marine Contractors Inc. v. Shell Petroleum Dev. Co of Nigeria, Ltd., [1984] 2 Lloyd's Rep. 77 (C.A.).

[9] Arbitration Act 1996, L. 1996 ch. 23.

[10] *Id.*, s. 69. A comparable provision permitting application to the court on a preliminary point of law appears as s. 45, also carried over in substance from the 1979 Act. Neither section contains a provision corresponding to s. 4 of the 1979 Act, *supra*, n. 9.

[11] As drafted and passed by Parliament, the 1996 Act did not extend the right to enter into exclusion agreements to parties to a domestic arbitration agreement. It was believed, however, that differentiating between domestic and nondomestic arbitration might be contrary to the duty set out in Article 6 of the Treaty of Rome not to discriminate against other members of the European Union, and accordingly, the sections making the distinction, ss. 85-87, were not brought into effect when the Secretary of State promulgated the Act. See S.I. 1996 No. 3146, s. 3 (Dec. 16, 1996).

[12] Pioneer Shipping Ltd. v. BTP Tioxide Ltd.: The Nema, [1982] A.C. 724. *See also* Antaios Compania Naviera v. Salen Rederierna: The Antaios, [1985] A.C. 191.

rights of one or more of the parties, (b) that the question is one which the tribunal was asked to determine, (c) that, on the basis of the findings of fact in the award-(i) the decision of the tribunal on the question is obviously wrong, or (ii) the question is one of general public importance and the decision of the tribunal is at least open to serious doubt, and (d) that, despite the agreement of the parties to resolve the matter by arbitration, it is just and proper in all the circumstances for the court to determine the question.[13]

In short, there is no more right to appeal from arbitral awards, and no presumption that the arbitrators lack the competence (in both senses of the term) to determine and apply the law to the controversy before them. But the opportunity to appeal remains, and the guidelines for granting leave are fairly broad.[14] If the court grants leave to appeal, it may confirm the award, vary the award, remand (remit) the award to the arbitral tribunal, or set the award aside in whole or in part.[15] The parties may, however, enter into an exclusion agreement, thereby eliminating the possibility of appeal.

Thus, the compromise in the current English law is the opposite of what the U.S. court upheld in the *LaPine* case. In the English practice for international arbitrations, the parties can opt out of the possibility of appeal. In the American practice, if *LaPine* becomes generally accepted, the parties will be able to opt in to an appeal procedure, indeed to a broader procedure than is available in England in that it seems to encompass facts as well as law and does not leave room for the court to decline to review the award as a matter of discretion.

The Traditional American Approach

The relation of courts to arbitration is another instance where the English model has not been followed in the United States. In *Burchell v. Marsh*,[16] decided three generations before passage of the FAA in 1925, the U.S. Supreme Court reversed a federal circuit court that had set aside an award of arbitrators rendered in a dispute between a New York

---

[13] Arbitration Act 1996 s. 69(3).

[14] Application for leave to appeal is to be made in writing, with notice to the other party and to the tribunal, but without a hearing unless the court finds that a hearing is required. *Id.* s. 69(1) and (5).

[15] *Id.* s. 69(7).

[16] 58 U.S. (17 How.) 344 (1855).

commercial house and an Illinois retailer. When one reads the Court's summary of the facts, one cannot help thinking that the arbitrators got it wrong. Nevertheless, the Court held that the lower court had been unjustified in setting the award aside.

> Arbitrators are judges chosen by the parties to decide the matters submitted to them, finally and without appeal. As a mode of settling disputes, it should receive every encouragement from courts of equity. If the award is within the submission, and contains the honest decision of the arbitrators, after a full and fair hearing of the parties, a court of equity will not set it aside for error, either in law or fact. A contrary course would be a substitution of the judgment of the chancellor in place of the judges chosen by the parties, and would make an award the commencement, not the end, of litigation.[17]

Well before the rise of comprehensive arbitration statutes, most courts in the United States took the same view. For instance, the New York Court of Appeals was faced in 1902 with an appeal from an order by a lower court confirming an arbitral award. The court held in *Wilkins v. Allen*[18] that such an appeal could raise only such questions as could be invoked in an application to vacate, modify, or correct an award, but not mere errors of judgment:

> The conclusiveness of awards is based upon the principle that the parties, having chosen judges of their own and agreed to abide by their decision, they are bound by their agreement and compelled to perform the award....If the legislature had intended to confer upon a defeated party the right to appeal from an award upon the merits and thus change the law as it has existed for

---

[17] To the argument that the arbitrators had obviously made a mistake, Judge Grier replied: "Courts should be careful to avoid a wrong use of the word 'mistake,' and, by making it synonymous with mere error of judgment, assume to themselves an arbitrary power over awards. The same result would follow if the court should treat the arbitrators as guilty of corrupt partiality, merely because their award is not such an one as the chancellor would have given. We are all too prone, perhaps, to impute either weakness of intellect or corrupt motives to those who differ with us in opinion." *Id.* at 350. Justice Nelson dissented, writing: "I think the damages allowed against the complainants, by the arbitrators, are so extravagant, disproportionate, and gross, as to afford evidence of passion and prejudice, and justified the judgment of the court below, in setting aside the award." *Id.* at 352.

[18] 169 N.Y. 494, 62 N.E. 575 (1902).

more than a century, that purpose would have been plainly stated in the statute, and the legislature would have employed language which would have clearly indicated its purpose, especially in view of the fact that no such right existed under the common law. To hold that any court, appellate or other, has the right to review the action of an arbitrator upon the merits of a controversy submitted to him, would entirely subvert the whole system and principle of arbitration and transfer to courts powers which the parties themselves have expressly confided to arbitrators, and that, too, without their consent.

There is a suggestion in the last quoted line that perhaps the parties might have consented to judicial review,[19] but none of the arbitration statutes in the 1920s and thereafter picked up on that idea. The message conveyed both by the courts and by the legislatures was clear. Choosing arbitration—whether to avoid delay in the courts, to preserve confidentiality, to secure decisions by experts, or whatever—meant excluding the courts, except to vacate the results of corruption or other misconduct.

When the FAA was adopted, the jurisdiction of the federal courts was limited to (i) enforcing agreements to arbitrate (§ 4), (ii) confirming awards (§ 9); (iii) vacating awards for arbitral misconduct (§ 10); and (iv) modifying or correcting an award if there was an evident material miscalculation or arbitrators have awarded upon a matter not submitted to them (§ 11). No provision was made for a case stated, as in England; no provision was made for judicial review of a finding of fact, even if "clearly erroneous"; no provision was made for correcting errors of law; and no provision was made authorizing the parties to vary the role of the courts by agreement.

In the early 1950s, in *Wilko v. Swan*,[20] the Supreme Court suggested, in a backhanded way, that courts might review arbitral awards made in "manifest disregard" of the law. In fact, the Court justified its holding—that an arbitration clause in a contract between a securities house and a customer violated the anti-waiver provision of the Securities Act of

---

[19] The suggestion also appears earlier: "Where the merits of a controversy are referred to an arbitrator selected by the parties, his determination, either as to the law or the facts, is final and conclusive, and a court will not open an award unless perverse misconstruction or positive misconduct upon the part of the arbitrator is plainly established, or there is some provision in the agreement of submission authorizing it." *Id.* 169 N.Y. at 496, 62 N.E. at 576.

[20] *Supra*, n. 2.

1933—by pointing out how little control the courts would be able to exercise over a Securities Act claim submitted to arbitration. The entire passage expressly drew the contrast between American and English law as it read at the time:

> While it may be true...that a failure of the arbitrators to decide in accordance with the provisions of the Securities Act would "constitute grounds for vacating the award pursuant to [FAA § 10]," that failure would need to be made clearly to appear. In unrestricted submissions, such as the present margin agreements envisage, the interpretations of the law by the arbitrators in contrast to manifest disregard are not subject, in the federal courts, to judicial review for error in interpretation. The [FAA] contains no provision for judicial determination of legal issues such as is found in the English law. As the protective provisions of the Securities Act require the exercise of judicial direction to fairly assure their effectiveness, it seems to us that Congress must have intended [the anti-waiver section] to apply to waiver of judicial trial and review.[21]

Whatever "manifest disregard" means, it is clear that the Supreme Court did not intend in the quoted passage to construct a system of judicial review of arbitral awards, and in fact no such system has grown up, though the scope of arbitration in the United States—including securities, antitrust, and patent controversies—has vastly expanded since the court considered lack of judicial review as a reason to disallow arbitration over disputes involving public law.

The LaPine Decision

With this background, we are ready to focus on the case that stimulated this essay. The contract in question involved a complicated relationship between LaPine, a California corporation formed to design and market a particular kind of computer disk drive, and Kyocera, a Japanese company that was to manufacture the device under license, as well as a third party, Prudential-Bache, that was supposed to supply financing for the venture. Following various disputes and revisions in the

---

[21] *Id.*, 346 U.S. at 436. Three years later in Bernhardt v. Polygraphic Co. of America, the Court reiterated: "Whether the arbitrators misconstrued a contract is not open to judicial review." 350 U.S. 198, 203 n.4 (1956).

arrangements, LaPine brought suit against Kyocera in the U.S. District Court for the Northern District of California. Kyocera invoked the arbitration clause in the contract, and the court ordered the parties to arbitrate.

The contract called for application of California law, and for arbitration "in accordance with the Rules of Conciliation and Arbitration of the International Chamber of Commerce and the Federal Arbitration Act." The clause went on as follows:

> The arbitrators shall issue a written award which shall state the bases of the award and include detailed findings of fact and conclusions of law. The U.S. District Court for the Northern District of California may enter judgment upon any award, either by confirming the award or by vacating, modifying, or correcting the award. The Court shall vacate, modify or correct any award: (i) based upon any of the grounds referred to in the Federal Arbitration Act, (ii) where the arbitrators' findings of fact are not supported by substantial evidence, or (iii) where the arbitrators' conclusions of law are erroneous.[22]

The arbitrators rendered an award with extensive findings of fact and conclusions of law, essentially favoring LaPine. LaPine moved in the district court to confirm the award. Kyocera opposed confirmation and applied to the court for an order modifying and vacating the award. No assertion was made that the arbitrators had engaged in misconduct such as is set out in § 10 of the FAA. Kyocera contended, however, that the arbitrators had made findings of fact not supported by substantial evidence, as well as erroneous conclusions of law, and that the arbitration clause in the agreement between the parties entitled it to review and correction by the court.

The district court rejected Kyocera's submission. It did not examine the specific challenges to either the findings of fact or the conclusions of law, on the ground that it lacked jurisdiction to do so.[23] Its jurisdiction, the court held, is determined by the FAA, and cannot be expanded by contract. "The role of the federal courts," Judge Ingram wrote, "cannot be subverted to serve private interests at the whim of contracting

---

[22] The terms of reference, agreed upon by the parties and the arbitrators in accordance with ICC rules, contained a paragraph tracking the provisions of the arbitration clause concerning judicial review.

[23] LaPine Technology Corp. v. Kyocera, 909 F. Supp. 697 (N.D. Cal. 1995).

parties." Reviewing the apparent split of authority in other circuits,[24] he wrote that "an even more serious obstacle to the validity of [the provision for judicial review in the arbitration clause] is grounded in public policy." The opinion went on to say:

> Judicial review of these proceedings...simply does not comply with the benefits usually contemplated by those who favor arbitration as an effective form of alternative dispute resolution.
>
> It appears to this court that the contractual provisions existing in this case wherein the parties choose and specify the scope of judicial review to pertain in their arbitration is offensive to the public policy which supports arbitration and those aspects of arbitration which are beneficial to the parties as well as to the courts whose responsibilities are eased by alternative forms of dispute resolution.

Finding that the challenges also brought by Kyocera under § 10 of the FAA were unsustainable, Judge Ingram confirmed the award and entered judgment for LaPine.[25]

The court of appeals reversed. It agreed that in the absence of any contractual terms regarding judicial review, nothing that the arbitrators had done would justify a court in modifying or vacating the award. But it went on to hold that the case "does not...fall neatly within the contours of the usual rule" since the parties contracted for "heightened judicial scrutiny of the arbitrators' award when they agreed that review would be for errors of fact or law." The court said:

> We hold that we must honor that agreement. We must not disregard it by limiting our review to the FAA grounds. To locate the principle that animates our holding, one need not look very much further than the Supreme Court's decisions applying

---

[24] In particular, *Chicago Typographical Union. v. Chicago Sun-Times*, 935 F.2d 1501 (7th Cir. 1991), rejecting expanded review of arbitral awards; *Gateway Technologies, Inc. v. MCI Telecommunications*, 64 F.3d 993 (5th Cir. 1995), accepting review on points of law when provided for in the arbitration agreement, and to the same effect, *Fils et Cables d'Acier de Lens v. Midland Metals Corp.*, 584 F. Supp. 240 (S.D.N.Y. 1984).

[25] As is common, the losing party tried to fit its appeal under § 10 by arguing that the arbitrators misapplied California law and thus "exceeded their powers." The district court properly rejected this effort as "nothing other than an attempt to bootstrap a 'legally erroneous' standard of review. The panel clearly did apply California law. It did not apply Texas or Wisconsin law...." *See supra*, n. 23, 909 F. Supp. at 708.

and interpreting the FAA. Those decisions make it clear that the primary purpose of the FAA is to ensure enforcement of private agreements to arbitrate, in accordance with the agreements' terms.

Quoting *Volt Information Sciences v. Board of Trustees*,[26] the court continued:

> Arbitration under the Act is a matter of consent, not coercion, and parties are generally free to structure their arbitration agreements as they see fit. Just as they may limit by contract the issues which they will arbitrate, so too may they specify by contract the rules under which that arbitration will be conducted.

Accordingly, the court sent the case back to the district court with instructions to conduct the review of the facts and law that the district judge had previously declined to undertake.

Some Reflections on LaPine

I. Impact on Arbitration Practice

Writing shortly after *LaPine* was decided, a prominent member of the New York arbitration community, Carroll Neesemann, hailed the outcome of the case on the ground that "within reason, parties may now craft their own standards for judicial review of arbitration awards, bringing to arbitration a major safeguard available in court."[27] He argued that though in the vast majority of cases arbitrators reach a fair and just result, "there also seems to be a fairly broadly held perception that, despite its otherwise attractive attributes, because of its unpredictability, arbitration should be avoided, especially in large cases where the stakes are high."

I must say that this is not my experience. I have been struck, particularly in international transactions, by the ever-increasing resort to arbitration, especially in very large transactions.[28] My impression is that

---

[26] 489 U.S. 468 (1989).
[27] Neesemann, *More Certainty Comes to Arbitration*, N.Y. LAW J., MAR. 26, 1998, p. 1, col. 2.
[28] A partner in a large New York law firm told me recently that 90% of the international transactions in which his firm is involved—including investments, joint ventures, technology licenses, and trade in goods—now contain arbitration clauses.

the bigger the transaction, the stronger is the pressure by foreign parties not to be trapped in litigation in the United States, and the stronger is the pressure by American parties not to be trapped in litigation in country X. But it is important to report Neesemann's view, because he regards *LaPine* as a pro-arbitration decision.

My reaction-as an academic and arbitrator, and only rarely as a practitioner-is different. My instinct is that it would not be good for arbitration, and in particular for arbitration in the United States, if the view of the Ninth Circuit in *LaPine* came to prevail generally.

For one thing, as the *LaPine* case (which was in litigation and arbitration for ten years) demonstrates, judicial review of the merits would inevitably prolong the process, negating the expeditiousness that is one of the important advantages of arbitration.[29] It was this consideration, plus the attendant expense, that led to the English decision to eliminate the case stated and sharply curtail the opportunity for appeal of arbitral awards.

For another, I wonder how counsel will cope with the quandary presented by *LaPine* when drafting or negotiating contracts with arbitral clauses: Shall we include a judicial review clause such as the one used in *LaPine*, calling for review both of findings of fact and of conclusions of law? Or stick to the traditional clause with no special mention of appeal or review? Or try something in between-for instance calling for review of conclusions of law only?

Further, I am all in favor of reasoned opinions, which are standard in international arbitrations and increasingly issued in domestic controversies. But would not the *LaPine* standard require complete records, transcripts and other baggage that arbitration was supposed to lighten? I speak not only of the paper generated, but also of the conduct of the case itself. Whenever I am sitting as an arbitrator and I hear a lawyer say "For the record...," I usually interrupt and say to counsel, "Never mind the record: your task is to persuade my colleagues and me, not a court that will never see this case." I am afraid that would change if

---

[29] The initial civil action in *LaPine* was filed in May 1987; the court ordered the parties to arbitrate in September 1987; the tribunal rendered its award in August 1994; Kyocera moved to vacate, modify and correct the award in November 1994; the district court issued its order declining to vacate or modify the award in December 1995, and the 9th Circuit reversed and remanded in December 1997. Presumably, when the district court renders its decision on the legal and factual challenges to the award, that decision will again be subject to appeal.

LaPine prevailed, and that arbitration, which is already becoming too much like litigation, would become even more so.

II. The Question of Jurisdiction

Judge Kozinski, as mentioned previously, expressed doubts about whether Congress had authorized the district courts to review arbitral awards, but wound up deriving a mandate to do so from the policy of the FAA.[30] I think that is unpersuasive, given the precise and limited role of the district courts set out in §§ 10 (see sidebar) and 11 of the FAA and the limited jurisdiction of district courts to hear appeals in other areas of federal civil procedure.[31]

Judge Fernandez's majority opinion in LaP*ine* treats the question of jurisdiction even more lightly. It refers to an opinion of the Seventh Circuit arising out of a labor dispute, in which Judge Posner wrote: "If the parties want, they can contract for an appellate arbitration panel to review the arbitrator's award. But they cannot contract for judicial review of that award; federal jurisdiction cannot be created by contract."[32]

Judge Fernandez quotes that passage, but rejects it. "If the court intended to refer to the FAA as a jurisdictional statute," he writes, "it would have been negating the established principle that the FAA is a regulation of commerce rather than a limitation on or conferral of federal court jurisdiction." With all respect, I do not understand that analysis.[33]

Of course, Congress could (i) confer jurisdiction on the district courts to review arbitral awards on the merits; or it could (ii) amend § 10

---

[30] *See supra*, text at n. 4.

[31] From 1979 until it was repealed in 1996, 28 U.S.C. § 636(c)(4) authorized appeals to the district courts from judgment of a magistrate judge when the parties have consented (i) to a trial before a magistrate judge; and (ii) to appeal to the district judge rather than to the court of appeals. District judges have jurisdiction under 28 U.S.C. § 158 to hear appeals from final judgments and some interlocutory orders issued by bankruptcy judges, and district judges have jurisdiction to review legal determinations of the Secretary of Health and Human Services under portions of the Social Security Act, 42 U.S.C. § 405(g). There may be a few other instances in which district judges have been authorized to hear appeals, but certainly not many.

[32] *Chicago Typographical Union, supra*, n. 24, 935 F.2d at 1505.

[33] Apparently Judge Fernandez considered the jurisdiction of the courts to flow from diversity of citizenship, not from the FAA. Of course if there were no arbitration clause and the jurisdictional amount were satisfied, a dispute between an American and a Japanese company could be heard in the federal district court. I do not see that it follows that when there is an agreement to arbitrate and the arbitration takes place, a grant of jurisdiction to review the resulting award can be dispensed with.

of the FAA to authorize judicial review when the parties have given their consent in the agreement to arbitrate. Further, Congress could limit either (i) or (ii) to questions of law; or it could make judicial review of arbitral awards available only upon leave of the court, as in England since the 1979 reforms. Without such legislative authorization, however, I do not think that the courts can assert jurisdiction to review awards of arbitrators on the basis of an implied grant, and I do not think the parties have it within their power to confer such jurisdiction on the courts.

A fair question is what a court should do with an arbitral award containing a *LaPine* clause, if it shares my view that it lacks jurisdiction to conduct the review called for in the agreement to arbitrate. Would the court find the judicial review provision so integral to the agreement to arbitrate that it would void the whole arbitration? That was the view taken by Kyocera in the district court in *LaPine*. Accepting that view, however, would give the losing party in the arbitration more than it could expect from the judicial review it sought, in that it would obtain annulment of the award without having to establish the soundness of its challenges to the arbitrators' findings.

Or would the court view the conduct of the arbitration as separate and severable from the review function, so that the award could stand, subject only to the challenges permitted by § 10? Judge Ingram took that view in the district court in *LaPine*, rejecting all speculation about whether the parties would have agreed to arbitration even without the enhanced judicial review or whether they would not have agreed to arbitration at all. I think Judge Ingram was right. But even raising the question shows that counsel seeking certainty is unlikely to find it in the example of *LaPine v. Kyocera*.

III. Impact on International Law

I have two other concerns, both related to international arbitration, one concerning the New York Convention,[34] and the other concerning the situs of the arbitration.

The New York Convention. Any commercial arbitration between a U.S. party and a foreign party (or between two foreign parties) falls under the New York Convention, even if it is conducted in the United States.[35] Accordingly, an award in such an arbitration is a Convention

---

[34] U.N. Convention on the Recognition and Enforcement of Foreign Arbitral Awards, 21 U.S.T. 2517; T.I.A.S. 6997; 330 U.N.T.S. 3, done at New York, June 10, 1958.

[35] *See* 9 U.S.C. § 202. The leading case confirming this statement is Bergesen v. Joseph Muller Corp., 710 F.2d 928 (2d Cir. 1983). The law is different in England, which, since the

award, which shall be recognized and enforced in each Contracting State under Article III, and may be set aside only on the grounds set out in Article V. Article V clearly excludes judicial review of the merits of an award-whether of findings of fact or of law.[36]

Though the formulations are somewhat different, as long as judicial oversight of arbitral awards rendered in the United States is limited by § 10 of the FAA or comparable state statutes, there is no danger of violating Articles III and V of the Convention. But once a court in the United States undertakes review of an award on the grounds stipulated in *LaPine*, it would seem to me to be acting contrary to the Convention. Can private parties waive commitments made by states in a multilateral treaty? Nothing in the New York Convention says so, and § 207 of the FAA, implementing the Convention says: "The court shall confirm the award unless it finds one of the grounds for refusal or deferral of recognition or enforcement of the award specified in the said Convention."[37]

The Situs of the Arbitration.

It ought to be true that if an American party and a foreign party enter into a contract containing an arbitration clause, it does not much matter where the arbitration takes place.[38] This is not quite true today, as the discussion of current English law illustrates, though the divergence of

---

United Kingdom adhered to the New York Convention in 1975, has defined a Convention award as "an award made...in the territory of a state (other than the United Kingdom) which is a party to the New York Convention. *See* Arbitration Act 1996 s. 100(1).

[36] For the reason this problem does not arise with regard to awards made in England, *see supra*, n. 35.

[37] A recent decision of the 2nd Circuit draws an elaborate distinction between confirmation of a Convention award, which is governed solely by the Convention and thus does not include implied grounds for refusing recognition and enforcement, such as "manifest disregard," and setting aside an award under the domestic law of the situs, which may well include manifest disregard. Yusuf Ahmed Alghanim & Sons v. Toys "R" Us, Inc., 126 F.3d 15 (2d Cir. 1997), *cert. denied*, 118 S. Ct 1042 (1998). I am not persuaded by the court's reasoning. Having participated in the drafting of Chapter 2 of the FAA, including § 202 (defining an award falling under the Convention), I do not recall any discussion of this anomaly. But the conclusion is not troubling if the only challenge to enforcement beyond those permitted in the Convention is manifest disregard, which can almost never be shown (and indeed was not shown in *Toys "R" Us*). If, however, more general review, as in *LaPine*, is permitted, the intended fit between the Convention and U.S. domestic law is indeed disturbed.

[38] For present purposes, I assume that provisions concerning the language of the arbitration, the applicable law, the appointment of arbitrators, and the rules of procedure are the same regardless of the chosen situs.

English law from the norm is much less than it was previously, and more and more countries are adopting the UNCITRAL Model Law.[39] But what happens if one party is American and a "*LaPine* clause" is included in the contract?

Does application of the clause depend on the situs of the arbitration in the United States? Or could the clause be adapted to refer to the High Court of Justice in London, the Tribunal de Grande Instance in Paris, the Tokyo District Court, etc., when the situs of the arbitration is in one of those cities? And if, as seems likely, the designated court does not carry out the review function ascribed to it in the contract, does that give a defense to the American party against enforcement of an award rendered in London, Paris, or Tokyo that has not been reviewed by the court, as called for in the contract?

Reversing the hypothetical, suppose the arbitration between an American and a foreign party takes place in the United States (as in *LaPine*), the award favors one party, and the court, in a merits review at the behest of the losing party, sets aside or modifies the award. Thereafter, enforcement is sought in the country of the foreign party or in a third country. May a foreign court enforce the award and disregard the action of the reviewing court?[40] Alternatively, may the foreign court enforce the award as modified by the court?

One need not pursue each of these variations to see that an option to include judicial review on the merits of arbitral awards would produce not certainty but a host of new burdens and puzzles. I do not contend that arbitration as presently practiced is perfect, either in domestic or in international controversies. The provision in the rules of the ICC for scrutiny of draft awards by the International Court of Arbitration (actually not a court but a committee) reflects recognition that in some instances oversight of the work of arbitrators may be in order. But the more I think about the decision of the Ninth Circuit in *LaPine v. Kyocera*, the less I like it. I hope "arbitration plus" does not catch on generally; I hope the Congress does not pick it up; and I hope that if the proposition ever gets that far, the Supreme Court will relegate it to a footnote and not a milestone in the history of arbitration.

---

[39] Adopted by the U.N. Commission on International Trade Law, June 21, 1985. The provision on recourse against an arbitral award is Article 34.

[40] *Compare* Chromalloy Aeroservices v. Arab Republic of Egypt, 939 F. Supp. 907 (D.D.C. 1996), *with* Arab Republic of Egypt v. Chromalloy Aeroservices, 22 YB. ICCA 691 (1997)(Cour d'Appel Paris, Jan. 14, 1997); *see also* Hilmarton Ltd. v. Omnium de Traitement et de Valorisation, 20 YB. ICCA 663 (1995) (Cour de Cassation, France, Mar. 23, 1964) and 22 YB. ICCA 696 (1997) (Cour de Cassation, France, June 10, 1997).

INDEX

A

AMERICAN ARBITRATION ASSOCIATION (AAA)
Administrative policy of, 98-101
Arbitrator selection, 101-102, 182, 184, 186-87
Commercial arbitration rules of, 103-05
Document production under, 267
Generally, 1-13, 28, 54, 84
Interim measures, 270-72
Rules, 354-55
Subpeona power, 260-61

ARBITRAL INSTITUTIONS
Administered arbitration, 153-63
American Arbitration Association (AAA). *See* AMERICAN ARBITRATION ASSOCIATION (AAA)
CPR Institute, 84
Independence, importance of, 165-74
Non-administered arbitration, 165-74
Role of, 84-88
Rules of vacancy, 216-18

ARBITRAL PARTIES. *See* PARTIES TO ARBITRATION

ARBITRATION
Developments in, 14-40
History of, 1-13
Procedural justice of, 41-49
Waiver of right to, 407-14

ARBITRATION AWARDS. *See* AWARDS

ARBITRATION CLAUSES
Effects of, 90-94. *See also* CLAUSES, DRAFTING OF

ARBITRATORS
Authority to grant remedies, 353-62
Conducting proceedings, 149-51
Jurisdiction of, 58-59
Non-attorney arbitrators, 189-98
Party-appointed, 199-210
Political correctness of, 211-14
Procedural and interim orders, power to issue, 263-73
Qualifications of, 53-56, 175-79
Questioning from, 223-28
Reassessing role of, 83-88
Selection of, 101-02, 181-88
Testifying in court, 229-38
Vacancy, 215-22

ATTORNEYS
Attorney-client privilege, 329-36
Presentation skills during arbitral proceedings, 299-310

AWARDS
Clarifications to, 377-82
Functus officio doctrine, 377-82, 387-89
Interim awards, 383-91
Judicial review of, 33-37, 383-86
Judicial vacatur of, 37-38, 200

Post-decision debriefing of, 393-402
Punitive damages, 363-76
Statute of limitations, 386-87
Writing requirement of, 337-52

C

CARRIAGE OF GOODS BY SEA ACT (COGSA), 32

CHOICE OF FORUM 21-24, 134-35

CHOICE OF LAW, 21-24

CLAUSES, DRAFTING OF
Collective bargaining agreements (CBA), 141-48
Consumer disputes, for, 115-26
Employment disputes, for, 115-26
Narrow arbitration clauses, 127-32
New York rule, 120-23, 367-68
Uniform Commercial Code (UCC), 116-20

COMMERCIAL AND BUSINESS ARBITRATION
Arbitrators in, 53-58
Benefits of, 51-53, 123-26
Internet and, 133-39
Managing complex cases, 107-14

CONSUMER ARBITRATION
Drafting arbitration agreements, 115-26
Generally, 25-26

E

EMPLOYMENT ARBITRATION
Drafting arbitration agreements, 115-24
Generally, 26-28

ENGLISH ARBITRATION ACT
Generally, 31, 102
Interim measures under, 270-72
Judicial review under, 464-67

F

FEDERAL ARBITRATION ACT (FAA)
Bankruptcy Code and, 92-94
Consolidation and joinder under, 97-105
Enactment of, 2
Judicial review under, 33-37, 435-62
Judicial vacatur under, 37-38, 200
Preemption of state law, 15-18, 90-91, 415-33,
Punitive damage awards under, 365-67, 421-24
Remedies under, 19-20
Revised Uniform Arbitration Act (RUAA) compared, 28-30
Scope of arbitrability, 18-19
Subpoenas issued under, 257-59
Venue, 403-05
Waiver, 407-14
Writing requirement, 74

INDEX

I

INTERNATIONAL COMMERCIAL ARBITRATION
Generally, 30-32
Party-appointed arbitrators, 205-09

J

JUDICIAL REVIEW OF ARBITRATION AWARDS
Contractual expansion, 435-62
Contractual limitation, 435-62
Federal Arbitration Act (FAA), 33-37, 435-62
Freedom of contract, 447-49
Integrity of process, 449-51
Manifest disregard of the law under, 444
New York Convention, 435-62
Procedural and substantive exceptions, 438-40
Public policy exception, 440-44
Reconciled with arbitration, 463-78

JURY TRIAL WAIVERS
Compared to arbitration, 51

N

NEW YORK CONVENTION
Enactment of, 30
Enforcement of awards under, 103, 135
Judicial review under, 435-62
Jurisdiction under, 69
Insurance matters under, 93-94

NEW YORK RULE, 120-23, 367-68

P

PARTIES TO ARBITRATION
Agency, 65-67, 78-79
Alter ego, 75-76
Assumption by conduct, 64, 77-78
Equitable estoppel, 67-69, 79-82
Identification of, 61-72
Incorporation by reference, 63-64, 77
Non-signatories, compelling to arbitrate, 61-72, 73-82
Piercing the corporate veil, 69-72
Third-party beneficiary, 64-65

PROCEEDINGS
Consolidation of, 89-106
Cross-examination of witnesses during, 293-97
Discovery in, 249-55
Expert testimony in, 281-88
Guidelines for, 107-14
Preliminary conferences, 239-48
Preparing witnesses for, 275-79
Presentation skills for advocates during, 299-310
Procedural and interim orders, 263-73
Subpoenas in discovery, 257-61
Tandem witnesses, 289-91

PROFESSIONAL RESPONISIBILITY
Attorney-client privilege, 329-36
Confidentiality, 311-20
Sanctions, 321-28

R

REVISED UNIFORM ARBITRATION ACT (RUAA)
Areas of concern, 29-30
Generally, 28
Goals of, 28-29
Judicial review under, 36
Subpoenas, 259
Writing requirement, 74

S

SECURITIES ARBITRATION
Generally, 33

SEPARABILITY DOCTRINE
Generally, 16

U

UNITED NATIONS COMMISSION ON INTERNATIONAL TRADE LAW (UNCITRAL)
Document production under, 267
Generally, 30, 103, 132-33
Interim measures, 270-72

UNITED NATIONS CONVENTION ON THE RECOGNITION AND ENFORCEMENT OF FOREIGN ARBITRATION AWARDS. *See* NEW YORK CONVENTION

W

WITNESSES
Cross-examination of witnesses, 293-97
Experts, 281-88
Preparing for arbitration proceeding, 275-79
Tandem witnesses, 289-291